PARLIAMENTARY BILLS OF RIGHTS

Both New Zealand and the United Kingdom challenge assumptions about how a bill of rights functions. Their parliamentary bills of rights constrain judicial review and also look to parliament to play a rights-protecting role. This arises from the requirement to inform parliament if legislative bills are not compatible with rights. But are these bills of rights operating in this proactive manner? Are governments encountering significantly stronger pressures to ensure legislation complies with rights? Are these bills of rights resulting in more reasoned deliberations in parliament about the justification of legislation from a rights perspective? Through extensive interviews with public officials and analysis of parliamentary debates where questions of compliance with rights arise (prisoner voting, parole and sentencing policy, counter-terrorism legislation and same sex marriage), this book argues that a serious gap exists between the promise of these bills of rights and the institutional variables that influence how these parliaments function.

JANET L. HIEBERT is a professor in the Department of Political Studies at Queen's University, Ontario.

JAMES B. KELLY is a professor in the Department of Political Science at Concordia University, Montréal.

CAMBRIDGE STUDIES IN CONSTITUTIONAL LAW

The aim of this series is to produce leading monographs in constitutional law. All areas of constitutional law and public law fall within the ambit of the series, including human rights and civil liberties law, administrative law, constitutional theory and the history of constitutional law. A wide variety of scholarly approaches is encouraged, with the governing criterion being simply that the work is of interest to an international audience. Thus, works concerned with only one jurisdiction will be included in the series as appropriate, while at the same time the series will include works which are explicitly comparative or theoretical - or both. The series editors likewise welcome proposals that work at the intersection of constitutional and international law, or that seek to bridge the gaps between civil law systems, the US and the common law jurisdictions of the Commonwealth.

Books in the series

Parliamentary Bills of Rights: The Experiences of New Zealand and the United Kingdom
Janet L. Hiebert and James B. Kelly

Lawyering for the Rule of Law: Government Lawyers and the Rise of Judicial Power in Israel
Yoav Dotan

Balancing Constitutional Rights: The Origins and Meanings of Postwar Legal Discourse
Jacco Bomhoff

Judges on Trial: The Independence and Accountability of the English Judiciary
Shimon Shetreet and Sophie Turenne

Proportionality and Constitutional Culture
Moshe Cohen-Eliya and Iddo Porat

The Politics of Principle: The First South African Constitutional Court, 1995–2005
Theunis Roux

The New Commonwealth Model of Constitutionalism, Theory and Practice
Stephen Gardbaum

Searching for the State in British Legal Thought: Competing Conceptions of the Public Sphere
Janet McLean

Judging Social Rights
Jeff King

Proportionality, Constitutional Rights and their Limitations
Aharon Barak

Parliamentary Sovereignty, Contemporary Debates
Jeffrey Goldsworthy

PARLIAMENTARY BILLS OF RIGHTS

The Experiences of New Zealand and the United Kingdom

JANET L. HIEBERT

and

JAMES B. KELLY

CAMBRIDGE
UNIVERSITY PRESS

CAMBRIDGE
UNIVERSITY PRESS

University Printing House, Cambridge CB2 8BS, United Kingdom

Cambridge University Press is part of the University of Cambridge.

It furthers the University's mission by disseminating knowledge in the pursuit of education, learning and research at the highest international levels of excellence.

www.cambridge.org
Information on this title: www.cambridge.org/9781107076518

First published 2015

A catalogue record for this publication is available from the British Library

Library of Congress Cataloguing in Publication Data
Hiebert, Janet, 1960- author.
Parliamentary bills of rights : the experiences of New Zealand and the United Kingdom experiences / Janet L. Hiebert, James B. Kelly.
pages cm – (Cambridge studies in constitutional law)
Includes bibliographical references and index.
ISBN 978-1-107-07651-8 (Hardback)
1. Civil rights–New Zealand. 2. Legislation–New Zealand. 3. Civil rights–Great Britain.
4. Legislation–Great Britain. I. Kelly, James B. (James Bernard), 1968- author. II. Title.
K3240.H54 2014
342.4108′5–dc23 2014027892

ISBN 978-1-107-07651-8 Hardback

For Wayne
For Michèle, Fiona and Liam

CONTENTS

TABLES AND APPENDICES

ACKNOWLEDGEMENTS

The idea to collaborate on this book occurred during a conversation one summer afternoon in 2003 in Parma, Italy, where we were both participating in a meeting of Research Committee 9 (Comparative Judicial Studies) of the International Political Science Association. After comparing notes on our independent research projects on whether, how and why the Canadian Charter of Rights and Freedoms has influenced legislative decision-making, we discovered we were both curious about what changes might arise elsewhere. More specifically, our curiosity arose from recent political reforms in New Zealand and the United Kingdom – two other Westminster-based systems that have chosen to marry a statutory bill of rights with a new statutory requirement to alert parliament when government is proceeding with a legislative bill despite being advised that it is inconsistent with protected rights. We had originally included Australia in this research project, as the first Rudd government began a national consultation on an Australian bill of rights. However, the Rudd government failed to act on the recommendations of the Brennan Commission, and thus our study focuses on the bills of rights in New Zealand and the United Kingdom.

Family and administrative responsibilities delayed the anticipated completion date of this project and, as one colleague has gently chided, the book has had a substantial gestation period. Fortunately, we have benefited from the extended opportunity to observe and reflect on how the New Zealand Bill of Rights Act and the United Kingdom's Human Rights Act have evolved, and the significance of changes that have occurred in how bureaucratic, executive and parliamentary actors engage in their new responsibilities to confront how legislative initiatives implicate rights.

A crucial element of understanding the significance of political reforms is discussion of how new statutory requirements are interpreted and how they influence the perspectives and responsibilities of those who help shape and advise on legislative policy developments. We are extremely grateful to the more than 70 public and political officials who met with us for interviews in Wellington and London. We also wish to express our sincere gratitude for the contributions of our dedicated research assistants, who helped with the time-intensive task of understanding how rights considerations influence the life of a legislative bill, and want to acknowledge our gratitude to Jeremy Clarke, Matthew Hodgetts, Matt Kersten, Emmett Macfarlane, Nazeer Patel, Kate Puddister, Arjun Tremblay, Nickolas Tzoulas and Tom Wilson.

We have both presented papers drawn from the research for this book at conferences and in other scholarly venues, and have also discussed the innovative and ambitious idea of a parliamentary-centred bill of rights in our classrooms. We appreciate and have benefited from the critical observations and questions of colleagues, research assistants and students. In particular, we would like to acknowledge and thank Andrew Byrnes, Tom Campbell, Fergal Davis, Fiona de Londras, Julie Debeljak, Rosalind Dixon, David Erdos, Keith Ewing, Stephen Gardbaum, Conor Gearty, Andrew Geddis, Claudia Geiringer, Marco Goldoni, Aileen Kavanagh, Francesca Klug, Christopher Manfredi, Christopher McCorkindale, Danny Nicol, Paul Rishworth, Francesca Scala, Richard Schultz, Alex Schwartz, Adrienne Stone, Adam Tomkins, Mark Tushnet and George Williams. We are also grateful to the opportunity to visit and share ideas with members and other visitors at the Centre for Comparative Constitutional Studies at University of Melbourne, the Gilbert and Tobin Centre of Public Law at the University of New South Wales, the New Zealand Centre for Public Law at Victoria University of Wellington and the New Zealand Centre for Human Rights Law Policy and Practice at University of Auckland.

We would also like to thank the three anonymous reviewers for their advice and constructive criticisms.

In addition, we are extremely proud and pleased to have worked with Cambridge University Press and want to thank Finola O'Sullivan, Rebecca Roberts, Richard Woodham, Bindu Vinod, and Kristy Barker.

We would like to acknowledge the financial support we received from the Social Sciences and Humanities Research Council.

As always, our greatest support came from our spouses. Thank you, Wayne and Michèle, for your unwavering support for us throughout this long project.

Janet L. Hiebert acknowledges the incorporation of arguments and ideas in this book from the following prior publications:

Janet L. Hiebert, 'Governing Under the Human Rights Act. The Limitations of Wishful Thinking', (2012) *Public Law*, 29–46.

Janet L. Hiebert, 'The HRA: Ambiguity about Parliamentary Sovereignty', (2013) 14 *German Law Journal*, 2253–74.

James B. Kelly acknowledges the incorporation of arguments and ideas in this book from the following prior publication:

James B. Kelly, 'Judicial and Political Review as Limited Insurance: The Functioning of the New Zealand Bill of Rights Act in "Hard" Cases', (2011) 49 *Commonwealth & Comparative Politics* 3, 295–317.

ABBREVIATIONS

BNA	British North America Act 1867
BORA	Bill of Rights Act vetting
BZP	Benzylpiperazine
CMP	Closed material proceedings
DCA	Department of Constitutional Affairs
EACD	Expert Advisory Committee on Drugs
ECHR	European Convention on Human Rights
ECtHR	European Court of Human Rights
FPP	First-past-the-post electoral system
HRA	United Kingdom's Human Rights Act 1990
ICCPR	International Covenant on Civil and Political Rights
JCHR	Joint Committee on Human Rights
MFAT	Ministry of Foreign Affairs and Trade
MMP	Mixed member proportional electoral system
ODPM	Office of Deputy Prime Minister
NZBORA	New Zealand Bill of Rights Act 1990
PBL	Parliament Business and Legislation Committee Secretariat
RIS	Regulatory impact statement
SCNZ	Supreme Court of New Zealand
SMP	Single member plurality electoral system
SO	Standing orders of the House of Representatives
SST	Sensible Sentencing Trust
TFMPP	trifluoromethylphenylpiperazine
TPIM	Terrorism Prevention and Investigation Measures

TABLE OF CASES

New Zealand

Belcher v. *Chief Executive of the Department of Corrections* [2007] NZSC 54
Belcher v. *Chief Executive of the Department of Corrections* [2007] 1 NZLR 507 (CA)
Boscawen v. *Attorney General* [2009] NZCA 12
Ngati Apa v. *Attorney General* [2003] 3 NZLR 643 (CA)
RE Bennett [1993] 2 HRNZ 358
R. v. *Hansen* [2007] NZSC 7
R. v. *Jeffries* [1994] 1 NZLR 290 (CA)
R. v. *Shaheed* [2002] 2 NZLR 377 (CA)
Taunoa v. *Attorney General* [2008] 1 NZLR 429 (NZSC)

European Court of Human Rights

A and others v. *Secretary of State for the Home Department* [2004] UKHL 56
A and others v. *United Kingdom*, Application no. 3455/05 [2009] ECHR 1 [GC]
Animal Defenders International v. *The United Kingdom*, No. 48876/08 (2013) [GC]
Animal Defenders International, R (on the application of) v. *The Secretary of State for Culture*
Chahal v. *UK* (1996) 23 EHRR 413
Ghaidan v. *Mendoza* [2002] EWC Civ 1533
Goodwin v. *The United Kingdom*, (2002) 35 EHRR 18
Greens and M.T. v. *The United Kingdom*, No. 60041/08 (23 Nov 2010)
Hirst v. *United Kingdom*, (2004) 38 EHRR 40
Hirst v. *Attorney General* [2001] EWHC Admin 239
Hirst v. *United Kingdom* (No. 2) [2005] ECHR 68, (2006) 42 EHHR 41, [GC]
Karner v. *Austria*, (2003) 38 EHRR 24
Media and Sport [2006] EWHC 3069 (Admin)
Schalk and Kopf v. *Austria*, No. 30141/04, [2010] ECHR 995
Scoppola v. *Italy (No. 3)* [2012] ECHR 868 [GC]
Secretary of State for the Home Department v. *AE* [2008] EWHC 585 (Admin)
Vgt Verein Gegen Tierfabriken v. *Switzerland*, No. 24699/94 (28 June 2001)
Wilkinson v. *Kitzinger* [2006] EWHC 2022 (Fam), [2007] 1 FLR 295

United Kingdom

Fitzpatrick v. *Sterling Housing Association Ltd* [2001] 1 AC 27
Ghaidan v. *Godin-Mendoza* (FC) [2004] UKHL 30
R (on the application of Chester) (appellant) v. *Secretary of State for Justice (respondent); McGeoch (AP) (Appellant)* v. *The Lord President of the Council and another (respondents)* (Scotland) (2013) UKSC 63
R v. *A* [2001] UKHL 25
Secretary of State for the Home Department v. *AF (No 3)* [2009] UKHL 28
Secretary of State for the Home Department v. *E* [2007] UKHL 47
Secretary of State for the Home Department v. *JJ and others* [2007] UKHL 45
Secretary of State for the Home Department v. *MB* [2007] UKHL 46
Willock v. *Muckle* [1951] 2 KB 844
William Smith (AP) v. *KD Scott Electoral Registration Officer* [2007] CSIH 9 XA33/04
YL v *Birmingham City Council and others* [2007] UKHL 27

TABLE OF LEGISLATION

Canada

Canadian Bill of Rights, S.C. 1960, c. 44, s. 2
Department of Justice Act, R.S.C., 1985, c. J-2

New Zealand

Children, Young Persons and their Families Amendment Act 2004
Citizens Initiated Referenda Act 1993
Criminal Investigations (Bodily Samples) Act 1995
Electoral Amendment Act 2002
Misuse of Drugs Act 1975
Misuse of Drugs Amendment Act 2005

United Kingdom

Local Government Act 1988, c. 9
Adoption and Children Act 2002, c.38
Communication Act 2003, c. 21
Gender Recognition Act 2004, c. 7
Prevention of Terrorism Bill, 2005
Terrorism Act 2006, c. 11, s. 23

1

Introduction

The marriage of a Westminster-based parliamentary system with a bill of rights represents a political path that, in the not too distant past, seemed implausible. Nevertheless, New Zealand enacted the New Zealand Bill of Rights Act (NZBORA) in 1990, and the UK passed the Human Rights Act (HRA) in 1998. By enacting these statutory bills of rights, both countries not only introduced a new domestic judicial authority to evaluate legislation for its consistency with protected rights; they also embarked on an ambitious attempt to use a bill of rights as an instrument to alter the norms of legislative decision-making.

Historically, few considered a bill of rights to be an attractive or viable option for either jurisdiction. This perspective was influenced by opinions that rights were adequately safeguarded by parliament, by a common law tradition that recognized the freedom of individuals to do as they wish unless expressly prohibited by law and by judicial enforcement of the rule of law. In any event, the conventional expectation that a bill of rights not only authorizes courts to review legislation but also imposes remedies that can veto the effects of otherwise duly enacted legislation is regarded as fundamentally incongruent with parliamentary sovereignty, which has long been considered an essential constitutional characteristic of Westminster-based parliamentary systems.

Two ideas borrowed from Canada helped shape New Zealand and UK reformers' assumptions that it was possible to conceive of a bill of rights to improve the protection of rights without contradicting the constitutional principle of parliamentary sovereignty. The first borrowed idea was to envisage judicial review with constrained remedial powers, or what Mark Tushnet refers to as 'weak form judicial review'.[1] The second idea was to introduce a new ministerial obligation to report to parliament

[1] M. Tushnet, 'New Forms of Judicial Review', (2003) 38 *Wake Forest Law Review* 813; M. Tushnet, *Weak Courts, Strong Rights. Judicial Review and Social Welfare Rights in Comparative Constitutional Law* (Princeton: Princeton University Press, 2008).

on whether bills are consistent with rights. Both ideas were expected to ensure the NZBORA and HRA function in a more parliamentary-centred manner than is associated with more conventional bills of rights (ironically, in ways in which the Canadian Charter of Rights and Freedoms, as it has evolved, does not).[2]

The concept of judicial review with constrained judicial remedial power was associated with the logic of Canada's 'notwithstanding clause'[3] – a power that allows provincial legislatures or the federal parliament to dissent from judicial interpretations of most sections of the Canadian Charter through ordinary legislation (or to pre-empt judicial review altogether) for periods of up to five years (and by implication until the next election). For reformers in New Zealand and the UK who were not prepared and/or lacked sufficient political support to relinquish the principle of parliamentary sovereignty, the notwithstanding clause demonstrated the possibility to design a bill of rights that introduces judicial review while nevertheless preserving parliament's ability to dissent from courts and preserve the legality of its legislation.[4]

[2] It is ironic that Canada gave birth to these ideas, neither of which has evolved in the way framers intended. The first idea, of legislative rights review, has not functioned particularly well because parliament rarely engages in review of whether the Charter is consistent with protected rights. The second idea, of allowing for political dissent from judicial rulings, has rarely been considered a political option for Canadian legislatures because of deep scepticism about the legitimacy of political judgment prevailing over judicial rulings. See J. Kelly, *Governing with the Charter. Legislative and Judicial Activism and Framers' Intent* (Vancouver: UBC Press, 2005); J. Hiebert, *Charter Conflicts. What is Parliament's Role?* (Montreal: McGill-Queen's University Press, 2002); J. Hiebert, 'Compromise and the Notwithstanding Clause: Why the Dominant Narrative Distorts our Understanding', in J. Kelly and C.P. Manfredi (eds.), *Contested Constitutionalism: Reflections on the Charter of Rights and Freedoms* (Vancouver: UBC Press, 2009), pp. 107–28.

[3] Although Canada's earlier experiment with a bill of rights, the 1960 statutory Canadian Bill of Rights, might be considered the first rights-protecting instrument to inspire subsequent experimentation, uncertainty about what remedies the Supreme Court was authorized to impose in circumstances where it was not possible to interpret legislation in a rights-compliant manner, and the meek judicial response interpreting the Canadian Bill of Rights, make it an unlikely subject for constitutional borrowing.

[4] The influence of the notwithstanding clause was at the idea level, rather than its being a specific mechanism to emulate or adapt. Political reluctance to conceive of judicial power as authorizing courts to invalidate inconsistent legislation negated the need to adopt an explicit mechanism to reverse the effect of a judicial ruling. Thus, the triggering mechanism for political dissent from judicial rulings in New Zealand and the UK differs from that in Canada, where parliament must act affirmatively to dissent from a judicial ruling by passing legislation that invokes the notwithstanding clause to either pre-empt judicial review or to justify legislation that dissents from a judicial ruling on the Charter. In contrast, in New Zealand and the UK, parliaments can voice their disagreement with

The NZBORA, in section 6, instructs judges that wherever an enactment can be given a meaning that is consistent with the rights and freedoms contained in the bill of rights, this 'meaning shall be preferred to any other meaning'. However, judges are not formally empowered to rule that other enactments have been impliedly repealed or revoked, or to decline to apply any provision considered inconsistent with any provision in the Bill of Rights. In the UK, section 3 of the HRA instructs judges that 'so far as it is possible', primary and subordinate legislation 'must be read and given effect in a way which is compatible with the Convention rights'. Where such interpretations are not possible, the HRA in section 4 empowers a superior court to make a 'declaration of incompatibility' if primary legislation cannot be interpreted in a manner that is consistent with Convention rights (a power which New Zealand courts lack). As is the case in New Zealand, UK judges lack the power to declare that inconsistent legislation is invalid. Thus, unlike the more traditional view that a bill of rights invokes 'the machinery of the courts to set binding constraints on political decision-making',[5] both the NZBORA and the HRA ensure parliament's judgement prevails in decisions about how rights will guide or constrain legislation.

However, the innovative character of these bills of rights goes well beyond their attempts to conceive of judicial power in a manner that is consistent with the principle of parliamentary sovereignty.[6] Equally significant is the second idea borrowed by reformers, which we refer to as legislative rights review (it is also referred to in the literature as political rights review).[7] Legislative rights review arises from the implications and

judicial rulings by ignoring these rulings, unless courts have used their interpretive powers to alter the intent or scope of legislation to arrive at rights-compliant interpretation, after which the legislatures could simply pass ordinary legislation to reinstate their preferred intentions with respect to the scope or effects of legislation.

5 S. Choudhry, 'Bills of Rights as Instruments of Nation Building in Multinational States: The Canadian *Charter* and Quebec Nationalism', in J. Kelly and C.P. Manfredi (eds.), *Contested Constitutionalism. Reflections on the Canadian Charter of Rights and Freedoms* (Vancouver: UBC Press, 2009) p. 239.

6 Stephen Gardbaum similarly emphasizes the potential of these bills of rights, and others associated with what he refers to as the Commonwealth model, to alter how political and judicial actors review legislation from a rights perspective. For Gardbaum, the Commonwealth model has the potential to represent the optimal techniques for protecting rights. S. Gardbaum, *The New Commonwealth Model of Constitutionalism. Theory and Practice* (Cambridge: Cambridge University Press, 2013).

7 Stephen Gardbaum refers to this practice as political rights review. S. Gardbaum, *The New Commonwealth Model of Constitutionalism. Theory and Practice* (Cambridge: Cambridge University Press, 2013), pp. 25–26. In previous work, Hiebert has referred to this concept

consequences of introducing a new statutory requirement that a government minister apprise parliament if a legislative bill is not consistent with protected rights. This ministerial requirement on compatibility was borrowed from the Canadian Bill of Rights in 1960,[8] and subsequently adapted for the Canadian Charter of Rights and Freedoms.[9] New Zealand and UK reformers anticipated that adopting this ministerial reporting obligation on compatibility would promote proactive engagement with rights when developing and approving legislation. If robustly interpreted, legislative rights review would prioritize the need to confront whether and how legislative initiatives implicate rights and assess their justification where protected rights are adversely affected, from the earliest phase of bureaucratic development and advice on a government's policy objectives, through to government's approach to and approval of its legislative agenda, and on to parliamentary deliberation and voting on bills. Viewed in this manner, the introduction of legislative rights review is tantamount to an attempt to fundamentally alter the norms of legislative decision-making.

in terms of both legislative rights review and political rights review. Upon continued reflection, we have decided to refer to the concept as legislative rights review to emphasize the institutional context in which these assessments are done, as we worry that the term 'political rights review' might misleadingly suggest these decisions are entirely based on the kinds of philosophical or political differences that distinguish political parties. Although judgment about compatibility will be inevitably influenced by different political views on the role of the state or the scope of rights, we worry that 'political rights review' diverts attention from the significant changes for assessing bills before and during cabinet, and after this in parliament (particularly in the UK where bills are assessed by a specialized rights committee), that arise from the requirements that the New Zealand Attorney General or the relevant UK Minister apprise parliament when bills are not consistent with protected rights.

[8] This idea originated in the 1960 statutory Canadian Bill of Rights. Then Progressive Conservative Prime Minister John Diefenbaker viewed a bill of rights as an instrument to revitalize parliament's role as a protector of Canadians' rights. Diefenbaker did not believe that rights were vulnerable because of inappropriate parliamentary intentions so much as to expedient bureaucratic actions that 'sacrificed [freedom] in favour of administrative or other advantages' and executive reliance (by the previous Liberal government) on order-in-council decisions that were inconsistent with rights, and which bypassed parliament. From his perspective, a key reform for improving the protection of rights was to reinvigorate Parliament's role as a custodian of rights: W.R. Jackett, 'Memorandum for the Minister of Justice', 21 April 1958; E.D. Fulton, 'Memorandum for the Prime Minister' 29 April 1958, as referred to by C. MacLennan, *Toward the Charter. Canadians and the Demand for a National Bill of Rights, 1929–1960* (Montreal: McGill-Queen's University Press, 2003), pp. 121–23.

[9] This requirement is contained in section 4(1) of the Department of Justice Act. *Department of Justice Act* R.S., 1985, c. J-2, s. 4.1(1); 1992, c. 1, s. 144(F)

The NZBORA requires (in section 7) that the Attorney General alert parliament when he or she is of the opinion that legislative bills are not consistent with the NZBORA. New Zealand borrowed this compatibility-reporting requirement in an attempt to strengthen the influence of the NZBORA on legislation, both with respect to how bills are developed and as they progress through parliament. As we argue in Chapter 2, then Prime Minister Geoffrey Palmer would have preferred to adopt a constitutional bill of rights that authorizes strong judicial remedial powers. However, when it became obvious that he lacked sufficient political support for such a radical constitutional reform and would have to settle for a statutory bill of rights with heavily constrained judicial remedial powers, Palmer thought it would be beneficial to adopt this reporting obligation, which he had learned about in an earlier visit to Canada. In his account of the reasons for adopting this mechanism, Palmer expected that this practice would serve two purposes. First, this reporting obligation would place a statutory obligation on government to act in accordance with the NZBORA, and cabinet would revise policy processes within the bureaucracy to ensure that bills were compatible with protected rights when introduced into parliament. Palmer's expectation was that this reporting requirement would function as 'a set of navigational lights for the whole process of Government to observe'.[10] Second, the requirement for the Attorney General to report to parliament when bills were inconsistent with rights would deter such practices because of the anticipated critical reaction in and beyond parliament.[11]

The UK similarly borrowed this idea of a statutory reporting obligation on compatibility, which is contained in section 19 of the HRA. However, rather than locate responsibility with the Attorney General, it is vested instead with individual ministers. UK political proponents of this reporting obligation similarly expected that this statutory obligation to report on the compatibility of legislative bills would discourage the introduction of inconsistent legislation, but thought that a more decentralized approach would better promote rights sensitivity throughout government and across departments. The UK reporting requirement also broadens the scope to cover all government bills (indicating either

[10] G. Palmer, *A White Paper for New Zealand* (New Zealand: House of Representatives, 1985), p. 6.

[11] G.W.R. Palmer, *New Zealand's Constitution in Crisis* (Dunedin, New Zealand: John McIndoe, 1992), pp. 59–60.

an affirmative claim of compatibility or inability to claim compatibility) and adapts this reporting requirement to the bicameral nature of the UK parliament. The UK has also created a specialized parliamentary rights committee, the Joint Committee of Human Rights (JCHR), to enhance parliament's capacity to scrutinize ministerial claims of compatibility.

Explaining our focus on legislative rights review

Both the NZBORA and HRA have garnered increasing attention from a largely sympathetic international scholarly community that is interested in the normative implications and sustainability of what they consider a new model for a bill of rights.[12] These bills of rights have been characterized in varied ways, including the Commonwealth model,[13] hybrid approach,[14] weak-form model[15] and parliamentary rights model.[16]

To date, the majority of scholarly attention has focused on the significance of constrained judicial power, which sympathetic commentators

[12] See for example, M.J. Perry, 'Protecting Human Rights in a Democracy: What Role for the Courts?', (2003) 38 *Wake Forest Law Review* 635–95; J. Goldsworthy, 'Homogenizing Constitutions', (2003) 23 *Oxford Journal of Legal Studies* 482–505; M. Tushnet, 'New Forms of Judicial Review'; M Tushnet, *Weak Courts, Strong Rights*; G. Williams, 'The Victorian *Charter of Human Rights and Responsibilities*: Origins and Scope', (2006) 30 *Melbourne University Law Review* 880–905.

[13] S. Gardbaum, 'The New Commonwealth Model of Constitutionalism', (2001) 49 *American Journal of Constitutional Law* 707; 'Reassessing the New Commonwealth Model of Constitutionalism', (2010) 8 *International Journal of Constitutional Law* 167; *The New Commonwealth Model of Constituitonalism*.

[14] P. Rishworth, 'The Birth and Rebirth of the Bill of Rights', in G. Huscroft and P. Rishworth (eds.), *Rights and Freedoms: The New Zealand Bill of Rights Act 1990 and the Human Rights Act* (Wellington: Brookers, 1995), p. 4; J. Goldsworthy, 'Homogenizing Constitutions', (2003) 23 *Oxford Journal of Legal Studies* 483.

[15] Mark Tushnet characterizes these bills of rights as incorporating weak form judicial review because judicial decisions do not determine the legal authority of legislation, and can be ignored or set aside through ordinary legislative means. He contrasts the scope of judicial powers in New Zealand and the UK with the American form of judicial review, which he describes as strong form review because it is assumed by the Supreme Court and others that this Court is supreme in the exposition of the law and the Constitution, and that its decisions impose a duty on legislatures to follow the Court's interpretation. M. Tushnet, 'New Forms of Judicial Review'; *Weak Courts, Strong Rights*.

[16] J. Hiebert, 'New Constitutional Ideas: Can New Parliamentary Models Resist Judicial Dominance When Interpreting Rights?', (2004) 82 *Texas Law Review* 1963; 'Constitutional Experimentation: Rethinking How a Bill of Rights Functions', in T. Ginsburg and R. Dixon (eds.), *Comparative Constitutional Law* (Cheltenham: Edward Elgar, 2011), pp. 298–320.

believe addresses democratic objections to judicial review.[17] We do not dispute the importance of understanding how courts interpret rights, the significance of how protected rights are formulated in legal language or how bills of rights conceive the scope of judicial authority, rules of standing or judicial remedies. However, we believe it is also important to appreciate how bills of rights influence legislative decision-making. Only a small portion of the legislation that parliaments pass will ever be subject to litigation. Thus, even under more conventional bills of rights, parliaments effectively have the final say for the majority of legislation passed, regardless of whether and how rights-based considerations have shaped legislative outcomes.

Although bills of rights are expected to influence how political actors and citizens assess the legitimacy of proposed state actions, the accumulated ways in which judicial rulings more generally influence political and societal debates over time, particularly around contested issues, cannot be equated with a deliberate intent to promote legislative engagement with questions of rights as a regular element in the day-to-day legislative decision-making process. The framers of the NZBORA and HRA envisaged a more substantive parliamentary role to protect rights, both in a proactive sense of holding government to account for decisions that potentially infringe upon rights and, in the UK, in a reactive sense by revisiting legislation upon a judicial finding that legislation is not compatible with protected rights. As such, the marriage of a bill of rights with an expectation of legislative rights review is potentially a far-reaching way of guarding against rights infringements by assuming that all legislation will have been subject to rights-based compatibility review, and not just the relatively small subsection that is litigated under more conventional bills of rights and eventually subject to judicial review.[18]

This parliamentary-centred focus to rights protection explains and justifies our interest in how the NZBORA and HRA are influencing legislative decision-making processes and outcomes. Moreover, we believe the best way to characterize the NZBORA and HRA is to refer to them as *parliamentary bills of rights*, which is the term that we will be

[17] Stephen Gardbaum is an exception and focuses on the significance of both ideas, which he characterizes as constituting 'novel, and arguably more optimal techniques for protecting rights within a democracy': S. Gardbaum, *The New Commonwealth Model of Constitutionalism*, p. 1.

[18] This argument was made earlier in J. Hiebert, 'Constitutional Experimentation'.

using hereon. Our judgement on this issue reflects the importance of the political and institutional contexts associated with the Westminster-based parliamentary systems in which these bills of rights operate. Our attention to political and institutional variables differentiates our approach from the more court-centred ones that generally focus on judicial review or on the structural or textual design of a bill of rights.

In the chapters that follow, we examine the extent to which the ministerial requirement of reporting on compatibility has influenced bureaucratic development, evaluation and advice about legislative initiatives prior to their approval by cabinet and introduction to parliament. We also examine parliament's willingness and capacity to demand better explanations or evidence to justify a government's intent to pursue legislation that implicates rights adversely and, where consensus does not exist, the extent to which deliberation reflects good-faith disagreements about the scope of rights or how rights considerations appropriately guide or constrain the legislative objective in question.

We are not alone in recognizing the potential significance of introducing a compatibility-based focus for legislative decision-making. Aileen Kavanagh characterizes the combined effects of constrained judicial remedies and legislative rights review as a collaborative approach to protect rights.[19] As she argues, the central purpose of the HRA was to 'strength[en] the ability of the courts to protect rights, whilst at the same time encouraging greater parliamentary sensitivity to, and engagement with, human rights concerns'.[20] Stephen Gardbaum also conceives of the combination of constrained judicial remedies and legislative rights review as a significant change in how rights are protected – a change that he believes has potential to provide the optimal way to protect rights, by reallocating powers between courts and legislatures in a more balanced manner than occurred under either parliamentary supremacy or what is associated with judicial supremacy. Gardbaum argues that this approach, which he refers to as the Commonwealth model, combines the strengths of both polar models while avoiding both of their principal weaknesses. As a result, citizens will benefit from improved legislative reasoning about rights, while also being protected by judicial oversight that will

[19] A. Kavanagh, *Constitutional Review under the UK Human Rights Act* (Cambridge: Cambridge University Press, 2009), pp. 406–11.

[20] A. Kavanagh, 'The Joint Committee on Human Rights: A Hybrid Breed of Constitutional Watchdog', in Murray Hunt, Hayley Hooper and Paul Yowell (eds.), *Parliament and Human Rights: Redressing the Democratic Deficit* (Oxford: Hart Publishing, 2015).

help counter legislative under-enforcement of rights.[21] David Feldman also emphasizes the significance of this shared responsibility for confronting how proposed legislation implicates rights, suggesting that 'systematic engagement with human rights in a democratic political process can come about only when it is seen as a goal of all institutions, executive, legislative and judicial, working towards a common goal when exercising their different but complementary functions'.[22]

This attempt to broaden responsibility for judgements about rights, and to focus bureaucratic and political attention on whether legislation is justified in light of its implications for rights, addresses a concern that has long been associated with bills of rights: the temptation for parliamentarians to avoid tackling contentious issues that implicate rights and threaten to undermine party cohesiveness and divide society and, through their inaction, to pass responsibility for the resolution of these issues to courts.[23] What makes this concern particularly potent is the frequently contested nature of judgements about how rights-based principles appropriately guide or constrain complex policy debates, which for many raises democratic concerns about why courts rather than parliament should resolve these thorny issues. However, a different concern is that since only a fraction of legislation will ever be subject to judicial review, if parliamentarians abdicate political responsibility for judgements about rights, this raises the distinct possibility that many contentious issues will not be subject to any form of reasoned deliberation about the justification of legislation in light of their impact on rights. Concerns about abdicating the public and political responsibility to work through contested issues about the meaning and scope of fundamental public norms have led to calls in the United States for a more 'populist constitutional law' that leaves 'a wide range open for resolution through principled political discussions', rather than equating judicial rulings with strict constitutional requirements.[24]

Although others have addressed the significance of the new statutory obligation for ministerial reports on compatibility, there is an absence in

[21] S. Gardbaum, *The New Commonwealth Model of Constitutionalism*, pp. 68–69.

[22] D. Feldman, 'The Impact of Human Rights on the UK Legislative Process', (2004) *Statute Law Review* 91.

[23] James Bradley Thayer warned of this problem more than a century ago: J.B. Thayer, *The Origin and Scope of the American Doctrine of Constitutional Law* (Boston: Little, Brown and Company, 1893).

[24] M. Tushnet, *Taking the Constitution Away from the Courts* (Princeton: Princeton University Press, 1999), p. 185.

the literature of substantive and qualitative research on the differences made by this concept of legislative rights review for how public officials evaluate and advise on bills, how governments broach their legislative decisions and how parliament evaluates bills. Our intent is to address the substantial gap between optimistic assessments of the significance of this concept and its practical effects for legislation.

Initially, we framed our research as a study of whether and how ministerial reporting obligations in the NZBORA and HRA are influencing legislative decision-making. However, as our research progressed and we sought to explain how the concept of legislative review was altering government and parliamentary behaviour, we realized our initial framing of the research questions was misplaced. The more appropriate way to frame our queries is to ask: how do Westminster parliamentary factors influence the nature and impact of legislative rights review?

Our study gives priority to the institutional and political contexts in which the NZBORA and HRA operate – Westminster-based parliamentary systems where the executive generally dominates parliament and where cohesive parties structure how parliament functions. As we argue, these Westminster factors constrain and ultimately complicate ambitious attempts to introduce a compatibility-based framework as a way of influencing how government decides its legislative agenda, or how parliament scrutinizes and votes on bills.

Westminster-based parliamentary systems generally operate on the basis of what Christopher Kam refers to as a 'double monopoly of powers', in the following two ways. First, cabinet has a near monopoly over executive and legislative power; second, a single party has monopoly over the cabinet. Where the electoral system fails to produce a majority government, coalition governments can change the dynamics of political behaviour by allowing party leaders to use the possibility of dissent to constrain the demands of coalition partners.[25] In New Zealand the adoption of MMP (mixed member proportional representation) makes electoral majorities highly improbable, and thus cabinet decision-making must maintain support from other parties or key players in parliament. Nevertheless, cabinet remains the central driver of political decision-making, for which the Prime Minister is the most important and influential member. As in Rhodes, Wanna and Weller's description of the political significance of cabinet in Westminster-based parliamentary systems, including both

[25] C.J. Kam, *Party Discipline and Parliamentary Politics* (Cambridge: Cambridge University Press, 2009), pp. 6–7.

the UK and New Zealand, a cabinet decision represents 'government policy, not opinion'.[26]

Government's monopoly over or control of legislative power is facilitated by strong party cohesion, whether in a majority or coalition situation. An essential mechanism for maintaining party cohesion is strong party discipline. The constraints that party discipline imposes on parliamentarians, and the consequences for government, were famously characterized almost 40 years ago by Lord Hailsham's use of the term 'elective dictatorship' to describe the UK parliament, because of government's relative certainty of getting its legislative agenda passed.[27] As Griffith and Ryle's classic text on parliament suggests, 'the principal consideration determining the way in which Parliament works is the party system'.[28]

The voting behaviour of MPs in Westminster-based systems has become so cohesive that their deviations from the party line are both infrequent and often inconsequential.[29] Where deviations occur, they are more common in larger parliaments such as the UK's, because the sheer size of parliament ensures that promises or threats to career progression are less effective ways to constrain elected members' behaviour. Where the government's electoral majority is sufficiently large, occasional backbench rebellions are more predictable yet less problematic with respect to government's capacity to pass its legislative agenda. There has been an increase in backbench rebellions in the UK in particular since the 1970s, occurring under the Conservative government over the issue of European integration, particularly during John Major's tenure, and under Blair's Labour government with respect to the invasion of Iraq, university tuition fees, foundational hospitals and the prevention of terror measures.[30]

[26] R.A. Rhodes, J. Wanna and P. Weller, *Comparing Westminster* (Oxford: Oxford University Press, 2009), p. 108.

[27] Lord Hailsham, 'Elective Dictatorship', (1976) *The Listener* 496.

[28] J. Griffith and M. Ryle, *Parliament: Functions, Practice and Procedures*, (London: Sweet & Maxwell, 1989), p. 17.

[29] C.E.S. Franks, *The Parliament of Canada* (Toronto: University of Toronto Press, 1987); K. Jackson, *The Dilemma of Parliament* (Auckland: Allen and Unwin, 1987); D. Jaensch, *The Politics of Australia* (Melbourne: Macmillan Australia, 1992).

[30] See P. Norton, *Dissention in the House of Commons: Intra-Party Dissent in the House of Commons Division Lobbies 1945–1974* (London: Macmillan, 1975); *Dissension in the House of Commons, 1974–1979* (New York: Oxford University Press, 1980); and 'Behavioural Changes: Backbench Independence in the 1980s', in Philip Norton (ed.), *Parliament in the 1980s* (Oxford: Basil Blackwell, 1985). See also Philip Cowley, *Revolts and Rebellions: Parliamentary Voting under Blair* (London: Politico's, 2002); and *The Rebels. How Blair Mislaid His Majority* (London: Politico's, 2005).

Nevertheless, although parliamentary parties are not perfectly monolithic entities and MPs can and do vote against their parties, occasionally to great effect, party cohesion remains a potent force in the UK parliament. Kam explains that although the size of the British parliament ensures that the vast majority of MPs will never attain a cabinet position, the combined effects of discipline – particularly in the earlier years of a member's career when career aspirations are stronger – and the longer term effects of socialization into the norms of party loyalty operate as effective limits on MPs' propensity to dissent from party-loyal behaviour.[31]

In smaller parliaments such as New Zealand's, members' behaviour is subject to even tighter, 'rigid and controlled party discipline', which helps to explain why 'there is no tradition of government back-benchers voting against the executive in large numbers (although individuals may occasionally dissent)'.[32] Moreover, as we will argue, the potential instability that MMP generates has encouraged inter-party agreements and changes in the Standing Orders that effectively muzzle or constrain intra-party dissent in parliament.

Although executive discipline and cohesive political parties are shared core characteristics of both political systems, we recognize the dangers of treating these political systems as monolithic or static entities. Three important variables distinguish New Zealand from the UK in ways that affect how these bills of rights influence legislative decisions: the electoral system, bicameralism and the UK expectation of compliance with relevant domestic and international court rulings, which is lacking in New Zealand. These factors can influence the internal political dynamics of how these political systems operate, particularly with respect to ideas of justifying and scrutinizing legislative bills in terms of their implications for protected rights.

New Zealand's MMP electoral system influences the dynamic between the executive and parliament in distinct ways. The Attorney General's section 7 reporting duty was conceived within a parliamentary dynamic based on New Zealand's earlier electoral system of SMP. However, with the adoption of MMP, a new set of rules has emerged that complicate the idea of legislative rights review. These changes were introduced to avoid government instability, which is a common feature in political systems with electoral systems based on proportional representation. Unlike the single member plurality voting system in the UK (SMP), which generally

[31] C.J. Kam, *Party Discipline and Parliamentary Politics*, pp. 189–204.

[32] Rhodes et al., *Comparing Westminster*, p. 202.

produces single-party majority governments, MMP has the potential for instability because no political party controls a majority of seats in parliament. To avoid instability, New Zealand changed its parliamentary Standing Orders and adopted the 'party vote', which exists in PR systems such as that in the Netherlands and allows the party leadership to cast a single vote for their MPs on bills before parliament. On its own, the party vote cannot address the issue of government instability, but in conjunction with the second important change under MMP – formalized agreements with minor parties – the party vote ensures the stability of government because these multi-party governing arrangements under MMP control a majority of seats in parliament.

Since New Zealand's transition from SMP to MMP, the composition of government has followed one of two paths. The most common formation has been a coalition government, supported by minor parties that negotiate 'confidence and supply' agreements with the lead coalition partner, such as the Labour party or the National party. Under these agreements, minor parties support the government in exchange for the introduction of specific legislation drawn from their election manifesto. The second type of formation has been minority government, also sustained in office by 'confidence and supply' agreements. The concern over government instability under MMP saw corresponding changes in the Cabinet Manual. The revised Cabinet Manual requires consultation and agreement between the multi-party partners before government legislation is introduced into parliament. Once this agreement is reached and the legislation is introduced it is generally passed, because the 'party vote' ensures its progression into law.

These changes have significant implications for the NZBORA, as well as for how parliament responds after the Attorney General has apprised parliament that he or she believes that legislative bills are not consistent with protected rights. As we argue in Chapter 4, many section 7 reports involve government bills that are based on 'confidence and supply' agreements with minor parties. More importantly, most of these bills have been passed without amendments to address potential NZBORA incompatibilities raised by the Attorney General. MMP has significantly complicated this reporting mechanism's ability to facilitate parliamentary engagement and review of government bills, for a simple reason – these bills are based on agreement reached before their introduction into parliament, and are necessary to sustain a government in office because they are based on policy commitments made to minor parties in the period immediately after an election which allow a major party or parties to form a government. Parliamentary engagement has been marginalized as a result, because of the party dynamics that have emerged under MMP and the need to sustain the ministry through multi-party governing arrangements.

A significant way in which the UK differs from New Zealand (apart from its electoral system) is its bicameral system. In 1999 a significant reform enhanced the authority of the House of Lords to challenge the executive by approving amendments that significantly alter the scope or effects of bills.[33] Moreover, the greater emphasis on scrutinizing bills associated with the House of Lords, as contrasted with the work of the Commons – attributed in large part to less restrictive time pressures, and also greater liberty from party pressures[34] – encourages more attention to how proposed legislation implicates rights. As discussed in Chapters 8 and 9, the House of Lords regularly engages JCHR reports and has frequently passed significant rights-protecting amendments. The UK's creation of a specialized and jointly constituted parliamentary rights committee, which New Zealand lacks, enhances the significance of bicameralism in terms of parliamentary scrutiny of legislative bills, from the perspective of their consistency with protected rights.

The HRA also differs from the NZBORA because the HRA's incorporation of the European Convention of Human Rights into domestic law creates a strong expectation of compliance with the judicial rulings of domestic courts and the European Court of Human Rights, arising from the treaty character of the ECHR. As discussed in Chapter 6, political framers expressed a strong presumptive belief that parliament would (and should) generally comply with rulings of the European Court of Human Rights, and reinforced this expectation by including a fast-track procedure for passing remedial measures in s. 10 of the HRA.

All three factors have a significant impact on the operation of legislative rights review in New Zealand and the UK, and thus make it difficult

[33] Analysis of the House of Lords after the 1999 reform that removed the majority of hereditary peers suggests this change is a significant factor in changing how the House of Lords performs. This reform not only created the confidence necessary for peers (and the public) to accept their legitimacy in the political process, but also reduced the ability of any party to control the chamber, which resulted in Liberal Democrats (the party most sympathetic to the ECHR) gaining more importance in British politics. M. Russell and M. Sciara, 'Why Does the Government Get Defeated in the House of Lords? The Lords, the Party System and British Politics', (2007) 2 *British Politics* 299–322.

[34] A. Renwick, 'House of Lords Reform. A Briefing Paper', Political Studies Association, 2011.

to talk about the NZBORA or HRA as if they function as a uniform model of a bill of rights. Thus, while both bills of rights share the Westminster characteristics of executive control of parliament and the centrality of cohesive political parties in structuring how parliament functions, our policy chapters on New Zealand and the UK account for how and why these distinct factors interact and influence political behaviour under each bill of rights.

How compatibility assessments might influence legislation

Although a bill of rights represents a statement of the normative values that are intended to guide the evaluation of state actions, bills of rights are not self-enforcing. Indeed, it is naïve to assume that a government will willingly subject itself to constraints that prevent it from pursuing actions it deems important to the public interest, and also profitable in a political or electoral sense, in the absence of strong external pressures to change (whether these pressures accrue from the individual or combined impacts of a realistic threat of judicial censure, political opposition or societal demands). Indeed, it is difficult to overstate the difficulty of altering political behaviour and assumptions, particularly in the short term. Encouraging legislative decision-makers to readjust political strategies to assess proposed legislation through the lens of rights-based compatibility is difficult because of the contested nature of judgements about rights, which ensures frequent contestation will occur with respect to the content and scope of protected rights and how consideration of rights should guide or constrain specific legislative initiatives.

Equally if not more challenging is the juxtaposition of this attempt to establish a compatibility-based framework for parliamentary review within the Westminster parliamentary context, in which disciplined political parties structure and give meaning to the parliamentary vote and the perpetual role of the opposition – to present itself as the alternative to government – encourages the reduction of complex issues to two viewpoints: in favour or opposed. Unless party leaders accept the merits of a compatibility-based framework (a proposition that is less likely if a bill of rights lacks strong public support), they are not likely to see the political utility in choosing this focus through which to criticize government. Nevertheless, it is within this highly charged political and partisan environment that ministers and parliamentarians are now being expected to integrate compatibility-based assessments of proposed legislation with more traditional foci on policy objectives, interpretations of the public interest, demands of political constituents, broader public opinion, partisan gamesmanship, the political stability of government and a range of cost–benefit political analyses. This ambitious goal of proactive legislative rights review requires a fundamental shift in how party leaders and parliamentarians operate. Stated more bluntly, it suggests the need for nothing short of a fundamental change to the very political culture that characterizes a competitive, parliamentary and adversarial system of government.[35]

We can anticipate three possible ways in which this reporting obligation on compatibility could influence cabinet and parliament, each with distinct implications for political behaviour. There is no reason to assume that any single approach will necessarily characterize government or parliamentary behaviour for all bills, and thus indications of each of these interpretations or responses to compatibility might be apparent within the same parliamentary session.

One approach would reflect government's and parliamentarians' willingness to engage in spirited normative debates about the scope of the right(s) implicated in legislative bills, the seriousness of the possible infringement and its relationship to the legislative objective in question, the justification of the government's reasons for pursuing a bill, or arguments for amendments intended to redress serious rights concerns. Under this scenario, legislative decision-makers would engage in good-faith judgements about how rights principles should guide or constrain the legislative objectives in question in a manner that is not necessarily derivative of or overly influenced by relevant case law.[36] Disagreements about the scope of rights or whether and how they are implicated for any particular legislative bill would occur fairly frequently, as anticipated in Jeremy Waldron's observation that persistent disagreement should be regarded 'as one of the elementary conditions of modern politics'.[37] In these circumstances, the majority principle would ultimately be relied upon to resolve contentious debates; a reflection of what Waldron

[35] This argument borrows from J. Hiebert, 'Governing Like Judges?', in T. Campbell, K.D. Ewing and A. Tomkins (eds.), *The Legal Protection of Human Rights: Sceptical Essays* (Oxford: Oxford University Press, 2011), pp. 40–65; J. Hiebert, 'Governing Under the Human Rights Act: The Limitations of Wishful Thinking', (2012) *Public Law* 27.

[36] Stephen Gardbaum articulates a similar view in his normative prescription for how these bills of rights should influence legislative decision-making. S. Gardbaum, *The New Commonwealth Model of Constitutionalism*, pp. 77–94.

[37] J. Waldron, *The Dignity of Legislation* (Cambridge: Cambridge University Press, 1999), p. 153.

characterizes as a respectful way of governing under the reality of differences of opinion about justice or the common good.[38]

A second possibility would be a more juridically influenced approach in which bureaucratic, governmental and parliamentary deliberations about compatibility are heavily influenced by interpretations of relevant case law, almost as if judges were looking over the shoulders of bureaucrats and politicians when developing and assessing legislative bills. Danny Nicol characterizes this approach as reflecting a culture of compliance, where parliament conceives of its role as that of an 'adjunct of the courts'.[39]

Reliance on case law to assess the merits of legislative initiatives would also resemble what Alec Stone Sweet has observed in France, Germany, Italy and Spain, where apprehension of judicial censure provides a strong incentive for compliant legislative behaviour. Stone Sweet argues that European legislative decision-makers react to the threat that legislation could be invalidated for violating rights by exercising self-restraint, or what has been referred to as auto-limitation.[40] As the prospect of constitutional censure 'hovers over the legislative process', public and political officials have adopted constitutional rules, discursive tools and modes of reasoning to insulate their activities from future constitutional censure. Legislators also express their policy differences in the vocabulary of constitutional judges, in that debates about the merits of policy take the form of debates about constitutional compliance. Thus, as Stone Sweet argues, 'governing with judges means governing like judges'.[41] Another factor that Stone Sweet identifies as influencing political behaviour in the European parliaments which he studied is the capacity of parliamentarians (usually from opposition parties) to utilize abstract review by constitutional courts, which he suggests is a popular and relatively cost-free way for opposition parties to bind the legislative majority and attain their own policy objectives.[42] However, it is important to recognize the

[38] Waldron, *The Dignity of Legislation*, pp. 159–60.

[39] D. Nicol, 'The Human Rights Act and the Politicians', (2004) 24 *Legal Studies* 453.

[40] Alec Stone Sweet uses this term, which he attributes to the earlier work of Favoreau, and which was also used by Chistine Landfried. See L. Favoreau 'Décentralisation et constitution', (1982) 98 *Revue du droit public* 1259; C. Landfried, 'Judicial Policymaking in Germany: The Federal Constitutional Court', (1992) 15 *West European Politics* 50; A Stone Sweet, *Governing with Judges: Constitutional Politics in Europe* (Oxford: Oxford University Press, 2000).

[41] Stone Sweet, *Governing with Judges*, p. 204.

[42] Ibid., pp. 74–75.

significance of how institutional factors influence political behaviour. Neither New Zealand nor the UK authorizes abstract review, and thus parliamentarians lack this opportunity to challenge proposed legislation as a form of political strategy to defeat bills they oppose. Moreover, the incentives to incorporate judicial norms into the legislative process are weaker in the UK than in the European jurisdictions Stone Sweet assesses, and are even weaker yet in New Zealand (where judicial remedial power is even more constrained than in the UK, and which lacks the UK's strong political expectation of compliance with domestic or international judicial norms).

A third possibility would be that government behaviour eschews any form of reasonable attempt to explain or justify legislation from a compatibility perspective, and parliament is either unwilling or incapable of engaging in good-faith debates about how rights guide or constrain legislative decisions. This is most likely to occur either when governments do not anticipate a serious judicial or political challenge for failing to acknowledge, confront or comply with notions of compatibility, or where senior government actors engage in cost–benefit analyses which suggest the anticipated political benefits of non-compliance exceed anticipated political and legal consequences. Failure to engage in reasonable attempts to justify or ensure compliance would reflect an extreme reaction to the challenges presented by a Westminster context, as previously discussed. It would also confirm Tushnet's thesis of the potential for instability of a model that both attempts to address questions of rights yet constrains the scope and effects of judicial remedial power.[43]

The ways in which scholars assess the significance or impact of legislative review will inevitably be influenced by normative views of constitutionalism, and whether these are orientated toward a more juridical or political perspective. Although we acknowledge the difficulty of escaping normative orientations when analysing how bills of rights function, our intent is not to enter into scholarly debates about whether courts or parliament are the better institution to protect rights. Instead, we interpret our mission as the presentation of a qualitative, empirical assessment of the impact of the procedural and substantive changes associated with the political architects of the NZBORA and HRA's attempts to introduce a compatibility-based framework for bureaucratic, governmental and parliamentary assessments of bills. Thus, we do not

[43] M. Tushnet, *Weak Courts.*

suggest that bureaucratic interpretations of relevant case law, ministerial reports on compatibility or JCHR reviews should necessarily be construed as the benchmark for determining whether bills are compatible with protected rights; instead, we focus on whether government is prepared to explain and justify its decisions, the extent to which a compatibility-based framework animates and informs parliamentary debate and, ultimately, whether the legislative decision reflected reasoned deliberations (even when consensus is not achieved) on how a compatibility framework appropriately guides or constrains the legislative bill in question.

Although we focus heavily on the extent to which ministerial reports on compatibility and their subsequent scrutiny by parliament influence parliamentary deliberations, we also recognize the importance of not omitting or discounting less obvious and more subtle ways in which compatibility-based assessments can influence legislative decision-making.[44] The requirement for ministerial reports on compatibility can be expected to precipitate bureaucratic engagement with rights principles to ascertain whether and how legislative initiatives implicate rights. Public servants tend to operate within a rule-bound orientation that accords strong attention to statutory obligations, such as those associated with assessing proposed legislation and advising on compatibility. Moreover, they have professional reputations which they wish to protect, and thus perceptions that the adequacy or expertise of their advice has been questioned not only represent potential embarrassment, but could also undermine good working relationships with their political ministers and staff. This potential vulnerability can arise regardless of whether parliament has a speciality rights committee, because legislative drafters will identify possible compatibility problems. However, it is increased when a specialized and robust rights committee evaluates compatibility issues, which can result in letters or informal questions about a bill's objectives or the choice of means to pursue the initiative. These queries not only pose concerns for public officials' sense of professionalism and reputation; they also potentially enhance workloads because of the need to

[44] We are particularly indebted to Aileen Kavanagh and one of the anonymous reviewers of an earlier draft of a chapter for bringing to our attention that we had underemphasized the significance of less obvious ways in which compatibility-based assessments impact on legislative decision-making. See for example A. Kavanagh, 'The Joint Committee on Human Rights: A Hybrid Breed of Constitutional Watchdog', in Murray Hunt, Hayley Hooper and Paul Yowell (eds.), *Parliament and Human Rights: Redressing the Democratic Deficit* (Oxford: Hart Publishing, 2015).

revisit issues and explain, justify and potentially reassess earlier advice. As we were told in our interviews, public officials are keenly interested in avoiding the prospect of having to explain, justify and possibly revise an opinion on compatibility.

To address the more subtle and less visible ways in which a compatibility framework influences legislative decision-making in the pre-parliamentary phase of a bill's life, we rely heavily on extensive interviews which we conducted with legal and policy officials whose responsibilities entail developing legislation and advising department and officials on possible compatibility problems. Although confidentiality requirements constrain public officials in terms of discussing specific legislative bills, we have been able to gain a clear understanding of how compatibility is generally assessed, how requirements to advise ministers or the Attorney General for statutory reporting purposes have altered policy processes, the kind of influences this advice exerts on policy options, the influences exerted by parliamentary or extra-parliamentary bodies such as the JCHR or the New Zealand Law Commission, the frequency or general nature of political resistance and whether political attitudes to the HRA or NZBORA impact on how legal advice is proffered or framed. Thus, we are able to assess not only the obvious indications of parliamentary deliberation and contestation of ministerial reports, but also the more subtle ways in which compatibility-based concerns help frame and influence government bills.

Our research focus on the significance and consequences of ministerial reports on compatibility leads to the following research questions: How does a pre-legislative focus on compatibility generally influence the development of legislation? How does the requirement to report on compatibility influence government's legislative decisions and parliament's evaluation of bills? In what ways and with what effects do Westminster factors influence the ways in which these bills of rights function? Do institutional variances between these systems affect parliament's capacity or willingness to address compatibility issues or hold government to account for decisions that adversely implicate rights?

The methodology we employ to address these questions centres on analysing the bureaucratic practices that relate to rights-based compatibility scrutiny and the nature of ministerial judgement about compatibility. We examine institutional changes in the policy development process within the bureaucracy, the role of policy and legal advisors, the role of lead departments and ministers with special responsibilities in relation to the bill of rights and institutional and rule changes within parliament that were introduced to accommodate the introduction of these parliamentary bills of rights.

This aspect of the research comprises more than 70 open-ended interviews with public and political officials,[45] which were conducted between 2004 and 2012, and which hereon will be referred to as Interviews. Questions asked of policy officials and legal advisors included:

- What kind of training was introduced to understand how the bill of rights relates to the department or agency's responsibilities?
- Was this training adequate?
- How has the NZBORA or HRA altered the processes or considerations for assessing legislative proposals?
- How is the NZBORA or HRA interpreted at the departmental or agency level?
- Are those evaluating policy knowledgeable about the bill of rights?
- How is compatibility determined?
- Who determines whether proposed legislation is compatible?
- Do lawyers dominate determinations of compatibility?
- Are determinations of compatibility a task that only lawyers can or should perform?
- Do policy officials participate in judgements about compatibility?
- Would the policy process be improved if more departmental officials (non-lawyers in particular) saw their role as requiring assessments of compatibility?
- How relevant is case law when determining the meaning and scope of rights?
- How difficult is it to determine whether a legislative initiative is consistent with case law?
- Does guidance on compatibility change as case law changes?
- Do other department officials or ministers resist advice about compatibility?
- How is resistance expressed?
- How much discretion do ministers have to proceed with an initiative that is inconsistent with case law?
- Does political criticism of the bill of rights affect policy evaluation or assessments of compatibility?

[45] These interviews were conducted under the condition of anonymity. However, those parliamentarians to whom we refer by name waived this condition.

- Are legal advisors pressured implicitly or explicitly to provide advice that allows a minister or the Attorney General to claim compatibility, even if so doing challenges their professional judgement?
- Will ministers or the Attorney General claim that a bill is compatible in the face of contrary legal advice?
- How have criteria or processes for assessing and advising on compatibility changed as the bill of rights has evolved?

In the UK, questions also include:

- Will a minister proceed to cabinet and sponsor a bill that would require a report of incompatibility?
- Do departments/ministers shop around for more favourable legal advice on compatibility?
- How influential are JCHR reports?
- Does anticipation of a JCHR report encourage a more robust approach to advising on compatibility?
- What explains whether JCHR reports influence government behaviour?
- How likely is government to change its assessment of compatibility and/or consider amendments following a critical JCHR report?
- What explains the willingness or reluctance of government to revise its assessment of compatibility following a negative JCHR report?
- What accounts for differences of opinion between government advisors and the JCHR on questions of compatibility?

In the UK we also interviewed parliamentarians and advisors who have served on the JCHR, which regularly assesses ministerial claims of compatibility and reports to parliament on whether legislative bills implicate rights in an adverse manner. Among the questions we asked are:

- Why did the committee decide to interpret its broad remit to focus so heavily on the issue of compatibility?
- To what extent does the committee engage with policy officials about government initiatives before legislative bills are drafted?
- Does the committee have sufficient time to review bills?
- Does the committee divide along partisan lines?
- Are there tensions between members from the Commons and those from the Lords?
- How do members assess compatibility?
- Do members who are also lawyers dominate the proceedings?

- Is the committee's focus sufficiently or excessively legalistic?
- Are ministerial reports of compatibility sufficiently compelling?
- Would it be beneficial if ministerial reports were more substantive?
- What kinds of arguments or information would be helpful for the JCHR?
- Do departments take the committee's work seriously?
- Does parliament take the committee's reports seriously?
- Do committee members use reports for partisan purposes?
- Are some departments more responsive to committee reports than others, and if so which ones?
- What are the most significant challenges the committee incurs in terms of how it conducts its review?
- Is the committee effective?
- How is effectiveness evaluated?
- What changes to the committee's procedures would be beneficial?
- Is government taking the HRA more seriously as the HRA evolves?

In New Zealand, we interviewed former Prime Minister Geoffrey Palmer, who conceptualized the NZBORA while in opposition, introduced it in 1985 as Minister of Justice in the fourth Labour government and oversaw its passage as Prime Minister in 1990. Although New Zealand does not have a specialized parliamentary committee such as the JCHR, we interviewed parliamentarians on the Justice and Electoral Select Committee, and the Law and Order Select Committee. In addition, we interviewed two Attorney Generals who served in the fifth Labour government, Margaret Wilson (1999–2005) and Michael Cullen (2006–2008), as well as Christopher Finlayson during his time as Shadow Attorney General, before becoming Attorney General.

We utilize government documents, parliamentary committee reports and House of Commons debates on legislative bills that raise significant and substantial questions about rights compatibility. Finally, we rely on secondary sources such as media reports of speeches or comments that relate to how political actors have interpreted their responsibilities under their respective bills of rights.

This institutional focus is complemented with process tracing that considers the passage of key legislative initiatives which raise serious questions about compatibility with rights. In short, we are interested in the impact of these political efforts on altering the norms of legislative decision-making. Examples include greater attention to rights-compliant ways of achieving a government's legislative agenda in the pre-parliamentary phase of policy development, governmental willingness to acknowledge and explain the reasons for pursuing bills that raise serious concerns about rights and parliamentarians' willingness and capacity to hold government responsible to justify legislation from the perspective of its consistency with rights and, where consensus is lacking, to engage in good-faith debates about the scope of rights or how rights appropriately guide legislative decisions.

In New Zealand, the policy debates we examine are drawn primarily from key government initiatives that the Attorney General reported to parliament under section 7 of the NZBORA. In addition, because of the importance of confidence and supply agreements under MMP, we also consider government bills that are based on agreements with minor parties, or members' bills introduced by parliamentarians who belong to parties in multi-party governing arrangements. We focus primarily on government bills that have triggered section 7 reports, as distinct from private members' bills, because a core ideal associated with these bills of rights is to strengthen parliament's capacity to hold government to account for decisions that implicate rights in an adverse manner. Other important reasons for emphasizing government rather than private member bills are the following: first, they represent the large majority of bills passed by parliament; second, the government's commitment to the passage of its own bills, as well as those of coalition partners or parties in formal confidence and supply agreements make these ideal scenarios to evaluate the impact of MMP on this broader attempt to alter the norms of legislative decision-making. However, we also consider one non-governmental bill (prisoner voting), which allows us to examine whether more independent rights-based deliberations occur in the absence of the potentially constraining effects of the party whip.

The policy issues examined in New Zealand centre on changes in criminal policy and consider the competition between two policy discourses that have attempted to co-exist since 1990: a rights-based discourse initiated by the Attorney General when reporting to parliament under section 7 of the NZBORA, and penal populism, which remains the dominant policy discourse in the area of criminal reform despite the introduction of the NZBORA in 1990. More importantly, the 1999 Citizen Initiated Referendum on criminal reform has generally been used by all subsequent governments to validate a victim-focused approach to criminal policy. The following issues are considered in order to understand the dominance of penal populism despite the introduction of the NZBORA: sentencing and parole reform, such as the 'three strikes' policy introduced by New Zealand National as part of its supply and confidence agreement with ACT New Zealand; extended parole supervision orders for child sex offenders; the creation of a compulsory DNA bank for individuals whom the police intend to arrest for a range of offences; the classification of 'party pills' or 'legal highs' as controlled substances under the Misuse of Drugs Act 1975; and finally, the blanket disenfranchisement of all prisoners in correctional facilities.

Our choice of case studies in the UK reflects three principal considerations. First, we select reasonably high-profile and contentious issues that seriously test governmental and parliamentary responses to the idea of legislating within a compatibility-based framework. Second, we believe it is appropriate to consider contemporary debates that are fairly common in western liberal democracies and which raise fundamental issues of human rights. Third, we trace the evolution of the HRA to consider whether and how more experience with the practices of reporting on compatibility have influenced the nature of ministerial reports or parliamentary scrutiny. In the UK, the policy issues include anti-terrorist measures, the introduction of closed material procedures in civil legal proceedings (CMP), restrictions on political advertising, the recognition of civil partnerships and the subsequent decision to introduce same sex marriage, and the creation of identity cards and a national registry scheme. We also look at how government and parliament have responded to pressure to enact remedial measures after the European Court of Human Rights ruled that the UK decision to deny all prisoners the right to vote violates the European Convention of Human Rights.

Organization of the book

We begin our analysis by focusing on New Zealand, which we assess in Chapters 2–5. Chapter 2 examines the origins of the NZBORA. We argue that it is apt to conceptualize the NZBORA as a parliamentary bill of rights because it was designed within the parliamentary setting, evolved as a result of the party and parliamentary dynamics of the fourth Labour government and was amended because of reluctance to jettison parliamentary supremacy. Ironically, the NZBORA was a product of the power dynamic that Palmer sought to check: prime ministerial dominance of the parliamentary arena. This chapter also considers the important institutional changes within the bureaucracy and how bills are evaluated for consistency with protected rights. The emergence of 'BORA vetting' by the Ministry of Justice and Crown Law Office ensures that all bills are assessed in light of the NZBORA before their introduction to parliament.

While this exercise differs from the process in Canada, where a prime motivation is based on risk-based assessments of the likelihood that legislation will be declared unconstitutional, BORA vetting in New Zealand is nevertheless modelled after the Canadian approach to reasonable limits under s. 1 of the Canadian Charter, despite New Zealand courts' inability to declare inconsistent legislation to be invalid. Further, bureaucratic risk assessment relies on domestic and Commonwealth judicial decisions when determining whether breaches of the NZBORA are demonstrably justified under section 5. It is these bureaucratic assessments that the Attorney General relies on when deciding whether to report to parliament under section 7 of the NZBORA, which suggests a degree of judicialization despite the absence of judicial remedies in the NZBORA.

Chapter 3 focuses on the changing parliamentary dynamic since the first MMP election in 1996, and the challenges created for substantive engagement of the Attorney General's reporting duty under section 7 of the NZBORA. As we argue, important rule changes to ensure government stability in a multi-party parliament have complicated the ability of parliamentarians to scrutinize government bills once the Attorney General has alerted them to potential incompatibilities. Despite political willingness on the part of the Attorney General to acknowledge that bills appear incompatible with NZBORA, these political statements do not have the effect on parliamentary deliberations that Palmer had expected. Every Attorney General since 1990 has approached the reporting duty in a robust fashion: 65 reports have been issued to parliament, almost half of which involve government bills. Yet parliament has passed most of these bills without amendments to address compatibility issues. The disconnect between robust reporting and limited parliamentary engagement is largely explained by the independent status of the Attorney General, who has a professional and statutory responsibility to dispense section 7 free from party or partisan consideration. However, as members of disciplined caucuses, parliamentarians are constrained by the policy choices of the leadership team and, unlike the Attorney General, do not approach the NZBORA as independent political actors. MMP has reinforced important party and parliamentary dynamics, as the need to construct multi-party governing arrangements prevents parliamentarians on the government side from engaging government bills that are accompanied by a section 7 report.

Chapter 4 presents two case studies: amendments to the Misuse of Drugs Act 1975, and the issue of prisoner disenfranchisement that emerged as a members' bill in 2010. In particular, this chapter examines the Misuse of Drugs Act 1975 and the passage of key amendments to this act despite the Attorney General, the New Zealand Supreme Court, the New Zealand Law Commission and the New Zealand Human Rights Commission raising serious questions about these amendments' compatibility with the NZBORA. In this sense, the Misuse of Drugs Act 1975 is a case study of the possibility of rights-based dialogue under a parliamentary bill of rights, as well as an example of the serious institutional constraints that prevent select committees from functioning as mechanisms of parliamentary oversight when the ministry introduces legislation with potential compatibility issues. Similarly, the issue of prisoner disenfranchisement demonstrates the importance of the party vote for a members' bill, and the significance of discretion under the Standing Orders as a way to prevent effective parliamentary oversight. While the select committee process under MMP is perhaps fertile ground for rights-based scrutiny of the ministry's legislative agenda, given that MMP has produced either minority coalition or minority single-party governments, we argue that the changes in the parliamentary Standing Orders introduced to accommodate MMP have been counterproductive to parliamentary oversight of the ministry's legislative agenda. Indeed, reports of the Attorney General under section 7 of the NZBORA in relation to the Misuse of Drugs Act 1975 did not see the Health Committee engage the substance of these reports, nor did it see the revision of the amendments to ensure greater compatibility with the NZBORA.

Chapter 5 considers a series of government bills introduced into parliament that were reported on by the Attorney General under section 7 of the NZBORA. Many of the bills are part of confidence and supply agreements negotiated with minor parties, and few have been amended to ensure compatibility with the NZBORA. In this chapter, we argue that government bills passed despite a section 7 report, or those based on confidence and supply agreements, clearly demonstrate the difficulty of promoting robust parliamentary evaluation of bills in the face of strong party discipline and limited incentives for parliamentarians to challenge the party leadership. In addition, we argue that the policy context is important, as is the rights-bearer in question. As the section 7 reports considered involve criminal policy changes that restrict the rights of the accused, the incarcerated or those under parole conditions, parliamentarians have not been receptive to the section 7 concerns raised by the Attorney General. As we argue, penal populism is the dominant policy discourse in criminal policy and negates the willingness of parliamentarians to engage the NZBORA issues raised by a section 7 report.

Thus, the desire to have a bill of rights-inspired policy discourse occur when the Attorney General reports under section 7 of the NZBORA has proven difficult in the criminal policy context.

In Chapters 6–9 we shift focus to the UK's Human Rights Act. Chapter 6 discusses the political reasons for adopting the HRA, and the bold political claims that the prudential structure of the HRA will significantly alter legislative decision-making by ensuring that a focus on compatibility with Convention rights becomes a fundamental factor in legislative decision-making. Political proponents defended the HRA as an effective rights-protecting instrument that, they suggested, would fundamentally transform bureaucratic and political assumptions and practices.

Chapter 7 analyses internal processes for evaluating whether bills are compatible with Convention rights and how government has broached its reporting obligation. We argue that the HRA is having a substantial impact on how bills are evaluated, both to aid ministers in their statutory reporting obligation to report on compatibility and to provide government with the necessary advice for managing the risks associated with possible judicial censure. Although government may have a strong incentive to avoid unnecessary litigation, ministers and cabinet exercise discretionary judgement about how much risk they are prepared to tolerate and almost always report that bills are compatible with Convention rights. However, the reporting obligation on compatibility has not been interpreted to convey the level of risk the government is prepared to accept, and thus parliament is heavily dependent upon independent scrutiny by the JCHR to advise it as to whether and why bills raise serious concerns of compatibility.

Chapters 8 and 9 shift the focus from the pre-legislative stage of compatibility review to the parliamentary arena, and examine how the political and institutional characteristics of the UK parliamentary system constrain legislative rights review. Although the bills we examined prompted rigorous and critical review by the JCHR, the government has incurred weak pressure from the House of Commons to explain or justify its claims of compatibility. Party leaders and whips have not incorporated an emphasis on compatibility into their political strategies for evaluating legislation. Thus, while opposition parties continue to define their role as one of demonstrating why they are the preferable alternative to government, compatibility-based assessments are neither part of their political vocabulary nor strategic considerations they employ. Although the House of Lords has demonstrated considerably stronger interest in both following up on JCHR concerns and promoting rights-improving amendments, government is often able to call upon its majority in the Commons (or, in the case of the Coalition government, a majority of the members from the two parties) to defeat Lords-based amendments. We also find that even in those circumstances where parliamentary debates in the House of Commons engage in rights-based arguments, the HRA itself is generally peripheral to these debates, as members emphasize civil liberties without explicit reference to Convention rights or to the HRA's emphasis on compatibility to justify their arguments.

We conclude that the introduction of legislative rights review in the NZBORA and HRA has significantly influenced the ways in which public officials broach policy development. Ministerial statements of compatibility have altered the development of legislation in a substantial manner. The requirement to confront how legislative bills implicate rights has generated greater awareness among policy officials of the importance of considering what evidence or reasons justify legislative objectives that potentially implicate rights in an adverse manner and of utilizing a rights-based framework when thinking about different ways of accomplishing a legislative objective. This focus is reinforced in the UK because of the practice of informal conversations between the JCHR's legal advisor and assistants and policy officials during the formative stages of developing legislation. The public officials we interviewed in both countries were remarkably consistent in their acknowledgement that the earlier rights-based considerations are addressed, the easier it is to conceive of ways to advise a department or minster on how legislative initiatives could be accomplished in a rights-compliant manner.

Although policy evaluation processes have changed because of the statutory obligation to advise parliament on compatibility, we conclude that it would be a serious mistake to assume that compatibility-reporting obligations have discouraged governments from knowingly promoting bills that may not be compatible with protected rights.

In New Zealand, contrary to Palmer's expectation that the requirement to report to parliament when bills are not consistent with rights would discourage government from willingly or frequently introducing inconsistent legislation, governments have not shied away from approving bills accompanied by an incompatibility report. Neither apprehension of parliamentary criticism nor serious concerns of judicial censure operate as strong deterrents to the promotion of bills that the Attorney General has identified as raising serious compatibility concerns which warrant a section 7 report.

In the UK, notwithstanding government and ministers' strong reluctance to acknowledge an inability to claim that bills are consistent with rights, an affirmative claim that a legislative bill is compatible with Convention rights is not necessarily a good indicator of compatibility. These reports generally mask the fact that the government has exercised substantial discretionary judgement about how much risk it is prepared to tolerate, which is not disclosed to parliament. Moreover, the relatively perfunctory statement of compatibility is rarely accompanied by substantive arguments or evidence to justify proceeding with a bill in light of its serious adverse implications for protected rights.

We argue that a key reason why these compatibility reports have not been strong deterrents for New Zealand or UK governments' pursuit of legislative bills that raise serious questions of compatibility is that attempts to use the NZBORA and HRA as instruments for altering the norms of legislative decision-making have had little impact on the substance or nature of political behaviour or parliamentary debates. Party leaders have not adopted a compatibility-based lens for assessing bills in their perpetual efforts to demonstrate why their party is the preferable alternative to government, and thus MPs regularly ignore section 7 reports (New Zealand) or JCHR reports (UK) and fail to press ministers to explain why they believe bills should be passed or amended to redress compatibility concerns. In the UK, although the House of Lords often passes rights-improving amendments, upon the bill's return to the Commons, government members will frequently support their leaders' missions to defeat or undermine these amendments.

The evolution of legislative rights review demonstrates a fundamental contradiction between the reasons for these bills of rights and assumptions as to how they were intended to operate. One of the key reasons why political reformers in both New Zealand and the UK looked to a bill of rights was to address concerns that parliament had become too weak to hold the executive to account. These bills of rights rely heavily on political willingness to enforce their provisions. Yet neither the NZBORA nor the HRA have augmented parliament's power vis-à-vis the executive; nor have they altered the dynamics of how parliament functions.

PART I

The New Zealand Bill of Rights Act 1990

2

Political Origins of the New Zealand Bill of Rights Act

The adoption of the New Zealand Bill of Rights Act 1990 (NZBORA) by the fourth Labour government (1984–1990) demonstrates the critical importance of a political actor – in this case, Geoffrey Palmer – functioning as a constitutional entrepreneur driving the bill of rights project, as well as the political constraints that determine the structure of the document ultimately accepted by parliament.[1] The attempt to introduce a bill of rights began as a commitment of New Zealand National in 1960 and was presented to parliament in 1963. However, this reform was abandoned in 1964 when the Constitution Reform Committee unanimously recommended that parliament should not proceed with the draft bill.[2] While the introduction of a bill of rights was initially viewed as a necessary institutional reform to complement New Zealand's unicameral parliament following the abolition of the Legislative Council in 1951,[3] the debate would remain of limited importance throughout the 1970s.

As argued by David Erdos, the trigger event that reignited the bill of rights debate in New Zealand, and convinced former sceptics such as Geoffrey Palmer and Kenneth Keith of its value,[4] was the prime ministership of Robert Muldoon, who headed the New Zealand National government (1975–1984) in the period immediately preceding the fourth Labour government.[5] Shortly before entering parliament in 1979, Palmer

[1] J. Kelly, 'Judicial and Political Review as Limited Insurance: The Functioning of the New Zealand Bill of Rights Act in "Hard" Cases', (2011) 49 *Commonwealth & Comparative Politics*, 299–300.

[2] D. Erdos, *Delegating Rights Protection: The Rise of Bills of Rights in the Westminster World* (Oxford: Oxford University Press, 2010), pp. 87–92.

[3] G. Palmer, *New Zealand's Constitution in Crisis* (Dunedin: McIndoe, 1992), pp. 45–7.

[4] G. Palmer, 'A Bill of Rights for New Zealand?', in K.J. Keith (ed.), *Essays on Human Rights* (Wellington: Sweet & Maxwell Ltd., 1968), pp. 125–31.

[5] D. Erdos, 'Aversive Constitutionalism in the Westminster World: The Genesis of the New Zealand Bill of Rights Act 1990', (2007) 5 *International Journal of Constitutional Law* 362.

published *Unbridled Power*, which focused on the growing concentration of power in the Office of the Prime Minister and the corresponding marginalization of parliament as an institution. Although the trend of prime ministerial dominance preceded Muldoon, *Unbridled Power* contended that it reached unprecedented levels during this period, characterized by Muldoon serving simultaneously as Prime Minister, Minister of Finance and Leader of the House during the government's first three years in office.[6] In response to 'Muldoonism', Palmer advocated constitutional and parliamentary reform to address what Erdos has since labelled 'aversive constitutionalism'.[7]

Erdos contends that the political origins of bills of rights in Westminster democracies such as Canada, New Zealand and the United Kingdom, are the result of negative – or aversive – experiences of political parties during periods in opposition,[8] and the belief that the incumbent government has failed to recognize established constitutional boundaries on their political authority.[9] In the case of New Zealand, the fourth Labour government implemented a statutory bill of rights in 1990 largely to prevent a reoccurrence of the authoritarian approach taken by Muldoon.[10] While the 1984 Labour party election manifesto committed the party to an entrenched bill of rights as supreme law, the NZBORA would be enacted as ordinary law because of widespread opposition within the Labour parliamentary party, New Zealand National and large segments of society, including the New Zealand Law Society, to an entrenched bill of rights. This opposition emanated largely from concerns about judicial empowerment and the implications for parliamentary supremacy as the dominant constitutional principle in New

Alternative theories include Ginsburg's 'judicial review as insurance policy': T. Ginsburg, *Judicial Review in New Democracies* (Cambridge: Cambridge University Press, 2003). As well, Hirschl argues that judicialization is an attempt to preserve power by temporal political elites, which he labels as 'hegemonic preservation theory': R. Hirschl, *Toward Juristocracy: The Origins and Consequences of the New Constitutionalism* (Harvard: Harvard University Press, 2004).

6 G. Palmer, 'Muldoon and the Constitution', in M. Clark (ed.), *Muldoon Revisited* (Palmerston North: Dunedin Press, 2004), p. 175.

7 G. Palmer, *Unbridled Power: An Interpretation of New Zealand's Constitution and Government* (Melbourne: Oxford University Press, 1979).

8 Erdos, 'Aversive Constitutionalism in the Westminster World', 361.

9 D. Erdos, 'Elite Supply 'Blockages' and the Failure of National Bill of Rights Initiatives in Australia: A Comparative Westminster Analysis', (2008) 46 *Commonwealth & Comparative Politics* 351.

10 Palmer, 'Muldoon and the Constitution', pp. 175–79.

Zealand if a bill of rights was enacted as supreme law.[11] Although the introduction of a constitutional bill of rights was the centrepiece of Palmer's prescription for unbridled power, Labour's constitutional agenda was much broader and included the reform of parliamentary select committees, regular parliamentary sittings, limitations on government by regulation and a review of the single member plurality electoral system.[12]

As will be argued in later chapters, the reporting duty of the Attorney General under section 7 demonstrates the weakness of the NZBORA when the cabinet is prepared to legislate notwithstanding the bill of rights. Indeed, despite Palmer's contention that parliament would rarely (if ever) pass legislation that was accompanied by a section 7 report, the Attorney General's reporting duty has had a limited impact on government bills once they are introduced, as parliament has largely passed such legislation without amendment.[13] Indeed, the Attorney General has reported on 32 government bills (1990 to 2014),[14] of which 28 have been passed into law, and only two bills have been amended to address NZBORA issues raised by the Attorney General.[15] As most section 7 reports have occurred in policy areas where parliament is least likely to seek amendments to ensure NZBORA compliance – sentencing provisions, parole reform, criminal policy, drug policy and prisoner disenfranchisement – the high political cost of defending the rights of the accused or those incarcerated has undermined the Attorney General's reporting duty as an effective mechanism of parliamentary oversight.

The constitutional and political origins of the NZBORA, as well as the functioning of judicial and political rights review in a 'weak-form' system,[16] are considered in this chapter. Unlike the Canadian Charter of Rights and Freedoms, which is a constitutional bill of rights that allows

[11] Erdos, *Delegating Rights Protection*, pp. 94–98.

[12] G. Skene, 'Parliamentary Reform', in J. Boston and M. Holland (eds.), *The Fourth Labour Government: Radical Politics in New Zealand* (Auckland: Oxford University Press, 1987), pp. 72–74.

[13] A. Geddis, 'The Comparative Irrelevance of the NZBORA to Legislative Practice', (2009) 43 *New Zealand Universities Law Review* 469–70.

[14] The last government bill considered with a section 7 report is the Parole (Extended Supervision Orders) Amendment Bill 2014, introduced by New Zealand National (17 April 2014).

[15] Four bills are presently progressing through parliament (see Appendix 1 for details).

[16] M. Tushnet, *Weak Courts, Strong Rights: Judicial Review and Social Welfare Rights in Comparative Constitutional Law* (Princeton: Princeton University Press, 2008), pp. 25–27.

for judicial remedy of rights violations, the NZBORA is a statutory or 'parliamentary' bill of rights that is enforced principally through parliamentary oversight mechanisms.[17] To consider the origins and functioning of this parliamentary bill of rights, this chapter is divided into three sections. The first section considers the modern bill of rights debate in New Zealand and focuses on the Muldoon era (1975–84) and the Labour governments of David Lange (1984–89) and Geoffrey Palmer (1989–90). The influence of Palmer, as the principal constitutional entrepreneur driving the bill of rights project, cannot be overstated,[18] although this section also considers the important parliamentary constraints that prevented Palmer from achieving his preference for an entrenched bill of rights as supreme law.

Part 2 considers the bureaucratic response to the NZBORA and the importance of the Bill of Rights Act (BORA) vetting that occurs before legislation is introduced into parliament. Focusing on the roles of the Ministry of Justice and the Crown Law Office, this section argues that an important benefit of the NZBORA has been a reformed policy process that attempts to address rights issues before legislation is introduced into parliament. However, a negative BORA vet by the Ministry of Justice or Crown Law simply requires the Attorney General to issue a section 7 report under the NZBORA, which does not prevent the introduction of a bill into parliament or its subsequent passage without amendments. The final section considers the judicial response to the NZBORA, as well as the institutional environment of the judiciary in New Zealand, which reinforces this rights instrument as a parliamentary enforced bill of rights.

Although this study focuses on the limitations of parliamentary reporting duties in statutory instruments such as section 7 of the NZBORA in the context of government bills, as well as limited engagement of statutes by the judiciary, it is acknowledged that judicial review involving the conduct of the police has resulted in important safeguards under the NZBORA.[19] Indeed, as Andrew Geddis has remarked, 'The claim advanced here – that the NZBORA has had little or no effect on Parliament's activities as lawmaker – is not the same as a claim that the

[17] J. Hiebert, 'Interpreting a Bill of Rights: The Importance of Legislative Rights Review', (2005) 35 *British Journal of Political Science* 240.

[18] A. Butler and P. Butler, *The New Zealand Bill of Rights Act: A Commentary* (Wellington: LexisNexis NZ, 2005), pp. 24–36; S. Levine, 'Bills of Rights in Parliamentary Settings: New Zealand and Israeli Experience', (1991) *Parliamentary Affairs* 337, 346.

[19] K.J. Keith, 'Concerning Change': The Adoption and Implementation of the New Zealand Bill of Rights Act 1990', (2000) 31 *Victoria University of Wellington Law Review* 735.

NZBORA either is toothless or represents no inflation in the relative power of the judiciary in other respects'.[20] Thus, the NZBORA has had an important impact on criminal process governed by common law principles, though a negligible effect on legislative outcomes after the Attorney General reports under section 7 of the NZBORA in the context of government bills.[21] While the streamlining of BORA vetting is now an established part of the legislative process, it has nonetheless proven limited protection when the cabinet or parliament legislates against unpopular rights-bearers such as the accused, the imprisoned or those groups disadvantaged by electoral politics.

I. The fourth Labour government and the bill of rights debate

The defeat of Muldoon in 1984 heralded the beginning of the fourth Labour government and its agenda of political reform under the direction of Deputy Leader and Minister of Justice Geoffrey Palmer. Although the concept of a bill of rights had been part of the constitutional discourse since 1960 and was formally part of the Labour party manifesto in 1984, according to Palmer, 'It must be said that there was no great enthusiasm for it by Labour MPs then or later.'[22] Convinced that there was a political market for a bill of rights, as 'there was a distinct feeling that the Muldoon government had been high-handed and repressive from a constitutional point of view', Palmer established a working group within the Ministry of Justice to draft a position paper on a New Zealand Bill of Rights Act.[23]

In 1985 Palmer presented *A Bill of Rights for New Zealand – A White Paper* to parliament, which represented the initial attempt at fulfilling Labour's 1984 election commitment. The bill of rights project was viewed within the Lange ministry as largely Palmer's brief: as former cabinet minister Michael Bassett has noted, 'few people demanded it, and nobody else in cabinet was an enthusiast'.[24] Indeed, the justification for a bill of

[20] Geddis, 'The Comparative Irrelevance of the NZBORA', 469–70.

[21] A. Geddis, 'Inter-institutional "Rights Dialogue" Under the New Zealand Bill of Rights Act', in T. Campbell, K.D. Ewing and A. Tomkins (eds.), *The Legal Protection of Human Rights: Sceptical Essays* (Oxford: Oxford University Press, 2011), pp. 98–100; H. McQueen, 'Parliamentary Business: A Critical Review of Parliament's Role in New Zealand's Law-Making Process', (2010) 32 *Auckland University Law Review* 15–16.

[22] Palmer, *New Zealand's Constitution in Crisis*, p. 52.

[23] Palmer, *New Zealand's Constitution in Crisis*, p. 53.

[24] M. Bassett, *Working with David: Inside the Lange Cabinet* (Auckland: Hachette Livre NZ, 2008), p. 189.

rights presented by Palmer suggests a tone of aversive constitutionalism and the belief that the excesses of Muldoonism required fundamental constitutional reform:

> The adoption of a Bill of Rights in New Zealand will place new limits on the powers of Government. It will guarantee the protection of fundamental values and freedoms. It will restrain the abuse of power by the Executive branch of Government and Parliament itself . . . It will provide a minimum set of standards to which public decision making must conform. In that sense a Bill of Rights is a mechanism by which governments are made more accountable by being held to a set of standards.[25]

Recognizing that a bill of rights as supreme law represented a major constitutional change and not simply a gradual one in the relationship between parliament and the courts, Palmer attempted to temper criticism that parliamentary supremacy would be displaced by judicial supremacy. Commenting on the ability of the courts to invalidate legislation as inconsistent with a bill of rights, the Minister of Justice cautioned: 'It is an important change but too much should not be made of it. Courts will only infrequently declare provisions in acts of parliament contrary to the Bill of Rights.'[26]

Palmer attempted to reconcile an entrenched bill of rights with the dominant constitutional principle of parliamentary supremacy, which he argued had been displaced by prime ministerial dominance under Muldoon – a bill of rights, according to Palmer, could ensure that parliament, and not the cabinet, was the supreme political institution in New Zealand. Specifically, the bill of rights project was justified as one of parliamentary reinvigoration, and thus consistent with Labour's broader project of institutional reform spearheaded by Palmer:

> In practical terms, a Bill of Rights is a most important set of messages to the machinery of Government itself. It points to the fact that certain sorts of laws should not be passed, that certain actions should not be engaged in by Government. In that way a Bill of Rights provides a set of navigation lights for the whole process of Government to observe. And in the end I believe that will be the greatest contribution a Bill of Rights will make to improving our system of government.[27]

[25] Parliament of New Zealand 1985, *A Bill of Rights for New Zealand – A White Paper* (Wellington: Government Printers), p. 5.

[26] *A Bill of Rights for New Zealand – A White Paper*, p. 6.

[27] Ibid.

The 1985 White Paper represents Palmer's preferred bill of rights, though the Minister of Justice indicated that it was simply a position paper, and that the Lange government would be very receptive to amendments to ensure a bill of rights with broad public acceptance: '[e]veryone involved in this issue must understand that the Government has no particular commitment to any particular provisions in this Bill of Rights ... Nothing has been set in concrete.'[28] The draft New Zealand Bill of Rights was to be established as supreme law: as Article 1 specified, 'any law (including existing laws) inconsistent with this Bill shall, to the extent of the inconsistency, be of no effect.'[29] In addition, the Treaty of Waitangi would be entrenched and included as Article 4 of the New Zealand Bill of Rights, thus constitutionalizing the status and position of the Māori people in the constitutional setting. Similar to the Canadian Charter of Rights, the New Zealand Bill of Rights would have an explicit limitations clause (Article 3), where 'The rights and freedoms contained in this Bill of Rights may be subject to only such reasonable limits prescribed by law as can be demonstrably justified in a free and democratic society.'[30] To emphasize the important judicial role in a supreme law bill of rights, Article 25 authorized judicial remedies for rights violations, as individuals 'may apply to a court of competent jurisdiction to obtain such remedies as the court considers appropriate and just in the circumstances'.[31] Finally, the 1985 White Paper would entrench the New Zealand Bill of Rights, as it established only two mechanisms for its repeal or amendment (Article 28): first, an express declaration for its repeal or amendment passed by 75 percent of the members of the House of Representatives; second, a simple majority vote in a national referendum conducted during an election campaign.[32]

The 1985 White Paper provided extensive justification for the need for a supreme bill of rights, as well as lengthy discussions on the preferred judicial approach to the NZBORA. In this sense, it attempted to clearly establish the framers' intention to set out a procedural bill of rights that would avoid the dangers of judicial activism and the paradox of liberal constitutionalism associated with the Canadian Charter of Rights and Freedoms.[33] The principal justification for an entrenched bill of rights

[28] *A Bill of Rights for New Zealand – A White Paper*, pp. 6–7. [29] Ibid., p. 10.
[30] Ibid., p. 11. [31] Ibid., p. 15. [32] Ibid., p. 16.
[33] C. Manfredi, *Judicial Power and the Charter: Canada and the Paradox of Liberal Constitutionalism*, 2nd edition (Toronto: Oxford University Press, 2001), pp. 21–4.

provided by Palmer centred on the limited checks on executive power in the New Zealand parliamentary setting: 'The power of the Government, alone and through Parliament, without the restraint or even the delay which would come from a second chamber, is enormous.'[34] For Palmer, an entrenched bill of rights would facilitate accountable and democratic government by placing procedural limitations on the Prime Minister and cabinet, while leaving parliament free to decide the substance of public policy, which would not be the domain of judicial review: 'For the most part it would not control the *substance* of the law and of the policy which would continue to be elaborated in, and administered by, present and future parliaments and governments.'[35]

Section 6 of the White Paper discusses the functioning of the bill of rights and the new role envisioned for the judiciary in enforcing a supreme law document. While the White Paper acknowledged that it contemplated a new judicial role, as '[t]here is no denying that to give the judges power to declare an Act of Parliament invalid does constitute a fundamental change in our constitutional arrangements',[36] it suggested that this judicial role was not absolute and was largely tempered by Article 3, which allows parliament to impose reasonable limitations on rights and freedoms and to disagree with judicial positions:

> In a great many cases where controversial issues arise for determination, there is no 'right' answer. The action taken by the Government of the day will depend upon its own political persuasions, and its assessments as to where the balance of the public interest lies. It is the very essence of democracy that it allows for people to hold differing views on controversial issues, and for the democratically elected Government of the day to adopt a standpoint thereon but for which of course it must take responsibility in the normal way at the next election. The basic test stated in Article 3 of the Bill of Rights means that in most cases the courts will leave it to Parliament to define the public interest, and to enact legislation encapsulating its decision.[37]

As such, the 1985 White Paper was developed in the context of Palmer's concern with unbridled power in the New Zealand parliamentary setting, his desire to address it through constitutional reform including, but not limited to, a supreme law bill of rights and his argument that the principles of parliamentary supremacy, in most cases, could be preserved despite the entrenchment of a bill of rights. In effect, Palmer argued for the need

[34] *A Bill of Rights for New Zealand – A White Paper*, p. 27. [35] Ibid., p. 28.
[36] Ibid., p. 40. [37] Ibid., p. 45.

to contain unbridled *executive* power and to prevent unbridled *judicial* power.

Interim report of the Justice and Law Reform Select Committee

Once the White Paper was presented to parliament in April 1985 by then Minister of Justice Geoffrey Palmer, it was sent to the Justice and Law Reform Select Committee, which held hearings over two years and presented an interim report in July 1987. The select committee would present a final report in October 1988; this was followed by the New Zealand Bill of Rights' introduction by Geoffrey Palmer as Prime Minister in October 1989, Palmer having succeeded David Lange as leader.[38] In many ways, the leadership transition from Lange to Palmer is the critical event in the modern bill of rights debate, as opposition within the Labour parliamentary party was significant, which prevented Palmer from overcoming internal and external opposition to the 1985 White Paper. Former cabinet minister Michael Bassett commented on the importance of Palmer's elevation to the premiership, as it revived the bill of rights as a viable political project: 'The bill was put aside, and it only re-emerged in emasculated form once Palmer became Prime Minister.'[39] Similarly, Paul Rishworth notes that the bill of rights did not become a central political objective of the fourth Labour government until Palmer replaced Lange as Prime Minister: 'with Geoffrey Palmer as Prime Minister there was no question but that the New Zealand Bill of Rights Bill would be introduced and in due course enacted.'[40]

In its interim report, the Justice and Law Reform Select Committee (hereafter 'select committee') noted that it received a large number of submissions (431), of which 243 opposed the bill (56 per cent), 35 supported the bill (8 per cent) and 56 provided qualified support (13 per cent).[41] Much of the content of the select committee's interim report was a report from the Department of Justice, which provided

[38] Butler and Butler, *The New Zealand Bill of Rights Act*, pp. 29–31.

[39] Bassett, *Working with David*, p. 189.

[40] P. Rishworth, 'The Birth and Rebirth of the Bill of Rights', in G. Huscroft and P. Rishworth (eds.), *Rights and Freedoms: The New Zealand Bill of Rights Act 1990 and the Human Rights Act 1993* (Wellington: Brooker's, 1995), p. 23.

[41] Parliament of New Zealand 1987. Interim Report of the Justice and Law Reform Select Committee. *Inquiry into the White Paper – A Bill of Rights for New Zealand.* Second Session, Forty-First Parliament (July), p. 8.

a summary of the submissions and outlined options available for proceeding with the bill of rights in the face of overwhelming opposition. Similar to the Canadian case, in which Pierre Trudeau faced strong opposition to the Charter of Rights among the provincial premiers – a critical constituency whose agreement was viewed as necessary for amendment to Canada's former constitution, the British North America Act, 1867 – and where Trudeau decided to gamble on unilateral patriation as a strategy to marginalize provincial opposition,[42] the Department of Justice recommended that the Minister of Justice proceed with a bill of rights despite the limited support for this political project.[43]

In its report, the Department of Justice noted that 'the power given to the judiciary by the White Paper was clearly the principal reason for opposition to the proposal',[44] followed by access to justice concerns, as 'those whose rights are infringed are the persons least likely to be able to afford to protect those rights'.[45] It is important to note that a significant number of submissions that opposed a supreme law bill of rights did believe that institutional reform was necessary, but preferred an elected upper house to address unbridled power in a unicameral parliamentary setting.[46] Finally, the remaining opposition to the 1985 White Paper centred on concerns about the uncertainty that a bill of rights would introduce into New Zealand's constitutional setting,[47] the possibility of increased litigation under a bill of rights,[48] arguments that it was premature to enact a bill of rights[49] and the possibility of constitutional development freezing because of the amendment process in Article 28.[50]

Despite significant opposition to the 1985 White Paper,[51] which the Department of Justice concluded was the result of 'a misunderstanding of the operation of our existing constitutional arrangements',[52] its

[42] Kelly, *Governing with the Charter*, pp. 60–63.

[43] D. F. Dugdale, 'Common sense about the Bill of Rights: A Criticism of Geoffrey Palmer's super-law', (2006) *New Zealand Law Journal* 127–28.

[44] Ibid., p. 8. [45] Ibid., p. 9. [46] Ibid., p. 12. [47] Ibid., p. 10. [48] Ibid., p. 11.

[49] Ibid., p. 12. [50] Ibid., p. 13.

[51] K. J. Keith, '"Concerning Change": The Adoption and Implementation of the New Zealand Bill of Rights Act 1990', (2000) 31 *Victoria University of Wellington Law Review*, 725; Paul Rishworth, 'A Canadian Bill of Rights for New Zealand? The Justice and Law Reform Committee's Final Report', (1989) *New Zealand Recent Law Review* 83.

[52] *Inquiry into the White Paper*, p. 22.

overarching position was that 'there is substantial merit in a bill of rights'.[53] Although the Department of Justice outlined seven options for a New Zealand Bill of Rights – the White Paper with minor amendments,[54] the White Paper with major amendments,[55] adopting the International Covenant approach,[56] a non-judicially enforceable bill,[57] a non-judicially enforceable bill scrutinized by parliament or some other body,[58] a bill of rights with a small number of rights[59] and, finally, complete abandonment of a bill of rights[60] – the Department of Justice reiterated its view that the 1985 White Paper simply had not been understood: 'We remain of the view that there is significant merit in a bill of rights and that the proposal has not been adequately examined by the community.'[61] Thus, its principal recommendation to the select committee was to proceed with a supreme law bill of rights; it added that 'greater effort should be made to engender interest in and debate on the bill of rights proposal'.[62]

Final report of the Justice and Law Reform Select Committee

In his personal writings, Geoffrey Palmer noted that he 'found the proceedings profoundly depressing. It was clear New Zealanders knew little about how government worked and the ordinary New Zealander did not seem to care much.'[63] Recognizing that the political context had been significantly altered by the negative reaction to the 1985 White Paper, which saw New Zealand National come out against an entrenched bill of rights,[64] Palmer consulted extensively with Labour's Justice Caucus Committee in an effort to salvage the bill of rights project before the select committee presented its final report to parliament.

The Final Report of the Select Committee was introduced in October 1988 and clearly reflected the context surrounding the bill of right as a viable political project. The committee report was passed by a majority of its members, as New Zealand National ultimately decided not to support a bill of rights in any form.[65] Although the majority of the select committee was drawn from the Labour party and supported an

[53] *Inquiry into the White Paper*, p. 23. [54] Ibid., pp. 23–76. [55] Ibid., pp. 76–9.
[56] Ibid., pp. 79–80. [57] Ibid., p. 80. [58] Ibid., pp. 81–3. [59] Ibid., p. 83.
[60] Ibid., p. 83. [61] Ibid., p. 84. [62] Ibid., p. 84.
[63] Palmer, *New Zealand's Constitution in Crisis*, p. 56. [64] Ibid., p. 57.
[65] Ibid., p. 57.

entrenched bill of rights, the committee recognized that this was not a possibility, as 'New Zealand is not yet ready, if it ever will be, for a fully fledged bill of rights along the lines of the White Paper draft.'[66] As such, the select committee recommended that a bill of rights should be introduced as an ordinary statute, 'that is not a supreme law and not entrenched'.[67] Other significant departures from the 1985 White Paper included the recommendation to remove the articles relating to the Treaty of Waitangi from the proposed bill of rights,[68] the inclusion of social and economic rights,[69] a certification process modelled after the Canadian Bill of Rights whereby the Attorney General would report to parliament whether bills introduced were consistent with the bill of rights,[70] and the creation of a parliamentary scrutiny committee to examine all bills of rights matters in legislation presented to the House of Representatives.[71]

By the time of the final report, it was clear that the Lange government had lost whatever interest it had in Palmer's bill of rights project, as the fourth Labour government was consumed by internal divisions associated with the radical market reforms and privatization policies undertaken under the Minister of Finance, Roger Douglas.[72] Indeed, Lange's second mandate was marked by deep divisions that 'Rogernomics' created within the Labour parliamentary party as Douglas advocated unorthodox economic policies for a Labour party, such as the privatization of state-owned industries and monetarist policies derived from the writings of Milton Friedman.[73] Tensions between the Minister of Finance and the Prime Minister over the pace of economic reforms resulted in Douglas' departure from cabinet in December 1988, only to see the former Minister of Finance reinstated by a vote of the Labour caucus on 3 August 1989.[74] This was interpreted as a loss of confidence in David Lange's leadership; he therefore announced his resignation as Prime Minister and party leader on 7 August, and was replaced by Geoffrey Palmer on 9 August 1989.

[66] Parliament of New Zealand 1988. Final Report of the Justice and Law Reform Committee. *A White Paper on a Bill of Rights for New Zealand* (October), p. 3.

[67] Palmer, *New Zealand's Constitution in Crisis*, p. 3.

[68] *A White Paper on a Bill of Rights for New Zealand*, p. 4. [69] Ibid., p. 10.

[70] Ibid., p. 10. [71] Ibid., p. 11. [72] Bassett, *Working with David*, pp. 449–80.

[73] J. Boston, 'Thatcherism and Rogernomics: Changing the Rules of the Game – Comparisons and Contrasts', (1987) 39 *Political Science* 130, 136.

[74] E. McLeay, *The Cabinet and Political Power in New Zealand* (Auckland: Oxford University Press, 1995), p. 189.

The New Zealand Bill of Rights Bill

Without this leadership transition, it is unlikely that the fourth Labour government would have introduced the New Zealand Bill of Rights Bill into parliament. Unlike Canada, where the Liberal ministry of Pierre Trudeau was committed to the introduction of a Charter of Rights, for which Minister of Justice Jean Chrétien had been responsible before parliament,[75] the New Zealand Bill of Rights Bill remained Palmer's responsibility after his emergence as Prime Minister and not that of his successor as Minister of Justice, Bill Jeffries. This unusual situation occurred because Palmer realized that 'there was not a great deal of enthusiasm for all this in the government. So when I became Prime Minister I retained responsibility for this legislation to ensure that it was passed.'[76]

The New Zealand Bill of Rights Bill was introduced into parliament by Palmer on 10 October 1989 and generally reflected the recommendations made in the Final Report of the Justice and Law Reform Select Committee. This statutory bill of rights, however, did not contain social and economic rights; Palmer successfully argued against their inclusion in caucus, convinced that '[t]o broaden a Bill of Rights so that it encompassed such broad policy questions would have made it unmanageable and opened it up to ridicule.'[77] Additionally, the New Zealand Bill of Rights Bill did not establish a Bill of Rights Select Committee, though it did include a parliamentary reporting duty for the Attorney General as section 7 of the NZBORA 1990.[78]

During the introduction of the New Zealand Bill of Rights, Prime Minister Geoffrey Palmer provided a summary of the evolution of the document, from the 1985 White Paper to the statutory bill of rights presented to parliament on 10 October 1989. Recognizing that the principal opposition to a supreme law bill of rights 'was the transfer of power the draft Bill was seen to entail from the elected representatives to the judiciary',[79] Palmer defended the draft bill of rights as a *parliamentary* bill of rights consistent with New Zealand's constitutional principles as a Westminster system. The parliamentary nature of the New Zealand Bill of Rights Bill was the result of three interrelated levels of scrutiny

[75] Kelly, *Governing with the Charter*, pp. 60–79.

[76] Palmer, *New Zealand's Constitution in Crisis*, p. 58. [77] Ibid., p. 57.

[78] Butler and Butler, *The New Zealand Bill of Rights Act*, p. 31.

[79] Rt. Hon. G. Palmer – Labour Party (10 October 1989) NZPD 13038.

required when a bill was reported to parliament or reviewed by the judiciary: first, the Attorney General's reporting duty to parliament under section 7;[80] second, the requirement under clause 5 that the judiciary must, wherever possible, interpret legislative intention as being consistent with the NZBORA;[81] and finally, the role of select committees to scrutinize legislation for consistency with the NZBORA.[82] Palmer concluded his introduction by defending the value of a parliamentary bill of rights: 'The Bill of Rights is a parliamentary Bill of Rights, but the protections it provides are, nevertheless, real.'[83]

Although New Zealand National was united in its opposition to the New Zealand Bill of Rights Bill, it did not provide a consistent position. Bill Graham, who would serve as Minister of Justice in the Bolger ministry (1990–97), delivered the response to Palmer:

> If it is not supreme law it is not worth having. It is as simple as that. We have ended up with a totally toothless Bill. It is a watered-down, Claytons version of a Bill of Rights. It is a bumper-sticker legislative measure that has little or no merit, and, because it is now to be deemed as only one other piece of legislation, it has downgraded those very basic freedoms that are so important and that we all want to try to retain.[84]

In contrast, Leader of the Opposition Jim Bolger indicated that New Zealand National would vote against the New Zealand Bill of Rights Bill because it transferred significant power to the judiciary, as 'the Prime Minister knows full well that even with an unentrenched Bill of Rights – a Bill that is not superior law – will be used by the courts to write new law.'[85] Palmer's defence of the bill of rights as a necessary check on executive power was refuted by Simon Upton, the New Zealand National member for Raglan, who concluded that it did not constrain the cabinet: 'Even if the courts came out and said that under the Bill something was in breach of the Bill of Rights, the Government is entitled to pass legislation to overcome that decision. Nothing in the Bill checks the power of the Executive. As long as it is legal it is OK; as long as it is within the Standing Orders it is OK.'[86]

[80] Rt. Hon. G. Palmer – Labour Party (10 October 1989) NZPD 13039. [81] Ibid.
[82] Rt. Hon. G. Palmer – Labour Party (10 October 1989) NZPD 13040.
[83] Rt. Hon. G. Palmer – Labour Party (10 October 1989) NZPD 13041.
[84] B. Graham – National Party (10 October 1989) NZPD 13043.
[85] Hon. J.B. Bolger – National Party (10 October 1989) NZPD 13046.
[86] S. Upton – National Party (10 October 1989) NZPD 13049.

The House of Representatives' voting over whether to introduce the New Zealand Bill of Rights Bill divided by 43 to 31, thus sending the bill to the Justice and Law Reform Committee purely along party lines. The select committee reported to parliament on 17 July 1990 and recommended that the New Zealand Bill of Rights Bill proceed with one minor amendment: clause 3A was inserted to clarify that the judiciary did not have the power to invalidate an enactment and could not refuse to apply a provision it considered inconsistent with the bill of rights.[87] This amendment now appears as Section 4 of the New Zealand Bill of Rights Act 1990. During the debate on the select committee report, Paul East, for New Zealand National, combined both strands of the official opposition's criticism of the bill of rights – stating that it was worthless *and* a transfer of power to the judiciary. According to East, it remained 'a Claytons Bill of Rights that is not enforceable; it is meaningless. The opposition is particularly opposed to the latest version because it is an attempt to introduce in the long term, by stealth, a full-scale Bill of Rights.'[88]

New Zealand National focused on practical limitations of the Attorney General's parliamentary reporting duty under section 7, which Prime Minister Palmer argued was an adequate substitution for judicial review, and evidence of the parliamentary mechanisms of rights protections: 'The significance of the Attorney-General's reporting requirement is that it will necessitate a careful examination of all Government Bills before introduction. That scrutiny will bolster the present lawmaking processes.'[89] In contrast, Douglas Kidd described the reporting duty as 'pantomime' because it required the executive, and not parliament, to hold the executive to account:

> The Bill proposes that not Parliament but the principal law officer of the Crown, the Executive, the would-be propellers of offending legislation into the House, will tell on the Crown – the Executive – to Parliament. Then presumably all Cabinet members, who have to act collectively, and all members of the governing party's caucus, who are bound by the Whips, will turn round and throw the Bill out. To describe the possible proceedings is to suggest that a pantomime is about to be enacted – it cannot be put any higher than that.[90]

[87] B. Dillon – Labour Party (17 July 1990) NZPD 2799.
[88] P. East – National Party (17 July 1990) NZPD 2800.
[89] Rt. Hon. G. Palmer – Labour Party (10 October 1989) NZPD 13039.
[90] D. Kidd – National Party (17 July 1990) NZPD 2805.

The description of Palmer's parliamentary bill of rights as a 'Trojan Horse', meaningless in its present form but to be transformed by the judiciary into a supreme law bill of rights through creative judicial review, has been the basis of James Allan's critique of the New Zealand Bill of Rights Act 1990. Allan contends that the judiciary has transformed a 'Clark Kent bill of rights' into 'Superman' despite parliamentary rejection of a supreme law document during the public and parliamentary review of the 1985 White Paper.[91]

As the New Zealand Bill of Rights Bill progressed through the remaining stages in the parliamentary process, the debate followed an established pattern. Palmer defended a statutory bill of rights as both necessary and effective, and New Zealand National described the New Zealand Bill of Rights Bill as a 'significant failure for the Prime Minister' but also a 'Trojan Horse' that, once passed, and once people were comfortable with it, 'will suddenly spring into its Mark IV form ... which will be the Bill of Rights that will allow the courts to strike down legislation'.[92] The New Zealand Bill of Rights Bill was read for a third time on 21 August 1990, and passed into law as the New Zealand Bill of Rights Act 1990 by a vote of 36 to 28. Royal Assent was granted on 28 August 1990, and the act came into force on 25 September 1990.[93] One of the ironies of the bill of rights debate in New Zealand is that its principal architect, Geoffrey Palmer, resigned as Prime Minister and Labour leader on 4 September 1990, as the caucus, which was never committed to the NZBORA, pressed Palmer to resign in favour of Mike Moore. The leadership change was largely due to the forthcoming election: Palmer was viewed as an electoral liability and Moore as the candidate with the highest likelihood of retaining office, or the one best able to minimize seat losses in parliament.[94] Mike Moore would serve as Prime Minister until 2 November 1990, having led the Labour party to its worst election result since 1935.

The implementation of NZBORA 1990 bears important similarities to that of the Canadian Charter of Rights and Freedoms. In both cases, a political actor in a senior leadership role functioned as a constitutional entrepreneur pushing a bill of rights as a legacy project. In addition,

[91] J. Allan, 'Turning Clark Kent into Superman: The New Zealand Bill of Rights Act 1990', (2000) 9 *Otago Law Review* 628–30.

[92] P. East – National Party (14 August 1990) NZPD 3459–60.

[93] Rishworth, 'The Birth and Rebirth of the Bill of Rights', p. 24.

[94] Bassett, *Working with David*, pp. 535–36.

important political and constitutional factors nearly succeeded in derailing both bills of rights projects. In the case of Canada, it was federalism, and the assumption that the Trudeau Liberals required unanimous provincial consent before requesting changes to the British North America Act (BNA Act) by the Westminster parliament. Further, the defeat of the Trudeau government in 1979 and his resignation as Liberal leader appeared to end the Charter project, as the former Prime Minister indicated he would return to private life in Montreal once his successor had been chosen. However, before this could occur, the minority government of Prime Minister Joe Clark was defeated over a confidence issue in December 1979; Trudeau rescinded his resignation and led the Liberal party to a majority government in the 1980 election.

Recognizing that the fulfilment of his 'magnificent obsession' had been rescued from certain defeat, Trudeau challenged the constitutional norm that unanimous provincial consent was necessary before changes to the BNA Act could be approved by Westminster. While the Supreme Court of Canada supported the legality of unilateral changes to the BNA Act, it recognized a constitutional convention that 'substantial provincial consent' was necessary before the Trudeau government could submit its request to Westminster. However, this constitutional constraint was significantly weakened by the Supreme Court of Canada, which stated that conventions could only be enforced by political mechanisms.[95] While the Charter of Rights was proclaimed into law in April 1982, it is easy to overlook, after several decades, that the Charter project nearly ended in failure. Its implementation was a result of the personal commitment of its principal sponsor, Pierre Elliot Trudeau; unforeseen political developments, such as Trudeau's return to the position of Prime Minister in 1980; and the Supreme Court of Canada's reluctant endorsement of unilateral patriation in 1981, which allowed Trudeau to overcome federalism as a constitutional impediment to realization of the Charter of Rights.

Although the genesis of the NZBORA 1990 did not encounter the same level of institutional resistance as the Charter of Rights, as New Zealand is a unitary system with a unicameral parliament, its successful implementation may be more surprising than its Canadian counterpart. Whereas the Trudeau Liberals were united in their support of the Charter of Rights, the New Zealand Labour Party was ambivalent regarding

[95] Kelly, *Governing with the Charter*, pp. 47–79.

whether a bill of rights was a necessary addition to the domestic constitutional framework. Further, civil liberty groups and members of the legal profession were strong supporters of the Canadian Charter of Rights, while the NZBORA was opposed overwhelmingly by civil society, including the New Zealand Law Society. Indeed, public support was used by the Trudeau Liberals to neutralize federalism as a barrier to successful implementation, conceptualizing the Charter as part of the 'people's package' that transferred power away from governments to citizens: the Trudeau Liberals used the possibility of a referendum on the Charter to neutralize political opposition from the provincial premiers, which resulted in all governments except that of the separatist Parti Québécois agreeing to patriation of the BNA Act.

In the case of New Zealand, a small number of Labour MPs, as well as senior members of the Department of Justice, supported the bill of rights. Ironically, what resulted in its adoption was the very thing that had motivated Geoffrey Palmer's entry into politics – unbridled power in the office of Prime Minister. Without his ascension to the prime ministership, which allowed Palmer to proceed with a constitutional agenda with limited political support, it is doubtful that the NZBORA would have been approved by parliament. The reinstatement of Roger Douglas to cabinet by the Labour parliamentary caucus, David Lange's interpretation of this as a loss of confidence and Palmer's unexpected ascension to Prime Minister cannot be overlooked as critical events that resulted in the successful adoption of the NZBORA in 1990.

II. The Bolger/Shipley government and the NZBORA 1990

Although New Zealand National opposed the NZBORA while in opposition, the governments of Jim Bolger (1990–97) and Jenny Shipley (1997–99) accepted it as an important statement of domestic rights obligations after defeating the Labour party in the 1990 election. Indeed, the bureaucratic and parliamentary architecture of the NZBORA was set by the New Zealand National government that preceded the fourth Labour government, as the Bolger ministry introduced important changes in the legislative process to ensure that bills submitted to parliament were developed in light of the NZBORA. While the NZBORA has proven to be a limited check on government legislation when the cabinet is committed to proceeding with legislation that appears to be inconsistent with the NZBORA, the emergence of a rights culture within the legislative process is the principal benefit of this parliamentary bill of rights. In this respect, Geddis' criticism of the NZBORA as 'irrelevant' to legislative practice is only correct in relation to the limited impact on legislative outcomes when the Attorney General reports to parliament under section 7 of the NZBORA.[96]

In 1991, then Attorney General Paul East established the practice that his successors have largely followed in relation to the NZBORA. In regard to government bills that have reached the drafting stage, the Parliamentary Counsels Office refers non-Justice bills to the Ministry of Justice and Justice bills to the Crown Law Office for review by departmental legal advisors. These 'BORA vets' are legal assessments presented to the Attorney General by the Ministry of Justice or the Crown Law Office indicating whether, in the opinion of these executive agencies, draft legislation for parliament's consideration is consistent with the NZBORA.[97] If a BORA vet by Crown Law or the Ministry of Justice concludes that draft government legislation appears to be inconsistent with the NZBORA, the responsible legal officer must notify the Attorney General and the Parliamentary Counsel who is drafting the bill; for non-government bills, the Attorney General and the Chief Parliamentary Counsel must be notified.[98]

Although it is the Attorney General's responsibility under section 7 of the NZBORA to report to parliament any bill that appears inconsistent with the Act, these reports are based largely on the assessments provided by the Ministry of Justice and the Crown Law Office to the Attorney General.[99] Further, the Attorney General only reports to parliament under section 7 when a limitation is not considered reasonable under section 5 of the NZBORA.[100] Initially, the full report of the Attorney General under section 7 was published in Hansard, but this practice was abandoned in favour of a significantly abridged report that was found in

96 Geddis, 'The Comparative Irrelevance of the NZBORA', 468–69.

97 P. East, 'Monitoring Bills for Compliance with the New Zealand Bill of Rights Act 1990', in M. Chen and G. Palmer (eds.), *Public Law in New Zealand* (Melbourne: Oxford University Press, 1993), p. 556.

98 East, 'Monitoring Bills for Compliance', p. 556.

99 Geddis, 'The Comparative Irrelevance of the NZBORA', 475; G. Huscroft, 'The Attorney-General's Reporting Duty', in P. Rishworth, G. Huscroft, S. Optican and R. Mahoney (eds.), *The New Zealand Bill of Rights Act* (Melbourne: Oxford University Press, 2003), p. 215.

100 P. Fitzgerald, 'Section 7 of the New Zealand Bill of Rights Act 1990: A Very Practical Power or a Well-intentioned Nonsense', (1992) 22 *Victoria University of Wellington Law Review* 137.

the Appendix to the House of Representatives by 1996.[101] By 2000, the Attorney General's report under section 7 of the NZBORA had come to lack explicit reasoning as Paul East and his successors invoked 'legal professional privilege' to jettison fulsome public reports, arguing that section 7 reports constituted protected communication with a client.[102]

However, this position became increasingly untenable and culminated with Attorney General Margaret Wilson's 2003 decision to release all BORA vets produced by the Ministry of Justice and Crown Law Office.[103] While the Attorney General had released BORA vets on a case-by-case basis before 2003, academic commentators such as Andrew Butler argued for the release of all of them, arguing that it would improve the scrutiny of legislation at select committee stage and facilitate parliamentary engagement with the NZBORA.[104] More critical commentators disputed that the section 7 reporting duty was protected by privilege, arguing that a compelling public interest was advanced by their release, as it would support greater transparency in the legislative process.[105]

The decision to release all BORA vets leading to a section 7 report, including advice where the Ministry of Justice and Crown Law Office concluded that the NZBORA was not engaged, occurred in the context of the Climate Change Response Bill introduced by the Labour government in 2003.[106] The Foreign Affairs, Defence, and Trade Committee noted the absence of a section 7 report by Attorney General Margaret Wilson, as well as the disagreement of the policy community affected by this issue. This created a practical difficulty for the committee, which it noted in its report to parliament: 'Without the benefit of the Attorney General's advice or the time to utilize independent advice for the Bill of Rights Act, we are in an impossible position to refute submitters' claims that the bill

[101] C. Archer and G. Burt, 'Section 7 of the Bill of Rights Act', (2004) *The New Zealand Law Journal* 320.

[102] Archer and Burt, 'Section 7 of the Bill of Rights Act', 320.

[103] G. Huscroft, 'Protecting Rights and Parliamentary Sovereignty: New Zealand's Experience with a *Charter*-inspired, Statutory Bill of Rights', (2002) 21 *Windsor Yearbook of Access to Justice* 122–24.

[104] A. Butler, 'Strengthening the Bill of Rights', (2000) 31 *Victoria University of Wellington Law Review* 145–46.

[105] Archer and Burt, 'Section 7 of the Bill of Rights Act', 320.

[106] G. Huscroft, 'Is the Defeat of Health Warnings a Victory for Human Rights? The Attorney General and Pre-legislative Scrutiny for Consistency with the New Zealand Bill of Rights', (2003) 14 *Public Law* 111.

is not compliant with the Bill of Rights Act.'[107] The current practice in New Zealand addresses this criticism, as since 2003 all BORA vets have been available on the Ministry of Justice website before a bill is considered at the select committee stage. In addition, the Ministry of Justice publishes all reports submitted by the Attorney General to parliament under section 7 of the NZBORA on its departmental website.[108]

The reporting duty under section 7 of the NZBORA varies depending on whether the legislation is a government or non-government bill. Because of BORA vetting within the executive branch, the Attorney General is required to make a statement at introduction for a government bill, whereas the Attorney General is only required to issue a section 7 report in regard to a non-government bill 'as soon as practicable after the introduction of the Bill'.[109] This practice occurs because non-government bills are not subject to BORA vetting by the Ministry of Justice or Crown Law before introduction,[110] and the Parliamentary Counsel Office – the agency that drafts all legislation passed into law – only provides drafting support for non-governmental bills that pass first reading.[111] Indeed, the Attorney General has issued 65 section 7 reports to parliament since 1990, and more than half (33 of 65) have involved non-government bills. This is not surprising, as non-government bills are vetted by the Crown Law Office and the Ministry of Justice only after they are introduced into parliament.[112] Indeed, of the 33 non-government bills about which the Attorney General has reported to parliament under section 7 of the NZBORA, only eight have been passed by parliament, of which six have been amended to address

[107] Climate Change Response Bill. As reported by the Foreign Affairs, Defence, and Trade Committee. www.parliament.nz/NR/rdonlyres/6B3A11DB-193A-41AB-969F-D43230FE3E17/47792/DBSCH_SCR_2203_2558.pdf (p. 14).

[108] A complete list of section 7 reports under the NZBORA 1990 can be accessed at www.justice.govt.nz/policy/constitutional-law-and-human-rights/human-rights/domestic-human-rights-protection/about-the-new-zealand-bill-of-rights-act/advising-the-attorney-general/section-7-reports-published-before-august-2002/section-7-reports-published-before-august-2002

[109] Parliament of New Zealand 2011. Standing Orders of the House of Representatives, SO 262(2)(b).

[110] Interview with senior departmental officials, Ministry of Justice, New Zealand, Wellington (4 May 2004 and 27 July 2006); interview with senior departmental officials, Parliamentary Counsels Office, New Zealand, Wellington New Zealand (12 May 2004).

[111] Interview with senior departmental officials, Ministry of Justice, Wellington, New Zealand (12 May 2004).

[112] Geddis, 'The Comparative Irrelevance of the NZBORA,' 475–76.

the concerns of the Attorney General under the NZBORA. This should not be viewed as evidence of the importance of the section 7 reporting duty and the reluctance of parliamentarians to pass such legislation, however; it simply indicates the overall small number of non-government bills that are passed by parliament.

The Crown Law Office and the Ministry of Justice

A highly institutionalized BORA vetting process has been established within the bureaucracy that supports the cabinet and its legislative agenda, with the Ministry of Justice and Crown Law Office playing a dominant role in vetting legislation's relationship to the NZBORA. Although the process is referred to as BORA vetting, an important distinction exists between BORA *policy advice* and BORA *legal advice* provided by the Ministry of Justice and Crown Law Office. In particular, BORA policy advice is provided to client departments by the Ministry of Justice and Crown Law, as the client departments have internal legal advisors on BORA issues that provide legal assessments of compatibility, whereas the Minister of Justice and Crown Law provide legal advice to the Attorney General in regard to the section 7 reporting duty.[113]

While the political responsibility for issuing section 7 reports to parliament is the Attorney General's, this is the end product of an institutionalized vetting system that exists at all stages of policy development. When developing policy proposals for possible inclusion in the cabinet's legislative agenda, the responsible minister is required to demonstrate to the Cabinet Legislation Committee (LEG) that the policy proposal has been considered in light of the NZBORA. Under chapter 7.19(c) of the Cabinet Manual, the sponsoring minister is required to engage in broad inter-departmental and inter-agency consultation on the proposed policy, and chapter 7.31 specifies the requirement to consult with both the Ministry of Law and the Crown Law Office on BORA implications: 'The Ministry of Justice must be consulted on all bills, so that it can vet them for consistency with the New Zealand Bill of Rights Act 1990. (See paragraph 7.62.) Bills

[113] Interview with senior government official, Ministry of Justice, Wellington, New Zealand (4 May 2004 and 26 July 2006); Interview with senior government official, Crown Law Office, Wellington, New Zealand (6 May 2004 and 25 July 2006).

developed by the Ministry of Justice are vetted by the Crown Law Office. The Ministry of Justice must also be consulted on all proposals to create new criminal offences or penalties or alter existing ones, to ensure that such provisions are consistent and appropriate.'[114] Additionally, under chapter 7.60, 'Ministers must confirm that bills comply with certain legal principles or obligations when submitting bids for bills to be included in the legislation programme. In particular, Ministers must draw attention to any aspects of a bill that have implications for, or may be affected by: (a) the principles of the Treaty of Waitangi; (b) the rights and freedoms contained the New Zealand Bill of Rights Act 1990 and the Human Rights Act 1993.'[115]

Although the Cabinet Manual 2008 outlines the process for submitting cabinet papers for possible inclusion in the government's legislative agenda, it is the Cabinet Guide – referred to as 'CabGuide' – which provides detailed descriptions outlining the precise types of consultations that must be conducted, as well as the appropriate documentation that must be included by those seeking to introduce a bill to parliament for approval by the Cabinet Legislation Committee.[116] Each cabinet paper must include a compliance statement that indicates whether the bill complies with, among other things, the NZBORA, and the reasons why a bill may not comply.[117] Indeed, under section 10 of the cabinet paper submission, the sponsoring minister must 'state the nature of any potential inconsistencies identified, or state that there are none; note the steps taken to address any issues, or include information on any justifications for the bill infringing a right or freedom'.[118]

Because of the decentralized nature of the legal profession within the New Zealand government, the responsibility for BORA compliance in the cabinet submission is that of the department's legal officers and not the Ministry of Justice or Crown Law Office. Geoffrey Palmer contends that the decentralized nature of the legal profession is a barrier to effective legal advice: 'Each department has its own solicitors providing advice. By the time a problem reaches the Crown Law Office, it is

[114] Cabinet Office (New Zealand) 2008, Department of the Prime Minster and Cabinet. *Cabinet Manual 2008*. Wellington: New Zealand.

[115] Cabinet Office (New Zealand) 2008, Department of the Prime Minster and Cabinet. *Cabinet Manual 2008*, 7.60 – Compliance with legal principles and obligations.

[116] See http://cabguide.cabinetoffice.govt.nz/procedures/legislation

[117] CabGuide – structure of a paper seeking to introduce a bill.

[118] Ibid.

sometimes too late to put the matter right.'[119] To address this 'Balkanization of the legal services with the New Zealand government',[120] Palmer has advocated the creation of a Law Department with sole responsibility for providing legal advise to all government departments.[121] To address the possibility of inconsistency in the approach to compliance procedures within a cabinet submission, the Bill of Rights Unit at the Ministry of Justice provides guidelines to assist departmental legal advisors in BORA assessment.[122] This document provides advice on how to approach the bill of rights, how to assess potential rights infringements and how to determine whether limitations are reasonable, as well as an overview of the reasonable limits test in section 5 of the NZBORA.

The *Guidelines on the New Zealand Bill of Rights Act 1990* (hereafter *Guidelines*) indicate that the Ministry of Justice has two roles in relation to the NZBORA: 'advising departments on the consistency of policy proposals and government bills with New Zealand's human rights laws' and 'advising the Attorney-General on the consistency of a bill with the Bill of Rights Act'.[123] In the context of bills sponsored by the Ministry of Justice, the Crown Law Office performs these roles. In regard to advising departments, the Ministry of Justice reiterates the requirement that all policy proposals must include a statement of consistency with the NZBORA. Further, the *Guidelines* emphasize that this is the responsibility of departmental legal advisors: 'Each government department has to make its own assessment and sign off on human rights implications in the department's area of responsibility.'[124] However, the *Guidelines* emphasize that higher-level BORA advice can be provided by the Ministry of Justice and Crown Law Office to client departments that are preparing statements of consistency: 'in carrying out this assessment, departments should, where appropriate, consult agencies with an interest or experience in human rights issues such as the Ministry of Justice (human rights policy and legal assistance), and the Crown Law Office (legal advice).'[125]

[119] G. Palmer, 'The Provision of Legal Services to Government', (2000) 31 *Victoria University of Wellington Law Review* 69.

[120] Ibid. [121] Ibid., 73.

[122] Ministry of Justice (New Zealand) 2004, *The Guidelines on the New Zealand Bill of Rights Act 1990: A Guide to the Rights and Freedoms in the Bill of Rights Act for the Public Sector.*

[123] Ibid. [124] Ibid. [125] Ibid.

Once the Cabinet Legislation Committee approves a cabinet paper, the sponsoring ministry prepares drafting instructions for the Parliamentary Counsel Office, which drafts all government legislation, with the exception of that related to the Inland Revenue Department.[126] Although the Ministry of Justice and Crown Law Office advise sponsoring departments on the consistency of policy proposals with the NZBORA and provide assistance in reconciling policy objectives with the NZBORA, the drafting instructions provided to the Parliamentary Counsel Office may contain BORA inconsistencies. It is the responsibility of the Parliamentary Counsel Office to circulate draft legislation to the Ministry of Justice and Crown Law Office for consideration. At this stage, the Ministry of Justice and Crown Law Office engage in BORA vetting, which concludes with advising the Attorney General whether a report under section 7 is required if the draft legislation is approved for introduction into the House of Representatives.

However, before BORA vetting is performed in relation to the Attorney General's reporting duty, the Ministry of Justice and Crown Law Office engage with the sponsoring department to reconcile policy objectives with the NZBORA. In the *Guidelines*, the two-week period before draft legislation is sent to the Cabinet Legislation Committee allows the Ministry of Justice and Crown Law Office to re-engage with the sponsoring department to resolve any outstanding BORA issues:

> In most cases, vetting a Bill involves members of the Ministry of Justice's Bill of Rights team working closely with the sponsoring agency to ensure that successive versions of the Bill comply with the Bill of Rights Act. If a provision appears to raise issues of consistency with the Bill of Rights Act you will be contacted to clarify the effect or purpose of that provision or justifications for it. This involves a process of ongoing consultation and negotiation between the agency and the Ministry. The Ministry may present different options for achieving a specific objective, particularly if it considers that the objective can be achieved in a way that does not give rise to Bill of Rights Act issues. This process of negotiation may lead to changes being made to the Bill to address particular concerns.[127]

The *Guidelines* emphasize that if a provision of a bill is considered inconsistent with the NZBORA and cannot be justified as a reasonable

[126] Cabinet Office 2008, Department of the Prime Minster and Cabinet. *Cabinet Manual 2008*. Wellington: New Zealand. Section 7.46 'Role of the Drafter'.

[127] Ministry of Justice (New Zealand) 2004, *The Guidelines on the New Zealand Bill of Rights Act 1990*.

limit under section 5, the Ministry of Justice and Crown Law Office will, in consultation with the sponsoring department, explore alternative approaches to guard against a BORA inconsistency: 'Failing that, the Ministry will ask you to consider whether the provision can be omitted from the Bill on the basis that the provision appears to be inconsistent with the Bill of Rights Act.'[128]

Once this consultation process ends, the Parliamentary Counsel Office prepares the final version of the bill that the sponsoring department will present to the Cabinet Legislation Committee for consideration as part of the government's legislative programme. The New Zealand Cabinet Manual requires that the final version of the draft bill must be submitted to the Ministry of Justice (non-Justice bills) or Crown Law Office (Justice bills) two weeks before it is to be considered by the Cabinet Legislation Committee. At this stage, the role of the Ministry of Justice and Crown Law Office transitions from providing BORA *policy* advice to departments to providing BORA *legal* advice to the Attorney General on the draft legislation to be presented to the Cabinet Legislation Committee.

In regard to non-Justice bills, the Ministry of Justice has an internal peer-review process regarding legal advice presented to the Attorney General that is posted on the ministerial website. Since 2003, under Attorney General Margaret Wilson, the Ministry of Justice has posted all BORA advice provided to the Attorney General by the Ministry of Justice and Crown Law Office.[129] To ensure that there is internal consistency in the BORA assessment of legislation to be submitted to the Cabinet Legislation Committee, legal advice presented by the Ministry of Justice to the Attorney General is signed by two legal advisors within the ministry: a member of the BORA unit and a member of the Office of Legal Counsel.[130] In regard to bills sponsored by the Ministry of Justice, the practice at the Crown Law Office is to have the legal advice drafted by a junior member of the Human Rights Team and reviewed by a senior team member before both team members sign it.[131] Further, if the legal advisors at the Ministry of Justice determine the Attorney

[128] Ibid.

[129] New Zealand Bill of Rights Act 1990 – Advice provided by the Ministry of Justice and the Crown Law Office to the Attorney-General on the consistency of Bills with the Bill of Rights Act 1990. www.justice.govt.nz/policy/constitutional-law-and-human-rights/human-rights/bill-of-rights

[130] Interview with senior departmental officials, Ministry of Justice, Wellington, New Zealand (4 May 2004 and 26 July 2006).

[131] Ibid., (25 July 2006).

General should be advised that proposed legislation is potentially inconsistent with the NZBORA and that a section 7 report should be issued, the Ministry of Justice will seek an opinion from the Crown Law Office as to whether to advise the Attorney General in regard to the parliamentary reporting duty under section 7 of the NZBORA.[132] Although this is not a formal requirement, a practice has developed of inter-departmental consultation between the Ministry of Justice and the Crown Law Office when it is concluded that the Attorney General should be briefed about a potential use of section 7 of the NZBORA.

Once the legal advice on the BORA implications of proposed legislation has been provided to the Attorney General, they decide whether, in the context of section 7, to accept the advice of the Crown Law Office and the Ministry of Justice or advise the cabinet that the proposed legislation is consistent with the NZBORA. Indeed, the support provided by Crown Law and the Ministry of Justice is simply advice, as it is the Attorney General that has the political responsibility for issuing a section 7 report to parliament, and the professional responsibility to advise the cabinet on the consistency of its legislative agenda.[133] In many respects, the BORA vetting process within government is an attempt to create a transparent and accountable dialogue should the government decide to proceed with legislation that the Attorney General has advised is potentially inconsistent with the NZBORA.[134] Once the Cabinet Legislation Committee and the full cabinet have approved the draft bill, it must be referred to the government caucus(es) and the confidence partners under New Zealand's mixed member proportional (MMP) system to ensure that it has the support to progress to introduction by the sponsoring minister.[135] At the conclusion of the caucus consultation process, the draft bill is introduced into parliament and must contain a section 7 report if the Attorney General concludes that it appears to be inconsistent with the NZBORA 1990.

[132] Ibid. [133] Archer and Burt, 'Section 7 of the Bill of Rights Act', 321.

[134] S. Jackson, 'Designing Human Rights Legislation: "Dialogue", the Commonwealth Model and the Role of Parliaments and Courts', (2007) 13 *Auckland University Law Review* 101–3. For a critical position on the section 7 reporting duty see P. Fitzgerald, 'Section 7 of the New Zealand Bill of Rights Act 1990: A Very Practical Power or Well-intentioned Nonsense?', (1992) 22 *Victoria University of Wellington Law Review* 135–58.

[135] Cabinet Office 2008, Department of the Prime Minster and Cabinet. *Cabinet Manual 2008* – section 7.54 (Wellington: New Zealand), p. 94.

There is disagreement as to whether pre-introduction of BORA vetting within the New Zealand bureaucracy has created a culture of rights that disciplines a government's legislative agenda to its domestic rights commitments, and thus acts as an adequate substitution for judicial enforcement and scrutiny of the NZBORA. Geddis notes:

> As a matter of formal constitutional theory, the NZBORA does not prevent a minister from introducing apparently inconsistent legislative proposals into the House of Representatives. Furthermore, as a matter of practice, successive governments have been quite prepared with legislative proposals after being told these contain apparently NZBORA-inconsistent measures. . .[136]

While Geddis is correct that successive governments have introduced legislation on which the Attorney General has issued a section 7 report – in 32 instances between 1990 and 2014 – this does not necessarily demonstrate the absence of a rights culture within the New Zealand bureaucracy developed in response to the NZBORA 1990. In comparison, the Minister of Justice in Canada has never issued a report to parliament that legislation appears to be inconsistent with the Canadian Charter of Rights under section 4.1.1 of the Department of Justice Act; in contrast, the New Zealand Attorney General has issued 65 reports (1990–2014) under section 7 of the NZBORA. This should not be taken as evidence of a more robust rights culture within the Canadian federal bureaucracy, given that the Supreme Court of Canada declared 72 statutes unconstitutional between 1982 and 2012. Indeed, the mechanisms for rights scrutiny in Canada and New Zealand are nearly identical within the bureaucracy, despite the more robust approach to section 7 reports in New Zealand and the failure by the Minister of Justice in Canada to report a Charter inconsistency to parliament.[137]

What the Attorney General's reporting duty in New Zealand (and the equivalent responsibility under the Department of Justice Act in Canada) demonstrates is that assessment of compatibility, and of whether to proceed with legislation containing potential inconsistencies, is the political responsibility of the cabinet introducing the legislation into

[136] Geddis, 'Inter-institutional 'Rights Dialogue' Under the New Zealand Bill of Rights Act', 95.

[137] J. Kelly, 'Legislative Activism and Parliamentary Bills of Rights: Institutional Lessons for Canada', in J. Kelly and C. Manfredi (eds.), *Contested Constitutionalism: Reflections on the Canadian Charter of Rights and Freedoms* (Vancouver: UBC Press, 2009), pp. 86–106.

parliament. Further, it demonstrates that despite a robust rights culture within the bureaucracy, the cabinet retains discretion over whether to proceed with its legislative agenda *despite* being advised by public servants that incompatibilities may exist. The mechanisms for rights compliance within the parliamentary approach to bills of rights, in the context of New Zealand, remain political mechanisms within the parliamentary setting employed once the Attorney General reports to the House of Representatives under section 7 of the NZBORA. Instead of demonstrating the absence of a rights culture within New Zealand, the decisions of successive governments to proceed with potentially incompatible legislation demonstrate the continued dominance of the cabinet in the New Zealand parliamentary setting, despite the introduction of a statutory bill of rights and the MMP electoral system's adoption in 1996.[138]

III. The NZBORA and the courts

Although Geoffrey Palmer's preference was for a judicially enforced bill of rights, the NZBORA adopted in 1990 in statutory form contains a number of important sections that limit judicial enforcement of the NZBORA in relation to acts passed by parliament. In particular, sections 4–7 of the NZBORA are the main provisions that outline judicial and parliamentary roles that reinforce it as a parliamentary bill of rights. Sections 4–6 provide guidance to judicial actors in interpreting the NZBORA and section 7 is a political 'trigger' that requires the Attorney General to notify parliament when, in the opinion of this law officer, legislation is inconsistent with the NZBORA. What is not provided for – and indeed is explicitly prohibited – is the ability of the judiciary to declare acts of parliament inconsistent with the NZBORA, or to issue remedies to correct these deficiencies. These provisions result in the NZBORA emerging as an interpretive bill of rights that relies on parliamentary enforcement. This interpretive characteristic of the NZBORA is reinforced by the judicial approach to this document, a political culture of parliamentary supremacy that is deeply embedded (and which greatly reduces the political cost

[138] For an analysis of the impact of MMP on criminal law issues in New Zealand, see N. Lacey, 'The Prisoners' Dilemma and the Political Systems: The Impact of Proportional Representation on Criminal Justice in New Zealand', (2011) 42 *Victoria University of Wellington Law Review* 615–38.

of passing legislation that is inconsistent with the NZBORA) and a parliamentary engagement of rights issues that cannot, with the best intentions, be characterized as dialogic or institutional interaction between judicial and political actors that ensures the passage of compatible legislation.[139]

These provisions – sections 4 to 7 – effectively prevent the judiciary from engaging in substantive review and enforcement of the NZBORA against acts of parliament. Also, the development of restrictive judicial approaches to the NZBORA, and the dominance of parliamentary supremacy as *the* constitutional principle in New Zealand, reinforces the importance of political triggers and the relative unimportance of judicial review of statutes passed by parliament to ensure NZBORA compliance. For instance, section 4 of the NZBORA establishes parliament's preferred approach to judicial interpretation and clearly establishes that courts cannot repeal or revoke statutory law 'by reason only that the provision is inconsistent with any provision of this bill of Rights'.[140] Unlike the Supreme Court of Canada, which has invoked the 'living tree metaphor' as a justification to engage in expansive judicial review, the judiciary in New Zealand, operating in a political culture where parliamentary sovereignty is 'an ultimate principle of New Zealand's constitution',[141] have accepted the limited role provided to the courts by parliament under section 4 of the NZBORA.[142]

Similar to the Canadian Charter of Rights and Freedoms, the NZBORA has an explicit limitations clause (section 5).[143] This limitation clause, however, is different as it is internally qualified by section 4 of the NZBORA, which prevents courts from declaring any provision to

[139] P. Butler, 'Human Rights and Parliamentary Sovereignty in New Zealand', (2004) 35 *Victoria University of Wellington Law Review* 341–66; P. Joseph, 'Parliament, the Courts and the Collaborative Enterprise', (2004) 15 *King's College Law Journal* 321–45.

[140] New Zealand Bill of Rights Act 1990, Section 4: '**Other enactments not affected**. No court shall, in relation to any enactment (whether passed or made before or after the commencement of this Bill of Rights), — a) Hold any provision of the enactment to be impliedly repealed or revoked, or to be in any way invalid or ineffective; or (b) Decline to apply any provision of the enactment — by reason only that the provision is inconsistent with any provision of this Bill of Rights.'

[141] M. Palmer, 'New Zealand's Constitutional Culture', (2007) *New Zealand Universities Law Review* 586.

[142] Butler, 'Strengthening the Bill of Rights', 130.

[143] New Zealand Bill of Rights Act 1990, Section 5: '**Justified limitations**. Subject to section 4 of this Bill of Rights, the rights and freedoms contained in this Bill of Rights may be subject only to such reasonable limits prescribed by law as can be demonstrably justified in a free and democratic society.'

be 'impliedly repealed or revoked, or to be in any way invalid or ineffective ... or [to] decline to apply any provision of the enactment'. Finally, section 6 of the NZBORA directs the courts to prefer an interpretation of a legislative enactment that is consistent with rights and freedoms.[144] As a result, there is much confusion over the boundaries of judicial review and the appropriate methodological approach to NZBORA inquiry. For instance, does section 4 constrain judicial review to such a degree that it is inappropriate for judges to engage in section 5 analyses? If judges are permitted to engage in section 5 analyses, and find an enactment constitutes an unreasonable limitation, must the courts then read the limitations consistent with the NZBORA under section 6? Finally, if judges cannot read an enactment consistent with the NZBORA, is the judiciary permitted to issue a 'declaration of inconsistency' under section 5? If the judiciary can issue a 'declaration of inconsistency' under section 5, does section 4 of the NZBORA require the court to adopt parliament's intended meaning, despite the declaration of inconsistency?

Although the Court of Appeal, before being replaced by the Supreme Court of New Zealand (SCNZ) as the highest domestic court in 2004 following the abolition of appeals to the Judicial Committee of the Privy Council, established an approach to section 5 in *Moonen*,[145] it was recently clarified in *Hansen* that the correct methodological approach to judicial review requires the courts to approach the NZBORA in the following manner: first, ascertain parliament's intended meaning; second, ascertain whether the meaning is inconsistent with the NZBORA; third, consider whether an apparent inconsistency is reasonable under section 5; fourth, if the inconsistency is unreasonable, consider whether an interpretation can be found that is consistent with the NZBORA under section 6. Finally, if this is not possible, section 4 requires that parliament's intended meaning be adopted despite the section 5 engagement.[146]

Despite segments of the academic community suggesting that the Court of Appeal established a judicial declaration of inconsistency in

[144] New Zealand Bill of Rights Act 1990, Section 6: '**Interpretation consistent with Bill of Rights to be preferred.** Wherever an enactment can be given a meaning that is consistent with the rights and freedoms contained in this Bill of Rights, that meaning shall be preferred to any other meaning.'

[145] *Moonen* v. *Film and Literature Board of Review* [2000] 2 NZLR 9.

[146] *R.* v. *Hansen*, [2007] NZSC 7 (Tipping J. at para 92).

Moonen,[147] a unanimous Court of Appeal (2009) reiterated in *Boscawen* v. *Attorney General* in 2009 that the 'question as to whether a declaration of inconsistency is an available remedy under the NZBORA is still to be resolved'.[148] As a result, the NZBORA is a politically, not judicially, enforced document in the context of acts passed by parliament. Unable to convince parliamentarians of the importance of judicial review and remedies, Prime Minister Palmer settled on what Hiebert refers to as 'political rights review'.[149] Indeed, the judiciary has not issued a declaration of inconsistency in relation to the NZBORA but has issued one in relation to the New Zealand Human Rights Act 1993, a statutory document addressing matters of discrimination. The Human Rights Act, unlike the NZBORA, provides for judicial declarations of inconsistency as an appropriate judicial remedy for discrimination.

As the judicial culture of New Zealand is deeply influenced by the principle of parliamentary supremacy,[150] the absence of an explicit parliamentary-created declaration of inconsistency has acted as a significant deterrent preventing judicial creation of this remedy power.[151] Indeed, parliament's intention was to authorize political declarations of inconsistency by the Attorney General under section 7 of the NZBORA and, unless it is established through parliamentary amendment of the NZBORA, judicial creation of a declaratory power is, according to Geiringer, 'a road to nowhere'.[152] In *Boscawen*, the Court of Appeal argued that it could not create a declaration of inconsistency in the abstract, and relied on the Attorney General's Advisory Group on the establishment of a Supreme Court rejection of a 'reference procedure' for this court as support. Although the SCNZ did not rule out the future creation of this remedy, it concluded: 'We prefer to leave the question to be decided in a case in which the outcome depends on the answer.'[153]

147 P. Rishworth, 'Changing Times, Changing Minds, Changing Law – Sexual Orientation and New Zealand Law, 1960 to 1985', (2007) 11 *International Journal of Human Rights* 85–107.

148 *Boscawen* v. *Attorney General* [2009] NZCA 12 (O'Regan J. at para 56).

149 Hiebert, 'Interpreting a Bill of Rights', 235–55.

150 Palmer, 'New Zealand's Constitutional Culture', 586; Erdos, 'Judicial Culture and the Politicolegal Opportunity Structure', 95–127.

151 C. Geiringer, 'On a Road to Nowhere: Implied Declarations of Inconsistency and the New Zealand Bill of Rights Act', (2009) 40 *Victoria University of Wellington Law Review* 613–47.

152 Geiringer, 'On a Road to Nowhere', 613–47.

153 *Boscawen* v. *Attorney General* [2009] NZCA 12 (O'Regan J. at para 56).

The absence of a judicial declaration of inconsistency, either authorized by parliament or created by the courts through section 5, suggests that the NZBORA is enforced, in the context of statutes passed by parliament, exclusively through political mechanisms. As such, the designation of the NZBORA as a parliamentary bill of rights is appropriate. Although section 5 provides for the possibility of judicial declarations of inconsistency, there are several factors that suggest that a judicially created one is rather unlikely: first, judicial discussions of declarations of inconsistency in the abstract, that, if a declaratory power was established, would render it rather ineffective because of the restrictive judicial test created in the abstract; second, a judicial culture that is shaped by New Zealand's political culture, with the courts reluctant to challenge the intention of parliament; finally, the minimalist nature of the NZBORA as a 'first generation' bill of rights focusing on civil and legal protections.

Although New Zealand courts have not established a judicial declaration of inconsistency, they have created judicial rules on its operation that would significantly hamper the transition to this judicial remedy if such a rule were established, either by parliament (unlikely) or the courts (highly unlikely). Geiringer has identified seven judicial hurdles created around implied declarations of inconsistency, with the three most significant being: a declaration of inconsistency must be raised at the court of first instance; a declaration of inconsistency is only a civil remedy and not a criminal remedy; a declaration of inconsistency is not available if parliament is 'engaged' with the issue.[154] Unlike Canada, where the equivalent of a 'declaration of inconsistency' via section 52(1) of the Constitution Act, 1982 and section 24(1) of the Charter applies to all breaches (civil and criminal) and does not need to be raised at the court of first instance, the New Zealand judiciary has severely reduced the possibility of a declaration of inconsistency functioning as a mechanism of rights-based dialogue between courts and legislatures if one were created, either by parliament or by the courts.

These judicial constraints on the application of a declaration of inconsistency are very significant, as bills of rights issues are generally not raised at courts of first instance, because the judicial proceedings centre on the establishment of guilt and the 'live issue' rather than abstract academic debates about rights infringements, reasonable limits and declarations of inconsistency as appropriate remedies. This approach to

[154] Geiringer, 'On a Road to Nowhere', 623–34.

declarations of inconsistency was established by the SCNZ in *Taunoa* v. *Attorney General*, where an attempt to declare the Prisoners' and Victims Claim Act inconsistent with the NZBORA was dismissed by the SCNZ because it had not been previously raised and would, in the opinion of the Court, represent a 'new' case and not an appealed decision of a lower court.[155] The implications of this procedural hurdle are significant, as the ability for declarations of inconsistency to be raised to the level of the Supreme Court is rather limited. Further, this judicial approach significantly undermines the development of a central objective of declarations of inconsistency in parliamentary bills of rights: an important mechanism to facilitate institutional dialogue between courts and legislatures, where courts notify parliament of legislative infringements and parliament decides whether and how to respond. Thus, an important aspect of dialogic constitutionalism has been significantly undermined by the *Taunoa* principle in the event that a declaration of inconsistency is established.

A more serious judicial hurdle was established by the Court of Appeal in *Belcher* v. *Chief Executive of the Department of Corrections*.[156] In *Belcher*, the Court of Appeal determined that a judicial declaration of inconsistency is a civil remedy that cannot be granted in criminal proceedings. This approach to declarations of inconsistency departs markedly from the practice of advanced Westminster systems with bills of rights, such as Canada, the United Kingdom and Victoria's modified remedies (declarations of inconsistent interpretation), where declarations are permitted in any area of law covered by the bill of rights. The *Belcher* principle will seriously undermine the value of a declaration of inconsistency if established, as criminal procedure represents the vast majority of NZBORA cases reviewed. Indeed, if a declaration of inconsistency is established, the remedial powers available under the NZBORA will be unavailable with regard to a large number of rights infringements because of the *Belcher* principle. According to Geiringer, this principle is likely to endure in the long term, as the SCNZ refused to grant leave to hear the jurisdictional issue raised by the Court of Appeal.

The final procedural hurdle to an effective judicial remedy power is the *Boscawen* principle, which states that the courts cannot consider declarations of inconsistency in the abstract. In *Boscawen*, a declaration

[155] *Taunoa* v. *Attorney General* [2008] 1 NZLR 429 (NZSC).

[156] *Belcher* v. *Chief Executive of the Department of Corrections* [2006] 1 NZLR 507 (CA).

of inconsistency was sought against the Electoral Finance Bill 2007, which was introduced into parliament without the Attorney General issuing a section 7 report. The plaintiffs contended that the Electoral Finance Bill 2007 clearly violated freedom of expression by imposing spending restrictions on third parties in election campaigns, and that the Attorney General's failure to notify parliament was a breach of statutory responsibility under the NZBORA. The SCNZ dismissed both arguments, claiming the Attorney General's discretion as to whether to report to parliament under section 7 must not be subjected to judicial oversight 'as it would place the Court at the heart of a political debate actually being carried on in the House. It would effectively force a confrontation between the Attorney General and the court, on a topic in which parliament has entrusted the required assessment to the Attorney General, not the courts.'[157] On the question of abstract review, as previously discussed, the SCNZ rejected it, claiming that the Attorney General's Advisory Group on the Supreme Court of New Zealand provided clear guidance: by rejecting advisory opinions for a future SCNZ, the courts had no authority to consider declarations of inconsistency in the abstract.

Erdos argues that judicial approaches do not operate in a vacuum, and that political culture and the development of a politico-legal opportunity structure are strong determinants of how a court approaches a bill of rights.[158] Evidence for the importance of political culture is found in judicial constraints placed on declarations of inconsistency established in *Taunoa*, *Belcher* and *Boscawen*. Matthew Palmer argues that constitutional realism in New Zealand – the beliefs and behaviour of constitutional actors – reinforce the principle of parliamentary supremacy, and act as a serious constraint on judicial creativity under the NZBORA as 'Suspicion of judges' ability to frustrate the will of a democratically elected government taps into a deep root in the New Zealand national constitutional culture.'[159] This is evident in the *Hansen* methodology established by the SCNZ for approaching judicial review under the NZBORA. Unlike the Supreme Court of Canada, which first investigates whether there is a rights violation in a legislative scheme and then

[157] *Boscawen* v. *Attorney General* [2009] NZCA 12 (O'Regan J. at para 36).
[158] Erdos, 'Judicial Culture and the Politicolegal Opportunity Structure', 95–127.
[159] Palmer, 'New Zealand's Constitutional Culture', 586.

considers the intention of parliament under the reasonable limits clause, as a violation must be based on a 'pressing and substantial' legislative objective, the SCNZ first attempts to discover the intention of parliament. Part of the methodological difference is related to the statutory nature of the NZBORA and the fact it is equal in status to other enactments.

In particular, the Interpretations Act 1999 states that '[t]he meaning of an enactment must be ascertained from its text and in light of its purpose' and this approach clearly signals to the judiciary, when interpreting the NZBORA, that the courts must defer to parliament's stated purpose and not the effect of legislative enactments on rights and freedoms. As governments generally legislate with the purpose of protecting rights and freedoms and the Interpretations Act 1999 limits judicial discovery of intention to 'the indications found in the enactment', the principle of parliamentary supremacy severely curtails judicial participation in rights protections when courts review statues passed by parliament.

The political culture limitations on judicial review are significant in New Zealand. Unlike the courts in Canada – which have engaged in limited forms of declarations of inconsistency since 1867, as the courts could declare government action *ultra vires* a violation of the division of powers, and this power was expanded to include declarations of unconstitutionality under the Charter of Rights and Freedoms in 1982 – no such judicial review function exists in New Zealand because of its unitary status and its largely unwritten constitution. Clearly, this has complicated the judicial function under the NZBORA. More importantly, it emphasizes the importance of explicit political triggers authorizing the courts to engage in substantive judicial review. Indeed, even with Canadian courts engaged in federalism review since 1867, the inclusion of explicit political triggers in the Canadian Charter empowering the courts to engage in substantive rights review was required in order to see the politico-legal culture of parliamentary supremacy within a federal framework replaced as *the* constitutional principle in Canada.

Geiringer concludes that the emergence of implied declarations of inconsistency represents 'a road to nowhere' because of restrictive judicial approaches to this issue, a judicial culture that avoids confrontations with parliament and a populace that embraces the principles of parliamentary supremacy without reservation. Indeed, Geiringer states that 'we cannot rely on the implied declaration of inconsistency jurisdiction to found a robust dialogue of the kind that is emerging in the United

Kingdom between the judicial and political branches of government.'[160] Short of parliament amending the NZBORA to include a declaration of inconsistency – an unlikely development, given that the NZBORA has only been amended once, in 1993, to expand the grounds for non-discrimination – it appears unlikely that the judiciary will engage in robust review of statutes through implied doctrines created by an activist judiciary any time soon. For these reasons, the NZBORA is an interpretive bill of rights that requires political actors to be vigilant in ensuring its application to legislation once the Attorney General reports to parliament under section 7. As the next chapters argue, parliamentary oversight of the government's legislative agenda has not lived up to former Prime Minister Palmer's expectation of this parliamentary bill of rights, due to changes to the Standing Orders of the House of Representatives to accommodate MMP, as well as the political realities of multi-party governing coalitions and 'confidence and supply' agreements with minor parties that have emerged under MMP, and which are essential to government stability.

Conclusion

The political origins of the NZBORA demonstrate that Geoffrey Palmer, first as Deputy Leader of the Labour Party and then as Prime Minister, viewed the NZBORA as part of a broader institutional configuration of the constitutional system intended to strengthen parliament by constraining the growing power of the cabinet and the Prime Minister. At first, Palmer believed that a judicially enforceable bill of rights was necessary to ensure a return to parliamentary government, as judicial review would require the cabinet to defend its legislative agenda as consistent with the rights and freedoms approved by parliament in the form of the NZBORA. As such, the NZBORA would establish parliament's intentions regarding rights and freedoms, and judicial review would ensure that the cabinet upheld parliament's stated intention in the NZBORA when acts of parliament were challenged before the courts.

Conceptualization of the NZBORA as an instrument of parliamentary control over the cabinet, however, found a sceptical audience that questioned how judicial empowerment could be reconciled with

[160] Geiringer, 'On a Road to Nowhere', 649.

parliamentary supremacy. Unable to transcend this principled opposition to a judicially enforced bill of rights, which nearly derailed the bill of rights project, the NZBORA gained momentum as a result of two interrelated, and unforeseen, developments: first, the decision to recast it as a statutory bill of rights simply enforced through parliamentary instruments such as section 7 of the NZBORA; second, the sudden resignation of David Lange and Geoffrey Palmer's surprising ascension to the prime ministership in August 1989. In this respect the Canadian Charter of Rights and the NZBORA were saved from certain defeat by unforeseen political events. In the case of Canada, Trudeau's return to the prime ministership after the short-lived Clark ministry, which held office for only nine months, saw the Charter of Rights and Freedoms return as the principal objective of the national government. It passed because it was the personal political legacy of Pierre Trudeau. In New Zealand, his prime ministership allowed Geoffrey Palmer to prioritize the NZBORA – which had not been the case under his predecessor – and to employ the authority of his office to ensure its passage by the majority Labour government. Although the NZBORA was passed as a statutory instrument without judicial enforcement, it was part of a larger project of institutional change, alongside electoral and parliamentary reform, that was designed to shift power away from the cabinet and back to parliament. In essence, Palmer was dedicated to parliamentary reform through extra-parliamentary instruments, and sought to ensure a return to parliamentary government by curtailing what he perceived as unbridled power on the part of the cabinet and the Prime Minister.

Although this chapter has questioned the ability of parliamentary oversight mechanisms to correct the empowerment of the ministry at the expense of parliament, the emergence of BORA vetting within the bureaucracy is perhaps the most important legacy of the NZBORA. In this respect, the incorporation of rights considerations during the design of legislation demonstrates a commitment by the ministry to parliament's decision to pass the NZBORA in 1990. Our criticism of the cabinet and its commitment to the NZBORA – as well as the effectiveness of parliamentary oversight mechanisms, such as the Attorney General's reporting duty under section 7 – is therefore based on the failure of parliamentarians or the ministry to amend government bills once a section 7 report is tabled before parliament under Standing Order 262 of the House of Representatives. As we will argue in the next chapters, the failure of this parliamentary bill of rights, as it relates to the government's legislative agenda, is largely the result of an unexpected development – the jettisoning of the SMP electoral system and its replacement with MMP in 1996. Indeed, the NZBORA was an attempt to address the problems of the SMP system and the empowerment of the cabinet and the prime minster. The emergence of MMP has created a new set of issues surrounding parliamentary government, which in turn have significant implications for a parliamentary bill of rights operating within an MMP electoral system.

3

The New Zealand Bill of Rights Act 1990 and MMP

The Attorney General's statutory reporting duty under section 7 of the New Zealand Bill of Rights Act (NZBORA) is an essential instrument for parliamentary engagement of rights and freedoms. It is an important public statement that identities potentially incompatible legislation introduced into New Zealand's unicameral parliament.[1] While this reporting duty does not prevent the passage of legislation,[2] it is intended to facilitate parliamentary engagement with legislation that may be inconsistent with the NZBORA.[3] Indeed, the Attorney General does not conclude that legislation is inconsistent with the NZBORA, but simply provides a reasoned opinion that legislation 'appears inconsistent', subject to parliamentary review of this report. However, by drawing this to the attention of parliamentarians, the Attorney General's disclosure has the potential to facilitate two important outcomes: first, parliamentary resolution of potentially incompatible legislation through amendments at the select committee stage; second, an informed parliamentary decision to proceed with legislation reported on by the Attorney General under section 7 of the NZBORA.[4]

Although there is debate about the value of section 7 reports,[5] all Attorney Generals have taken this responsibility seriously under the

[1] S. Gardbaum, *The New Commonwealth Model of Constitutionalism: Theory and Practice* (Cambridge: Cambridge University Press, 2013), pp. 132–33.

[2] C. Archer and G. Burt, 'Section 7 of the Bill of Rights Act', (2004) *New Zealand Law Journal* 320–21.

[3] P. Fitzgerald, 'Section 7 of the New Zealand Bill of Rights Act 1990: A Very Practical Power or Well-intentioned Nonsense', (1992) 22 *Victoria University of Wellington Law Review* 136–37.

[4] S. Jackson, 'Designing Human Rights Legislation: "Dialogue", the Commonwealth Model and the Roles of Parliaments and Courts', (2007) 13 *Auckland University Law Review* 100–3.

[5] G. Huscroft, 'Is the Defeat of Health Warnings a Victory for Human Rights? The Attorney General and Pre-legislative Scrutiny for Consistency with the New Zealand Bill of Rights', (2003) 14 *Public Law* 109–21; A. Geddis, 'The Comparative Irrelevance of the NZBORA to

NZBORA. Since 1990, 65 reports have been issued to parliament, of which 33 involved non-government bills (local and members' bills) and 32 government bills.[6] In Canada, by comparison, the Minister of Justice has never issued a similar report under section 4.1.1 of the Department of Justice Act.[7] Given that the Supreme Court of Canada invalidated 45 statutes enacted by the Parliament of Canada as unconstitutional violations of the Charter of Rights and Freedoms between 1984 and 2012, the Minister of Justice's failure to report any inconsistency to parliament is rather curious.[8] Indeed, there appears to be an inverse relationship between risk of judicial invalidation and the robustness of the parliamentary reporting duty. The most robust use of reporting obligations by the Attorney General is seen with regard to statutory bills of rights such as the NZBORA, whereas rarely, if ever, are reports of inconsistency sent to parliament by the Minister of Justice with regard to constitutional bills of rights such as the Canadian Charter of Rights and Freedoms.[9]

Legislative Practice', (2009) 43 *New Zealand Universities Law Review* 465–88; J. Hiebert, 'Rights Vetting in New Zealand and Canada: Similar Ideas, Different Outcomes', (2005) *New Zealand Journal of Public and International Law* 63–105.

6 Of the 32 government bills with section 7 reports, 28 bills have been passed into law and four are currently progressing through the parliamentary process (17 April 2014). The last government bill included is Parole (Extended Supervision Orders) Amendment Bill 2014. Of the 33 non-government bills, eight have been passed into law and two are presently before parliament.

7 *Department of Justice Act*, R.S.C., 1985, c. J-2:

> **4.1** (1) Subject to subsection (2), the Minister shall, in accordance with such regulations as may be prescribed by the Governor in Council, examine every regulation transmitted to the Clerk of the Privy Council for registration pursuant to the *Statutory Instruments Act* and every Bill introduced in or presented to the House of Commons by a minister of the Crown, in order to ascertain whether any of the provisions thereof are inconsistent with the purposes and provisions of the *Canadian Charter of Rights and Freedoms* and the Minister shall report any such inconsistency to the House of Commons at the first convenient opportunity.

8 This figure only includes legislation passed into law by the Parliament of Canada that was subsequently invalidated by the Supreme Court of Canada. In the same period, 1984–2012, the Supreme Court of Canada invalidated 27 acts passed by the provincial legislatures. Thus, Supreme Court of Canada has invalidated 72 statutes passed by Parliament and the provincial legislatures.

9 Mark Tushnet categorizes alternative models of judicial review in Westminster systems as the interpretive mandate (New Zealand), where the judiciary cannot enforce guarantees; the augmented-interpretive mandate (United Kingdom), where the judiciary may issue non-binding declarations of incompatibility; and the dialogic mode of review (Canada), which combines strong-form judicial review (declarations of unconstitutionality) with

Plausible explanations for this variance may be the distinct historical context of these law officers in different parliamentary settings,[10] or simply parliamentarians' discretionary interpretations of these statutory responsibilities.[11] However, as we go on to argue, an alternative explanation that accounts for the frequency of reporting when bills are inconsistent with bills of rights (or anticipated judicial interpretations of them) is a rational calculation of risk assessment by the cabinet. Indeed, the most robust reporting occurs when the cabinet's legislative agenda cannot be overturned by legislative or judicial rights review, as in the case of New Zealand. In contrast, parliamentary systems with robust legislative and judicial review generally see few, if any, reports of inconsistency. What has been interpreted as transparency and evidence of a flourishing rights culture,[12] therefore, may simply be a political calculation that reporting an inconsistency to parliament has no impact on a government's ability to pass its legislative agenda. Thus, the risks associated with reporting inconsistencies may be so low, as in the case of New Zealand, that disclosure becomes part of the legislative calculation on how to govern with rights instruments. In contrast, in Canada, where the risk of disclosure is significant because the courts can declare legislation unconstitutional, political actors are reluctant to disclose possible breaches of the Charter of Rights and Freedoms to parliament.

Similar to the experience of the UK House of Commons under the Human Rights Act (HRA) 1998, we argue that section 7 reports by the Attorney General have failed to generate meaningful and substantive engagement of the NZBORA once legislation is introduced into parliament. Section 7 reports have not advanced the principal goal of parliamentary oversight of the political executive and its legislative agenda.[13] Indeed, a total of 28 government bills accompanied by section 7 reports have been passed into law since 1990 and four are presently before

strong-form legislative responses such as formal political reversal of judicial decisions through constitutional instruments such as the Charter's notwithstanding clause, section 33. See M. Tushnet, *Weak Courts, Strong Rights* (Princeton: Princeton University Press, 2008), pp. 25–33.

[10] J. Hiebert, 'Rights Vetting in New Zealand and Canada: Similar Ideas, Different Outcomes', (2005) *New Zealand Journal of Public and International Law* 90–3.

[11] G. Huscroft, 'Reconciling Duty and Discretion: The Attorney General in the Charter Era', (2009) 34 *Queen's Law Journal* 14.

[12] P. Butler, 'Human Rights and Parliamentary Sovereignty in New Zealand', (2004) 35 *Victoria University of Wellington Law Review* 341–66.

[13] J. Hiebert, 'Governing Under the Human Rights Act: The Limitations of Wishful Thinking', (2012) *Public Law* 26–49.

parliament; only two government bills have been amended to address compatibility issues raised by the Attorney General.[14] This is one of the central paradoxes of parliamentary bills of rights and the attempt to substitute judicial oversight with enhanced parliamentary oversight of the political executive. Mechanisms such as the Attorney General's reporting duty are designed to address the issue of judicial power through parliamentary reflection and enforcement. However, these mechanisms require parliamentary willingness to directly challenge legislation introduced by the cabinet with the full knowledge that, in the opinion of the Attorney General, the legislation is incompatible with the NZBORA.

This demonstrates a serious disconnect between constitutional projects intended to facilitate enhanced protection of rights through the combined effects of parliamentary oversight and weak-form judicial review (or what Stephen Gardbaum characterized as constitutional engineering) and the functioning of constitutional instruments such as section 7 of the NZBORA. Specifically, parliamentary parties are disciplined institutions in which members of the government support the cabinet and its legislative agenda in the parliamentary arena. As a rule, backbench government members do not hold the cabinet to account, as this is the role of opposition parties. While designed to facilitate parliamentary scrutiny, the Attorney General's statutory section 7 reporting duty requires – and is premised on – members of the government benches holding the cabinet to account when incompatible legislation is introduced into parliament; however, this is not likely to happen because of the disciplined political parties in the Westminster tradition, as well as the principle of responsible government, where it is the duty of opposition parties to scrutinize the government's legislation agenda and hold it to account. As a result, the theory behind section 7 of the NZBORA does not conform to the reality of Westminster parliamentary democracy and disciplined political parties that support their respective leadership teams in parliament.

While few non-government bills with section 7 reports have been passed, this is not evidence of the effectiveness of section 7 as a check

[14] The two government bills amended to address compatibility issues raised by the Attorney General are (1) Children, Young Persons and their Families Amendment Act 1994 and (2) Electoral Amendment Act 2002. Thus, 93 per cent of all government bills that the Attorney General has reported to parliament under section 7 of the NZBORA have passed without amendment.

on incompatible legislation. Indeed, very few non-government bills are passed in any parliamentary session and those with section 7 reports are dispensed with before first reading for reasons other than the compatibility issues identified by the Attorney General.[15] A notable exception to this is the passage of the Electoral (Disqualification of Sentenced Prisoners) Amendment Act 2010, introduced as a members' bill by Paul Quinn of New Zealand National and the subject of a section 7 report by Attorney General Christopher Finlayson; however, this members' bill is consistent with the 'law and order' agenda of National and its confidence and supply partner ACT New Zealand, and was unanimously supported by both caucuses. As the vast majority of bills passed are government bills, the effectiveness of section 7 as a mechanism of parliamentary oversight must be evaluated in relation to its effect on potentially incompatible legislation introduced by the cabinet.

There are important similarities between the Westminster and New Zealand parliaments that account for parliamentarians' inability to sufficiently engage the HRA and the NZBORA in regard to government bills, such as executive dominance and party discipline that are structural determinants of parliamentary behaviour. However, a number of unique institutional features exist in New Zealand that further contribute to the unrealized possibilities of section 7 and parliamentary oversight of government bills. First, New Zealand's mixed member proportional (MMP) electoral system has important implications for the NZBORA and section 7 reports by the Attorney General. Second, because MMP has generally resulted in minority parliaments, the formation of governing coalitions based on confidence and supply agreements with minor parties has clear implications for the NZBORA in the parliamentary setting. This is not unique to New Zealand: the 2010 General Election in the United Kingdom produced the first hung parliament since 1974, and at the time of writing, in 2014, the UK is governed by a Conservative–Liberal Democrat coalition.[16] This may simply be an aberration in the United Kingdom, however, whereas it has been an enduring aspect of MMP in New Zealand.[17] Finally, New Zealand does not have a dedicated parliamentary

[15] A. Geddis, 'The Comparative Irrelevance of the NZBORA to Legislative Practice', (2009) 42 *New Zealand Universities Law Review* 471, 478.

[16] V. Bogdanor, *The Coalition and the Constitution* (Oxford: Hart Publishing, 2011), pp. 45–60.

[17] P. Joseph, 'MMP and the Constitution', (2009) 7 *New Zealand Journal of Public and International Law* 118.

committee like the Joint Committee on Human Rights (JCHR) in Westminster, which engages executive certification of legislation as compatible with domestic rights instruments.

What this suggests, therefore, is that the structural variables of parliamentary democracy – executive dominance, party discipline, electoral systems, coalition agreements and the committee system within parliament – are the most significant determinants of the effective functioning of the HRA 1998 and the NZBORA 1990 because they are *parliamentary* bills of rights. Finally, MMP has necessitated rule changes in the Standing Orders of the House of Representatives to ensure stability and efficiency in a multi-party parliament. While the standard explanation for the weakness of parliamentary bills of rights is a lack of judicial enforcement, as well as constrained judicial review,[18] our explanation is decidedly parliament-centred, as we focus on the structural conditions of Westminster parliamentary democracy in New Zealand and the United Kingdom. The puzzle of parliamentary failure to effectively engage section 7 reports, as this chapter will argue, is largely explained by the introduction of MMP, the rule changes made to accommodate MMP and the challenges the new system posed to government stability and effectiveness within the parliament of New Zealand. These changes have significant implications for the NZBORA because it is a parliamentary bill of rights and must be assessed in light of the structural variables determining parliamentary government, such as the electoral system and the Standing Orders of the House of Representatives. Perhaps more significant (and so far largely ignored) is that these structural variables can undermine the ability of parliamentary bills of rights to promote rights-based dialogue and parliamentary resolution of rights-based incompatibilities.

I. Parliamentary bills of rights and the Commonwealth model

In his assessment of parliamentary bills of rights in Canada, New Zealand, the United Kingdom and Australia, Stephen Gardbaum concludes that New Zealand functions in the way that the new Commonwealth model of constitutionalism envisions – strong-form political review coupled with (but not subordinated) to weak-form judicial review.[19] While judicial review has been augmented by the NZBORA, Gardbaum concludes that it is rather constrained, and this has mitigated concerns

[18] M. Tushnet, *Weak Courts*, pp. 48–9.
[19] S. Gardbaum, *The New Commonwealth Model of Constitutionalism*, p. 151.

about judicial power in New Zealand. Unlike Canada, where concerns about judicial supremacy have long been present because of parliamentary reluctance to challenge judicial interpretation through the override provision of the Charter of Rights, section 33,[20] the New Zealand parliament retains full sovereignty over the constitutionality of legislation. This legislative sovereignty is not curtailed by the Attorney General's statutory reporting duty under section 7 or by the limited nature of judicial review under sections 4 and 6 of the NZBORA. While parliament remains responsible for the *enforcement* of the NZBORA once the Attorney General reports, the cabinet remains *accountable* for the introduction of legislation that may be inconsistent with rights and freedoms, as well as retaining the ability to *ignore* rights-based critiques raised within parliament or by the courts.[21]

While Gardbaum's assessment of the NZBORA is consistent with Erdos' statement that judicial activism has resulted in important safeguards when dealing with state authorities such as the police,[22] this was not the principal intention of the NZBORA.[23] Courts in the common law tradition have historically placed constraints on the police. While this has been augmented by the introduction of the NZBORA, a positive assessment of the NZBORA should not be based on a judicial role that existed before its implementation. In defending the NZBORA in draft form before parliament, Geoffrey Palmer was explicit that the NZBORA was conceptualized principally as a constraint on prime ministerial government and executive supremacy *in the legislative context*. Palmer considered the NZBORA as a check on adversarial constitutionalism within the parliamentary setting and a way to re-invigorate parliamentary democracy through rights-based analysis of the cabinet's legislative agenda by ordinary parliamentarians. Thus, the NZBORA was a crucial aspect of attempts at parliamentary reform by the fourth Labour government (1984–90) in order to check the trend toward prime ministerial dominance that had intensified under Robert Muldoon of New Zealand National (1975–84). The NZBORA was also an attempt to address the

[20] S. Gardbaum, *The New Commonwealth Model of Constitutionalism*, p. 123.

[21] C. Charters, 'Responding to Waldron's Defence of Legislatures: Why New Zealand's Parliament Does Not Protect Rights in Hard Cases', (2006) *New Zealand Law Review* 621–63.

[22] S. Gardbaum, *The New Commonwealth Model of Constitutionalism*, pp. 147–49. See also D. Erdos, 'Judicial Culture and the Politicolegal Opportunity Structure: Explaining Bill of Rights Legal Impact in New Zealand', (2009) 34 *Law and Social Inquiry* 96, 102.

[23] S. Gardbaum, *The New Commonwealth Model of Constitutionalism*, p. 135.

deficiencies of a unicameral parliament in controlling the cabinet, which had become more acute because of the flaws of the single member plurality (SMP) electoral system that emerged in New Zealand from the 1970s where a plurality of the vote by the first *or* second place party always translated into a majority of seats in parliament.[24]

Palmer rationalized that section 7 of the NZBORA would be a powerful mechanism of legislative self-restraint, arguing that the cabinet would be very reluctant to introduce legislation that produced a section 7 report.[25] Indeed, Palmer sincerely believed that the Attorney General would rarely use section 7, as the threat of being associated with incompatible legislation would discipline the cabinet to only introduce rights-compatible legislation.[26] In effect, section 7 would be a serious deterrent and would serve as an adequate substitution for judicial review, given that Palmer had failed to convince parliamentarians, including his own Labour colleagues, of the need for an entrenched constitutional bill of rights with expansive judicial remedial powers. A parliamentary bill of rights, enforced through political mechanisms such as section 7 reports by the Attorney General, was the compromise that Palmer accepted as Minister of Justice and later as Prime Minister.

While Gardbaum acknowledges that parliament has generally ignored section 7 reports by the Attorney General,[27] he contends that a fair appreciation of the NZBORA must include a consideration of legislative responses to judicial decisions. For Gardbaum, this is the essence of the new Commonwealth model of constitutionalism, as the judiciary extends invitations to reconsider legislation in light of the NZBORA and parliament decides whether to accept these invitations and revisit legislation. In the case of New Zealand, Gardbaum argues that parliament has been receptive to these judicial invitations, and has responded to most judicial decisions involving the NZBORA.[28] Gardbaum highlights the *Quilter* decision in which the Court of Appeal declined to interpret the gender-neutral language of the 1955 Marriage Act as allowing judicial recognition of same sex marriage, and parliament's revisiting

[24] G. Palmer, 'Muldoon and the Constitution', in M. Clark (ed.), *Muldoon Revisited* (Palmerston North: Dunedin Press, 2004), pp. 208–10; interview with Sir Geoffrey Palmer, New Zealand Law Commission, Wellington, New Zealand (6 May 2004).

[25] G. Palmer, *New Zealand's Constitution in Crisis* (Dunedin: McIndoe, 1992), p. 59.

[26] G. Palmer, *A Bill of Rights for New Zealand – A White Paper* (Wellington: Government Printers, 1985), p. 5.

[27] S. Gardbaum, *The New Commonwealth Model of Constitutionalism*, p. 134.

[28] Ibid., p. 149.

the definition of marriage with the Civil Union Act 2004. Similarly, in *Poumoka* the Court of Appeal invited parliament to revisit the penalty provisions of the 1999 Criminal Justice Amendment Act, and parliament responded with the Sentencing Act 2002.[29]

We disagree with this assessment of NZBORA. Having refused the Attorney General's invitation to consider the implications of potentially inconsistent legislation by issuing a section 7 report, it is unclear why parliament would receive a judicial invitation more favourably. As Geiringer has argued, the constraints on robust judicial review imposed by the courts,[30] as well as by sections 4 and 6 of the NZBORA, present a strong rebuke to Gardbaum's defence of the NZBORA. Like Geiringer, we prioritize the political rather than legal mechanisms that enforce the NZBORA, and base our assessment on how well these parliamentary oversight mechanisms function in regard to checking the cabinet's legislative agenda.[31] While parliament may revisit legislation, as it did in the case of the Civil Union Act 2004 and the Sentencing Act 2004, it is unclear whether these episodes represent parliamentary acceptance of a judicial invitation to reconsider in light of the NZBORA. In the case of Canada this dynamic does exist, as legislative amendment has generally been the dialogic response to judicial declarations of unconstitutionality.[32] However, it is unclear whether dialogue theory captures the New Zealand dynamic because parliament is under no obligation to accept a judicial invitation to revisit legislation. This has been the main criticism of dialogic constitutionalism, as developed by Hogg and Bushell[33] and adopted in other jurisdictions.[34] Specifically, this approach is problematic because it considers any legislative response to a judicial decision

29 S. Gardbaum, *The New Commonwealth Model of Constitutionalism*, p. 149.

30 C. Geiringer, 'On a Road to Nowhere: Implied Declarations of Inconsistency and the New Zealand Bill of Rights Act', (2009) 40 *Victoria University of Wellington Law Review* 613–47.

31 C. Geiringer, 'The Dead Hand of the Bill of Rights? Is the New Zealand Bill of Rights Act 1990 a Substantive Legal Constraint on Parliament's Power to Legislate?', (2007) 11 *Otago Law Review* 390.

32 E. MacFarlane, 'Dialogue or Compliance? Measuring Legislatures' Policy Response to Court Rulings on Rights', (2013) 34 *International Political Science Review* 39–56.

33 P. Hogg, A. Bushell Thorton and W. Wright, 'Charter Dialogue Revisited – or "Much Ado About Metaphors"', (2007) 45 *Osgoode Hall Law Journal* 2–65.

34 P. Butler, 'Human Rights and Parliamentary Sovereignty in New Zealand', (2004) 35 *Victoria University of Wellington Law Review* 341–66; P. Joseph, 'Parliament, the Courts and the Collaborative Enterprise', (2004) 15 *King's College Law Journal* 321–345; A. Young, 'Is Dialogue Working Under the Human Rights Act 1998?', (2011) *Public Law* 773–800.

as evidence of the new judicial–parliamentary relationship that emerges under a parliamentary bills of rights.[35]

There is, however, a more serious reservation we have regarding Gardbaum's defence of the NZBORA. A parliamentary bill of rights is defined by the presence of institutional mechanisms that allow parliamentarians to engage in rights-based assessments of the cabinet's legislative agenda. Such a bill of rights is principally, if not exclusively, enforced in the parliamentary setting. The failure to engage section 7 reports by the Attorney General is both significant and puzzling, and cannot be compensated for by judicial invitations to reconsider legislation in light of the NZBORA. It is significant, because it questions how effectively the NZBORA functions as a parliamentary bill of rights if the chief instrument of parliamentary engagement has failed to transform the scrutiny of legislation identified by the Attorney General as potentially incompatible. It is puzzling, simply because a serious disconnect exists between the stages of legislative rights review and the commitment to BORA vetting: specifically, pre-introduction scrutiny by the bureaucracy is robust and transparent, as all BORA advice by the Ministry of Justice and Crown Law Office is accessible to the public and parliamentarians via the Ministry of Justice website.[36]

The Attorney General's reporting duty is also robust and transparent: all section 7 reports are posted on the Ministry of Justice website, as well as being available on the parliament of New Zealand's website. While parliamentary reference to the Attorney General's section 7 reports does occur, in the case of government legislation it does not see the cabinet introduce amendments to address the rights-based concerns raised at the select committee stage.[37] Indeed, nearly all government legislation introduced with a section 7 report has been passed without NZBORA-friendly amendments. Simply referring to the NZBORA and the Attorney

[35] C. Manfredi and J. Kelly, 'Six Degrees of Dialogue: A Response to Hogg and Bushell', (1999) 37 *Osgoode Hall Law Journal* 513–27; J. Kelly, 'A Difficult Dialogue: Statements of Compatibility and the Victorian *Charter of Human Rights and Responsibilities Act*', (2011) 46 *Australian Journal of Political Science* 257–79; L. McDonald, 'Rights, "Dialogue" and Democratic Objections to Judicial Review', (2004) 32 *Federal Law Review* 1–28.

[36] www.justice.govt.nz/policy/constitutional-law-and-human-rights/human-rights/bill-of-rights

[37] A. Geddis, 'Inter-institutional "Rights Dialogue" under the New Zealand Bill of Rights Act', in T. Campbell, K.D. Ewing and A. Tomkins, (eds.), *The Legal Protection of Human Rights: Sceptical Essays* (Oxford: Oxford University Press, 2011), pp. 98–100.

General's report does not constitute 'dialogue' in any meaningful sense, despite assertions of an emerging parliamentary discourse on the NZBORA.[38] Specifically, section 7 was designed to provide parliamentary oversight as a way to facilitate the amendment of legislation to ensure its compatibility – or, at a minimum, fulsome justification by the cabinet of the need to proceed with incompatible legislation. As we argue in this chapter, neither condition for parliamentary dialogue presently exists in relation to the NZBORA.

II. The NZBORA 1990 and electoral reform

Although the NZBORA was an institutional response to address prime ministerial dominance within a unicameral parliament, it was not the only reform to address the danger of unbridled power within New Zealand's parliamentary setting.[39] What has generally escaped analysis when the NZBORA is evaluated for its effectiveness as a parliamentary bill of rights is consideration of perhaps the most significant constitutional change engineered by the fourth Labour government – the transition from the SMP to the MMP electoral system in 1993. In 1985, the Lange ministry established the Royal Commission on the Electoral System, which reported in 1986 and recommended changing the electoral system from SMP to MMP after approval in a national referendum.[40] According to the Royal Commission, all post-war majority governments had been elected simply with a plurality of votes, and this questioned the fairness of the SMP system.[41] Indeed, the Labour party had won a plurality of votes in the 1978 and 1981 elections, yet the New Zealand National party secured office because of a more efficient distribution of its vote. This motivated Palmer as Minister of Justice to appoint the Royal Commission to review the SMP system, which he considered

[38] P. Butler, 'It Takes Two to Tango: Have They Learned Their Steps?', University of Sydney Workshop on 'Judicial Supremacy or Inter-institutional Dialogue? Political Responses to Judicial Review' (18–19 May 2010), 24–29.

[39] G. Palmer, *Unbridled Power* (Auckland: Oxford University Press, 1987); see also G. Palmer, *New Zealand's Constitution in Crisis* and D. Erdos, 'Aversive Constitutionalism in the Westminster World: The Genesis of the New Zealand Bill of Rights Act 1990', (2007) 5 *International Journal of Constitutional Law* 343–69.

[40] J. Boston, S. Levine, E. McLeay and N. Roberts, *Electoral and Constitutional Change in New Zealand: An MMP Source Book* (Palmerston North: Dunmore Press, 1999), p. 13.

[41] Royal Commission on the Electoral System, *Toward a Better Democracy*, cited in G. Palmer and M. Palmer, *Bridled Power*, 4th edition (Melbourne: Oxford University Press, 2004), pp. 12–13.

a major cause of unbridled power given the growing inefficiency of the electoral system that facilitated and sustained the Muldoon ministry.[42] In this respect, MMP was viewed as an appropriate response to the deficiencies of the SMP system in adequately translating votes into seats. As a modified system of proportional representation, MMP would preserve the constituency basis of the SMP system and augment it with List MPs allocated to political parties that garnered at least 5 per cent of the popular vote.

The recommendations of the Royal Commission would result in two referendums. The first occurred in 1992, when New Zealanders were asked two significant questions: first, did they favour changing the electoral system; second, which of four electoral systems presented as alternatives to SMP did they favour? This resulted in 84.7 per cent of voters supporting a change in the electoral system and 70.5 per cent favouring the MMP electoral system.[43] The second referendum occurred in 1993 and was a binding choice between retaining the SMP electoral system or replacing it with MMP. The 1993 referendum saw a narrow majority of 53.9 per cent supporting the electoral change to MMP over SMP.[44] The first MMP election occurred in 1996, and it has since been noted that: 'As expected, the move to proportional representation has brought an end to the long era of single-party majority government. All the administrations since the first MMP election have involved at least two parties. Indeed, most governments have included, in one way or another, the participation of at least three parties. . .'.[45]

One of the central ironies of the NZBORA is that it was designed to address the deficiencies of the SMP system and its contribution to cabinet domination of parliament, the party caucus and the legislative process. Yet, soon after the introduction of the NZBORA in 1990, SMP was replaced by MMP without consideration of this major constitutional change's implications for a parliamentary bill of rights designed in response to the parliamentary configuration resulting from SMP. This is an important point, as the transition to MMP – and indeed the electoral system in general – has not been considered as a structural variable that

42 G. Palmer and M. Palmer, *Bridled Power*, p. 12.

43 R. Malone, *Rebalancing the Constitution: The Challenge of Government Law-Making under MMP* (Wellington: Milne Printers, 2008), pp. 39–40.

44 Ibid., p. 41.

45 J. Boston and D. Bullock, 'Experiments in Executive Government under MMP in New Zealand: Contrasting Approaches to Multi-party Governance', (2009) 7 *New Zealand Journal of Public and International Law* 39–75.

affects the performance of parliamentary bills of rights.[46] There are a number of significant changes associated with MMP that have implications for the NZBORA and the effectiveness of parliamentary scrutiny of legislation introduced into the House of Representatives. Clearly, the MMP system has resulted in a more proportional distribution of seats in the House of Representatives, as individuals vote twice: a constituency vote and a party vote. There are generally 120 seats in the House of Representatives, with 70 constituency seats won by a plurality of the vote and roughly 50 seats allocated in proportion to votes received by political parties that win at least 5 per cent of the national vote.[47] Thus, MMP has produced two distinct members of parliament: the constituency MP and the List MP (individuals who enter parliament based on their ranking on party lists submitted to the Electoral Commission before an election). Indeed, political parties that are unsuccessful at the constituency level yet secure at least 5 per cent of the vote, such as the Green party, are represented in parliament as List MPs. This is an improvement on SMP, as it does ensure greater and fairer representation in parliament.

MMP has changed the character of government, substituting single-party majority governments with, for the most part, multi-party minority coalitions sustained by confidence and supply agreements with minor parties.[48] However, it has seen the continued domination of government by New Zealand National and Labour, alternating in office and supported by formalized agreements with minor parties such as United Future,

[46] Despite the important contribution made by S. Gardbaum in *The New Commonwealth Model of Constitutionalism* and his analysis of the NZBORA (Chapter 6), the implications of MMP for the effectiveness of NZBORA are not considered. While MMP is considered by G. Palmer and M. Palmer in *Bridled Power*, it is largely considered in the context of its impact on parliament, as an institution, and not the NZBORA, as a parliamentary bill of rights. Indeed, this is a general characteristic of the academic analysis of the NZBORA, with only a few exceptions, such as C. Charters, 'Responding to Waldron's Defence of Legislatures'.

[47] The size of the House of Representatives varies depending on the number of parties securing the 5 per cent threshold for representation in Parliament. Indeed, the House of Representatives generally has 120 members divided between 70 constituency MPs and 50 List MPs. However, this total number may be higher or lower than 120, depending on the number of parties that reach the 5 per cent threshold for seats as List MPs under MMP.

[48] J. Boston and D. Bullock, 'Experiments in Executive Government under MMP in New Zealand: Contrasting Approaches to Multi-party Governance', (2009) 7 *New Zealand Journal of Public and International Law* 46; R. Malone, '"Who's the Boss?" Executive-Legislature Relations in New Zealand Under MMP', (2009) 7 *New Zealand Journal of Public and International Law* 5–6.

Table 3.1 *New Zealand government formation, 1975–2014*

Year	Vote	Government	Parties	Confidence and Supply Agreement(s)
1975–1984	SMP	majority	New Zealand National	n/a
1984–1990	SMP	majority	New Zealand Labour	n/a
1990–1994	SMP	majority	New Zealand National	n/a
1994–1996	SMP	minority coalition	New Zealand National, Right of Centre party, United party	n/a
1996–1999	MMP	minority coalition	New Zealand National and New Zealand First	none
1999–2002	MMP	minority coalition	New Zealand Labour and Alliance party	Green party
2002–2005	MMP	minority coalition	New Zealand Labour and Progressive party	United Future
2005–2008	MMP	minority coalition	New Zealand Labour and Progressive party	New Zealand First, United Future, Green party
2008–2011	MMP	Minority	New Zealand National	ACT New Zealand, Māori party, United Future
2011–2014	MMP	Minority	New Zealand National	ACT New Zealand, Māori party, United Future

ACT New Zealand, the Green party or New Zealand First. Indeed, the New Zealand National ministry led by Prime Minister John Key since 2008 is a minority government supported by confidence and supply agreements with ACT New Zealand, the Māori party and United Future. These agreements are formalized arrangements which specify policy commitments that will be introduced as legislation by the governing partners and ministerial positions that will be allocated to senior members of minor parties that support the government. Further, they outline the general contours of parliamentary arrangements between the political parties, issues such as confidence and ministerial responsibility and the relationship between the Prime Minister and the leaders of confidence and supply parties.[49]

According to Boston and Bullock, despite MMP changing the character of cabinet government to one of multi-party composition,

> the advent of MMP has not fundamentally altered the nature of Cabinet government, the role and responsibilities of individual ministers, the role of party caucuses in the policy process or the conventions surrounding the operations of the public service. There is but one major exception. Without doubt, the convention of Cabinet collective responsibility has been affected by the introduction of MMP.[50]

Malone disputes the suggestion that the character of cabinet government has generally remained consistent under MMP, as policy implementation requires the support of several parties – a significant change from the case for a single-party government under SMP.[51] This position is echoed by Elizabeth McLeay, who suggests that the transition from first-past-the-post (FPP) to MMP has altered the role of the Prime Minister: from 'a situation of having no partisan veto players under FPP, prime ministers had to learn to cope with one or more'.[52]

[49] Cabinet Office 2012, 'National-led Administration: Consultation and Operating Arrangements', Circular (1 May); Confidence and Supply Agreement 2008, *Confidence and Supply Agreement*, National and United Future (14 November); Confidence and Supply Agreement 2008, *Confidence and Supply Agreement*, National and ACT New Zealand (14 November); Confidence and Supply Agreement 2008. *Confidence and Supply Agreement*, Relationship Accord, National and Māori Party (16 November).

[50] J. Boston and D. Bullock, 'Experiments in Executive Government under MMP in New Zealand: Contrasting Approaches to Multi-party Governance', (2009) 7 *New Zealand Journal of Public and International Law* 46.

[51] R. Malone, ''Who's the Boss?' Executive-Legislature Relations in New Zealand Under MMP', (2009) 7 *New Zealand Journal of Public and International Law* 5.

[52] E. McLeay, 'Leadership in Cabinet under MMP', in R. Miller and M. Mintrom, (eds.) *Political Leadership in New Zealand* (Auckland: Auckland University Press, 2006), p. 108.

While it is clear that the transition to MMP has impacted cabinet government and the executive–legislature relationship,[53] we suggest that this debate on the electoral system has neglected to consider the implications of MMP for the NZBORA as a parliamentary bill of rights. While MMP has altered the composition of governing arrangements, it has not addressed the problem of executive domination of the parliamentary arena. Instead of single-party dominance through disciplined political parties, MMP has resulted in multi-party executive supremacy and dominance of parliament through agreements with several disciplined political parties. Perhaps more importantly, stable governing coalitions are predicated on agreements with minor parties that generally represent single issues, such as sentencing policy in the case of ACT New Zealand, parole reform in the case of United Future and New Zealand First's focus on crime rates and immigration policy. What has been ignored is that the search for stable governing arrangements under MMP, where minority multi-party governments enter into formal agreements with minor parties, can undermine the parliamentary mechanisms of rights-based scrutiny within the NZBORA. Indeed, a critical reason why section 7 reports have generally been ignored in relation to government bills – or members' bills sponsored by MPs from confidence and supply parties – may be that the legislation cannot be revisited or amended at the select committee stage, given that it is part of a formalized agreement with a minor party.

While the democratic legitimacy of legislation under MMP may be stronger, as it must be passed by political parties that represent a majority of votes cast in the preceding general election, this has come at the expense of transparency and the ability of parliamentarians, under section 7 of the NZBORA, to engage in rights-based parliamentary scrutiny.[54] Because confidence and supply agreements are reached before legislation is designed, drafted and introduced into parliament, this has negated the dialogic potential of the NZBORA when a section 7 report is

[53] In addition to the work of Boston and Bullock, Malone, and McLeay, see G. Palmer and M. Palmer, *Bridled Power*, 4th edition (Melbourne: Oxford University Press, 2004), pp. 13–18; J. Boston, S. Church and T. Bale, 'The Impact of Proportional Representation on Government Effectiveness: The New Zealand Experience', (2003) 62 *Australian Journal of Public Administration* 7–22; J. Bradbury, 'The Best of Both Worlds? MMP Electoral Reform and Constitutional Development in Scotland and Wales', (2009) 7 *New Zealand Journal of Public and International Law* 157–83.

[54] T. Bromwich, 'Parliamentary Rights-vetting Under the NZBORA', (2009) *New Zealand Law Journal* 191.

issued in relation to legislation that originates as part of an agreement with a minor party. As this chapter will argue, many of the section 7 reports issued in relation to government bills under MMP have involved legislation in the criminal policy context that find their origin in governing agreements with minor parties such as New Zealand First, United Future and ACT New Zealand. Indeed, one of the concerns with MMP was government stability due to minority parliaments, as well as government efficiency resulting from multiple veto points in the legislative process. However, as Boston, Church and Bale have argued, in general the negative implications associated with proportional representation have not emerged in New Zealand.[55] Indeed, confidence and supply agreements can ensure stability and legislative efficiency, as most agreements have run the course of an entire parliament in New Zealand under MMP and have ensured the passage of the government's legislative agenda, with the support of minor parties.

Yet, and most problematically for section 7 of the NZBORA, important procedural changes to ensure stability under MMP, in addition to formalized agreements, have significantly depreciated the possibility of parliamentary scrutiny in relation to the NZBORA and the potential for rights-friendly amendments at the select committee stage. These include changes to the Standing Orders of the House of Representatives and to the consultation requirements in the Cabinet Manual. While Standing Order (SO) 262 specifies the reporting duty of the Attorney General under section 7 of the NZBORA,[56] two procedural modifications were introduced to accommodate MMP which complicate the effectiveness of the Attorney General's reporting duty and SO 262. Significant changes to the Standing Orders occurred in 1996 after an examination of parliamentary procedures in European countries with proportional representation.[57] This fact-finding expedition was largely motivated by the desire to adopt 'best practices' in PR systems to avoid government instability once New Zealand transitioned from single-party government to multiparty government under MMP. The most significant change introduced is SO 138, the party vote, which was inspired by parliamentary practice in

[55] J. Boston, S. Church and T. Bale, 'The Impact of Proportional Representation on Government Effectiveness'.

[56] Parliament of New Zealand 2011, Standing Orders of the House of Representatives, SO 262.

[57] J. Boston, S. Levine, E. McLeay and N. Roberts, *Electoral and Constitutional Change in New Zealand: An MMP Source Book* (Palmerston North: Dunmore Press Ltd., 1999), p. 228.

the Netherlands.[58] Under SO 138, 'where further vote is called for, a party vote is held unless the subject of the vote is to be a treated as a conscience issue'.[59] While this may appear an insignificant change, as disciplined parties produce party votes in Westminster systems, the procedures for registering a party vote are unique. Instead of individual members of parliament being present in the chamber to cast a vote, SO 140(1)(a) allows the casting of a single party vote by a designated party member, such as the leader or the Chief Whip.[60] Waldron finds this procedure particularly problematic and concludes that several of the Standing Order reforms introduced in response to MMP do not show sufficient respect for deliberative democracy, as 'the whips for each party, upon a division simply call out a number representing their parliamentary strength, whether their members are around to walk through the lobbies or not. Theoretically they have to be in the precincts of parliament where their offices are, but if they are away their vote can still be counted through a proxy system.'[61]

The party vote has important implications for parliamentary scrutiny of legislation introduced into the House of Representatives when the Attorney General has reported under section 7 of the NZBORA. With regard to government bills, this requires the Attorney General to vote for legislation via the party vote despite having issued a section 7 report that the legislation may be inconsistent with the NZBORA. More significantly, it means that votes on the floor of the House of Representatives during first, second and third readings of legislation cannot facilitate dialogic engagement with the NZBORA in any meaningful way. Indeed, the party vote negates the need to provide ministerial justification for proceeding with legislation that may be inconsistent, given that the party vote ensures its passage, most likely in the form in which it was introduced into parliament. This further complicates the possibility of rights-friendly amendments at the select committee stage, as party votes and confidence and supply agreements can ensure the passage of legislation. As Waldron critically notes, 'The result is that often only a handful of MPs grace the chamber with their presence. If it is a controversial

58 D. McGee, *Parliamentary Practice in New Zealand* (Wellington: Dunmore Publishing, 2005), p. 204.

59 Parliament of New Zealand 2011, Standing Orders of the House of Representatives, SO 138.

60 Ibid., SO 140(1)(a).

61 J. Waldron, *Parliamentary Recklessness: Why We Need to Legislate More Carefully* (Maxim Institute John Graham Lecture, 2008), pp. 24–5.

measure, the opposition benches may be packed. But the Government benches will have only the minister supporting the bill, one member to move for closure as soon as a certain number of opponents have spoken, and a whip to call out the parliamentary strength of the party.'[62]

Claire Charters has provided a strong critique of parliament's ability to adequately protect rights, and uses the passage of the Foreshore and Seabed Act by the Labour-led government in 2004 to illustrate how MMP has not facilitated dialogic engagement within parliament. According to Charters, 'MMP has not increased the airing of disagreement in Parliament. The executive does not secure other parties' support for its position within the legislature by utilizing a transparent and inclusive process. Instead, it makes deals away from public scrutiny and input.'[63] Indeed, the importance of 'confidence and supply' agreements has been recognized by the Cabinet Manual, along with the requirement that legislation must be referred to the relevant party caucuses by the sponsoring minister to ensure support before the legislation is introduced into the House of Representatives.[64] Further, section 7.57 requires consultation with 'confidence and supply' parties before legislation is introduced to ensure that bills introduced by the government and supported by minor parties can be passed.[65] Indeed, once multi-party agreement is secured, this ensures the passage of legislation because of the party vote and SO 140(1)(a).

While MMP has altered the complexion of cabinet and the parliamentary calculation to pass legislation, the cabinet retains important discretionary power under the Standing Orders implemented in response to MMP. This questions whether executive dominance of parliament, the party caucuses that form or support the ministry and the legislative process in general have been altered by the introduction of MMP. In effect, all continue under MMP, albeit in a more complex structure without noticeable depreciation of the potential for unbridled power in New Zealand's parliamentary setting. Under SO 283(1)(a), the member moving a bill at first reading determines which select committee will

[62] J. Waldron, *Parliamentary Recklessness*, p. 25.

[63] C. Charters, 'Responding to Waldron's Defence of Legislatures' 636.

[64] Cabinet Office (New Zealand) 2008, Department of the Prime Minister and Cabinet, *Cabinet Manual 2008* (Wellington, New Zealand). In particular, see 7.53–7.56 (Reference to caucus(es)) and 7.57–7.59 (Consultation with non-government parliamentary parties).

[65] Ibid., 7.57(a).

consider the bill.[66] In the case of legislation introduced by the government this is an important discretionary power, given that under MMP, the parties supporting legislation through confidence and supply agreements may not posses a majority on every select committee. As Charters has demonstrated, SO 283 has been used strategically by the cabinet to assign legislation to select committees where a majority exists to guarantee the passage of legislation, as well as to prevent the introduction of amendments that the government cannot support.[67]

In regard to the Foreshore and Seabed Act, introduced to mitigate the Court of Appeal decision *Ngatia Apa* v. *Attorney General* – which determined that the Māori Land Court had jurisdiction to determine that the foreshore and seabed was Māori customary land – Charters argues that the choice of select committee demonstrates the significant discretion available to the cabinet to protect its legislation from parliamentary scrutiny and amendment.[68] Instead of sending the Foreshore and Seabed Bill to the Māori Affairs Committee, which was the appropriate venue for this legislation, the sponsoring minister, Michael Cullen, sent it to the Fisheries Committee. This occurred despite the bill involving neither fish nor any subject matter considered by the Fisheries Committee. It was a strategic calculation to send the Foreshore and Seabed Bill to a select committee that was sympathetic to the government, where it controlled a majority of its members with the support of parties that participated in confidence and supply agreements with the Labour party.[69]

In addition, a select committee can decide which government department will serve as the lead agency advising the committee. This has resulted in significant disagreement across party lines on the appropriateness of such allocations in regard to several changes involving sentencing and parole policy. In the case of the Sentencing and Parole Reform Bill 2009, which saw the New Zealand National ministry of John Key honour its 'confidence and supply' agreement with ACT New Zealand by introducing ACT's 'three strikes' sentencing policy as New Zealand National legislation,[70] the issue of executive supremacy and its

[66] Parliament of New Zealand 2011, Standing Orders of the House of Representatives, SO283(1)(a).

[67] C. Charters, 'Responding to Waldron's Defence of Legislatures' 640.

[68] Ibid., 633. [69] Ibid., 640–41.

[70] Confidence and Supply Agreement 2008, *Confidence and Supply Agreement*, National and ACT New Zealand (14 November).

undiminished nature under MMP is readily apparent. The Minister of Justice, Simon Power, originally introduced the bill, and the lead government department assigned to the Law and Order Committee was the Ministry of Justice. As noted in the minority report by the New Zealand Labour Party, 'this made sense because this bill aims to changing sentencing laws which are clearly under the jurisdiction of the Ministry of Justice through the Court'.[71] The Sentencing and Parole Reform Bill 2009 was accompanied by a section 7 report by Attorney General Christopher Finlayson, and the Law and Order Committee was originally provided with a critical analysis of the bill by the Ministry of Justice that questioned the rationale of the 'three strikes' policy.[72]

However, before the select committee reported, two important procedural changes were instituted by New Zealand National, supported by ACT New Zealand: first, responsibility for this bill was transferred from the Minister of Justice to the Minister of Police and Corrections Minister, Judith Collins; second, the government department providing advice was shifted from the Ministry of Justice and the New Zealand Police became lead advisor, supported by the Department of Corrections as secondary advisor.[73] In effect, advisory authority was transferred from the government department with responsibility for BORA scrutiny within government to the state actor responsible for ensuring law and order, as well as the department responsible for the maintenance of correctional facilities. Perhaps more significantly, members of New Zealand National and ACT New Zealand on the Law and Order Committee denied a request by the Labour party to allow the Ministry of Justice to continue to provide advice on the Sentencing and Parole Reform Bill 2009.[74] As noted in the Labour minority report, 'It is disgraceful that the committee is being denied the right to receive advice from the agency that clearly has the most knowledge and experience of sentencing laws.'[75]

The Sentencing and Parole Reform Bill will be considered in greater detail in Chapter 5, but this brief introduction questions the transformative

[71] Parliament of New Zealand 2010, Sentencing and Parole Reform Bill. As reported from the Law and Order Committee (26 March), 11.

[72] Ministry of Justice (New Zealand) 2009, Initial Briefing to Law and Order Select Committee, Sentencing and Parole Reform Bill (29 April), 10–11.

[73] Parliament of New Zealand 2010, Sentencing and Parole Reform Bill. As reported from the Law and Order Committee (26 March), 11–12.

[74] Ibid. As reported from the Law and Order Committee (26 March), 12.

[75] Ibid.

potential of MMP to address the danger of cabinet dominance attributed to SMP when the ministry, for a variety of reasons, is committed to the passage of legislation without substantive parliamentary scrutiny. Further, it demonstrates the ability of multi-party governing arrangements to marginalize the mechanisms of rights-based scrutiny within the NZBORA, as neither the section 7 report issued by the Attorney General, nor the initial briefings by the Ministry of Justice, nor the minority select committee report issued by the Labour party had any discernable impact on the final bill passed into law as the Sentencing and Parole Reform Act 2010.

III. Citizen-initiated referendums and penal populism

Unlike a constitutionally entrenched bill of rights, where judicial norms and approaches to policy considerations such as reasonable infringements or the appropriate boundaries of judicial review are significant structural variables that determine the parameters of a bill of rights, parliamentary bills of rights – in statutory form – respond to different structural considerations. Simply put, parliamentary bills of rights are driven by political calculations as to whether a stable governing coalition exists to pass legislation identified as incompatible, whereas constitutional bills of rights are driven by political calculations as to whether legislation will withstand judicial scrutiny and remedy. In effect, parliamentary bills of rights without significant judicial oversight have lower thresholds to achieve policy outcomes, given that the actor that initiates legislation, the cabinet, generally controls the parliamentary setting. As we have argued and will argue throughout this book, parliamentary bills of rights are distinct approaches to the protection of rights and freedoms that are structured, shaped and contained by the political configurations of the parliamentary setting in which they operate.

As many of the section 7 reports issued by the Attorney General are in relation to criminal policy, it is important to discuss a change instituted in 1993 by the New Zealand National ministry of former Prime Minister Jim Bolger. The Citizens Initiated Referenda Act allows for non-binding questions to be considered by voters if the sponsor collects the signatures of 10 per cent of the electorate.[76] In 1999, a Citizen Initiated Referendum (CIR) posed the following question: 'Should there be a reform of our justice system placing greater emphasis on the needs of victims,

[76] Parliament of New Zealand 1993, Citizens Initiated Referenda Act 1993.

providing restitution, and compensation for them and imposing minimum sentences and hard labour for all serious violent offences?' This CIR saw an 85 per cent turnout rate, with 91.75 per cent of voters in favour of a 'tough on crime' approach to criminal policy.[77]

John Pratt and Marie Clark have argued that the 1999 CIR referendum is an illustration of the emergence of 'penal populism' as a significant framework to understand criminal policy reform in New Zealand. Closely related to Taylor's concept of 'populist punitiveness', where 'politicians encourage punitive law and sentences and thereby improve their chances of re-election by making such responses to indicators of public mood and sentiments',[78] penal populism is a more formalized approach to the incorporation of non-traditional actors as policy entrepreneurs and advocates the following:

> Indeed, rather than trying to find resonance with the public mood when it suits them, politicians may be led by extra-parliamentary forces which claim to speak on behalf of the public at large. In these respects, various lobby and pressure groups, usually coalescing around single-issue politics and drawing on grass roots support, while deliberately eschewing advise from academics or penal officials, represent something more substantive than mere ethereal sentiment or mood: they can become, under certain circumstances, part of the democratic process itself, ensuring that law and order issues become central to political agendas.[79]

In New Zealand, penal populism emerged in two distinct forms in the parliamentary setting after 1999:[80] first, policy competition between the Labour and National parties to outbid each other as 'law and order' parties irrespective of the policy constraints which the NZBORA posed for this policy agenda; second, MMP as a welcoming environment for penal populism by making it easier for single-issue political parties, such as ACT New Zealand with its law and order agenda, to enter parliament.

Although CIR results are non-binding, successive Labour and New Zealand National governments have used the 1999 referendum to justify legislative changes to sentencing and parole legislation that defy the

[77] The 1993 question and results can be found at www.elections.org.nz/voting-system/referenda

[78] J. Pratt and M. Clark, 'Penal Populism in New Zealand', (2005) 7 *Punishment & Society* 304.

[79] J. Pratt and M. Clark, 'Penal Populism in New Zealand'.

[80] Pratt fully develops the concept of penal populism in J. Pratt, *Penal Populism* (London: Routledge, 2007), especially in Chapter 4.

NZBORA. In response to the 1999 CIR, the Labour-led government of Helen Clark introduced a series of sentencing reforms to establish its penal populist credentials: the Sentencing Act 2002, Parole Act 2002 and Victims' Rights Act 2002.[81] In supporting the Sentencing and Parole Reform Bill 2001, which led to the passage of these three acts, Minister of Justice Phil Goff stated: 'This legislation is considered and thorough. It also reflects the concerns of the 92 per cent of New Zealanders who voted in favour of the 1999 referendum on law and order.'[82] Goff was clear that these policies would see an increase in the prison population in a period of declining crime rates, but justified such policies based on their consistency with the wishes of New Zealanders:

> The public referendum in 1999 showed New Zealanders wanted tougher measures taken against criminals, and the government has acted on that. These figures are the proof.
>
> The forecast confirms that since the Sentencing Act 2002 came into force, the average sentences have increased across the board. We have also abolished the nonsense of serious violent offenders being automatically released at two thirds of their sentences.
>
> New Zealand's worst offenders are also now receiving the harshest sentences ever handed down.[83]

Although the 2011 Labour party manifesto questions the continued approach to penal populism, noting that the approach to law and order issues during the past four decades has been driven by the need to get tough on crime, it does not repudiate this approach.[84] Instead, the 2011 manifesto stresses that a future Labour government will approach this issue in a smarter fashion, but notes that this does not mean the party has gone soft on crime – it simply wants to be 'smarter' about its penal populism agenda. Thus, it appears that penal populism is a paradigm that is difficult to jettison, for fear that political opponents will exploit this for partisan effects.

Similarly, the minority government of John Key's New Zealand National and its partner, ACT New Zealand, has continued a law and order agenda. New Zealand National literature during the 2011 election

[81] These acts, before being divided, were introduced as the Sentencing and Parole Reform Bill 2001 by Minister of Justice Phil Goff.

[82] P. Goff 2001, 'Goff Introduces Sentencing and Parole Reform Bill', (7 August).

[83] P. Goff 2004, 'Tougher Laws Driving Up Prison Populations' (9 March). See also P. Goff 2005, 'Tougher Laws, Better Policing Push Up Jail Numbers' (23 January).

[84] New Zealand Labour Party 2011, *Labour Party Manifesto – Own our Future*, 389.

confirmed its commitment to be 'tough on crime': 'National will stay tough on criminals. We will screen parole applications to reduce unnecessary hearings, increase penalties for child pornography, and introduce civil detention orders for the most high-risk offenders who are at imminent risk of serious sexual or violent re-offending.'[85] This policy competition between the two main political parties, Labour and National, has been sustained by MMP and the ability of single-issue political parties to enter into 'confidence and supply' agreements that create multi-party governing arrangements. In particular, ACT New Zealand has pressured New Zealand National to maintain law and order policies:

> The ACT Party has always had a strong focus on law and order. It is the prime responsibility of government to keep its citizens safe.
>
> With the ACT Party in Government under National, we have ensured that National puts this responsibility at the top of its list.[86]

A central element of the confidence and supply agreement between New Zealand National and ACT New Zealand in 2008 was the introduction of the 'three strikes' law, passed as the Sentencing and Parole Reform Act 2010. Modelled on California's 'three strikes' law, this ACT New Zealand-inspired act provides, in the case of 40 offences, for sentences ranging from a minimum of 25 years in prison without parole to life in prison.[87]

In summary, a number of structural variables have tremendous influence on whether the NZBORA, as a parliamentary bill of rights, can fulfil its principal objective of greater parliamentary oversight of the cabinet's legislation agenda and its relation to the NZBORA. The first is the endurance of a cabinet-dominated parliamentary setting, despite the introduction of MMP. While this feature of Westminster systems has been affected by the introduction of MMP, it has not been replaced to such a degree that the issue of unbridled cabinet power in New Zealand's parliamentary setting has abated. Second, the structural reality of MMP in terms of government instability and effectiveness has been addressed by important changes to the Standing Orders of the House of Representatives and the Cabinet Manual. These changes – the party vote and the

[85] New Zealand National Party 2011, 'Law & Order: Protecting Communities. Building a Safer New Zealand', Policy 2011, 1.

[86] ACT New Zealand 2011, *Law and Order*.

[87] W. Brookbanks, 'Punishing Recidivist Offenders in New Zealand Using Three Strikes Legislation: Sound Policy or Penal Excess?', (2012) 9 *US-China Law Review* 3–6.

requirement of consultation with supply and confidence partners to ensure the passage of legislation – work against the idea that the NZBORA will significantly enhance parliament's role as a protector of rights, because they make it exceedingly difficult, if not impossible, for parliamentarians outside of the executive to engage in substantive rights-based scrutiny when the Attorney General reports under section 7 of the NZBORA.

Additionally, the 1999 CIR poses a particular challenge for section 7 reports by the Attorney General when legislation involves criminal policy, as Labour and New Zealand National governments have justified potentially inconsistent legislation by referring to popular demand for tougher sentences. Thus, instead of facilitating rights-based dialogue on sentencing provisions that necessitate the Attorney General reporting to parliament under section 7 of the NZBORA, the 1999 CIR has become the justification for passing legislation, despite the presence of glaring breaches of the NZBORA. These are serious impediments to the effectiveness of section 7 of the NZBORA and the dialogic potential of this parliamentary bill of rights.

IV. Report of the Attorney General

Since 1990, the Attorney General has submitted to the House of Representatives 65 section 7 reports under the NZBORA, 36 of which have been passed into law (Appendix 1). This would suggest that that Attorney General's section 7 reporting duty has been a significant instrument of rights-based scrutiny, as parliament has passed slightly more than half of the legislation (36/65) on which the Attorney General has dispensed his or her statutory responsibility under the NZBORA. However, the data overstates the importance of section 7 reports, as it combines all categories of legislation introduced into the House of Representatives, such as local, members' and government bills.

The effectiveness of section 7 reports, however, must be evaluated in relation to bills introduced by those political parties that are involved in multi-governing arrangements under MMP. Indeed, these are bills that are the product of multi-party consultation and agreement before their introduction into parliament and may very well be a central aspect of a confidence agreement under MMP, as was the case for New Zealand National and ACT New Zealand with the Sentencing and Parole Reform Bill 2009. Further, legislation sponsored by the government or its confidence partners is introduced with full knowledge that the Attorney

Table 3.2 *Section 7 reports to parliament by bill category, 1990–2014*

Type	Bills	Passed	In Progress	% Passed
Government	32	28	4	87.5
Members'	27	4	2	14.82
Local	6	4	0	66.67
	65	36	6	55.38

General has reservations about its consistency with the NZBORA and will be issuing a report to parliament. The cabinet is made aware of the Attorney General's position on draft legislation at the Cabinet Legislation Committee meeting which precedes a bill's approval and introduction into parliament.[88] If the Attorney General's reporting duty has the ability to facilitate parliamentary scrutiny and amendment, it would occur in relation to government bills, which constitute the overwhelming type of legislation reviewed by parliament.

As Table 3.2 indicates, there is tremendous variance in the type of bills passed into law that are accompanied by a section 7 report. Local bills are those sponsored by parliamentarians on behalf of local authorities, such as the Eden Park Trust Amendment Bill;[89] and members' bills refer to those introduced by parliamentarians outside of the ministry, such as the Electoral (Disqualification of Convicted Prisoners) Amendment Bill 2010.[90] Very few members' bills with a section 7 report have been passed by parliament (4/27). The large number of section 7 reports on defeated non-government bills (local and members'), however, does not demonstrate the importance of section 7 as an instrument of rights-based parliamentary scrutiny. Indeed, most, if not all, non-government bills are dispensed with after their introduction into parliament and do not proceed to the select committee stage, where the section 7 report may serve as an important instrument of dialogic engagement of the NZBORA. In effect, they are defeated *before* the section 7 report can be an instrument of parliamentary engagement. Many of the defeated non-government bills

[88] D. Parker 1985, *The Attorney General's Reporting Function under Section 7 of the New Zealand Bill of Rights Act 1990*, www.justice.govt.nz/policy/constitutional-law-and-human-rights/human-rights/bill-of-rights/the-attorney-generals-reporting-function-under-section-7-of-the-new-zealand-bill-of-rights-act-1990

[89] Report of the Attorney General under the New Zealand Bill of Rights Act 1990 on the Eden Trust Amendment Bill.

[90] Report of the Attorney General under the New Zealand Bill of Rights Act 1990 on the Electoral (Disqualification of Convicted Prisoners) Amendment Bill.

reported on by the Attorney General are dispensed with simply because the bills are not vetted by the Ministry of Justice and Crown Law Office before their introduction and are of questionable quality.[91] Further, as non-government bills, they are not the product of pre-introduction consultation and support by multi-party caucuses, and cannot rely on the party vote to facilitate their progression through parliament.[92] Therefore, non-government bills are generally dispensed with at first reading for reasons other than their potential incompatibility with the NZBORA.

In contrast, nearly every government bill with a section 7 report (28/32) has been passed despite the Attorney General reporting potential NZBORA inconsistencies. Indeed, parliament has yet to defeat a government bill introduced with a section 7 report, as the four remaining government bills are presently at the select committee stage and will most likely be passed, resulting in 100 per cent of all government bills with a section 7 report being passed by the House of Representatives. Their passage is not surprising, given the significance of the party vote and the Cabinet Manual requirement that multi-party agreement be secured before legislation is introduced into parliament. What is surprising, from the perspective of how this statutory reporting obligation was intended to function (that is, to facilitate parliamentary oversight), is the limited number of government bills that have been amended to address the NZBORA issues raised by the Attorney General when issuing a section 7 report to parliament.

Only two of the 28 government bills passed into law, or 7 per cent, have been amended to address the concerns raised by the Attorney General.[93] Further, the last government bill amended in relation to a section 7 report became law in 2002, and this was the eighth section 7 report issued on a government bill since the inception of the NZBORA in 1990 (see Appendix 1).[94] Thus, the past decade has seen 20 government bills with section 7 reports passed into law without amendment, suggesting a strong ability of the cabinet to resist any changes to its legislation.

[91] Interview with senior government official, Ministry of Justice, Wellington, New Zealand (26 July 2006).

[92] A. Geddis, 'Inter-institutional "Rights Dialogue" Under the New Zealand Bill of Rights Act', p. 97.

[93] The following government bills have been amended in light of section 7 reports by the Attorney General: Children, Young Persons and their Families Amendment Act 2004; Electoral Amendment Act 2002.

[94] The last government bill amended to address a reported inconsistency with the NZBORA was the Electoral Amendment Act 2002.

As we have argued in this book, the principles embedded in parliamentary democracy have a strong, determining effect, that complicates the ability of institutional reforms such as the NZBORA to produce prescribed policy design outcomes.

The limited parliamentary engagement of the Attorney General's section 7 report strongly suggests that the attempt at constitutional design in the NZBORA has not been successful. Indeed, a parliamentarian's career progression is determined by their standing in the parliamentary caucus and not their skill as a legislator who critically engages the NZBORA via a section 7 report. In truth, critical engagement of NZBORA inconsistencies of government bills is counterproductive to the career progression of members of the governing party or parties that reside outside of cabinet. The section 7 reporting duty, therefore, is premised on critical engagement of government bills by members outside the cabinet, as the party vote and coalition agreements offer opposition parties little ability to influence the outcome of legislation. This is a seriously flawed premise that discounts the importance of the party caucus and its centrality to the career progression of a parliamentarian, as well as overstating the willingness of parliamentarians to question the legislative choices of the party leadership. The near unanimous passage of government bills without amendments addressing the section 7 issues raised by the Attorney General, therefore, is largely explained by the design of constitutional instruments such as section 7 of the NZBORA being derailed by the reality of parliamentary democracy.

Table 3.3 presents the 36 bills passed into law with section 7 reports under SMP and MMP, as well as the six bills presently before parliament. Of the 25 government bills passed into law with section 7 reports under MMP, 17 are directly related to the confidence and supply agreements that have characterized New Zealand's Parliament under MMP. None of the government bills related to these agreements were amended to address the NZBORA before their passage. Further, two local bills are based on confidence and supply agreements,[95] and one members' bill.[96] Thus, 63 per cent of bills with section 7 reports are directly related to such agreements and only one act, the Wanganui District Council (Prohibition of Gang Insignia) Act 2009 which originated as a local bill,

[95] Manukau City Council (Control of Graffiti) Bill 2005; Wanganui District Council (Prohibition of Gang Insignia) Bill 2008.

[96] Electoral (Disqualification of Convicted Persons) Amendment Bill 2010.

Table 3.3 *Section 7 reports, 1990 to 2014, bills passed or presently before parliament*

I. Bills Passed into Law (n=36)

#	Bill	SMP/MMP	Type	Year	Amended*	Government	Partner	Confidence and Supply Agreement(s)	Policy Area
1	Transport Safety Bill	SMP	Govt	1991	No	**Majority** – New Zealand National	n/a		Criminal policy
2	Kumeu District Agricultural and Horticultural Bill	SMP	Members'	1991	Yes	**Majority** – New Zealand National	n/a		Environmental
3	Films, Videos, and Publications Classification Bill	SMP	Govt	1992	No	**Majority** – New Zealand National	n/a		Criminal policy
4	Children, Young Persons and their Families Amendment Bill	SMP	Govt	1993	Yes	**Majority** – New Zealand National	n/a		Social policy
5	Trade in Endangered Species Amendment Bill	MMP	Members'	1997	Yes	**Majority Coalition** – New Zealand National and New Zealand First	none		Environmental
6	Casino Control (Moratorium) Amendment Bill	MMP	Govt	1997	No	**Majority Coalition** – New Zealand National and New Zealand First	none		Economic policy
7	Land Transport Bill	MMP	Govt	1997	No	**Majority Coalition** – New Zealand National and New Zealand First	none	2006 agreement with New Zealand First outlines steps to address drinking and driving, breathalyzer tests, and criminal sanctions	Criminal policy
8	Housing Restructuring (Income Related Rents) Amendment Bill	MMP	Govt	2000	No	**Minority Coalition** – New Zealand Labour and Alliance party	Green Party	New Zealand Labour and Alliance party minority coalition agreed, in general terms, to	Social policy

Table 3.3 (*cont.*)

I. Bills Passed into Law (n=36)								
							introduce legislation to reduce inequality and to improve social and economic equality	
9 Summit Road (Canterbury) Protection Bill	MMP	Local	2000	Yes	**Minority Coalition** – New Zealand Labour and Alliance party	Green party		Environmental
10 Social Security (Residence of Spouses) Amendment Bill	MMP	Govt	2001	No	**Minority Coalition** – New Zealand Labour and Alliance party	Green Party	New Zealand Labour and Alliance party minority coalition agreed, in general terms, to introduce legislation to reduce inequality and to improve social and economic equality	Social policy
11 War Pensions Amendment Bill	MMP	Govt	2001	No	**Minority Coalition** – New Zealand Labour and Alliance party	Green party	New Zealand Labour and Alliance party minority coalition agreed, in general terms, to introduce legislation to reduce inequality and to improve social and economic equality	Economic policy
12 Electoral Amendment Bill (No.2)	MMP	Govt	2001	Yes	**Minority Coalition** – New Zealand Labour and Alliance party	Green Party		Electoral policy
13 Income Tax Bill 2002	MMP	Govt	2002	No	**Minority Coalition** – New Zealand Labour and Alliance party	Green Party		Economic policy

14	Land Transport (Street and Illegal Drag Racing) Amendment Bill	MMP	Govt	2002	No	**Minority Coalition** – New Zealand Labour and Progressive party	United Future	2004 agreement between New Zealand Labour and United Future specifies policies that protect the rights of victims	Criminal policy
15	Social Security (Long-term Residential Care) Amendment Bill	MMP	Govt	2003	No	**Minority Coalition** – New Zealand Labour and Progressive party	United Future	The agreement between United Future and Labour/Progressive specifies United Future's priorities regarding family-based policies	Social policy
16	Taxation (Annual Rates, GST, Trans-Tasman Imputation and Miscellaneous Provisons) Bill 2003	MMP	Govt	2003	No	**Minority Coalition** – New Zealand Labour and Progressive party	United Future		Economic policy
17	Care of Children Bill	MMP	Govt	2003	No	**Minority Coalition** – New Zealand Labour and Progressive Party	United Future	The agreement between United Future and Labour/Progressive specifies United Future's priorities regarding family-based policies	Social policy
18	Parole (Extended Supervision) and Sentencing Amendment Bill	MMP	Govt	2003	No	**Minority Coalition** – New Zealand Labour and Progressive party	United Future	2004 agreement between New Zealand Labour and United Future specifies policies that protect the rights of victims	Criminal policy
19	Future Directions (Working for Families) Bill	MMP	Govt	2004	No	**Minority Coalition** – New Zealand Labour and Progressive party	United Future	The agreement between United Future and Labour/Progressive specifies United Future's priorities regarding family-based policies	Social policy

Table 3.3 (*cont.*)

I. Bills Passed into Law (n=36)								
20 Relationships (Statutory References) Bill	MMP	Govt	2004	No	**Minority Coalition** – New Zealand Labour and Progressive party	United Future		Social policy
21 Criminal Procedure Bill	MMP	Govt	2004	No	**Minority Coalition** – New Zealand Labour and Progressive party	United Future	2005 agreement between New Zealand Labour and United Future specifies policies that protect the rights of victims	Criminal policy
22 Manukau City Council (Control of Graffiti) Bill 2005	MMP	Local	2005	No	**Minority Coalition** – New Zealand Labour and Progressive party	New Zealand First, United Future, Green party	2005 agreement with New Zealand First committed to developing new initiatives to reduce youth offending and involvement in criminal gangs	Criminal policy
23 Misuse of Drugs (Classification of BZP) Amendment Bill	MMP	Govt	2007	No	**Minority Coalition** – New Zealand Labour and Progressive party	New Zealand First, United Future, Green party	2005 agreement with United Future enacts prohibition against decriminalizing recreational drug use involving cannabis	Criminal policy
24 Auckland Regional Amenities Funding Bill	MMP	Members'	2007	Yes	**Minority Coalition** – New Zealand Labour and Progressive party	New Zealand First, United Future, Green party		Economic policy
25 Wanganui District Council (Prohibition of Gang Insignia) Bill	MMP	Local	2008	Yes	**Minority Coalition** – New Zealand Labour and Progressive party	New Zealand First, United Future, Green party	2005 agreement with New Zealand First committed to developing new initiatives to reduce youth offending and involvement in criminal gangs	Criminal policy

26 Eden Park Trust Amendment Bill	MMP	Local	2009	Yes	**Minority** – New Zealand National	ACT New Zealand, United Future, Māori party		Environmental
27 Criminal Investigations (Bodily Samples) Amendment Bill	MMP	Govt	2009	No	**Minority** – New Zealand National	ACT New Zealand, United Future, Māori party	2008 agreement between New Zealand National and ACT New Zealand specifies getting tough on sentencing, bail, and parole	Criminal policy
28 Sentencing and Parole Reform Bill	MMP	Govt	2009	No	**Minority** – New Zealand National	ACT New Zealand, United Future, Māori party	2008 agreement between New Zealand National and ACT New Zealand specifies getting tough on sentencing, bail, and parole. New Zealand National agrees to introduce ACT New Zealand's 'Three Strikes Bill' and support it until select committee stage	Criminal policy
29 Parole (Extended Supervision Orders) Amendment Bill	MMP	Govt	2009	No	**Minority** – New Zealand National	ACT New Zealand, United Future, Māori party	2008 agreement between New Zealand National and ACT New Zealand specifies getting tough on sentencing, bail, and parole	Criminal policy
30 Misuse of Drugs Amendment Bill	MMP	Govt	2010	No	**Minority** – New Zealand National	ACT New Zealand, United Future, Māori party	2008 New Zealand National party Post-election Plan committed to a clamp down on the drug trade. United Future agrees to this provision, consistent with its 2005 supply and confidence agreement with New Zealand National	Criminal policy

Table 3.3 (*cont.*)

I. Bills Passed into Law (n=36)								
31 Criminal Procedure (Reform and Modernization) Bill	MMP	Govt	2010	No	**Minority** – New Zealand National	ACT New Zealand, United Future, Māori party	2008 agreement between New Zealand National and ACT New Zealand specifies getting tough on sentencing, bail, and parole	Criminal policy
32 New Zealand Bill of Rights section 24(e) Amendment Bill 2010	MMP	Govt	2010	No	**Minority** – New Zealand National	ACT New Zealand, United Future, Māori party	2008 agreement between New Zealand National and ACT New Zealand specifies getting tough on sentencing, bail and parole	Criminal policy
33 Electoral (Disqualification of Convicted Persons) Amendment Bill	MMP	Members'	2010	No	**Minority** – New Zealand National	ACT New Zealand, United Future, Māori party	2008 agreement between New Zealand National and ACT New Zealand specifies getting tough on sentencing, bail and parole	Criminal policy
34 Social Assistance (New Work Tests, Incentives, and Obligations) Amendment Bill	MMP	Govt	2010	No	**Minority** – New Zealand National	ACT New Zealand, United Future, Māori Party		Social policy
35 Alcohol Reform Bill	MMP	Govt	2010	No	**Minority** – New Zealand National	ACT New Zealand, United Future, Māori party		Criminal policy
36 New Zealand Public Health and Disability Amendment Bill (No2) 2013	MMP	Govt	2013	No	**Minority** – New Zealand National	ACT New Zealand, United Future, Māori party		Social policy

II. Bills before Parliament (n=6)

#	Bill	SMP/MMP	Type	Year	Amended *	Government	Partner	Confidence and Supply Agreements	Policy Area
37	Taxation (Income-sharing Tax Credit) Bill	MMP	Govt	2010		**Minority** – New Zealand National	ACT New Zealand, United Future, Māori party	2008 agreement with United Future commits the New Zealand National ministry to support income splitting as tax reform to first reading	Economic policy
38	Prisoners' and Victims' Claims (redirecting Prisoner Compensation) Amendment Bill	MMP	Govt	2011		**Minority** – New Zealand National	ACT New Zealand, United Future, Māori party	2011 agreement between New Zealand National and ACT New Zealand specifies getting tough on sentencing, bail and parole	Criminal policy
39	Lobbying Disclosure Bill	MMP	Members'	2011		**Minority** – New Zealand National	ACT New Zealand, United Future, Māori party		Electoral policy
40	Land Transport (Admissibility of Evidential Breath Test) Amendment Bill	MMP	Members'	2012		**Minority** – New Zealand National	ACT New Zealand, United Future, Māori party	2011 agreement between New Zealand National and ACT New Zealand specifies getting tough on sentencing, bail, and parole	Criminal policy
41	Land Transport Amendment Bill	MMP	Govt	2013		**Minority** – New Zealand National	ACT New Zealand, United Future, Māori party	2011 agreement between New Zealand National and ACT New Zealand specifies getting tough on sentencing, bail, and parole	Criminal policy

Table 3.3 (*cont.*)

I. Bills Passed into Law (n=36)								
42 Parole (Extended Supervision Orders) Amendment Bill	MMP	Govt	2014		**Minority** – New Zealand National	ACT New Zealand, United Future, Māori party	2011 agreement between New Zealand National and ACT New Zealand specifies getting tough on sentencing, bail, and parole	Criminal policy

*Amended to address NZBORA concerns in Attorney General's section 7 report.

was amended to address issues raised in the Attorney General's section 7 report.

The large number of section 7 reports issued by the Attorney General and the limited number of bills amended to address potential NZBORA consistencies raise an important question: why would successive Attorney Generals continue to approach section 7 in a robust fashion, given that parliamentarians have been not used these reports to scrutinize, engage and amend government bills to ensure greater consistency with the NZBORA? Indeed, why the contradictory approach of robust reporting by the Attorney General and weak engagement by parliamentarians? The answer to this is a combination of professional responsibility on the part of the Attorney General and statutory obligation under the NZBORA. Further, this mixed record is a reflection of parliamentary rules and processes that directly influence whether the NZBORA can facilitate parliamentary engagement by private members, who are conditioned by the party caucus to support the parliamentary leadership, and as a result may not be predisposed to accept the arguments raised by the Attorney General's section 7 report.

These important parliamentary variables work against the logic of section 7 despite the attempt to constitutionally design parliamentary engagement under the NZBORA. The present Attorney General, Christopher Finlayson, has issued 21 section 7 reports since the New Zealand National ministry of John Key assumed office in 2008, and 13 reports have been issued in relation to government bills. Many of Finlayson's section 7 reports have involved a key campaign issue for New Zealand National – law and order, an issue that is also at the core of the 'confidence and supply' agreements between National and ACT New Zealand. When questioned as to why he issued section 7 reports against key government legislative initiatives, Finlayson argued this was the professional responsibility of the Attorney General who, as 'the Government's lawyer', must act independently and 'must not be swayed by party political considerations but must objectively come to certain conclusions'.[97] In effect, it is the statutory and professional responsibility of the Attorney General to simply advise the government of the compatibility of its legislative agenda. In this respect, the constitutional design of section 7 has been successfully employed by the Attorney General because of the unique status and role which allows this law officer to

[97] P. Gower 2009, 'Finlayson "Just Doing My Duty" on Crime Bills', *The New Zealand Herald* (4 May).

be free from partisan considerations when executing the statutory obligation under the NZBORA. However, as we have argued in this chapter, when constitutional design confronts the principles of parliamentary democracy, the overall success of section 7 varies greatly for a statutory bill of rights such as the NZBORA.

Conclusion

In evaluating the NZBORA from the perspective of structuring a bill of rights to facilitate greater parliamentary responsibility to protect rights, we have approached the assessment of bills of rights from a perspective that has not previously been adopted. As the New Zealand Bill of Rights Act 1990 and the United Kingdom's Human Rights Act 1998 are parliamentary bills of rights, we have prioritized the importance of the principles of parliamentary democracy and how they structure, shape and ultimately complicate constitutional engineering's ability to produce legislative design outcomes. Indeed, the standard approach to assessing bills of rights is principally textual and judicial, as this approach prioritizes the inclusion of domestic rights commitments that are protected through judicial review and remedial powers. This is an acceptable approach in systems based on the principle of constitutional supremacy, as the constitution is the structural principle that shapes the actions of judicial and political actors. However, as we have argued in this chapter, and will argue throughout this book, the NZBORA and the UK HRA take their cue from the principles that underlie parliamentary democracy, despite the attempt to engage in institutional design to facilitate parliamentary engagement of the government's legislative agenda from a bill of rights perspective.

In designing parliamentary bills of rights such as the NZBORA, the principal architects of these documents, such as Geoffrey Palmer, sincerely believed that the inclusion of provisions such as section 7 and the Attorney General's reporting duty would facilitate parliamentary engagement of legislation and serve as an adequate alternative to judicial review. While this attempt at institutional design has been successful in the bureaucratic realm, as the NZBORA has been incorporated into the policy design process and the Ministry of Justice and the Crown Law Office are the lead agencies that vet the government's legislative agenda, it has been significantly less effective in the parliamentary arena. The difference between the success of constitutional design in the bureaucratic realm and its failure in the parliamentary arena illustrate the premise underlying this study of parliamentary bills of rights – bureaucrats and parliamentarians are structured by the principles of parliamentary democracy, as they seek to advance the policy goals determined by the party leadership and the cabinet.

The failure to design a bill of rights that effectively alters legislative outcomes is evident in the limited engagement of section 7 reports by parliamentarians and the cabinet's ability to pass its legislative agenda without amendment despite the Attorney General's reports to parliament on possible NZBORA incompatibilities. The introduction of MMP has the potential to ensure the success of the NZBORA, as it was intended by Geoffrey Palmer to address the principal feature of parliamentary democracy considered counterproductive to democratic governance – the growing concentration of power in the cabinet and the emergence of adversarial constitutionalism. Indeed, MMP had the ability to weaken cabinet dominance, as it substitutes single-party majority governments with either minority governments dependent on parliament for the continuation of a ministry or multi-party coalition governments in which a ministry is maintained by formalized agreements. In essence, there is the potential for adversarial politics under SMP to be replaced by consensual politics under MMP, and this may see a reinvigoration of parliament as a legislative body.

As this chapter argued, the possibilities which lie in MMP have yet to be realized in relation to the NZBORA because of important changes in the Standing Orders of the House of Representatives to prevent a common characteristic of systems based on proportional representation – government inefficiency and instability because of the absence of single-party government. Important changes to the Cabinet Manual that require inter-party agreement on legislation before its introduction into parliament, and changes in the Standing Orders to allow party votes, have maintained the dominance of the cabinet in much the same way that it existed under SMP. These formalized rule changes have been augmented by informal developments, such as confidence and supply agreements negotiated between political parties that construct multi-party governing arrangements under MMP. As this chapter has demonstrated, many of the section 7 reports by the Attorney General involved government bills based on confidence and supply agreements with minor parties that support the ministry in office. The irony is that the NZBORA was introduced to address the growth of cabinet dominance under SMP, and section 7 reports were considered an element of constitutional design to address this trend. The introduction of MMP, and the rule changes introduced to accommodate this electoral system within a unicameral parliamentary system, have largely prevented the NZBORA from achieving its principal design objective – parliamentary engagement of the cabinet's legislative agenda as a substitute for judicial review.

4

The Misuse of Drugs Act 1975 and Prisoner Disenfranchisement

The bill of rights experience in New Zealand is significantly different from that in the United Kingdom because of important institutional variations that exist in this Westminster parliamentary democracy. These institutional distinctions involve: the New Zealand parliament as a unicameral body,[1] as the Legislative Council was abolished in 1951; the mixed member proportional (MMP) electoral system, which replaced the single member plurality (SMP) in 1996; and the absence of a dedicated parliamentary committee, such as the JCHR in the United Kingdom, that considers the relationship between the ministry's legislative agenda and the NZBORA. The absence of such a parliamentary committee is notable, given that this was a recommendation made by the Law and Electoral Reform Committee when it reported back to parliament on the draft New Zealand Bill of Rights Bill introduced by the Minister of Justice in 1985;[2] however, the fourth Labour government (1984–1990) did not accept this recommendation and, similar to the Canadian case, New Zealand's statutory bill of rights does not have a dedicated parliamentary committee that considers whether bills are compatible with the NZBORA.

In this chapter we present two case studies: amendments to the Misuse of Drugs Act 1975 and prisoner disenfranchisement. While this chapter focuses on government bills introduced into parliament regarding which the Attorney General has reported potential inconsistencies under section 7 of the NZBORA, it also considers a significant members' bill – the Electoral (Disqualification of Sentenced Prisoners) Amendment Act 2010. This is for a very important reason – members' bills require the support of parliamentary parties to proceed to royal assent. Given that

[1] G.A. Wood, 'New Zealand's Single Chamber Parliament: An Argument for an Impotent Upper House?', (1983) 36 *Parliamentary Affairs* 334.

[2] Parliament of New Zealand 1988, Final Report of the Justice and Electoral Reform Committee. *A White Paper on a Bill of Rights for New Zealand*, (New Zealand: House of Representatives), 3.

the prisoner disenfranchisement bill was passed with the support of the minority government led by New Zealand National, supported by its 'confidence and supply' partner ACT New Zealand, it is a members' bill in name only. For instance, it was introduced by a member of New Zealand National, was supported by this caucus and ACT New Zealand and is consistent with the broader 'law and order' policy approach of these parties since the formation of the current New Zealand National ministry in 2008.

The Misuse of Drugs Act 1975 is an important case study through which to understand the unique experience of the NZBORA under MMP and the scrutiny of legislation at the select committee stage in a multi-party parliament. Since the introduction of the NZBORA in 1990, the reverse-onus provision in section 6(6) of the Misuse of Drugs Act has been determined by the courts in *Hansen* to be inconsistent with the right to be presumed innocent guaranteed by section 25(c) of the NZBORA. In response, parliament has amended the Misuse of Drugs Act 1975 on two separate occasions, with the full benefit of *Hansen* and the constitutional parameters suggested by the judiciary. In light of the *Hansen* decision, the Attorney General reported to parliament in 2007 and 2010 that proposed amendments to the Misuse of Drugs Act 1975 are inconsistent with the NZBORA and are at odds with *Hansen*. In both instances, the Health Committee ignored the report of the Attorney General under section 7 of the NZBORA and preserved the reverse-onus provision in section 6(6) of the Misuse of Drugs Act 1975. The amendments to the Misuse of Drugs Act 1975 passed despite the inconsistencies identified by the Supreme Court of New Zealand (SCNZ), the Attorney General and the New Zealand Law Commission. Further, the Health Committee received submissions by the New Zealand Human Rights Commission and the New Zealand Law Society that reinforced the position of the judiciary in *Hansen*, as well as that of the Attorney General, that a reverse-onus provision cannot be reconciled with section 25(c) of the NZBORA. Further still, the Law Commission was directed by parliament to recommend changes to the Misuse of Drugs Act 1975 to ensure compliance with the NZBORA, and this occurred in 2011. However, the recommendation by the New Zealand Law Commission to remove the reverse-onus provision has yet to be acted upon by the Minister of Health, who has responsibility for the Misuse of Drugs Act 1975.

In some respects, the legislative history of the Misuse of Drugs Act 1975 in light of *Hansen* complies with the process labelled as 'institutional dialogue' that is suggested to be a defining feature of parliamentary bills of rights.[3] A public dialogue on the merits of section 6(6) of the Misuse of Drugs Act 1975 occurred between the 48th and 50th parliaments (2007–2013), producing two section 7 reports by the Attorney General involving the Misuse of Drugs (Classification of BZP) Amendment Bill 2007 and the Misuse of Drugs Amendment Bill 2010 and seeing a substantive report released by the New Zealand Law Commission recommending the repeal of section 6(6) because it cannot be reconciled with the NZBORA. Yet, despite this extensive rights-based dialogue, the Health Committee was not swayed by the suggested deficiencies in the proposed changes to the Misuse of Drugs Act. Clearly, the process of dialogue has been evident during parliamentary review of amendments to the Misuse of Drugs Act 1975 at the select committee stage, yet this dialogue has failed to result in substantive amendments to address deficiencies in the proposed amendments to the Act. This demonstrates both the possibility of dialogue under a parliamentary bill of rights and the limitations due to the marginal effectiveness of parliamentary oversight mechanisms. Indeed, these limitations are the result of the dominant characteristics of parliamentary government, and the MMP variation that exists in New Zealand: party discipline; the importance of supply and confidence agreements among multi-party coalition partners that generally preclude substantive parliamentary oversight;[4] changes in the parliamentary Standing Orders to ensure government stability under MMP; and the limited ability of MMP to address government control of select committees, despite the transition from single-party majority government under SMP to multi-party government, supported by confidence partners, under MMP.[5]

The following analysis of the Misuse of Drugs Act 1975 and Electoral (Disqualification of Sentenced Prisoners) Amendment Act 2010 demonstrate Geiringer's general point that 'select committee reports and parliamentary debates provide little evidence of systematic and comprehensive parliamentary scrutiny of the Bill of Rights implications of legislation'.[6] As noted previously, Standing Order 283(1)(a) allows the

[3] S. Gardbaum, *The New Commonwealth Model of Constitutionalism: Theory and Practice* (Cambridge: Cambridge University Press, 2013), p. 111.

[4] A. Kaiser, 'MMP, Minority Governments and Parliamentary Opposition', (2009) 7 *New Zealand Journal of Public and International Law* 79.

[5] D. McGee, 'Concerning Legislative Process', (2007) 11 *Otago Law Review* 429–31.

[6] C. Geiringer, 'The Dead Hand of the Bill of Rights? Is the New Zealand Bill of Rights Act 1990 a Substantive Legal Constraint on Parliament's Power to Legislate?', (2007) 11 *Otago Law Review* 400.

member moving a bill to determine which select committee will review the bill.[7] This has proven to be an important power that allows the ministry, despite the introduction of MMP, to offset parliamentary oversight at the select committee stage by the strategic use of this discretionary power. While the ministry under MMP rarely controls a majority of members on each select committee, the ministry and its supply and confidence partners generally control the key select committees that receive the vast majority of legislation with section 7 reports, such as the Health, Law and Order, Justice and Electoral and Social Services select committees. The strategic control of key committees, combined with strategic designation of the select committees that will review the ministry's legislative agenda, largely explains why parliamentary committees under MMP have failed to emerge as effective instruments of parliamentary oversight and rights-based compatibility.

I. Unicameralism and executive dominance

Recognizing that a single-chamber parliament and the SMP electoral system had contributed to prime ministerial dominance of the parliamentary setting, Geoffrey Palmer argued that the absence of an upper house would be addressed by a series of reforms introduced by the fourth Labour government. Indeed, Palmer suggested that these reforms would advance the goal of the NZBORA in the parliamentary setting, which centred on the perceived need to establish appropriate limits on the power of the Prime Minister and to address the ministry's dominance of parliament through control of the legislative process.[8] In addition to establishing the Royal Commission on the Electoral System in 1985, which led to the introduction of MMP during the 1996 general election, the fourth Labour government introduced significant parliamentary reforms to address unbridled power by the ministry: first, the establishment of permanent select committees with defined policy mandates to examine all bills introduced into parliament; second, limiting select committee membership to those outside of the ministry.[9] With the

[7] Parliament of New Zealand 2011, Standing Orders of the House of Representatives, SO 283(1)(a).

[8] D. Erdos, *Delegating Rights Protection: The Rise of Bills of Rights in the Westminster World* (Oxford: Oxford University Press, 2010), pp. 94–8.

[9] G. Palmer, *New Zealand's Constitution in Crisis: Reforming our Political System* (Dunedin: John McIndoe, 1992), pp. 110–17.

addition of MMP in 1996, it has been argued that select committees have become more powerful, as single-party majority government is now a rare occurrence in New Zealand and committee membership is based on party standings in the House of Representatives.[10] Thus, the proportional allocation of membership is suggested to constrain the ministry's ability to control the select committee system through party discipline. This, in turn, is suggested to limit the ministry's overall control of parliament, as this element of executive dominance through disciplined parliamentary parties is significantly less relevant in New Zealand because of the proliferation of parties under MMP.[11] This is also suggested to offset the implications of unicameralism in New Zealand as adversarialism has been replaced with consensus politics, attributed to a culture shift produced by MMP and the need for multi-party support in order to pass legislation.[12]

Although New Zealand lacks an upper house, it does have extra-parliamentary bodies that can provide scrutiny on government bills and may ensure that legislation is consistent with the NZBORA. For instance, as Minister of Justice, Geoffrey Palmer established the Legislation Advisory Committee (LAC) in 1986; its main objective is to ensure the passage of 'good quality legislation' by publishing guidelines, such as those involving the NZBORA, that policy actors incorporate when drafting legislation.[13] The Ministry of Justice supports the LAC, and its membership is composed of public servants, academics and legal practitioners. Although the LAC regularly makes presentations to parliamentary select committees, it rarely comments on the substantive implications of legislation, such as compliance with the NZBORA, and restricts its scrutiny to procedural compliance with the LAC guidelines to ensure well-drafted legislation. The lack of substantive engagement

[10] G. Palmer and M. Palmer, *Bridled Power: New Zealand's Constitution and Government*, 4th edition (Melbourne: Oxford University Press, 1996), p. 175.

[11] R. Malone, '"Who's the Boss?" Executive-Legislature Relations in New Zealand Under MMP', (2009) 7 *New Zealand Journal of Public and International Law* 13–14.

[12] For a critical assessment of MMP, see N. Aroney and S. Thomas, 'A House Divided: Does MMP Make an Upper House Unnecessary for New Zealand?', (2002) *New Zealand Law Review* 403–40; T. Carl Lundberg, 'Politics is Still an Adversarial Business: Minority Government and Mixed-Member Proportional Representation in Scotland and New Zealand', (2013) 15 *British Journal of Politics and International Relations* 609–25.

[13] Legislation Advisory Committee (New Zealand), Legislation Advisory Committee Annual Report 2012, 6.

may simply be a reflection of the LAC as an extra-parliamentary body housed in the Ministry of Justice, and the reality that substantive BORA scrutiny is already the responsibility of public servants within the Ministry of Justice and Crown Law Office. While the LAC has the appearance of an extra-parliamentary body that could review legislation for compliance with the NZBORA, it has never performed this role. Thus, the scrutiny of legislation in New Zealand is almost exclusively the responsibility of parliamentarians that sit on select committees drawn from a range of parties that have emerged under MMP.

II. Select committees, MMP, and Standing Orders

The Attorney General's report under section 7 of the NZBORA has the greatest potential to influence the design of legislation at the select committee stage, for a number of important reasons. The Standing Orders of the House of Representatives set strict guidelines regarding the number of speeches that may be made at any stage of the legislative process, with the exception of proceedings at the select committee stage. For instance, speeches at first, second, and third readings are limited to 12 members, who may speak for a maximum period of 10 minutes.[14] Standing Order (SO) 103 requires that, if possible, representatives of all parliamentary parties are permitted to speak, and that 'overall participation in a debate should be approximately proportional to party membership in the House'.[15] Although parliamentarians have access to the Attorney General's report when a bill is introduced into parliament, under SOs 281(1)(a) and 281(1)(b), the first reading debate on a bill generally occurs within three sitting days following its introduction into the House of Representatives. Whether or not parliamentarians have the ability to fully digest the report of the Attorney General in a meaningful way at first reading debate, therefore, is open to speculation. Indeed, the section 7 report may simply not be a factor at the first reading debate, given that a maximum of three sitting days exist between introduction of a bill, the tabling of a section 7 report by the Attorney General and

[14] Parliament of New Zealand 2011, Standing Orders of the House of Representatives, Appendix A: Time Limits of Speeches and Debates.

[15] Parliament of New Zealand 2011, Standing Orders of the House of Representatives, SO 103(a).

the first reading debate, which is limited to 12, speeches allocated by party standings in the House of Representatives.

The value of section 7 reports and their ability to act as an instrument of parliamentary oversight of the ministry's legislative agenda is potentially most effective at the select committee stage. This is a result of the time frame provided by SO 286(2), where select committees have a period of 4–6 months to conduct hearings, receive submissions and seek evidence under SO 192,[16] and report to parliament.[17] In addition, the Business Committee may, under SO 291(2), extend the reporting time for any bill beyond 6 months.[18] Thus, the select committee stage may provide the best opportunity for section 7 reports to facilitate rights-based dialogue and parliamentary oversight of the ministry's legislative agenda, given that select committee proceedings allow the participation of the broader policy community engaged with the NZBORA and the legislative process, such as the New Zealand Law Society and the New Zealand Human Rights Commission. Further, given that MMP was designed to address the dominance of the legislative agenda by the ministry, and SO 182(1) determines that 'the overall membership of select committees must, so far as reasonably practicable, be proportional to party membership in the House', single-party domination of a select committee is an unlikely occurrence, although multi-party domination by the ministry and its 'confidence and supply' partners is still a likely possibility.

Despite the failure of any party to secure a majority of seats in parliament under MMP since 1996,[19] a noticeable trend since the change in the electoral system is growing control of key select committees by the ministry, either on its own or in tandem with its 'confidence and supply' partners. This is a surprising development, as select committee membership should be allocated under SO 182 in proportion to party membership, and no single party has controlled a majority of seats since the first MMP election in 1996. The growing control of the select committee process under MMP is consistent with Boston, Church, and

[16] Parliament of New Zealand 2011, Standing Orders of the House of Representatives, SO 192.

[17] Ibid., SO 286(2). [18] Ibid., SO 291(2).

[19] At the time of writing, the 2014 New Zealand election had just concluded and the New Zealand National Party did secure a majority of seats in Parliament (61/120). However, this seat figure is based on List seat allocations before 300,000 special votes have been considered, which may result in New Zealand National falling slightly short of forming the first single party majority government under MMP.

Bale's general position that MMP has not generally affected government effectiveness in New Zealand.[20]

Table 4.1 provides the composition of four select committees, from the 45th (1996–1999) to the 50th parliaments (2011–2014), that have reviewed the lion's share of government legislation (18/22) passed with section 7 reports: Health, Justice and Electoral, Law and Order and Social Services.[21] An important trend is the growing control of these select committees enjoyed by the ministry – either on its own, or in combination with its 'confidence and supply' partners. Indeed, the composition of these key select committees generally only conformed to party standings in the House of Representatives during the 45th parliament, the first to see the ministry formed under the MMP electoral system. The outcome of the 1996 election saw the New Zealand National-led majority coalition with New Zealand First control 51 per cent of the seats in parliament (61/120), and this corresponded to 50 per cent of the seats on the Health, Justice and Law Reform and Social Services select committees. However, beginning with the 46th parliament (1999–2002) and the emergence of minority coalition governments that lasted until the 48th parliament (2005–08), we see the development of minority governments and their 'confidence and supply' partners having committee membership that exceeds their parties' share of seats in the House of Representatives.

In particular, during the 46th parliament, the minority government of New Zealand Labour and the Alliance Party controlled 49 per cent of the seats in parliament (59/120); when their supply and confidence partners are considered, this multi-party governing arrangement increases to 55 per cent (66/120). However, as Table 4.1 demonstrates, their membership and control of the four select committees that receive the lion's share of section 7 reports involving the ministry's legislative agenda exceeds the proportion of seats they hold in parliament. For instance,

[20] J. Boston, S. Church and T. Bale, 'The Impact of Proportional Representation on Government Effectiveness: The New Zealand Experience', (2003) 62 *Australian Journal of Public Administration* 12–13.

[21] A total of 25 government bills have been passed into law with section 7 reports since the introduction of MMP at the 45th Parliament (1996–9). However, only 22 of these bills were sent to select committee, as two bills were passed under urgency – Parole (Extended Supervision Orders) Amendment Bill and New Zealand Public Health and Disability Amendment Bill (No 2) – and one bill was not sent to the select committee despite the absence of urgency – Future Directions (Working for Families) Bill.

Table 4.1 *Select committees and party standings under MMP, 45th to 50th parliaments (1996–2014)*

45th Parliament (1996–1999)							**46th Parliament (1999–2002)**						
Committee	**Size**	**Government**	**%**	**C+S Partners**	**G, C+S Partners**	**%**	**Committee**	**Size**	**Government**	**%**	**C+S Partners**	**G, C+S Partners**	**%**
Health	10	5	50%	none	5	50%	Health	8	4	50%	1	5	63%
Justice and Law Reform	10	5	50%	none	5	50%	Justice and Electoral	10	5	50%	1	6	60%
Social Services	10	5	50%	none	5	50%	Law and Order	10	5	50%	0	5	50%
							Social Services	10	5	50%	1	6	60%
Parliament	120	61	51%	none	61	51%	Parliament	120	59	49%	7	66	55%
47th Parliament (2002–2005)							**48th Parliament (2005–2008)**						
Committee	**Size**	**Government**	**%**	**C+S Partners**	**G, C+S Partners**	**%**	**Committee**	**Size**	**Government**	**%**	**C+S Partners**	**G, C+S Partners**	**%**
Health	11	5	45%	1	6	55%	Health	11	5	45%	2	7	64%
Justice and Electoral	11	5	45%	1	6	55%	Justice and Electoral	7	3	43%	1	4	57%
Law and Order	8	4	50%	1	5	63%	Law and Order	7	3	43%	1	4	57%
Social Services	10	4	40%	1	5	50%	Social Services	11	4	36%	2	6	55%
Parliament	120	54	45%	8	62	52%	Parliament	121	51	42%	16	67	55%
49th Parliament (2008–2011)							**50th Parliament (2011–2014)**						
Committee	**Size**	**Government**	**%**	**C+S Partners**	**G, C+S Partners**	**%**	**Committee**	**Size**	**Government**	**%**	**C+S Partners**	**G, C+S Partners**	**%**
Health	9	5	56%	0	5	56%	Health	10	5	50%	0	5	50%
Justice and Electoral	9	5	56%	0	5	56%	Justice and Electoral	9	5	56%	0	5	56%
Law and Order	9	5	56%	1	6	67%	Law and Order	9	5	56%	0	5	56%
Social Services	9	5	56%	0	5	56%	Social Services	9	5	56%	0	5	56%
Parliament	122	58	48%	11	69	57%	Parliament	121	59	49%	5	64	53%

G = Government
C+S Partners = Confidence and Supply Partners
G, C+S = Government plus Confidence and Supply Partners

the Labour-led government and its supply and confidence partners controlled a significant majority of seats on the Health (63%), Justice and Electoral (60%) and Social Services (60%) select committees, above their share of seats in parliament (55%). This pattern is consistent from the 46th to the 48th parliaments, in which minority-led coalition governments, with the support of 'supply and confidence' partners, controlled a proportion of seats on these important select committees that exceeded the proportion of seats they held in the House of Representatives. This suggests that SO 182(1) is not a hard-and-fast rule, as multi-party governing arrangements have greater influence over these key select committees than their numbers in parliament warrant under MMP.

This is a significant trend, and a powerful reason why these select committees have not functioned as mechanisms of parliamentary oversight that scrutinize the ministry's legislation by relying on the Attorney General's section 7 report under the NZBORA. While concern regarding the growing use of urgency in the legislative process is warranted,[22] as it may allow the ministry to bypass the select committee stage – a development that occurred in relation to the Parole (Extended Supervision Orders) Amendment Bill and the New Zealand Public Health and Disability Amendment Bill (No 2) 2013 – this is not the most pressing development that allows the ministry to re-assert a controlling influence over the legislative process. This, quite simply, is the evolution of the committee system under MMP and the re-emergence of the defining characteristic of the New Zealand parliament that existed under SMP: the dominance of critical select committees by the ministry, which has been evident since the 49th parliament (2008–2011). While Malone is correct that the ministry has rarely controlled many select committees since the advent of MMP in 1996,[23] since the 46th parliament (1999–2002) it has controlled key select committees that review the vast majority of government legislation reported on by the Attorney General under section 7 of the NZBORA.

[22] C. Geiringer, P. Higbee and E. McLeay, *What's the Hurry? Urgency in the New Zealand Legislative Process 1987–2010* (Wellington: Victoria University of Wellington Press, 2011), pp. 5–6; S. Mueller, 'Where's the Fire? The Use and Abuse of Urgency in the Legislative Process', (2011) 17 *Canterbury Law Review* 316–30; S. Mueller, 'The Busy House: Alternatives to the Urgency Motion', (2011) 9 *New Zealand Journal of Public and International Law* 167–91.

[23] R. Malone, '"Who's the Boss?"' 13.

The New Zealand National government led by Prime Minister John Key since the 49th parliament is unique for two reasons. First, John Key has led a minority government since 2008 and has not conformed to the MMP pattern of coalition governments seen since the 1996 election. Second, despite holding a minority of seats in parliament – 48 per cent, or 58/122 – New Zealand National has controlled a majority of seats (56 per cent) on Health, Justice and Electoral, Law and Order, and Social Services select committees. This has created an unusual paradox, wherein parliament is multi-party and structured by MMP, whereas the key select committees that have considered the lion's share of section 7 reports have come to resemble parliamentary committees under SMP.

In particular, the New Zealand National minority government has controlled a majority of members of the Health, Justice and Electoral, Law and Order, and Social Services select committees, despite having a minority of seats in parliament. Although SO 182(1) mandates that select committee membership should reflect party standings in the House of Representatives, it is clear that this rule is malleable and does not prevent a minority government from securing a majority of seats on key select committees. This malleable rule, in conjunction with SO 283(1)(a), which allows a member moving a bill to indicate which select committee will review a bill, demonstrates the tremendous discretionary power available to the ministry under MMP. Perhaps more importantly, it questions whether MMP has addressed the ministry's dominance of parliament,[24] as the MMP-inspired rule changes have clear implications for select committees' ability to scrutinize the ministry's legislative agenda once alerted to compatibility concerns by the Attorney General under section 7 of the NZBORA. While a notable feature of the select committee process under MMP has been the frequency of legislative amendment of government bills, which may be viewed as a loss of legislative control by the ministry, very few bills have been amended in relation to NZBORA concerns raised by the Attorney General.

III. Misuse of Drugs (Classification of BZP) Amendment Act 2008

The main statutory instrument for the criminalization and regulation of controlled substances in New Zealand is the Misuse of Drugs Act 1975.

[24] T. Carl Lundberg, 'Politics is Still an Adversarial Business: Minority Government and Mixed-Member Proportional in Scotland and in New Zealand', (2013) 15 *British Journal of Politics and International Relations* 620–21.

Under section 3A of the Misuse of Drugs Act 1975, controlled substances are categorized into three classes of harm: Class A (very high risk); Class B (high risk); and Class C (moderate risk).[25] In addition, the Misuse of Drugs Act 1975 contains a reverse-onus provision, section 6(6), that presumes individuals are engaged in supply involving a controlled substance if found in possession of a specified quantity.[26] Schedule 5 of the Misuse of Drugs Act 1975 specifies the quantities of controlled substances that trigger the presumption of supply under section 6(6).[27] While the authority to determine both the classification of controlled substances and the quantity that serves as the 'trigger amount' for the presumption of supply under section 6(6) rests with the Minister of Health, section 5AA of the Misuse of Drugs Act 1975 establishes an Expert Advisory Committee on Drugs (EACD). Under the Act, the Minister of Health can only amend the list of controlled substances, the classification of controlled substances and the quantity of controlled substances that engages section 6(6) if first recommended to do so by the EACD.

Originally introduced into New Zealand in 1999 as dietary supplements and marketed as herbal products consistent with a healthy lifestyle, benzylpiperazine (BZP) soon became the main ingredient used in the production of what came to be known as 'party pills' or 'social tonics' because of their ability to produce 'legal' highs.[28] With toxicity levels similar to amphetamine, and 10 per cent as potent, BZP quickly became a popular and legal synthetic stimulant unregulated by the Misuse of Drugs Act 1975.[29] In a 6-year period (1999 to 2005) it was estimated that 20 million 'party pills' were consumed, which prompted the Minister

[25] Parliament of New Zealand, Misuse of Drugs Act 1975, Section 3A – Classification of Drugs, 9.

[26] Ibid., Section 6 – Dealing with Controlled Drugs, 21.

6(6) For the purposes of subsection (1)(f), a person is presumed until the contrary is proved to be in possession of a controlled drug for any of the purposes in subsection (1)(c), (d), or (e) if he or she is in possession of the controlled drug in an amount, level, or quantity at or over which the controlled drug is presumed to be for supply (see section 2(1A)).

[27] Ibid., Schedule 5 – Amount, Level, or Quantity At and Over Which Controlled Drugs are Presumed to be for Supply, 103.

[28] Expert Advisory Committee on Drugs 2006, 'The Benzylpiperazine (BZP)/Trifluoromethylphenylpiperazine (TFMPP) and Alcohol Safety Study', Report for the Ministry of Health (24 November), 3.

[29] Hon. J. Anderton – Progressive Party (11 September 2007), 642 NZPD 11714.

of Health to authorize an investigation by the EACD into the health implications of BZP and related products such as trifluoromethylphenylpiperazine (TFMPP) under section 5AA(2) of the Misuse of Drugs Act 1975.[30]

In its April 2004 report to the Minister of Health, the EACD concluded that it was unable to recommend how BZP should be classified as a controlled substance under the Misuse of Drugs Act 1975, as the evidence was inconclusive regarding the health effects of BZP and TFMPP.[31] The EACD did recommend to the Minister of Health, however, that BZP should be classified as a restricted substance under Schedule 4 of the Misuse of Drugs Act 1975 and only available to individuals 18 years and older.[32] In addition, the EACD recommended further study on BZP and related products, and on 6 December 2006 it reported its subsequent health-related findings to the Minister of Health.[33] In the interim, the Labour-led government passed the Misuse of Drugs Amendment Act 2005, which introduced a number of significant changes to the Misuse of Drugs Act 1975. First, the Minister of Health accepted the EACD recommendation and classified BZP as a restricted substance that could only be purchased by individuals aged 18 years and over.[34] Second, the amendments passed by the Misuse of Drugs Amendment Act 2005 created a presumption of supply in respect to possession of 5 grams or more of methamphetamine. As a Class A controlled substance, the 'trigger amount' of presumption of supply in regard to methamphetamine operated as a reverse-onus provision under section 6(1)(f) of the Misuse of Drugs Act 1975. If convicted of presumption of supply in regard to a Class A controlled substance, an individual faced a maximum sentence of life imprisonment unless they were able to prove that they were not engaged in the trafficking of this controlled substance.[35]

In December 2006, the EACD reported to the Minister of Health that emerging scientific evidence required the reclassification of BZP from a

[30] Expert Advisory Committee on Drugs 2006, 'BZP/TFMPP and Alcohol Safety Study', 3.

[31] Expert Advisory Committee on Drugs 2004, 'The Expert Advisory Committee on Drugs (EACD) Advice to the Minister on Benzylpiperazine (BZP)', (April), 3.

[32] Expert Advisory Committee on Drugs 2004, 'EACD Advice on BZP', 4.

[33] Ibid.

[34] Parliament of New Zealand 2005. Misuse of Drugs Amendment Act 2005, 'Schedule 4 – Restricted Substances', 54.

[35] Parliament of New Zealand 2005, Misuse of Drugs Amendment Bill (No 3), As Reported from the Health Committee (23 May).

regulated to a controlled substance under the Misuse of Drugs Act 1975. The EACD now considered that BZP and related substances posed a moderate risk of harm and recommended to the Minister of Health that BZP be labelled as a Class C controlled substance, along with all analogues and derivatives of this product.[36] Similarly, in April 2007 the EACD recommended to the Minister of Health that the quantity of 5 grams or 100 tablets of BZP and related controlled substances should be the trigger amount for the presumption of supply under section 6(6) of the Misuse of Drugs Act 1975.[37]

The New Zealand Supreme Court and Hansen

During the period in which the Minister of Health was conducting consultations with policy stakeholders over the EACD recommendations, the SCNZ delivered its judgment in *R.* v. *Hansen* regarding section 6(6) of the Misuse of Drugs Act 1975 and the trigger amount necessary to demonstrate presumption of supply.[38] The SCNZ delivered *Hansen* on 7 February 2007; the EACD presented its recommendation to the Minister of Health to set the quantity for the presumption of supply of BZP at 5 grams on 24 April 2007. The time sequence involving *Hansen* and the EACD recommendation is important, as BZP would be listed as a Class C controlled substance (moderate risk) when the Minister of Health introduced the Misuse of Drugs (Classification of BZP) Amendment Bill in August 2007.

At issue in *Hansen* was a reverse-onus provision in the Misuse of Drugs Act 1975 that, under section 6(6), provided that a person found in possession of a prescribed amount of cannabis was engaged in trafficking 'until the contrary is proven'.[39] This reverse-onus provision was determined by the SCNZ, in a 4:1 decision, to be inconsistent with section 25 (c) of the NZBORA – the right to be presumed innocent until proved guilty according to law – and, further, section 25(c) was considered an unreasonable limitation under section 5 of the NZBORA.[40] A majority of

[36] Expert Advisory Committee on Drugs 2006, 'Advice to the Minister on Benzylpiperazine (BZP)', (9 December), 5.

[37] Expert Advisory Committee on Drugs 2007, 'Advice to the Minister on Benzylpiperazine (BZP)', (24 April), 3.

[38] *R.* v. *Hansen*, [2007] NZSC 7.

[39] *R.* v. *Hansen*, [2007] NZSC 7 at para 1 (Elias C.J.)

[40] C. Geiringer, 'The Principle of Legality and the Bill of Rights Act: A Critical Examination of R. v. Hansen', (2008) 6 *New Zealand Journal of Public and International Law* 68–73.

the court considered that, in its application to cannabis possession over 28 grams, section 6(6) was not rationally connected to the legislative objective and was not a proportional response to the objective and the level of rights infringement. However, unlike the House of Lords in the United Kingdom, which read an equivalent reverse-onus provision to be consistent with the Human Rights Act 1998, the SCNZ refrained from adopting a similar remedy: Justice Tipping concluded that 'whether (such an approach) is appropriate in England is not for me to say, but I am satisfied that it is not appropriate in New Zealand.'[41] Therefore, the SCNZ simply indicated that it could not give the Misuse of Drugs Act 1975 a consistent reading with the NZBORA and refrained from either issuing an implied declaration of inconsistency under section 5 or 'reading' the provision as consistent via section 6 of the NZBORA. In essence, the SCNZ left it to parliament to remedy the NZBORA issues identified in *Hansen* regarding the level of possession that indicated a willingness to engage in supply of a Class C controlled substance such as cannabis.

In determining whether the reverse-onus provision in section 6(6) of the Misuse of Drugs Act 1975 was a reasonable limit on section 25(c) of the NZBORA, the SCNZ established judicial suggestions for demonstrating that possession was for the purposes of supply. Justice Tipping accepted that the presumption of supply would be a reasonable limit on section 25(c) if the level of possession demonstrated a high probability that supply was the purpose of possession.[42] Although *Hansen* did not involve a challenge to the Misuse of Drugs Amendment Act 2005 or the Minister of Health's decision to set the quantity of possession for the purposes of supply at 5 grams for methamphetamines, Tipping commented that the quantity currently established for Class A controlled substances was not a proportional limitation on section 25(c) of the NZBORA:

> But for the future, and in relation to drugs for which the level, amount or quantity was set before the 2005 Amendment Act came into force, there is, in my view, too much risk that the level may be set, or has been set, at a point which does not reflect the necessary high probability that possession at that level is for supply.[43]

The significance of Tipping's concern that possession of 5 grams of a Class A controlled substance did not demonstrate a high probability of

[41] *R.* v. *Hansen*, [2007] NZSC 7 at para 158 (Tipping J.)

[42] Ibid., at para 147–148 (Tipping J.) [43] Ibid., at para 148 (Tipping J.)

possession for the purposes of supply is instructive, given that the EACD recommended a similar quantity to the Minister of Health in relation to BZP, a Class C controlled substance (moderate risk). Indeed, a related Class C controlled substance, cannabis, had a trigger amount of 28 grams under Schedule 5 of the Act. In justifying the quantity of 5 grams of BZP as the trigger amount for section 6(6) of the Misuse of Drugs Act, the EACD noted that this amount is generally the level set for most controlled substances in Schedule 5.[44] It stated that it was reasonable to conclude that possession of 5 grams of BZP demonstrated possession for the purposes of supply.[45]

The Misuse of Drugs (Classification of BZP) Amendment Bill 2007

The attempt to regulate and control the distribution of 'party drugs' such as BZP saw the introduction of the Misuse of Drugs (Classification of BZP) Amendment Bill in 2007 by the minority coalition government led by New Zealand Labour and its partner, the Progressive Party. Although this bill was sponsored by the Associate Minister of Health, Jim Anderton of the Progressive party, it was closely related to the 'confidence and supply' agreement between Labour and United Future in 2005 that pledged not to decriminalize recreational drugs such as cannabis. Further, while this proposed amendment was not a direct legislative response to *Hansen*, the EACD recommendations that informed the Misuse of Drugs (Classification of BZP) Amendment Bill 2007 were made after the SCNZ commented on the constitutional standard necessary to demonstrate that possession was for the purposes of supply, and thus acted as a reasonable limitation on section 25(c) of the NZBORA.

The *Hansen* decision can be viewed as an illustration of Gardbaum's position that the NZBORA demonstrates the distinctiveness of the Commonwealth model and its attempt to decouple judicial review from judicial supremacy. Further, one of the redeeming qualities of the new Commonwealth model, according to Gardbaum, is that the judiciary simply invites the legislature to respond to its conception of the NZBORA, and leaves it to parliament to decide whether to accept judicial

[44] Expert Advisory Committee on Drugs 2007, Advice to the Minister on Benzylpiperazine (BZP) (24 April), 2.

[45] Ibid., 1.

invitations to revisit legislation.[46] Despite the majority decisions in *Hansen* that considered section 6(6) an unreasonable limit under section 5, none of the justices were prepared to give this section an interpretation under section 6 of the NZBORA that established its compatibility through judicial re-interpretation of parliamentary intention.[47]

The Misuse of Drugs (Classification of BZP) Amendment Bill 2007 contained the EACD's main recommendations to the Minister of Health between 2006 and 2007: first, BZP would cease to be a restricted product under Schedule 4 of the Misuse of Drugs Act 1975 and would be listed as a Class C controlled substance under Schedule 3 of the Act; second, the trigger amount of BZP possession for the purposes of supply would be set at 5 grams or 100 tablets.[48] As BZP would now be classified as a controlled substance with a specified quantity under Schedule 5, the reverse-onus provision under section 6(6) of the Misuse of Drugs Act 1975 was extended to BZP and related products. The proposed legislative change occurred after the *Hansen* decision in which a majority of the justices determined that section 6(6) was an unreasonable limitation on section 25(c) of the NZBORA, as well as providing clear judicial guidance on the trigger level necessary to demonstrate the reasonableness of the limitation under section 5 of the NZBORA. Indeed, the legislative standard suggested by the justices in *Hansen* did not have any influence on the quantity established by the Misuse of Drugs (Classification of BZP) Amendment Bill 2007 introduced by the Associate Minister of Health, Jim Anderton; nor did *Hansen* have any influence on the EACD, which recommended this quantity to the Minister of Health in 2007. Specifically, the EACD did not refer to the *Hansen* decision in its recommendation to the Minister of Health, despite the court delivering its judgment before the EACD reported to the Minister of Health.

The report of the Attorney General

In his report to parliament under section 7 of the NZBORA, Attorney General Michael Cullen indicated that the extension of BZP to section 6(6)

[46] S. Gardbaum, *The New Commonwealth Model of Constitutionalism*, pp. 153–54.

[47] A. Geddis, 'Inter-institutional 'Rights Dialogue' Under the New Zealand Bill of Rights Act', in T. Campbell, K.D. Ewing and A. Tomkins (eds.), *The Legal Protection of Human Rights: Sceptical Essays* (Oxford: Oxford University Press, 2011), p. 101.

[48] Parliament of New Zealand 2007, Misuse of Drugs (Classification of BZP) Amendment Bill. Explanatory Note, 1.

of the Misuse of Drugs Act 1975 was a breach of section 25(c) of the NZBORA, the right to be presumed innocent until proven guilty according to law, and was not a reasonable limitation under section 5.[49] In reaching this conclusion, the Attorney General juxtaposed the *Hansen* standard – a threshold possession set at a very high level to make it 'highly probable or nearly certain that the purpose of possession is supply' – with the EACD-recommended quantity demonstrating a reasonable presumption of possession for supply.[50] In his conclusion, the Attorney General endorsed the *Hansen* standard as necessary to justify a limitation on section 6(6) of the Act, as the quantity of BZP and related products set out in Schedule 5 'are not sufficiently high that it is safe to conclude that there is a high probability that the purpose of the possession of the drug is supply'.[51]

Although the Attorney General accepted the EACD recommendation that BZP should be classified as a controlled substance 'without delay', Michael Cullen concluded that the level of possession recommended by the EACD and included in the Misuse of Drugs (Classification of BZP) Amendment Bill 2007 was insufficient to establish that possession was for the purposes of supply. Noting that the Labour-led coalition government had invited the Law Commission to conduct a review of the Misuse of Drugs Act 1975,[52] which would likely result in a reconsideration of section 6(6) as a reverse-onus provision, the Attorney General reported to parliament under section 7 that the quantity established under the Act for BZP and related products did not, in the opinion of the Attorney General, constitute a reasonable limitation of section 25(c) of the NZBORA.

The parliamentary debate and select committee proceedings

As a parliamentary enforced bill of rights, in NZBORA theory the Attorney General's section 7 report is the mechanism that brings compatibility issues to the attention of the House of Representatives for

49 Report of the Attorney General under the New Zealand Bill of Rights Act 1990 on the Misuse of Drugs (Classification of BZP) Amendment Bill 2007, 3.

50 Ibid., 4.

51 Ibid., 5.

52 The Law Commission released a position paper (February 2010) and presented its final report to Parliament on 3 May 2011: *Controlling and Regulating Drugs. A Review of the Misuse of Drugs Act 1975.*

possible resolution.[53] In effect, section 7 is the trigger mechanism of parliamentary engagement that follows the introduction of a bill, as it may result in the sponsoring minister defending the decision to proceed with a government bill reported on by the Attorney General and, further, may function as a resource for opposition parties to demand changes to the bill to ensure greater consistency with the NZBORA. The Misuse of Drugs (BZP Classification) Amendment Bill is unique in an important sense. Unlike many government bills introduced without judicial review of closely related legislative initiatives, the proposed amendments to the Misuse of Drugs Act 1975 were designed in light of *Hansen*, as well as the Attorney General's report that borrowed heavily from the constitutional standard that the SCNZ suggested to parliament in *Hansen*.

During the first reading debate on the Misuse of Drugs (Classification of BZP) Amendment Bill, Associate Minister of Health Jim Anderton referred to the section 7 report by Attorney General Michael Cullen, and noted that the Attorney General identified an inconsistency with the Act's reverse-onus provision and section 25(c) of the NZBORA.[54] While the Associate Minister of Health referred to the section 7 report by the Attorney General, he ignored the *Hansen* decision and disputed the finding of inconsistency by the Attorney General. Specifically, the Associate Minister of Health countered that the purpose of the bill was to enhance young people's human rights by providing clear guidelines for the consumption and possession of BZP.[55] On the issue of possession for the purposes of supply, the Associate Minister of Health noted that the Health Committee would consider the amount, and the trigger amount would be revisited once the committee reported back to the House of Representatives.

Instead of structuring the debate on the Misuse of Drugs (BZP Classification) Amendment Bill, or resulting in a reasoned argument why the government had decided to proceed with a bill reported on by the Attorney General, the NZBORA inconsistencies identified by the section 7 report were largely ignored as the bill proceeded through the House of Representatives and the select committee stage. Indeed, the last time the Attorney General's section 7 report was referred to by a government

[53] C. Archer and G. Burt, 'Section 7 of the Bill of Rights Act', (2004) *New Zealand Law Journal* 321; T. Bromwich, 'Parliamentary Rights-vetting Under the NZBORA', (2009) *New Zealand Law Journal* 189–90.

[54] Hon. J. Anderton – Progressive Party (11 September 2007) 642 NZPD 11715.

[55] Ibid.

minister was at the introductory debate, and this simply involved a cursory reference by Associate Minister of Health Jim Anderton. The parliamentary debate that followed is not an illustration of dialogue theory that is suggested to be a defining feature of parliamentary bills of rights,[56] but rather evidence of Pratt's paradigm of penal populism, as most parliamentarians supported the need to introduce harsh penalties for the possession of BZP.[57]

After the cursory treatment of the Attorney General's report by the Associate Minister of Health, the parliamentary debate focused almost exclusively on the dangers of drug use and the need to criminalize BZP as it was argued to be a gateway drug.[58] Barbara Stewart reminded parliament that New Zealand First attempted to have BZP and related products designated as a controlled substance when it was first classified as a regulated product by the Misuse of Drugs Amendment Act 2005.[59] The only exception to this pattern of parliamentary neglect of Michael Cullen's section 7 report was the Green Party List MP Nandor Tanczos, who engaged the NZBORA inconsistencies at all stages of the debate and called for fulsome justification by the Associate Minister of Health for proceeding with a bill that ignored *Hansen* and the Attorney General's report.[60] However, with a parliamentary caucus of six List MPs, the Green Party was unable to influence the debate on the Misuse of Drugs (Classification of BZP) Amendment Bill, or generate other political parties' parliamentary engagement with the inconsistencies reported by the Attorney General.

After first reading, this bill was reviewed by the Health Committee, which recommended its passage without amendment by majority vote, despite receiving 38 submissions opposed to the bill and only 14 supporting it.[61] Although the Health Committee referred to the Attorney General's section 7 report, the majority report did not engage the substantive

[56] A. Young, *Parliamentary Sovereignty and the Human Rights Act* (Oxford: Hart Publishing, 2009), pp. 115–44; J. Varahus, 'Courts in the Service of Democracy: Why Courts Should Have a Constitutional (But Not Supreme) Role in Westminster Legal Systems', (2009) *New Zealand Law Review* 484, 508.

[57] J. Pratt, *Penal Populism* (New York: Routledge, 2007), p. 157.

[58] J. Dean – National Party (11 September 2007) 642 NZPD 11716–17.

[59] B. Stewart – NZ First (11 September 2007) 642 NZPD 11721–22.

[60] N. Tancsos – Green Party (11 September 2007) 642 NZPD 11724–11726.

[61] Parliament of New Zealand 2007, Misuse of Drugs (Classification of BZP) Amendment Bill. Report of the Health Committee (15 November), 10.

concerns raised by the Attorney General. Instead, the report indicated that a majority of the presentations before the Health Committee agreed that the quantity of BZP used to demonstrate possession for the purposes of supply contravened the NZBORA.[62] This is significant, as the Associate Minister of Health viewed the select committee as an important arena to debate the level of possession for BZP's inclusion under Schedule 5 and a place where NZBORA inconsistencies could be addressed when the committee reported back to the House of Representatives. This did not occur at the select committee stage, as the majority of the committee accepted the EACD-recommended level of 5 grams without reservation.

The Health Committee's majority report accepted the government's position that a 'pressing' public health issue was addressed by the BZP classification and that the Act should 'not be delayed to address concerns about the presumption for supply provisions of the Act'.[63] Further, the committee report sidestepped the issue of the reverse-onus provision in section 6(6) of the Act, and simply noted that the Law Commission had been tasked with a review of the Misuse of Drugs Act 1975. According to the Health Committee, 'The majority of us are satisfied that the review will address the New Zealand Bill of Rights Act 1990 issues associated with this bill.'[64] In effect, parliamentarians were satisfied that the Law Commission would identify any outstanding NZBORA issues at some later stage. The only parliamentary party to engage the Attorney General's report at the select committee stage was the Green Party and its representative Sue Kedgley, who did not support classifying BZP under the Misuse of Drugs Act 1975, suggesting that there was no evidence of a public health concern associated with this product: '[w]e are alarmed that Parliament is allowing this significant breach of the New Zealand Bill of Rights Act 1990 on the basis of such flimsy evidence. In our view, setting a presumption of supply at five grams – or possession of one hundred tablets – is arbitrarily low, and cannot be justified rationally.'[65]

At second reading, the Associate Minister of Health noted he was pleased that the Health Committee had reported back to parliament without amendments to the bill.[66] Similar to the debate at the intro-

[62] Parliament of New Zealand 2007, Misuse of Drugs (Classification of BZP) Amendment Bill. Report of the Health Committee (15 November), 6.

[63] Ibid. [64] Ibid., 7. [65] Ibid., 8.

[66] Hon. J. Anderton – Progressive Party (5 March 2008) 645 NZPD 14647.

duction of the bill, the remaining parliamentary debate on the Misuse of Drugs Act (Classification of BZP) Amendment Bill 2007 simply focused on whether to criminalize BZP and related products; this was advocated by Labour, National, New Zealand First, United Future and the Progressive Party. The debate also considered whether BZP should be simply a regulated and not a controlled substance, as the Māori party and ACT New Zealand suggested. At no time did the parliamentary debate deviate from the public policy objective of criminalizing BZP under the Misuse of Drugs Act, resulting in the neglect of two significant issues: first, consideration of the *Hansen* decision and the Attorney General's report that the reverse-onus provision of section 6(6) was incompatible with the NZBORA for the quantity of possession specified; second, whether the trigger amount should be raised from its existing level of 5 grams to address the concerns raised by the Attorney General that this level was an unreasonable limitation on section 25(c) of the NZBORA.

Despite the design of section 7 as a trigger for parliamentary oversight of the NZBORA, the Attorney General's report did not lead the Associate Minister of Health, as the sponsor of this government bill, to engage the Attorney General's criticism beyond cursory reference to this report once the bill was introduced into parliament. This is consistent with Tessa Bromwich's analysis that 'Parliament's most significant failing in its engagement with human rights is its frequent omission to address the substance of a s.7 report.'[67] Thus, the government failed to provide any justification for proceeding with a bill identified by the Attorney General as incompatible with the NZBORA, and failed to refer to the SCNZ's recent *Hansen* decision. Further, the Associate Minister of Health deferred these issues to the Health Committee, arguing that this was the appropriate forum to consider potential NZBORA inconsistencies identified by the Attorney General. In turn, the Health Committee accepted the bill without amendment and deferred the question of the constitutionality of the reverse-onus provision in section 6(6) of the Act to the Law Commission review of the Misuse of Drugs Act 1975. In reference to Gardbaum and his defence of the Commonwealth model, we see a series of invitations by parliamentary actors to consider the NZBORA implications of section 6(6) of the Misuse of Drugs Act 1975; unfortunately, there is

[67] T. Bromwich, 'Parliamentary Rights-vetting Under the NZBORA', 191.

no evidence of these invitations being accepted or considered, which accounts for the passage of the Misuse of Drugs (Classification of BZP) Amendment Act 2008 without amendments addressing the identified NZBORA inconsistencies. This has led Geddis to lament: 'If this is what inter-institutional dialogue rights-dialogue-in-action looks like, then it is hardly an edifying spectacle.'[68]

A number of explanations account for the limited engagement with the Attorney General's report throughout all stages of review of the Misuse of Drugs (Classification of BZP) Amendment Bill 2007. The institutional explanation centres on it being a government bill that secured the support of its 'confidence and supply' partners before being introduced into parliament, as required by the New Zealand Cabinet Manual.[69] Although the Green Party ultimately voted against the bill in later parliamentary stages, the Labour-led ministry and its 'confidence and supply' partners still possessed a narrow majority to pass the bill, with a combined party vote of 61 in a 121-seat parliament. As a result, there was never any danger of the bill being defeated, given that the party vote guaranteed its passage before it was introduced into parliament and before the Attorney General reported to parliament. Similarly, the Labour-led ministry and its 'confidence and supply' partners possessed a majority of members on the Health Committee, which reviewed the 2007 amendments to the Misuse of Drugs Act 1975.[70] Indeed, the Labour party and New Zealand First controlled 6 of 11 party votes on the Health Committee.

These institutional explanations are important, as they illustrate a central point made by David Feldman in his analysis of government receptivity to human rights critiques by parliament in the context of the United Kingdom's HRA 1998 – a government is generally unwilling to accept human rights critiques of its legislation once it is introduced into parliament, as the ministry is committed to its passage in the form in which it is introduced.[71] Feldman's conclusion is even more relevant in

[68] A. Geddis, 'The Comparative Irrelevance of the NZBORA to Legislative Practice', (2009) 43 *New Zealand Universities Law Review* 487.

[69] T. Carl Lundberg, 'Politics is Still an Adversarial Business: Minority Government and Mixed-Member Proportional in Scotland and in New Zealand', (2012) *British Journal of Politics and International Relations* (First View – July 2012), 10–11.

[70] For an elaboration on this point, see A. Kaiser, 'MMP, Minority Governments and Parliamentary Opposition', (2009) 7 *New Zealand Journal of Public and International Law* 88.

[71] D. Feldman, 'The Impact of Human Rights on the UK Legislative Process', (2004) 25 *Statute Law Review* 110.

the context of New Zealand and the parameters of multi-party governing arrangements – here the party vote and 'confidence and supply' agreements make it difficult to revise legislation, as it has been agreed to before its introduction into parliament. Further, these events question whether MMP has addressed executive dominance of a unicameral parliament, as Aroney and Thomas suggest that MMP has not been an adequate substitute for an upper house that functions as an essential check on the government's legislative agenda.[72] Further, Lundberg argues that MMP has simply been a 'movement away from the excesses of the Westminster model' and not, as its advocates believed it would be, a 'decisive break'.[73]

While the institutional explanation offers a strong account of why parliamentarians from multi-party governing agreements under MMP fail to engage potential NZBORA inconsistencies identified by the Attorney General, this does not explain why opposition parties fail to use the section 7 report as a resource to challenge government legislation. Indeed, in a highly partisan environment such as New Zealand's parliament, the Attorney General's report would appear to be a valuable tool for the opposition to embarrass the government and question its commitment to human rights. This would be particularly relevant in the case of the Labour party, as the NZBORA was designed and passed by the fourth Labour government. The puzzle as to why opposition parties do not use a section 7 report to challenge a government bill is largely explained by two variables: the capacity and willingness of parliamentarians to engage in rights-based scrutiny and the policy context of many bills with NZBORA incompatibilities identified by the Attorney General. As Geiringer has concluded, 'there is little evidence of systemic and comprehensive parliamentary scrutiny of the Bill of Rights implications of legislation.'[74] Although Geiringer does not explore the reasons for this lack of engagement, research by Evans and Evans reveals a fundamental flaw in the design of parliamentary bills of rights such as the NZBORA – the failure to understand the significance of the party caucus as a constraint on parliamentarians' willingness to engage in rights-based scrutiny. In their interviews with 55 Australian parliamentarians, Evans and Evans found that the demands of the party caucus and executive dominance were both significant constraints that limited the willingness

[72] N. Aroney and S. Thomas, 'A House Divided: Does MMP Make an Upper House Unnecessary in New Zealand?', (2012) *New Zealand Law Review* 431.

[73] T. Carl Lundberg, 'Politics is Still an Adversarial Business' 21.

[74] C. Geiringer, 'The Dead Hand of the Bill of Rights' 400.

Table 4.2 *Section 7 reports and policy context, government bills passed into law under MMP*

					POLICY AREA OF SECTION 7 REPORT			
Parliament	Government	Type	Confidence and Supply Partners	Section 7 reports	Criminal	Social	Economic	Electoral
1996–1999	New Zealand National and New Zealand First	majority coalition	none	2	1	0	1	0
1999–2002	New Zealand Labour and Alliance party	minority coalition	Green party	5	0	2	2	1
2002–2005	New Zealand Labour and Progressive party	minority coalition	United Future	8	3	4	1	0
2005–2008	New Zealand Labour and Progressive party	minority coalition	New Zealand First, United Future, Green party	1	1	0	0	0
2008–2011	New Zealand National	minority	ACT New Zealand, Māori party, United Future	8	7	1	0	0
2011–present	New Zealand National	minority	ACT New Zealand, Māori party, United Future	1	0	1	0	0
Total				**25**	**12**	**8**	**4**	**1**

of parliamentarians to critically assess legislation in terms of its relation to domestic rights instruments.[75]

Turning to the importance of policy context and how it can undermine parliamentary engagement with compatibility issues identified by the Attorney General, as outlined in Table 4.2, 25 government bills with section 7 reports have been passed into law since the introduction of MMP in New Zealand, and 12 of these involve criminal policy. In effect, these section 7 reports involve legislation in which the Attorney General has concluded that provisions unfairly undermine the right of the accused or those convicted of crimes to legal rights provisions in the NZBORA. Criminal policy is the very issue where political parties are unlikely to use section 7 reports to challenge the government on its commitment to rights, or to demand amendments to ensure NZBORA compatibility, given that it would require political parties to defend the rights of the accused or those convicted of serious crimes.[76] This is unlikely to occur because of the entrenchment of penal populism in New Zealand, where political parties are unwilling to appear weak on crime for fear of this issue being exploited electorally by their competitors. This means they engage in what Roberts refers to as a 'penal arms race', in which political parties offer ever harsher punishment policies in an attempt to attract voters and to protect themselves from the electorally fatal charge that they are 'soft on crime'.[77]

The challenge of rights-based engagement of the NZBORA has been particularly acute in the past decade, as a large majority of section 7 reports involving government bills have been classified as criminal policy (11/18). From 2002 to 2008, Labour-led governments passed nine bills into law with section 7 reports, four of which involved criminal policy; since 2008 New Zealand National have passed nine bills into law with section 7 reports, seven of which involve criminal policy. Despite the Misuse of Drugs (Classification of BZP) Amendment Bill being in conflict with *Hansen* and at odds with the section 7 report issued by the

[75] C. Evans and S. Evans, 'Messages from the Front Line: Parliamentarians' Perspectives on Rights Protection', in T. Campbell, K.D. Ewing and A. Tomkins (eds.), *The Legal Protection of Human Rights: Sceptical Essays* (Oxford: Oxford University Press, 2011), pp. 329–46.

[76] J. Kelly, 'Judicial and Political Review as Limited Insurance: The Functioning of the New Zealand Bill of Rights Act in 'Hard' Cases', (2011) 49 *Commonwealth & Comparative Politics* 308–9.

[77] J. Roberts, 'Sentencing Reform in New Zealand: An Analysis of the Sentencing Act 2002', (2003) 36 *The Australian and New Zealand Journal of Criminology* 252.

Attorney General, it passed without amendment and with overwhelming parliamentary support – 109 votes were in favour and 11 opposed. Further, the opposition to the bill from the Greens (6 votes), Māori Party (3 votes) and ACT New Zealand (2 votes) was related not to the issues raised by the Attorney General, but rather disagreement as to whether BZP should be reclassified from a restricted to a controlled substance under the Misuse of Drugs Act 1975. Thus, the theory of section 7 reports acting as a trigger for parliamentary engagement and rights-based oversight of the government's legislative agenda failed to consider the importance of policy context. For instance, parliamentarians are very reluctant to seek amendments when criminal policy changes result in a section 7 report because of the political risk associated with supporting rights claimants such as criminals. While Pratt has argued that the approach to penal populism has shifted in New Zealand to a greater concern with the rights of victims and is not simply about appropriate punishment,[78] this modest shift is unrelated to the NZBORA, as there is limited evidence of rights-based criticisms of penal policy in the parliamentary setting.

IV. Misuse of Drugs Amendment Act (no 2) 2011

In 2009 the EACD made the further recommendation to the Associate Minister of Health that ephedrine and pseudoephedrine should be reclassified as controlled substances (Class B2) under the Misuse of Drugs Act 1975,[79] and suggested a trigger amount of 10 grams for the presumption of supply under section 6(6) of the Act.[80] Both are decongestants commonly used to treat upper respiratory tract conditions and were restricted products under the Misuse of Drugs Act 1975. However, pseudoephedrine is an essential ingredient for the production of methamphetamine and ephedrine can be converted into pseudoephedrine.[81] The reclassification of both products, which had previously been over-the-counter

[78] J. Pratt, 'When Penal Populism Stops: Legitimacy, Scandal and the Power to Punish in New Zealand', (2008) 41 *The Australian and New Zealand Journal of Criminology* 377–78.

[79] Expert Advisory Committee on Drugs 2009, 'Classification of pseudoephedrine and ephedrine under the Misuse of Drugs Act 1975', (15 July), 4.

[80] Expert Advisory Committee on Drugs 2009, 'EACD Recommendations in Relation to Pseudoephedrine and Ephedrine', (6 November), 3.

[81] Expert Advisory Committee on Drugs 2003, 'Advice to the Minister of Health on Ephedrine', (November), 3; Expert Advisory Committee on Drugs 2003, 'Advice to the Minister of Health on Pseudoephedrine', (June), 5.

medications, meant they would now require a prescription issued by a medical practitioner, with strict amounts and time limits per prescription. The EACD recommended possession of 10 grams for the presumption of supply for individuals without exemptions, such as chemists and legitimate suppliers, based on advice provided by the Ministry of Health in its October 2009 report to the EACD. The Ministry of Health suggested the trigger amount of 10 grams for the presumption of supply as this represented twice the amount a medical practitioner could prescribe in a one-month period; for the Ministry of Health, this was sufficient to demonstrate possession for the purposes of supply.[82] This level was set despite the Attorney General's 2007 report considering the reclassification of BZP which accepted the *Hansen* principle that a reverse-onus provision could only be considered a reasonable limit on section 25(c) of the NZBORA if there was a high probability or near certainty that possession was for the purposes of supply.

In February 2010, before the Minister of Health acted on the Ministry of Health-inspired EACD recommendations, the Law Commission released an interim review of the Misuse of Drugs Act 1975. In *Controlling and Regulating Drugs*, the Law Commission tentatively recommended that section 6(6) of the Misuse of Drugs Act should be repealed and an 'aggravated possession offence' created with a specified quantity of drugs for controlled substances that are generally inconsistent with personal use.[83] (This would become the final recommendation of the Law Commission in its *Controlling and Regulating Drugs: A Review of the Misuse of Drugs Act 1975*, released in May 2011, before the amendments to the Act proposed in 2010 were passed as the Misuse of Drugs Amendment Act (No 2) 2011.) In reaching this tentative conclusion, the Law Commission concluded that it could not conceive of how a reverse-onus provision such as section 6(6) of the Misuse of Drugs Act could be reconciled with the NZBORA:

> On balance we consider the difficulties associated with any attempt to achieve a reverse-onus provision that is consistent with the Bill of Rights Act outweigh its possible advantages. Given the different approaches of the judges in Hansen, it would be impossible to predict with any certainty

[82] Ministry of Health (New Zealand) 2009, 'Advice to the Expert Advisory Committee on Drugs on: The Presumption of Supply of Pseudoephedrine and Ephedrine', (October), 3.

[83] New Zealand Law Commission 2010, 'Controlling and Regulating Drugs', Issue Paper 16 (11 February), 208.

> that the presumption would be found by a court to be consistent with the Bill of Rights Act unless it was set at a level which is unlikely to be effective.[84]

Although the Law Commission released an interim position, it did provide clear guidance to parliament and the Health Committee when considering future amendments to the Misuse of Drugs Act. The interim recommendation to replace the reverse-onus provision with an aggravated possession offence was endorsed by the Ministry of Health 'on the grounds that it removes the NZBORA concerns whilst concentrating on the quantity of drugs possessed regardless of intended use'.[85] Indeed, the very reason that the Health Committee refused to reconsider the reverse-onus provision during its review of the Misuse of Drugs Act (BZP Classification) Amendment Bill 2007 was *because* of the forthcoming review by the Law Commission.

Misuse of Drugs Amendment Bill 2010

When the Associate Minister of Health Peter Dunne introduced amendments to the Misuse of Drugs Act 1975 recommending that ephedrine and pseudoephedrine be classified as controlled drugs under Schedule 5 of the Act, with the trigger level for possession for the purposes of supply set at 10 grams, he did so with the full knowledge that this was inconsistent with *Hansen* and the interim recommendations of the Law Commission charged with reviewing the Misuse of Drugs Act 1975. The proposed amendments included a punishment not exceeding 8 years' imprisonment when convicted of possession for the purposes of supply. In his report under section 7 of the NZBORA, Attorney General Christopher Finlayson noted that the proposed amendments were inconsistent with *Hansen* and took issue with the trigger amount of 10 grams, as this amount was simply 'more than a person with a cold or flu could reasonably use'.[86] Further, the Attorney General concluded that the proposed amendments appeared inconsistent with section 25(c) of the NZBORA, as 'it is therefore apparent the threshold of 10 grams was not

[84] New Zealand Law Commission 2011, 'Controlling and Regulating Drugs: A Review of the Misuse of Drugs Act 1975', (26 April), 208.

[85] Ministry of Health (New Zealand) 2010, 'Regulating and Controlling Drugs, Ministry of Health Submission to the Law Commission', (April), 12.

[86] Report of the Attorney General under the New Zealand Bill of Rights Act 1990 on the Misuse of Drugs Amendment Bill, 3–4.

selected on the basis that possession above this level would correspond with a high probability or near certainty that the ephedrine or pseudoephedrine was possessed for the purposes of supply'.[87] Finally, the Attorney General brought to parliament's attention the Law Commission's tentative position that section 6(6) of the Act should not be retained, though Finlayson recognized this was for parliament to consider at a later time once the Law Commission released its final report on the Misuse of Drugs Act 1975.[88]

At first reading, the Associate Minister of Health referred to the Attorney General's section 7 report, acknowledged that there were continued concerns with the reverse-onus provision in the Act, but indicated that 'it is not the intention of this bill to second-guess the outcome of the Law Commission's review'.[89] Similar to the defence of the BZP classification amendment introduced in 2007 by then Associate Minister of Health Jim Anderton, the current minister acknowledged, but did not engage, the Attorney General's report that raised concerns about the 2010 amendments proposed to the Misuse of Drugs Act 1975. In an apparent effort to respect the independence of the Law Commission, the Associate Minister reserved the right to comment when the final report was released.

While the Associate Minister of Health did not engage the report of the Attorney General, several members of parliament attempted during the first reading to consider the NZBORA implications raised by the Attorney General. However, these episodes question whether parliamentarians can properly digest constitutional assessments that are intended to facilitate rights-based dialogue.[90] Indeed, this is one of the central assumptions of advocates of parliamentary enforced bills of rights – an uncritical belief that parliamentarians can engage in rights-based dialogue and possess the skills to utilize parliamentary oversight mechanisms to ensure that government bills have greater respect for domestic rights instruments.[91]

[87] Report of the Attorney General, 4. [88] Report of the Attorney General, 4.

[89] Hon. P. Dunne – United Future (24 August 2010) 666 NZPD 13528.

[90] C. Evans and S. Evans, 'Messages from the Front Line', p. 344.

[91] B. Galligan and F.L. Morton, 'Australian Exceptionalism: Rights Protections Without a Bill of Rights', in T. Campbell, J. Goldsworthy, and A. Stone (eds.), *Protecting Rights Without a Bill of Rights* (London: Ashgate, 2006), pp. 27–30; J. Uhr, 'The Performance of Australian Legislatures in Protecting Rights', in T. Campbell, J. Goldsworthy and A. Stone (eds.), *Protecting Rights Without a Bill of Rights* (London: Ashgate, 2006), pp. 41–59; T. Campbell, 'Parliamentary Review with a Democratic Charter of Rights', in T. Campbell, K.D. Ewing

While parliamentarians have the democratic legitimacy to define the content of rights, as Galligan, Morton, Uhr and Campbell correctly contend, whether they have the capacity to perform this task is open to debate. Speaking in support of the Misuse of Drugs Amendment Bill 2010 introduced by the National-led ministry, Paul Hutchinson of the National party erroneously suggested that the section 7 report found the 2010 amendments consistent with the NZBORA.[92] After concluding that section 6(6) of the Misuse of Drugs Act was a limitation on section 25(c) of the NZBORA, the Attorney General's report considered whether the limitation was reasonable through an assessment of the complex *Moonen* test. The *Moonen* test requires that for a limitation to be reasonable, all stages must be satisfied to support a finding of consistency under section 5 of the NZBORA. While Hutchinson was correct that the Attorney General considered the amendments 'pressing and substantial' legislative objectives sufficient to justify section 25(c),[93] the reverse-onus provision ultimately failed to satisfy the *Moonen* test because the supply level of 10 grams was not considered a proportional response to the legislative objectives pursued.[94]

Consistent with its opposition to the BZP amendments introduced in 2007, the Green party opposed the 2010 amendments to the Misuse of Drugs Act 1975. The party considered the amendments inconsistent with the NZBORA and were highly critical of the New Zealand National government's refusal to engage the interim report of the Law Commission.[95] However, as the Misuse of Drugs Amendment Bill was designated as a party vote, and was supported by New Zealand National (57 seats), United Future (1 seat) and the Māori party (4 seats), the New Zealand National-led ministry and its 'confidence and supply' partners had sufficient votes to pass the 2010 amendments, as this multi-party governing arrangement controlled 62 seats in the 122-seat House of Representatives. Further, as New Zealand Labour supported the Misuse of Drugs Amendment Bill, these changes easily passed on a combined party vote of 104 to 14, with

and A. Tomkins (eds.), *The Legal Protection of Human Rights: Sceptical Essays* (Oxford: Oxford University Press, 2011), 464–70.

92 Dr. P. Hutchinson – National Party (24 August 2010) 666 NZPD 13532.

93 Ibid. 94 Report of the Attorney General, 3–4.

95 M. Turei – Green Party (24 August 2010) 666 NZPD 13534.

only the Green Party (9 votes), ACT New Zealand (4 votes) and an independent member of parliament opposing the changes.

The Health Committee report added very little to the debate, and ignored the Attorney General's concern about extending section 6(6) of the Misuse of Drugs Act 1975 to ephedrine and pseudoephedrine for possession of 10 grams or more.[96] Instead, the Health Committee focused on amendments to the Act that would allow the Ministry of Health, through notices in the Gazette, to prohibit the advertisement or display of drug paraphernalia. Under the legislative scheme of the time, it was an offence to sell or purchase drug paraphernalia; the Health Committee was advised, on the recommendation of the New Zealand Police, to change the phrase 'drug paraphernalia' to 'drug utensils', as this was argued to make the law clearer and close a loophole that allowed the importation of incomplete drug paraphernalia without legal consequence.[97] Although the Labour party supported the 2010 amendments, arguing that the bill 'would do no harm', the minority view included in the Health Committee report questioned any amendments to the Misuse of Drugs Act 1975 while the Law Commission was conducting its review. Indeed, the minority report noted that a long-standing government practice was to 'suspend or oppose legislative change while a review is under way'.[98] Finally, the Health Committee report ignored the New Zealand Human Rights Commission's brief supporting the interim recommendation of the Law Commission to repeal the reverse-onus provision in the Misuse of Drugs Act 1975, noting that a similar provision had recently been determined inconsistent with the Victorian Charter of Human Rights and Responsibilities Act.[99]

While it can be argued that rights-based dialogue occurred at the select committee stage, it had no practical impact on the Misuse of Drugs Amendment Bill, as it was raised either by policy stakeholders such as the Human Rights Commission or parliamentary parties such as the Greens which lacked the ability to secure NZBORA-consistent amendments. As this legislation was passed on a party vote where the two dominant parties, National and Labour, supported the underlying

[96] Parliament of New Zealand 2010, Misuse of Drugs Amendment Bill. Report of the Health Committee (29 November), 1.

[97] Ibid., 2. [98] Ibid., 3.

[99] New Zealand Human Rights Commission 2010. Misuse of Drugs Amendment Bill. Submission by the Human Rights Commission to the Health Committee (27 September), 2.

policy intention, the legislation was essentially protected against amendment because its passage was secured before its introduction into parliament.

The final report of the Law Commission

In 2007, the Associate Minister deferred a fuller consideration of the reverse-onus provision in the Misuse of Drugs Act 1975 until the Law Commission had reported, arguing this was necessary to ensure the independence of the review and the impartiality of the recommendations presented to parliament. By 2010, when the Associate Minister of Health introduced the Misuse of Drugs Amendment Bill with the benefit of the Law Commission's interim recommendations, this position had been modified, with the argument that it would be inappropriate to comment until the Law Commission had released its final report. As noted, this report, *A Review of the Misuse of Drugs Act 1975*, was released in May 2011, nearly three months before the second reading debate resumed on the Misuse of Drugs Amendment Bill in July 2011, thus satisfying the conditions established by the Associate Minister of Health for engaging in rights-based dialogue with an independent agency created by parliament. In its final report, the Law Commission confirmed its earlier recommendation that the reverse-onus provision in section 6(6) of the Misuse of Drugs Act 1975 should be repealed and replaced with an 'aggravated' possession offence, which would be differentiated from 'simple' possession based on quantity of supply, in order to target those individuals engaged in supply and not personal use.[100]

During the second reading debate, the Associate Minister of Health referred to the 144 recommendations made by the Law Commission and indicated that the government welcomed the report, but did not comment on the issue central to the Misuse of Drugs Amendment Bill and the Attorney General's section 7 report – whether the reverse-onus provision in section 6(6) of the Act should be repealed because of clear inconsistencies with section 25(c) of the NZBORA.[101] The 2010 amendments to the Misuse of Drugs Act 1975 received Royal Assent in August 2011 and the Misuse of Drugs Amendment Act (No 2) 2011 was proclaimed. While the bill was amended during the parliamentary hearings

[100] New Zealand Law Commission 2011, 'Controlling and Regulating Drugs', *A Review of the Misuse of Drugs Act 1975* (3 May), 12.

[101] Hon. P. Dunne – United Future (12 July 2011) 674 NZPD 20019.

and debates, the amendments were not made to address the concerns raised by the Attorney General.

What is striking about the parliamentary debate that followed the release of the Law Commission's report is the complete failure to refer to the central recommendation of the report – the reverse-onus provision and its incompatibility with the NZBORA, as interpreted by the SCNZ in *Hansen* and the Attorney General in his 2007 and 2010 section 7 reports to parliament. While it is understandable that the Associate Minister requested a period of reflection before responding, as the Law Commission's report was extensive and made wide-ranging recommendations regarding the Misuse of Drugs Act 1975, the party vote procedure under MMP allowed the New Zealand National government to completely ignore the central issue of the 2010 amendment to the Misuse of Drugs Act 1975 – whether to repeal the reverse-onus provision. Clearly, the party vote mechanism largely negates the possibility of meaningful dialogue on the NZBORA, and can explain why section 7 reports by the Attorney General have not generated substantive parliamentary engagement of rights-based compatibility issues. In effect, the party vote muzzles parliamentary debate and renders the Attorney General's report a largely meaningless exercise, given that the outcome of the legislative process is decided before a government bill is introduced into parliament.

However, the party vote cannot fully explain the lack of parliamentary engagement of the NZBORA, though it is a significant constraint on rights-based dialogue in New Zealand. What should not be discounted is that many section 7 reports involve criminal policy, and this is also a serious impediment to parliamentary willingness to demand amendments in order to ensure greater compatibility with the NZBORA. Generally speaking, this is not an area in which political parties that contend for power, such as the New Zealand Labour party and New Zealand National, demand amendment to legislation to ensure greater consistency with the NZBORA. Such engagement of the NZBORA would require these parties to support the rights of the accused and those convicted of serious criminal offences, which is a risky electoral strategy, as many section 7 reports in the area of criminal policy are clear examples of the endurance of penal populism in New Zealand. Indeed, the entrenchment of penal populism as the shared policy framework in New Zealand is evident in the parliamentary vote on the Misuse of Drugs Amendment Bill 2010, where the two main political parties, National and Labour, accepted the policy rationale of extending the Misuse of Drugs Act 1975 to ephedrine and pseudoephedrine despite inconsistencies with

Table 4.3 *Section 7 reports: voting results under NZBORA, 1990–2014, bills passed into law under MMP*

	Bill	Type	Year	Policy Area	Party Vote	% of Vote	YEAS	NOES
1	Land Transport Bill	Govt	1997	Criminal policy	78–40	66.10	New Zealand National 44; New Zealand Labour 8; Alliance 3; ACT New Zealand 8; New Zealand First 6; Independents 9	New Zealand Labour 29; Alliance party 9; United New Zealand 1; Independent 1
2	Land Transport (Street and Illegal Drag Racing) Amendment Bill	Govt	2002	Criminal policy	97–17	85.09	New Zealand Labour 52; New Zealand National 24; New Zealand First 13; United Future 8	ACT New Zealand 8; Green party 9
3	Parole (Extended Supervision) and Sentencing Amendment Bill	Govt	2003	Criminal policy	91–25	78.45	New Zealand Labour 51; New Zealand National 27; Green party 5; United Future 8	New Zealand First 13; Green party 4; ACT New Zealand 8

Table 4.3 (*cont.*)

	Bill	Type	Year	Policy Area	Party Vote	% of Vote	YEAS	NOES
4	Criminal Procedure Bill	Govt	2004	Criminal policy	108–11	90.76	New Zealand Labour 49; New Zealand National 48; New Zealand First 7; United Future 2; Progressive party 1; Independent: Copeland	Green party 6; Māori party 4; Independent; Field
5	Misuse of Drugs (Classification of BZP) Amendment Bill	Govt	2007	Criminal policy	109–11	90.83	New Zealand Labour 49; New Zealand National 48; New Zealand First 7; United Future 2; Progressive party 1; Independents: Copeland, Field	Green party 6; Māori party 3; ACT New Zealand 2

6	Criminal Investigations (Bodily Samples) Amendment Bill	Govt	2009	Criminal policy	108–14	88.52	New Zealand National 58; New Zealand Labour 43; ACT New Zealand 5; Progressive party 1; United Future 1	Green party 9; Māori party 5
7	Sentencing and Parole Reform Bill	Govt	2009	Criminal policy	63–58	52.07	New Zealand National 58; ACT New Zealand 5	New Zealand Labour 43; Green party 9; Māori party 5; United Future 1
8	Parole (Extended Supervision Orders) Amendment Bill	Govt	2009	Criminal policy	113–9	92.62	New Zealand National 58; New Zealand Labour 43; ACT New Zealand 5; Māori party 5; Progressive party 1; United Future 1	Green party 9
9	Misuse of Drugs Amendment Bill	Govt	2010	Criminal policy	104–14	88.14	New Zealand National 57; New Zealand Labour 42;	Green party 9; ACT New Zealand 4; Independent: C. Carter

Table 4.3 (*cont.*)

	Bill	Type	Year	Policy Area	Party Vote	% of Vote	YEAS	NOES
							Māori party 3; Progressive party 1; United Future 1	
10	Criminal Procedure (Reform and Modernization) Bill	Govt	2010	Criminal policy	110–10	91.67	New Zealand National 57; New Zealand Labour 42; ACT New Zealand 5; Māori party 4; Progressive party 1; United Future 1	Green party 9; Mana 1
11	New Zealand Bill of Rights section 24(e) Amendment Bill 2010	Govt	2010	Criminal policy	110–10	91.67	New Zealand National 57; New Zealand Labour 42; ACT New Zealand 5; Māori party 4; Progressive party 1; United Future 1	Green party 9; Mana 1
12	Alcohol Reform Bill	Govt	2010	Criminal policy	108–13	89.26	New Zealand National 59;	New Zealand Labour 2

						New Zealand Labour 32; Green party 14; ACT New Zealand 1; Mana 1; United Future 1	(Robertson R, Sio); New Zealand First 7; Māori party 3; Independent: Horan 1
13	Manukau City Council (Control of Graffiti) Bill 2005	Local	2005	Criminal policy	109–11	90.83	New Zealand Labour 49; New Zealand National 48; New Zealand First 7; United Future 2; Progressive party 1; Independents: Copeland, Field	Green party 6; Māori party 3; ACT New Zealand 2
14	Wanganui District Council (Prohibition of Gang Insignia) Bill	Local	2008	Criminal policy	62–59	51.24	New Zealand National 58; ACT New Zealand (Boscawen, Garrett, Hide) 3; United Future 1	New Zealand Labour 42; Green party 9; ACT New Zealand (Roy, Douglas) 2; Māori party 5; Progressive party 1

Table 4.3 (*cont.*)

	Bill	Type	Year	Policy Area	Party Vote	% of Vote	YEAS	NOES
15	Electoral (Disqualification of Convicted Persons) Amendment Bill	Members'	2010	Criminal policy	63–58	52.07	New Zealand National 58; ACT New Zealand 5	New Zealand Labour 42; Green party 9; Māori party 5; Progressive party 1; United Future 1
					79.95	**Party Vote Average (Criminal Policy)**		
16	Trade in Endangered Species Amendment Bill	Members'	1997	Environmental	no vote recorded			
17	Summit Road (Canterbury) Protection Bill	Local	2000	Environmental	no vote recorded			
18	Eden Park Trust Amendment Bill	Local	2009	Environmental	no vote recorded			
19	Casino Control (Moratorium) Amendment Bill	Govt	1997	Economic policy	71–49	59.17	New Zealand National 44; New Zealand First 17; ACT New Zealand 8; United New Zealand 1; Independent 1	New Zealand Labour 37; Alliance party 12; Independent 1

20	War Pensions Amendment Bill	Govt	2001	Economic policy	no vote recorded			
21	Income Tax Bill 2002	Govt	2002	Economic policy	109–8	93.16	New Zealand Labour 52; New Zealand National 25; New Zealand First 13; Green party 9; United Future 8; Progressive party 2	ACT New Zealand 7; Independent 1
22	Taxation (Annual Rates, GST, Trans-Tasman Imputation and Miscellaneous Provisions) Bill 2003	Govt	2003	Economic policy	69–49	58.47	New Zealand Labour 52; Green party 9; United Future 8	New Zealand National 27; New Zealand First 13; ACT New Zealand 8; Independent: Awatere Huata
23	Auckland Regional Amenities Funding Bill	Members'	2007	Economic policy	113–7	94.17	New Zealand Labour 49; New Zealand National 48; Green party 6; Māori party 3; United Future 2;	New Zealand First 7

Table 4.3 (*cont.*)

	Bill	Type	Year	Policy Area	Party Vote	% of Vote	YEAS	NOES
							ACT New Zealand 2; Progressive party 1; Independents: Copeland, Field	
					76.24	**Party Vote Average (Economic Policy)**		
24	Housing Restructuring (Income Related Rents) Amendment Bill	Govt	2000	Social policy	71–39	59.17	New Zealand Labour 49; Alliance party 10; Green party 7; New Zealand First 5	New Zealand National 30; ACT New Zealand 8; United New Zealand 1
25	Social Security (Residence of Spouses) Amendment Bill	Govt	2001	Social policy	70–49	58.82	New Zealand Labour 49; Alliance party 9; Green party 7; New Zealand First 5	New Zealand National 39; ACT New Zealand 9; United New Zealand 1
26	Social Security (Long-term Residential Care) Amendment Bill	Govt	2003	Social policy	68–49	58.12	New Zealand Labour 50; New Zealand First 7; Green party 5;	New Zealand National 48; ACT New Zealand 1

							Māori party 2; United Future 3; Progressive party 1	
27	Care of Children Bill	Govt	2003	Social policy	62–58	51.67	New Zealand Labour 51; Green party 9; Progressive party 2	New Zealand National 27; New Zealand First 13; ACT New Zealand 8; United Future 8; Māori party 1; Independent: Awatere Huata
28	Future Directions (Working for Families) Bill	Govt	2004	Social policy	78–26	75	New Zealand Labour 51; New Zealand First 13; Green party 6; United Future 8	New Zealand National 21; ACT New Zealand 4; Independent: Awatere Huata
29	Relationships (Statutory References) Bill	Govt	2004	Social policy	PERSONAL VOTE 74–45			
30	Social Assistance (New Work Tests, Incentives, and Obligations) Amendment Bill	Govt	2010	Social policy	65–55	54.17	New Zealand National 58; ACT New Zealand 5; Māori party 1 (Turia); United Future 1	New Zealand Labour 42; Green party 9; Māori party 3 (Flavell, Harawira, Katene); Progressive party 1

Table 4.3 (*cont.*)

	Bill	Type	Year	Policy Area	Party Vote	% of Vote	YEAS	NOES
31	New Zealand Public Health and Disability Amendment Bill (No2) 2013	Govt	2013	Social policy	63–55	53.39	New Zealand National 59; Māori party 2: ACT New Zealand 1: United Future 1	New Zealand Labour 33; Green party 13; New Zealand First 7; Mana 1; Independent 1
					58.62	**Party Vote Average (Social Policy)**		
32	Electoral Amendment Bill (No.2)	Govt	2001	Electoral policy	70–45	60.87	New Zealand Labour 49; Alliance party 10; Green party 6; New Zealand First 5	New Zealand National 38; ACT New Zealand 6; United Future 1
					73.17	**Party Vote Average (All Policy Areas)**		
PV = Party Vote								

the NZBORA.[102] As previously argued, section 7 reports by the Attorney General can only function as parliamentary oversight mechanisms of the government's legislative agenda if they are engaged by parliamentarians and, in particular, by the opposition parties that use section 7 reports to demand amendments to ensure greater consistency with the NZBORA.

Table 4.3 considers the voting results of bills passed into law under MMP in which the Attorney General reported to parliament under section 7 of the NZBORA. In this period (1990 to 2014), a total of 32 bills were passed, but only 27 have recorded votes. The average parliamentary vote for bills passed with section 7 reports is 73.16 per cent of the sitting members, or approximately 89 of the 121 available votes in parliament. This voting percentage varies between policy areas, with criminal policy legislation having the highest level of support (79.9%), followed by economic policy (76.3%) and electoral policy (60.9%); social policy has the lowest level of support (58.6%), which is not a surprising development given that National is a right-of-centre party whereas Labour is left-of-centre. In contrast, the party or parties forming the ministry in each parliament have constituted a minority of sitting members, averaging 47.3 per cent or 57 of the 121 seats in parliament. When 'confidence and supply' partners are considered, these multi-party governing arrangements increase slightly, to 52.9 per cent, or 64 of the 121 members in each parliament under MMP. The passage with large legislative majorities of bills with section 7 reports is indeed significant, as it illustrates the dilemma facing parliamentary oversight mechanisms when there is broad cross-party agreement on the underlying policy *irrespective* of the NZBORA implications raised by the Attorney General. Simply put, the party vote and the policy area determines whether legislation is passed under MMP, and largely explains why parliamentarians do not engage in rights-based analysis of legislative proposals – they are disciplined by the party vote to support the measure, and perhaps more importantly, they agree with the underlying policy and instruments chosen, regardless of the Attorney General's report of inconsistency.

Focusing simply on criminal policy, there is clear cross-party agreement among the dominant political parties on the policy paradigm that informs this issue, penal populism, and this is a serious problem with regard to section 7 reports' ability to generate parliamentary engagement

[102] J. Pratt, 'The Dark Side of Paradise: Explaining New Zealand's History of High Imprisonment', (2006) 46 *British Journal of Criminology* 557–58; J. Pratt, *Penal Populism* (Routledge: New York, 2007), pp. 27–8.

to address NZBORA inconsistencies as bills progress through the House of Representatives. With few exceptions, Labour and the National party have voted together to pass these criminal policy bills with massive legislative majorities. For instance, the Misuse of Drugs (Classification of BZP) Amendment Act 2008 passed on a party vote of 109 to 11, the Misuse of Drugs Amendment Act 2011 by 104 to 14 and the Criminal Investigations (Bodily Samples) Amendment Bill by 108 to 14. While the Green Party has been receptive to the concerns raised by the Attorney General and has relied on section 7 reports to oppose legislation with potential NZBORA inconsistencies, its caucus is simply too small to ensure rights-based changes.

The government response to the Law Commission's report

The Associate Minister of Health, Peter Dunne, tabled the government's formal response to the Law Commissions review of the Misuse of Drugs Act 1975 on 8 September 2011, one month after the Misuse of Drugs Amendment Act (No 2) 2011 received royal assent.[103] The only recommendation upon which the government would immediately act was the suggestion to create a new legislative scheme for regulating psychoactive substances outside of the Misuse of Drugs Act 1975. In 2013, the New Zealand National minority government passed the Psychoactive Substances Act. Unlike the Misuse of Drugs Act 1975, which requires the EACD to recommend to the Minister of Health that a specific substance be regulated by the Act, the Psychoactive Substances Act 2013 bans all psychoactive substances and requires the industry to demonstrate that a product poses a low risk of harm before the Ministry of Health will issue a licence for sale and consumption.[104] Thus, the onus is on the importer to demonstrate low risk for the purposes of a licence, whereas the Misuse of Drugs Act 1975 places the onus on the EACD to recommend to the Minister of Health restrictions on a particular substance based on its perception of a moderate to high risk. The government argued this was a more efficient policy approach to party pills, an area in which new products regularly appear. The process under the Misuse of Drugs Act

[103] Ministry of Health (New Zealand) 2011, 'Controlling and Regulating Drugs – a review of the Misuse of Drugs Act 1975', Government Response to the Law Commission's Report (8 September).

[104] Ministry of Health (New Zealand) 2013, 'Psychoactive Substances Bill', Initial Briefing to the Health Committee (17 April), 3.

required the EACD to study the implications of new party pills before making recommendations to the Minister of Health; this created long delays before new party pills could be classified under the Misuse of Drugs Act 1975. The Psychoactive Substances Act 2013 was an important recommendation of the Law Commission that would allow parliament, and not the industry, to control the area of party pills.

In his report to parliament, the Associate Minister of Health stated that the next government would overhaul the Misuse of Drugs Act 1975. The minority government led by New Zealand National was returned to office after the general election on 26 November 2011, but at the time of writing has yet to act on this commitment. As a result, the reverse-onus provision in section 6(6) of the Misuse of Drugs Act 1975 continues, despite a long debate that generally concludes it cannot be reconciled with the NZBORA. This rights-based dialogue began in 2005 when the Court of Appeal took issue with section 6(6) of the Misuse of Drugs Act 1975 and its relationship to the NZBORA. The Attorney General agreed with this position in 2007 and 2008, as did the New Zealand Supreme Court in 2007. Finally, the Law Commission agreed that section 6(6) cannot be reconciled with section 25(c) of the NZBORA and recommended its removal from the Misuse of Drugs Act in its final report in 2011. While this may be viewed in some quarters as evidence of the new Commonwealth model of constitutionalism being fully engaged in New Zealand, it does raise questions as to whether the NZBORA has made a noticeable difference to legislative outcomes, given that the government has continued to take its preferred policy approach despite serious and widespread concerns with section 6(6) of the NZBORA over the life of three parliaments.

V. Electoral (Disqualification of Sentenced Prisoners) Amendment Act 2010

Although the right to vote is protected under section 12(a) of the NZBORA, the issue of prisoner disenfranchisement preceded the adoption of the bill of rights in 1990: the Royal Commission on the Electoral System that recommended the adoption of MMP also suggested that the blanket disenfranchisement of all prisoners should be reconsidered. Reporting in December 1986, the Royal Commission argued that the blanket restriction on prisoner voting – which had existed since 1956, with a brief repeal between 1975 and 1977 – should be abandoned. This approach was considered inconsistent with contemporary penal theory that argued certain classes of prisoners should retain ordinary rights of citizenship to ensure their reintegration into society once released from prison.[105] Indeed, the Royal Commission recommended that only prisoners serving sentences for serious offences should be disenfranchised, and recommended that the right to vote should be rescinded for sentences of three years or more.[106]

The New Zealand National government led by Prime Minister Jim Bolger passed the Electoral Act 1993, which implemented the recommendation of the Royal Commission on the Electoral System in regard to prisoner voting. Under section 80(1) of the Electoral Act 1993, the right to vote was changed from a blanket restriction under section 42(1)(d) of the Electoral Act 1956 to restrictions simply on those prisoners serving sentences of three years or more.[107] The Royal Commission's recommendation was important, but the position released by the Solicitor General on 17 November 1992 also had a significant influence on the Electoral Act 1993 and section 80(1). Commenting on the proposed changes to the Electoral Act, Solicitor General McGrath considered the blanket restriction on prisoner voting in section 42(1)(d) of the Electoral Act 1956 as a violation of the right to vote in section 12(a) of the NZBORA.[108] Further, the Solicitor General endorsed the Royal Commission's recommendation that prisoner disenfranchisement should be limited to those serving sentences of three years or more, arguing this approach would represent a reasonable limitation on the right to vote, as it would be limited to serious offences only.[109]

In 1993, the High Court of New Zealand also considered whether the blanket restriction on prisoner voting in the Electoral Act 1956 was a violation of the right to vote in section 12(a) of the NZBORA, and further, in the event of a conflict between the Electoral Act 1956 and the NZBORA, which act should prevail.[110] Although the High Court viewed the blanket approach to prisoner disenfranchisement as a violation of section 12(a) of the NZBORA, the Court

[105] Report of the Royal Commission on the Electoral System. *Toward a Better Democracy* (December 1986), 237.

[106] Ibid., 238.

[107] G. Robins, 'The Right of Prisoners to Vote: A Review of Disenfranchisement in New Zealand', (2006) 4 *New Zealand Journal of Public and International Law* 169–70.

[108] Department of Justice (New Zealand) 1992. Consistency between the Bill of Rights Act 1990 and Restrictions on Prisoners Voting Rights (17 November), para 3.

[109] Department of Justice. para 26.

[110] *RE Bennett* 2 HRNZ 358.

ruled that the Electoral Act 1956 must prevail because the NZBORA was not a supreme law bill of rights but simply an ordinary statute equal in status to the Electoral Act 1956. Further, as section 4 prevented the courts declaring acts invalid when they conflicted with the NZBORA, a unanimous ruling by Justice Greig concluded that the NZBORA did not, and could not, take precedence over other legislative enactments:

> There is no room for any other interpretation of the provision of the Electoral Act and the clear conflict with the Bill of Rights. The provision of the Electoral Act therefore must prevail and Mr. Bennett and others detained in penal institutions under convictions remain disqualified for registration and are unable, notwithstanding the declaration in the Bill of Rights, to exercise any right to vote.[111]

Between 1993 and 2010 a general consensus existed among the main parties of government, Labour and New Zealand National, that a blanket restriction on prisoner voting was a violation of the right to vote protected in section 12(a) of the NZBORA. Further, both Labour and New Zealand National considered a total ban as an unreasonable limitation on section 12(a), and supported a partial ban on prisoners serving sentences of three years or more.

This consensus was challenged in 2010 when a members' bill sponsored by Paul Quinn of New Zealand National was placed on the Order Papers and subsequently introduced into the House of Representatives. During the period in which parliament is in session in New Zealand, precedence is given every second Wednesday to members' bills, where under SO 277(1) a maximum of eight members' bills can be on the Order Papers at any given time. When a vacancy occurs and several members lodge notices of proposals with the Clerk of the House of Representatives, a ballot is held that randomly selects one for inclusion on the Order Papers for the next members' day. Although the Electoral (Disqualification of Sentenced Prisoners) Amendment Bill was selected through a lottery system, a members' bill can only succeed if it is supported by party caucuses.[112] Once a members' bill is introduced into parliament, it is at

[111] *RE Bennett*, 361.

[112] The bill was originally introduced as the Electoral (Disqualification of Convicted Prisoners) Amendment Bill and was changed, at the recommendation of the Law and Order Committee, to the Electoral (Disqualification of Sentenced Prisoners) Amendment Bill.

the mercy of parliamentary parties and the party vote under SO 138 unless it is designated as a conscience vote. The party vote was used in relation to the Electoral (Disqualification of Sentenced Prisoners) Amendment Bill, and it was supported by New Zealand National and its 'confidence and supply' partner ACT New Zealand throughout all stages of the parliamentary process.

In the Explanatory Note, the sponsoring member proposed amending section 80(1)(d)(ii) of the Electoral Act 1993 to remove the right of any prisoner serving a sentence of less than three years to register as an elector.[113] In effect, this members' bill would disenfranchise all prisoners by preventing their inclusion on the electoral rolls, and sought to reinstate the approach that existed under the Electoral Act 1956.[114] Paul Quinn justified this significant policy change as minor and consistent with contemporary thinking on the issue of prisoner disenfranchisement. Indeed, Quinn argued that the approach advanced by the Royal Commission on the Electoral System was no longer acceptable, as contemporary sentencing policy in New Zealand considered most, if not all, of those incarcerated as serious offenders, even if they were serving sentences of less than three years.[115]

The report of the Attorney General

As this was a members' bill, the Attorney General did not review the Electoral (Disqualification of Sentenced Prisoners) Amendment Bill until it was introduced into the House of Representatives on 10 February 2010. Indeed, the Attorney General reported to parliament under section 7 of the NZBORA on 17 March, when the bill was moved at first reading.[116] In his section 7 report, Attorney General Christopher Finlayson concluded that the Electoral Amendment Bill 2010 appeared to be an unjustified violation of section 12 of the NZBORA.[117] Finlayson based this assessment on *Re Bennett* and the

[113] Parliament of New Zealand 2010. Electoral (Disqualification of Convicted Prisoners Amendment Bill. Explanatory Note (10 February), 1.

[114] Parliament of New Zealand 2010. Electoral (Disqualification of Convicted Prisoners) Amendment Bill, 1.

[115] Ibid., 2.

[116] P. Quinn – National Party (17 March 2010) 661 NZPD 9610.

[117] Report of the Attorney General under the New Zealand Bill of Rights Act 1990 on the Electoral (Disqualification of Convicted Prisoners) Amendment Bill, 1.

High Court of New Zealand's decision that the blanket disenfranchisement of prisoners was a violation of the right to vote. However, the Attorney General did acknowledge that the High Court failed to consider whether a ban on all prisoners voting would be a reasonable limitation under section 5 of the NZBORA.[118] However, Finlayson noted that the European Court of Human Rights, in *Hirst* v *the United Kingdom (No 2)*, and the Supreme Court of Canada, in *Sauvé* v *Canada*, considered the disenfranchisement of all prisoners to be inconsistent with electoral rights.[119]

In his assessment of reasonable limitations under section 5 of the NZBORA, Attorney General Finlayson noted that the objective of the members' bill 'appears to be that a person convicted for serious crimes against the community should forfeit the right to vote as part of their punishment'.[120] While the Attorney General accepted that disenfranchising serious offenders advanced a significant and important objective, the proposed amendment to the Electoral Act 1993 was not rationally connected, and thus constituted an unreasonable limitation on section 12 of the NZBORA. Specifically, the Attorney General objected to the characterization of all those incarcerated as serious offenders, as 'It is questionable that every person serving a sentence of imprisonment is necessarily a serious offender',[121] and took issue with 'irrational inconsistencies' in the proposed amendment: 'The Bill would therefore introduce irrational inconsistencies in the law where mentally impaired prisoners detained in a hospital or secure facility for less than 3 years could vote while all prisoners serving sentences less than three years in prison would be disenfranchised.'[122]

Although the Attorney General did not explicitly comment on the Electoral Act 1993, his section 7 report echoed the 1992 assessment by Solicitor General McGrath, the 1993 decision of the High Court of New Zealand in *Re Bennett* and the viewpoints of all governments that accepted the Electoral Act 1993. Specifically, the Attorney General advocated the status quo that informed the Electoral Act 1993 – that a blanket approach to prisoner disenfranchisement could not be considered a reasonable limitation, whereas restricting criminal disenfranchisement to serious offences would satisfy section 5 of the NZBORA.

[118] Report of the Attorney General, 2. [119] Ibid. [120] Ibid., 1.
[121] Ibid. [122] Ibid., 3.

Standing Orders and select committee allocations

The ability of the Attorney General's report to influence the parliamentary debate – and, more importantly, parliamentary scrutiny at the select committee stage – is compromised by the unfettered discretion provided to members under the Standing Orders of the House of Representatives to determine which select committee receives a bill after first reading. Although the members' bill fell under the subject matter of legislation normally assigned to the Justice and Electoral Committee under SO 185, the sponsoring member moved under SO 283 (1)(a) that the Law and Order Committee would consider the bill.[123] This is an important strategic allocation with substantive implications for the NZBORA as a parliamentary enforced bill of rights, as the Law and Order Committee is advised by the Department of Corrections and not the Ministry of Justice.[124] In addition, New Zealand National, the minority government, controlled a majority of members on the Law and Order Committee (5/9) and, in collaboration with its 'confidence and supply' partner, ACT New Zealand, had a commanding majority of committee membership (6/9). This supra majority, combined with the party vote, ensured that the Electoral (Disqualification of Sentenced Prisoners) Amendment Bill would pass into law despite noted inconsistencies with the NZBORA.

The Department of Corrections does not administer the Electoral Act, as this is the responsibility of the Ministry of Justice; nor does the Department of Corrections have any expertise as it relates to the NZBORA. As a result, the select committee's principal departmental advisor on this bill – as well as on the NZBORA implications of blanket disenfranchisement of all prisoners – was a department with limited experience in human rights, the right to vote as protected under section 12(a) of the NZBORA and the Electoral Act 1993. The decision to send the Electoral (Disqualification of Convicted Prisoners) Amendment Bill 2010 to the Law and Order Committee was not justified by Paul Quinn; however, as presently constituted, the Standing Orders of the New Zealand parliament do not require a member to justify the select committee allocation of a bill, even when the subject matter outlined in SO 185 is not part of the committee's mandate.

[123] P. Quinn – National Party (17 March 2010) 661 NZPD 9610.

[124] A. Geddis, 'Prisoner Voting and Rights Deliberation: How New Zealand's Parliament Failed' (2011) *New Zealand Law Review* 463.

Parliamentary attempts at section 7 engagement and scrutiny

While this procedural limitation is problematic, given that the proposed amendment to the Electoral Act 1993 constituted a substantive change in public policy, a more troubling aspect of the proposed amendment emerged during the first reading. According to Quinn, this change was necessitated 'because a large number of ordinary folk have asked me to introduce it'.[125] Further, the sponsoring member downplayed the significance of the contemplated policy change, which was, according to the High Court of Australia, the Supreme Court of Canada and the European Court of Human Rights, an unreasonable limitation that could not be justified in a free and democratic society.

These judicial findings were, despite Quinn's characterization, based on contemporary approaches to penal theory and citizenship. Whereas the Electoral Act 1993 was a government bill that responded to the findings of the Royal Commission on the Electoral System in 1986, which in turn was a policy recommendation stemming from the Report of the Penal Policy Committee in 1981, the Electoral (Disqualification of Sentenced Prisoners) Amendment Act was simply a populist measure introduced by a private member without a compelling justification, rationale or public policy context. Perhaps more importantly, a members' bill is developed without the support of the Ministry of Justice and its specialized human rights unit specifically tasked with developing legislation in the context of the NZBORA. Given the absence of BORA scrutiny, to which government bills are subjected before their introduction into parliament, a members' bill relies on the parliamentary setting for critical engagement of its consistency with the NZBORA, as well as the Attorney General's section 7 report.

In contrast to the 2007 and 2010 amendments to the Misuse of Drugs Act 1975, a lively parliamentary debate involving the NZBORA and the Attorney General's section 7 report took place in relation to the Electoral (Disqualification of Sentenced Prisoners) Amendment Act. We do see the presence of rights-based dialogue and attempts at parliamentary oversight through engagement with the Attorney General's section 7 report; parliamentary engagement with the NZBORA and the Attorney General's report is evident in the contributions made by opposition parties such as Labour and the Greens. However, this engagement is absent in the contributions of the sponsoring member and the

125 P. Quinn – National Party (17 March 2010) 661 NZPD 9610.

parliamentary caucuses that supported it through the party vote, New Zealand National and ACT New Zealand.

As the combined party votes of National and ACT New Zealand were sufficient for the bill to proceed to the select committee stage, as the Electoral (Disqualification of Convicted Prisoners) Amendment Bill secured 63 party votes in a 122-seat parliament at all stages of debate, the NZBORA engagement by the opposition parties, while significant, had no discernible influence as the bill progressed through parliament. For instance, the opposition members focused on the NZBORA limitations of the proposed bill, with Lianne Dalziel of the Labour Party relying heavily on the Attorney General's recommendation that the disenfranchisement of all prisoners was an unreasonable limitation as it was arbitrary and did not consider the seriousness of the offence.[126] Similarly, Charles Chauvel echoed the section 7 report's conclusion that the proposed amendment 'breaches the New Zealand Bill of Rights Act because it is inconsistent with the International Covenant on Civil and Political Rights, the High Court decision in *Re Bennett*, and the decisions of the Supreme Court of Canada and the European Court of Human Rights'.[127] The Green Party argued that the bill should not proceed as its core principles violated the NZBORA.[128]

Members of New Zealand National and ACT New Zealand who participated in the parliamentary debate simply ignored the rights-based arguments raised by the opposition parties. Instead, the debate descended into a partisan attempt to portray the Labour and Green parties as soft on crime. David Garrett of ACT New Zealand stated that this members' bill was supported because 'it is part of a sea change that this Government has embarked upon in the law and order field. Along with measures to combat drug abuse and the other drivers of crime, the National-ACT Government is making it very clear that prison ought to be a place that people do not want to return to'.[129]

A surprising development during the first reading, and one that foreshadowed the impending difficulties of parliamentary oversight at the select committee stage for the opposition parties, was the participation by the Chair of the Law and Order Committee, Sandra Goudie of the National party. Similar to the sponsoring member, the Chair of the Law

[126] Hon. L. Dalziel - Labour Party (21 April 2010) 662 NZPD 10340.
[127] C. Chauvel - Labour Party (21 April 2010) 662 NZPD 10343.
[128] D. Glendon - Green Party (21 April 2010) 662 NZPD 10345.
[129] D. Garrett - ACT New Zealand (21 April 2010) 662 NZPD 10342.

and Order Committee portrayed the amendment as a simple policy change, as well as viewing the loss of political rights as an acceptable component of penal policy.[130] In regard to the NZBORA and concerns raised by the Labour and Green parties about the reasonableness of blanket prisoner disenfranchisement, Goudie concluded: 'the moment they commit a crime they abdicate their rights.'[131] Further, Goudie heaped praise on the Minister of Corrections, Judith Collins, and the efforts to advance New Zealand National's law and order policy: 'We have given the police Tasers, we have given them more police on the front line, and we have given them more powers to deal with crime and methamphetamine.'[132]

The Law and Order Committee

At the conclusion of the first reading debate, the bill was referred to the Law and Order Committee on a party vote (63 to 59), supported by New Zealand National (58 votes) and ACT New Zealand (5 votes). The Department of Corrections' initial briefing to the Law and Order Committee did not engage the Attorney General's report, but simply referred to the NZBORA issues raised by Christopher Finlayson. The Department of Corrections noted that the proposed changes would have a disproportionate impact on Māori, who are overrepresented in prison populations.[133] The engagement of the NZBORA and the Attorney General's report at select committee followed the same pattern as the first reading debate – a lively debate led by the opposition parties, joined by groups such as the New Zealand Law Society and the New Zealand Human Rights Commission, which was simply ignored by the members of National and ACT New Zealand, which had a commanding majority on the Law and Order Committee.

For instance, a total of 55 individuals and organizations made written submissions to the Law and Order Committee. Only two written submissions supported the proposed changes to the Electoral Act 1993, and one was submitted by the bill's sponsor, Paul Quinn. In effect, 93 per cent

[130] S. Goudie – National Party (21 April 2010) 662 NZPD 10345.

[131] S. Goudie – National Party (21 April 2010) 662 NZPD 10346. [132] Ibid.

[133] Department of Corrections (New Zealand) 2010. Electoral (Disqualification of Convicted Prisoners) Amendment Bill. Initial Briefing for the Law and Order Committee (26 June), executive summary – point 6.

(51/55) of the written submissions did not support the bill and two submissions did not take a position on whether the bill should be passed into law.[134] The New Zealand Human Rights Commission and the New Zealand Law Society strongly opposed the bill because it was inconsistent with international standards and the NZBORA 1990, and represented indirect discrimination because it would have a disproportionate impact on Māori.[135]

In its report to the Law and Order Committee, the Department of Corrections noted that there were serious risks with proceeding with the current version of the draft bill. As comparable jurisdictions had determined that blanket prisoner disqualification could not be considered a reasonable violation of the right to vote, it was noted that a strong possibility existed that this issue would be litigated before the New Zealand Supreme Court. Indeed, papers were filed with the High Court in Auckland in September 2013 to challenge the blanket disenfranchisement of all prisoners.[136] In addition, as the ability to issue a declaration of inconsistency as a judicial remedial power had been left open in *R.* v *Hansen*, the Department of Corrections cautioned the Law and Order Committee that the criminal disenfranchisement bill, if passed into law, could serve as a test case that may lead to the establishment of this judicial remedy under the NZBORA.[137] However, despite the noted risks connected to the passage of this members' bill, the Department of Corrections recommended only two minor changes: that the title be changed from 'convicted prisoners' to 'sentenced prisoners' to ensure only those serving prison sentences would be disenfranchised, with the amendment to section 80(i)(d)(iii) reworded to reflect this change.[138]

[134] Department of Corrections (New Zealand) 2010. Electoral (Disqualification of Convicted Prisoners) Amendment Bill. Departmental Report for the Law and Order Committee (16 August).

[135] New Zealand Human Rights Commission 2010. Submission by the Human Rights Commission to the Law and Order Committee. Electoral (Disqualification of Convicted Prisoners) Bill (11 June), 1.6; New Zealand Law Society 2010. Submission on Electoral (Disqualification of Convicted Prisoners) Amendment Bill 2010 (16 June), 2.

[136] K. Johnston 2013, 'Criminals Seek to Overturn Voting Ban', *Stuff.co.nz* (6 September), www.stuff.co.nz/national/crime/9134868/Criminals-seek-to-overturn-voting-ban

[137] Department of Corrections (New Zealand) 2010. Electoral (Disqualification of Convicted Prisoners) Amendment Bill. Departmental Report for the Law and Order Committee (16 August), 3.

[138] Department of Corrections (New Zealand) 2010. Electoral (Disqualification of Convicted Prisoners) Amendment Bill. Departmental Report for the Law and Order Committee (16 August), 16.

Despite near unanimous opposition to the proposed amendment to disenfranchise all prisoners, the Department of Correction recommended only technical amendments to the Law and Order Committee.

Majoritarianism and the Law and Order Committee

The Law and Order Committee reported the bill back to parliament on 17 September 2010, and a majority of its members accepted the two changes proposed by the Department of Corrections. The report contained the minority views by the Labour and Green parties arguing that the bill was constitutionally flawed, 'that no substantive case has been but forward in favour of this change'[139] and, further, that 'The bill offers remarkably little in the way of any evidence or arguments as to why this would be a good or desirable change.'[140] While the committee report was being finalized, the opposition members walked out in protest against the committee chair, Sandra Goudie, and her decision to prevent Ministry of Justice officials from appearing before the Law and Order Committee.[141] As will be discussed in Chapter 5, a similar complaint about the exclusion of the Ministry of Justice from advising the Law and Order Committee would be included in Labour's minority report on the Sentencing and Parole Reform Bill 2010.

Frustration with the Law and Order Committee's proceedings and Chair is evident during the second and third reading debates. Recognizing that the Department of Corrections was not the ideal committee advisor on a bill where the Attorney General had reported to parliament, Labour committee members requested that the committee chair allow officials from the Ministry of Justice to be appointed as secondary advisors. Under SO 208, a select committee has the discretion to appoint additional advisors, and SO 192 provides the chairperson with the ability to request the appearance of any person before the select committee.[142] The committee chair refused this request by the Labour

139 Parliament of New Zealand 2010. Electoral (Disqualification of Convicted Prisoners Amendment Bill). As Reported from the Law and Order Committee (17 September). New Zealand Labour party minority view, 3.

140 Parliament of New Zealand 2010. Electoral (Disqualification of Convicted Prisoners Amendment Bill). As Reported from the Law and Order Committee (17 September). Green Party minority view, 6.

141 D. Cheng 2010, 'Upset MPs Stage Walkout', *The New Zealand Herald* (1 July); *The New Zealand Herald* 2010, 'Labour Views Left Out of Law and Order Reports' (2 July).

142 Parliament of New Zealand 2011, Standing Orders of the House of Representatives, SOs 192, 208.

party, which was in the minority on this New Zealand National–ACT New Zealand-dominated committee[143] – a request which was made after the Department of Corrections, under questioning from Labour members of the committee, admitted that it lacked competency in the area of electoral law.[144] Lianne Dalziel of the Labour party suggested that the bill's allocation to the Law and Order Committee was a strategic decision to protect it against the careful scrutiny that would have taken place before the Justice and Electoral Committee, as well as to prevent the Ministry of Justice advising the Law and Order Committee negatively.[145]

In response to these criticisms, committee chair Sandra Goudie countered that 'the Law and Order Committee is run in accordance with the Standing Orders, and if a decision is made, it is made by majority.'[146] While this is correct, under MMP, the composition of select committees under SO 182 must, 'so far as [is] reasonably practicable, be proportional to party membership in the House'.[147] New Zealand National, a minority government, had majority control over the critical Law and Order Select Committee. This, in combination with the party vote and the 'confidence and supply' agreement with ACT New Zealand, allowed the committee chair to exercise unbridled power to marginalize the opposition parties' efforts to engage in parliamentary scrutiny of the bill, and to disregard the significance of the Attorney General's report to parliament under section 7 of the NZBORA. As Geddis notes, at the Committee of the Whole House stage, the failure to engage the substantive criticisms of the opposition members and the Attorney General was evident: only three members of New Zealand National participated in the debate, and ACT New Zealand – the party that controlled five votes critical to the passage of the bill – did not participate.[148] The limited participation is an indication of the importance of the party vote which shows the inability of the opposition parties, despite strong criticism of the bill, to prevent its passage into law.

143 Hon. C. Cosgrove – Labour Party (20 October 2010) 667 NZPD 14681.
144 Ibid.
145 Hon. L. Dalziel – Labour Party (20 October 2010) 667 NZPD 14684.
146 S. Goudie – National Party (8 December 2010) 669 NZPD 15965.
147 Parliament of New Zealand 2011, Standing Orders of the House of Representatives, SO 182.
148 A. Geddis, 'Prisoner Voting and Rights Deliberation' 464.

Conclusion

As a parliamentary bill of rights, the enforcement mechanisms of the NZBORA are directly influenced by the rules that structure parliament as an institution, such as the electoral system and the Standing Orders of the House of Representatives. These rules have been augmented by governing practices such as 'confidence and supply' agreements with minor parties that have entered parliament under MMP, which are essential requirements that allow a government to advance its legislation in a multi-party parliament. In this regard, we have argued that an unexplored issue in the study of the NZBORA has been the transition from SMP to MMP, and the corresponding changes in the Standing Orders to accommodate the implications of government formation in New Zealand. Indeed, MMP has yet to produce a single-party majority government, instead offering multi-party coalition or single-party minority governments – both of which governmental configurations have been supported by 'confidence and supply' agreements with minor parties. The implications of these governing arrangements and rule changes are profound for a parliamentary enforced bill of rights.

The case studies presented in this chapter demonstrate the tremendous discretionary authority that continues to be exercised by the cabinet and by those MPs sponsoring members' bills, despite the transition to MMP and a new policy context. These rule changes have profound implications for legislative scrutiny of bills and the efficacy of parliamentary oversight mechanisms such as the Attorney General's reporting duty. In the case of amendments to the Misuse of Drugs Act 1975, the cabinet was able to achieve its preferred policy outcome despite clear statements by the Attorney General, on a number of occasions, that the reverse-onus provision in section 6(6) of the Act could not, in its present form, be viewed as compatible with the NZBORA. Further, the position of the Attorney General was confirmed by the courts in *Hansen*, as well as being supported by the Law Commission when it released its 2010 report before parliament passed the Misuse of Drugs Amendment Act (No. 2) 2011. The fascinating element of the legislative history of the amendments to the Misuse of Drugs Act 1975 considered in this chapter is that, despite consistent criticism of the amendments by the Attorney General, the courts and the Law Commission – as well as condemnation of the changes before the Health Committee by organizations such as the New Zealand Law Society – these changes passed without amendments to address the NZBORA incompatibilities flagged by the Attorney General.

The same pattern of parliamentary refusal to act on warnings that a bill presently before the House of Representatives is incompatible with the NZBORA was evident in the prisoner disenfranchisement bill introduced by a private member, Paul Quinn. Despite the section 7 report by the Attorney General that relied on the High Court decision in *Bennett* and comparable jurisprudence, as well as intense criticism at select committee stage, the New Zealand parliament removed all prisoners' right to vote in 2010, and thus reverted to the pre-NZBORA approach to voting as a privilege and not a protected civil right, as it is under the NZBORA.

The legislative outcomes in both case studies demonstrate the importance of rule changes introduced to accommodate MMP, and the implications of these changes for a parliamentary enforced bill of rights. Because both bills were supported by the party vote, which in turn were reinforced by 'supply and confidence' agreements with minor parties, the government or sponsoring member was able to withstand opposition efforts to leverage the Attorney General's report as a instrument of parliamentary oversight of stated incompatibilities. The two case studies demonstrate that the NZBORA operates within the parliamentary setting under two competitive policy discourses: the discourse initiated by the Attorney General when tabling a section 7 report, and the discourse of penal populism that emerged as a result of the 1999 Citizen Initiated Referendum on criminal policy reform. Although the party vote and 'confidence and supply' agreements largely explain why controversial bills are passed without NZBORA-inspired amendments, the dominance of penal populism explains whey opposition parties are for the most part reluctant to challenge criminal law reform that is incompatible with the NZBORA.

Indeed, a dominant characteristic of penal populism is a jettisoning of the professional bureaucracy for policy inspiration, and the emergence of populist actors as policy initiators. The cases of prisoner disenfranchisement and the amendments to the Misuse of Drugs Act 1975 demonstrate that, despite the absence of majority government under MMP, the cabinet (or sponsoring member) has been able to apply the discretionary rules of parliamentary procedure to marginalize the influence of traditional policy actors. In the case of prisoner disenfranchisement, the bill's allocation to the Law and Order Committee, despite its subject matter (elections and voting) falling under the mandate of the Justice and Electoral Committee, was significant, as it resulted in the marginalization of an effective policy advisor, the Ministry of Justice, and the appointment of the Department of Corrections – an organization without any expertise in electoral law, and unsuited to serve as a lead advisor on an electoral reform bill. The referral to the Law and Order Committee was noteworthy as New Zealand National and its 'confidence and supply' partner, ACT New Zealand, controlled 63 per cent of the voting members (6/9) on the Law and Order Committee, thus ensuring that the bill would pass, supported by the New Zealand National and ACT New Zealand party vote, in the form that the member wished.

Although the changes to the Misuse of Drugs Act 1975 depart from this principle of penal populism, as the Ministry of Health was required to rely on the EACD before submitting changes to parliament, the composition of the Health Committee allowed the 2008 amendments under the Labour-led ministry and the 2011 amendments by the New Zealand National minority government to withstand parliamentary oversight and to pass without amendment to ensure NZBORA compatibility. What has been revealed, therefore, is the importance of the parliamentary setting, the rules that structure it and the discretionary choices that continue to be exercised by the cabinet under the NZBORA. Because the cabinet continues to control the parliamentary setting, albeit in a different way under MMP, the parliamentary enforcement of the NZBORA has generally conformed to the policy outcomes preferred by the cabinet, despite the Attorney General's regular tabling of section 7 reports on government bills.

5

The Attorney General, Select Committees and Penal Populism

As we have argued throughout our analysis of the New Zealand Bill of Rights Act (NZBORA), the procedural and parliamentary changes introduced in response to the mixed member proportional (MMP) electoral system have had a significant impact on the ability for this statutory bill of rights to act as an instrument to improve parliamentary oversight of the ministry's legislative agenda. Indeed, with few exceptions, cabinets have been able to achieve their legislative programmes without serious parliamentary constraints, despite the introduction of the NZBORA in 1990 and MMP in 1996.[1] The continuation of cabinet-centred government has occurred despite no single party capturing sufficient seats to form a majority in any parliament subsequent to the MMP system's introduction in 1996.[2] In this regard, the parliamentary process under MMP, as it relates to the NZBORA, is only marginally different from that which existed under SMP, despite an empowered parliamentary committee system resulting from the modified proportional representation electoral system.[3] While select committees are more effective under MMP and parliamentarians have a greater ability to secure amendments to government bills through Supplementary Order Papers (SOPs) at the Committee of the Whole House stage, these amendments have generally

[1] For a critique of the BORA scrutiny processes in New Zealand, see New Zealand Law Society (Human Rights and Privacy Committee), *Submission to the 18th Session of the Human Rights Council – Shadow Report to New Zealand's 2nd Universal Periodic Review* (17 June 2013), 3–5.

[2] The outcome of the 2014 New Zealand election that occurred on 20 September may result in the first single-party majority government for New Zealand National once over 300,000 special votes are counted.

[3] E. McLeay, 'Scrutiny and Capacity: An Evaluation of the Parliamentary Committees in the New Zealand Parliament', (2006) 21 *Australasian Parliamentary Review* 163–64; J. Boston and D. Bullock, 'Experiments in Executive Government under MMP in New Zealand: Contrasting Approaches to Multi-party Governance', (2009) 7 *New Zealand Journal of Public and International Law* 46.

not been made in relation to the NZBORA and the Attorney General's reports under section 7.

Where SMP resulted in single-party dominance, MMP has resulted in multi-party dominance of parliament and the legislative process.[4] Indeed, the common feature of both systems is disciplined political parties that facilitate executive dominance in an adversarial parliamentary setting, either as a single party under SMP or as multi-party ministries supported by minor parties that negotiate confidence and supply arrangements under MMP. Instead of ushering in a 'new politics' of consensual decision-making, MMP has ushered in a new approach to adversarial politics through multi-party executive dominance.[5] Specifically, the government caucuses have replaced the government caucus, and the disciplining nature of confidence votes under both SMP and MMP have been augmented by the disciplinary nature of confidence and supply agreements under MMP.[6]

From the perspective of parliament and the legislative process, these are marginal differences that have not changed, and cannot change, the underlying nature of Westminster parliamentary democracy. In New Zealand, the House of Representatives remains an adversarial and partisan system based on party competition in which parliament is divided between government and opposition, where parties compete for control of the government benches and thus control of parliament itself.[7] MMP has not transferred control of the legislative process from ministry to parliament; nor has the NZBORA, despite the best intentions underlying its section 7, allowed parliamentarians to scrutinize and hold the ministry to account. Executive dominance is the defining feature of Westminster-inspired parliamentary democracies. Changes to the electoral system and the addition of statutory bills of rights cannot alter its internal logic predicated on party control, despite efforts to theorize that a new

[4] T. Carl Lundberg, 'Politics is Still an Adversarial Business: Minority Government and Mixed-Member Proportional in Scotland and in New Zealand', (2013) 15 *British Journal of Politics and International Relations* 619; S. Levine, 'Parliamentary Democracy in New Zealand', (2004) 75 *Parliamentary Affairs* 658.

[5] H. Kumarasingham, 'Executive Power 60 Years On: Has Anything Changed?', (2010) 6 *Policy Quarterly* 47–8; H. Kumarasingham, 'Exporting Executive Accountability? Westminster Legacies of Executive Power', (2013) 66 *Parliamentary Affairs* 584.

[6] A. Kaiser and T. Brechtel, 'Party System, Bargaining Power and Coalition Formation After the 1999 New Zealand Election', (1999) 51 *Political Science* 182; F. Barker and E. McLeay, 'How Much Change? An Analysis of the Initial Impact of Proportional Representation on the New Zealand Parliamentary Party System', (2000) 6 *Party Politics* 139.

[7] F. Barker and E. McLeay, 'How Much Change?', 132.

type of politics is possible through electoral reform[8] or institutional modifications such as the introduction of the NZBORA.

While the NZBORA has had a positive impact on the design of legislation within the bureaucratic arena, and is perhaps the most important and enduring change associated with the introduction of this statutory bill of rights,[9] the influence of the NZBORA becomes less clear once legislation is introduced into the House of Representatives and subjected to parliamentary scrutiny at the select committee stage. This is equally true in regard to members' bills that are supported by the ministry and its supply and confidence partners – for example, the Electoral (Disqualification of Sentenced Prisoners) Amendment Bill 2010 considered in Chapter 4 – as members' bills are only passed if supported by a majority of the whips casting a 'party vote' under SO 139. This represents the paradox of the NZBORA, as it is primarily, if not exclusively, a parliamentary bill of rights enforced against the ministry or ministry-supported legislative agenda. Specifically, despite the introduction of MMP as an attempt to address executive dominance of the parliamentary setting, and notwithstanding the serious approach to section 7 reports taken by the Attorney General, the House of Representatives has been unable, or perhaps simply unwilling, to require the ministry to reconsider legislation that may breach the NZBORA. In effect, a statutory bill of rights that is principally enforced through parliamentary mechanisms has not, in practice,[10] lived up to the theory of the new model of constitutionalism present in Canada, New Zealand, Australia and the United Kingdom.[11]

This chapter discusses the select committee process in New Zealand and the important discretionary choices available under the Standing Orders of the House of Representatives. It then presents a discussion of penal populism and its emergence as the dominant policy discourse in

[8] For a favourable account of MMP and its impact on the legislative process and empowerment of parliament vis-à-vis the ministry, see R. Malone, *Rebalancing the Constitution: The Challenge of Government Law-Making under MMP* (Wellington: Milne Printers, 2008). While Malone demonstrates the growing importance of parliamentarians under MMP, his study does not consider section 7 reports before select committees, nor does he include consideration of any bill with NZBORA implications.

[9] J. Hiebert, 'Rights-vetting in New Zealand and Canada: Similar Ideas, Different Outcomes', (2005) *New Zealand Journal of Public and International Law* 63–105.

[10] A. Geddis, 'The Comparative Irrelevance of the NZBORA to Legislative Practice,' (2009) 43 *New Zealand Universities Law Review* 465–88.

[11] S. Gardbaum, 'Reassessing the New Commonwealth Model of Constitutionalism', (2010) 8 *International Journal of Constitutional Law* 183–88.

New Zealand, competing with a NZBORA-inspired discourse evident in the Attorney General's section 7 report to parliament. The dominance of penal populism, in addition to the discretionary choices available under the Standing Orders, largely explains why government bills are rarely subjected to substantive parliamentary oversight for their relationship to the NZBORA. The chapter concludes with four case studies that demonstrate the importance of penal populism for the effectiveness of this parliamentary bill of rights: the Parole (Extended Supervision) Amendment Act 2004; the Parole (Extended Supervision Orders) Amendment Act 2009; the Criminal Investigations (Bodily Samples) Amendment Act 2009; and finally the Sentencing and Parole Reform Act 2010.

I. The Select Committee process and the NZBORA

The NZBORA is an important constitutional instrument, yet it is shaped by rules governing parliamentary procedure in New Zealand that are outlined in the Standing Orders of the House of Representatives – rules that were revised to accommodate MMP in 1996,[12] but were not, incidentally, significantly revised to accommodate the NZBORA in 1990. These MMP-inspired rule changes sought to balance two competing objectives: government efficiency, which would be compromised by the emergence of minority or coalition governments under MMP, and government stability, which required changes to the Standing Orders to ensure that multi-party governing arrangements retained control over the legislative process. The NZBORA was designed with the intention of changing parliamentary practices and facilitating a culture of rights within the legislative process. Yet, despite this important intention, the NZBORA's application has instead been altered by established parliamentary practices such as partisanship and executive dominance derived from party politics, as well as reformed parliamentary practices to accommodate MMP.

As we only consider government bills reported on by the Attorney General under section 7 of the NZBORA, controversial government bills in which opposition members asserted that section 7 reports should have been issued are not analysed. For instance, the absence of section 7 reports on the Foreshore and Seabed Bill 2004 and the Electoral Finance Bill 2007 generated heated debate as to why the Attorney General

[12] J. Boston, *Governing Under Proportional Representation: Lessons from Europe* (Wellington: Institute of Policy Studies, Victoria University of Wellington, 1998), pp. 94–121.

considered these controversial measures compatible with the NZBORA. Indeed, the judicial challenge in *Boscawen* v. *Attorney General* considered whether the section 7 reporting duty had been breached because the Attorney General failed to report that the Electoral Finance Bill 2007 was in breach of the NZBORA.[13] Although the Attorney General's discretion to report under section 7 was upheld in *Boscawen*, the Electoral Finance Bill 2007 remains an important illustration that the reporting duty is exercised by a legal actor that functions within the parameters of party politics in the parliamentary setting.

Similarly, we do not consider important legislative changes involving sexual equality, such as the Civil Union Amendment Act 2007 or the Marriage (Definition of Marriage) Amendment Act 2013, as these bills were not reported to parliament by the Attorney General under section 7 of the NZBORA. Specifically, the analysis is limited to section 7 as a potential trigger for rights-based dialogue and considers whether, in fact, there is parliamentary engagement of the Attorney General's report.

Although briefly mentioned in Chapter 4, Standing Order (SO) 283(1)(a) has proven significant, as it allows the member introducing a bill to nominate which select committee will consider it.[14] While SO 185 specifies the subject matters that fall under the jurisdiction of each select committee, the discretion to nominate remains with the member, and a bill can be directed to a select committee that may be more receptive to the underlying policy. As previously noted, this occurred in the context of the Foreshore and Seabed Bill introduced by the Labour-led ministry in 2004, which responded to the Court of Appeal's decision in *Ngati Apa* v *Attorney General* that determined the Māori Land Court had the jurisdiction to determine that the foreshore and seabed was Māori customary land.[15] The Foreshore and Seabed Bill, under SO 185, should have been referred to the Māori Affairs Committee; however, the minister responsible for the bill, Michael Cullen of the Labour party, referred the bill to the Fisheries and Other Sea-related Legislation Committee. Claire Charters has argued that referring the Foreshore and Seabed Bill to a committee other than Māori Affairs was a strategic decision to ensure

[13] *Boscawen* v. *Attorney General* [2009] NZCA 12.

[14] Parliament of New Zealand 2011, Standing Orders of the House of Representatives, SO 283(1)(a).

[15] C. Charters, 'Responding to Waldron's Defence of Legislatures: Why New Zealand's Parliament Does Not Protect Rights in Hard Cases', (2006) *New Zealand Law Review* 632–33.

that the government's response to the Court of Appeal's decision was passed without serious parliamentary oversight, which would have occurred had the bill been referred to the Māori Affairs Committee because a majority of its members were Māori and held Māori-designated seats in parliament.[16]

In the context of the NZBORA and section 7 reports, the appropriate committee to review legislation reported on by the Attorney General is the Justice and Electoral Committee, as the subject matter outlined in SO 185 for this select committee specifies 'courts, Crown legal and drafting services, electoral matters, human rights, and justice'.[17] Most bills with section 7 reports have not been reviewed by the Justice and Electoral Committee, however, which leads to a further complication for select committees as agents of parliamentary oversight in the context of the NZBORA. Specifically, select committees are assigned advisors that correspond to the subject area of the committee specified in SO 185. For instance, the Justice and Electoral Committee is advised by the Ministry of Justice and Crown Law Office, the Health Committee is advised by the Ministry of Health and the Law and Order Committee is advised by the Department of Corrections and New Zealand Police. Because the subject matter of the legislation determines which select committee it is assigned to – and not the fact that it has a section 7 report identifying potential human rights violation – a select committee reviewing a bill reported on by the Attorney General will not generally be advised by the Ministry of Justice or Crown Law Office unless it is referred to the Justice and Electoral Committee. Thus, the NZBORA implications of legislation will be the responsibility of the specific select committee's departmental advisor, irrespective of whether this department has the experience or competence to advise on human rights issues.

While each department or ministry has its own legal counsel that may advise on NZBORA issues,[18] this is not their principal departmental responsibility, whereas the Ministry of Justice and the Crown Law Office have units dedicated solely to the consideration of NZBORA compatibility issues. Therefore, it is not surprising that that consideration of NZBORA issues varies greatly at the select committee stage. Those select

[16] Charters, 'Responding to Waldron's Defence of Legislatures', 640–41.

[17] Parliament of New Zealand 2011, Standing Orders of the House of Representatives, SO 185.

[18] G. Palmer, 'The Provision of Legal Services to Government,' (2000) 31 *Victoria University of Wellington Law Review* 69.

Table 5.1 *Section 7 reports sent to select committee under MMP, 1996–2014, bills passed into law or before parliament*

Select Committee	# s. 7 Reports	% of Total s. 7 Reports
Finance and Expenditure Committee	3	9.1%
Foreign Affairs, Defence, and Trade Committee	1	3.0%
Government Administration Committee	3	9.1%
Health Committee	2	6.1%
Justice and Electoral Committee	8	24.2%
Law and Order Committee	4	12.1%
Local Government and Environment Committee	3	9.1%
Planning and Development Committee	1	3.0%
Social Services Committee	5	15.2%
Transport and Industrial Relations Committee	3	9.1%
	33	

Note: (n=33: 1 bill passed under urgency, 1 bill bypassed select committee, and 3 bills yet to be assigned to a select committee: 38–5=33)

committees advised by the Ministry of Justice and the Crown Law Office will have a higher level of compatibility scrutiny and advice, whereas committees that rely on departmental legal advisors with limited experience with the NZBORA will be at a serious disadvantage when considering reports of the Attorney General under section 7 of the NZBORA.

As demonstrated in Table 5.1, the Ministry of Justice and Crown Law Office have been principal departmental advisors on the largest number of bills before select committees with section 7 reports (8/33), which represents 24.2 per cent of all bills reported on by the Attorney General to parliament considered at the select committee stage.[19] Indeed, the vast majority of bills with section 7 reports considered before select committees are not advised on by either the Ministry of Justice or the Crown Law Office, demonstrating a serious procedural defect in the Standing Orders

[19] Under MMP a total of 38 bills have been passed into law, or currently before Parliament, with section 7 reports, but only 33 have been considered at the select committee stage at the time of writing. Specifically, one bill was passed under Urgency and bypassed the select committee stage, one bill was not assigned to a select committee by parliamentary consent and three bills have yet to be assigned to a select committee. The total figure is 42 bills, if the former SMP system is considered.

of the New Zealand Parliament. Standing Order 208 does allow select committees to appoint additional departmental advisors, and this may allow the Ministry of Justice, if requested by a majority of committee members, to advise on section 7 issues. However, a more reasonable approach would be to change the Standing Orders in the following way: to ensure that select committees are properly advised on NZBORA issues, the Ministry of Justice should be appointed as a secondary advisor to all select committees when reviewing a bill reported on by the Attorney General under section 7 of the NZBORA.

The significance of the Ministry of Justice or Crown Law Office advising on a small minority of bills passed into law that had been reported on by the Attorney General is evident in Table 5.2, which considers the basis of the section 7 reports. As demonstrated, the section 7 reports fall into two broad categories of rights and freedoms protected under the NZBORA: civil and political rights, which constitute 50 per cent of all reported inconsistencies by the Attorney General (22/44); and legal rights, which also represent 50 per cent (22/44) of section 7 reports considered at the select committee stage involving bills passed into law or currently being considered by parliament.[20] These are highly specialized areas of law, and the section 7 reports presented by the Attorney General are based on assessments made by the dedicated NZBORA vetting units within the Ministry of Justice and the Crown Law Office. However, when a select committee engages in parliamentary oversight of bills presently before it, it generally does not have the benefit of consulting the government agencies that produced the advice on which the Attorney General reported to parliament under section 7 of the NZBORA. The reluctance of select committees to engage in strict scrutiny of government bills is largely explained by the continued importance of party discipline and supply and confidence agreements under MMP. The ways in which the Standing Orders assign departmental advisors may also explain why select committees are unable to engage the Attorney General's section 7 reports presently before them, given that they rely on departmental legal advisors who do not generally advise on NZBORA issues.

The relevant bills considered in Chapter 4 and 5 are presented in Table 5.3. This table considers which select committee a bill should have

[20] There are a total of 38 section 7 reports of bills passed into law (n=32) or presently being considered by Parliament (n=6) under MMP. However, several section 7 reports involve multiple provisions of the NZBORA, resulting in a total of 44 reported inconsistencies under section 7 by the Attorney General.

Table 5.2 *Subject matter of Section 7 reports under MMP, bills passed or before select committees, 1996–2014*

Section		Provision	Category	#	%
Civil and Political Rights (n=22)					
	Section 12	Electoral rights	Democratic and civil rights	1	2%
	Section 14	Freedom of expression	Democratic and civil rights	6	14%
	Section 19(1)	Freedom from discrimination	Non-discrimination and minority rights	15	34%
Legal Rights (n=22)					
	Section 9	Right not to be subjected to torture or cruel punishment	Life and security of the person	1	2%
	Section 21	Unreasonable search and seizure	Search, arrest and detention	3	7%
	Section 22	Liberty of the person	Everyone has the right not to be arbitrarily arrested or detained	2	5%
	Section 23	Rights of person arrested or detained	not specified	1	2%
	Section 24(d)	Rights of person charged	shall have the right to adequate time and facilities to prepare a defence	1	2%
	Section 25	Minimum standards of criminal procedure	not specified	2	5%

Section 25(a)	Minimum standards of criminal procedure	the right to a fair and public hearing by an independent and impartial court	1	2%
Section 25(c)	Minimum standards of criminal procedure	the right to be presumed innocent until proven guilty	6	14%
Section 25(e)	Minimum standards of criminal procedure	the right to be present at the trial and to present a defence	1	2%
Section 26	Retroactive penalties and double jeopardy	not specified	2	5%
Section 27	Right to justice	not specified	1	2%
Section 27(3)	Right to justice	Every person has the right to bring civil proceedings against, and to defend civil proceedings brought by, the Crown, and to have those proceedings heard, according to law, in the same way as civil proceedings between individuals	1	2%

N = 44. Multiple NZBORA issues were raised in the 38 section 7 reports considered at the select committee stage.

Table 5.3 *Standing orders and select committee allocations, select Section 7 reports*

#	Bill	Type	SO 55	SO 185	SO 283(1)(a)
1	Parole (Extended Supervision) and Sentencing Amendment Bill 2003	Govt	×	Justice and Electoral Committee	Justice and Electoral Committee
2	Misuse of Drugs (Classification of BZP) Amendment Bill 2007	Govt	×	Health Committee	Health Committee
3	Criminal Investigations (Bodily Samples) Amendment Bill 2009	Govt	✓	Justice and Electoral Committee	Justice and Electoral Committee
4	Sentencing and Parole Reform Bill 2009	Govt	×	Justice and Electoral Committee	Law and Order Committee
5	Parole (Extended Supervision Orders) Amendment Bill 2009	Govt	×	Justice and Electoral Committee	Bypassed without using SO 55
6	Misuse of Drugs Amendment Bill 2010	Govt	×	Health Committee	Health Committee
7	Electoral (Disqualification of Convicted Persons) Amendment Bill 2010	Members'	×	Justice and Electoral Committee	Law and Order Committee
8	Parole (Extended Supervision Orders) Amendment Bill 2014	Govt	×	Justice and Electoral Committee	not yet allocated (17/4/2014)

SO 55 (urgency invoked by the Minister sponsoring the bill)
SO 185 (subject matter select committee)
SO 283(1)(a) (designated select committee by member proposing bill)

been assigned to based on its subject matter (SO 185), which committee a bill was actually referred to under SO 283(1)(a), whether a minister used urgency to bypass the select committee stage (SO 55) and whether the Attorney General reported to parliament under section 7 of the NZBORA (SO 262). These are important aspects of the Standing Orders that, when used strategically by the cabinet minister or private member introducing a bill, can significantly undermine select committees' ability to thoroughly engage the NZBORA implications of proposed legislation. Also, given that New Zealand lacks a specialized rights scrutiny committee such as the United Kingdom's Joint Committee on Human Rights, the ability to decide which committee reviews a bill is clearly an important strategic choice available to the government or member introducing a bill, which can marginalize parliamentary oversight of the NZBORA.

In regard to the bills considered in Chapters 4 and 5, one bill was passed under urgency (SO 55) by the sponsoring minister – the Criminal Investigations (Bodily Samples) Amendment Bill 2009 – and one bill bypassed the select committee stage by parliamentary agreement without using urgency: the Parole (Extended Supervision Orders) Amendment Bill 2009. Two bills were referred under SO 283(1)(a) to select committees that would not normally be assigned such bills based on their subject matter under SO 185: the Sentencing and Parole Reform Bill 2009 and the Electoral (Disqualification of Convicted Persons) Amendment Bill 2010. Thus, a total of four key legislative initiatives reported on by the Attorney General under section 7 saw the use of parliamentary tactics to aid their passage without substantive scrutiny. These are important parliamentary tactics that, when employed strategically, can effectively neutralize select committees' ability to address the NZBORA implications raised by the Attorney General.

In the remainder of this chapter, we consider the ability of select committees and parliamentarians to enforce the NZBORA in the context of government bills containing incompatibilities reported to parliament by the Attorney General. What is revealed is the co-existence of two competitive policy discourses – penal populism and the rights-based discourse advanced by the Attorney General's section 7 reports – that have significant implications for the NZBORA as a parliamentary bill of rights.

II. Penal populism and the New Zealand Bill of Rights Act

As a policy discourse, penal populism has a tendency to conflict with the legal rights protections afforded to the accused and convicted in the

NZBORA. Indeed, two distinct policy discourses generally occur during parliamentary debate on the merits of criminal policy amendments identified by the Attorney General as potentially inconsistent with the NZBORA. The first, represented by the Attorney General's section 7 report,[21] is a rights-based discourse that prioritizes the accused, considers the nature of the rights violation, determines whether a reasonable basis exists for limiting a protected right and considers whether the infringement is a proportional attempt to achieve the pressing and substantial legislative objectives identified by the Attorney General.

The second policy discourse is derived from penal populism. It focuses on victims' rights as the overriding policy objective of criminal policy, articulates a retributive approach to criminal policy, jettisons the professional bureaucracy as the actor that develops this penal policy and relies on extra-parliamentary forces such as single-issue interest groups for policy inspiration and validation.[22] The 1999 Citizen Initiated Referendum (CIR) that saw 92 per cent of New Zealanders vote in favour of a 'reform of our criminal justice system placing greater emphasis on the needs of victims, providing restitution and compensation for them and imposing minimum sentences and hard labour for all serious violation offences' is generally viewed as representing the emergence of penal populism as the dominant discourse on criminal policy.[23] The 1999 CIR has had an important influence on minor political parties that have entered parliament under New Zealand's MMP electoral system and, because of multi-party governing arrangements, the main political parties such as Labour and National that have led MMP-constructed ministries.

New Zealand has been identified by Nicola Lacey as an outlier among proportional representation systems in regard to criminal policy, as most tend to depoliticize this issue through a reliance on the professional bureaucracy, as well as demonstrating 'moderate penal politics'.[24] Lacey

[21] G. Huscroft, 'Protecting Rights and Parliamentary Sovereignty: New Zealand's Experience with a *Charter*-Inspired, Statutory Bill of Rights', (2002) 21 *Windsor Yearbook of Access to Justice* 120–22.

[22] J. Pratt and M. Clark, 'Penal Populism in New Zealand', (2005) 7 *Punishment and Society* 304; J. Pratt, *Penal Populism* (London: Routledge, 2007), pp. 12–20; N. Lacey, 'The Prisoners' Dilemma and Political Systems: The Impact of Proportional Representation on Criminal Justice in New Zealand', (2011) 42 *Victoria University of Wellington Law Review* 617–18.

[23] S. Parry, 'The Road to Nowhere: An Account of the Increase in New Zealand's Rate of Incarceration between 1999 and 2009', (2011) 17 *Auckland University Law Review* 89.

[24] N. Lacey, 'Political Systems and Criminal Justice: The Prisoners' Dilemma After the Coalition', (2012) 65 *Current Legal Problems* 217.

argues that New Zealand is an outlier because the smaller parties that have emerged under MMP are not organized around the traditional cleavage of proportional representation systems, which is the socio-economic divide along a left–right axis. Instead, smaller parties that have emerged under MMP in New Zealand have largely been concerned with specific issues such as crime and the need for a tougher approach to 'law and order'.[25] Further, the strong parliamentary presence of the Green party since the 1999 election suggests the importance of postmaterialist issues such as environmentalism in the House of Representatives. The smaller 'law and order' parties, such as ACT New Zealand, tend to be heavily influenced by populist pressure groups such as the Sensible Sentencing Trust,[26] and are attractive coalition partners for major parties that need to construct multi-party governing arrangements 'because their specific focus means that a bargain can be struck with them without the larger party having to negotiate across a range of issues'.[27] ACT New Zealand is presently the natural 'supply and confidence' partner of the National party, and has supported New Zealand National since its return to office in 2008. New Zealand First and United Future New Zealand have, on different occasions, supported both Labour and National-led ministries through 'confidence and supply' agreements, and also exhibit populist approaches to law and order issues.

A review of these smaller parties' election manifestos demonstrates the significance of penal populism as a policy discourse in coalition politics and its subsequent structuring influence on the NZBORA. In 2002, ACT New Zealand declared that 'New Zealand is now crime ridden. Under Labour violent crime has risen by over 10%. No one is safe from callous violence. We are suffering from a failed 30-year experiment of being nice to criminals, hoping they will be nice back to us.' This viewpoint was still present in its 2011 election manifesto.[28] Similarly, New Zealand First declared in 2002 that 'New Zealand has changed from being safe to a crime-ridden, ill-disciplined and violent society'[29] and, along with ACT

[25] N. Lacey, 'Political Systems and Criminal Justice' 219.

[26] J. Pratt and M. Clark, 'Penal Populism in New Zealand', 306; J.V. Roberts, 'Sentencing Reform in New Zealand: An Analysis of the Sentencing Act 2002', (2003) 36 *The Australian and New Zealand Journal of Criminology* 251–252; N. Lacey, 'The Prisoners' Dilemma and Political Systems: The Impact of Proportional Representation on Criminal Justice in New Zealand', (2011) 42 *Victoria University of Wellington Law Review* 633–34.

[27] N. Lacey, 'Political Systems and Criminal Justice', 219.

[28] ACT New Zealand 2002, *Policy 2002: Our Vision*.

[29] New Zealand First 2002, *Keeping New Zealand First 2002*.

New Zealand, advocated sentencing principles such as 'three strikes' legislation and mandatory minimum sentences for violent offences.[30]

While 'confidence and supply' agreements provide minor parties with disproportionate influence over criminal policy, as Lacey contends, larger parties accept this disparate influence in a single policy area because these agreements ensure the ministry's stability, as well as providing the largest party in the government with a disproportionate influence over all remaining policy areas not subject to a supply and confidence agreement.[31] In effect, the political cost of advancing a 'law and order' agenda on behalf of a minor party is rather low for a minority government, as penal populism resonates with the broader public, whereas the political benefit for a minority single-party or coalition government supporting this populist agenda is significant. Indeed, it allows a minority government – either a single party, in the case of New Zealand National (2008–present), or Labour-led minority coalitions – to function as a *de facto* majority government through 'confidence and supply' agreements that require a populist approach to criminal policy in exchange for control over all other legislative initiatives. Indeed, as both Labour and New Zealand National also engaged in penal populist rhetoric in their respective election manifestos since 2002, albeit that the Labour party called for a rethinking (but not an abandonment) of the 'tough on crime' approach in its 2011 election manifesto,[32] the disproportionate influence of minor parties over criminal policy has not in fact been inconsistent with the policy tendencies of the major political parties.[33] This policy tradeoff between parliamentary parties is significant in the context of the NZBORA and the competing policy discourses that are evident when the Attorney General reports to parliament under section 7 of the NZBORA. While the Attorney General initiates a rights-based discourse on the impact of proposed criminal policy changes under section 7 of the NZBORA, this has not been a significant feature of parliamentary debates that consider such bills.

The framers of the NZBORA intended that the parliamentary debate surrounding the NZBORA would be heavily influenced by the Attorney

[30] New Zealand First 2011, *New Zealand First Election Manifesto 2011.*

[31] N. Lacey, 'The Prisoners' Dilemma and Political Systems', 632.

[32] New Zealand Labour Party 2011, *Labour Party Manifesto 2011 – Own our Future*, p. 389.

[33] J. Varuhas, 'Courts in the Service of Democracy: Why Courts Should have a Constitutional (But Not Supreme) Role in Westminster Legal Systems', (2009) *New Zealand Law Review* 494.

General's section 7 report, and that it would structure parliamentary deliberation on whether to proceed with legislation that appeared inconsistent with rights and freedoms.[34] However, the parliamentary response to section 7 reports since 1990 suggests that this rights-based discourse has not emerged, for a variety of reasons.[35] According to Andrew Geddis, a 'section 7 report attached to a government bill almost always has negligible impact, as the government already has committed substantial policy resources and political capital by introducing it into the House, so has a vested interest in pushing it to enactment'.[36] While this is clearly an important constraint on parliamentary oversight, the policy context of the legislation under review and the fact that penal populism is the dominant policy discourse in the area of criminal policy are perhaps more serious impediments that complicate the emergence of a NZBORA-inspired parliamentary discourse. Thus, penal populism structures the parliamentary debate on the merits of criminal policy reform, and not, as was intended, the Attorney General's section 7 report alerting parliament to potential inconsistencies with the NZBORA.

III. Parole (Extended Supervision) Amendment Act 2004

In 2003 the Labour-led coalition government introduced an extended supervision regime that, among other measures, allowed convicted child sex offenders to be monitored for up to 10 years after serving prison sentences. The influence of penal populism as a dominant policy discourse was evident in the announcement by the Minister of Justice, Phil Goff, who presented the Parole (Extended Supervision) and Sentencing Amendment Bill 2003 to parliament in November 2003. This bill was presented as a 'management system' to supervise high-risk offenders once they were released from prison. Acknowledging that the Attorney General had reported that the extended supervision regime was inconsistent with the NZBORA, the Minister of Justice declared: 'I make no apologies for insisting that protection of children takes priority over those convicted sex offenders who the court believes are likely to

[34] G. Palmer, *New Zealand's Constitution in Crisis: Reforming our Political System* (Dunedin: John McIndoe, 1992), pp. 58–60.

[35] T. Bromwich, 'Parliamentary Rights-vetting Under the NZBORA', (2009) *New Zealand Law Journal* 190–91.

[36] A. Geddis, 'Inter-institutional 'Rights Dialogue' Under the New Zealand Bill of Rights Act', in T. Clark, K.D. Ewing and A. Tomkins (eds.), *The Legal Protection of Human Rights: Sceptical Essays* (Oxford: Oxford University Press, 2011), p. 98.

re-offend.'[37] Under the proposed legislation, the Chief Executive of the Department of Corrections could request, in the period before a convicted child sex offender was released from prison, that a court grant an extended supervision order (ESO) to monitor a convicted child sex offender for up to 10 years after their release from prison.[38] The request would be accompanied by a health assessor's report that concluded a convicted child sex offender 'is likely to commit further relevant offences on ceasing to be an eligible offender'.[39]

Once the request was granted, a high-risk child sex offender would be subject to home detention during the first 12 months after being released from prison, would be required to regularly report to a parole officer under 'parole-type conditions', and 'may be required to submit to electronic monitoring to check compliance with conditions prohibiting offenders from going to specific places or areas'.[40] Failure to comply with the conditions of an ESO after serving a prison sentence would see a convicted child sex offender return to prison for an additional two-year sentence. Finally, the Parole (Extended Supervision) and Sentencing Amendment Bill 2003 would have a retroactive application: those convicted of child sex offences and imprisoned before the passage of the bill would be released under the conditions allowed by the proposed ESO regime.

The report of the Attorney General

The Attorney General's report on the Parole (Extended Supervision) and Sentencing Amendment Bill 2003 is written in a way that is not typical of section 7 reports to parliament. Generally speaking, a section 7 report is presented as simply an opinion to consider, and written to convey that parliament has the ability to dispute the assertions made by the Attorney General.[41] Indeed, most section 7 reports refrain from

[37] P. Goff 2003, 'Goff Unveils Supervision Regime for Sex Offenders', (11 November).

[38] New Zealand Parliamentary Library 2003. Bills Digest No 1039. Parole (Extended Supervision) and Sentencing Amendment Bill 2003 (11 November), 2.

[39] Ibid.

[40] Parliament of New Zealand 2003. Parole (Extended Supervision) and Sentencing Amendment Bill – Explanatory Note, 1.

[41] G. Huscroft, 'Protecting Rights and Parliamentary Sovereignty: New Zealand's Experience with a *Charter*-inspired, Statutory Bill of Rights', (2002) 21 *Windsor Yearbook of Access to Justice* 122; C. Archer and G. Burt, 'Section 7 of the Bill of Rights Act', (August 2004) *The New Zealand Law Journal* 321; S. Jackson, 'Designing Human Rights

providing an authoritative conclusion that legislation is inconsistent with the NZBORA, and are couched in language which simply notes that legislation *appears* inconsistent with the NZBORA.

As outlined in Table 5.4 and previously noted, the dominant approach to assessments of inconsistency by all Attorney Generals who have issued section 7 reports in relation to government bills has been to refrain from issuing authoritative statements on their consistency with the NZBORA.[42] Indeed, more than 80 per cent (26/32) of section 7 reports issued in relation to government bills have concluded that the bill 'appears inconsistent' with the NZBORA. The first Attorney General to report to parliament under section 7 of the NZBORA, Paul East, issued 67 per cent (4/6) of the reports that concluded that government sponsored legislation was inconsistent, while Margaret Wilson authored two such assessments. Margaret Wilson (New Zealand Labour) and Christopher Finlayson (New Zealand National) are the Attorney Generals who have authored the most section 7 reports on government bills (25/32), at 12 and 13 respectively. In the case of Finlayson, who has served as Attorney General in the fifth National government from 2008 to the time of writing, he has always reported to parliament that legislation 'appears inconsistent' with the NZBORA, and has never concluded that legislation *is*, in fact, inconsistent with the NZBORA.[43]

Attorney General Wilson identified two aspects of the proposed ESO regime as clearly inconsistent with the NZBORA: the retrospective application of the ESO, and statutory authority to engage in electronic monitoring of high-risk sex offenders for 24 hours a day.[44] The Attorney General considered the retrospective application of the ESO as inconsistent with section 26(2) of the NZBORA, which protects against double jeopardy: 'No one who has been finally acquitted or convicted of, or pardoned for, an offence shall be tried or punished for it again.'[45] Although the Minister of Justice viewed the ESO as a 'preventative measure' and not an additional criminal penalty, the Attorney General

Legislation: 'Dialogue', the Commonwealth Model and the Role of Parliaments and Courts', (2007) 13 *Auckland University Law Review* 100–1.

42 This pattern holds in relation to members' and local bills with section 7 reports attached.

43 The two bills in which Attorney General Margaret Wilson concluded that the legislative measures were inconsistent with the NZBORA are the following: Income Tax Bill 2002; Parole (Extended Supervision) and Sentencing Amendment Bill 2003.

44 Report of the Attorney General under the New Zealand Bill of Rights 1990 on the Parole (Extended Supervision) and Sentencing Amendment Bill, para 1.

45 Report of the Attorney General, para 6.

Table 5.4 *Attorney General conclusions on NZBORA inconsistency*

1990–2014	I					II				
		GOVERNMENT BILLS					MEMBERS' AND LOCAL BILLS			
Attorney General	S.7 Reports	Inconsistent	%	Appears Inconsistent	%	S.7 Reports	Inconsistent	%	Appears Inconsistent	%
East	4	4	100	0	0	7	7	100	0	0
McGrath	0	0	0	0	0	1	0	0	1	100
Graham	1	0	0	1	100	2	0	0	2	100
Wilson	12	2	16.67	10	83.33	8	0	0	8	100
Hodgson	1	0	0	1	100	0	0	0	0	0
Cullen	1	0	0	1	100	5	1	20	4	80
Parker	0	0	0	0	0	2	1	50	1	50
Finlayson	13	0	0	13	100	8	0	0	8	100
Total	**32**	**6**	**18.75**	**26**	**81.25**	**33**	**9**	**27.27**	**24**	**72.73**

concluded that, in fact, the ESO regime was a criminal penalty, and thus a serious violation of section 26(6) of the NZBORA that could not be considered a reasonable limitation:

> The possible imposition of significant movement restrictions, electronic monitoring and home detention, strengthens the argument that the retrospective imposition of these aspects of the ESO on an individual who has been convicted of a relevant offense prior to the Bill coming into force should be viewed as a 'punishment' for the purposes of s.26(2) of the Bill of Rights Act.[46]

If the ESO had contained less intrusive measures to manage high-risk child sex offenders and their rehabilitation, such as mandated counselling sessions, the Attorney General argued there would not be a violation of section 26(2), as the ESO regime would have been 'fairly described as plainly rehabilitative and not punitive, thereby avoiding inconsistency with s.26(2)'.[47]

The ESO regime amended the Parole Act 2002 by introducing section 15(3)(f), which allows the Parole Board to order that a high-risk child sex offender be equipped with electronic monitoring devices as part of the conditions surrounding their 10-year supervised release from prison. This represents the second aspect of the ESO regime considered by the Attorney General to be inconsistent with the NZBORA, as '24 hour electronic monitoring of an individual in a criminal law enforcement context (even if there is a rehabilitative element to the scheme) interferes with a person's reasonable expectation of privacy and hence is a *prima facie* of section 21 of the Bill of Rights Act (right to be secure against unreasonable search or seizure).'[48] The use of electronic monitoring devises was considered unreasonable because of 'the uncertainty regarding the accuracy of current electronic monitoring technology and its potentially experimental nature'.[49] The ESO regime allowed for additional prison sentences of two years if a high-risk child sex offender violated the terms of his or her release, and the Attorney General expressed concern that technological limitations of electronic devices raised questions as to whether, in fact, they represented a reasonable limit on section 21 of the NZBORA. Finally, in a rare departure from section 7 reports as policy-neutral documents, Attorney General Wilson suggested that the government needed to provide more information on

[46] Report of the Attorney General, para 12. [47] Ibid., para 15.
[48] Ibid., para 18. [49] Ibid., para 21.

why 'alternative means of monitoring would be less effective' than 24-hour electronic monitoring.[50] In this regard, the Attorney General questioned whether the government had pursued the least restrictive legislative means, as she did not consider the ESO regime a reasonable limit under section 5 of the NZBORA.

Although the Attorney General determined that the government had a legitimate interest in preventing re-offending by high-risk child sex offenders, she stated that 'preventative measures based solely on predictions of offending ... should be carefully constrained and reviewed in order to prevent potential abuse, disproportionate social stigma and infringements of basic rights and freedoms.'[51] As the measures contained in the ESO regime went further than comparable legislation in the United Kingdom and Canada, the Attorney General reported to parliament that the Parole (Extended Supervision) and Sentencing Amendment Bill was inconsistent with the NZBORA.

Parliament and the dominance of penal populism

At first reading, the Minister of Justice reiterated his disagreement with the Attorney General's section 7 report, defending the ESO system as a choice between the protection of children from recidivist sex offenders and the 'right to total freedom of a child sex offender released from prison who is deemed likely to offend again'.[52] Although New Zealand National supported the ESO regime, it was critical of the policy approach by the Labour-led ministry and its attempt to establish its 'law and order' credentials. With few exceptions, such as the contributions of the Green party and United Future New Zealand, the parliamentary debate on the ESO regime was not influenced by the rights-based discourse of the Attorney General's report but by the predominance of penal populism as the structuring discourse of criminal policy in New Zealand. There was strong criticism from the main opposition parties, but New Zealand National and United Future supported the bill and it passed by a party vote of 91–25 at third reading.[53] At the first reading debate, Tony Ryall of

[50] Report of the Attorney General, para 20. [51] Report of the Attorney General, para 4.

[52] Hon. P. Goff – Labour party (19 November 2003) 613 NZPD 10195.

[53] The party vote on the Parole (Extended Supervision) and Sentencing Amendment Bill – AYES 91: New Zealand Labour (51), New Zealand National (27), Green party (5), United Future (8); NOES 25: New Zealand First (13), Green party (4), ACT New Zealand (8).

the National party questioned whether the use of electronic bracelets would protect children from paedophile sex offenders: 'I ask Mr. Goff how an electronic bracelet and a quarterly visit from a parole officer will stop a paedophile from abusing a child. It will not do so.'[54] Instead, the National party argued that high-risk sex offenders should 'never be released from jail, and that extends preventive detention for those sorts of individuals'.[55]

New Zealand First did not support the ESO regime as it argued the bill was 'fundamentally flawed' and would not provide adequate protection against recidivist paedophile sex offenders. Instead, New Zealand First argued that if there was to be 24-hour supervision of paedophile sex offenders, 'let us have it in a mental institution or a proper asylum where the staff can give the person good medical care'.[56] ACT New Zealand opposed the bill for two reasons. First, it did not believe that the bill would be effective and would not deter high-risk paedophile sex offenders from re-offending. Second, and more consistent with its party philosophy, ACT New Zealand did not support the retrospective application of any law. Adopting the discourse of penal populism, ACT New Zealand ignored the basis of the Attorney General's section 7 report and reiterated its view that New Zealand had become a crime-ridden society in which paedophile sex offenders posed a serious risk to society if released into the general population.[57] Similar to New Zealand First, ACT New Zealand argued that such offenders should never be released from prison: 'we see that there are some people who commit offences against children and who should not be out in the community ever. They should be on preventative detention. They should never be released.'[58]

The only serious engagement of the Attorney General's section 7 report occurred during the parliamentary debate by Nandor Tanczos (Green party) and Marc Alexander (United Future). Although the Green party was divided on whether to support the ESO, Tanczos identified problems with the 10-year supervision regime and noted that the 'Green party is concerned that those provisions do not comply with the New Zealand Bill of Rights Act, and that there are issues around double jeopardy.'[59]

[54] Hon. T. Ryall - National party (19 November 2003) 613 NZPD 10197.

[55] Ibid.

[56] R. Mark - New Zealand First (19 November 2003) 613 NZPD 10200.

[57] Dr M. Newman - ACT New Zealand (19 November 2003) 613 NZPD 10203.

[58] Ibid.

[59] N. Tanczos - Green party (19 November 2003) 613 NZPD 10201.

However, the Green party expressed confidence in the parliamentary process and the political commitment to the NZBORA, arguing that the legislation attempted to balance the NZBORA with competing interests but simply failed to strike the correct balance. According to Tanczos, the correct balance would be struck at the select committee stage, as 'the job of select committees is to work through those details'.[60] Similarly, United Future engaged the Attorney General's section 7 report, but disagreed with the statement that the ESO was not a reasonable limitation on the NZBORA as 'such limitations on offenders are completely and utterly justifiable, given the severity of the offences committed.'[61]

Although there were attempts to engage the Attorney General's section 7 report, this discourse was displaced by the dominance of penal populism. Indeed, the nature of the parliamentary debate centred on whether electronic monitoring and parole-like conditions would be sufficient to prevent high-risk sex offenders from committing future crimes against children. As such, the rights violations that ESOs presented to sex offenders released into the general public were of little interest to most parliamentarians, given that rights-based critiques would require parliamentarians to defend convicted paedophile sex offenders by questioning the appropriateness of further restrictions. Indeed, the Attorney General's report was either ignored – as in the case of the Labour party, the National party, New Zealand First, and ACT New Zealand – because the affected audience was convicted paedophile sex offenders; engaged in an effort to dispute the concerns raised by the Attorney General (United Future); or embraced as part of a process for rectifying NZBORA concerns at the select committee stage (Green party). What drove the debate was the framework of penal populism, as summarized by ACT New Zealand: 'The bill was written by a Labour party that wants to pretend it is tough on crime, when all of us in the Opposition know that it is soft on crime and just talks tough.'[62] While the Attorney General had a professional responsibility to evaluate the ESO in relation to convicted child sex offenders and their NZBORA rights, most parliamentary parties ignored this report and instead focused on the need to protect future victims of crime.

[60] N. Tanczos – Green party (19 November 2003) 613 NZPD 10201.

[61] M. Alexander – United Future (19 November 2003) 613 NZPD 10202.

[62] Dr M. Newman – ACT New Zealand (19 November 2003) 613 NZPD 10205.

The Justice and Electoral Committee

In its submission to the Justice and Electoral Committee, the New Zealand Law Society opposed the Parole (Extended Supervision) and Sentencing Amendment Bill, largely agreeing with the section 7 report issued by the Attorney General.[63] To address the section 26 violations of the NZBORA, the New Zealand Law Society recommended that ESOs be part of the original sentence to avoid the violation of double jeopardy[64] and, further, that retrospective application of ESOs be eliminated.[65] In an important discussion on process, the New Zealand Law Society focused on the significance of the Attorney General having issued a section 7 report that strongly concluded that the NZBORA had been violated, and cautioned parliament to only pass the ESO regime if it fundamentally disagreed with the Attorney General's assessment: 'In the context of *this* case, that would require a judgment that the bill does not authorize a second punishment, is not retrospective, and does not authorize an intrusive monitoring regime contrary to s 21.'[66]

While the Justice and Electoral Committee disagreed with the Attorney General's assessment of the ESO regime as 'punishment' and disputed that double jeopardy existed, the basis of the disagreement is rather tenuous and unsatisfactory:

> Some eligible offenders may welcome the protection afforded by the extended supervision order. They may recognize that the intensive monitoring will assist them to remain in the community, and provide an element of self-protection. They may consider the restrictive conditions of any order to be rehabilitative rather than punitive.[67]

Thus, the Justice and Electoral Committee opted to disagree with the Attorney General based on the possibility that paedophile sex offenders would recognize the rehabilitative value of the proposed ESO regime. This was not a principled disagreement with the Attorney General rooted in a fundamental difference over whether the ESO regime was further punishment of convicted child sex offenders, as argued by the Attorney General. Instead, it was a weak response that characterized the ESO regime as a

[63] New Zealand Law Society 2003. Submissions on the Parole (Extended Supervision) and Sentencing Amendment Bill at para 3.

[64] New Zealand Law Society, para 11. [65] Ibid., para 15. [66] Ibid., para 23.

[67] Parliament of New Zealand 2004. Parole (Extended Supervision) and Amendment Bill. As reported from the Justice and Electoral Committee (14 June), 5.

potential management scheme if recognized this way by convicted child sex offenders, who may recognize the rehabilitative value of ESO use for 10 years after their release from prison.

The resumption of the parliamentary debate

Before the parliamentary debate resumed at the Committee of the Whole House stage, the New Zealand Parliamentary Library released an assessment of the Justice and Electoral Committee report. In Bills Digest No. 1115, provided to parliamentarians, the New Zealand Parliamentary Library disagreed with the select committee and instead supported the Attorney General's assessment that the ESO regime was an additional penalty and inconsistent with section 26 of the NZBORA.[68]

Instead of engaging the section 7 report or the independent assessment in the Bills Digest, the parliamentary debate largely returned to the theme of victims' rights and the opposition claims that the Labour party remained weak on issues of law and order, despite introducing a bill identified by the Attorney General as inconsistent with the NZBORA. When the Attorney General's report was referred to, as it was sporadically in the parliamentary debate that followed the Select Committee report, the opposition parties simply noted their disagreement with the Attorney General's concern that the rights of convicted child sex offenders had been limited. For the National party, the section 7 concerns were ignored because the ESO regime advanced greater societal objectives designed to protect children from recidivist sex offenders.[69] Similarly, United Future disregarded the section 7 report through a penal populist discourse that made reference to the 1999 Citizen Initiated Referendum (CIR), arguing that 'The rights of the victim must take supreme position over those of the offender.'[70]

Dail Jones of New Zealand First referred to the importance of the 1999 CIR and how penal populism had become a policy discourse that could not be discounted, despite the concerns raised by the Attorney General, as 'We cannot go against the views of the 92 per cent of the public who want tougher sentences than those supported by this

68 New Zealand Parliamentary Library 2004. Bills Digest No. 1115. As reported from the Justice and Electoral Committee (14 June), p. 3.

69 R. Worth – National Party (29 June 2004) 618 NZPD 14143.

70 M. Alexander – United Future (29 June 2004) 618 NZPD 14195.

Government.'[71] Jones alluded to the influence of extra-parliamentary forces such as the Sensible Sentencing Trust,[72] which has been identified as a characteristic of policy development consistent with penal populism.[73] Indeed, New Zealand First refused to support the ESO regime, arguing that a party committed to law and order could not support such a weak approach to high-risk sex offenders.[74]

The influence of penal populism extended to the National party: Judith Collins dismissed the concerns raised by the Attorney General rather abruptly, stating that 'The only people I noticed who are against this bill are those who are constantly concerned with the rights of child sex abusers.'[75] In a clear illustration of the limited impact of section 7 reports, Lianne Dalziel of the Labour party attributed the conclusion of NZBORA inconsistency to the National party, and not, as was the case, to the section 7 report presented to parliament by Attorney General Margaret Wilson of the Labour party: 'I reject the assertion of the National Opposition spokesperson that this legislation in fact offends against the New Zealand Bill of Rights Act.'[76] As a member of the select committee that disputed the Attorney General's characterization of the ESOs as inconsistent with section 26 of the NZBORA, Dalziel reiterated that 'some people do not regard that as punishment',[77] but rather as a sensible policy designed to protect against re-offending by high-risk paedophile sex offenders.

The Parole (Extended Supervision) and Sentencing Amendment Bill was passed with minor amendments, but none were made in response to the concerns raised by the Attorney General. Indeed, the party vote in support of the bill represented nearly 79 per cent of the votes cast (91–25); votes against the bill as a result of the Attorney General's report were cast only by four members of the Green party, while both New Zealand First (13 votes) and ACT New Zealand (8 votes) voted against the bill because it was considered a weak attempt to protect children – these parties consistently argued that paedophile sex offenders should remain under preventative detention and should never be paroled, and argued that the Labour party was simply attempting to appear tough

[71] D. Jones – New Zealand First (29 June 2004) 618 NZPD 14145. [72] Ibid.

[73] J. Pratt and M. Clark, 'Penal Populism in New Zealand', (2005) 7 *Punishment & Society* 306; N. Lacey, 'Political Systems and Criminal Justice' 222.

[74] D. Jones – New Zealand First (29 June 2004) 618 NZPD 14176.

[75] J. Collins – National party (29 June 2004) 618 NZPD 14178.

[76] L. Dalziel – Labour party (29 June 2004) 618 NZPD 14190. [77] Ibid.

on crime. The party vote, therefore, does not truly represent the dominance of penal populism and how it can negate the rights-based discourse represented by the Attorney General's section 7 report to parliament. Of the 116 party votes cast in the parliamentary debate, nearly 97 per cent (112/116) were conducted within the paradigm of penal populism, as only the contributions of members of the Green party could be characterized as part of a rights-based discourse influenced by the NZBORA.

Belcher v. Chief Executive of the Department of Corrections

The Parole (Extended Supervision) Amendment Act 2004 was challenged as a violation of the NZBORA by Joseph Belcher, an individual convicted of sexually assaulting a child in 1996 and sentenced to a 10-year prison term. Belcher was released on parole in November 2001, and in October 2004 the Chief Executive of the Department of Corrections applied for an ESO, which was granted by a court in April 2005.[78] In effect, the Chief Executive sought a retrospective application of an ESO, as Belcher had been released before the passage of the Parole (Extended Supervision) Amendment Act 2004. The Court of Appeal decision is important, as it addressed the crux of the disagreement between the Attorney General, the select committee and those members of parliament that supported the ESO regime – whether an ESO is a form of punishment and a violation of section 26 of the NZBORA because of its retrospective nature (the Attorney General's view), or whether it is a management scheme that is rehabilitative in character and consistent with the NZBORA (the view of the Minister of Justice, the select committee and most members of parliament, save four members of the Green party).

Justice Young for a unanimous Court of Appeal concluded that the ESO regime is a form of punishment, and provided 14 elements of the ESO regime that supported this position.[79] As the ESO order was granted after Belcher was paroled in 2001, the retrospective application of the Parole (Extended Supervision) Amendment Act 2004 was determined to violate section 26 of the NZBORA. Further, as the Crown did not attempt

[78] *Belcher* v. *Chief Executive of the Department of Corrections* [2007] 1 NZLR 507 (CA) at paras 12–17.

[79] Ibid., at para 47.

to defend the ESO regime as a reasonable limit under section 5 of the NZBORA, the Court of Appeal concluded that it should approach the issue 'on the basis that the retrospective nature of the ESO scheme is not justified for the purpose of s 5'.[80] As it was not possible to read the ESO provisions consistent with the NZBORA under section 6, the Court of Appeal considered whether to issue a declaration of inconsistency.[81] However, the Court of Appeal decided that it did not have the jurisdiction to consider this issue, and reserved it for future consideration.[82] Upon appeal to the Supreme Court of New Zealand, the decision that the ESO regime could not be read as consistent with the NZBORA was upheld, though the Supreme Court concluded that in fact the Court of Appeal had the jurisdiction to issue a declaration of inconsistency.[83] As a result, the characterization of the ESO as a penalty with retrospective application that violated section 26 of the NZBORA was confirmed by the highest court of New Zealand in 2007.

IV. Parole (Extended Supervision Orders) Amendment Act 2009

The 2008 election in New Zealand saw the defeat of the fifth Labour government (1999–2008) and its replacement with a minority government composed solely of New Zealand National. As part of the confidence and supply agreements negotiated between the New Zealand National and ACT New Zealand, as well as National's agreement with United Future, the National party made a commitment within the first 100 days to introduce legislation that it characterized as its 'first actions on law and order'.[84] In particular, two commitments in National's Post-Election Action Plan resulted in the Attorney General reporting to parliament under section 7 once the National minority government had submitted legislation to the House of Representatives: the commitment to 'remove the right of the worst repeat offenders to be released on

[80] *Belcher* v. *Chief Executive of the Department of Corrections* at para 52.

[81] C. Geiringer, 'On a Road to Nowhere: Implied Declarations of Inconsistency and the New Zealand Bill of Rights Act', (2009) 40 *Victoria University of Wellington Law Review* 624–25.

[82] *Belcher* v. *Chief Executive of the Department of Corrections* at paras 57–59.

[83] *Belcher* v. *Chief Executive of the Department of Corrections* [2007] NZSC 54 at para 8.

[84] National's Post-Election Action Plan. This document is part of the ACT New Zealand and United Future New Zealand 2008 confidence and supply agreements. See *National-ACT Confidence and Supply Agreement* (16 November 2008) and *National Party – Supply and Confidence Agreement with United Future* (14 November 2008).

parole',[85] introduced as the Sentencing and Parole Reform Bill 2009,[86] and the commitment to 'introduce legislation to require DNA testing for every person arrested for an imprisonable offence',[87] introduced as the Criminal Investigations (Bodily Samples) Amendment Bill 2009.[88] The Sentencing and Parole Reform Bill 2009 would be modified to include, as part of National's 'confidence and supply' agreement with ACT New Zealand, the 'three strikes' sentencing policy endorsed by the Sensible Sentencing Trust.

The Parole (Extended Supervision Orders) Amendment Bill 2009 was introduced by the Minister of Justice during the initial 100 days of the New Zealand National ministry as part of its 'first actions' on law and order. New Zealand National characterized the legislation targeting convicted child sex offenders as minor amendments to close 'the two potential loopholes that were inadvertently introduced into the Parole Act 2002 through an amendment in 2007'.[89] In light of this characterization, the National government was given permission by all parliamentary parties to fast-track the passage of the bill without the use of urgency, which allowed the bill to circumvent the select committee stage and pass into law in a single day.[90]

There are several problems with the National government's request to bypass the normal parliamentary process without requesting urgency in the context of the Parole (Extended Supervision Orders) Amendment Bill 2009. First, these amendments were introduced with the benefit of judicial clarification on whether ESOs were criminal punishment or a management scheme designed to rehabilitate child sex offenders. Although parliament is under no statutory obligation to respond to divergent judicial conceptions of the NZBORA,[91] the fact that the Attorney General's view was endorsed suggests the importance of a full parliamentary

[85] National's Post-Election Action Plan. Cited in *National-ACT Confidence and Supply Agreement* (16 November 2008), First Actions on Law and Order.

[86] Report of the Attorney General under the New Zealand Bill of Rights Act 1990 on the Sentence and Parole Reform Bill 2009.

[87] National's Post-Election Action Plan. Cited in *National-ACT Confidence and Supply Agreement* (16 November 2008), First Actions on Law and Order.

[88] Report of the Attorney General under the New Zealand Bill of Rights Act 1990 on the Criminal Investigations (Bodily Samples) Amendment Bill 2009.

[89] P. Goff 2009, 'Government Closes Loopholes in Child-sex Law', (2 April).

[90] A. Geddis, 'Inter-institutional 'Rights Dialogue' Under the New Zealand Bill of Rights Act', in T. Campbell, K.D. Ewing and A. Tomkins (eds.), *The Legal Protection of Human Rights: Sceptical Essays* (Oxford: Oxford University Press, 2011), pp. 87–107.

[91] S. Gardbaum, 'Reassessing the New Commonwealth Model of Constitutionalism' 187.

discussion of ESOs. Second, as this was a government bill sponsored by the Minister of Justice and subjected to pre-introduction scrutiny by the Crown Law Office, the fifth National government was fully aware that the Attorney General would issue a section 7 report once the bill was introduced into parliament.

After informing the House of Representatives that the Business Committee had agreed to quickly pass the bill,[92] and the Speaker noting that there was no opposition to this request, the Attorney General issued his section 7 report to parliament.[93] Presumably, this was the first notification that the opposition parties received in regard to apparent NZBORA inconsistencies in legislation that the government considered as merely housekeeping in nature. The reaction to the section 7 report by ACT New Zealand and the Green party, as will be discussed, strongly suggests that the opposition parties agreed to fast-track the bill without first being informed of the Attorney General's forthcoming report to parliament.

In the Explanatory Note, the Minister of Justice suggested that prior to 2007, 'the Parole Board could impose conditions similar to full-time residency restrictions for the first 12 months of an extended supervision order' and the 'Parole Amendment Act 2007, which created residential restrictions, inadvertently extended the 12-month limit to part-time residency restrictions'.[94] As such, the Parole (Extended Supervision Orders) Amendment Bill, according to the Explanatory Note, simply re-established 'the pre-2007 status quo', also clarifying 'that part-time residential restrictions can be imposed at any time during the order'.[95]

The report of the Attorney General

In a strongly worded report to parliament, the Attorney General disagreed that the amendments to the ESO regime simply re-established the pre-2007 status quo. Instead, the Attorney General concluded, 'this Bill has the appearance of introducing a new power', as the proposed amendments extended electronically monitored residential restrictions on convicted child sex offenders from the first 12 months to the full period of

[92] Hon. G. Brownlee – National Party (2 April 2009) 653 NZPD 2377.
[93] Hon. C. Finlayson – National Party (2 April 2009) 653 NZPD 2377.
[94] Parliament of New Zealand 2009, Parole (Extended Supervision Orders) Amendment Bill. Explanatory Note, 1–2.
[95] Ibid., Explanatory Note, 2.

the ESO.[96] Thus, the National government's 'first action on law and order' allowed paedophile sex offenders to be subject to residential restrictions for up to 10 years after their release from prison. In the opinion of the Attorney General, the Parole (Extended Supervision Orders) Amendment Bill repeated the constitutional violations first identified in 2004 by Attorney General Margaret Wilson and recently confirmed by the Supreme Court of New Zealand (SCNZ) in *Belcher* v. *Chief Executive of the Department of Corrections.*[97] Specifically, the amendments to residential restrictions violated section 26 of the NZBORA, as the proposed ESO regime continued to be a penalty with retrospective application.

The Attorney General did, however, identify an additional inconsistency with the NZBORA that did not exist in the Parole (Extended Supervision) Amendment Bill 2004. Because the bill provided for electronic home detention for the entire duration of an ESO, short of 24 hours a day, with potential application for 10 years, the Attorney General concluded that the proposed amendments raised apparent inconsistencies with section 22 of the NZBORA, which protects against arbitrary detention.[98] According to Finlayson, the proposal allowed for 'long term detention without charge or trial'; further, 'detention which is imposed solely on the basis of possible future offending, rather than proved past offending, is inherently problematic'.[99] This assessment was based on jurisprudence from the European Court of Human Rights and the United States Supreme Court that determined that preventative detention, outside of strict guidelines not present in the Parole (Extended Supervision Orders) Amendment Bill, was 'repugnant' to constitutional principles surrounding arbitrary detention.[100]

In the conclusion to the section 7 report, Attorney General Finlayson offered policy advice similar to that of his predecessor, Margaret Wilson – that long-term detention would survive constitutional review and would be considered a reasonable limit if it is was part of the original sentence. As this was not part of the proposed amendments, the Attorney General was unrestrained in his insistence that 'The state should not detain citizens solely on the basis of preventing future offending, nor should it punish offenders twice for the same offence.'[101]

[96] Report of the Attorney General under the New Zealand Bill of Rights Act 1990 on the Parole (Extended Supervision Orders) Amendment Bill, 2.
[97] Report of the Attorney General, 2–3. [98] Ibid., 3–4. [99] Ibid., 4.
[100] Ibid., 4. [101] Ibid., 6.

Parliamentary fast-tracking and section 7 backtracking

Because the opposition parties had agreed to fast-track the bill, the first opportunity to read the Attorney General's section 7 report occurred during the only debate on the bill, at second reading. Though the debate was quite brief, and only the Minister of Justice and five other parliamentarians participated, the influence of penal populism as a policy discourse is evident. For instance, the Minister of Justice defended the bill as presenting only minor amendments and reiterated that the 'public has the right to know that serious child sex offenders are being managed effectively once they are released from prison'.[102] Similarly, the sole Labour member to participate in the debate, Clayton Cosgrove, accepted the need to quickly pass the amendments to the ESO regime, this being 'an issue of public safety'.[103] However, neither the Minister of Justice nor Cosgrove made reference to the Attorney General's section 7 report, instead focusing on the need to protect against potential recidivist behaviour by paedophile sex offenders.

The Green party acknowledged that it had agreed to fast-track the legislation on the understanding that the bill represented technical amendments;[104] as it had done so before it was aware of the Attorney General's concerns with the residential requirement changes in the proposed bill, it was decided that 'the Green party will have to cast a vote of abstention, because we have not been given the full information to be able to consider, on behalf of the New Zealand public, exactly which course we should take'.[105] In this respect, the Green party acted consistently: it has always been strongly influenced by the Attorney General and reluctant to support legislation with a section 7 report. ACT New Zealand supported the bill despite the participating member, David Garrett, conceding that he had yet to read the section 7 report;[106] however, as this policy was part of the 'confidence and supply' agreement ACT New Zealand had negotiated with the National party, it supported the bill because 'The State does not monitor people in the community for up to 10 years for no good reason.'[107]

[102] Hon. S. Power – National Party (2 April 2009) 653 NZPD 2379.
[103] Hon. C. Cosgrove – Labour Party (2 April 2009) 653 NZPD 2379.
[104] K. Locke – Green Party (2 April 2009) 653 NZPD 2380. [105] Ibid., 2381.
[106] D. Garrett – ACT New Zealand (2 April 2009) 653 NZPD 2381.
[107] Ibid., 2382.

The bill passed on a party vote of 113–9, as only the Green party was swayed by the section 7 report of the Attorney General. In his 2008 Maxim Institute lecture, Jeremy Waldron raised serious concerns about the legislative process in New Zealand, which he described as 'parliamentary recklessness' because its unicameral chamber 'has evolved procedures for fast-track legislation which are quite disgraceful by world standards, and which is by and large the play-thing of the executive'.[108] Waldron's comments were made in the context of the use of urgency, the party vote and quorum, which he considered to have substituted parliamentary sovereignty with the 'sovereignty of a parliamentary executive'.[109] The Parole (Extended Supervisions Orders) Amendment Bill 2009 was introduced by a minority government presumably at the mercy of the House of Representatives.

In theory, a section 7 report should result in a cautious approach to legislation reported on by the Attorney General. However, by characterizing changes to the ESO regime as re-establishing the pre-2007 approach, and securing the agreement to fast-track the legislation before the Attorney General reported to parliament, the National ministry demonstrated a central argument advanced in this book – that parliamentary bills of rights are structured, shaped and influenced by the norms, rules and incentives that structure party politics in a partisan chamber.

Parole (Extended Supervision Orders) Amendment Bill 2014

Corrections Minister Anne Tolley indicated in January 2014 that new amendments to the ESO regime would be introduced to parliament that extend its application to child sex offenders beyond the current 10 year period, as well as extending the ESO regime to 'a small number of high risk sex offenders against adults, as well as very high risk violent offenders'.[110] Indeed, the 2014 amendments recently introduced expand the range of qualifying offences that may be subject to the an ESO regime, as well as allowing for their application to 'equivalent offences committed overseas'.[111] The Parole (Extended Supervision Orders) Amendment Bill

108 J. Waldron, *Parliamentary Recklessness: Why We Need to Legislate More Carefully*. Maxim Institute 2008 Annual John Graham Lecture, 20.

109 Waldron, 20–23.

110 A. Tolley 2014, 'Extended Supervision Orders to be Expanded', (17 January).

111 Report of the Attorney General under the New Zealand Bill of Rights Act 1990 on the Parole (Extended Supervision Orders) Amendment Bill 2014, para 4.

2014 was tabled before parliament (17 April 2014), and the Attorney General prepared a section 7 report (dated 27 March 2014) that was also tabled when the Corrections Minister presented the bill. In his section 7 report, Attorney General Christopher Finlayson noted that the bill did not violate section 22 (the right not to be arbitrarily detained) despite allowing for residential restrictions that 'could be imposed for an unlimited number of consecutive ten-year periods, if the offender continues to meet the criteria for the ESO'.[112] Because the 2014 amendments included 'mandatory five yearly reviews' for ESOs applied after the initial 10-year period,[113] the Attorney General concluded 'These biennial reviews in combination with the existing review provisions constitute an effective procedural safeguard against arbitrary detention'.[114] However, because of the retrospective application, as well as the ESO regime constituting an additional criminal penalty, the Attorney General decided that the proposed amendments violated section 26 of the NZBORA (the right against the imposition of retrospective penalties and double jeopardy).[115]

In reaching this conclusion, the Attorney General made reference to his 2009 report on ESO regimes, as well as the 2003 report by then Attorney General Margaret Wilson, and supported this conclusion by reference to principles established by the Court in *Belcher*.[116] At the time of writing (19 April 2014), the first reading debate has not commenced on the Parole (Extended Supervision Orders) Amendment Bill 2014, nor has the bill been referred to a select committee. However, once the legislative process begins, the 2014 changes to the ESO regime will most likely pass without any amendments to address the NZBORA inconsistencies outlined in the Attorney General's report, as well as submissions that will be made by organizations such as the New Zealand Law Society and the New Zealand Human Rights Commission. Further, these amendments will pass on the basis of a strong party vote, and will most likely be opposed simply by the Green party, the parliamentary party that has viewed the Attorney General's report as reason to oppose government legislation. What explains the continued passage of legislation with strong parliamentary support despite the presence of a section 7 report? The answer is simple – the policy context (criminal reform), the affected rights-bearer (convicted criminals) and the dominant policy discourse (penal populism) largely explain why NZBORA-incompatible legislation passes with strong parliamentary support.

[112] Report of the Attorney General, para 7. [113] Ibid., para 4. [114] Ibid., para 11.
[115] Ibid., para 20. [116] Ibid., para 16.

V. Criminal Investigations (Bodily Samples) Amendment Act 2009

The Criminal Investigations (Bodily Samples) Amendment Bill 2009 was introduced under urgency as part of New Zealand National's 'first actions on law and order'. According to Geiringer, Higbee and McLeay, 'urgency is a technique for extending the House's sitting hours and for prioritizing certain items of government business within those hours. In some cases, the way urgency is taken will result in reduced opportunities for reflection and deliberation; in others, it is simply a case of more House time being freed up for that legislative deliberation to occur'.[117] Arguing that DNA samples are the 'modern-day fingerprint',[118] the Minister of Justice introduced key changes to the collection of DNA samples to 'help police solve more crimes'.[119] Although New Zealand has allowed for the collecting of DNA samples since 1995,[120] the proposed amendments greatly expanded the number of offences in regard to which DNA samples could be collected, removed the need for judicial authorization for the gathering of DNA without consent, allowed DNA samples to be collected from individuals the police simply 'intend to charge' and provided, if necessary, for the forceful collection of samples.[121] This marked a policy shift away from due process and toward penal populism as, previously, only individuals *convicted* or *suspected* of a narrow range of relevant offences could be compelled to provide a DNA sample if authorized by judicial review.

The proposed changes to the gathering of DNA samples would occur in two stages. During the first stage (enactment until July 2010), the police would be able to collect DNA samples from individuals they intended to charge with any relevant offence within the expanded schedule of offences in the Criminal Investigations (Bodily Samples) Amendment Act. Under stage 2, which would fully commence in December 2011, the police would be able to collect DNA samples for those they intended to charge for any imprisonable offence. Further, the amendments provided for different treatment of young persons between 14 and 17 years. Finally, the Minister defended the proposal by employing

117 C. Gieringer, P. Higbee and E. McLeay, *What's the Hurry? Urgency in the New Zealand Legislative Process* (Wellington: Victoria University Press, 2011), p. 21.

118 S. Power 2009, 'Government Introduces Bill for Modern-day Fingerprint', (10 February).

119 Ibid.

120 Criminal Investigations (Bodily Samples) Act 1995.

121 Parliament of New Zealand 2009, Criminal Investigations (Bodily Samples) Amendment Bill – Explanatory Note, 1.

penal populism, arguing that 'The Government regards this legislation as critical in the fight against the escalating rate of crime'.[122]

The report of the Attorney General

Christopher Finlayson reported to parliament that the proposed amendments appeared inconsistent with section 21 of the NZBORA, which protects against unreasonable searches and seizures.[123] Noting that the bill 'represents a substantial expansion of the current scheme under which such samples are taken only from certain convicted offenders',[124] the Attorney General concluded that the legislative changes challenged the following protections guaranteed by section 21: 'There must be a specific and sufficient basis for taking the sample' and 'Absent emergency or other special circumstances, there must be prior independent approval of the taking of the sample, most commonly by judicial warrant.'[125]

The Attorney General was concerned that New Zealand had decided to model its DNA bank after the United Kingdom, where the absence of judicial safeguards for DNA collection was found to breach the European Convention on Human Rights.[126] While the Attorney General recognized that the proposed changes would result in greater rates of conviction, as well as acknowledging that the Explanatory Note indicated that guidelines were to be developed to govern the gathering of DNA samples by the police, the Attorney General did not consider this 'a sufficiently clear or reliable substitute for statutory safeguard'.[127] Indeed, the Attorney General disputed the central proposition of the Minister of Justice – that DNA samples are the 'modern fingerprint'. Although the Attorney General noted judicial disagreement over this issue on the part of several high courts, Finlayson agreed with the positions of the Canadian and American courts that disputed 'that DNA samples are equivalent to the taking of fingerprints'.[128] Relying on the jurisprudence of these courts, where DNA samples can be taken only from convicted serious offenders and are accorded a high level of privacy protection, the Attorney General

122 S. Power 2009, 'Government introduces Bill'.

123 Report of the Attorney General under the New Zealand Bill of Rights Act 1990 on the Criminal Investigations (Bodily Samples) Amendment Bill, para 1.

124 Report of the Attorney General, para 2.1.

125 Ibid., paras 2.2.1, 2.2.2.

126 Ibid., para 2.4.

127 Ibid., para 2.5.

128 Ibid., para 13.

concluded that the 'taking of samples from suspects for databank purposes is inconsistent with the search and seizure rights'.[129]

The Attorney General's second major disagreement concerned whether police guidelines and judicial remedies are in fact adequate substitutions for judicially authorized search warrants to obtain DNA samples. The Explanatory Note argued that, once developed, these guidelines would provide adequate safeguards; the Attorney General disagreed, however, 'as it has been emphasized both in New Zealand and more broadly that intrusive search regimes require express, external and prior safeguard'.[130] While the Attorney General concluded that the bill 'appears inconsistent' with the NZBORA, the section 7 report represents a strong condemnation of the Criminal Investigations (Bodily Samples) Amendment Bill proposed by the fifth National government, generally imploring the government to maintain the status quo represented by the Criminal Investigations (Bodily Samples) Act 1995.

Parliamentary considerations at first reading

Although the Minister of Justice made passing mention of the Attorney General's report, the dominance of penal populism quickly emerged during his summation at first reading: 'The priority of this Government in the justice portfolio is public safety, and this bill contributes to that goal by giving the police tools to resolve more crime. . .'.[131] In addition, the participating National members also failed to engage the Attorney General's report and instead reiterated the government's rationale for the proposed policy changes: that DNA samples are the 'modern fingerprint'[132] and that the Ministry of Justice would develop guidelines to ensure adequate safeguards existed when the police gathered DNA samples.[133]

The dominance of penal populism is evident, as well, in the complex position adopted by the Labour party and ACT New Zealand. At all stages of parliamentary consideration, the Labour party noted serious reservations with proceeding with a bill reported to parliament by the

[129] Ibid., para 16.1. [130] Ibid., para 20.

[131] Hon. S. Power – National Party (10 February 2009) 652 NZPD 1118.

[132] Ibid.: C. Borrows – National Party (10 February 2009) 652 NZPD 11121; S. Bridges – National Party (12 February 2009) 652 NZPD 1277.

[133] Hon. S. Power – National Party (10 February 2009) 652 NZPD 1118.

Attorney General, yet voted to support the bill at each stage of the parliamentary process. For instance, Clayton Cosgrove and Lianne Dalziel noted serious NZBORA limitations with the bill,[134] but supported its passage to the select committee stage so that the section 7 report could lead to future amendments to ensure greater NZBORA consistency. Referring to the Attorney General's report, Lianne Dalziel noted: 'That is a very worthy report, but it cannot end just there. It cannot be just brushed off in Parliament as having been prepared and tabled. We need to debate the seriousness of actually making such a change to the law that breaches our obligations under the New Zealand Bill of Rights Act'.[135] In this respect, Labour attempted to embrace both policy discourses – the Attorney General's and penal populism – despite the contradictory views represented by these distinct policy discourses. Similarly, ACT New Zealand, as a law and order party with a libertarian orientation, was concerned with forced production of DNA samples of people whom the police simply intended to charge.[136] However, as ACT New Zealand was in a confidence and supply agreement with the National party, it supported the bill being sent to select committee for further consideration.

As we have seen in other bills considered in Chapters 4 and 5, the Attorney General's section 7 report has had the strongest influence on the Green party. At first reading, Keith Locke was clear that 'The Green party will be voting against this bill, in line with the report to the House of the Attorney General, Christopher Finlayson, that this measure is not justified under section 21 of the New Zealand bill of Rights Act'.[137] Both the Greens and the Māori party were alarmed by the forceful collection of DNA samples by the police without judicial authorization, and the Māori party raised a series of fundamental objections to this proposed practice. Specifically, the Māori party argued that racial profiling by the police targeted this community, resulting in higher levels of Māori in the judicial system and correctional facilities. Thus, the ability of the police to forcefully extract DNA samples would disproportionally affect Māori people, as 'the research demonstrates that systemic factors operate at

[134] Hon. C. Cosgrove – Labour Party (10 February 2009) 652 NZPD 1118–9; Hon. L. Dalziel – Labour Party (10 February 2009) 652 NZPD 1123.

[135] Hon. L. Dalziel – Labour Party (10 February 2009) 652 NZPD 1123.

[136] D. Garrett – ACT New Zealand (10 February 2009) 652 NZPD 1127–1128.

[137] K. Locke – Green Party (10 February 2009) 652 NZPD 1125.

one or more steps of the criminal justice process, which make it more likely for Māori people to be apprehended, arrested, charged, convicted, and imprisoned'.[138]

The Justice and Electoral Committee

The first reading debate concluded with a party vote that sent the bill to the Justice and Electoral Committee with a strong majority (107 to 13), with only the Greens and Māori party voting against.[139] At select committee, 18 submissions were received; only six supported the proposed changes to collection of DNA samples, with, not surprisingly, the New Zealand Police Association, the Sensible Sentencing Trust and the Sensible Sentencing Trust Nelson supporting the government bill.[140] The briefs submitted by the New Zealand Human Rights Commission and the New Zealand Law Society generally represent the nature of the opposition to the proposed changes. Specifically, the New Zealand Law Society's general position is that a bill reported on by the Attorney General 'ought generally not to be enacted' and should only be enacted if parliamentarians explicitly and publically disagree with the section 7 report.[141] For the Law Society, the expansion of the range of offences under which DNA samples could be compelled by the police without judicial warrant was concerning, as 'These expansions essentially place all offences listed in Part 3 in the same category as murder, rape or serious violent offending. Examples of offences that trigger the power to take samples include willful ill-treatment of animals, disorderly behavior and a wide range of regulatory offences in areas such as resource management, transport, customs, fisheries, revenue, immigration and company law.'[142]

138 Te Ururoa Flavell – Māori Party (10 February 2009) 652 NZPD 1129.

139 The party vote for the Criminal Investigations (Bodily Samples) Amendment Bill – AYES 107: New Zealand National (58), New Zealand Labour (43), ACT New Zealand (5); United Future (1); NOES 13: Green Party (9), Māori Party (4).

140 Office of the Clerk of the House of Representatives (New Zealand) 2009. Criminal Investigations (Bodily Samples) Amendment Bill: Summary of Submissions (7 May).

141 New Zealand Law Society 2009. Submission on Criminal Investigations (Bodily Samples) Amendment Bill (9 May) at para 3.

142 New Zealand Law Society at para 5.

The Human Rights Commission reiterated the concerns of the Law Society[143] and raised the potential discriminatory application of the proposed changes and the issue of racial profiling and the Māori people, given that the Department of Corrections reported in 2007 that Māori are more likely to be apprehended than non-Māori New Zealanders: 'As the legislation would apply to people who the police have good reason to suspect of committing a relevant offence and whom they intend to bring a complaint against, it is highly likely that Māori would be disproportionately represented among those whose DNA is taken.'[144] Indeed, both the Law Society and the Human Rights Commission recognized the importance of DNA samples as an investigative tool, but argued that the status quo represented by the Criminal Investigations (Bodily Samples) Act 1995 should be retained, as 'the Bill significantly alters the balance struck between "law and order" requirements and "personal freedoms" within existing law'.[145]

The composition of the Justice and Electoral Committee is significant: New Zealand National, as a minority government, controlled a majority of the committee members (5/9) who reviewed this government bill. Two members of the National party were also List MPs with very low rankings, which has clear implications for parliamentary engagement of the Attorney General's report and their willingness to challenge the government's legislative agenda. In particular, National List MPs Kanwaljit Singh Bakshi and Paul Quinn were ranked 38th and 48th, respectively, on National's list during the 2008 election. The total number of List MPs in the 49th parliament (2008–2011) was 52, and National was awarded 17 positions under the MMP allocation of additional seats. While parliamentarians are members of disciplined political parties, List MPs are further tied to the party leadership as their ranking – and subsequent reentry into parliament – is determined by their placement on the party list. As the two National List MPs were ranked near the bottom of the party list, this serves as a further deterrent against parliamentary engagement of the Attorney General's report particularly for members of the governing party.

[143] New Zealand Human Rights Commission 2009. Submission of the Human Rights Commission on Criminal Investigations (Bodily Samples) Amendment Bill to the Justice and Electoral Committee (6 April), at paras 6.1 to 6.4.

[144] Ibid., at para 5.4 and footnote 20.

[145] New Zealand Law Society at Part 2b, para 3.

Despite the concerns raised by the Attorney General and the large majority of briefs submitted to the committee that did not support the proposed changes, the Justice and Electoral Committee recommended that the bill be passed with minor amendments to address simply technical issues, not the NZBORA issues raised in the section 7 report. Although the report noted the strong opposition to the absence of judicial oversight, the expansion of the offences under which DNA samples could be gathered and the increased powers accorded to the police, it argued that administrative efficiency was more important than judicial authorization. Specifically, the committee argued that because 'many arrests are made outside of standard court hours', requiring judicial authorization 'would create judicial inconvenience if the Police were required to apply for a judicial order to enable a bodily sample to be taken from a person who had been arrested'.[146] Further, the committee report, unlike the Attorney General, accepted that Police Operational Guidelines 'would render judicial oversight prior to the taking of a sample unnecessary'.[147]

Although the report was issued in the name of the Justice and Electoral Committee, it outlined the separate views of the Labour and Green parties. Labour members were directly influenced by the Attorney General's report and argued there should be an amendment to provide for judicial oversight for the collection of DNA samples; they disagreed that this would place an onerous requirement on the police, as the current legislation required judicial authorization and 'there does not appear to be a problem in gaining after-hours search warrants'.[148] The report indicated that Labour members intended to propose amendments to the bill during the Committee of the Whole House. Similarly, the Green party endorsed the current DNA collection scheme, 'which requires judicial approval for the taking of DNA samples and where they are taken only from certain convicted offenders'.[149]

The Committee of the Whole House and third reading debate

At the Committee of the Whole House stage, Charles Chauvel of the Labour party proposed two amendments to the bill. The first

[146] Parliament of New Zealand 2009. Criminal Investigations (Bodily Samples) Amendment Bill. As reported from the Justice and Electoral Committee, 2.
[147] Ibid. [148] Ibid. [149] Ibid., 3.

amendment, if passed, would have addressed some of the concerns raised by the Attorney General, as Chauvel proposed that section 24J(1) of the Criminal Investigations (Bodily Samples) Amendment Bill include subsection 1A, which would require judicial authorization: 'A constable may only require a bodily sample to be given in accordance with a suspect compulsion order.'[150] Indeed, this amendment would not address all of the concerns raised by the Attorney General, as the central aspects of the bill with NZBORA implications – expanding the range of offences under which DNA samples could be included, as well as authorizing the collection of DNA from those the police intend to charge – were not part of the amendment proposed by the Labour party. This modest amendment was defeated by a party vote of 64 to 57, as New Zealand National, ACT New Zealand and United Future voted against the proposed requirement of judicial authorization.[151] The second amendment would require parliamentary review of the proposed act after five years, and was defeated by a similar party vote.

The bill proceeded to third reading with minor technical amendments, and the Associate Minister of Justice did acknowledge that opposition to the bill still existed because of the NZBORA concerns raised by the Attorney General. However, the Associate Minister of Justice continued to defend DNA samples as the 'modern fingerprint', and thus representing a 'minimal physical intrusion' that would be regulated by Police Operational Guidelines that 'have been developed to avoid the arbitrary application of the power. . .'.[152] The bill was commended to the House with a restatement of the influence of penal populism in this policy area: 'The Government has made public safety its top priority in the law and order portfolio. This bill will be a crucial tool in the fight against violent crime. . .'[153]

Throughout the parliamentary debate on the Criminal Investigations (Bodily Samples) Amendment Bill, the Labour, Green and Māori parties opposed the bill because of the section 7 report issued by the Attorney General. However, only the Labour party took a contradictory approach: it criticized the bill as a violation of the NZBORA, but supported the passage of the bill at every critical parliamentary vote. What can explain this complex approach by the Labour party – supporting the Attorney

[150] C. Chauvel – Labour Party (15 October 2009) 658 NZPD 7160.
[151] The party vote is recorded at 658 NZPD 7160.
[152] Hon. N. Guy – National Party (27 October 2009) 658 NZPD 7486–7487.
[153] Ibid., 7487.

General while also supporting the passage of the bill criticized by the Attorney General? Indeed, despite unswerving criticism of the bill, Labour voted with the government and the bill passed at third reading on a strong party vote of 108 to 14.[154] The explanation is largely electoral strategy and the recognition that appearing strong on the NZBORA would see the Labour party appear weak on law and order. Given the dominance of penal populism as the principal, if not exclusive, policy discourse structuring law and order in New Zealand, the Labour party made a strategic calculation to support a bill with clear and unresolved NZBORA issues.

VI. Sentencing and Parole Reform Act 2010

Similar to the bills already considered, the Sentencing and Parole Reform Bill 2009 was accompanied by a section 7 report issued by the Attorney General.[155] It too was passed without amendment to address the issues raised by the Attorney General, and saw the section 7 report largely ignored during the parliamentary debates by New Zealand National and ACT New Zealand. The bill was defended by the Minister of Justice within the paradigm of penal populism, and viewed as an important policy to address the perceived criminal policy imbalance that favoured the criminal at the expense of victims. The bill saw the influence of non-traditional policy advocates such as the Sensible Sentencing Trust; the limited influence of key groups such as the New Zealand Law Society, the New Zealand Human Rights Commission and the New Zealand Privacy Commissioner; and the marginalization of the key bureaucratic actors, such as the Ministry of Justice. Finally, the bill saw the elevation of bureaucratic actors, such as the Corrections Department and New Zealand Police, as lead advisors despite these government agencies lacking any policy expertise in criminal policy reform.

In this respect, the Sentencing and Parole Reform Bill 2009 is an excellent example of the policy context labelled by Pratt as penal populism.[156] Specifically, the government responded to populist pressures,

154 The party vote is recorded at 658 NZPD 7506. AYES 108: New Zealand National (58), New Zealand Labour (43), ACT New Zealand (5); Progressive (1); United Future (1). NOES 14: Green party (9), Māori party (5).

155 Report of the Attorney General under the New Zealand Bill of Rights Act 1990 on the Sentence and Parole Reform Bill 2009.

156 J. Pratt, 'When Penal Populism Stops: Legitimacy, Scandal and the Power to Punish in New Zealand', (2008) *The Australian and New Zealand Journal of Criminology* 370–71.

marginalized civil actors and departmental advisors that questioned this policy direction, and appointed departmental advisors that could not challenge the populist policy direction set by New Zealand National in collaboration with ACT New Zealand. The 'confidence and supply' agreement between New Zealand National and ACT New Zealand prioritized law and order issues, and National agreed 'to introduce the ACT Three Strikes Bill as part of this package' and, further, 'to give the ACT bill a fair hearing in the committee based on the evidence and give due weight to the submissions received'.[157] ACT New Zealand's sentencing policy was modelled after California's 'three strikes' rule and was designed to address repeat serious offenders through an approach that significantly increased the penal sanction with each new offence as a way to improve confidence in the justice system:

> On first conviction of one of the qualifying offences – a relatively wide range of offences against the person including robbery – a court issues a warning; on the second conviction of such an offence, the offender receives a final warning, must serve the full sentence given, and is not eligible for parole; on the third conviction for such an offence, the court must impose the maximum sentence for the offence, and the offender will be ineligible for parole unless the court decides that this is 'manifestly unjust'. Strikes do not lapse over time.[158]

The 'three strikes' sentencing policy demonstrates the influence of non-traditional policy actors and penal populism, as the Sensible Sentencing Trust (SST) first advocated this policy following the 1999 Citizen Initiated Referendum, which is viewed as representing the emergence of penal populism as the dominant criminal policy discourse in New Zealand. This populist organization was formed in 2001 and had an immediate effect on criminal policy in New Zealand, as well as having a direct relationship with ACT New Zealand. For instance, the toughening of penal policy under the fifth Labour government (1999–2008), which saw the introduction of the Victims' Rights Act 2002 and the Sentencing Act 2002, were policy responses to address the pressure exerted by the SST outside of parliament and advocated within parliament by ACT New Zealand.[159]

[157] Confidence and Supply Agreement 2008, *Confidence and Supply Agreement*. National and ACT New Zealand (16 November).

[158] N. Lacey, 'Political Systems and Criminal Justice' 225.

[159] J.V. Roberts, 'Sentencing Reform in New Zealand: An Analysis of the Sentencing Act 2002', (2003) *The Australian and New Zealand Journal of Criminology* 251–54.

The SST–ACT New Zealand relationship is significant, as it led to the inclusion of the 'three strikes' sentencing policy as part of the Sentencing and Parole Reform Bill introduced into parliament in 2009. To cement its relationship with the SST, ACT New Zealand added David Garrett to its party list for the 2008 election, and ranked this individual, who had served as legal advisor to the SST, high enough to ensure his entry into parliament as a List MP. With the exception of former ACT New Zealand leader Rodney Hide, who was elected as a constituency MP for Epsom during the 2008 election,[160] all remaining ACT New Zealand members of parliament entered as List MPs after the 2008 election.[161]

A related part of the 2008 agreement between New Zealand National and ACT New Zealand involved the composition of select committees and inter-party coordination, where 'ACT and National will consult on the make-up and operation of select committees with a view to reaching an agreed position'.[162] During his brief career in parliament (2008–2010),[163] David Garrett was appointed to the Law and Order Committee, thereby significantly increasing New Zealand National's control of a key committee despite its status as a minority government during the 49th parliament. Indeed, New Zealand National had an outright majority on the Law and Order Committee (5/9 members), which increased to a two-thirds majority with the appointment of David Garrett as the ACT New Zealand committee member (6/9 members).

Before considering the Sentencing and Parole Reform Bill 2009, it is important to understand the key developments that preceded its introduction into parliament, as well as critical developments that occurred as it progressed to royal assent. The bill was originally assigned to the Minister of Justice, Simon Power, who presided over the cabinet deliberations in December 2008 that approved the introduction of the bill into parliament on 18 February 2009. As the bill was the responsibility of the Minister of Justice, it was developed by the Ministry of Justice, which

[160] New Zealand National agreed not to run a candidate against the former ACT New Zealand leader in Epsom, thereby ensuring Hide's entry into parliament as a constituency MP and a stronger ACT New Zealand caucus that would have been produced under MMP during the 2008 election.

[161] N. Lacey, 'Political Systems and Criminal Justice' 224–225.

[162] Confidence and Supply Agreement 2008, *Confidence and Supply Agreement*, National and ACT New Zealand (16 November).

[163] David Garrett resigned from the ACT New Zealand caucus, and subsequently from Parliament, when it was revealed he had used the identity of a dead child to receive a false passport.

acted as the lead departmental advisor from December 2008 until January 2010. At a cabinet meeting in February 2009 in which the ministry agreed to introduce the Sentencing and Parole Reform Bill into parliament during the week of 17 February, it was recommended by the Minister of Justice that the bill be referred to the Justice and Electoral Committee for consideration.[164] However, at first reading the Minister of Justice referred the bill to the Law and Order Committee.[165] The Minister of Justice remained responsible for the bill and the Ministry of Justice served as the lead departmental agency advising the Law and Order Committee until 19 January 2010, when responsibility was transferred to the Minister of Police and Minister of Corrections, Judith Collins.

In a letter to the Chair of the Law and Order Committee, Sandra Goudie, Judith Collins informed the committee that cabinet decided on 17 December 2009 to transfer the bill from the Minister of Justice to the Corrections Minister.[166] In an unusual move, as SO 201 gives parliamentary committees discretion over the appointment of departmental advisors, the Corrections Minister requested that the New Zealand Police 'be the lead advisers on this Bill during the remainder of your consideration of it ... the Department of Corrections is also invited to be an adviser to the Committee'.[167] Both requests were complied with, and the Ministry of Justice ceased to have any responsibility for the bill it developed on behalf of the Minister of Justice. If the composition of the Law and Order Committee was consistent with party standings in parliament, the request for specific agency advisor by the Correction Minister may not have been acted upon, as New Zealand National did not command a majority in the House of Representatives. However, the fact that New Zealand National commanded a majority of the membership of this select committee and the Corrections Minister requested new departmental advisors suggests the government considered it prudent to appoint more favourable advisors than the Ministry of Justice.

The Sentencing and Parole Reform Bill demonstrates the strengths of the legislative process developed in light of the NZBORA, as well as the limitations of a parliamentary bill of rights operating in an MMP electoral

164 Office of the Minister of Justice (New Zealand) 2009. Cabinet. Sentencing and Parole Reform Bill: Final Approval for Introduction (February 12), 6.

165 Hon. S. Power – National Party (18 February 2009) 652 NZPD 1420.

166 Office of Hon Judith Collins 2010. Letter to Sandra Goudie MP, Chair, Law and Order Committee (19 January), 1.

167 Office of Hon Judith Collins 2010, 1–2.

environment. Specifically, because the bill was developed by the Ministry of Justice, it was scrutinized for its BORA compliance by the Crown Law Office, saw the Minister of Justice outline to cabinet the outstanding NZBORA issues that could not be addressed, and finally saw the Minister of Justice introduce a bill into parliament although the cabinet had full knowledge that it was inconsistent with the NZBORA, as well as New Zealand's international treaty obligations. The Attorney General confirmed this assessment of incompatibility when issuing a section 7 report before first reading commenced on the Sentencing and Parole Reform Bill.

For academics such as Stephen Gardbaum, this process demonstrates the value of the 'Commonwealth model', as it preserves the final judgement on incompatible legislation for parliament and not the courts.[168] Gardbaum suggests that the 'weakness of the NZBORA from the new model perspective is arguably less clear than this strength. . . '.[169] We respectfully disagree. The new model is premised on full parliamentary debate, scrutiny and engagement of legislation introduced with known rights-based incompatibilities. Indeed, the theory of the new model is premised on the assumption that legislation is passed into law only after a fulsome debate whereby parliament passes it with full knowledge – as well as acceptance – that it is incompatible with domestic rights instruments. As we will argue, the Sentencing and Parole Reform Bill 2009 demonstrates the ability of the executive to employ the Standing Orders of the House of Representatives to prevent parliamentary oversight of legislation identified by the Attorney General as inconsistent with the NZBORA. Further, this bill demonstrates the continuation of what Erdos described as 'aversive constitutionalism' and Palmer labelled 'unbridled power' in New Zealand,[170] as MMP has not significantly limited the cabinet's control over the policy process.[171]

NZBORA scrutiny and cabinet deliberations

The Sentencing and Parole Reform Bill 2009 was first discussed at the Cabinet Business Committee on 5 December 2008, and originally

[168] S. Gardbaum, *The New Commonwealth Model of Constitutionalism: Theory and Practice* (Cambridge: Cambridge University Press, 2013), pp. 151–52.

[169] Ibid., p. 151.

[170] D. Erdos, *Delegating Rights Protection: The Rise of Bill of Rights in the Westminster World* (Oxford: Oxford University Press, 2010), pp. 94–8.

[171] G. Palmer and M. Palmer, *Bridled Power: New Zealand's Constitution and Government*, 4th Edition (Melbourne: Oxford University Press, 2004), pp. 13–14.

included changes to the Sentencing Act 2002 and the Parole Act 2002 to deny parole for the 'worst repeat violent offenders and worst murder cases'.[172] The bill was modified at the Cabinet Domestic Policy Committee (5 February 2009) to incorporate 'aspects of the ACT party's "three strikes" policy in line with the National-ACT Confidence and Supply Agreement'.[173] The cabinet approved these changes (12 February 2009), and the Minister of Justice was authorized to introduce the bill into parliament during the sitting week of 17 February 2009.[174]

The documentation presented to cabinet and the relevant cabinet committees by the Minister of Justice demonstrate that the Ministry of Justice had serious reservations about the bill and its compatibility with the NZBORA. For instance, parts of the discussion paper written by the Minister of Justice and circulated to the Cabinet Business Committee (5 December 2008) are heavily redacted under the 'Human rights implications' section. Paragraphs 41 to 43 are completely redacted, and the document only provides concerns raised by the Ministry of Foreign Affairs and Trade (MFAT) that the bill is not compliant with New Zealand's international human rights obligations.[175] During the 11 December 2008 meeting of the cabinet, the Minister of Justice confirmed that the bill complied with the principles of the Treaty of Waitangi, the Privacy Act 1993 and the Legislation Advisory Committee (LAC) Guidelines.[176] However, the Minister of Justice did not inform Cabinet that the bill complied with the NZBORA, and the document forwarded to the Cabinet Business Committee (22 January 2009),[177] as well as the document submitted to the cabinet (29 January 2009), 'directed that further consideration be given to options for addressing New Zealand Bill of Rights Act concerns about the proposals for

[172] Office of the Minster of Justice (New Zealand) 2008. Cabinet Business Committee. 'No Parole for Worst Repeat Offenders and Worst Murder Cases' (5 December), 1.

[173] Office of the Minister of Justice (New Zealand) 2009. Cabinet Domestic Policy Committee. 'Worst Repeat Violent Offender Policy' (5 February), 1.

[174] Office of the Minister of Justice (New Zealand) 2009. Cabinet. Sentencing and Parole Reform Bill: Final Approval for Introduction (12 February), 6.

[175] Office of the Minister of Justice (New Zealand) 2008. Cabinet Business Committee. 'No Parole for Worst Repeat Offenders and Worst Murder Cases (5 December), 9–10.

[176] Office of the Minister of Justice (New Zealand) 2008. Cabinet. Sentencing and Parole Reform Bill: Approval for Introduction (11 December), 2.

[177] Office of the Minister of Justice (New Zealand) 2009. Cabinet Business Committee. Final Approval for Introduction of Sentencing and Parole Reform Bill (22 January), 1.

sentences of life without parole for the worst repeat offenders and those convicted of the worst murders'.[178] Indeed, the cabinet document granting final approval (29 January 2009), before the policy was modified to include the 'three strikes' approach, states that the bill only complies with 'New Zealand's obligations under international human rights agreements' and does not provide a similar claim in regard to the NZBORA.[179]

The 'three strikes' sentencing approach was added to the Sentencing and Parole Reform Bill at the Cabinet Domestic Policy Committee meeting (5 February 2009) and opposition to the bill, which was initially led by the Ministry of Justice, now included the Ministry of Māori Development (Te Puni Kōkiri) as well as the New Zealand Treasury:

> Te Puni Kōkiri does not support this proposed legislation as US research has shown that the deterrent effect of 'three strikes' legislation on violent crime is minimal in the context of overall crime trends; that violence may increase; and that criminals rather than reducing their criminal activity, seek to mitigate risk of arrest by murdering or injuring police officers and their victims. The legislation is also likely to have a disproportionate effect on Māori as Māori are more likely to be victims of crime than non Māori.[180]

Further, the Regulatory Impact Statement (RIS) prepared by the New Zealand Treasury questioned whether the bill would advance one of the central objectives, which was to improve public safety, as 'offenders who commit serious violent offences do not necessarily have previous sentences for serious violent offences'.[181] The RIS also questioned whether the bill would satisfy the objective of increasing confidence in the justice system, arguing that it could have the opposite effect among Māori because 'The policies have the considerable potential to affect the confidence of Māori in the criminal justice system, as they will impact on Māori most. Māori are more likely than other ethnic groupings to be convicted of violent offences.'[182] Finally, the RIS noted that the proposed changes generated opposition within the bureaucracy, as several

[178] Office of the Minister of Justice (New Zealand) 2009. Cabinet. Final Approval for Introduction of Sentencing and Parole Reform Bill (29 January), 1.

[179] Ibid., 7.

[180] Office of the Minister of Justice (New Zealand) 2009. Cabinet Domestic Policy Committee. Worst Repeat Violent Offender Policy (5 February), 6.

[181] New Zealand Treasury 2009. Regulatory Impact Statement. Sentencing and Parole Reform Bill (February), 3.

[182] Ibid., 4.

government departments and agencies had raised serious concerns 'about the possibility for disproportionate impacts as between offenders and between ethnic groups, but the policy has not been revised'.[183]

The position paper submitted to cabinet seeking final approval to introduce the bill clearly demonstrates significant inter-departmental disagreement on two issues: first, whether the bill would achieve the stated objectives of increased confidence in the justice system and improved public safety; second, whether the bill was compliant with the NZBORA and international obligations. The document presented to cabinet concluded: 'The Bill does not comply with BORA or relevant international obligations for the reasons outlined in paragraphs 7 and 8, and 14.'[184] Paragraph 7 concluded that life sentences without parole 'appear to breach' the NZBORA and several international treaties signed by New Zealand, and the revised approach to 'compassionate release' for those sentenced to life imprisonment without parole was considered by the Ministry of Justice as insufficient to be compatible with the NZBORA. Similarly, paragraph 14 concluded that the minimum non-parole period of 25 years at the third-strike offence unless it was considered by a court to be 'manifestly unjust' would likely breach the NZBORA and international treaties, because it would result in disproportionate sentences that would not be redeemed through the 'manifestly unjust' exception.[185]

What is significant in the cabinet paper presented by the Minister of Justice – in addition to acknowledgement that the proposed bill is incompatible with the NZBORA, as well as the significant opposition to the policy rationale by key agencies (the Treasury, the Ministry of Justice, and the Ministry of Māori Development) – is the disclosure that key government agencies 'were informed but not consulted on this paper or the draft bill'.[186] This is a key dimension of the policy process characterized as 'penal populism' – a jettisoning of the professional bureaucracy and the reliance on non-traditional policy actors such as populist policy advocates for inspiration, development and validation.[187] Indeed, 'time constraints' and the government's desire to honour its election commitment to introduce a series of 'tough on crime' measures during its first 100 days in office were used as justification for the failure to consult key

[183] The New Zealand Treasury, 5.

[184] Office of the Minister of Justice (New Zealand) 2009. Cabinet. Sentencing and Parole Reform Bill: Final Approval for Introduction (12 February), 4.

[185] Ibid., 2–3. [186] Ibid., 4. [187] J. Pratt, *Penal Populism*, p. 17.

government agencies. Thus, the need to respond to populist pressures, as well as the National–ACT 'confidence and supply' agreement, saw the Sentencing and Parole Reform Bill 2009 introduced into parliament despite significant opposition from the professional bureaucracy and the lead agency responsible for criminal policy, the Ministry of Justice.

Control the rules, control the outcome

In addition to disregarding the advice presented by the Minster of Justice, cabinet recommended that the bill be referred to the Law and Order Committee, despite the subject matter of the bill falling under the mandate of the Justice and Electoral Committee under SO 185. In an unusual move, the Explanatory Note provided to parliament reproduced, in its entirety, the RIS prepared by the New Zealand Treasury that outlined the NZBORA incompatibilities, as well as inter-agency disagreement with the proposed policy.[188] The section 7 report by the Attorney General echoed the assessment provided by the Ministry of Justice: Christopher Finlayson concluded that the penalty for a third-strike offence 'may raise an inconsistency with the right against disproportionately severe treatment affirmed by s.9 of the Bill of Rights Act'.[189] The Attorney General determined that the 'three strikes' sentencing regime, particularly the third offence sentencing approach, 'may result in gross disproportionality in sentencing',[190] as 'Absent manifest injustices, the sentencing court is obliged to impose a sentence on a qualifying offender that may be significantly more severe than that imposed on a more culpable, but non-qualifying, offender'.[191]

At first reading, New Zealand Labour opposed the bill, but not because of the reported inconsistencies with the NZBORA. Clayton Cosgrove argued that the 'three strikes' policy was unnecessary because of the changes introduced by the previous Labour-led ministry, which led to a '72 per cent decline rate for parole applications'.[192] Indeed, the Labour party opposed the bill because it believed that the changes would have negligible effects in terms of improving public safety or increasing

[188] Parliament of New Zealand 2009. Sentencing and Parole Reform Bill. Explanatory Note, 5–11.

[189] Report of the Attorney General under the New Zealand Bill of Rights Act 1990 on the Sentencing and Parole Reform bill, para 4.

[190] Ibid., para 16. [191] Ibid., para 13.3.

[192] Hon. C. Cosgrove - Labour party (18 February 2009) 652 NZPD 1423.

confidence in the justice system. Thus, Labour argued against the policy by relying on the success of its previous penal populism-influenced 'law and order' amendments. Similarly, the Māori party ignored the section 7 report and focused on the disproportionate impact that the 'three strikes' sentencing policy would have on Māori people as its reason for opposing the bill.[193] Only the Green party framed its opposition to the bill in relation to the section 7 report of the Attorney General, as well as the negative findings of the RIS reproduced within the Explanatory Note.[194] However, the three opposition parties noted the negative influence of the Sensible Sentencing Trust in the bill's development, as well as the important role played by ACT New Zealand in pressuring New Zealand National to include the 'three strikes' sentencing policy as part of its criminal policy agenda.[195]

The bill was read for the first time on a party vote of 64 to 58, and was referred to the Law and Order Committee (18 February 2009).[196] Under SO 291, a select committee is required to report to the House of Representatives within six months after a bill is referred, unless the Business Committee extends the timeframe. The Law and Order Committee released an interim report after nearly a year (17 February 2010) and a final report on 26 March 2010. Several changes within this period are important, as they demonstrate the ability of New Zealand National, despite its status as a minority government, to use the Standing Orders of the House of Representatives to effectively marginalize opposition to the bill, within both the bureaucracy and important segments of civil society. As is evident from the parliamentary debate after second reading, the opposition parties largely focused on the manipulation of the rules by New Zealand National at the select committee stage to introduce a controversial bill without amendment or serious parliamentary oversight. As previously discussed, New Zealand National functioned as a de facto majority government in the context of this bill as a result of its 'confidence and supply' agreement with ACT New Zealand, as the two parties controlled a majority of seats in parliament (63/121), as well as on the Law and Order Committee (6/9).

193 Hon. T. Turia - Māori party (18 February 2009) 652 NZPD 1432.

194 M. Turei - Green party (18 February 2009) 652 NZPD 1433.

195 Hon. C. Cosgrove - Labour party (18 February 2009) 652 NZPD 1422; M. Turei - Green party (18 February 2009) 652 NZPD 1433.

196 The party vote is recorded at 652 NZPD 1440. AYES 64: New Zealand National (58), ACT New Zealand (5), United Future (1); NOES 58: New Zealand Labour (43), Green party (9), Māori party (5), Progressive (1).

The Ministry of Justice provided an initial briefing to the Law and Order Committee before being replaced by New Zealand Police and Corrections New Zealand as departmental advisors. In its report, the Ministry of Justice reiterated the concerns raised by the Attorney General in his section 7 report, and attached a copy of this report as Appendix 4.[197] Further, the Ministry of Justice reiterated MFAT's concern that the bill did not comply with New Zealand's human rights obligations, and strongly cautioned against proceeding with it:

> Enacting legislation contrary to international human rights obligations would pose risks to New Zealand's international reputation through international criticism and increased complaints against New Zealand before the United Nations (UN) monitoring committees for the International Covenant on Civil and Political Rights and the Convention Against Torture and Other Cruel, Inhuman or Degrading Treatment or Punishment. It may result in those committees formally finding New Zealand in breach of its international obligations, which is a serious matter due to the general international law obligation to comply with treaty commitments in good faith.[198]

This report represents the last time the Ministry of Justice formally advised the Law and Order Committee, as the cabinet transferred responsibility for the bill to the Minister of Police and Corrections Minister in December 2009. As a result of the request by Judith Collins, the Corrections Department and New Zealand Police were given responsibility for the Sentencing and Parole Reform Bill, despite the bill being developed by the Ministry of Justice and the recommended advisors lacking any capacity in sentencing policy.

The importance of New Zealand National having a majority on the Law and Order Committee is evident in regard to the reports issued by the committee. An interim report was released (17 February 2010), at which time Labour members were prevented from including a minority report.[199] At this time, the Law and Order Committee called for new submissions on the bill, but limited participation to those individuals and groups that had previously made submissions, with a closing date of 5 March 2010. New Zealand Police submitted its departmental report to

[197] Ministry of Justice (New Zealand) 2009. Sentencing and Parole Reform Bill – Initial Briefing to the Law and Order Committee (29 April), paras 55–8.

[198] Ministry of Justice (New Zealand) 2009, para 60.

[199] 'Labour Questions Minister's Commitment to Bill', *Otago Daily Times* (17 February 2010).

the Law and Order Committee (12 March 2010), which simply reviewed the submissions without engaging in any analysis of the outstanding human rights issues. In its report, New Zealand Police noted that there were 1075 submissions on the bill, and 94 per cent (1009/1075) supported the bill.[200] On 26 March 2010 the Law and Order Committee released its final report to parliament, which included a minority report by New Zealand Labour.

The minority report by Labour is significant as it demonstrates the ability of New Zealand National, through its control of the Law and Order Committee, to prevent parliamentary oversight and critical bureaucratic engagement of the Sentencing and Parole Reform Bill. As noted in the minority report, New Zealand National and ACT New Zealand passed resolutions to prevent the Ministry of Justice from continuing as advisors to the Law and Order Committee. Further, despite introducing a revised 'three strikes' policy that changed sentencing from a qualifying offence to a relevant offence (10 February 2010), the committee did not hold oral hearings on this change, and limited written briefs to those individuals and organizations that had made previous submissions. Finally, New Zealand National and ACT New Zealand members that controlled the Law and Order Committee provided a two-week period for submissions to be received on the changes to the bill.[201]

In the minority report, Labour noted that it opposed all of these changes, and in particular the committee's decision to appoint new departmental advisors at the request of the Corrections Minister:

> New Zealand Police advisors told the committee that this is only the second time Police have been the lead agency on a sentencing bill – the other occasion being the Vehicle Confiscation and Seizure Bill – and further admitted to the committee that the Police would not have the expertise to lead a review of this legislation, should a review clause be undertaken. They said that the Ministry of Justice would be the more appropriate agency to lead a review. If the Police do not have the expertise to lead a review of the legislation, how can they have the expertise to lead the formation and implementation of the legislation?[202]

200 New Zealand Police Association 2010. Sentencing and Parole Reform Bill. Departmental Report (12 March), 3.

201 Parliament of New Zealand 2010. Sentencing and Parole Reform Bill. As reported by the Law and Order Committee (26 March), 11.

202 Ibid., 12.

For the Labour party this was counterproductive, as the Ministry of Justice developed the bill and possessed the institutional capacity to properly advise the committee, whereas New Zealand Police admitted that they had rarely served as the principal advisor on a bill and, further, that this agency could not properly advise the committee on sentencing policy.

Given that New Zealand Police admitted a limited capacity to serve as the lead advisor to the Law and Order Committee, why would New Zealand National and ACT New Zealand use its voting power to weaken the effectiveness of this select committee? The answer is clearly revealed during the second reading debate led by the Corrections Minister, in which the importance of penal populism is evident:

> I would also like to thank all those members of the public who took the time to make a submission on the bill. Ninety-four percent of submitters supported the bill. They stated their concerns about violent crime, public safety, and the need to hold offenders to account. Many supporters wanted to address what they described as the disparity between the rights of the offenders and those of the victims, and to spare victims the stress associated with repeated parole hearings.[203]

In her closing remarks at second reading, Judith Collins noted: 'This bill is tangible evidence that the Government is delivering on its election promise to toughen up on criminals.'[204] However, to do so, New Zealand National had to overcome significant bureaucratic resistance to the Sentencing and Parole Reform Bill, which proved more significant than parliamentary attempts by the opposition parties to block the passage of the bill. Although opposition members made reference to the Attorney General's section 7 report at the Committee of the Whole House,[205] as well at third reading,[206] the Labour party focused its criticism on the resolutions passed at the Law and Order Committee that barred the Ministry of Justice from advising the committee.[207] Ruth Dyson felt it was 'an absolute outrage that the proper officials – the Ministry of Justice

[203] Hon. J. Collins – National party (4 May 2010) 662 NZPD 10674. [204] Ibid., 10675.

[205] C. Hipkins – Labour party (18 May 2010) 663 NZPD 10920.

[206] G. Robertson – Labour party (25 May 2010) 663 NZPD 11228.

[207] Hon. C. Cosgrove – Labour party (18 May 2010) 663 NZPD 10932; G. Robertson – Labour party (25 May 2010) 663 NZPD 11229; Hon. R. Dyson – Labour party (25 May 2010) 663 NZPD 11233; C. Sepuloni – Labour party (25 May 2010) 663 NZPD 11241.

officials – who are entitled to give their opinion to the executive and to Parliament through the select committee process – were stopped by Minister Judith Collins from giving their advice on this bill to the Law and Order Committee'.[208]

The Sentencing and Parole Reform Bill 2009 passed third reading on a party vote of 63 to 58.[209] It passed without amendments to address the NZBORA concerns raised by the Ministry of Justice and the Attorney General, as well as the concerns raised by MFAT that it breached New Zealand's international human rights obligations. This bill passed without amendment despite the concerns raised by the Ministry of Māori Development that it would unfairly target Māori, and thus was discriminatory and would breach the NZBORA. This significant bureaucratic opposition was augmented by presentations made by the New Zealand Law Society and the New Zealand Human Rights Commission.[210] Yet this opposition did not result in any concessions by New Zealand National to address concerns that the bill was in breach of the NZBORA and, more importantly, would not achieve the goals of increased security and confidence in the justice system outlined in the Explanatory Note. The design and implementation of the Sentencing and Parole Reform Bill 2009 demonstrate the influence of penal populism and the importance of 'confidence and supply' agreements under MMP that allowed New Zealand National to control the rules and, thereby, marginalize parliamentary and bureaucratic oversight of legislation as it relates to the NZBORA.

Conclusion

The importance of penal populism as a policy discourse – and one that restricts the ability of section 7 reports to facilitate parliamentary oversight of government bills – has been considered in this chapter. Indeed, New Zealand National's '100 days of action on law and order', supported by its 'confidence and supply' partner ACT New Zealand, had clear penal

[208] Hon. R. Dyson – Labour party (25 May 2010) 663 NZPD 11234.

[209] The party vote is recorded at 663 NZPD 11247: AYES 63: New Zealand National (58), ACT New Zealand (5); NOES 58: New Zealand Labour (43), Green party (9); Māori party (5), United Future (1).

[210] New Zealand Law Society 2010. Submission on Sentencing and Parole Reform Bill (23 March); New Zealand Human Rights Commission 2010. Sentencing and Parole Reform Bill (5 March).

populist undertones and saw the introduction of several controversial initiatives, such as parole reform in the guise of an expanded ESO regime and a 'three strikes' sentencing policy implemented as a concession to ACT New Zealand. In addition, this compressed policy timeframe, as New Zealand National wanted policy deliverables within 100 days of assuming office to demonstrate its penal policy credentials, also saw the expansion of the range of offences under which DNA samples can be demanded by the police, with the simultaneous reduction of the statutory and judicial criteria under which compelled production of these samples can be gathered. All of these initiatives were flagged by the Attorney General as in breach of the NZBORA; the ESO regime was confirmed by the SCNZ, in *Belcher*, to be a criminal penalty, and thus a retrospective application of a sentencing provision that also violated the protection against double jeopardy in the NZBORA. As we have argued, penal populism and its 'crime control' objective has clearly displaced the 'due process' requirements that exist under the NZBORA, as well as those statutory protections that occurred in earlier legislation such as the Criminal Investigations (Bodily Samples) Act 1995.

The legislative initiatives passed by both Labour and New Zealand National governments demonstrate the cross-party appeal of penal populism, and how it has come to dominate the policy discourse that informs criminal policy reform. This is an important reason why the Attorney General's reporting duty has failed to generate parliamentary oversight of government bills that involve sentencing provisions deemed incompatible with the NZBORA. While all the acts of parliament considered in this chapter demonstrate the effect of penal populism on this parliamentary bill of rights, the Sentencing and Parole Reform Act 2010 clearly illustrates the unfettered power that remains with the cabinet despite the introduction of the MMP and the absence of single-party majority governments that occurred under SMP. It also reveals the dominance of penal policy discourse, most clearly in the second reading debate by Corrections Minister Judith Collins after her assumption of responsibility for the bill, as she thanked the '94 per cent' of submitters that supported the bill. What the Corrections Minister did not acknowledge, however, was the near-universal opposition to this bill by the human rights community, as well as significant departmental opposition from the Minister of Justice and the Ministry of Māori Development.

The passage of the Sentencing and Parole Reform Act 2010 calls into question whether aversive constitutionalism has been addressed in New

Zealand. Further, it questions whether MMP has contained unbridled power, which was the intention of electoral reform and the NZBORA by Geoffrey Palmer. Because New Zealand National, through its 'confidence and supply' partner ACT New Zealand controlled the critical rules outlined in the Standing Orders of New Zealand – the allocation of the select committee, the ability to pass resolutions at select committee that marginalized the Ministry of Justice and the appointment of departmental advisors without policy capacity in this area, such as Corrections New Zealand and New Zealand Police – the Attorney General's report under section 7 of the NZBORA was of limited significance. Finally, because the Prime Minister retains the discretion to designate a lead minister on a bill, which was relevant in the context of reassigning the Sentencing and Reform Act 2010 from the Minister of Justice to the Corrections Minister, this effectively ended the bureaucratic resistance to the 'three strikes' policy that originated in the Ministry of Justice.

What the Sentencing and Parole Reform Act 2010 demonstrates, therefore, is the continued importance of ministerial control of key Standing Orders, the bureaucracy that develops legislation and the allocation of critical select committees that review bills which have received a section 7 report by the Attorney General. Indeed, given that select committees operate under the party vote system, ministerial control extends to the very parliamentary institution that is critical for parliamentary oversight mechanisms such as section 7. What has been overlooked, or simply not enforced, is the Standing Orders requirement that select committee membership should reflect, where possible, party standings in the House of Representatives. As we demonstrated in the chapters that considered the NZBORA, this important rule has not been enforced, as both Labour-led ministries and New Zealand National governments have had majority control over the select committees that receive the vast majority of bills reported on by the Attorney General. Thus, a critical parliamentary institution necessary for substantive enforcement of the NZBORA has yet to perform the role of parliamentary oversight of the cabinet's legislative agenda.

While the NZBORA has changed the internal policy process within government, the case studies considered in Chapters 4 and 5 demonstrate the limited ability within the parliamentary process to require amendment if a government decides to proceed with a bill with acknowledged NZBORA incompatibilities. Thus, a parliamentary bill of rights is only as robust as parliament's ability to hold the cabinet to account through oversight mechanisms that, at a minimum, require the government to justify proceeding with a bill containing NZBORA incompatibilities. Unfortunately, this is not the New Zealand experience of a parliamentary bill of rights, despite the policy development virtues of BORA scrutiny by the Ministry of Justice and Crown Law Office since 1990.

PART II

The United Kingdom's Human Rights Act 1998

6

Political Origins of the Human Rights Act

The United Kingdom's Human Rights Act (HRA) is the product of a conscious attempt to envisage the protection of rights occurring in a less court-centred manner than is usually associated with a bill of rights, where courts are given authority to impose binding constraints on legislation. The HRA came into effect in 2000 and authorizes a domestic judicial role that significantly exceeds that which had earlier existed. Before this, judges could protect rights through their interpretation of the common law but parliament was not required to justify legislation before domestic courts in terms of its consistency with Convention rights. Although the UK ratified the European Convention of Human Rights (EHCR) in 1951, and accepted the jurisdiction of the Court of Human Rights with respect to individual complaints in 1966,[1] UK courts were unable to rely directly on Convention rights in domestic proceedings prior to the HRA's enactment.[2]

The HRA allows citizens to challenge legislation for violating Convention rights in domestic courts while withholding a remedial power for judges to set aside inconsistent legislation. If judges deem legislation to be inconsistent with Convention rights, when possible they can rely on their interpretive powers to construe and interpret the scope or effects of legislation in a rights-compliant manner, or they can engage a new power to declare that legislation is incompatible with protected rights. However, parliament retains authority for determining the legality of legislation and can respond to a judicial declaration of incompatibility by either maintaining the legislation as is, or passing remedial measures to give effect to judicial concerns. If a court alters the scope or effects of legislation in the effort to interpret it in a rights-compliant manner,

1 D. Oliver, *Constitutional Reform in the UK* (Oxford: Oxford University Press, 2003), p. 111.

2 I. Leigh and R. Masterman, *Making Rights Real. The Human Rights Act in its First Decade* (Oxford: Hart Publishing, 2008), pp. 5–8.

parliament can accept this interpretation or legislate to overrule it. Thus, regardless of the nature of the judicial remedy, parliament has the final say on the legality of legislation.

Notwithstanding the political decision to adopt a bill of rights that constrains the scope of judicial remedies, the political architects of the HRA went out of their way to emphasize that the HRA would not be weak or ineffective. One reason for this assertion was the decision to include a dedicated process for enacting remedial legislation in section 10 of the HRA, which recognizes the strong presumptive expectation of compliance with judicial interpretations of Convention rights, flowing from the UK's treaty obligations to respect the ECHR.[3] A second reason for insisting that constrained judicial remedial power would not undermine the effectiveness of the HRA – and the one on which we focus – was the suggestion that by introducing a new statutory obligation to alert parliament about whether proposed legislation is consistent with Convention rights, the HRA would encourage public and political officials to assess whether legislative bills are compatible with Convention rights and would also facilitate parliamentary engagement about the justification of legislation from a rights perspective. Stated differently, a focus on compatibility was expected to alter the very norms of legislative decision-making.

Although government was already in the practice of assessing whether proposed legislation was consistent with Convention rights before the HRA was adopted, this pre-HRA form of self-evaluation was neither robustly performed nor accountable to parliament.[4] The HRA envisages legislation being subject to as many as four stages of rights review, three of which are centred on the legislative process. The first of these four stages is pre-legislative review and arises from the requirement to fulfil the new ministerial reporting obligation in section 19 to apprise parliament either that a minister reports the legislative bill is compatible with Convention rights or, alternatively, that he or she is not able to affirm compatibility. The requirement to confront how bills implicate rights for purposes of this new statutory reporting obligation was expected to precipitate assessments of legislative initiatives by the policy officials and legal advisors who apprise ministers of potential rights problems and consider alternative and more rights-compliant ways to achieve the legislative objective.[5] This emphasis on ensuring legislative initiatives

[3] Interviews. [4] Interviews.

[5] J. Straw, 'Building a Human Rights Culture', address to Civil Service College Seminar (19 December 1999), www.nationalarchives.gov.uk/ERORecords/HO/415/1/hract/cscspe.htm

are compatible with Convention rights was also expected to influence legislative drafters' work to ensure legislation is drafted in a manner that is compliant with protected rights.[6] The second stage is parliamentary review, which is facilitated by a specialized parliamentary rights committee that was created shortly after the HRA took effect (the Joint Committee on Human Rights). The third stage is judicial review, which occurs as a result of a new judicial authority for domestic courts to consider whether legislation is consistent with Convention rights and recognizes judicial censure for inconsistent legislation. This judicial role encompasses an interpretive form under section 3 of the HRA that could result in judges altering the scope or effects of legislation to render legislation compatible with Convention rights, or engages judges in a more explicit form of censure by declaring under section 4 that the legislation is incompatible with Convention rights. The fourth stage arises from the creation of a legislative procedure for implementing remedial legislation in section 10 that reflects the political framers' expectations that parliament will generally comply with domestic and European Court of Human Rights (ECtHR) rulings of incompatibility.[7]

We use the term 'legislative rights review' to refer, generally, to the collective practices of pre-legislative scrutiny of whether bills are compatible with rights, the act of ministerial reporting on compatibility and parliamentary scrutiny and deliberation about whether legislation is justified, notwithstanding its potential implications for rights.[8] This concept of legislative rights review reflects a proactive vision of rights protection by imposing an obligation on government to report to

[6] Parliament of the United Kingdom, *Hansard*, HL, vol 582, col 1233, 3 November 1997 (Lord Irvine); Parliament of the United Kingdom, *Hansard*, HC, vol 307, col 780, 16 February 1998 (Jack Straw); Straw, 'Building a Human Rights Culture'.

[7] This argument of four stages of rights engagement was earlier made by the author in J. Hiebert, 'The HRA: Ambiguity about Parliamentary Sovereignty', (2013) 14 *German Law Journal* 2254.

[8] Stephen Gardbaum refers to this practice as political rights review: S. Gardbaum, *The New Commonwealth Model of Constitutionalism: Theory and Practice* (Cambridge: Cambridge University Press, 2013), pp. 25–6. In earlier works, Hiebert used both terms when characterizing this practice. However, upon continued reflection, we believe that the term 'legislative rights review' best captures the idea of assessing whether and how legislative initiatives implicate rights in the pre- and parliamentary phases of legislative development. It also reflects both the inevitable judgement this entails about whether the legislative objective is warranted despite its potentially adverse implications for rights, and the dynamics of parliamentary decision-making: J. Hiebert, 'New Constitutional Ideas. But Can New Parliamentary Models Resist Judicial Dominance when Interpreting Rights?', (2004) 82 *Texas Law Review* 1963.

parliament on whether bills are compatible with Convention rights, which helps guard against rights being restricted unknowingly, as well as by focusing parliament's attention on questions of compatibility and justification.

In its first part, this chapter examines the origins of the HRA. Its second part analyses political architects' claims that the prudential structure of the HRA will significantly alter legislative decision-making by ensuring that a focus on compatibility with Convention rights becomes a fundamental norm in legislative decision-making.

1. Overcoming political resistance to a bill of rights

Despite the relatively recent passage of the HRA, questions of whether the UK requires a bill of rights and, if so, what form this bill of rights should take remain controversial, as was evident in the divided report issued late in 2012 by a commission struck to address the question of a new bill of rights for the UK,[9] as well as by persistent political criticisms of the HRA extending as far as calls for its repeal. After initial arguments about the virtues of the HRA around the time it came into force, the Labour government's enthusiasm for it soon waned; then Prime Minister Tony Blair and senior ministers became openly critical of the ways in which the HRA was being interpreted.[10] Conservative

[9] The Commission on a Bill of Rights, *A UK Bill of Rights? The Choice Before Us*, 18 December 2012, www.justice.gov.uk/cbr/index.htm

[10] The most blatant criticism from a political minister came from then Home Secretary David Blunkett, who indicated he was 'fed up with having to deal with a situation where Parliament debates issues and the judges overturn them': F. Gibb, 'Blunkett vs. the Bench: The Battle has Begun', *The Times*, 4 May 2003, www.thetimes.co.uk/tto/law/article2208546.ece. Blunkett characterized passage of the HRA as the Blair government's 'biggest mistake' in its first term of office: www.independent.co.uk/opinion/commentators/bruce-anderson/bruce-anderson-dont-pity-those-foreigners-who-exploit-our-generosity-616625.html. Blair did little to rebut this impression, and a year after the HRA came into effect suggested he would seek to amend the HRA if it were interpreted so as to prevent the government from proceeding with its anti-terrorist legislation. See B. Brogan, 'Blunkett Puts War before Concerns for Human Rights', *The Daily Telegraph*, 24 September 2001, www.telegraph.co.uk/news/uknews/1341426/Blunkett-puts-war-before-concerns-for-human-rights.html. Four years later, in the wake of the London bombings of 7 July 2005, the government's anti-Human Rights Act rhetoric intensified. Blair stated publicly that the 'rules of the game are changing', again indicating a willingness to amend the Human Rights Act if necessary to allow terrorist suspects to be deported, and suggesting that he was prepared to renounce aspects of the ECHR if the judiciary blocked these decisions. S. Jeffrey, 'The Rules of the Game are Changing', *The Guardian*, 5 August 2005, www.guardian.co.uk/attackonlondon/story/0,16132,1543359,00.html; G. Jones,

Prime Minister David Cameron and his predecessor Michael Howard have both called for repeal of the HRA.[11]

Historically, the UK's lack of interest in a bill of rights reflected both a deep confidence in how the nation's political constitution functions and a strong belief that a bill of rights is not compatible with the constitutional principle of parliamentary sovereignty. This view of incompatibility arose from conventional expectations that judicial review of a bill of rights necessarily encompasses a judicial remedial capacity to set aside inconsistent legislation, thus contradicting the principle that parliament should have the final say on the legality of duly enacted legislation.

However, Britain's long-standing and continued unease with the idea that parliament should be constrained by judicial review does not mean that considerations of rights are deemed irrelevant to the ways in which the legal and political systems operate. Rights have long been thought of as already protected by the nation's political constitution.[12] This belief was heavily influenced by famed nineteenth-century legal constitutional theorist A.V. Dicey's arguments that rights are safeguarded by the flexibility in the common law, by judicial enforcement of the rule of law and by a sovereign parliament.[13] The common law was thought to provide considerable freedom because it treats rights in residual terms, as the ability of citizens to do as they wish unless law expressly prohibits the activity in question. Dicey's definition of the rule of law assumed that the decisions and discretion of government officials must be consistent with the law, and thus governments and public officials are as constrained by the law as are all other subjects, law is made known by accepted procedures and law is binding only if these procedures are followed. In other words, parliament can exercise its sovereign power

'Blair to Curb Human Rights in War on Terror', *The Telegraph*, 6 August 2005, www.telegraph.co.uk/news/uknews/1495605/Blair-to-curb-human-rights-in-war-on-terror.html

[11] 'Cameron Calls for Repeal of Human Rights Act', *The Guardian*, 12 May 2006, www.guardian.co.uk/politics/2006/may/12/immigrationpolicy.immigration; M. Tempest, 'Howard Warns Against "Judicial Activism"', *The Guardian*, 10 August 2005, www.guardian.co.uk/politics/2005/aug/10/uksecurity.terrorism

[12] For two compelling interpretations of this idea of political constitutionalism, see A. Tomkins, *Our Republican Constitution* (Oxford: Hart Publishing, 2005); R. Bellamy, *Political Constitutionalism: A Republican Defence of the Constitutionality of Democracy* (Cambridge: Cambridge University Press, 2007).

[13] I. Leigh and R. Masterman, *Making Rights Real: The Human Rights Act in its First Decade* (Oxford: Hart Publishing, 2008), p. 9.

only through law.[14] Parliament was also expected to safeguard liberties by holding government to account for illiberal or unwarranted intrusions into rights.[15] If citizens were dissatisfied with how parliament performed, this assessment could be conveyed during general elections by electing different parliamentarians (and through this process choosing an alternative government). Thus, the legitimacy of British legislation rested on the general right to participate in the political deliberations associated with representative government.

Historically, British constitutional principles did not conceive of rights as dependent upon judicial interpretations of a legal statement of norms, but instead emphasized what Jeremy Waldron characterizes as the 'right of rights',[16] where 'large numbers of rights-bearers act together to control and govern their common affairs'.[17] Stated differently, this political conception of British constitutionalism did not construe constraints on political decisions in the legal and external language of constitutional rights because politics and the constitution were not considered separate but were, in the words of Keith Ewing, two sides of the same coin.[18] Conor Gearty describes how rights relate to this concept of the political constitution:

> In the traditional model, parliamentary sovereignty functioned as a kind of empty vessel into which the (temporary) victors in the endless political fray could pour their ever-contingent versions of right and wrong. Even the process of determining who won the electoral game could be changed, but then changed back again if subsequent elected representatives had the chance and the desire.[19]

Confidence in the Westminster model to protect rights resulted in a lack of interest in a bill of rights. As one long-time proponent of a bill of rights observed, 'even a perceptive and critical student of government

[14] A.V. Dicey, *An Introduction to the Study of the Law of the Constitution*, 10th edition (London: Macmillan, 1960), pp. 55–7. For a persuasive interpretation of his work for Westminster parliamentary systems, see J. Ajzenstat, 'Reconciling Parliament and Rights: A.V. Dicey Reads the Canadian Charter of Rights', (1997) 30 *Canadian Journal of Political Science* 645, p. 653.

[15] A.W. Bradley and K.D. Ewing, *Constitutional and Administrative Law*, 13th edition (New York: Pearson Education Limited, 2003), pp. 404–5.

[16] J. Waldron, *Law and Disagreement* (Oxford: Clarendon Press, 1999), p. 282. See generally chs. 10–11.

[17] Ibid., p. 233 (note omitted).

[18] K.D. Ewing, 'The Politics of the British Constitution', (2000) *Public Law* 436.

[19] C. Gearty, *Principles of Human Rights Adjudication* (Oxford: Oxford University Press, 2004), p. 23.

and law could be forgiven [as recently as the 1960s] for giving our constitution . . . a clean bill of health'.[20]

Yet for many, confidence in protecting rights through the combined effects of the common law and parliamentary sovereignty began to erode in the face of a perceptible and increasing gap between theories of parliamentary power and a substantial decline in parliamentary power. Many lament the decline of parliament not only for the erosion of good governance[21] but also for its inability to protect rights in the way envisaged by Dicey in his classic defence of the Westminster-based principle of parliamentary sovereignty.[22] As Bradley and Ewing argue, Dicey was writing about the virtues of parliament in the late nineteenth century, a period considered the 'high-water mark' of parliamentary power, where an independent parliament could scrutinize government effectively and where parliament 'operated as an intermediary between the electorate and the executive'. Yet, as they argue, the 'inexorable growth of the party system and its attendant discipline' has undermined parliament's power and influence, while the executive has 'increasingly gain[ed] control of the House of Commons'.[23]

Concerns about parliament's inability to control the executive spawned new interest in constitutional reforms, including a bill of rights.[24] Some highlight initial attention to a bill of rights occurring as a result of 'blatantly racist' immigration policies in the 1960s.[25]

[20] Anthony Lester, as referred to by K. Harrison and T. Boyd, *The Changing Constitution* (Edinburgh: Edinburgh University Press, 2006), p. 84.

[21] See e.g. C. Foster, *British Government in Crisis* (Portland: Hart Publishing, 2005).

[22] Dicey, *An Introduction*.

[23] Bradley and Ewing, *Constitutional and Administrative Law*, p. 405.

[24] A. Lester, *Democracy and Individual Rights* (London: Fabian Society, 1968); J. Macdonald, *Bill of Rights* (London: Liberal Publications Department, 1969); J. Jaconelli, *Enacting a Bill of Rights: The Legal Problems* (London: Oxford University Press, 1980); C.L. Black Jr., 'Is There Already a British Bill of Rights?', (1973) 89 *Law Quarterly Review* 173; P. Wallington and J. McBride, *Civil Liberties and a Bill of Rights* (London: Cobden Trust, 1976); R. Jenkins, *Legislation on Human Rights with Particular Reference to the European Convention on Human Rights* (June 1976), Home Office, as referred to by Lester and Pannick (eds.), *Human Rights Law and Practice*, 2nd edition (London: LexisNexis, 2004), pp. 11–12, note 3; M. Zander, *A Bill of Rights* (London: Barry Rose Publishers, 1975), as referred to by M. Lippman, 'The Debate Over a Bill of Rights in Great Britain: The View from Parliament', (1980) 2 *Universal Human Rights* 25, at 27, note 7.

[25] See for example, M. Zander, *A Bill of Rights*, 3rd edition (London: Sweet & Maxwell, 1985), pp. 1–2; A. Lester, 'Democracy and Individual Rights', (1968) *Fabian Tract* no 390, p. 4.

The ease with which the Wilson government was able to pass the 1967 Commonwealth Immigrants Act that denied Asian–British subjects their citizenship precisely when they needed it,[26] and the inability of these vulnerable minorities to have their rights enforced in the domestic courts, are said to have contributed to a consciousness (albeit slumbering) about the need for a different and more explicit approach to protect rights.[27]

However, more than a quarter of a century would pass before a bill of rights attained sufficient parliamentary support.[28] Initially, only the Liberal party (which later become the Liberal Democrats) supported a bill of rights; it included a bill of rights in its political manifesto as early as the 1970 election.[29] The Labour or Conservative parties both opposed a bill of rights, despite each having small numbers of members who supported this reform (Labour members Roy Jenkins and Shirley Williams and Conservative members Sir Keith Joseph, Sir Michael Havers, Leon Brittan and Lord Hailsham).[30] In the two decades before the HRA's introduction, legislation was introduced in the House of Lords on more than ten occasions to either incorporate the European Convention of Human Rights into domestic law or construct a domestic bill of rights.[31] However, each proposal was poorly received in the House of Commons.[32] Proposals for a bill of rights originating in the House of Commons fared no better. Conservative MP Edward Gardner introduced a private member's bill to incorporate the ECHR into British law in 1987 without success[33] while Liberal Democrat MP Robert Maclennan attempted to generate debate about a bill of rights

[26] For more about the Act see D. Steel, *No Entry: The Background and Implications of the Commonwealth Immigrants Act 1968* (London: C. Hurst & Co., 1969), as referred to by F. Klug, *Values for a Godless Age: The Story of the United Kingdom's New Bill of Rights* (London: Penguin Books, 2000), p. 259, ch 6, note 2.

[27] Klug, *Values for a Godless Age*, p. 153.

[28] For discussion of parliamentary debates in the late 1960s and 1970s on the idea of a bill of rights, see Lippman, 'The Debate Over a Bill of Rights', 25.

[29] D. Erdos, 'Ideology, Power Orientation and Policy Drag: Explaining the Elite Politics of Britain's Bill of Rights Debate', (2009) 44 *Government and Opposition* 20, pp. 21–2.

[30] F. Klug, 'A Bill of Rights: What For?', in C. Bryant (ed.), *Towards a New Constitutional Settlement* (London: Smith Institute, 2007), p. 32, www2.lse.ac.uk/humanRights/articlesAndTranscripts/FK_SmithInstitute_07.pdf

[31] A. Reidy, 'The House of Lords in Defence of Human Rights?', UCL Constitution Unit, October 1999, pp. 5–7, www.ucl.ac.uk/constitution-unit/publications

[32] Ibid.

[33] Parliament of the United Kingdom, *Hansard*, HC, vol 109, c. 1224 6 February 1987 (Edward Gardner).

in 1989.[34] Anthony Lester introduced proposals in 1994 and 1997, both of which failed to pass. Lester's first proposal to incorporate the ECHR into domestic law would have given courts remedial powers to set aside inconsistent legislation, and had a rough ride in parliament.[35] His second bill did not fare any better, despite preserving parliament's legal authority for legislation.[36]

Conservative opposition to a bill of rights emphasized the importance of retaining parliamentary sovereignty while also positing that rights were already adequately safeguarded by British constitutional principles.[37] The Labour party opposed a bill of rights on ideological and democratic grounds, reflecting the view that it is undemocratic to allow judges to invalidate the wishes of the people. Labour was also sceptical about trusting to courts decisions regarding whether legislation respects rights, and considered that the judicial record on civil liberties did not support a bill of rights that is subject to judicial review.[38] Conservative party dominance in four successive general elections (1979, 1983, 1987, 1992) ensured a bill of rights would not be introduced in this period, despite a soon-forgotten 1979 election manifesto[39] that included a commitment to an all-party discussion of a bill of rights.[40]

The Conservative government's opposition to a bill of rights did not dissuade prominent non-parliamentary groups from advocating a bill of rights. Such groups included Charter 88 (a group formed to demand constitutional reform), Liberty (formerly known as the National Council for Civil Liberties), the Institute of Public Policy Research (a think-tank with close connections to the Labour party), the Scottish Council for Civil Liberties and the Committee for the Administration of Justice in Northern Ireland.[41] Incorporation of the ECHR into domestic law

[34] Parliament of the United Kingdom, *Hansard*, HC, vol 155, cols. 76–117, 19 June 1989 (Robert Maclennan).

[35] Lester says of the bill that it had a 'turbulent passage through the Lords' and was 'mutilated by wrecking amendments supported by Conservative ministers': Lester and Pannick, *Human Rights Law and Practice*, p. 13.

[36] Ibid., p. 13.

[37] F. Klug, 'A Bill of Rights: What For?'

[38] A. Lester et al., *A British Bill of Rights*, 2nd edition (London: Institute of Public Policy Research, 1996), p. vi.

[39] F. Klug, 'A Bill of Rights: Do We Need One or Do We Already Have One?' (2007) *Public Law* 701.

[40] Conservative general election manifesto, 1979, www.margaretthatcher.org/document/110858

[41] F. Klug, *Values for a Godless Age*, p. 158.

was also supported publicly by two former Lord Chancellors (Lord Gardiner and Lord Hailsham), the Lord Chief Justice (Lord Taylor), the Master of the Rolls (Sir Thomas Bingham), several Law Lords, the Bar Council, the Law Society and two former Home Secretaries (Lord Jenkins and Sir Leon Brittan).[42]

Fuelling this growing interest in a bill of rights was the governance style and policies of the Thatcher government, which scholars have criticized for displaying an 'imperious attitude towards democratic checks and balances'[43] and treating democracy as little more than a 'periodic plebiscite to decide who should rule rather than address how they should rule'.[44] Ewing and Gearty argue that the Thatcher period revealed traditional political checks on executive power were inadequate because of the government's willingness to exploit the full scope for 'untrammelled power latent in the British constitution but obscured by the hesitancy and scruples of previous consensus-based political leaders'.[45] Francesca Klug characterizes confidence in parliament's ability to check the executive as having reached an all-time low in 1987:

> The turning point was the 1987 general election. The failure of the political system to brook virtually any challenge to a Conservative government which, on the basis of three elections on a minority vote, could bring in almost any measures it wished, was hitting home. The reputation of Parliament as a bulwark against the executive was pretty much in tatters. It became obvious that the government of the day could control Parliament through the party whip and the tantalizing carrot of promotion to ministerial office.[46]

Support for a bill of rights was also fuelled by growing concern about 'the impotency of the common law in the face of the sovereign Parliament',[47] notwithstanding judicial willingness to recognize 'fundamental common law rights' and to expound a stronger statement of

[42] Lester and Pannick, *Human Rights Law and Practice*, p. 12.

[43] Erdos, 'Ideology, Power Orientation and Policy Drag', p. 33.

[44] P. Hirst, *After Thatcher* (London: Collins, 1989), p. 45, emphasis in original.

[45] K.D. Ewing and C.A. Gearty, *Freedom under Thatcher: Civil Liberties in Modern Britain* (Clarendon Press: Oxford, 1990), p. 7.

[46] Klug, *Values for a Godless Age*, p. 158, notes omitted.

[47] J. Laws, 'Is the High Court the Guardian of Fundamental Constitutional rights?', (1993) *Public Law* 50; T. Bingham, 'The European Convention on Human Rights: Time to Incorporate', (1993) 109 *Law Quarterly Review* 390; Lord Woolf, 'Droit Public – English Style', (1994) *Public Law* 57; S. Sedley, 'Human Rights: A Twenty-First Century Agenda', (1995) *Public Law* 385; all as referred to by Leigh and Masterman, *Making Rights Real*, p. 10, n. 46.

positive rights, in comparison to the largely residual way in which liberty had previously been construed.[48]

In the early 1990s some senior members of the Labour party began to reassess their historic opposition to a bill of rights. Neil Kinnock's Labour party manifesto committed the party to a democratically enforceable bill of rights.[49] However, Labour's defeat in the 1992 election, its fourth in a row, meant a lack of substantial parliamentary support for a bill of rights, as the Conservative majority government remained highly critical of this kind of reform. In 1993, new opposition leader John Smith committed his party to incorporating the European Convention into domestic law, as part of a larger reform package intended to 'restore democracy to our people'. Smith considered that incorporation represented the 'quickest and simplest' way to introduce human rights into British law.[50] Tony Blair, then shadow Home Secretary, set aside his earlier objection to a bill of rights and worked on policy options that would give effect to incorporation.[51] Labour continued to pursue the idea of incorporating the ECHR into domestic law after Smith's unexpected death in 1994. Shadow ministers Jack Straw and Paul Boateng published a consultation paper, *Bringing Rights Home*, in 1997, setting out Labour's proposals for incorporation.[52] The proposal to incorporate the European Convention of Human Rights into domestic law was part of a larger constitutional reform agenda that proposed to 'modernise British politics' and to 'increase individual rights', to 'decentralise power' and to 'open up government and ... reform Parliament'.[53]

David Erdos explains Labour's new-found support for a bill of rights as an example of 'power orientation', whereby an opposition party becomes more supportive of the idea of constraining executive power via the transfer of greater responsibilities to the judiciary after having been shut

[48] Leigh and Masterman, *Making Rights Real*, pp. 10–12.

[49] Labour Party manifesto, 1992, 'It's Time to Get Britain Working Again', www.politicsresources.net/area/uk/man/lab92.htm1992

[50] Klug, 'A Bill of Rights: What For?'

[51] Klug, *Values for a Godless Age*, p. 160, referring to debates about unpublished papers of the Policy Commission on Constitutional Reform, 17 February 1993.

[52] J. Straw and P. Boateng, 'Bringing Rights Home: Labour's plans to Incorporate the European Convention on Human Rights into UK Law', (1997) *European Human Rights Law Review* 71.

[53] Home Office, *Rights Brought Home: The Human Bill of Rights*, Cm. 3782 (1997), preface by the Prime Minister.

out of power for a considerable duration (in contrast to the party in power, which is more likely to oppose constraints that will affect its exercise of power). His theory also helps explain why a party that supported a bill of rights while in opposition is less enamoured with it when its opposition status changes and it forms the government.[54]

The Labour party included a commitment to incorporate the ECHR into UK law in its 1997 election manifesto. Once it had been elected, debate intensified about what form incorporation should take. Along with Labour party members, this debate included a small group of academics, lawyers and NGOs who were also sympathetic to the idea.[55] A few months later, the government published a White Paper, *Rights Brought Home: The Human Rights Bill*, which made the case for incorporation of the ECHR into domestic law.[56]

As the name of the consultation paper suggests, proponents of incorporation argued that incorporating Convention rights into domestic law would 'bring rights home' and respond to the problem of 'justice being exported', with citizens required to pursue their claims in Strasbourg.[57] They also argued that incorporation, along with other constitutional reform projects such as devolution, would 'strengthen representative and democratic government ... by enabling citizens to challenge more easily actions of the state if they fail to match the standards of the European Convention'.[58]

The decision to incorporate the ECHR into domestic law mitigated the impetus for broader philosophical and political debates about the content of the HRA. Although some disputed the idea that Convention rights provided a sufficient foundation for a contemporary bill of rights,[59]

54 Erdos, 'Ideology, Power Orientation and Policy Drag', 40.

55 F. Klug, 'The United Kingdom Experience', www.lse.ac.uk/humanRights/articlesAndTranscripts/The_UK_Experience.pdf at para 3.

56 Home Office, *Rights Brought Home*.

57 Straw and Boateng, 'Bringing Rights Home', 74–5.

58 Parliament of the United Kingdom, *Hansard*, HC, vol 306, col 769, 16 February 1998 (Jack Straw).

59 Some critics believe the decision to incorporate the European Convention of Human Rights into domestic law, instead of develop a homegrown bill of rights results in incomplete protection for rights, due to the omission of social and economic rights. See for example K.D. Ewing, 'The Case for Social Rights', in T. Campbell, J. Goldsworthy and A. Stone (eds.), *Protecting Human Rights: Instruments and Institutions* (Oxford: Oxford University Press, 2003), p. 323; K. D. Ewing, 'The Unbalanced Constitution', in T. Campbell, K.D. Ewing and A. Tomkins (eds.), *Sceptical Essays on Human Rights* (Oxford: Oxford University Press, 2001, p. 103.

others were either content with this decision because they interpreted the ECHR as already representing the UK's bill of rights,[60] broached incorporation as a pragmatic way to deal with what could be a more explosive issue and/or interpreted it as a first step toward developing a home-grown or British bill of rights.[61]

Although the decision to incorporate Convention rights into domestic law resolved much of the debate about the content of which rights to codify, the question of whether and how codified rights should alter judicial and political responsibilities remained a serious political issue. Labour's support for incorporation did not mean it was prepared to repudiate the idea that parliament should retain final authority for the legality of duly enacted legislation. In its White Paper, the government described its intent to withhold a remedial judicial power to invalidate inconsistent legislation as both respectful of democratic principles and necessary to preserve the principle of parliamentary sovereignty:

> The Government has reached the conclusion that courts should not have the power to set aside primary legislation, past or future, on the ground of incompatibility with the Convention. This conclusion arises from the importance which the Government attaches to Parliamentary sovereignty. In this context, Parliamentary sovereignty means that Parliament is competent to make any law on any matter of its choosing and no court may question the validity of any Act that it passes. In enacting legislation, Parliament is making decisions about important matters of public policy. The authority to make those decisions derives from a democratic mandate. Members of Parliament in the House of Commons possess such a mandate because they are elected, accountable and representative. To make provision in the Bill for the courts to set aside Acts of Parliament would confer on the judiciary a general power over the decisions of Parliament which under our present constitutional arrangements they do not possess, and would be likely on occasions to draw the judiciary into serious conflict with Parliament. There is no evidence to suggest that

[60] Lord Steyn, a senior law lord, characterized the ECHR as representing 'our Bill of Rights': Bradley and Ewing, *Constitutional and Administrative Law*, p. 422.

[61] Lester clearly equated incorporation with the first step in developing a bill of rights: Lord Lester, 'First Steps Towards a Constitutional Bill of Rights', (1997) 2 *European Human Rights Law Review* 124. Another prominent commentator, John Wadham (then director of Liberty), argued that incorporation was a necessary and essential first step in protecting rights, but on its own was not enough. What the UK needed, he argued, was a domestic bill of rights. J. Wadham, 'Why Incorporation of the European Convention on Human Rights is Not Enough', in R. Gordon and R. Wilmot-Smith (eds.), *Human Rights in the United Kingdom* (Oxford: Oxford University Press, 1996), p. 25.

> they desire this power, nor that the public wish them to have it. Certainly, this Government has no mandate for any such change.[62]

Thus, the serious challenge to overcome was the potential impact of judicial review for the principle of parliamentary sovereignty.[63] As Klug observes, political leaders lacked a popular mandate to expand the scope of judicial review: this view was influenced by the belief that the judiciary's 'narrow class, race, and gender composition has historically made them appear unlikely champions of the rights of dispossessed individuals or oppressed minorities. It seemed to most observers that the obvious benefits of a statement of fundamental rights in practice brought power to judges rather than power to the people'.[64]

In wrestling with the issue of how to conceive of judicial power and also preserve the principle of parliamentary sovereignty, Labour leaders and other supporters of human rights legislation took advantage of the opportunity to reflect on the recent decisions to adopt a bill of rights taken by two other countries with a shared heritage of Westminster-based parliamentary government. Canada and New Zealand had earlier addressed what had previously been considered an insurmountable obstacle: the question of how to introduce a judicially reviewable bill of rights within a parliamentary system that emphasizes parliament has final legal authority for the validity of duly enacted legislation (as altered in Canada by federalism, which gave rise to judicial review to resolve division of power conflicts). Although political framers of these bills of rights addressed this conundrum in different ways, both countries drew a greater distinction between judicial review and judicial remedies than exists for more conventional bills of rights.[65]

In 1960 Canada adopted a statutory bill of rights. However, ambiguity about the nature of the judicial role,[66] and the meek Canadian judicial

[62] Home Office, *Rights Brought Home*, 2.13.

[63] Klug, *Values for a Godless Age*, pp. 160–1.

[64] Klug, 'The United Kingdom Experience'.

[65] For discussion of this alternative form, see S. Gardbaum, 'The New Commonwealth Model of Constitutionalism', (2001) 49 *American Journal of Comparative Law* 707; M. Tushnet, 'New Forms of Judicial Review and the Persistence of Rights – and Democracy – Based Worries', (2008) 38 *Wake Forest Law Review* 813; M.J. Perry, 'Protecting Human Rights in a Democracy: What Role for the Courts?', (2003) 38 *Wake Forest Law Review* 635; J. Hiebert, 'Parliamentary Bills of Rights: An Alternative Model?', (2006) 69 *Modern Law Review* 7; J. Hiebert, 'New Constitutional Ideas: Can New Parliamentary Models Resist Judicial Dominance when Interpreting Rights?' (2004) 82 *Texas Law Review* 1963.

[66] Courts were instructed that unless it is expressly declared that legislation will act notwithstanding the Canadian Bill of Rights, every law of Canada should be 'construed and

approach that evolved, rendered the Canadian Bill of Rights an unlikely target for emulation. The 1982 Canadian Charter of Rights and Freedoms was far more explicit about the nature and scope of judicial remedial power. Both the Charter and the Supreme Court jurisprudence that evolved under this constitutional bill of rights are far better known internationally, and had a more substantial impact on political thought about whether it would be possible for a Westminster-based parliamentary system to adopt a bill of rights without repudiating parliament's legal authority for legislation. The Charter authorizes strong judicial remedial powers that allow for the invalidation of inconsistent legislation and yet tempers the force of these by including a power referred to as the 'notwithstanding clause', which allows legislatures to either pre-empt judicial review altogether or to set aside the effects of an adverse judicial ruling for most sections of the Charter, on a temporary but renewable basis. Yet ultimately the Charter had a negative influence on how the relationship between judicial and political power was conceived in the UK. Although the notwithstanding clause represents the idea of constrained judicial remedies, at least in the short term, UK supporters of incorporation had serious concerns about emulating how the Charter envisages the resolution of political disagreements with judicial rulings. In Canada, political actors are reluctant to invoke the notwithstanding clause because of the broad public disdain generated by its use. In the UK, the worry was that if parliament's capacity to disagree with courts relies on enacting an override power, apprehension of similar criticism would dissuade politicians from using it and, as a result, court rulings would effectively displace parliament's judgement in cases of disagreement. This would diminish the practical and political significance of a constitutional design intended to preserve parliament's final authority over legislation. Although a 1993 Labour policy contemplated use of a notwithstanding mechanism based on Canada's notwithstanding power,[67] this proposal was subsequently dropped as discussion about a bill of rights evolved. However, if UK proponents of reform considered the Canadian conception of judicial power under the Charter of Rights as being too strong, the New Zealand model was likely interpreted as having the opposite problem of being too weak.

Although Labour supporters approved of the idea of distinguishing between judicial review and strong judicial remedial powers, they

applied as not to abrogate, abridge or infringe or to authorize the abrogation, abridgment or infringement' of protected rights. Canadian Bill of Rights, S.C. 1960, c. 44, s. 2.

67 Wadham, 'Bringing Rights Half-way Home', (1997) 2 *EHRLR* 141–2.

rejected the specific approaches to this idea taken by Canada and New Zealand and, in so doing, developed a new variation on the relationship between judicial review and judicial remedies (which has subsequently influenced how the parliamentary/judicial relationship is conceived in the statutory bills of rights adopted by the Australian jurisdictions of Australian Capital Territory and Victoria).[68]

Labour supporters of the HRA struck a position that is both more constrained than in Canada and yet more authoritative than in New Zealand. The HRA authorizes the judiciary to interpret legislation 'so far as possible so as to be compatible with Convention rights' but where primary legislation does not permit this, the HRA empowers a superior court to make a 'declaration of incompatibility'. This declaration does not change the status of legislation, which remains in place unless or until parliament amends the law. However, as will be discussed presently, the framers fully expected that a declaration of incompatibility would put pressure on parliament to consider remedial measures.

The proposed Human Rights Act was subject to extensive parliamentary debate,[69] and drew strong criticism from the Conservative front bench and from some media outlets.[70] The HRA was enacted on 9 November 1998 and came into effect on 2 October 2000.

2. Legislative rights review

Although the decision to incorporate the European Convention of Human Rights reduced the significance of framers' intentions with respect to the particular content of the HRA, Labour supporters nevertheless had a distinct vision of how the HRA would operate. They conceived the HRA as embodying a less court-centred approach for protecting rights than is normally associated with a bill of rights, and anticipated that public and political officials would engage in proactive

[68] For more discussion on the significance of this example of constitutional borrowing, see Gardbaum, *The New Commonwealth Model of Constitutionalism*, pp. 204–10.

[69] For a range of the parliamentary debates see J. Cooper and A. Marshall-Williams (eds.), *Legislating for Human Rights: The Parliamentary Debates on the Human Rights Bill* (Oxford: Hart Publishing, 2000).

[70] For a discussion of the media reaction, see F. Klug, 'Target of the Tabloids', *The Guardian*, 14 July 2000..

rights-based assessments of whether legislation is compatible with Convention rights,[71] a practice we refer to as legislative rights review.

The two institutional changes associated with promoting legislative rights review were a new requirement that ministers apprise parliament whether bills are compatible with Convention rights and the creation of a specialized parliamentary rights committee (the JCHR). Although the JCHR was not specifically mandated by the HRA, it was discussed in conjunction with proposals to adopt HRA and was conceived, politically, as a way to improve parliamentary rights-based scrutiny of legislative bills.[72] The political architects of the HRA argued that these two institutional changes would help 'weave acceptance and understanding of the ECHR into the democratic process', rather than 'isolat[ing] it as the preserve of judges, remote from the general public.'[73]

In defending this bold claim about how the HRA would affect parliamentary decision-making, Jack Straw insisted that this proactive emphasis on rights consistency was not 'mere jargon' or 'empty words' because the HRA would change habits of mind, intellectual reflexes and professional sensibilities of public and political authorities. As he proclaimed, Convention principles were not incorporated as 'playthings for the lawyers'; instead, Convention principles and norms would be 'all-pervasive' because 'Ministers and all public authorities will need to be ready to show that they have had them constantly in mind in making decisions affecting people's civil and political rights'.[74] Moreover, the requirement to make a report to parliament was expected not only to influence the scrutiny of draft legislation within government but also to 'greatly assist Parliament's consideration of Bills by highlighting the potential implications for human rights'.[75] Blair similarly echoed the idea that the HRA would facilitate proactive rights engagement, stating that the HRA 'requires all of us in public service to respect human

[71] Home Office, *Rights Brought Home*, 3.4; J. Straw, 'Building a Human Rights Culture', address to Civil Service College Seminar (19 December 1999), www.nationalarchives.gov.uk/ERORecords/HO/415/1/hract/cscspe.htm.

[72] Home Office, *Rights Brought Home*, 3.6–3.7); Straw and Boateng, 'Bringing Rights Home', 79.

[73] F. Klug, submission to the JCHR, Twenty-Second Report, Session 2001–2002, HC 160/HL 1142, appendix 18, para 5.

[74] Straw, 'Building a Human Rights Culture'.

[75] Parliament of the United Kingdom, *Hansard*, HC, vol 306, col 780, 16 February 1998 (Jack Straw).

rights in everything we do'.[76] As one commentator notes, 'the sales pitch accompanying the Human Rights Act 1998 was impressive: from the Labour party's briefing paper in 1996 to the Lord Chancellor's flourishes during its second reading we were told that it would "nurture a culture of understanding of rights and responsibilities at all levels in our society" and result in a human rights culture developing across the country'.[77]

2.1 *Ministerial reports on compatibility*

The first of the institutional changes intended to facilitate proactive rights engagement is the new statutory reporting responsibility,[78] in which the minister introducing a bill must indicate one of two things: that he or she is of the view that the proposed legislation is compatible with Convention rights (section 19(1)(a)) or that no such statement of compatibility can be made but the government nevertheless wishes the House to proceed with the bill (section 19(1)(b)).

As discussed earlier, this idea of ensuring greater parliament attention to how legislative bills implicate rights is an example of constitutional borrowing. The idea was first developed in Canada in the 1960 Bill of Rights and was later adapted for the New Zealand Bill of Rights Act. When first introduced, expectations were that this reporting requirement would improve political awareness about how legislative initiatives implicate rights and compel cabinet, and eventually parliament, to deliberate carefully about the merits of potentially rights-offending actions.[79] A senior Canadian Department of Justice official once proclaimed

[76] Home Office, *Conventional Behaviour, Questions about the HRA, and Introduction for Public Authorities* (1999) as referred to by F. Klug, 'The Long Road to Human Rights Compliance', (2006) 57 *Northern Ireland Legal Quarterly* 189.

[77] L. Clements, 'Winners and Losers', (2005) 32 *Journal of Law and Society* 35 (notes omitted).

[78] The HRA encompasses only government bills. However, during second reading debate, ministers are expected to express the government's view on whether private members' bills are compatible with Convention rights. David Feldman suggests that the expectation that a minister will express his or her view about the promoters' statement of compatibility is sufficiently strong as to amount to a constitutional convention. D. Feldman, 'Institutional Roles and Meanings of "Compatibility"', in H. Fenwick, G. Phillipson and R. Masterman (eds.), *Judicial Reasoning Under the UK Human Rights Act* (Cambridge: Cambridge University Press, 2007), p. 99.

[79] See J. Hiebert, 'Parliamentary Bills of Rights: An Alternative Model?', (2006) 69 *Modern Law Review* 7; J. Hiebert, 'Interpreting a Bill of Rights: The Importance of Legislative Rights Review', (2005) 35 *British Journal of Political Science* 235; J. Hiebert, 'New

proudly that the 'whole machinery of government' would now be enlisted in the project of safeguarding rights, and that because of this, the Canadian Bill of Rights represented the world's most 'comprehensive, powerful and effective' rights instrument.[80] Notwithstanding such unbridled optimism, the intention of creating more robust Canadian parliamentary scrutiny has never been realized.[81] Although a reporting obligation on compatibility also exists for the Charter of Rights, no reports of incompatibility with the Charter have ever been made to the Canadian parliament. Thus, it would be surprising if British framers were interested in emulating Canadian practices associated with this concept – if they were even aware that a reporting obligation on Charter inconsistency exists in Canada.

Supporters of the HRA more likely looked to the similar statutory reporting obligation in New Zealand, whose framers consciously borrowed from Canada when adopting this requirement. As previously discussed, New Zealand Attorneys-General have not shied away from reporting that government bills implicate rights adversely, and affirmations of an inability to claim compatibility have not presented serious obstacles for government achieving its legislative objectives. Whether or not consciously motivated by perceived shortcomings in how this ministerial reporting obligation has evolved in Canada and New Zealand, the framers of the HRA made four significant changes to how this practice would function in the UK. First, instead of only reporting where bills are inconsistent with rights, ministers are required to report on all bills by either affirming that the bill is compatible with Convention rights or acknowledging an inability to claim compatibility. Second, the reporting requirement was modified from the New Zealand practice to reflect the bicameral nature of the UK parliament.[82] When a bill passes from one house to the other a

Constitutional Ideas: Can New Parliamentary Models Resist Judicial Dominance when Interpreting Rights?', (2004) 82 *Texas Law Review* 1963.

80 E.A. Driedger, 'The Meaning and Effect of the Canadian *Bill of Rights*: A Draftsman's Viewpoint', (1977) 9 *Ottawa Law Review* 316.

81 J. Hiebert, *Charter Conflicts: What is Parliament's Role?* (Montreal: McGill-Queen's University Press, 2002); J. Hiebert, 'Parliamentary Engagement with the Charter: Rethinking the Idea of Legislative Rights Review', (2012) 58 *Supreme Court Law Review* 87; J. Kelly, *Governing with the Charter: Legislative and Judicial Activism and Framers' Intent* (Vancouver: UBC Press, 2005).

82 Although Canada's parliament is bicameral, the report on compatibility is only made to the House of Commons.

second statement is required, which must take into account earlier amendments made. Third, unlike the centralizing responsibility for reports held by the Minister of Justice (Canada) or Attorney General (New Zealand), the HRA imposes this reporting obligation on any minister responsible for a bill. This decentralized approach was considered a beneficial way to ensure that a rights culture is broadly dispersed and that questions of compatibility are not considered the exclusive domain of one department.[83] Finally, the drafters signalled their intention to create a specialized parliamentary committee, the JCHR, with a broad mandate to examine the rights dimension of legislative bills and thus enhance parliament's capacity to assess these ministerial reports on compatibility.

The idea of striking a parliamentary human rights scrutiny committee was earlier proposed by Liberty, previously known as the National Council for Civil Liberties (NCCL).[84] In its White Paper, *Rights Brought Home. The Human Rights Bill*, the government suggested that although parliament should determine how best to scrutinize government actions under the HRA, it considered the 'best course would be to establish a new Parliamentary Committee with functions relating to human rights'. The White Paper was not specific about the mandate or structure of the committee, but suggested three possibilities: a joint committee of both houses of parliament; a separate committee in each house; or a committee that meets jointly for some purposes and separately for others. With respect to the new committee(s)'s mandate, the White Paper suggested it 'might conduct enquiries on a range of human rights issues relating to the Convention' and that the new committee(s) could produce reports 'so as to assist the Government and Parliament in deciding what action to take'. Finally, the White Paper suggested the committee (s) might also 'examine issues relating to the other international obligations of the UK' including 'proposals to accept new rights under other human rights treaties'.[85] The government announced its intention to create the JCHR in December 1998,[86] but it was two years before the JCHR was actually established and held its first meeting (on 31 January 2001).

[83] Interviews. [84] Klug, 'The United Kingdom Experience', at para 3.

[85] Home Office, *Rights Brought Home*, 3.6–3.7.

[86] The Rt Hon Margaret Beckett MP, Leader of the House of Commons, indicated that both houses would be asked to appoint a Joint Committee on Human Rights. *Hansard*, HC, vol 332, col 604, 14 December 1998.

2.2 *Different conceptions of parliamentary scrutiny*

Despite sweeping claims that the HRA will facilitate 'a culture of rights and responsibilities in the UK',[87] little was said about how government or parliament should broach the task of reporting or reviewing legislation from the perspective of whether it is compatible with Convention rights. As previously discussed, we can imagine three different ways in which government and parliament could interpret this task. One approach would engage parliamentarians in normative debates about the scope of rights and the justification for decisions that implicate these in a restrictive manner. As Stephen Gardbaum characterizes this approach, these judgements would involve 'political and moral deliberation and not only or primarily legal reasoning', which he says should bring a 'freer perspective of principle to the issue than is typical of judicial reasoning'.[88] Danny Nicol suggests a non-legally driven approach could lead to a culture of controversy and contestation, in which parliamentarians deliberate the merits of a bill without necessarily framing the debate to reflect legal considerations for compatibility.[89] Thus, instead of exercising deference to judicial interpretations of Convention rights, parliamentarians would 'seize control of the very power to interpret rights' when deciding on 'the prioritisation between rights'. Under this version, although the judicial role might 'prompt Parliament to dwell on the rights implications of impugned measures' parliament itself would 'ponder, deliberate, and resolve whether the Convention right was to be interpreted as permitting the measure under scrutiny'.[90]

A second approach would reflect what Nicol characterizes as a culture of compliance, where political actors act as if parliament was little more than an adjunct of the court when issues of rights arise, and thus take their cues from relevant case law.[91] This view is consistent with Alec Stone Sweet's characterization of political behaviour in several European jurisdictions, which he captures succinctly in the phrase: 'governing with judges means governing like judges.'[92]

Robert Blackburn adds another perspective that could be integrated into either or both of these first two forms of judgement: an emphasis on justifying decisions that implicate rights. As he suggests, 'human

[87] Straw, 'Building a Human Rights Culture'.
[88] Gardbaum, *The New Commonwealth Model of Constitutionalism*, p. 80.
[89] D. Nicol, 'The Human Rights Act and the Politicians', (2004) 24 *Legal Studies* 451, at 454.
[90] Ibid. [91] Ibid.
[92] A. Stone Sweet, *Governing with Judges* (Oxford: Oxford University Press, 2000), p. 204.

rights should form part of the "rules of the game" under which the system of politics and government is conducted'.[93] Murray Hunt similarly emphasizes the importance of justification, arguing that 'all exercises of powers which infringe upon fundamental rights, interests or values require public justification by reference to reasons'. For Hunt, this reference to reasons is a requirement of rational explanation of why a particular action or decision has been taken, or why no action has been taken.[94]

A third way in which government or parliament might broach the new emphasis on compatibility would be to ignore or minimize the obligation to focus, justify or defend the rights-impacting aspects of legislative bills. This possibility would demonstrate the instability that Mark Tushnet identifies as a possibility for this model, particularly if a lack of political engagement coincides with overly deferential judicial rulings that neither challenge political actors to reassess their rulings nor inspire bureaucrats and political actors to pursue and promote rights-compliant ways of achieving legislative objectives.[95]

These different possible responses have distinct implications for how compatibility considerations might influence legislative decisions. For example, a culture of legal compliance would emphasize assessing bills in terms of their consistency with relevant case law, and also anticipate future judicial rulings. Approached robustly, it could encourage government and parliament to support risk-averse legislation in an attempt to minimize the possibility of a judicial ruling that the legislation is inconsistent with Convention rights, in the event that legislation is subject to human rights litigation. In contrast, a culture of controversy

[93] R. Blackburn, 'Towards a Constitutional Bill of Rights for the United Kingdom', p. xxxii, (London: Pinter Publishers, 1999), as referred to by J. Croft, 'Whitehall and the Human Rights Act', The Constitution Unit, UCL, September 2000, www.ucl.ac.uk/spp/publications/unit-publications/61.pdf

[94] M. Hunt, 'Reshaping Constitutionalism', in J. Morrison, K. McEvoy and G. Anthony (eds.), *Judges, Transition, and Human Rights* (Oxford: Oxford University Press, 2007), p. 470.

[95] Tushnet's thesis of the instability of this model is premised on the expectation that weak court systems could mimic strong-form systems of judicial review, where courts dominate judgement about the legitimacy of legislation from a rights perspective, or, alternatively, will revert back to parliamentary supremacy, where Westminster-based governments encounter weak pressures to change or justify decisions that implicate rights adversely. M. Tushnet, *Weak Courts, Strong Rights: Judicial Review and Social Welfare Rights in Comparative Constitutional Law* (Princeton: Princeton University Press, 2008), pp. 18–42.

could prompt government and parliament to engage in independent judgement about the merits of legislation, without necessarily worrying about whether this political judgement is likely to lead to litigation and judicial censure. This approach could also encourage parliament to approve more risky legislative initiatives, and could affect parliament's decisions regarding whether remedial measures are warranted in the event of a judicial declaration of incompatibility. To the extent that either of these approaches are influenced by an emphasis on justifying decisions, this perspective would place a premium on the quality of the evidence or explanations the government offers for decisions that implicate rights adversely, and could discourage parliament from approving initiatives where persuasive arguments or evidence about justification are lacking. The third response, in which compatibility considerations are not a pressing factor in explaining or justifying legislation, would suggest politics as usual in the pre-HRA sense.

2.3 Parliamentary sovereignty

In addition to a lack of clarity about how government and parliament would interpret their respective responsibilities for legislative rights review, another reason for uncertainty about how the HRA would influence political behaviour is lingering ambiguity arising from political claims that the HRA does not fundamentally alter the principle of parliamentary sovereignty. As Aileen Kavanagh writes, it is widely believed among judicial and academic commentators that the HRA preserves parliamentary sovereignty, and does so in an ingenious fashion.[96] However, Kavanagh, among others, also argues that although the HRA preserves the doctrine of parliamentary sovereignty in formal terms, it nevertheless limits parliament's capacity in a substantive manner.[97] Similarly, Alison Young suggests that, notwithstanding constraints on judicial power that prevent courts from setting aside inconsistent legislation, the capacity to interpret rights 'so far as possible' to ensure that rights are respected is so malleable that it has little meaning.[98] Another reason for questioning the practical consequences of having

[96] A. Kavanagh, *Constitutional Review Under the UK Human Rights Act* (Cambridge: Cambridge University Press, 2009) p. 313.

[97] Ibid., p. 336.

[98] A.L. Young, 'Judicial Sovereignty and the Human Rights Act 1998', (2002) 61*Cambridge Law Journal* 53, at 64–5.

formally retained the principle of parliamentary sovereignty is that regardless of how the HRA construes judicial remedial power, the UK's treaty obligation to respect European Court of Human Rights rulings constrains parliament's political capacity to ignore negative ECtHR rulings. Moreover, some argue that parliamentary sovereignty had already been compromised because the UK's membership of the European Union means that EU law takes priority over UK laws.[99]

Ambiguity about the political significance of having formally retained the principle of parliamentary sovereignty muddies the issue of how parliament should broach legislation or respond to judicial declarations of incompatibility. Ambiguity with respect to these issues is a logical consequence of a political attempt to construct a bill of rights that emphasizes a juridical approach for interpreting liberal constitutional values and yet also relies on political willingness to enact remedies.[100] The HRA is said to have created an expectation of compliance with judicial interpretations of liberal constitutional norms.[101] Yet the political architects of the HRA also characterized the principle of parliamentary sovereignty as a key virtue of the HRA.[102]

Senior Labour proponents of the HRA did not dispute this expectation of compliance with ECtHR rulings. Thus, notwithstanding Jack Straw's insistence that parliamentary sovereignty had been preserved, he acknowledged that if the UK parliament disagreed with the ECtHR it would have little option but to comply with judicial rulings, unless it decides to withdraw from the Convention. However, he strongly qualified the likelihood of withdrawing, acknowledging that the Convention

[99] M. Elliott, 'United Kingdom: Parliamentary Sovereignty Under Pressure', (2004) 2 *International Journal of Constitutional Law* 545, at 547–8; M. Elliott, 'Parliamentary Sovereignty and the New Constitutional Order: Legislative Freedom, Political Reality and Convention', (2002) 22 *Legal Studies* 340; J.L. Black-Branch, 'Parliamentary Supremacy or Political Expediency?: The Constitution Position of the Human Rights Act Under British Law', (2002) 23 *Statute Law* 59, at 72; J. Laws, 'Law and Democracy', (1996) *Public Law* 72; W. Wade, 'Sovereignty: Revolution or Evolution?', (1996) 112 *LQ Review* 568; T. Allan, 'Parliamentary Sovereignty: Law, Politics, and Revolution', (1997) 113 *LQ Review* 443.

[100] This argument draws from earlier work by Hiebert: see 'The HRA: Ambiguity about Parliamentary Sovereignty' (2013) 14 *German Law Journal* 2254–74 and 'Legislative Rights Review: Addressing the Gap between Ideals and Constraints', in M. Hunt, H. Hooper and P. Yowell (eds.), *Parliament and Human Rights: Redressing the Democratic Deficit* (Hart Publishing), 2015.

[101] Interviews.

[102] Parliament of the United Kingdom, *Hansard*, HC, vol 317, col 1357, 21 October 1998 (Jack Straw).

will likely 'enjoy a high degree of permanence in UK Law' and that unilateral withdrawal by the UK was improbable.[103] However, the issue of withdrawal has not been settled. Tony Blair was reported to have considered the possibility of withdrawal in 2003 while Prime Minister, even if on a short-term basis to deport terror suspects, while the Cameron Conservative government has also floated this idea.[104]

Whatever the political reasons for emphasizing the HRA's retention of parliamentary sovereignty, political debates about the HRA lack clarification about how to reconcile the formal retention of the principle of parliamentary sovereignty with the strong expectation of compliance with the ECtHR, whether and how the concept of legislative rights review should direct this reconciliation and what criteria or processes might help distinguish reasonable from unreasonable parliamentary judgements about rights.

3. Conclusion

The HRA envisages an ambitious model of rights protection that entrusts government with responsibility to evaluate whether and how proposed legislative initiatives implicate rights, and to report to parliament when bills are consistent with Convention rights as well as when ministers cannot confirm such consistency. It also relies heavily upon parliament to hold government to account for decisions that implicate rights adversely and to engage in reasoned judgement about the justification of legislative bills from a rights perspective. In short, this concept of legislative rights review suggests a fundamentally different norm for legislative decision-making that emphasizes rights-based evaluations and justifications for bureaucratic, governmental and parliamentary decision-making.

If this ambitious idea of proactive rights-based assessments significantly alters bureaucratic, governmental and parliamentary behaviours it could well provide a more comprehensive form of rights protection than that associated with a more conventional bill of rights. All bills of rights can stimulate political debate about the meaning of a polity's public norms and values. However, more conventional bills of rights emphasize

[103] Straw and Boateng, 'Bringing Rights Home', 77.

[104] 'Can Britain Withdraw from the European Human Rights Convention?', *The Guardian*, 24 April 2013, www.guardian.co.uk/world/2013/apr/24/withdrawal-human-rights-convention-price; 'Theresa May: Tories to Consider Leaving European Convention on Human Rights', *BBC News*, 9 March 2013, www.bbc.co.uk/news/uk-politics-21726612

the institutionalization of this debate as occurring primarily at the judicial rather than legislative level, notwithstanding the effects judicial review has on political and societal characterization of rights. Public and political 'rights talk' is not the same thing as having legislative actors utilize a rights framework to consciously and critically assess the ways in which legislative initiatives are conceived or consider the rights-impacting effects of the means chosen to pursue them when debating and voting on legislative bills. Consequently, a post-legislative emphasis on judicial review (and what is essentially a reactive approach to rights protection) offers limited coverage because only a fraction of legislation will ever be litigated or subject to judicial oversight. Under this approach, unless legislative decision-makers incorporate rights-based evaluations at the time that legislation is developed and scrutinized, and insist on rights-based justifications when determining whether to amend or pass legislation, little assurance can be provided that the majority of the legislation passed will be assessed in terms of its potentially adverse implications for rights.[105]

However, regardless of the political intentions and/or rhetorical claims made about the benefits of a bill of rights, it is difficult to anticipate how a recently introduced bill of rights will alter political behaviour. It is also unrealistic to assume the mere fact that the HRA envisages proactive rights-based review will ensure that a government willingly accepts constraints that could prevent it from pursuing legislative initiatives which it deems not only important but also profitable in a political or electoral sense. Independent of qualitative research about how the HRA has influenced the ways in which government evaluates, revises and approves its legislative initiatives, and how parliament scrutinizes and votes on these, it would be a serious mistake to make an uncritical and unjustified pronouncement on the importance or significance of legislative rights review such as that opined after this concept was introduced in Canada.[106] The mere fact that ministers have a reporting obligation will not necessarily change the dynamics of a Westminster-based parliamentary system's functioning.

As discussed earlier, the HRA is a parliamentary bill of rights, and thus how and to what extent it shapes or constrains governmental and

[105] J. Hiebert, 'Constitutional Experimentation: Rethinking how a Bill of Rights Functions', in T. Ginsburg and R. Dixon (eds.), *Comparative Constitutional Law* (Cheltenham, UK; Northampton, MA: Edward Elgar Publishing, 2011), pp. 298–320.

[106] Driedger, 'The Meaning and Effect of the Canadian *Bill of Rights*'.

parliamentary behaviour will be influenced by the central features that characterize how the UK parliamentary system functions, which are executive dominance of parliament and the centrality of cohesive political parties in organizing and structuring how parliament functions and votes. Unless members of the governing party adopt a rights-based framework to justify rebellions against government, or opposition political leaders see value in utilizing a rights-based compatibility lens when assessing government in their perpetual role of showing why the opposition party is the better alternative to government, it is unlikely that government power will be substantially checked or that assessments of bills will focus heavily on the issue of compatibility. However, even if government and parliament are prepared to alter the norms that influence how they operate, it is a mistake to assume that disagreements about rights will centre on intent; for example, whether a government intends to restrict rights as distinct from contested political judgements about the scope of rights, the role of the state in redressing social problems, and the appropriate way of reconciling compelling policy objectives that implicate rights.

The next three chapters pursue the issue of how government and parliament engage with the HRA, and whether and how the political and institutional factors that characterize Westminster parliaments interact with and constrain this idealized notion of proactive legislative rights review.

7

Pre-legislative Compatibility Assessments under the HRA

Bills of rights are expected to elevate the attention paid to whether legislation is reasonable and justifiable when rights are implicated in an adverse manner. In more conventional bills of rights, critical analysis of whether legislative decision-makers have acted inappropriately occurs principally in the post-legislative and legal contexts of judicial review. However, the political architects of the HRA were determined to depart from conventional expectations about how a bill of rights functions. Not only did they decide against authorizing courts to determine the legal validity of duly enacted legislation, they also envisaged proactive rights-based assessments throughout the various stages of the life of a legislative bill – a concept we refer to as *legislative rights review*. As a former Lord Chancellor said of the HRA, 'we didn't bring in the Human Rights Act to get a litigation culture. We brought it in to get a human rights culture.'[1]

As discussed earlier, two institutional changes were charged with the responsibility to facilitate legislative rights review. These changes were the introduction of a new statutory reporting obligation in section 19 of the HRA, requiring ministers to report on whether bills are compatible with Convention rights, and the creation shortly after the HRA came into effect of a specialized parliamentary rights committee, the Joint Committee on Human Rights (JCHR). This reporting requirement on compatibility was expected to encourage the use of more compliant ways to achieve the legislative objective in question, and also to prevent government from unknowingly introducing rights-infringing legislation. The public act of reporting on compatibility, along with rights-based review by the JCHR, was also intended to augment parliament's attention to the rights dimension of bills in order to pressure government to justify decisions or amend bills that appear to implicate rights in an adverse and unreasonable manner.

[1] Lord Falconer, Speech to the Law Society and Human Rights Lawyers' Association, London, 17 February 2004.

The first part of this chapter focuses on legislative rights review in the pre-parliamentary stage in the life of a bill, where legislative initiatives are evaluated for their compatibility with Convention rights, cabinet decides whether to approve these as part of the government's legislative agenda, and cabinet approves whether the sponsoring minister can affirm that the bill is compatible under section 19(1)(a) or must instead indicate an inability to make this claim under section 19(1)(b).[2] The second part of the chapter examines the JCHR's role and influence in the pre-parliamentary phase of legislative development.

I. Government reactions to new responsibilities

As argued earlier, the idea of altering the norms of legislative decision-making to confront whether and how legislative bills implicate rights is complicated by the contested nature of judgements about both how rights considerations appropriately guide specific legislative objectives and also whether the proposed method of pursuing a legislative objective is compatible with Convention rights. However, it is also complicated by the ways in which a Westminster-based parliamentary system influences political behaviour. The central role that cohesive political parties play in organizing the parliamentary vote provides government relatively strong confidence in its ability to pass its legislative agenda (although this is the case to a lesser degree in relatively rare minority situations, unless coalitions are stable). The centrality of cohesive political parties also has an important effect on how parliamentarians engage with legislative bills. The perpetual role of the opposition to present itself as the alternative to government, and high expectations that members will generally support their leaders' political agenda, leads to a parliamentary culture of 'us vs. them' in which debates often boil down to two viewpoints – in favour or opposed. This orientation encourages political players and the media to interpret amendments to legislative bills as political losses for government.

The concept of legislative rights review envisages members scrutinizing bills from a compatibility perspective and focusing on the justification of

[2] The analysis of how bills are evaluated from a compatibility perspective draws upon earlier works by J. Hiebert: 'Governing under the Human Rights Act. The Limitations of Wishful Thinking', (2012) *Public Law* 29; 'Legislative Rights Review: Addressing the Gap between Ideals and Constraints', in M. Hunt, H. Hooper and P. Yowell (eds.) *Parliament and Human Rights: Redressing the Democratic Deficit* (Oxford: Hart Publishing), 2015.

bills where rights are implicated. However, this emphasis does not simply represent a new set of considerations for parliamentarians. It implies a fundamental change from more conventional and party-centred forms of political behaviour that reflect intense partisan gamesmanship oriented towards parties' preferred legislative agendas, ideological views of the role of the state and the public interest, political demands of core and courted constituents, ensuring party cohesion, demonstrating which party should form the next government, broader public opinion and a range of cost/benefit analyses centred on either retaining or achieving government status. The tension between the idea that members assess bills in terms of their compatibility with rights and more conventional political expectations that members generally take their lead from party leaders' positions on any legislative bill is especially acute for members from the governing party, who have career-related pressures and cultural incentives to support the government, and who see their own political futures closely linked to the success of government. As suggested earlier, if approached robustly, the concept of legislative rights review presumes nothing short of a fundamental change to the very political culture that characterizes the competitive, parliamentary and adversarial system of Westminster government.

Incentives for government to confront how bills implicate rights

If newspaper headlines were the principal way to gauge political behaviour under the HRA, the impression drawn would likely be that governments wilfully challenge or resist legislative rights review and the expectation of compliance with Convention rights at almost every step. The Labour government's professed enthusiasm for the HRA wore remarkably thin very early in the life of the HRA. Less than two years after the HRA came into effect, then Home Secretary David Blunkett dismissed rights-based criticisms of the government's decision to detain foreign terrorist suspects indefinitely without trial as 'airy fairy' fears,[3] pronounced that politicians and not judges are the true defenders of liberty,[4] proclaimed the government was 'fed up with having to deal with a situation where Parliament debates issues and the judges overturn

[3] P. Wintour, 'Blunkett Rejects 'Airy Fairy' Fears', *The Guardian*, 2 November 2001, www.guardian.co.uk/politics/2001/nov/12/uk.september11/print

[4] H. Young, 'David Blunkett Holds Liberty and the Judges in Contempt', *The Guardian*, 15 November 2001, www.guardian.co.uk/world/2001/nov/15/september11.britainand911

them'[5] and characterized passage of the HRA as the Blair government's 'biggest mistake' in its first term of office.[6] The Labour government's anti-Human Rights Act rhetoric intensified after the London bombings of 2005 when then Prime Minister Tony Blair challenged judicial authority on questions involving national security by pronouncing that the 'rules of the game are changing'[7] and threatened to renounce aspects of the ECHR if the judiciary blocked deportation decisions.[8] Not to be outdone, Conservative leader David Cameron pledged to repeal the HRA[9] and later, as Prime Minister, blamed the HRA for the riots that occurred in some metropolitan areas in summer 2011. According to Cameron, human rights laws have a 'corrosive influence on behaviour and morality'.[10] Cameron has also criticized the idea of having to comply with judicial rulings in his discussions of prisoner voting, stating publicly that the idea of extending the franchise to prisoners had left him 'physically ill'.[11] In 2013, the Conservatives ramped up their rhetoric against HRA-based constraints on legislation when Home Secretary Theresa May announced that in the next election, the Conservative party would campaign on withdrawing from the European Convention on Human Rights.[12]

Although headline-grabbing anti-HRA statements might make for lively political theatre, they do not explain whether, how or why the HRA influences the way legislative initiatives are evaluated or what

[5] As cited in F. Gibb, 'Blunkett vs. the Bench: The Battle has Begun', *The Times*, 4 May 2003, http://business.timesonline.co.uk/tol/business/law/article1115351.ece

[6] As quoted by B. Anderson, 'Don't Pity Those Foreigners who Exploit our Generosity', *The Independent*, 12 November 2001, www.highbeam.com/doc/1P2-5206859.html.

[7] S. Jeffrey, 'The Rules of the Game are Changing', *The Guardian*, 5 August 2005, www.guardian.co.uk/attackonlondon/story/0,16132,1543359,00.html

[8] G. Jones, 'Blair to Curb Human Rights in War on Terror', *The Telegraph*, 6 August 2005, www.telegraph.co.uk/news/uknews/1495605/Blair-to-curb-human-rights-in-war-on-terror.html

[9] A. Travis, 'Cameron Pledges Bill to Restore British Freedoms', *The Guardian*, 28 February 2009, www.guardian.co.uk/politics/2009/feb/28/conservatives-human-rights

[10] T. Shipman and K. Walker, 'Cameron's War on Feckless Families: PM Attacks the Human Rights Laws and Backs National Service', *The Daily Mail*, 17 August 2011, www.dailymail.co.uk/news/article-2026163/David-Cameron-UK-riots-speech-PM-attacks-human-rights-laws-backs-national-service.html

[11] 'Prison Votes Will Be Kept to a Minimum', *BBC News*, 20 January 2011, www.bbc.co.uk/news/uk-politics-12233938

[12] S. Walters, 'A Great Day for British Justice: Theresa May Vows to Take UK out of the European Court of Human Rights', *The Mail Online*, 4 March 2013, www.dailymail.co.uk/news/article-2287183/A-great-day-British-justice-Theresa-May-vows-UK-European-Court-Human-Rights.html

considerations shape cabinet decisions to approve initiatives to go forth as bills to parliament when these implicate rights in an adverse manner.

The section 19 ministerial obligation to report on whether bills are compatible with Convention rights has resulted in more attention to how legislation implicates rights, for two reasons. The first reason, and the one articulated by the framers of the HRA, is the need to govern in a more rights-sensitive manner by confronting how bills implicate rights for the purposes of revising and reassessing legislative choices, and also to foster greater parliamentary responsibility for judgements about rights. The requirement to acknowledge an inability to claim a bill is compatible with Convention rights, and the likely negative attention this kind of report would generate, was expected to dissuade government from frequently approving a bill that would require a section 19(1)(b) report. The second reason has more to do with a government's inherent interest in managing the risks of judicial censure that arise from the HRA's authorization of a new domestic judicial role for interpreting and applying Convention rights. Public officials whom we interviewed emphasize strong political expectations of compliance with negative judicial rulings, and the significance this has for how legislative bills are evaluated.[13]

Our research reveals that the HRA has significantly altered bureaucratic processes for developing and assessing legislative initiatives. Proposed legislation is systematically evaluated for compatibility with Convention rights. Advice to ministers is framed in terms of a risk assessment of the government's likely chances of succeeding or failing if litigation occurs, and is based on legal assessments of relevant case law. Public officials confirm that although ministers do not like being informed that their initiatives might be vulnerable to judicial censure if the legislation were to be litigated, they nevertheless want to fully understand the legal consequences of their decisions, because government has a strong interest in avoiding unnecessary litigation – particularly if potential problems could have been addressed at the time legislation was developed.[14]

This interest in identifying the risks of judicial censure is consistent with Alec Stone Sweet's research on European legislatures, where apprehension of judicial censure operates as a strong incentive for proactive, compliant legislative behaviour.[15] At first glance, the idea that the UK

[13] Interviews. [14] Interviews.

[15] A. Stone Sweet, *Governing with Judges: Constitutional Politics in Europe* (Oxford: Oxford University Press, 2000), pp. 75–9. As previously noted, Stone Sweet refers to

government should also be concerned about the prospects of judicial censure might seem a puzzle, given that constraints on judicial remedial power do not allow courts to set aside the effects of inconsistent legislation. However, the assumption that the prospects of judicial censure do not exert a substantial influence on political behaviour in the UK underestimates the significance of political expectations of compliance with judicial norms, which are reinforced by the treaty character of the ECHR[16] and reflected in the HRA through the inclusion of a fast-track approach for passing remedial legislation in section 10. It also underestimates the influence that judicial interpretations of the HRA can have on legislation.

Domestically, the strongest form of judicial censure is a judicial declaration of incompatibility under section 4 of the HRA. This kind of judicial outcome is not easily ignored by politicians, because the expectation of compliance with judicial rulings also extends to the domestic realm.[17] A second form of domestic judicial censure is for courts to use their interpretive power in section 3 to render legislation compliant with Convention rights where possible, which can have a substantial impact on the scope or effects of legislation. As Danny Nicol argues, this form of judicial remedy occurs in a less confrontational manner than if the judiciary were to render a declaration of incompatibility, because judicial 'rewrites of legislation' under section 3(1) of the HRA 'constitute relatively invisible means of changing the law in contrast to headline-grabbing declarations of incompatibility'.[18] Nevertheless, this remedial power can have a direct and substantial effect on legislation by significantly altering its scope or effects. An example of judicial willingness to alter legislative intentions so as to render an interpretation that the court deems compatible with Convention rights, and which was not subsequently amended by parliament, occurred in *R* v. *A* when the Law Lords altered parliament's clear intention about how the rules of evidence are interpreted in the context of sexual assault

autolimitation, which he attributes to the earlier work of Favoreau; it was also used by Christine Landfried. See L. Favoreau, 'Décentralisation et Constitution', (1982) 98 *Revue du droit public* 1259; C. Landfried, *Bundesverfassungsgericht und Gesetzgeber* (Baden-Baden: Nomos, 1984) and 'Judicial Policymaking in Germany: The Federal Constitutional Court', (1992) 15 *West European Politics* 50.

16 Interviews. 17 Interviews.

18 D. Nicol, 'The Human Rights Act and the Politicians' (2004) 24 *Legal Studies* 451.

trials.[19] Another significant example of the legislative impact of this interpretative power was the decision to 'read down' the relevant provisions of the Prevention of Terrorism Act 2005 to address the issue of whether the presence of Special Advocates is a sufficient substitute for the open adversarial hearing required for fair trials.[20] The House of Lords ruled that where disclosed materials consist of general assertions in circumstances in which the case against the subject of the order is based solely or primarily on 'closed materials' to which the subject is not privy, the right to a fair trial under Article 6 is not satisfied.[21] By the court's own acknowledgement, this reliance on the section 3 interpretative power in the HRA 'may well destroy the system of control orders which is a significant part of this country's defences against terrorism'.[22] Thus, commentators caution against underestimating the potential political influence of either form of judicial censure from domestic courts.[23]

Quite apart from an interest in avoiding the expenses and human resources associated with litigation, another reason to consider compatibility concerns when developing and evaluating legislative initiatives is the political consequence of having to address a negative judicial ruling. Once government has determined its policy objectives, consulted with relevant stakeholders, finessed internal disagreements and signified its political position by introducing legislation, senior political

[19] *R* v. *A* (2001) UKHL 25. At issue was rape shield legislation, which denied the admissibility of evidence relating to the sexual history of an alleged victim. The prohibition reflected parliamentary intention to reduce judicial discretion because of previous concerns of judicial gender bias against female victims of assault, which influenced the uses and interpretation of evidence related to a woman's sexual past. However, the Law Lords ruled that the ban on evidence that the accused had a previous sexual relationship with the accuser breached the right to a fair trial. Instead of declaring the legislation incompatible under section 4 of the HRA, the Law Lords restored some of the judicial discretion the legislation had removed, thus conflicting with parliament's clear intention. The effect of the ruling allows judges to decide if the evidence the accused wants to put forward is relevant to the issue of whether the alleged victim had consented to sex on the occasion in question. Parliament did not override this judicial decision.

[20] A. Kavanagh, 'Special Advocates, Control Orders and the Right to a Fair Trial', (2010) 73 *Modern Law Review*, 836, 848.

[21] *Secretary of State for the Home Department* v. *AF (No 3)* [2009] UKHL 28.

[22] Ibid., at 70 per Lord Hoffmann.

[23] A. Kavanagh, 'Constitutionalism, Counterterrorism, and the Courts: Changes in the British Constitutional Landscape' (2011) 9 *I-CON* 172; T. Campbell, 'Incorporation through Interpretation', in T. Campbell, K.D. Ewing and A. Tomkins (eds.), *Sceptical Essays on Human Rights* (New York: Oxford University Press, 2001), p. 80.

leaders will be understandably reluctant to be placed in the position of having to revisit these decisions. This may be required either to enact remedial measures if a court rules that legislation is not compatible with Convention rights or in situations where government deems a legislative response necessary to set aside the effects of a section 3 interpretation that fundamentally alters the meaning or scope of legislation in ways which government opposes. Not only would the return of a contentious issue compete with other initiatives in an often crowded parliamentary calendar; it could also reopen internal disagreements that risk undermining delicate compromises between competing factions of the party or coalition.

Yet despite an obvious interest in risk aversion – and the incentive to develop and adopt compliant ways to achieve legislative objectives[24] – our research suggests that governments are also willing to be significant risk takers as well, in the sense of approving bills despite having been advised that they incur a relatively high degree of risk for judicial censure or, as shown in Chapters 8 and 9, by rejecting subsequent calls for amendments by the JCHR or the House of Lords in the face of contested claims of compatibility.

Although governments appear to have a reasonably healthy appetite for risk, they are not generally prepared to acknowledge to parliament circumstances in which it can be reasonably anticipated that judgement about compatibility will be contested, or to explain their reasons for concluding that bills justify an affirmative claim of compatibility under section 19. The overwhelming majority of bills introduced to parliament are accompanied by affirmative claims of compatibility. Nevertheless, as we will explain, affirmative section 19 HRA reports to parliament are a poor indicator of whether or not proposed legislation raises serious questions about compatibility. Section 19 (1)(a) reports often mask substantial political judgement that may not be based solely on interpretations of relevant case law. Instead, political judgements appear to reflect a range of considerations relating to whether the political benefits of passing risky legislation outweigh the desire to avoid the risk of being subject to a negative JCHR report, criticized in the House of Lords, or pressured to pass remedial legislation in the wake of a negative judicial ruling should litigation occur.

[24] Interviews.

Bureaucratic evaluations and advice on compatibility

Preparations for governing under the HRA included extensive training for pubic officials on how to assess proposed legislation from a human rights perspective. An audit of existing legislation was also conducted to identify areas of vulnerability to judicial censure. Officials suggest these processes helped instil acceptance of and awareness about the implications of the HRA. Yet several concerns were identified about the adequacy of the training provided. Some who were interviewed suggest that the initial guidelines were overly technical and lacked sufficient information to help officials assess the implications of specific legislative initiatives for protected rights, while others expressed concern that the training was not broad enough to provide public authorities with necessary knowledge about how to incorporate HRA considerations in their daily functions. In the period following this initial training, some of those interviewed suggested the need for more refresher training and questioned the lack of follow-up training in light of the evolution of case law, other human rights developments and turnover in the public service.[25]

The HRA did not introduce the idea of evaluating legislation for its consistency with Convention rights. Before the HRA was adopted, the Foreign Office addressed basic issues and principles associated with compliance with ECHR decisions, assisted by guidance developed by the Treasury Solicitor's Department and the cabinet office.[26] The Department of Constitutional Affairs was created in 2003 under the responsibility of the Lord Chancellor, both in recognition of the consequences associated with a new domestic judicial authority to review legislation and determine whether it is compatible with Convention rights and in order to assist ministers with their new statutory obligation, in section 19, to report on compatibility. The DCA's mission was to promote compliance with fundamental rights instruments to which the UK is party. The DCA had two central divisions: a legal division that focused on compatibility with human rights and a human rights policy division that considered the implications of legislation that derogates from human rights, ministerial statements acknowledging an inability to claim compatibility with rights and other issues involving possible tension between

[25] Interviews.

[26] Treasury Solicitor's Department in conjunction with the Cabinet Office (MPO) Training Division, *The Judge Over Your Shoulder: Judicial Review of Administrative Decisions* (London: Cabinet Office, 1987).

the HRA and specific legislation. The department was disbanded in 2007, and responsibility for the HRA was transferred to the Department of Justice.

The DCA offered a suite of guidelines ranging from more technical documents aimed at mid-level management to those intended for more general audiences. The DCA saw its role as providing the basic materials that could then be applied and developed by other departments, agencies and public authorities in their own training programmes. Although the DCA's role was to promote compliance with the HRA throughout government, it was neither expected nor had sufficient resources to regularly provide advice to all departments about whether bills are compatible with Convention rights.[27] Instead, responsibility for evaluating proposed legislation and advising on compatibility with the HRA rests principally with departments. The idea of centralizing legal advice about compliance with the HRA was considered counterproductive to one of the essential political purposes of the HRA, which was to ensure that all departments confront whether legislative initiatives are compatible with Convention rights and to consider rights-compliant ways to achieve them.[28] Some of those interviewed suggest that having legal advisors employed by specific departments is also beneficial for ensuring that a compatibility perspective reflects the policy objectives of the department. As one official suggested, having a legal advisor working within a department enables him or her to identify with the policy goals and the institutional culture of that particular department, which allows greater sensitivity in achieving the policy goals of the department while still satisfying questions of compliance.[29]

An obvious question about reliance on decentralized advice is whether it leads to inter-departmental differences in the standards and criteria used to assess whether legislative initiatives are compatible with Convention rights. Officials interviewed offered several reasons why this is not the case. First, the DCA's central mission was to promote consistent legal advice between departments, and thus its guidance sought to engage departments in similar ways of thinking about and evaluating compatibility. Second, the informal yet frequent rotation of lawyers ensures that ideas about compatibility are widely shared, as few lawyers spend their career in one department and therefore legal interpretations do not

[27] Interviews. [28] Interviews. [29] Interviews.

become localized or subject to particular departmental norms. Finally, some department lawyers are on loan from the government legal services team in the Treasury Solicitor's Department, which also helps ensure consistency in the criteria and standards used for evaluating compatibility. To the extent that centralization does occur, it is with respect to litigation. The Treasury Solicitor's Department handles most of the litigation across government. The department also has a series of legal teams that provide legal advice to departments without their own in-house lawyers.[30]

Some of the lawyers interviewed admit they did not initially anticipate that the HRA would make a substantial difference in how proposed legislation is evaluated, because pre-HRA practices already considered whether bills are compatible with Convention rights. However, those familiar with the processes both before and after the HRA was adopted suggest the standard for legal evaluations of compatibility has become considerably more robust and sophisticated than was the case prior to the HRA's adoption. This change is attributed to two factors. One is greater concern about the political consequences of legislation being deemed incompatible with Convention rights now that domestic courts have the responsibility to interpret and apply Convention rights. The second is the new statutory ministerial reporting requirement on compatibility, which increases both the immediacy of having to confront whether and how bills implicate rights and the regularity of this kind of policy focus when developing bills. Both conditions are said to provide stronger incentives for more rigorous review.

One lawyer referred to a situation before the HRA was adopted in which little more was done other than quickly reading a copy of the bill and pronouncing that it satisfied Convention rights, despite the virtual absence of substantive scrutiny. The same lawyer suggested that under the HRA, this kind of casual confirmation of compatibility no longer occurs.[31] However, some of the lawyers we interviewed acknowledge growing pains during the development and application of criteria to advise departments on questions of compatibility. In the early days of the HRA, they suggest that the legal advice provided was overly risk-averse because of uncertainty about the kind of rights claims that would be made and how jurisprudence would evolve. Some suggest that in hindsight their assessments of possible compatibility

[30] Interviews. [31] Interviews.

issues far exceeded what was required in the circumstances, and indicate that this extreme form of risk-averse advice is no longer provided. Moreover, some admit that in the early period of adapting to the HRA, the nature of the advice given was not as helpful as it could have been, because it failed to direct more attention to ways of conceiving of the legislative objective in a rights-compatible manner.[32] However, the lawyers we interviewed uniformly agree that the legal advice provided has improved substantially since the early experiences with the HRA. Whereas in the early days there was a tendency toward phrasing such as 'there could be a human rights problem' and 'to be on the safe side you had better not do this', government lawyers say that they are now more likely to provide specific advice about how a legislative goal can be achieved in a way that is compatible with judicial interpretations of rights.[33]

Legal advice on compatibility is based upon interpretations of relevant domestic and European case law. Legal officials indicate that the most significant changes to the legal advice provided under the HRA include a considerably higher standard for what kind of argument is necessary to recommend that a bill is compatible with the Convention, and a clearer and more detailed explanation of the reasons for pursuing policy objectives that implicate rights. This focus on justification is said to have helped rationalize policy decisions and imposed stronger discipline on the development of legislative bills. Officials indicated that prior to the HRA, there was not the same focus on the relationship between policy objectives and means in terms of proportionality considerations.[34] Another important change is the increased depth of expertise on human rights issues within departments. Before the HRA was adopted, a department might have had only a single expert on its legal team for Convention issues (or perhaps no expert, in which case it would have to rely on the Foreign Office), whereas departments now have access to multiple experts.[35] Officials suggest that as case law evolves, it has become easier for government lawyers to define the scope of rights and the standards for

[32] Interviews. [33] Interviews.

[34] However, some officials noted that there is still a tendency to put too much detail into secondary legislation, while ensuring that the primary framework is compliant. But they recognized this is inadequate because there is no section 19 equivalent for secondary legislation, and this form of delegation imposes considerable responsibility on public authorities to ensure power is exercised in compliant ways.

[35] Interviews.

determining discrimination, and to draw inferences about the degree of judicial deference that can be expected.[36]

As suggested earlier, the introduction of a ministerial reporting obligation on compatibility was expected to facilitate engagement with rights at all stages of the legislative process.[37] Although legal advisors help department officials identify ways to pursue legislative goals in a rights-compliant manner and articulate the substantive reasons for whether a particular policy approach satisfies or is inconsistent with proportionality standards,[38] many of those interviewed suggest that this ideal of intra-departmental engagement with rights has not been fully realized. This gap is attributed in large part to an implicit division of labour within departments and agencies for conducting rights-based assessments, with many policy officials treating compatibility issues as distinct legal considerations that are addressed almost exclusively by human rights lawyers, and often late in the policy process. Moreover, some legal advisors suggest that policy officials can be reluctant to challenge a minister when an initiative seems obviously inconsistent with Convention rights, and instead leave it for the lawyers to present the legal reasons for considering revisions.[39] However, some legal officials suggest there is a problem with this division of labour with respect to assessing compatibility, as the most common compatibility concerns arise over questions of proportionality – the relationship between a legislative goal and the means utilized to achieve it – which involve policy-laden assessments with regard to which policy officials have important insights.[40]

Relationship between legal advice and cabinet decisions

Interviewees indicated that the policy environment in which they work is characterized by a strong presumption against introducing a legislative initiative that would require a minister to report inability to claim a bill is compatible with Convention rights.[41] However, this presumption does not address the issues of how compatibility is interpreted for policy approval or statutory reporting purposes, or whether different standards for compatibility are invoked for legislative approval vs. reporting purposes.

[36] Interviews.

[37] Parliament of the United Kingdom, *Hansard*, HL, vol 593, col 1163, 27 November 1997 (Lord Irvine).

[38] Interviews. [39] Interviews. [40] Interviews. [41] Interviews.

The most recent cabinet guidelines (2014) require ministers to inform the Parliamentary Business and Legislation Committee (PBL) if it appears likely that any provisions of a bill will not allow the minister to declare it compatible with Convention rights.[42] Proposed bills must also be accompanied by a memorandum declaring whether rights will be adversely implicated before the bill can be approved for introduction or publication in draft form. This ECHR memorandum must be vetted by the Attorney General's office before being circulated to the PBL committee. The memorandum is expected to address the human rights issues raised and include a 'frank assessment by the department of the vulnerability to challenge in legal and policy terms'.[43] The Law Officers within the Attorney General's office evaluate the HRA memorandum and may request additional analysis if they identify legal compatibility issues regarding which they have serious questions. The Attorney General has the final word on the legal opinion about whether a bill is compatible with Convention rights. Once the PBL committee gives its approval, a statement for parliament is finalized declaring whether or not a minister can claim compatibility, and the bill is approved for introduction or publication in draft.[44] We were advised that if the Attorney General concludes legislation is not compatible, it is unlikely the Minister will be allowed to claim compatibility should the measure be approved to proceed as a bill.[45]

This multi-layered process of evaluating whether proposed legislation is compatible with the HRA – along with the Attorney General's judgement which, we were told, is authoritative in cases of disagreement – makes it highly unlikely that a bill will proceed to parliament without the government being fully aware of the legal concerns or contested issues regarding its provisions' compatibility with Convention rights. As it is unlikely that government would be unaware that proposed bills implicate rights before introducing bills to parliament, and the overwhelming majority of bills have been accompanied by an affirmative claim of compatibility, one might be tempted to conclude that government is taking an extremely risk-averse approach to governing under the HRA, by only approving those legislative initiatives which it is confident will be

[42] Cabinet Office. *Guidelines for Making Legislation*. July 2014, s. 11, https://www.gov.uk/government/uploads/system/uploads/attachment_data/file/328408/Guide_to_Making_Legislation_July_2014.pdf

[43] Cabinet Office. *Guidelines for Making Legislation*. July 2014, pp. 100–6

[44] Interviews. [45] Interviews.

successfully defended should litigation arise. However, as we argue presently and in Chapter 8 and 9, this inference is not supported by our research and does not take into account the scope and role of political judgement about whether and how compatibility concerns constrain cabinet decisions, as well as how to interpret the statutory reporting obligation of ministers under section 19 of the HRA.

Although ministers might be required to alert the PBL committee about the nature or seriousness of any potential threat that could undermine legislation, including the risk of judicial censure, the statutory compatibility reporting requirement has not been interpreted as an obligation to inform parliament about how or why a bill is vulnerable to judicial censure, or the level of risk attached. Moreover, Cabinet Office guidelines for reporting under section 19 and claiming a bill is compatible with Convention rights have changed considerably as the HRA has evolved and now make it easier for ministers to claim bills are compatible, despite the prospect of potentially adverse litigation. Early guidelines as to how ministers were to broach their section 19 reporting responsibility emphasized the primacy of legal opinion. Initially, ministers were advised they were only to issue a positive assurance of compatibility if 'the balance of [legal] argument supports the view that the provisions are compatible'. Moreover, ministers were instructed that even if they consider a policy objective to be compatible with Convention rights, their reasons do not constitute a 'sufficient basis' to claim compatibility if legal advisors do not believe that these arguments would 'ultimately succeed before the courts'.[46]

This emphasis on the primacy of legal advisors' opinions on compatibility was subsequently displaced by guidelines suggesting considerable latitude for political judgement when determining if a minister can claim a bill is compatible with Convention rights.[47] At the time of writing, the relevant cabinet guidelines authorize a minister to make a statement that in his or her view, the bill's provisions are compatible with Convention rights. This focus on ministerial judgement when determining compatibility has been in effect since at least 2007.[48] Some construe this new

[46] Department for Constitutional Affairs, 'Guidance Section 19 Statements: Revised Guidance for Departments', www.humanrights.gov.uk/guidance/guide-updated.htm (no longer on the web; accessed 8 June 2006).

[47] The guidelines were withdrawn shortly before the DCA was disbanded in May 2007.

[48] This rule change occurred sometime after 8 June 2006, the last time we accessed the guidance. Another colleague doing research on the subject was advised in 2007 that the

emphasis on ministerial judgement to mean that ministerial statements of compatibility reflect little more than ministers' personal views. This is the interpretation of David Feldman, who served as the first legal secretary for the Joint Committee on Human Rights, and who argues that '[t]he Minister takes legal advice, but ultimately makes his or her own assessment, and does not purport to offer more than a personal opinion.'[49]

Some of the legal advisors we interviewed dispute the interpretation that ministers' reports on compatibility simply reflect ministers' personal views and, by implication, ignore the legal advice received from their advisors. They suggest it is extremely unlikely that a minister will claim a bill is compatible if this contradicts the clear legal advice received, and even more unlikely that a minister will be permitted to report to parliament that a bill is compatible if the Attorney General disagrees with this view.[50] Nevertheless, as we argue presently, the relationship between the legal advice provided and ministers' interpretation of it is muddied by how this advice is framed. Moreover, there is evidence that the former Labour government claimed an activity was legally valid despite receiving contrary legal advice.[51] Although the context did not pertain to compatibility for section 19 purposes (the issue was the legality of the Iraq war), the incident nevertheless raises the question of whether the Attorney General is subject or is susceptible to pressure to abandon independent legal judgement to support the government's political position on an issue.[52]

guidelines had been withdrawn. For the most recent version authorized see Cabinet Office, *Guidelines for Making Legislation.*

49 D. Feldman, 'Institutional Roles and Meanings of "Compatibility"', in H. Fenwick, G. Phillipson and R. Masterson (eds.), *Judicial Reasoning Under the UK Human Rights Act* (Cambridge: Cambridge University Press, 2007), p. 99.

50 Interviews.

51 The example is the government's claim about the legality of the Iraq war, despite consistent legal advice from its own advisers (and the initial judgment of the Attorney General) that it was not lawful to use force against Iraq without a second Security Council resolution to revive earlier authorization. http://news.bbc.co.uk/1/hi/uk_politics/4377605.stm; www.globalpolicy.org/security/issues/iraq/attack/law/2005/0324wilmshurst.htm

52 M. Wolf, 'Was the Attorney General Leant On to Change His Mind?', *The Independent*, 24 March 2005, www.independent.co.uk/news/uk/politics/was-the-attorney-general-leant-on-to-change-his-mind-6149914.html

This argument was made earlier in J. Hiebert, 'Governing Like Judges?', in T. Campbell, K.D. Ewing and A. Tomkins (eds.), *The Legal Protection of Human Rights: Sceptical Essays* (Oxford: Oxford University Press, 2011), pp. 40–65, at p. 58.

Section 19(1)(b) reports to date

Ministers have acknowledged the inability to report a bill as compatible with Convention rights at the time of its introduction on only two occasions, and in two other instances have indicated the inability to claim compatibility following a bill's return to the House of Commons after amendments were made in the House of Lords. The first occasion in which government was not prepared to confirm the bill it was introducing was compatible with Convention rights occurred early in the life of the HRA, and reflected political acceptance of short-lived cabinet guidelines that, at the time, emphasized the primacy of legal opinion over political judgement on issues of compatibility. The report was made in the context of the Labour government's Communications Bill, in which the sponsoring minister defended the bill as promoting goals the government strongly supported, but indicated that the legal advice her department received did not allow for a positive report of compatibility to be made (discussed in Chapter 9).

The only other acknowledgement that a bill, as introduced, prevents an affirmation of compatibility occurred with the House of Lords Reform Bill 2012–13,[53] which sought to make the provision for the franchise for House of Lords elections identical to elections to the House of Commons.[54] The compatibility issue arose from the disenfranchisement of prisoners and both the Labour and Coalition governments' failure to implement remedies after the ECtHR had ruled that the UK practice violates the right to vote (Article 3 of Protocol No. 1 of the ECHR).[55] Given this context, it would have been extremely difficult for the government to suggest to parliament that the continued denial of the vote to all prisoners allows for a positive affirmation of compatibility. Moreover, the sponsoring minister was Deputy PM Nick Clegg, leader of the Liberal Democrat party, which strongly supports repeal of the ban on prisoner voting (discussed in Chapter 9). It is difficult to imagine how Clegg could have both claimed the bill was compatible with Convention rights and avoided rebellion within his party and accusations of hypocrisy from supporters.

[53] Parliament of the United Kingdom, House of Lords, Reform Bill 2012–13, Explanatory Notes, Bill 52–EN, www.publications.parliament.uk/pa/bills/cbill/2012–2013/0052/en/13052en.htm

[54] www.publications.parliament.uk/pa/bills/cbill/2012–2013/0052/13052.pdf

[55] Parliament of the United Kingdom, House of Lords, Reform Bill 2012–13, Explanatory Notes, Bill 52–EN.

Section 19(1)(b) reports of an inability to claim compatibility have also been made on two occasions of a bill moving from the House of Lords to the Commons. In both instances the reports served the Labour government's political interest: challenging the legitimacy of House of Lords attempts to block reform measures intended to recognize the moral legitimacy of same sex relationships. The first occurred after the House of Lords tried to block the government's attempt to repeal a particularly controversial aspect of the Local Government Act 1988 (section 28), passed under Thatcher's Conservative government, which sought to prevent local authorities from promoting the acceptability of lesbian and gay relationships.[56] This provision had labelled same sex relationships as 'pretend' unions, and led to substantial protest rallies by activist groups such as OutRage! and Stonewall.[57] In 1999, Labour introduced a bill to reform local government that also included a clause to repeal this homophobic provision. After a majority in the House of Lords voted to defeat the repeal, the government included a statement of its inability to report that the legislation was compatible with Convention rights under section 19(1)(b) when the bill returned to the House of Commons.[58] When asked to explain the decision, Hilary Armstrong indicated that the bill could only be considered as compatible with Convention rights if this section were repealed.[59] Three years later, the government was able to repeal the ban. The second instance in which a section 19(1)(b) report was made when a bill returned from the Lords to the House of Commons arose after a majority in the Lords approved the family members amendment in the civil partnership legislation, which the government interpreted as undermining the bill's purpose of redressing inequality (discussed in Chapter 9). In both circumstances, these section 19(1)(b) reports did not present potential obstacles or embarrassment to the Labour government, but instead helped to demonstrate the government's support for gay and lesbian issues and differentiate its policy from Conservative positions on these issues in the House of Lords.

[56] A. Thorp, 'The *Local Government Bill* [HL]: The "Section 28" Debate', (2000) House of Commons Library, Research Paper 00/47 6 April, summary.

[57] A. Gillan, 'Section 28 Gone ... But Not Forgotten', *The Guardian*, 17 November 2003, www.guardian.co.uk/politics/2003/nov/17/uk.gayrights

[58] Local Government Bill, (Session 1999–2000), House of Commons, www.publications.parliament.uk/pa/cm199900/cmbills/087/2000087.htm

[59] Parliament of the United Kingdom, *Hansard* HC, vol 346 c 622W, 23 March 2000 (Hilary Armstrong).

The puzzle of frequent contestation about compatibility claims

Despite routinely positive claims to parliament that bills are compatible with Convention rights, these judgements are frequently challenged by the JCHR, which provides regular and detailed reports that identify serious potential rights infringements (discussed in more detail in Chapters 8 and 9). The frequency with which the JCHR contests ministerial claims of compatibility presents an interesting puzzle about the nature of legal advice that ministers receive with regard to compatibility and its relationship to ministerial and cabinet judgement on whether to proceed with a bill, and how to interpret the statutory reporting obligation on compatibility.

We asked officials the following three questions in an attempt to understand and explain the frequency with which the JCHR contests ministerial claims of compatibility:

1) What criteria are used to advise a minister that a bill is not compatible with Convention rights?
2) Does strong political criticism of the HRA influence how compatibility is assessed and what advice is provided to ministers?
3) How do legal advisors explain the frequency with which the JCHR disagrees with ministerial claims of compatibility?

Legal advisors emphasize that evaluating whether bills are compatible with Convention rights involves the interpretation and application of principles in relevant case law, and that changes in case law influence the advice they provide. The standard approach to providing legal advice takes the form of a risk assessment, for which the criterion is whether the bill presents a higher than 50 per cent chance of being declared incompatible with Convention rights. Advisors say they recommend that a minister should not claim a bill is compatible if there is a stronger than 50 per cent chance that the government would lose if legislation is subject to litigation.[60] However, some advisors admit that ministers and cabinet have approved initiatives where the risk level is higher than that which is generally accepted.[61]

We followed up by asking legal advisors if they have ever been subject to overt or implicit political pressure to alter the legal advice they provide in order to support a minister's desire to report that a bill is compatible with Convention rights. As previously discussed, the Labour government's enthusiasm for the HRA soon waned as ministers confronted critical reports from the JCHR and rebuke from others arguing that key

[60] Interviews. [61] Interviews.

elements of legislative bills which the government strongly supported, were not compatible with Convention rights. Political criticism of the HRA has not relented under the Conservative-led Coalition government and in December 2012, seven former ministers called on David Cameron to live up to his earlier pledge to repeal the HRA.[62]

Despite strong anti-HRA rhetoric from political leaders, the officials we interviewed deny that they have been subject to overt or implicit political pressure to alter their advice so as to allow a positive statement of compatibility. They also categorically reject any suggestion that anti-HRA sentiment influences their assessments of compatibility or the advice they provide. We were also told that even if legal advisors were subject to political pressure to alter their advice on compatibility, they would put their professional reputation as lawyers ahead of good working relationships with ministers, and therefore were not prepared to alter or abandon their professional judgement about compatibility.[63] Yet despite repeated and unwavering assurances that the legal advice they provide is unaffected by explicit or implicit political pressure or political anti-HRA sentiment, upon further probing we learned that the force of this legal advice is at times tempered by the way it is framed. Some officials acknowledged that on occasion their advice allows for different interpretations on the essential compatibility question. As they explained, legal advice is not presented as a singular or straightforward conclusion that a proposed measure is or is not compatible with Convention rights; instead, it is presented as a thought process about the arguments on either side of the compatibility issue, and where legal advisors believe the balance lies. Framing legal advice in a manner that allows for differing interpretations of whether the measure can be claimed to be compatible with Convention rights is most likely when case law is not settled, when it has not addressed critical issues raised by a legislative initiative or when questions of compatibility turn on assessments of proportionality.[64] Some officials acknowledge that ministers have interpreted advice received to support a positive claim of compatibility even when advisors believed and indicated that the proposed legislation incurred a high risk of not succeeding if litigated.[65]

[62] 'Tories Turn Up Heat on Human Rights Act as Seven Former Ministers Call on Cameron to Repeal the Law', *Mail Online*, 5 December 2012, www.dailymail.co.uk/news/article-2243161/Tories-turn-heat-Human-Rights-Act-seven-ministers-Cameron-repeal-law.html

[63] Interviews. [64] Interviews.

[65] This argument was made earlier by J. Hiebert, 'Governing under the Human Rights Act', 37–8.

As questions of compatibility frequently turn on the issue of proportionality, it is important not to understate the significance of this admission that legal advice on compatibility is framed in a manner that allows the minister to choose between different judgements on this essential question. Although public officials did not state so explicitly, it is reasonable to assume that this method of framing legal advice about compatibility has the benefit of diffusing the tension that might otherwise occur if they were to flatly advise a minister that his or her preferred initiative is not compatible with Convention rights, and therefore unless revised requires a section 19(1)(b) report acknowledging an inability to claim compatibility. As discussed earlier, apprehension about telling a minister that departmental legislative objectives are not compatible with Convention rights for reporting purposes has encouraged some policy advisors to avoid these discussions, leaving delivery of this news as the responsibility of legal advisors.[66]

We also asked legal advisors to help us understand the frequency with which the JCHR disputes ministerial reports of compatibility. In asking this question, our intention was to elicit a response that supported one or more of the following hypotheses: legal advice provided to ministers is not overly robust, the JCHR's concerns are exaggerated, misplaced or poorly formed, or the answer to this conundrum lies somewhere else.

We were given two explanations for the frequent disagreement between affirmative ministerial claims of compatibility and subsequent critical JCHR reports that contest these assurances of compatibility. The first is the subjective nature of interpreting proportionality criteria, which legal advisors characterize as a key consideration in judgements about compatibility.[67] Legal officials indicate they believe there is considerable scope for legitimate disagreement both about the relative importance of the legislative objective when compared to its deleterious effects and about the efficacy of alternative means to accomplish the objective. Advisors indicated that the JCHR's views on proportionality are not interpreted as trumping or invalidating departmental legal advice, but instead are generally regarded simply as offering a different opinion on an issue that is prone to conflicting interpretations. Moreover, officials state that by the time the JCHR has reported its concerns, the relevant considerations have likely already been thoroughly evaluated and debated within the complex process through which legislative initiatives are reviewed at the

[66] Interviews. [67] Interviews.

departmental level, and also after as they proceed for cabinet consideration and drafting.[68] As one official stated:

> If a department looks carefully at these issues, and takes advice from its lawyers, sometimes from external counsel, and even consults the Attorney General, and has faced the possibility of being challenged in court, having gone through that whole process, it may rethink its policy in terms of political arguments, but there is little the committee will say that it hasn't already agonized about beforehand.[69]

This interpretation of JCHR views on compatibility – as representing just another opinion on the issue, which does not warrant the government's reassessing or reversing its earlier judgement about compatibility – is strongly reinforced by the candid statement made before the JCHR in 2006 by Harriet Harman, then Minister of State of Constitutional Affairs. Harman advised the JCHR that she did not consider its emphasis on legal questions about compatibility as representing 'added value' to the parliamentary process, particularly as the government already had access to extensive legal advice before deciding whether to proceed with its bill, and that the government would not change its mind on the compatibility issue on the basis of a JCHR report:

> I think there is a distinction in our minds between the question of legal compliance, and that is what the courts would be dealing with, and your view more widely about whether it is going in the spirit of the human rights approach . . . [W]e have got the Government Legal Service backed up by the Treasury solicitors if they need them, backed up by the advice of independent counsel, backed up, if they cannot find their way through, by the law officers, and because of the Human Rights Act and the proximity of the courts out there we are highly legally tooled up. We are tooled up to the point at which we believe we can rely on that legal advice, so that basically, if we finally get the advice from the Attorney General that something can be done, then I do not think there is anybody else who can trump that in the Government's mind. The Government is not likely to think again about the legal issues once it has had all the legal advice going up as far up as the Attorney General if it needs to . . . When you are doing stuff which really is very much like legal advice I am not sure that that is terribly helpful because we are likely to be in court and dealing with it in front of the courts and will be found to be right or wrong, and we feel we have got enough legal advice.[70]

[68] Interviews. [69] Interviews.

[70] Parliament of the United Kingdom, JCHR, Session 2005–2006, Oral Evidence and Memoranda given by Harriet Harman, Minister of State Department of Constitutional Affairs, Jan 16 2006, HL 143/HC 830-i

The second explanation for frequent disagreements between JCHR opinions and ministerial claims of compatibility is the difference of opinion on whether a lack of safeguards to ensure public officials interpret legislation or regulations in a compatible manner requires a section 19(1)(b) report acknowledging an inability to claim compatibility. The JCHR believes legislation is not compatible where these safeguards are lacking.[71] However, governments draw a sharp distinction between the intention to authorize compliant legislation and the possibility of it being interpreted by public authorities in a non-compliant manner. Thus, the mere possibility that legislation could be interpreted or applied in a non-compliant manner because of a lack of express safeguards does not factor into assessments of whether a legislative bill is considered to be compatible with Convention rights for ministerial reporting purposes. The rationalization for this interpretation is that since section 6 of the HRA requires all public authorities to exercise their powers in accordance with the HRA, the mere fact that legislation authorizes broad powers does not mean it is incompatible. Public officials are expected to broach their powers in a compliant manner.[72] This approach places a high premium on knowledge and good faith in public officials to act in a compliant manner. However, some argue this expectation is not warranted, because public officials have an inadequate knowledge of the HRA and their responsibilities under it.[73] The JCHR disagrees that a bill should be claimed to be compatible with Convention rights when safeguards are lacking. It also does not feel that governments should rely so heavily on faith in public servants to act in a compliant manner.

These differences with regard to inadequate safeguards in legislation and their relationship to compatibility reports build upon a larger disagreement between the JCHR and government on the treatment of public authorities. In 2004, the JCHR warned of a 'serious gap' in the HRA's protection of rights because of the narrow interpretation being used by public authorities, which could have particularly serious implications for those who are most vulnerable in society, such as elderly people in private care homes, people in housing association

[71] J. Hiebert, 'Governing under the Human Rights Act' 41. [72] Interviews.

[73] J. Watson, 'Something for Everyone: The Impact of the Human Rights Act and the Need for a Human Rights Commission', (2002) The British Institute of Human Rights, December. www.bihr.org.uk/sites/default/files/something_for_everyone.pdf

accommodation and children who receive services provided by private or voluntary sector bodies, or who study outside the regular education sector. The JCHR concluded it would be unsatisfactory to leave this matter to the present state in case law and urged the government to intervene as a third party to press the judiciary to adopt 'a broad, functional interpretation of the meaning of public authority under the Human Rights Act' so to ensure a 'careful application of the current section 6 test so as to prevent any diminution in human rights protection arising from the contracting out of public services'.[74] The government indicated it would intervene in suitable cases in which the meaning of public authority was at issue and would try to persuade the courts to adopt a wider definition of public authority;[75] however, this effort was not successful.[76]

In 2005 the Office for the Deputy Prime Minister (ODPM) published guidelines to assist public authorities with contracting obligations in light of the HRA.[77] The guidelines state that where a 'provider that is not a public authority provides a service to the public under contract to a public authority, that service needs to be provided in a way that takes account of the content of the Human Rights Act 1998, relevant to that contract'.[78] However, the JCHR was extremely critical of that guidance, describing it as difficult to understand, insufficiently attentive to the difficulties that contracting out services to the private sector can have for ensuring rights are protected, and having little or no influence on the procurement policies of local authorities.[79] The JCHR also argued that if government relies on contracting out it must ensure that rights are respected by those performing public functions,[80] and characterized as 'unacceptable' situations in which those who provide public services are uncertain about the scope of their responsibilities and obligations under the HRA.[81]

[74] Parliament of the United Kingdom, JCHR Seventh Report, Session 2003–2004, HL 339/HC 382 para 155.

[75] Parliament of the United Kingdom, JCHR, Nineteenth Report, Session 2004–2005, HL 112/HC 552, para 149.

[76] *YL* v. *Birmingham City Council and others* [2007] UKHL 27.

[77] *Guidance on Contracting for Services in Light of the Human Rights Act 1998*, ODPM, November 2005, www.communities.gov.uk/index.asp?id=1161370

[78] Parliament of the United Kingdom, JCHR, Ninth Report, Session 2006–2007, HL 77 HC 410, para 36.

[79] Ibid., paras 45–60. [80] Ibid., para 59. [81] Ibid., paras 67–69.

Our answer to the puzzle of frequent contestation

The two reasons just given help to explain the frequency with which the JCHR contests ministerial claims of compatibility. Disagreements about proportionality, and the political decision not to construe effective safeguards as necessary to claim a bill is compatible with Convention rights, go a considerable way in explaining why the government and JCHR so frequently disagree about compatibility. However, we believe there are two other significant reasons for the frequency with which affirmative claims of compatibility are contested.

We believe a third reason explaining why the JCHR frequently contests ministerial statements of compatibility is the relatively low threshold legal advisors use in advising ministers that it is appropriate to report a bill as compatible with Convention rights. As discussed, the standard for advising against a report on compatibility is if there is a stronger than 50 per cent chance that the government would lose if legislation is subject to litigation. In addition, advice on compatibility is occasionally framed in a malleable way that permits different judgements to be reached. These two factors support the interpretation that compatibility advice given to ministers does not represent an overly rigorous threshold for recommending whether a bill should be interpreted as compatible with Convention rights for statutory reporting purposes. Thus it is hardly surprising that judgements on this issue are frequently contested, particularly as the method used by the JCHR to assess compatibility appears to be substantially more rigorous.

We believe there is a fourth reason explaining the substantial discrepancy between ministerial and JCHR assessments of compatibility: that governments engage in strategic decision-making when deciding whether and how to address compatibility concerns, and also how to interpret the statutory obligation to report on compatibility. In so doing, they have adopted a relatively low standard for claiming compatibility and are rarely prepared to acknowledge to parliament when their interpretations of compatibility are likely to be contested, or to revisit their judgement when contestation occurs.

As discussed earlier, legal advice on compatibility serves two purposes. One is to assist ministers in fulfilling their statutory obligations to report to parliament on the compatibility status of bills, all as part of the broader goal Labour claimed for the HRA, of legislating in a more rights-compliant manner. The second purpose relates to policy development and approval requirements, as governments want to know about the prospects of judicial censure when managing their legislative agendas. Apprehension of possible judicial censure, and whether and how this will affect the cabinet approval stage, operates as a strong incentive to address possible problems at earlier stages in the policy process. Considerations of more rights-compliant ways to pursue or conceive of a legislative objective are most likely to occur, and are likely to be considered more politically palatable to ministers and government, early in the policy process, and also when they do not prevent government from pursuing legislative objectives to which it is strongly committed. This was conveyed frequently in our interviews, and this perspective also influenced a former chair of the JCHR to try and reform JCHR practices so as to scrutinize government initiatives much earlier in the process, before bills are actually introduced, as will be discussed later.

However, risk aversion is not the only consideration that shapes a government's legislative decisions under the HRA. Governments are frequently risk takers as well. Yet there appears to be little relationship between advice given about risks of judicial censure for policy approval purposes and the advice used for determining what kind of compatibility report is required under section 19 of the HRA. Thus, while governments appear willing to be risk takers – in the sense of introducing legislation which they are likely to have been warned is vulnerable to judicial censure if litigated – the nature or level of this risk is not conveyed to parliament via a section 19(1)(b) report indicating an inability to claim compatibility or, alternatively, in a substantive explanation for a section 19(1)(a) report indicating why the government believes the bill should be considered compatible, despite being vulnerable to a negative judicial ruling.

Our interpretation of a significant gap between knowing about and reporting on compatibility concerns is derived from the cumulative impact of the following four factors. First, legal advisors emphasized that their advice about compatibility is based on relevant case law and is framed as a risk-based assessment of the likelihood that government would lose if the legislation were litigated, and that it is then left to ministers and cabinet to decide how much risk they are prepared to tolerate. Second, officials confirm that ministers have approved bills with high levels of risk for which no section 19(1)(b) report has been made. Third, cabinet guidelines envisage considerable opportunity for political judgement when determining the nature of the section 19 report required, as ministers are authorized to state whether 'in his or her view' the bill's provisions are compatible with Convention rights.[82] Fourth, it is unlikely that government is unaware that it is introducing risky legislation; this is underscored by public officials' acknowledgement that JCHR compatibility concerns are rarely unexpected or come as a surprise,[83] by the multi-layered approaches for assessing compatibility issues and by the fact that ECHR memorandum must be sent to the Attorney General's office before being circulated to the PBL committee. When they are considered together, the force of the preceding four factors supports our interpretation that governments: 1) are prepared to approve legislative bills despite having been forewarned that the legislation is vulnerable to judicial censure; 2) have approved a low threshold for claiming that a bill is compatible with Convention rights for section 19 purposes; and 3) have not interpreted their section 19 responsibilities as requiring that they disclose to parliament the seriousness or nature of compatibility concerns of which they have been fully apprised, or their reasons for believing that their contrary judgement about compatibility is justified.

Affirmative section 19 reports frequently mask considerable discretionary political judgements about why government has approved risky bills, or the nature or level of anticipated risk. Risk aversion and risk-taking occupy either end of a continuum of political considerations of how to govern under the HRA. Both positions shape decisions about how policy goals are integrated into legislation, the choice of different ways of accomplishing these goals, decisions about whether the necessary ministerial report for parliament should claim compatibility or acknowledge an inability to claim compatibility and, ultimately, whether and how to respond to parliamentary and extra-parliamentary pressure to amend bills. The high stakes associated with government 'winning' parliamentary skirmishes, and the perpetual efforts of opposition parties to demonstrate they are the preferable alternative to government, help explain why governments are not anxious for ministers to make section 19(1)(b) reports affirming inability to claim a bill is compatible with Convention rights. Governments can reasonably anticipate that the JCHR and the House of Lords will seize upon such a situation to pressure them into revising the bill or providing justification for why parliament should knowingly pass legislation whose compatibility with Convention rights is uncertain. Yet governments are anxious to avoid or minimize possible

[82] Cabinet Office, *Guidelines for Making Legislation* (July 2014), para 11.107.
[83] Interviews.

obstacles or delays to the passage of legislation. The tendency for the opposition and media to portray government concessions as a sign of weakness also discourages governments from openly acknowledging awareness that legislation might be risky in terms of the possibility of judicial censure.

Strategic behaviour is evident in how and when governments respond to parliamentary concerns that elements of a bill are not compatible with Convention rights. Public officials confirm that once the government has approved the bill for parliament, the only thing likely to compel the government to revisit issues that give rise to compatibility concerns is if parliamentary opposition is sufficiently robust that the government is seriously concerned it will lose the vote or incur significant delays. These concerns are not directly associated with JCHR reports, but instead with subsequent calls for amendments in parliament (which occur primarily in the House of Lords, where peers regularly utilize JCHR reports to substantiate and reinforce the claimed importance of proposed changes).[84] However, as we demonstrate in Chapters 8 and 9, not only do governments not revise their earlier affirmative claims of compatibility, they also rely on their capacity to ensure cohesive voting from party members resulting in their frequent ability to dominate the House of Commons, so as to overturn the amendments upon the bill's return to the Commons.

The lack of transparency in cabinet decision-making, and norms of client confidentiality that prohibit public officials from disclosing the particular advice they provide, make it difficult to specify what particular considerations have influenced governments' decisions to forge ahead with risky legislation in any particular circumstance, or the specific reasons for them to decide against acknowledging uncertainty about compatibility to parliament in a section 19 report. Nevertheless, the considerations that shape political judgement about risk can be reasonably inferred from the kinds of strategic considerations that more generally influence electoral and party politics in Westminster-based parliamentary systems.

Political considerations about how to broach the HRA almost certainly include:

- If it were reported to parliament that government is not confident the bill is compatible with Convention rights under section 19(1)(b), what

[84] Interviews.

effects would this have on the government's ability to pass the legislation without substantive amendments?

- How will risky or risk-averse legislation play out for caucus?
- What effects will risky or risk-averse legislation have on the government's political and electoral constituencies and the media (and in particular the tabloid press)?
- Will government be able to leverage losing a case to subsequently argue to caucus or its electoral base that it was forced to adopt controversial measures that earlier lacked sufficient support?
- What is the estimated strength of lobbying efforts in support or in opposition to the legislative initiative in question?
- Would acknowledging an inability to claim compatibility undermine the government's ability to successful defend the legislation if subject to litigation?
- How long would government likely have from the time of passage and pressure to introduce remedial measures?
- How much deference will courts exercise when reviewing any remedial measures?

In addition to these strategic considerations, judgements about pursuing risky legislation and how to interpret the section 19 reporting obligation on compatibility are also likely shaped by philosophical differences about what constitutes the public interest (often involving contested views about what comprises an appropriate balance between security and liberty), as well as political and philosophical views about the nature of a social problem, the role of the state in redressing it and the appropriate division of labour between courts and parliament in resolving particular contested issues.[85]

In short, the fact that the overwhelming majority of compatibility reports are affirmative should not be interpreted as assurance that compatibility issues have been resolved, or that the four section 19(1)(b) reports acknowledging an inability to claim compatibility are indications of governments' commitment to transparency. Governments have not interpreted the statutory reporting requirement as an obligation to acknowledge or disclose the potentially contested nature of its political judgements about compatibility. The four section

[85] J. Hiebert, 'Legislative Rights Review: Addressing the Gap between Ideals and Constraints', in M. Hunt, H. Hooper and P. Yowell (eds.), *Parliament and Human Rights: Redressing the Democratic Deficit* (Oxford: Hart Publishing), 2015.

19(1)(b) reports to date are best explained by the timing and context in which these respective reports were made.

II. The role of the Joint Committee on Human Rights

As discussed earlier, the lack of transparency in the inner workings of cabinet makes it extremely difficult to identify how legal advice influences any specific ministerial or cabinet decision where questions of compatibility arise. Unlike in New Zealand, where legal advice is publicly available, advice in the UK is provided on a confidential basis with no statutory obligation or political interest to advise parliament about the nature of this advice or whether and how a minister or cabinet's response to this advice influenced a legislative bill.

The JCHR was created to help overcome the limitations of a non-transparent process for evaluating whether and how bills implicate rights that would otherwise rely predominantly upon government checking itself.[86] The JCHR's remit is extremely broad, but the committee decided early on to focus primary attention to whether bills are compatible with Convention rights and, by implication, to ascertain whether ministerial claims of compatibility are persuasive.[87] JCHR reports analyse legislative provisions which the committee identifies as raising compatibility issues and generally report concerns and recommendations to parliament while the bill is still being debated in at least one house. These reports also include copies of written correspondence with departmental officials and ministers (for bills, draft bills or White/Green Papers, as distinct from informal communications), the committee's assessments of these ministerial and departmental responses and testimony from oral hearings the committee has

[86] The JCHR's remit includes (a) matters relating to human rights in the United Kingdom (but excluding consideration of individual cases); (b) proposals for remedial orders, draft remedial orders and remedial orders made under section 10, schedule 2 of the Human Rights Act 1998; and (c) with respect to draft orders and remedial orders, whether the special attention of the House of Commons should be drawn to them.

[87] JCHR, First Report, Session 2000–2001, HL 69/HC 427 at Annex 1. In a subsequent report, the committee indicated in a letter sent to the secretary of state for the Home Department, 'our starting-point is of course the statement made under s. 19(1)(a) of the Human Rights Act 1998; but . . . the committee's remit extends to human rights in a broad sense, not just the Convention rights under the Act'. Parliament of the United Kingdom, JCHR, Third Report, Session 2003–2004, HL 23/HC 252, Appendix 1, p. 23.

conducted, and/or submissions from civil liberty organizations, academics and other non-governmental individuals or groups with concerns and opinions about the legislation in question. The committee follows up with progress reports, which include its assessment of ministerial and departmental responses to its earlier queries.[88] The committee also conducts thematic assessments that focus on serious rights issues.

Although the committee has characterized itself as the parliamentary guardian of the HRA,[89] the JCHR has broached its scrutiny and reporting obligations with three principal audiences in mind: department officials who help develop and evaluate legislative initiatives; the executive (ministers, who are responsible for the bills they introduce and who report on whether these are compatible with Convention rights, and cabinet, which approves which initiatives will be approved as bills for introduction to parliament); and parliamentarians who evaluate, debate and vote on legislation. Occasionally the JCHR targets a fourth audience for its reports, the judiciary – as discussed in Chapter 8 (describing the JCHR's criticism of the court's deference to parliament on control orders because it viewed this as an abdication of the judiciary's responsibility under the HRA). The remainder of this chapter considers the influence of JCHR reports on the first two audiences. The JCHR's influence on parliament is discussed in Chapters 8 and 9.

A serious challenge to the committee when assessing legislative bills is the lack of information explaining or supporting ministerial reports that legislative bills are compatible with Convention rights.[90] A proposed amendment during parliamentary debate on the HRA would have required that section 19 statements be accompanied by a report outlining any issues the minister considered relevant for the determination of

[88] Adam Tomkins makes the important observation that this perseverance, keeping an issue on the agenda through updated and thematic reports, is the way to win in politics by not letting an issue die or being dependent on an accident of litigation. Adam Tomkins, 'Parliament, Human Rights and Counter-Terrorism', in T. Campbell, K.D. Ewing and A. Tomkins (eds.), *The Legal Protection of Human Rights: Sceptical Essays* (Oxford: Oxford University Press, 2011), pp. 44–65.

[89] Parliament of the United Kingdom, JCHR, Second Report, Session 2001–2002, HL 37/HC 372, para 5.

[90] The Committee also recommended that in rare occasions that a government does acknowledge the need for a 19(1)(b) report, this should also be accompanied by full explanation of why the government considers the legislation to be sufficiently compelling. Parliament of the United Kingdom, JCHR, First Report, Session 2002–2003, HL 24/HC 191.

compatibility. The failed amendment was an attempt to ensure that parliament is aware of the substantive reasoning for ministerial reports on compatibility, to provoke more critical questioning and to avoid the potential for statements of compatibility to act as a rubber stamp for legal advice.[91] In speaking against the amendment, the government argued this additional report was not required, and that parliamentary debate 'would provide the best forum in which the Government's thinking could be fully explained'.[92]

However, despite initially acknowledging parliament's important role in evaluating the persuasiveness of the government's reasons for assuming a bill is compatible with Convention rights, early ministerial compatibility reports provided little explanation to support positive claims that bills are compatible with Convention rights, and ministers demonstrated little interest in parliament's perspective on this issue.[93]

The JCHR has persistently criticized the lack of explanation in support of compatibility claims and has pressured ministers and departments to provide more substantive explanations about the justification for contentious legislative provisions.[94] The Labour government was not sympathetic to the JCHR's position and argued that additional information about compatibility would conflict with the confidentiality of the government's legal advice.[95] However, the JCHR continued to press for

[91] Parliament of the United Kingdom, Hansard, HC, col 1349–2350, 21 October 1998.

[92] Ibid., col 1351, 21 October 1998.

[93] Interviews. See also Parliament of the United Kingdom, JCHR, Second Special Report, Session 2000–2001, HL 66-I/HC 332-I, appendices.

[94] One member of the committee characterized compatibility statements as 'random and haphazard', and suggested that a system should be established so that whenever a government publishes a bill, or a draft bill, the reasons why it is compatible or justified should accompany the bill in explanatory notes. Parliament of the United Kingdom, JCHR, Minutes of Evidence Taken on Monday, March 26 2001, Session 2000–2001, HL 66-i/HC 332-I, at Q26–28 (Lord Lester).

[95] As Jack Straw, then Home Secretary, replied to committee questioning: 'To go down the road that you suggest would … either mean that we were repeating what was in the explanatory memorandum … or it would require extensive disclosure of the legal advice available to ministers, either directly or indirectly. The first we do already and the second I am powerfully against. I would not be in favour of it and you would not get my colleagues in favour of it because it is a long standing rule that ministers are no more required to disclose legal advice given to them by law officers than any individual or corporation has to make available publicly or to any potential respondent or defendant to an action for the legal advice they have received. The law protects that very closely by professional privilege.' Parliament of the United Kingdom, JCHR, Minutes of Evidence Taken on Monday, March 26 2001, Session 2000–2001, HL 66-i/HC 332-I, Q27. The JCHR disagreed with the inference that it was seeking confidential legal information, and

information, suggesting the value of a freestanding or dedicated human rights memorandum to explain the government's conclusions that a bill is or is not compatible with Convention rights,[96] and in particular to explain why an infringement 'is justifiable and proportionate'.[97]

The JCHR's concerted attempts to improve the accountability and transparency of the government's decision-making have led to improvements to the explanations that support section 19 reports. Although the Labour government rejected the suggestion for a dedicated human rights memorandum,[98] it subsequently changed the Cabinet Office guidelines and instructed departments to provide detail of the most significant Convention issues that arise in a bill and also for the minister's conclusions on compatibility in the explanatory notes to a bill.[99] The JCHR noted modest improvement to some department reports under the Labour government, but indicated it was still not satisfied with the overall quality of the arguments and explanations provided to support positive claims of compatibility.[100] Moreover, some officials we spoke to believe that the use of explanatory notes is not a particularly useful medium for these explanations. By convention, explanatory notes are intended to be descriptive and not used for political arguments because they are published on behalf of parliament, and therefore should be neutral in as far as they pertain to political arguments. However, the task of explaining why a minister (and cabinet) believes that a bill is compatible with Convention rights can blur the line between explanation and argument.[101]

reminded the government that when promoting the HRA it had stressed the importance of involving parliament in judgments about rights: Ibid., Lord Lester, Q28.

96 Parliament of the United Kingdom, JCHR, Annual Report 2007, para 24; Parliament of the United Kingdom, JCHR, Thirty-first Report, Session 2007–2008, HL 173/HC 1078, para 43.

97 Interview. An example that demonstrates the nature of these explanations, including one of the rare instances of the government revealing the legal advice it has relied upon, is the Civil Contingencies Bill.

98 Officials we interviewed offered three explanations for failing to address the JCHR's concerns: workload demands; the failure of some departments to consider human rights considerations early enough in the policy process; and concerns that providing more detailed explanations about compatibility claims could be used to support litigation against the Crown (Interviews).

99 This undertaking was maintained in new Cabinet Guidelines under the Coalition government. Cabinet Office, *Guidelines for Making Legislation*, July 2014, para 11.122.

100 Interviews.

101 Interviews.

The relevant Cabinet Office guidelines changed again under the Coalition government, reflecting a commitment 'to provide more detailed information on the human rights aspects of government bills' in explanatory notes so as to 'assist Parliament, both in debates and through the Joint Committee on Human Rights'.[102] The guidelines advise departments that the JCHR is 'likely to examine closely the arguments put forward by the department justifying interference with a Convention right', and also warn department officials and ministers that if the JCHR believes explanatory notes to a bill 'do not adequately set out the Convention issues' it will ask the responsible minister for a memorandum on particular points, 'which will need to be produced extremely quickly'. The guidelines emphasize that it is 'clearly advantageous if the JCHR reports favourably early in the bill's passage' and that departments 'should attempt to identify areas likely to concern the Committee and prepare briefing ahead of time, if possible'. In a pre-emptive attempt to reduce ongoing correspondence with the JCHR, the guidelines also suggest that departments 'volunteer' a memorandum at the time of introduction that advises the JCHR of human rights issues a bill might raise, particularly if the issues are too substantial to be addressed in explanatory notes.[103] Finally, cabinet guidelines for drafting legislation identify the explanatory notes to the Criminal Justice and Immigration Bill (passed under the Labour government) as illustrating 'a comprehensive approach to human rights analysis that was noted with approval by the Joint Committee on Human Rights' which can be used as guidance for future bills.[104]

When speculating on reasons why more substantive explanations are provided than in the past, one official suggested the improvement is likely to have been influenced by public officials' growing acceptance of the idea that these explanations should accompany bills as a matter of prudent policy-making (or at least as a pragmatic response to the likelihood that the JCHR will continue to pressure departments to provide these), rather than being due to specific ministerial directives.[105] Like all busy professionals, the public servants who help develop and advise on bills have no interest in having to spend valuable time responding to queries that could have been avoided, and which detract from fulfilling other responsibilities.

[102] Cabinet Office, *Guidelines for Making Legislation*, July 2014, para 11.121.
[103] Ibid., paras 11.125–11.126. [104] Ibid., para 11.122. [105] Interviews.

Assessing the JCHR's influence before bills are introduced

The JCHR influences legislative initiatives at the pre-parliamentary stage in at least three ways, as government policy objectives evolve from general propositions to their consideration and eventual conception as legislative bills approved by cabinet for introduction to parliament. The first arises from the JCHR's record and reputation for critical reports on and substantive questions asked of ministers and departments, which encourages department officials to anticipate JCHR queries about how proposed policy objectives might implicate rights prior to these being formalized as legislative bills.[106] Policy officials and legal advisors we spoke to were remarkably consistent in their assessment that departments have a strong interest in avoiding mention in a critical JCHR report. This is understandable, particularly if the problematic provision is revisable without significant alteration to the scope of the legislative objective.[107] Public servants not only have to take into account ethical considerations about how to comply with statutory requirements; they also have professional reputations they wish to protect. Thus, legal advisors' failure to advise on serious compatibility issues subsequently identified by the JCHR raises concerns about whether their earlier judgement will be a source of embarrassment. The prospect of failing to advise on an issue that is subsequently subject to a critical JCHR report also raises issues regarding good working relationships with ministers and their staff. A letter from the JCHR to a minister requiring additional information not only requires that the minister and his or her staff devote time to respond to these queries but also engages departmental officials in the act of explaining or justifying earlier decisions and, depending on the interpretation or force of the JCHR's queries, potentially admitting that earlier advice needs to be re-evaluated and revised.

The JCHR's firmly established practice of persistent questioning of departments and ministers in pursuit of explanations, and following up when not convinced or where questions go unanswered, has compelled public servants and ministers to find ways to minimize the extent to which they will be called upon to explain and justify decisions to the committee. The attention accorded to the JCHR in Cabinet Office guidelines attests to this anticipatory effect, advising departments and ministers that they should provide more substantive explanations to support

[106] Interviews. [107] Interviews.

positions that rights are not implicated and/or that legislative objectives and means are compatible with Convention rights. It is not simply a time management issue – in the sense of having to make time to respond to the committee's queries – which has enhanced the committee's role and impact on policy development. The committee's practice of publishing a thorough and transparent record of its proceedings as an aid for parliament's subsequent scrutiny reduces the likelihood that correspondence left unanswered or weakly addressed responses will go unnoticed by parliamentary critics (most likely coming from the House of Lords) or non-governmental actors who are critical of the government's proposals. Both anticipation of JCHR objections and the need to explain reasons and provide justifications suggests the committee's focus on compatibility is having a significant prophylactic effect on how legislative bills are developed and the bureaucratic and political tasks of explaining assumptions about how and why they are compatible with Convention rights.

A second way in which the JCHR influences bills is more substantive in terms of altering initial conceptions of how to pursue a particular legislative objective, and even the nature of the policy objective itself. In those circumstances in which committee advisors engage in informal conversations with policy officials at the early stages of policy development, or where the committee engages in substantive review of policy proposals that are the subject of Green or White Papers, the JCHR can influence whether and how government decides to pursue a particular initiative. A critical factor that influences the JCHR's capacity to influence legislative initiatives at the pre-bill stage is that government has not yet invested as much political capital in the issue, and thus is more willing to adjust how it intends to proceed with the measure, because revisions at this stage are less likely to be portrayed in the media or in parliament as a sign of political weakness. It was this potential to influence government that motivated Andrew Dismore, former chair of the JCHR, to consider how the committee could more regularly become involved earlier in the policy process, for example by shifting its priorities to accord more time to reviewing government Green Papers (government-initiated consultation documents that explain a government initiative and function to elicit public reaction and encourage reflection on the merits of the initiative and different ways in which it can be achieved). His assumption was that if rights-based scrutiny could occur before the government had high political stakes associated with a particular legislative bill, the government would be more amenable to changes, because agreeing to rights-inspired amendments would not carry the same political liabilities.[108]

The JCHR's assessment of the government's Justice and Security Green Paper provides a good example of the committee's influence on the scope and effects of a government initiative through its evaluations of government proposals in this pre-bill period. The Green Paper proposed the use of closed material proceedings (CMP) in a wide range of civil proceedings (the actual bill is examined in more depth in Chapter 8). In this case, the JCHR's extremely critical assessment of the government's initiatives influenced the government to narrow the scope of its proposals to extend the availability of closed material procedures in civil proceedings.[109] When the legislative bill was introduced it differed significantly from the Green Paper proposal. Changes made in response to JCHR concerns included excluding inquests from the scope of the bill, allowing a more substantial role for the judiciary and allowing use of a CMP only in cases involving national security, as contrasted with the initial proposal that a CMP could be used in the broad context of the public interest.

A third way of influencing legislative initiatives is through the JCHR's evidence-based approach to assessing bills, particularly when these invoke new coercive powers that implicate liberty and which depart from judicial norms and/or constitutional principles. The JCHR's approach to the Justice Security Bill is again being called upon, which demonstrates the significance of the JCHR's emphasis on the importance of evidence to justify potentially rights-infringing actions. In its hearing process, the committee received evidence from a wide range of non-governmental organizations, civil liberty organizations and legal scholars who suggested the government had failed to justify the case for introducing closed material procedures into civil proceedings, and criticized the lack of safeguards and the lack of judicial oversight as significant departures from common law principles of justice and fairness. The JCHR also took

[108] Interviews (attribution authorized).

[109] This argument was made by J. Hiebert in 'Legislative Rights Review: Addressing the Gap between Ideals and Constraints', in M. Hunt, H. Hooper and P. Yowell (eds.) *Parliament and Human Rights: Redressing the Democratic Deficit* (Oxford: Hart Publishing), 2015. The minister responsible for the bill, Kenneth Clarke, indicated he had been influenced by the JCHR's criticisms and proposed amendments: Justice and Security Bill, Research Paper 12/80, House of Commons Library, 14 December 2012, p. 13. See also discussion by Parliament of the United Kingdom, JCHR, Fourth Report, Session 2012–2013, HL 59/HC 370, paras 21–22.

evidence from Kenneth Clarke, the minister in charge of the bill, who stated publicly that he had been unsettled by the evidence of Special Advocates who had indicated their strong critical reaction to the proposals.[110] Clarke subsequently confirmed that the government made substantive changes to the Green Paper proposal based on the JCHR's criticisms.[111]

It is difficult to discount the significance of the JCHR's reputation for critical commentary. Robust, frequent and critical reports serve as constant reminders to public officials, ministers and cabinet that unresolved compatibility queries will be questioned. JCHR reports encourage them to anticipate critical reviews and be prepared to respond to JCHR queries. Moreover, informal correspondence and review of White and Green Papers reinforce the importance of utilizing more compliant ways to achieve complex legislative initiatives before policy proposals become formalized as legislative bills. Finally evidence-based hearings maintain pressure on ministers to ensure their reasons are justified for pursuing legislative initiatives that implicate rights in an adverse manner.

However, notwithstanding these significant ways in which the JCHR increases pressure on department officials and ministers to anticipate, justify and address compatibility issues, it is important not to exaggerate its influence on legislation, whether before a bill has been introduced or after, while subject to parliamentary review (as discussed in Chapters 8 and 9). The JCHR's well-earned reputation as a respected and persistent thorn in a government's side does not ensure that government will necessarily reassess its views on compatibility (as Harman confirmed) or that parliament will take up the issues with sufficient force or conviction to require government to accept amendments, as will become more clear in the following two chapters.

As argued earlier, legal advisors' acknowledgement that government is prepared to proceed with risky legislation, and the frequency with which the JCHR contests these ministerial assertions of compatibility, serve as important arguments against the assumption that government will necessarily prioritize compliance with legal perspectives about compatibility, or subordinate its internal decision-making about compatibility to the

[110] O. Bowcott and I. Cobain, 'Ken Clarke Unsettled by Criticism of Secret Court Plan', *The Guardian*, 6 March 2012, www.guardian.co.uk/politics/2012/mar/06/ken-clarke-secret-courts-plan-criticised

[111] Parliament of the United Kingdom, *Hansard*, HC, vol 555, col 721, 18 December 2012 (Kenneth Clarke).

JCHR's or others' views on this issue. Anticipation of a negative JCHR report does not appear to regularly divert government from pursuing a bill for which it is deeply committed, or influence its judgements about compatibility. We were told repeatedly that once government has decided to introduce a bill and has reached a judgement about how to interpret the statutory reporting obligation, this judgement will not be revised once a bill is introduced regardless of what the JCHR has to say,[112] which was strongly confirmed by Harman in her appearance before the JCHR.

We will focus more specifically on the JCHR's influence on legislation in the next two chapters when examining how parliament evaluates legislation that has been subject to critical JCHR assessments.

Conclusion

Our interviews with public officials and assessment of cabinet guidelines and JCHR involvement in the pre-parliamentary phases of legislative development suggest that governments act strategically when deciding how the HRA should shape and influence their legislative agenda and how to interpret the statutory reporting obligation on compatibility. An important part of the process of developing and approving a government's legislative agenda is attention to potential obstacles that could alter, delay or defeat a government bill. The HRA introduces an additional set of considerations that enter into governments' assessments of the vulnerability of their political agenda. Political strategies for managing vulnerability associated with the HRA operate on a continuum ranging from risk aversion to risk-taking, and influence the scope of the government's policy objectives and means adopted for accomplishing these, as well as decisions about whether the necessary ministerial report to parliament on compatibility should affirm consistency with Convention rights or acknowledge an inability to claim compatibility.

Governments have every reason to want to be apprised of possible obstacles to the successful pursuit of their legislative agendas before introducing bills to parliament. Judicial review is a potentially potent obstacle, particularly where judicial remedial powers can alter the scope or effects of legislation, and where a strong expectation of compliance occurs that can compel a government to promote remedial measures

[112] Interviews.

which differ from its initial policy preferences and, if contested, can undermine party cohesion and reopen unwelcome controversies among relevant stakeholders and the broader public. This interest in anticipating and redressing unnecessary risk likely influences the way policy objectives are conceived and drafted as legislative bills, by focusing more attention on proportionality and compliant ways to achieve government objectives. Public officials confirm that assessments of legislative initiatives and advice to ministers about whether they are compatible with Convention rights are significantly more robust than was the case before the HRA was adopted, and emphasize the significance of proportionality considerations and their influence on the means adopted for pursuing legislative initiatives. This suggests that risk-averse incentives and, in particular, the reluctance to provoke unnecessary litigation have a significant influence on legislation by identifying and pursuing more compliant ways of implementing a government's legislative objectives, particularly where so doing does not sufficiently hinder a government's policy objectives.

The JCHR also exerts a prophylactic effect on legislation by emphasizing rigorous standards when evaluating proposed legislation's compatibility with Convention rights. The JCHR's persistence and tenacity when raising compatibility queries has resulted in the requirement to anticipate and address JCHR concerns being formalized in cabinet guidelines. The committee has also been able to influence the scope and nature of legislative initiatives through informal meetings with policy officials in the early stages of the policy process and through reviewing initiatives that are the subject of governmental White or Green papers.

However, risk aversion is not the only way in which governments respond to the HRA. At the other end of the continuum is the competing political strategy of risk-taking, which most likely occurs when government is strongly committed to a policy objective and interprets a more compliant approach as undermining the effectiveness of the proposed initiative and/or party and public support for its preferred approach.

A risk-taking strategy does not simply consider the gamble of whether or not the government will elude successful litigation, but also the consequences and political implications of losing. The considerations that likely influence governments' strategic calculus were described previously.

It is reasonable to assume that pursuing risky legislation is likely to be considered a more palatable option if the rights that are implicated affect unpopular minorities or other segments of society who do not evoke strong public sympathy, such as those labelled a threat to national security, or prisoners. Risk-taking involves political assessment by government leaders as to whether the anticipated societal and political benefits of pursuing risky legislative initiatives sufficiently outweigh the adverse consequences that could arise if legislation is eventually ruled inconsistent with Convention rights.

It goes without saying that in order to adopt either strategy, a government must have the capacity to anticipate the likelihood that legislation will be litigated, and also to assess how proposed legislation will likely fare if challenged. The resources required for these evaluations do not substantially increase demands on the policy process because compatibility assessments for section 19 purposes are framed as risk-based assessments of the government's prospects of defending legislation if subject to litigation. Moreover, depending on the issue, ministers might be well aware of JCHR concerns at this pre-legislative stage, whether as a result of informal advice or through review at draft stage.

However, risk-based assessments of legislative initiatives are not necessarily the same thing as compatibility-based assessments. Although a risk-based approach can identify possible inconsistencies with judicial rulings and lead to more compliant legislation, the extent to which concerns are identified and addressed will be heavily influenced by whether the relevant jurisprudence is sufficiently robust or settled. Where this is not the case, rights infringements might go unaddressed. Moreover, a risk-based approach that focuses on what a government can get away with is a substantively different exercise from a more substantial assessment of whether legislative bills or the actions of public authorities comply with the normative values reflected in the HRA. The distinction between risk-based and compatibility-based assessment is particularly apparent in the dispute between government and the JCHR on the importance of safeguards to ensure public authorities exercise power and make decisions in a rights-compliant manner.

Finally, the frequency with which the JCHR contests government claims of compatibility leads us to conclude that government behaviour frequently lies closer to the risk-taking than the risk-aversion end of the continuum of strategic responses to the HRA. This interpretation is reinforced by interviews with legal advisors who confirm that governments have approved bills when the level of risk identified is high (although without interpreting this as an obligation to present a section 19(1)(b) report acknowledging an inability to claim compatibility), and by the change in cabinet guidelines from the primacy of legal opinion to ministers' opinions. However, although governments might have a political appetite or tolerance for introducing a bill that is risky in terms of the possibility of judicial censure, there is no corresponding willingness to inform parliament about the nature or degree of risk, or to explain the assumptions or reasons for proceeding with a bill that stands a reasonable chance of being subject to judicial censure.

8

Parliamentary Review of National Security Measures

This chapter shifts the focus from how the HRA influences political behaviour in the pre-parliamentary phase of developing, evaluating and approving legislative initiatives to its influence on parliamentary deliberation and decisions about whether to amend, support or defeat bills. We begin with parliamentary assessments of legislative bills developed in the context of national security concerns, which is the focus of this chapter.

It is safe to assume that some legislative objectives provoke more resistance than others to the idea of being subject to rights-based constraints. Legislation directed at national security is a prime example.[1] Governments have particularly strong incentives to legislate during periods of real or apprehended risks to national security. While this impulse might be influenced by sincere intentions to protect the security of the nation and to soothe public concerns by giving the appearance that government is capable of exercising some modicum of control in these circumstances, it is also influenced by the government's political objective of demonstrating to the public that its record justifies continued support and re-election. However, as Fiona De Londras and Fergal Davis argue, political responses in times of periods of violent instability and high terrorist threats have resulted in a 'security bias' and political claims by the executive that new laws should not be subject to strong legislative or judicial checks, despite their potentially adverse implications for individual rights.[2]

[1] Fiona de Londras characterizes political behaviour in this context as the politics of 'panic'. She argues that terrorism-related panic is both a bottom-up and top-down phenomenon, where political actors incur pressure to protect the public but also reinforce this fear in a manner that 'habitually enables expansions of state power' in the name of national security. She argues that public pressures and political desires for extensive security measures combine to create a 'significant space within which to introduce laws and policies that result in an expansion of state power'. F. de Londras, *Detention in the 'War on Terror'. Can Human Rights Fight Back?* (Cambridge: Cambridge University Press, 2011).

[2] De Londras and Davis provide a persuasive critique of claims that the executive is uniquely suited or justified to 'make decisions about how to manage a risk that threatens national

This chapter examines parliamentary review of national security measures introduced after the HRA came into effect, including the Blair government's Anti-Terrorism, Crime and Security Bill (2001), which introduced indefinite detention of foreign terrorist suspects without charge and required a derogation from the ECHR; the Prevention of Terrorism Bill (2005), which introduced control orders as a replacement for indefinite detention after the Law Lords ruled that indefinite detention was incompatible with Convention rights; the Terrorism Bill (2005–06), introduced in the aftermath of the London bombing; the Counter-Terrorism Bill (2008), in which the Brown government sought to extend the period of detention without charge after parliamentary pressure forced the Labour government to reduce the period from its initial proposal of 90 days to 28; the Conservative-led Coalition government's Terrorism Prevention and Investigation Measures (TPIMs) Bill of 2011, containing measures conceived as a replacement for control orders; and the same government's Justice and Security Bill of 2012, which introduced closed procedures for civil trials involving national security issues.

The JCHR has strongly contested Labour and Coalition government claims that these respective bills are compatible with Convention rights. However, contrary to the framers' stated expectation that parliament should ask questions related to the 'reasoning behind a statement of compatibility' and that parliament is the forum where 'the Government's thinking [about its judgement on compatibility] can be fully explained',[3] the House of Commons has demanded relatively little of government in this regard. The House of Lords has been far more interested in engaging JCHR reports and using compatibility concerns to pressure government to amend bills. Yet, while the House of Lords has been able to secure important rights-protecting amendments, the significance of many of these has been diminished by their character. For example, rather than defeat controversial measures such as control orders, these powers were passed while subject to a requirement for parliamentary review in order to be renewed. However, renewal has not proven onerous for

security and that, as a result, neither the Legislature nor the Judiciary ought to limit Executive action, even on rights-protection grounds'. F. de Londras and F. F. Davis, 'Controlling the Executive in Times of Terrorism: Competing Perspectives on Effective Oversight', (2010) 30 *Oxford Journal of Legal Studies* 21.

[3] Parliament of the United Kingdom, *Hansard* HL, vol 583, vol 1163–1164, 27 November 1997 (Lord Chancellor (Lord Irvine)).

government. Moreover, the cohesive character of party membership has enabled both Labour and Coalition governments to defeat other rights-improving amendments in the Commons and, in the case of the Justice and Security Bill, to effectively whip peers as well.

Although neither Labour nor Coalition governments have achieved the full scope of their legislative agendas in the national security sphere and have had to accept significant amendments, the expectation of justifying compatibility to parliament has not generally been a substantial hurdle preventing governments from passing their principal policy goals of indefinite detention of foreign terrorist suspects, control orders that have weak judicial oversight, long periods of detention without charge (with the exception of Labour's second attempt under Brown) and closed material procedures for civil trials.

I. Anti-terrorism legislation

The Labour government introduced the Anti-Terrorism, Crime and Security Act soon after the terrorist events of 11 September 2001 in the United States. The government framed its legislative objective as responding to the following serious dilemma:[4] how should the UK deal with persons suspected of being international terrorists who cannot be deported because of concerns they will be tortured, but also cannot be subject to trial because of the sensitivity of the evidence and the high standard of proof in a criminal proceeding?[5]

The government's response was to create a new power to subject foreign nationals to indefinite detention if they are suspected of having links to international terrorism and are perceived to be a risk to national security.[6] The obvious conflict between indefinite detention without criminal trial and the protection of liberty under Article 5.1 of the ECHR required the government to either declare that the legislation was not

[4] The government attributed this dilemma to the *Chahal* ruling, that Article 3 of the ECHR is breached if a country deports anyone to a country while knowing that the individual in question faces a substantial risk of being tortured or subject to inhuman and degrading treatment: *Chahal* v. *UK* (1996) 23 EHRR 413.

[5] H. Fenwick and G.P. Phillipson, 'Legislative Over-breadth, Democratic Failure and the Judicial Response: Fundamental Rights and the UK's Anti-terrorist Legal Policy', in V. Ramraj, M. Hor and K. Roach (eds.), *Global Anti-Terrorism Law and Policy* (Cambridge: Cambridge University Press, 2005), pp. 455–90, p. 463.

[6] Ibid., p. 463.

compatible with Convention rights, or to make a derogation order under section 14 of the Human Rights Act 1998. The government chose the latter course and interpreted its decision to derogate from the ECHR as allowing it to claim that the bill was otherwise compatible with the HRA for section 19 reporting purposes.

Many disputed the necessity for additional powers,[7] characterizing them as 'panic measures' to address public concern,[8] and argued that the proposed measures were not a proportionate response to the actual level of threat facing the UK.[9] Critics also disputed the ministerial claim that the bill was compatible with Convention rights, arguing that despite the bill's 'clearly rights-abridging' powers,[10] parliament was being given the misimpression that the bill had undergone 'a process of Human Rights Act auditing' and therefore was assuming that 'the Bill met Convention standards'.[11] For example, Helen Fenwick and Gavin Phillipson criticized the government for ignoring the importance of the 'sustained, careful scrutiny' necessary for a country that respects the rule of law and human rights and characterized the legislation as containing 'draconian powers'.[12]

Then Home Secretary David Blunkett disputed allegations that the legislation was both unnecessary and inconsistent with a commitment to rights. He insisted that the Anti-Terrorism, Crime and Security Bill was a 'rational, reasonable and proportionate response' to security concerns,[13] and criticized what he referred to as the 'civil liberties lobby' for 'vitriolic

[7] For a comprehensive discussion, see C. Walker and S. Osborne (eds.), *Blackstone's Guide to The Anti-Terrorism Legislation* (Oxford: Oxford University Press, 2009). Non-governmental organizations have also been critical of the legislation: see in particular Liberty, www.liberty-human-rights.org.uk/issues/2-terrorism/index.shtml

[8] C. Walker, 'Clamping Down on Terrorism in the United Kingdom', (2006) 4 *Journal of International Criminal Justice* 1137.

[9] D. McKeever, 'The Human Rights Act and Anti-Terrorism in the United Kingdom: One Great Leap Forward by Parliament, But Are the Courts Able to Slow the Steady Retreat that has Followed?', (2010) *Public Law* 117; H. Fenwick and G. P. Phillipson, 'Legislative Over-breadth, Democratic Failure and the Judicial Response', p. 459.

[10] *Chahal* v. *UK* (1996) 23 EHRR 413.

[11] H. Fenwick, 'Anti-Terrorism, Crime and Security Act 2001: A Proportionate Response to 11 September?', (2002) 65 *Modern Law Review* 724, at pp. 727–28; see also C. Gearty, 'Terrorism and Human Rights: A Case Study of Impending Legal Realities', (1999) 19 *Legal Studies* 367, at p. 379.

[12] H. Fenwick and G.P. Phillipson, 'Legislative Over-breadth, Democratic Failure and the Judicial Response', p. 457.

[13] Parliament of the United Kingdom, *Hansard*, HC, vol 375, col 25, 19 November 2001 (David Blunkett).

abuse' rather than providing a helpful contribution to informed debate.[14] He also indicated that the government was prepared to amend the HRA if judicial review prevented strong anti-terrorism legislation.[15]

Parliamentary review

It was not merely the government's perceived lack of commitment to the HRA that some found troubling. Many were also concerned about the House of Commons' refusal to engage in rights-based scrutiny of the proposed measures, despite several parliamentary reports that identified substantial potential rights infringements.[16] The Anti-Terrorism, Crime and Security Bill was one of the first bills scrutinized by the JCHR. Despite some members' initial uncertainty about the scope or implications of the committee's mandate,[17] the gravity of the potential rights infringements helped galvanize the committee's understanding of its scrutiny function.[18] The JCHR reported it was not convinced that the Home Secretary had presented a justifiable case for why derogation and indefinite detention were required.[19] It also criticized the overly broad definition of 'terrorist' that was given, the lack of due process for authorizing indefinite detention, new powers to fingerprint immigrants and the retention of this data even after cases were solved and insufficient safeguards against abuse of the fingerprint database and for newly created police powers to detain and search suspects.[20]

Notwithstanding the JCHR's critical assessment of the bill, the government found it easy to get the legislation through the House of Commons. Although more than a dozen Labour members voted against the decision to derogate from Convention rights and authorize indefinite

[14] A. Travis, 'Blunkett to Face Rough Ride Over Terror Law', *The Guardian*, 19 November 2011, http://politics.guardian.co.uk/attacks/story/0,1320,597231,00.html

[15] 'Blunkett Puts War Before Concerns for Human Rights', *The Telegraph*, 24 September 2001, www.telegraph.co.uk/news/main.jhtml?xml=/news/2001/09/24/nblunk24.xml

[16] These included the House of Commons Home Affairs Select Committee, First Report, Session 2001–02 The Anti-Terrorism, Crime and Security Bill 2001, HC 351; The House of Lords Constitution Committee, Second Report, Session 2001–02, The Anti-Terrorism, Crime and Security Bill, HL Paper 41; and The House of Lords Delegated Powers and Regulatory Review Committee, Seventh Report, Session 2001–02, November 27 2001, HL 45

[17] Interviews. [18] Interviews.

[19] Parliament of the United Kingdom, JCHR, Second Report, Session 2001–2002, HL 37/HC 372, para 5.

[20] Ibid., paras 17–68.

detention without trial and more than 30 Labour members voted against the lack of judicial review of terrorist certifications,[21] the government's sizeable majority ensured passage of the bill without a single amendment. The relative speed and ease with which the Commons passed the legislation prompted the following harsh criticism from a political columnist in the *Guardian*: 'In a long record of shaming fealty to the whips, never have so many MPs showed such utter negligence towards so impressive a list of fundamental principles.'[22]

The government had a considerably more difficult time in the House of Lords, which subjected the bill to far more rigorous scrutiny – a factor at least one member attributed to the cavalier manner in which the House of Commons had dealt with the bill. Lord Stoddart rebuked the House of Commons for its lack of critical review of the bill:

> It is a matter of concern that a Bill containing 126 clauses should be sent to this House without most of them having been properly considered. It is no good the Home Secretary or any other Cabinet Minister complaining about this House, when it has done its job—a job which should have been done by the House of Commons in the first place, it having been elected to do so. It is entirely reprehensible that an elected House of Commons should have less concern than this House for the freedoms and the rights of the people of this country.[23]

The House of Lords called for significant rights-protecting amendments, such as deleting the creation of a new crime of inciting religious hatred, introducing a sunset clause whereby powers to detain without trial would lapse after a specific period and restricting the scope of provisions to retain communications data.[24] The House of Lords triggered 12 report stage defeats,[25] although many of these amendments were subsequently defeated in the House of Commons.[26]

[21] 'Labour MPs Rebel on Terror Bill', *BBC News*, 22 November 2001, http://news.bbc.co.uk/2/hi/uk_news/politics/1669175.stm

[22] H. Young, 'Once Lost, These Freedoms will be Impossible to Restore', *The Guardian*, 11 December 2001, www.guardian.co.uk/politics/2001/dec/11/britainand911.september11

[23] Parliament of the United Kingdom, *Hansard*, HL, vol 629, col 1155, 10 Dec 2001, Lord Stoddart.

[24] H. Fenwick and G. P. Phillipson, 'Legislative Over-breadth, Democratic Failure and the Judicial Response', p. 458.

[25] C. Nicholls, 'The UK Anti-Terrorism Crime & Security Act 2001: Too Much ... Too Soon', (2002) 9 *Commonwealth Human Rights Initiative Newsletter*, February.

[26] H. Fenwick and G. P. Phillipson, 'Legislative Over-breadth, Democratic Failure and the Judicial Response', p. 458.

Home Office Minister Lord Rooker was critical of these amendments, claiming they would 'wreck the bill'.[27] Blunkett was even more outspoken, rejecting arguments that rights-based concerns justify changes to the bill, dismissing those who moved amendments as 'naïve' and characterizing the proposed amendments as 'disembowelling' vital aspects of the legislation.[28] This criticism was hardly a surprise in light of Blunkett's earlier pronouncement that the HRA was 'the biggest mistake' the Blair government had made in its first term in office.[29]

Notwithstanding Blunkett's willingness to denounce those who claimed amendments were necessary to minimize the rights-offending aspects of the bill, fear of delay or defeat in the Lords prompted the government to eventually agree to several changes, the most important of which would: create a Special Immigration Appeals Commission in which a senior judge would hear challenges to the Home's Secretary's orders to declare suspicious foreign nationalists as 'international terrorists', with a right of appeal to the Court of Appeal on points of law;[30] obtain parliamentary approval to renew the indefinite detention scheme; require periodic reviews for the continued use of detention; and subject the legislation to comprehensive review by a committee of Privy Counsellors (the Newton Committee) by December 2003.

Conor Gearty interprets the government's forced acceptance of these amendments as an indication that the HRA contributed to less draconian legislation than might otherwise have been adopted;[31] an interpretation with which the legal advisors we interviewed concurred.[32] However, despite these important changes, the government was able to pass the core element of its new anti-terrorist initiative: the indefinite detention of foreign terrorist suspects without trial. Moreover, as will become evident, the government's forced concession to subject indefinite detention to future parliamentary review would not prove a substantial obstacle to

[27] 'Anti-Terror Defeats for Government', *BBC News*, 6 December 2001, http://news.bbc.co.uk/2/hi/uk_news/politics/1696047.stm

[28] M. Tempest, 'No. 10: Antiterror Bill Opponents are Naïve', *The Guardian*, 7 December 2011, www.guardian.co.uk/world/2001/dec/07/september11.usa1

[29] B. Anderson, 'Don't Pity Those Foreigners Who Exploit Our Generosity', *Independent*, November 12 2001, www.independent.co.uk/opinion/commentators/bruce-anderson/bruce-anderson-dont-pity-those-foreigners-who-exploit-our-generosity-616625.html.

[30] C. Nicholls, "The UK Anti-Terrorism Crime & Security Act 2001: Too Much ... Too Soon'. (2002) 9 *Commonwealth Human Rights Initiative Newsletter*, February

[31] C. Gearty, 'Human Rights in an Age of Counter-Terrorism: Injurious, Irrelevant or Indispensable?' (2005) 58 *Current Legal Problems* 25.

[32] Interviews.

its ability to renew this power, despite serious concerns on the part of the committee established to conduct the review, as well as the JCHR.

Ongoing debate about indefinite detention

The forced concession for comprehensive review and parliamentary approval for renewing indefinite detention ensured that this issue would retain a high public and political profile.[33] The Newton committee, established as a result of the demand for comprehensive review expressed by a majority of the House of Lords, concluded that the shortcomings of the indefinite detention policy were so serious that they should be replaced as a 'matter of urgency'. The committee recognized the continuing need for special counter-terror legislation, but recommended that these powers be subject to greater safeguards.[34] The JCHR supported the Newton committee's conclusions[35] and also warned parliament that because the indefinite detention provisions applied only to foreign nationals, this could constitute an unjustified violation of the right to be free from discrimination.[36] The JCHR also advised parliament that even if the judiciary accepted that derogation was justifiable, indefinite detention was nevertheless 'deeply undesirable'.[37] The JCHR would have preferred that parliament not renew these powers; it urged it to allow renewal for no more than six months, and only on the condition that government provide a firm undertaking to develop a new legal basis for its anti-terrorism law.[38] In a follow-up report the JCHR criticized the government's framing of the relevant issues as involving a choice

[33] The indefinite detention provision would cease in March 2003 unless the government received affirmative resolution for its continuance from each House. JCHR, Sixth Report, Session 2003–2004, HL 38/HC 381, para 20.

[34] Parliament of the United Kingdom, Report from the Privy Counsellor Review Committee (2003 HC 100), para 203.

[35] Parliament of the United Kingdom, JCHR, Sixth Report, Session 2003–2004, HL 38/HC 381, para 36.

[36] The government also claimed that it was 'defensible to distinguish between foreign nationals and our own citizens' because of their 'different rights and responsibilities'. It went on to suggest that while it 'would be possible to seek other powers to detain British citizens who may be involved international terrorism' this would be a 'very grave step' and that it believed 'such draconian powers would be difficult to justify'. Secretary of State for the Home Department, Reconciling Security and Liberty in an Open Society, Cm 6147, para 46 (2004).

[37] Parliament of the United Kingdom, JCHR, Sixth Report, Session 2003–2004, HL 38/HC 381, para 34.

[38] Ibid., para 37.

between national security and public safety,[39] warned parliament about the negative consequences that long-term derogations from human rights obligations would have on the nation's political culture[40] and urged parliament to evaluate anti-terrorist measures within an appropriate human rights framework.[41]

The government flatly rejected the Newton Committee and JCHR assessments that indefinite detention of foreign nationals is not a justifiable response to concerns of terrorism.[42] Moreover, parliament did not heed the JCHR's warnings and twice renewed the indefinite detention provisions, without any assurance that the government would try to find a more rights-compliant manner of dealing with international terrorist suspects.[43]

Although the government was willing to disregard the Newton Committee and JCHR arguments that rights principles require finding an alternative to indefinite detention, it was not prepared to ignore the Law Lords' ruling in *A* v. *Secretary of State for the Home Department*, in December 2004, that indefinite detention of foreign terrorist suspects is not compatible with Convention rights.[44] This judicial decision caught the government off guard.[45] The government had become accustomed to judicial deference with respect to its treatment of national security issues. As Gearty argues, the government had previously had good reason to be confident that the judiciary would be deferential when reviewing issues relating to national security:

> Time and again, the [British] judges have shown their true colours by upholding war-time emergency powers, extending police powers of arrest, extending powers of search and seizure, and legitimizing executive attacks on freedom of political association. Crises such as the industrial disputes that racked the 1980s and the ongoing conflict in Northern Ireland have shown the English senior judiciary at least to be invariably on the side of the executive ... The protection of civil liberties in Britain's non-rights based, unwritten constitution has been based on two false premises. The

39 Parliament of the United Kingdom, JCHR, Eighteenth Report, Session 2003–2004, HL 158/HC 713, para 7.

40 Ibid., HL 158/HC 713, para 5.

41 Ibid., para 10.

42 The government's position was revealed in a discussion paper. See Secretary of State for the Home Department, 'Reconciling Security and Liberty in an Open Society', Cm 6147, para 46 (2004).

43 The first renewal occurred on 3 March 2003 and the second occurred on 3 March 2004.

44 *A and others* v. *Secretary of State for the Home Department* [2004] UKHL 56.

45 Interviews.

> first is that Parliament would be careful about restricting civil liberties, and the second is that the judiciary would be vigilant in their support. Neither being the case, those seeking to assert their civil liberties in controversial circumstances have had next to nothing with which to defend themselves from executive aggression.[46]

However unhappy with the ruling it might have been, the Labour government did not ignore the decision. It was under strong pressure to introduce alternative measures, and to do so quickly. This pressure to consider remedial measures arose from the prevailing assumption that the government should comply with a judicial declaration of incompatibility,[47] and also from the imminent lapse of the indefinite detention provisions, unless renewed by parliament.[48] In February 2005, the government introduced the idea of control orders in its Prevention of Terrorism Bill, to replace indefinite detention.

II. Control orders

Control orders authorize restrictions on the liberty of any individual whom the Secretary of State has reasonable grounds to suspect is or has been involved in terrorism-related activity. Two kinds of control orders were created: one form that explicitly derogated from the ECHR by imposing obligations that are incompatible with an individual's right to liberty under Article 5; and a less restrictive form that nevertheless authorized electronic tagging, extended curfews, restrictions on individuals' abilities to visit certain locations or meet others and restrictions on movement and travel, employment and use of phones and computers.[49] The government insisted that both forms of control orders were fully compatible with the ECHR.[50] The JCHR disputed this claim.[51]

46 C. Gearty, 'Reflections on Human Rights and Civil Liberties in Light of the United Kingdom's Human Rights Act 1998', (2001) 35 *University of Richmond Law Review* p. 17.

47 Interviews.

48 The existing detention provisions would otherwise expire on 14 March 2005.

49 The conditions would vary depending on the particular order. For an example of the specific conditions applied in one particular case, see *Secretary of State for the Home Department* v. *AE* [2008] EWHC 585 (Admin).

50 Parliament of the United Kingdom, (UK) HC, Bill 61, *Prevention of Terrorism Bill*, 2005.

51 Parliament of the United Kingdom, JCHR, Twelfth Report, Session 2004–2005, HL 77/ HC 437, para 39.

The JCHR warned parliament that the legislation would create 'unprecedented power' for the executive to interfere with a wide range of Convention rights[52] and expressed strong reservations about the power to deny liberty without prior judicial involvement.[53] The House of Lords Select Committee on the Constitution also reported rights-based concerns arising from the withholding of relevant evidence from the individual subject to a control order and the potential for control orders (even non-derogating kinds) to have 'a drastic effect on the rights and liberties of the individual'.[54]

Despite these critical reports, the government rejected judicial authorization as a condition for obtaining a control order.[55] Blair also rejected the portrayal of the legislation as inconsistent with rights, side-stepping the issue of how the legislation treated those who were subject to control orders and arguing instead that 'no greater civil liberty' exists than to 'live free from terrorist attack'.[56] The government also dismissed the importance of judicial oversight as a condition for interfering with the liberty of those subject to control orders. The government explained its rejection of prior judicial authorization as a condition for imposing restrictions on an individual's liberty by insisting that government has 'prime responsibility to protect the nation's security' and that it was not prepared to abdicate this responsibility,[57] a response the JCHR characterized as representing an 'eccentric interpretation of the constitutional doctrine of the separation of powers'.[58]

As was the case with the 2001 anti-terrorist legislation, the government rushed the new scheme through the House of Commons,[59] clearing all

[52] Parliament of the United Kingdom, JCHR, Ninth Report session 2004–2005, HL 61/HC 389, paras 5–13, 15–17.

[53] Ibid., paras 5–17. These concerns raised again in JCHR, Twelfth Report, Session 2004–2005, HL 77/HC 437, para 25.

[54] Parliament of the United Kingdom, Select Committee on the Constitution, Second Report, Session 2004–2005, HL 66, paras 11–13.

[55] Parliament of the United Kingdom, Hansard, HC, vol 431, col 151–155, 22 February 2005 (Charles Clarke, Secretary of State for the Home Department).

[56] G. Jones, 'We Must Put Safety Before Liberty, Says Blair', *News Telegraph*, 24 February 2005, www.telegraph.co.uk/news/uknews/1484284/We-must-put-safety-before-liberty-says-Blair.html

[57] Parliament of the United Kingdom, *Hansard*, HC Deb vol 431, col 151–155, 22 February 2005 (Charles Clarke, Secretary of State for the Home Department).

[58] Parliament of the United Kingdom, JCHR, Ninth Report, Session 2004–2005, JCHR, HL 61/HC 389, para 12.

[59] The JCHR stated 'regret that the rapid progress of the Bill through Parliament has made it impossible for us to scrutinise the Bill comprehensively for human rights

parliamentary stages in the House of Commons in less than a week.[60] However, in contrast to the ease with which the bill passed in the House of Commons, the legislation received a rocky reception in the House of Lords. The government anticipated difficulty getting the legislation through the Lords[61] and signalled its willingness to consider limited judicial oversight of control orders that derogate from the Convention to ensure passage of the bill – a concession Keith Ewing characterizes as a 'brilliant manoeuvre', giving control orders a presumed respectability they would otherwise lack while also invoking a standard for review (determining whether the Home Secretary's decision is not 'obviously flawed') that would not significantly curtail actual decisions to issue control orders.[62]

This agreement for limited judicial oversight did not satisfy the JCHR, which warned parliament about the low threshold for making a control order.[63] The JCHR also drew parliament's attention to candid statements made by the Home Secretary and Prime Minister, in which they explained their support for the legislation as motivated by a desire to avoid any accusation that they might have done more to protect the public in the event of a terrorist attack succeeding.[64] From the JCHR's viewpoint, such political motivations reinforce the importance of having 'independent safeguards for individual liberty'.[65]

The Prevention of Terrorism Bill eventually passed a marathon session in the House of Lords, but only after the government promised annual review of the control order regime, regular reports by the Secretary of State on the exercise of this power and appointment of an independent reviewer to review the operation of the Act and present the report to parliament (the Home Secretary appointed Lord Carlisle to perform this

compatibility in time to inform debate in Parliament': Parliament of the United Kingdom, Tenth Report of Session 2004–2005, Prevention of Terrorism Bill, HL Paper 68, HC 334, para 1.

60 Parliament of the United Kingdom, JCHR, Ninth Report of Session 2004–2005, HL 62/ HC 389, para 1.

61 Interviews.

62 K.D. Ewing, *Bonfire of the Liberties: New Labour, Human Rights, and the Rule of Law* (Oxford: Oxford University Press, 2010), pp. 241–42. As he argues, the 'diluted standard' for judicial review of control orders 'falls some way below the normal standard for judicial review'.

63 Parliament of the United Kingdom, JCHR, Tenth Report, Session 2004–2005, HL 68/HC 334, paras 6–15.

64 As referred to by the JCHR, Ibid., paras 6–15.

65 Ibid., paras 6.

review). However, as will be argued, just as the review for renewal of indefinite detention did not subsequently lead to any difficulty for government in maintaining these powers, the renewal obligation for control orders would prove to be similarly unproblematic, despite strong and persistent criticism by the JCHR.

The Council of Europe's Commissioner for Human Rights rejected the proposition that the level of judicial oversight was sufficient because the judge would be required to determine the reasonableness of suspicions on the basis of secret evidence, and therefore would have difficulty determining the veracity or relevance of the evidence.[66] The government also incurred harsh criticism from academics who chastised it for 'playing games' in its warnings to opposition MPs and rebellious backbenchers that dangerous terrorists could 'walk free' if control orders were not passed, and its threatening those who opposed new powers that they would bear responsibility for atrocities committed by these suspects.[67] Critics were particularly troubled that despite the 'devastating impact' that control orders could have on individuals, they could be imposed by the Secretary State on a low standard of proof – 'reasonable grounds for suspicion'.[68] Moreover, although the legislation authorized judicial review regarding the question of whether the substantive conditions for control orders were met, it would be possible for the government's case to rely on information that was not disclosed to the subject of the order, raising concerns about the fairness of the proceedings. Many were critical of the legislative response to this problem, which was the appointment of a Special Advocate to represent the interests of the affected party, who nevertheless could not act on the basis of informed instructions from the individual whose liberty was in jeopardy.[69] As Aileen Kavanagh characterizes the tension between the legislation and principles of justice:

> Under the [Prevention of Terrorism Act] Special Advocates have both a 'disclosure' function and a 'representation' function. The disclosure function is 'to test to the full the cogency of the case put forward by the Home

[66] 'UK Criticized Over Human Rights', *BBC News*, 8 June 2005, http://news.bbc.co.uk/2/hi/uk_news/politics/4071968.stm.

[67] G.P. Phillipson, 'Defence, Discretion, and Democracy in the Human Rights Era', (2007) 60 *Current Legal Problems* 40, pp. 49–50.

[68] A. Kavanagh, 'Constitutionalism, Counterterrorism, and the Courts: Changes in the British Constitutional Landscape', (2011) 9 *I-CON* 172, p. 187.

[69] A. Kavanagh, 'Special Advocates, Control Orders and the Right to a Fair Trial', (2010) 73 *Modern Law Review* 836, pp. 837–38.

> Secretary for non-disclosure of material'. The representation function is 'to represent the Appellant's interests in relation to that part of the hearing held *in camera*, which entails making the best case possible from all the available evidence -both open and closed – but without informed instructions from the Appellant. One of the most severe disadvantages under which Special Advocates labour is that once they have seen the closed material, they cannot communicate with, or take instructions from the persons they are representing... Therefore, the normal lawyer-client relationship does not obtain. Moreover, Special Advocates have no access to independent expertise and evidence, they lack the resources of an ordinary legal team for the purposes of conducting a full defence in secret and they have no power to call witnesses. The combined effect of these restrictions on the work of the Special Advocate means that individuals are undoubtedly placed at a 'grave disadvantage' in control order proceedings.[70]

Both Labour and the Conservative-led coalition government regularly sought and received renewal of the control order scheme. In all instances, the JCHR reported serious concerns about the scheme and recommended amendments to try and mitigate rights-based problems, but without success.[71] However, legal challenges and growing political unease with control orders would eventually result in pressure to replace the control order scheme with an alternative arrangement (to be discussed presently).

III. The London bombing and the Terrorism Bill 2005–06

In the immediate aftermath of the July 2005 bombing in London that killed 56 people, the Labour government announced it was considering a new range of coercive anti-terrorist measures. Blair used the occasion to publicly proclaim that his government would not abide by judicially imposed constraints on its attempts to deal with terrorism,

[70] A. Kavanagh, 'Special Advocates, Control Orders and the Right to a Fair Trial', p. 838 (notes omitted).

[71] Parliament of the United Kingdom, JCHR, Twelfth Report, Session 2005–2006, HL 122/HC 915; Parliament of the United Kingdom, JCHR, Eighth Report of Session 2006–2007, HL 60/HC 365; Parliament of the United Kingdom, JCHR, Tenth Report, Session 2007–2008, HL 57/HC 356; Parliament of the United Kingdom, JCHR, Fifth Report, Session 2008–2009, HL 37/HC 282; Parliament of the United Kingdom, JCHR, Ninth Report, Session 2009–2010, HL 65/HC 395; Parliament of the United Kingdom, JCHR, Sixteenth Report of Session 2009–2010; HL 65/HC 395.

and expressed his government's irritation with the Law Lords' earlier ruling that indefinite detention was incompatible with Convention rights. Whether motivated by an intent to intimidate the judiciary with the hope of encouraging deferential rulings on similar issues in the future or to gain public support for legislation that might eventually be ruled incompatible with Convention rights, Blair publicly questioned whether the Law Lords would have reached the same outcome (in *A* v. *Secretary of State for the Home Department*) if this decision had been made after the London bombing.[72] Blair also declared that the 'rules of the game are changing'[73] and called upon judges to respect public concerns by upholding new laws to deport or detain Islamic extremists.[74] He indicated that his government would consider amending the HRA should 'legal obstacles' undermine the government's capacity to protect national security,[75] that it was prepared to renounce aspects of the European Convention on Human Rights if necessary and that it was considering a refusal to abide by a 1996 European Court ruling that effectively blocked the deportation of individuals to countries where they might face torture.[76] Blair's statements were followed by then Home Secretary Charles Clarke's appearance before the European Parliament in Strasbourg calling for the EU's judicial system to be 'rebalanced' to allow for deportation of extremists.[77] Conservative leader Michael Howard chimed in on this rhetorical anti-judicial review campaign by warning judges not to thwart the will of parliament in its fight

[72] G. Jones, 'Blairs on Collision Course Over Laws to Beat Terrorism', *The Telegraph*, 27 July 2005, www.telegraph.co.uk/news/uknews/1494869/Blairs-on-collision-course-over-laws-to-beat-terrorism.html

[73] S. Jeffrey, 'The Rules of the Game are Changing'.

[74] His statements promoted a public judicial response in which senior judges stated they would take 'not the slightest notice' of Blair's remarks and would not alter their behaviour 'one bit'. G. Jones, 'Blairs on Collision Course Over Laws to Beat Terrorism'; F. Gibb and P. Webster, 'We Won't Heed Blair, Say Judges' (quoting Lord Donaldson, a former Master of the Rolls, and Lord Ackner, a retired law lord), *The Times*, 28 July 2005, www.thetimes.co.uk/tto/news/uk/article1936100.ece

[75] 'Full Text of Blair Statement on Extremism', *The Times*, 5 August 2005, www.thetimes.co.uk/tto/news/uk/article1936508.ece

[76] G. Jones, 'Blair to Curb Human Rights in War on Terror', *The Telegraph*, 6 August 2005, www.telegraph.co.uk/news/uknews/1495605/Blair-to-curb-human-rights-in-war-on-terror.html

[77] P. Johnston, 'Clarke Urges EU to Rethink Rights Laws on Deportation', *The Telegraph*, 20 October 2005, www.telegraph.co.uk/news/1497789/Clarke-urges-EU-to-rethink-rights-laws-on-deportation.html

against terrorism, while also blaming the Labour government for having adopted the HRA in the first place.[78]

Academic commentators have become increasingly critical of political attempts to frame the legislative debate in binary terms such as liberty vs. security that suggest a polity and its citizens will inevitably be vulnerable unless priority is accorded to normal constitutional principles associated with the criminal justice system. As Davis and De Landros argue, this binary approach masks a deep 'murkiness' that distorts assessments of the proportionality of responses to attacks and perceived threats, and thus produces inadequate evaluation of the merits of state actions.[79]

Blair's statements were criticized by some Labour MPs, who feared he was catering to tabloid criticism of the HRA,[80] and also by other commentators due to his willingness to denounce the 'foundations' of democratic society to appease public insecurity.[81] His comments also provoked judicial reaction: senior judges indicated that they would take 'not the slightest notice' of Blair's remarks,[82] stating that the comments betrayed a lack of understanding of judicial responsibility.[83]

Blair's rhetorical backlash against judicial review was a prelude to the announcement of new anti-terrorism measures that would include

[78] 'Howard Warns Judges Over Terror', *BBC News*, 10 August 2005, http://news.bbc.co.uk/1/hi/uk_politics/4136940.stm; Brenden Carlin, John Steele and Duncan Gardham, 'Howard Attacks Courts on Terrorism', *The Telegraph*, 16 August 2005, www.telegraph.co.uk/news/uknews/1495880/Howard-attacks-courts-on-terrorism.html

[79] F.F. Davis and F. de Londras, 'Counter-Terrorist Judicial Review: Beyond Dichotomies', in F.F. Davis and F. de Londras (eds.), *Critical Debates on Counter-Terrorist Judicial Review* (Cambridge: Cambridge University Press, 2014).

[80] M. White, 'Labour MPs Attack Blair's 12-point Plan', *The Guardian*, 9 August 2005, politics.guardian.co.uk/terrorism/story/0,15935,1545190,00.html

[81] S. Chakrabarti, 'The Price of a Chilling and Counterproductive Recipe', *The Guardian*, 8 August 2005, www.guardian.co.uk/comment/story/0,,1544581,00.html

[82] F. Gibb and P. Webster, 'We Won't Heed Blair, Say Judges'.

[83] Lord Bingham described the statements of Blair and Howard as representing 'a complete misunderstanding' of their role, stating that the 'ultimate treason for any judge is to uphold as lawful that which is unlawful' and adding that the role of the judiciary was that of 'auditors of legality'. The newspaper story quoting Lord Bingham indicated that judges were not prepared to rubber-stamp political agreements between Britain and countries with poor human rights records which promised not to torture deportees or subject them to inhuman treatment once returned. Lord Bingham also questioned the government's willingness to criticize the judiciary in the media and characterized the government's willingness to use the press 'to try to bring pressures to bear [on the judiciary] instead of using legal arguments' as a 'very bad way to govern'. C. Dyer, 'Law Lord Hits Back at Politicians After Attacks on Judges', *The Guardian*, 15 September 2005, http://politics.guardian.co.uk/homeaffairs/story/0,11026,1570247,00.html

making it a criminal offence to condone or glorify terrorism, refusing asylum to anyone who has participated in or has been associated with terrorism, extending powers to strip citizenship for British or dual citizens who act contrary to the interests of the country, imposing new time limits for speedier extradition to other countries, extending detention periods for pre-charge terrorist suspects, increasing the use of control orders for British nationals and introducing new criteria for acquiring British citizenship.[84]

Parliamentary consideration of the Terrorism Act 2006

Despite initial cross-party consensus for many of Blair's proposals, likely influenced by their announcement so soon after the London bombings and the accompanying public anxiety, support diminished considerably upon closer parliamentary scrutiny. One particularly contentious element of the government's proposed scheme was a new power to criminalize any statements that 'glorify, exalt or celebrate' terrorism. Critics and opposition members argued that since incitement to commit terrorism is already a criminal offence, there was no need to create a new offence, particularly one so vague[85] that it would have a chilling effect on political debate.[86] The government amended the clause in response to this criticism, and removed the words 'exalt and celebrate'. But the word 'glorify' survived in a new clause, resulting in continued criticism and pressure to make it clear that speech could only be prosecuted where there was clear intent to incite terror.[87] The government barely managed to defeat a Labour-sponsored amendment in the Commons that would require 'intent' to be established (300–299)[88] and was subsequently able to pass the new offence by a vote of

[84] PM's Press Conference, 5 August 2005, http://webarchive.nationalarchives.gov.uk/20040105034004/number10.gov.uk/page8041

[85] A. Blick and S. Weir, 'The Rules of the Game. The Terrorism Bill 2005', *Democratic Audit*, 27 June 2005, www.jrrt.org.uk/publications/rules-game-terrorism-bill-2005-scoping-report.

[86] 'New Anti Terror Bill Published', Liberty, 15 September 2005, www.liberty-human-rights.org.uk/media/press/2005/new-anti-terror-bill-published.php – arguing its chilling effect on political debate, and that its breadth could result in the criminalization of speech despite the speaker having no intention of encouraging terrorism.

[87] G. Crossman, 'Terrorism Bill: Liberty's Briefing for Second Reading in the House of Lords', November 2005, www.liberty-human-rights.org.uk/pdfs/policy05/terrorism-bill-2nd-reading-lords.pdf

[88] 'Terror Bill Rebellion Defeated by One Vote', *The Guardian*, 2 November 2005, http://politics.guardian.co.uk/terrorism/story/0,15935,1607043,00.html

315 to 277, with 17 Labour MPs opposing the measure.[89] The government had considerably more difficulty with the House of Lords, which twice defeated the bill, before finally passing it despite continued criticism by Liberal Democrats that the wording was too vague.[90]

Even more contentious was the proposal to increase the period of detention without charge for terrorist suspects from 14 to 90 days. Police have been authorized in certain circumstances to arrest individuals suspected of being terrorists and detain them without charge for extended periods. This power was authorized in the Terrorism Act 2000, which allowed a period of seven days; the period was doubled to 14 days under the Criminal Justice Act 2003.[91] The Labour government's proposal to substantially extend the period in which terrorist suspects can be detained without charge became even more controversial upon comments from recently retired senior judge Lord Steyn that the proposal would be a breach of Article 5(3) of the ECHR and was an 'exorbitant and unnecessary power'.[92] Controversy was also fuelled by published reports of uncertainty regarding the government's legal advice on compatibility. Political confusion about whether the Attorney General believed that the proposed measures were compatible with Convention rights arose when Charles Clarke recanted earlier suggestions that the Attorney General had approved the legality of the provision. The Home Secretary advised MPs that he had spoken to the Attorney General and had received advice from him that the provisions were compatible with country's human rights obligations; however, in a subsequent statement to parliament, Clarke told MPs that he needed to clarify his earlier statement, and that the 'clear legal advice' he received about the compatibility of the bill 'did not come from the attorney personally'.[93]

The Liberal Democrat party insisted it would not support extending the detention without charge period more than 14 days, while the

[89] 'Blair Wins Vote on 'Glorification' of Terror', *The Scotsman*, 16 February 2006, http://thescotsman.scotsman.com/index.cfm?id=240182006

[90] 'Lords Back Down on Glorification', *BBC News*, 22 March 2006, http://news.bbc.co.uk/2/hi/uk_news/politics/4834738.stm

[91] A. Horne and G. Berman, 'Pre-Charge Detention in Terrorism Cases', (2012) House of Commons Library, 15 March, SN/HA/5364.

[92] J. Rozenberg, '90-day Detention of Suspects "Unlawful"', *The Telegraph*, 21 October 2005, www.telegraph.co.uk/news/uknews/1500305/90-day-detention-of-suspects-unlawful.html

[93] Parliament of the United Kingdom, *Hansard*, HC, vol 438, col 1071, 3 November 2005 (Charles Clarke).

Conservative party indicated it would not support any period longer than 28 days. Blair reacted by warning that if the government was forced to compromise on this issue, the result would undermine the nation's security.[94] Nevertheless, despite this attempt to elicit support, MPs defeated the proposal (322–291) – the Blair government's first defeat in the House of Commons since it came to power. A total of 49 Labour MPs (including 11 former ministers) defied a three-line whip and voted against the government, leading to suggestions by former cabinet minister Clare Short and opposition leader Michael Howard that Blair should resign.[95] When the government finally managed to pass the Terrorism Act 2006, police were given the power to detain suspects for up to 28 days without charge.[96] However, this power would be subject to annual renewal by parliament and, in the absence of subsequent approval, the detention period would revert back to 14 days.[97]

Notwithstanding the extensive criticism of long periods of detention without charge during the initial parliamentary debate, approval to renew this power was subsequently sought and obtained, even in the face of repeated warnings by the JCHR that parliament lacked adequate information to assess the need for this period of detention and should not approve the power without independent review.[98]

IV. Failed attempt to increase length of detention without charge

In January 2008 the Labour government, now under the leadership of Gordon Brown, introduced the Counter-Terrorism Act, which sought to extend the pre-charge detention period from 28 to 42 days (where the director of public prosecution and a chief police officer deemed that such

[94] O. King and M. Tempest, 'Government to Offer Terror Bill Compromise', *The Guardian*, 7 November 2005, www.guardian.co.uk/politics/2005/nov/07/uksecurity.terrorism1

[95] P. Wintour, 'After Eight Years in Power Tony Blair Hears A New Word: Defeat', *The Guardian*, 10 November 2005, http://politics.guardian.co.uk/terrorism/story/0,15935,1639028,00.html

[96] Terrorism Act 2006 (UK), c. 11, s. 23. The legislation also created new offences of preparing or encouraging terrorism, disseminating terrorist publications and giving or receiving training in terrorist techniques.

[97] Ibid., s. 25.

[98] Parliament of the United Kingdom, JCHR, Nineteenth Report, Session 2006–2007, HL 157/HC 790, paras 42–44; Parliament of the United Kingdom, JCHR, Twenty-Fifth Report, Session 2007–2008, HL 132/HC 825, paras 17–18; Parliament of the United Kingdom, JCHR, Eighteenth Report, Session 2008–2009, HL 119/HC 726, para 25; Parliament of the United Kingdom, JCHR, Sixteenth Report, Session 2009–2010, HL 86/HC 111, para 68.

extension was warranted).[99] A Home Office paper based the case for lengthening the pre-charge detention on the seriousness of the threat from international terrorism and the trend for increasingly complex plots involving increasing amounts of evidence and data.[100] Then Home Secretary Jacqui Smith had a more sensationalist explanation for the change, suggesting that a 'serious and consistent threat from terrorism' necessitated new powers to 'prosecute people who want to cause murder and mayhem on our streets'.[101]

The JCHR was extremely critical of the proposal, particularly in the absence of evidence to support increasing the period of detention without charge to 42 days.[102] It warned parliament the bill was not compatible with the right to liberty or the right of any detained person to be informed promptly of any charge, and was an unnecessary and disproportionate way to protect the public.[103] The JCHR also questioned the government's 'perfunctory dismissal' of alternatives to extending pre-charge detention.[104] Prominent civil liberties groups[105] and the Council of Europe criticized the proposal as a breach of the right to liberty and security and a fair trial.[106] Nevertheless, the detention provision narrowly passed in the House of Commons (315–306), with 36 Labour members voting against the bill.[107] To ensure passage of the bill, the government

99 The bill also sought to enable adverse inferences to be drawn from silence in post-charge questioning of terrorist suspects. Other elements would impose requirements on people convicted of terrorist offences to let authorities know where they are living and any changes to their circumstances, enhance the sentences of offenders who commit offences with a terrorist connection, extend powers to gather and share information for counter-terrorism and other purposes and amend the law relating to asset-freezing procedures.

100 Home Office, 'Pre-Charge Detention of Terrorist Suspects', December 2007 www.loc.gov/law/help/uk-pre-charge-detention.php

101 'Smith Plans 42-day Terror Limit', *BBC News*, 6 December 2007, http://news.bbc.co.uk/1/hi/uk_politics/7130072.stm

102 Parliament of the United Kingdom, JCHR, Second Report, Session 2007–2008, HL 23/HC 156, para 40.

103 Parliament of the United Kingdom, JCHR, Ninth Report, Session 2007–2008, HL 50/HC 199, paras 17–21.

104 Parliament of the United Kingdom, JCHR, Second Report, Session 2007–2008, HL 23/HC 156, para 46.

105 Liberty, 'Charge or Release', July 2010, www.liberty-human-rights.org.uk/sites/default/files/comparative-law-study-2010-pre-charge-detention.pdf

106 D. Campbell and A. Hirsch, 'Council of Europe Report Criticizes 42-day Detention', *The Guardian*, 1 October 2008, www.guardian.co.uk/uk/2008/oct/01/civilliberties.justice/print

107 'Brown Wins Crunch Vote on 42 Days', *BBC News*, 11 June 2008, http://news.bbc.co.uk/2/hi/uk_news/politics/7449268.stm

engaged in last-minute negotiations with Democrat Unionist MPs from Northern Ireland, which prompted calls that the Prime Minister had engaged in pork-barrel politics, focusing on a £200 million concession over water rates to be spent by the devolved administration in the province.[108] The media were particularly critical of Brown's efforts to pass the legislation, suggesting that politicians had been bribed and parliament's reputation seriously damaged in the process.[109]

Brown was forced to abandon the plan for an extended period of pre-charge detention, after the House of Lords overwhelmingly rejected the bill: it criticized the government for a lack of evidence that the extension was required;[110] for the absence of any international precedent for this kind of measure;[111] and for violating the separation of powers.[112] This was Brown's first serious defeat as Prime Minister.

Parliament subsequently renewed authorization for the 28-day period until the Coalition government allowed it to lapse in 2011. It has now

[108] 'Brown Survives Labour Revolt on 42-day Detention', *The Scotsman*, 12 June 2008.

[109] In a particularly scathing attack, the Times wrote:

> Last night Gordon Brown faced personal humiliation over his plan to extend detention without charge. In his effort to avoid this fate, he has humiliated Westminster instead. The most contentious vote of Mr Brown's premiership was won by browbeating MPs on what should have been an issue of conscience, and with thinly disguised bribery when browbeating did not work. He has won a tactical victory that will be presented as proof of his seriousness about national security. Would that it were. The reality this morning is a prime minister willing to erode ancient freedoms with cataclysmic threats to shore up his position; a government willing to write unworkable legislation for the sake of a hollow political gesture; and MPs on both sides of the aisle demeaned by the worst sort of horse-trading for their support. The currency of Parliament is the integrity of its Members. It has seldom been so willfully devalued . . .

'42 Days: Westminster for Sale', *The Times*, 12 June 2008, www.thetimes.co.uk/tto/opinion/leaders/article2091189.ece

[110] Parliament of the United Kingdom, *Hansard*, HL, vol 480, col 492, 13 October 2008.

[111] As Lord West of Spithead stated (Parliamentary Under-Secretary of State, Home Office):

> No other country in the western world that has a common law system like ours—an accusatorial rather than an inquisitorial system—has extended detention without charge to 42 days. In fact, no country has gone as far as 28 days. The nearest comparison is Australia with 12 days, and all the rest of the comparable countries operate with single figures. I need hardly remind your Lordships that in America it is two days and in Canada it is one day.

Parliament of the United Kingdom, *Hansard*, HL, vol 480, col 492, 13 October 2008.

[112] Parliament of the United Kingdom, *Hansard*, vol 480, col 493, 13 October 2008.

reverted to 14 days; the period is authorized by the Protection of Freedoms Act 2012.

V. TPIMS, an alternative to control orders

As argued earlier, the government's forced acceptance that control orders would be subject to annual parliamentary review did not represent a substantial burden on its ability to renew these, notwithstanding repeated JCHR warnings to parliament about the dangers of renewal. Although parliament may not have been unduly troubled by the extended reliance on these powers, the JCHR, civil liberties organizations and academic commentators remained critical of their continued use. Critics continued to question the necessity of these orders, and asked how many people pose such a threat to the state that they would (or should) be subject to a control order. Moreover, judicial review would become an increasingly potent force in securing control orders as courts began to question their earlier deference toward legislation addressing security issues.

In 2007 the Director of the Security Service reported that as many as 4,000 people could pose a direct threat to national security and that MI5 knew of as many as 2,000 individuals who supported al Qaeda and were actively engaged in terrorist activities in the UK.[113] However, only 15 control orders were in force at the end of 2008, and the number had dropped to 12 by 2010.[114] Clive Walker and Adam Tomkins both argue that judicial review is a significant factor in explaining the small number of control orders issued.[115] This view is consistent with Aileen Kavanagh's assessment that a subtle but significant change in judicial attitudes has

[113] C. Brown, 'MI5 Chief: Children are Being Taught to Become Terrorists', *The Independent*, 6 November 2007, www.independent.co.uk/news/uk/politics/mi5-chief-children-are-being-taught-to-become-terrorists-399171.html

[114] Home Office, 'Written Ministerial Statement on Control Orders: 11 March – 10 June 2010', www.homeoffice.gov.uk/publications/written-ministerial-statement/control-orders-june2010-wms/?view=Standard&pubID=818801

[115] C. Walker, 'The Threat of Terrorism and the Fate of Control Orders', (2010) *Public Law* 6. See also A. Tomkins, 'National Security and the Role of the Court: A Changed Landscape?', (2010) 126 *Law Quarterly Review* 543–67. Walker and Tomkins have argued that lower court and tribunal decisions mitigate the scope and effects of control orders, and help explain why relatively few control orders are in place, see C. Walker, 'The threat of terrorism and the fate of control orders', (2010) *Public Law*, p. 6. See also A. Tomkins, 'National Security and the Role of the Court: A Changed Landscape?', (2010) 126 *Law Quarterly Review* 543–67.

occurred, and there is no longer unquestioned support for the proposition that issues relating to national security are non-justiciable.[116]

Several control orders were appealed in a single hearing before the Law Lords, whose decisions in 2007 demonstrated considerable deference toward parliamentary approval of the control order scheme. A majority of the Law Lords ruled that a control order imposing an 18-hour curfew sufficiently infringed the liberty of the controlled persons as to constitute a deprivation of liberty under Article 5, and thus quashed the relevant orders. However, the Law Lords also ruled that if the curfew lasts no longer than 16 hours a day (as distinct from the 18 hours as authorized by the control order), the order would not be considered a deprivation of liberty for Article 5 purposes.[117]

The Law Lords also had to consider whether the control order scheme's authorization of a Special Advocate regime was consistent with the right to a fair hearing. On this issue, the Law Lords interpreted the control order proceedings as not constituting a criminal charge; thus the criminal trial guarantees in Article 6(1) did not apply. A majority of the Law Lords did indicate that the relevant procedures authorized in the Prevention of Terrorism Act 2005 would not be compatible with the right to a fair hearing in Article 6(1) if they allowed the essence of the case to proceed against someone subject to a control order without any disclosure being made to him or her.[118] Nevertheless, the House of Lords also ruled that the legislation should be interpreted under section 3 of the HRA where possible, rather than being declared incompatible with Article 6(1) under section 4 of the HRA.[119]

For government, the immediate significance of these outcomes was that the House of Lords' rulings left the basic control scheme intact. By not ruling that the legislation authorizing control orders was incompatible with Convention rights under section 4 of the HRA and instead relying on section 3, meaning that control orders would be 'read and given effect except where to do so would be incompatible with the right

[116] A. Kavanagh, 'Constitutionalism, Counterterrorism, and the Courts'.

[117] The decisions in three cases were delivered in a single day: *Home Secretary* v. *JJ* [2007] UKHL 45; *MB and AF* v. *Home Secretary* [2007] UKHL 46; and *Home Secretary* v. *E* [2007] UKHL 47. For analysis of the different judicial positions taken, see K.D. Ewing, *Bonfire of the Liberties: New Labour, Human Rights, and the Rule of Law* (Oxford: Oxford University Press, 2010), pp. 247–49.

[118] *Secretary of State for the Home* Department v. *MB* [2007] UKHL 46 (31 October 2007).

[119] Lord Bingham disagreed on this issue and indicated that a declaration of incompatibility was appropriate (para 44).

of the controlled person to a fair trial',[120] this judicial approach relieved government of the immediate pressure to consider remedial measures. However, this approach also meant that courts would be required to determine the conditions necessary to properly respect the right to a fair hearing on a case-by-case basis.[121]

The government announced that despite being pleased that the Law Lords had upheld the basic control order scheme, it was disappointed that the court had difficulty with long curfews.[122] However, the JCHR had a very different response, and tacitly criticized the Law Lords because it believed the judicial interpretation was contrary to the spirit of the HRA. From the JCHR's perspective, parliament had already grappled with the question of how to strike an appropriate balance between the right to a fair hearing and keeping sensitive information secret and, contrary to the JCHR's advice, had decided to place a duty on courts to rule even if 'the gist' of the case was not disclosed to the affected person. The JCHR interpreted the Law Lords' approach to the HRA as being inappropriately deferential to parliament and inconsistent with the structure or logic of the HRA, which the committee argued was intended to require parliament to reassess legislation if the judiciary concludes it is incompatible with Convention rights:[123]

> The scheme of the Human Rights Act deliberately gives Parliament a central role in deciding how best to protect the rights protected in the ECHR. Striking the right balance between sections 3 and 4 of the Human Rights Act is crucial to that scheme of democratic human rights protection. In our view it would have been more consistent with the scheme of the Human Rights Act for the [Law] Lords to have given a declaration of incompatibility, requiring Parliament to think again about the balance it struck in the control order legislation between the various competing interests.[124]

The Law Lords' approach has also been criticized by some scholars, who interpret the judiciary's refusal to rule that control orders are

[120] Aileen Kavanagh, 'Special Advocates, Control Orders and the Right to a Fair Trial', p. 840, referring to *Secretary of State for the Home* Department v. *MB* [2007] UKHL at 72, per Baroness Hale.

[121] This is the interpretation of the JCHR, which precipitated its critical response to how the Law Lords broached their interpretative duties under the HA. JCHR, Ninth Report, Session 2007–2008, HL 50/HC 199, paras 41–47.

[122] M. Herman and PA, 'Judges Order Rethink on Control Orders', *Times Online*, 31 October 2007, www.thetimes.co.uk/tto/law/article2210262.ece

[123] Parliament of the United Kingdom, JCHR, Ninth Report of Session 2007–2008, HL 50/HC 199, para 46.

[124] Ibid., para 47.

incompatible with human rights as a strong sign of the weakness of the HRA to protect rights.[125]

However, any relief the government felt with respect to the legal validity of its control order scheme was short-lived. Increasingly, concerns were expressed that the court had taken 'too sanguine' a view of the protection that Special Advocates could provide someone subject to a control order. Special Advocates challenged key assumptions underpinning the judgement in *MB* that closed procedures allow judges to adequately perform their review function, because they 'have no means to gainsaying the Government's assessment that disclosure could cause harm to the public interest'.[126] Moreover, the House of Lords' ruling in *MB* was difficult for courts of first instance to follow. As Kavanagh argues, clear differences of opinion among the five judges deciding the case made it difficult for lower courts to discern the full impact of the Court's reasons. Opinions ranged from the view that Article 6 requires a 'core, irreducible minimum of procedural protection' that is not satisfied if the case against the affected party relies upon closed material, to the dissenting opinion that use of closed materials along with reliance on Special Advocates is compatible with a fair trial.[127]

Two years after the Law Lords upheld the basic gist of the control order scheme, a majority clarified its opinion on whether the reliance on security-cleared Special Advocates in control order proceedings is a sufficient safeguard to protect a fair trial for Article 6 purposes.[128] In *Secretary of State for the Home Department* v. *AF (No. 3)*, the House of Lords ruled that if the disclosed materials consist only of general assertions, and the case against the 'controlled person' is based solely or primarily on closed material, the right to a fair trial under Article 6 is not satisfied.[129] The ruling represented what has been characterized as a 'considerable blow' to the validity of the control order scheme.[130]

[125] K.D. Ewing and J. C. Tham, 'The Continuing Futility of the Human Rights Act', (2008) *Public Law* 670.

[126] M. Chamberlain, 'Special Advocates and Procedural Fairness in Closed Proceedings' (2009) Civil Justice Quarterly 314 at 320, as referred to by A. Kavanagh, 'Special Advocate, Control Orders and the Right to a Fair Trial', pp. 840–41.

[127] A. Kavanagh 'Special Advocates, Control Orders and the Right to a Fair Trial', p. 839.

[128] [2009] UKHL 28.

[129] A. Kavanagh, 'Special Advocates, Control Orders and the Right to a Fair Trial', p. 838.

[130] A. Kavanagh, 'Constitutionalism, Counterterrorism, and the Courts: Changes in the British Constitutional Landscape', (2011) 9:1 International Journal of Constitutional Law, p. 187, 172–99.

The ruling followed upon the heels of the Grand Chamber ruling in *A* v. *UK*[131] that fairness requires that individuals who are subject to a control order be provided the gist of the materials that support the allegation made against them.[132] This is a position that the JCHR had earlier argued and the government rejected.[133] The timing was sufficiently close that both the Appellant and the Secretary of State were required to revise their written submissions before the House of Lords so as to reflect the Grand Chamber's decision.[134]

Kavanagh attributes the difference between the ruling in *AF* and the more deferential outcome two years earlier in large part to exposure to submissions by Special Advocates, which 'highlighted a "mosaic" quality of the closed material on which the Home Secretary's case' had been based, and thus encouraged judicial re-examination of the 'optimistic assessment' earlier held about the extent to which controlees could effective challenge the allegations against them. A second important factor explaining the less deferential approach in *AF* is the impact of the Grand Chamber ruling in *A* v. *UK* on this very issue, which the Law Lords considered themselves bound to accept.[135]

After the ruling, the Secretary of State decided that the control order against AF should be revoked because the closed evidence was too sensitive to be disclosed so as to satisfy the House of Lords' ruling. Lower courts subsequently quashed a number of other control orders.[136]

Kavanagh suggests the potential significance of the *AF* ruling for the future of the control order scheme should not be underestimated. By enhancing procedural fairness for those affected by control orders and strengthening the hand of Special Advocates when arguing for disclosure, the ruling could either lead to more disclosure or force the government to revoke a control order for which it was not prepared to disclose intelligence information. Moreover, reluctance to disclose

[131] *Secretary of State for the Home Department* v. *AF (No 3)* [2009] UKHL 28.

[132] *A and Others* v. *United Kingdom*, Application no. 3455/05 [2009] ECHR 1 at paras 193–224 [GC].

[133] Government Reply to the Report by the Joint Committee on Human Rights on the Annual renewal of Control Order Legislation 2009, Cm 7625 (2009) p. 1.

[134] A. Kavanagh, 'Special Advocates, Control Orders and the Right to a Fair Trial', p. 843.

[135] Ibid., pp. 840–42.

[136] A. Kavanagh, 'Constitutionalism, Counterterrorism, and the Courts'.

sensitive information could result in a weaker argument for a control order that courts would not find persuasive.[137]

The future of the control order scheme was placed in greater doubt after the 2010 defeat of the Labour government. The issue presented a serious tension for the new Conservative–Liberal Democrat coalition government. A sizeable wing of the Conservative party supported control orders;[138] however, Liberal Democrats had earlier indicated their strong opposition to the renewal of the measures and the party's 2010 election manifesto called for repeal of the control order legislation.[139] Nick Clegg, while Shadow Home Affairs spokesman, criticized control orders in a 2007 Guardian article, arguing:

> It is true that the nature of modern terrorism poses huge challenges to our criminal justice system. But our response should be to reform, streamline and strengthen our system to bring terror suspects before court, rather than circumvent due process altogether. A battery of curfews and tags, imposed in a legal limbo at the behest of politicians, is no surrogate for the aggressive use of the full force of the law. Would-be terrorists are criminals, and should be treated as such.[140]

Shortly after the election, the Coalition government indicated it would 'urgently review control orders'[141] and indicated that the control order regime would continue to operate until replacement measures were passed.[142] These included one that the Court of Appeal ruled to be so flawed that it could not be justified.[143]

137 A. Kavanagh, 'Special Advocates, Control Orders and the Right to a Fair Trial', pp. 839, 851–52.

138 P. Wintour, 'Control Orders Set to Split All Three Parties', *The Guardian*, 6 January 2011, www.guardian.co.uk/politics/wintour-and-watt/2011/jan/06/control-orders-split-all-three-parties

139 A. Travis, 'Control Order Ban Central to Coalition Civil Rights Policy, Warn Lib Dems', *The Guardian*, 29 October 2010, www.guardian.co.uk/law/2010/oct/29/control-order-ban-coalition-rights; 'Coalition Faces Major Problem on Control Orders – Davis', *BBC News*, 1 November 2010, www.bbc.co.uk/news/uk-politics-11664408

140 N. Clegg, 'This Is a Fork in the Road', (2007) *The Guardian*, 21 February, www.guardian.co.uk/commentisfree/2007/feb/21/comment.terrorism

141 Home Office, 'Written Ministerial Statement on Control Orders'.

142 Theresa May, then Home Secretary, informed the House of Commons that she had renewed the control order powers in the 2005 Act until 31 December 2011. *Hansard*, HC Deb 17 March 2011,v. 527, col 27WS.

143 A. Travis, 'Judges Tell Theresa May to Revoke 'Flawed' Control Order on Terror Suspect', *The Guardian*, 5 April 2011, www.guardian.co.uk/law/2011/apr/05/judges-theresa-may-control-order

In January 2011, the Coalition government announced it would repeal the control order scheme and introduce new terrorism prevention investigation measures (TPIMs).[144] The decision arose after a review of control orders, which included independent oversight by Lord Macdonald,[145] who disagreed with imposing restrictions on the liberty of individuals not subject to an ongoing criminal investigation. As Lord Macdonald reported, 'the government should not be permitted to direct house arrest in any form in the absence of criminal investigation or pending proceedings. This is simply to distinguish the rule of law from totalitarianism.'[146]

The government was not persuaded by Macdonald's position on this issue, and based the authorization of these coercive powers on executive rather than judicial oversight. The government introduced the Terrorism Prevention and Investigation Measures (TPIMs) Bill to the House of Commons in May 2011. The new measures would require individuals to reside at a specified residence and seek permission from the Secretary of State for an exemption from the residency requirement. Individuals would also have to surrender any travel documents, including passports or tickets for transportation, and would be subject to restrictions on use of or access to certain financial transactions. They would be prohibited from possession or use of electronic communication devices, denied freedom of association, required to report to a police station and have their photographs taken at particular times and locations as determined by the Secretary of State, and be subject to electronic monitoring of their movements, communications or other activities.[147]

The TPIMs regime would continue to allow closed hearings, where evidence is withheld from the suspect and their lawyer, while a Special Advocate would be appointed to act in the interests of the individual. The principal differences between TPIMs and control orders are as follows:

- the higher threshold required to authorize the former (a reasonable belief the individual is or has been involved in terrorism-related

[144] Parliament of the United Kingdom, Review of Counter-Terrorism and Security Powers. Review Findings and Recommendations (Cm 8004).

[145] Parliament of the United Kingdom, Review of Counter-Terrorism and Security Powers. A Report by Lord Macdonald of River Glaven QC, January 2011, Cm 8003.

[146] Parliament of the United Kingdom, Review of Counter-Terrorism and Security Powers, para 26.

[147] Parliament of the United Kingdom, Draft Enhanced Terrorism Prevention and Investigation Measures Bill, CM 8166, September 2011, www.gov.uk/government/uploads/system/uploads/attachment_data/file/98424/etpim-draft-bill.pdf

activity, as contrasted with reasonable suspicion of involvement in such activity);

- TPIMs authorize more tightly prescribed powers because the Prevention of Terrorism Act 2005 included a non-exhaustive list of measures that could be imposed;
- TPIMs do not include a power to relocate a suspect without consent;
- the 16-hour curfew associated with control orders is replaced by an 'overnight residence measure';
- TPIMs measure are subject to a two-year limit after which they cannot be renewed if the individual has not been involved with any terrorism-related activity;
- TPIMs are not subject to annual renewal, as were control orders.[148]

In September 2011, the government published the Draft Enhanced Terrorism Prevention and Investigation Measures Bill. The Draft Enhanced Bill addressed exceptional circumstances in which the Home Secretary would be given powers to impose even more severe restrictions on individuals that were not authorized by the earlier bill. To utilize these powers, the Secretary of State would be required to demonstrate that 'on the balance of probabilities' the individual was or had been involved in terrorism-related activity, a more stringent threshold than that authorized for the regular TPIMs scheme.

Both the regular and enhanced versions of TPIMs were heavily criticized. Critics argued that differences between TPIMs and control orders were negligible with respect to their adverse effects for civil liberties. Critics described the new TPIMs scheme as 'control orders lite',[149] because authority for imposing these coercive measures is given by the executive and outside the normal criminal justice system, and characterized the intent to gain parliamentary approval for additional restrictive measures as 'anti-terrorism powers for a rainy day'.[150] Other critics argued that as problematic as control orders are, they are preferable to TPIMs, because control orders were conceived as a radical but temporary

[148] J. Tobin, 'Terrorism Prevention and Investigation Measures Bill (HL Bill 91 of 2010–12)', House of Lords, Library Notice, 19 September 2011, LLN 2011/027, p. 1.

[149] Ibid.; see also M. Ryder, 'Control Orders Have Been Rebranded. Big Problems Remain', *The Guardian*, 11 January 2011, www.guardian.co.uk/commentisfree/libertycentral/2011/jan/28/control-orders-protection-of-freedoms-bill

[150] A. Wagner, 'Anti-terrorism Powers for a Rainy Day', UK Human Rights Blog, 4 September 2011, http://ukhumanrightsblog.com/2011/09/04/anti-terrorism-powers-for-a-rainy-day/

derogation from democratic and criminal justice principles, whereas TPIMs are 'one step closer to the normalisation of preventative administration detention'.[151]

The JCHR questioned the very justification for the measures, which it characterized as a 'watered down version' of control orders.[152] The committee indicated that although it accepted the UK faced a serious threat from terrorism, it was questionable whether the country still faced a 'public emergency threatening the life of the nation' more than eight years after the government first declared this to be case in 2001. The JCHR also questioned the reliance on this claim as continued justification for such coercive measures.[153] The committee warned parliament that despite the importance of access to information about the scale and nature of the threat posed by terrorism, neither parliament nor the JCHR were any closer to fully understanding the threat posed by international terrorism than they had been at the outset. As a consequence, it was difficult to make a reasonable judgement about the necessity and proportionality of the legislative response.[154] Moreover, this 'permanent state of emergency. . . inevitably has a deleterious effect on public debate about the justification for counter-terrorism measures'.[155]

The JCHR's concern about the continued reliance on government claims that circumstances justify continued reliance on exceptional powers, where coercive treatment is authorized outside the normal criminal justice system, is consistent with ongoing academic concern that governments are normalizing the use of exceptional measures.[156]

The JCHR urged parliament to 'bring human rights back in' when assessing and approving counter-terrorism legislation,[157] and recommended amendments to ensure that TPIMs can only be used as part of an active, ongoing criminal investigation.[158] The JCHR flatly rejected the

[151] Liberty News, 'Anyone for TPIMs – Control Orders with a Twist?', 2 September 2011, www.liberty-human-rights.org.uk/news/2011/anyone-for-tpims-control-orders-with-a-twist-.php

[152] Parliament of the United Kingdom, JCHR, Sixteenth Report of Session 2010–2012, para 1.11.

[153] JCHR, Sixteenth Report of Session 2010–2012, HL 86/HC 111, para 17.

[154] Ibid., para 18. [155] Ibid., summary.

[156] F. F. Davis and F. de Londras, 'Counter-Terrorist Judicial Review: Beyond Dichotomies'.

[157] Parliament of the United Kingdom, JCHR, Sixteenth Report of Session 2010–2012, HL 86/HC 111, para 6.

[158] Parliament of the United Kingdom, JCHR, Twentieth Report of Session 2010–2012, HL 204/HC 1571, para 1.

government's claim that civil preventative restrictions are an appropriate exercise of executive power, arguing:[159]

> There is no 'well established principle' across our legal system of executive-imposed restrictions on individuals who are not subject to any ongoing criminal process. On the contrary, the well-established principle is that executive restrictions on liberty are such a radical departure from our common law tradition that they always require prior judicial authorisation after proper legal process.[160]

The JCHR recommended a long list of suggested amendments, including using TPIMs only as long as an active criminal investigation is continuing, authorizing courts to determine whether the conditions for imposing TPIMs have been met, requiring the Secretary of State to provide those subject to TPIMs sufficient information to be able to give effective instructions to their representatives in relation to these allegations, creating a statutory obligation that the Home Secretary give reasons for imposing TPIMs and requiring annual renewal of the authority to issue TPIMs.[161] In its second report on the issue, the committee also recommended that the standard for imposing TPIMs be increased from reasonable belief to 'the balance of probabilities'.[162]

The government disagreed with the JCHR's concerns on most aspects of the bill but did agree to subject TPIMs to periodic review, although the period chosen was five years rather than the JCHR's recommended annual review.[163] The government also rejected the JCHR and Lord Macdonald's recommendation of using an alternative approach that links the imposition of coercive restrictions on individuals to an ongoing criminal investigation, indicating this approach would not provide adequate protection, and characterized the 'cumulative difficulties' of linking the imposition of restrictions to an ongoing criminal investigation as 'insurmountable'.[164]

[159] The Government Reply to the Sixteenth Report from the Joint Committee on Human Rights, Session 2010–2012 HL Paper 180, HC 1432, Legislative Scrutiny: Terrorism Prevention and Investigation Measures Bill, (Cm 8167, September 2011).

[160] Parliament of the United Kingdom, JCHR, Twentieth Report of Session 2010–2012, HL 204/HC 1571, para 1.6.

[161] Parliament of the United Kingdom, JCHR, Sixteenth Report of Session 2010–2012, pp. 19–21.

[162] Parliament of the United Kingdom, JCHR, Twentieth Report of Session 2010–2012, HL 204/ HC 1571, para 1.14.

[163] The Government Reply to the Sixteenth Report from the Joint Committee on Human Rights. Session 2010–2012 HL Paper 180, HC 1432, Cm 8167, p. 12.

[164] Ibid., pp. 1–2, 6–7

Much of the debate in the House of Commons focused on the persuasiveness of the government's claim that this legislation was fundamentally different from control orders and also whether it would provide sufficiently strong protection from terrorist threats, rather than on the substance of the JCHR's reported concerns. The fact that control orders originated under a Labour government helps explain why many Labour members were reluctant to address questions of compatibility, particularly in light of widespread claims that the adverse effects which TPIMs pose for liberty are not substantively different from those arising from control orders. Instead, several Labour critics accused the government of doing what was necessary to appease Liberal Democrats so as to allow them to maintain their election pledge while simply reenacting control orders and house arrest under the same name,[165] and also suggested that deals 'done to save face for the Deputy Prime Minister' were being put at the expense of public safety.[166]

Although the emphasis in the Commons debate was disproportionately on effectiveness and whether the government was being disingenuous in characterizing the effects of TPIMs as substantively different from those of control orders, a small minority of members expressed concerns about the justification of TPIMs from a civil liberties perspective[167] and criticized those who justify these measures on the basis of 'lazy assumption[s] that all people who are suspects in these circumstances are dangers'.[168] Nevertheless, the government had little difficulty getting approval for its regular TPIMs regime in the House of Commons.

However, the House of Commons did not support the government's proposal to authorize enhanced measures outside the regular TPIMs powers. One critic characterized the government's approach as asking parliament to authorize 'exceptional legislation to exceptional legislation in exceptional circumstances', which she described as the 'most convoluted, awkward, difficult and strange way of legislation' she had ever seen.[169] Other criticisms addressed ambiguity about the threshold for triggering

[165] Parliament of the United Kingdom, *Hansard* HC Deb vol 532, col 75–76.7 June 2011 (Yvette Cooper).

[166] Ibid., cols 111–12, 5 September 2011 (Hazel Blears).

[167] Ibid., col 81, 5 September 2011 (Jeremy Corbyn).

[168] Ibid., col 68, 5 September 2011 (Dr Huppert).

[169] Ibid., col 91, 5 September 2011 (Hazel Blears).

emergency legislation and whether it would take a national catastrophe before emergency legislation was considered appropriate, as suggested by Lord Macdonald in evidence before the JCHR, or something considerably less substantial;[170] whether parliament would have sufficient information or time to make careful judgements about whether these measures are appropriate and justified;[171] and the difficulties that could occur if an emergency situation arose while parliament was in recess.[172] A joint committee struck to examine the Draft Enhanced Terrorism Prevention and Investigation Measures Bill cautiously approved these measures, but reported that no compelling reason justified introducing these measures as a separate bill at some unspecified time or unspecified circumstance.[173]

After the TPIMs bill was introduced to the House of Lords, the government approved several amendments that did not fundamentally alter the scheme, and which the government characterized as technical changes that reflected its policy intentions.[174] The legislation received royal assent on 14 December 2011. In keeping with the JCHR's emphasis on evidence to justify coercive measures that restrict rights, the committee initiated post-legislative review of TPIMs and in December 2012, called to provide evidence on their necessity and impact.[175]

VI. Justice and Security Bill[176]

The Justice and Security Bill was introduced in 2012 and proposed the authorization of closed material procedures (CMP) in civil proceedings

170 Parliament of the United Kingdom, *Hansard* HC Deb vol 532, col 97 5 September 2011 (Paul Goggins).

171 Ibid., col 103, 5 September 2011 (Shabana Mahmood).

172 Ibid., col 97 5 September 2011 (Paul Goggins).

173 Parliament of the United Kingdom, Joint Committee on the Draft Enhanced Terrorism Prevention and Investigation Measures Bill, session 2012–2013, HL 70, HC 495, p. 34.

174 Parliament of the United Kingdom, *Hansard* HC Deb vol 536, col 855, 29 November 2011 (James Brokenshire).

175 Parliament of the United Kingdom, JCHR, Call for Evidence on Review of Terrorism Prevention and Investigation Measures, 20 December 2012, www.parliament.uk/business/committees/committees-a-z/joint-select/human-rights-committee/news/call-for-evidence-on-review-of-terrorism-prevention-and-investigation-measures/

176 J. Hiebert, 'Legislative Rights Review: Addressing the Gap between Ideals and Constraints', in M. Hunt, H. Hooper and P. Yowell (eds.), *Parliament and Human Rights: Redressing the Democratic Deficit* (Oxford: Hart Publishing), 2015.

where the use of sensitive materials arises;[177] a concept the media and other critics characterized as the equivalent to establishing secret courts.[178] Parliamentary debate on this bill reinforced substantive differences in the priority accorded to HRA and JCHR reports in the two houses of parliament. As was the case in earlier debates on anti-terrorist measures, the House of Commons paid minimal attention to HRA compliance or JCHR reports, while the Lords focused heavily on compatibility issues and used JCHR reports to support calls for amendments. However, the Lords' treatment of this bill also demonstrates the vulnerability of pursuing compatibility-inspired amendments in the face of strong party pressure. Thus, despite having identified serious rights-based concerns and passing rights-protecting amendments that were subsequently overturned in the House of Commons, concerns about compatibility yielded, in the final vote in the House of Lords, to more base political considerations of preserving the stability of the Coalition government.

The legislative process began with a Green Paper in which Kenneth Clarke, the minister responsible for this initiative, emphasized the problem of civil claims being initiated against government or state agencies which involve sensitive materials that cannot be publicly disclosed for fear of undermining national security or threatening relationships with other nations with whom the UK shares intelligence.[179] As a result, the government argued that taxpayers are liable for the costs associated with these cases, because 'security and intelligence agencies have had no way of presenting their evidence in court without putting their methods at risk and their agents in danger'.[180] The government's proposal to address this situation was to introduce closed material procedures into civil proceedings where the use of sensitive materials is required.[181]

The use of closed procedures for hearing sensitive evidence relating to national security dates back to changes made to the Special Immigration Appeals Commission Act of 1997 after the ECtHR called into question

177 Ministry of Justice, Justice and Security Green Paper, Cm 8194 (2011).

178 L. Davies and N. Watt, 'David Cameron Defends Secret Courts and Surveillance Plans', *The Guardian*, 4 April 2012, www.guardian.co.uk/law/2012/apr/04/clarke-defends-secret-courts-plans-clegg; A. Tomkins, 'Justice and Security in the United Kingdom', (2014) v. 47:3 Israel Law Review pp. 305–329.

179 Ministry of Justice, Justice and Security Green Paper, Cm 8194 (2011).

180 Ibid., foreword by Ken Clarke.

181 Ministry of Justice, Justice and Security Green Paper, Cm 8194 (2011).

the compatibility of the Home Secretary's discretion to rely on classified materials to deport non-nationals on security grounds, without any right of appeal.[182] The ruling led to the introduction of the Special Advocate system, in which lawyers with security clearance are appointed to represent the interests of those whose cases involve classified materials.[183] However, the Justice and Security Bill sought to extend closed material proceedings to civil actions, which prompted extensive criticism from the JCHR, parliamentarians (particularly those in the Lords), judges, constitutional scholars and prominent non-governmental organizations.

The JCHR initiated hearings to assess the implications and potential justification for the legislation,[184] reported on the proposals contained in the Justice and Security Green Paper and issued two subsequent reports on the bill as introduced and amended.[185] Based on the evidence it generated, and analysis of the government's proposals, the JCHR disputed the government's claim that the legislation was justified and criticized its case as being based on 'vague predictions' that do not come close to the compelling evidence required to justify closed material proceedings.[186] The JCHR advised parliament that the government had not duly assessed the implications of CMPs for the common law principle of a right to fair hearing, which requires 'the right to an open and adversarial trial on equal terms and reasons for the court's decisions',[187] and urged that parliamentary consideration of the bill be guided by attention to whether the government had compelling evident that justifies the necessity 'for such a serious departure from the fundamental principles of open justice and fairness'.[188]

[182] *Chahal* v. *UK* (1997) 23 EHRR 413; Constitutional Affairs Committee, 'The Operation of the Special Immigration Appeals Commission and Special Advocates', Seventh Report, Session 2004–05, HC 323-I, para 45.

[183] House of Commons Library, Research Paper, 12/80, Justice and Security Bill, 14 December 2012, pp. 4–8.

[184] Parliament of the United Kingdom, JCHR, The Justice and Security Green Paper, Oral Evidence, HC 1777–i–v, 24 January 2012.

[185] Parliament of the United Kingdom, JCHR, Twenty-Fourth Report of Session 2010–2013, HL 286/HC 1777; JCHR, Fourth Report, Session 2012–2013, HL 59/HC 370; JCHR Eighth Report, Session 2012–2013, HL 128/ HC 101.

[186] Parliament of the United Kingdom, JCHR, Twenty-Fourth Report of Session 2010–2013, HL 286/HC 1777, para 10.

[187] Parliament of the United Kingdom, JCHR, Fourth Report, Session 2012–2013, HL 59/ HC 370, para 16.

[188] Ibid., para 18.

The legislative bill differed significantly from the Green Paper proposals by excluding inquests from the scope of the bill, allowing a more substantial role for the judiciary and allowing use of a CMP only in cases involving national security, as contrasted with the proposal that they be used in the public interest.[189] However, the changes did little to quell criticism of the bill's adverse human rights implications.

When reviewing the bill, the JCHR reported that, notwithstanding its assessment that the government had failed to demonstrate the justification for CMPs, it would nevertheless focus on how to improve the bill to accommodate human rights concerns, because of the committee's belief that the government was likely to succeed in passing this legislation.[190] The JCHR outlined an extensive list of recommendations to narrow the scope for invoking a CMP and to ensure scrutiny of the justification for these uses, which included giving judges the discretion and power to decide applications for a closed material proceeding and instructing judges that when exercising discretion about the availability of CMP in civil proceedings, they should decide whether a claim for Public Interest Immunity (PII) could have been made in relation to the material.[191] In a PII the balancing exercise is between the public interest in non-disclosure and the public interest in the administration of justice, whereas in a CMP there is no equivalent balancing exercise by the court, whose task is to ensure that material is not disclosed if so doing would harm the public interest.[192]

The JCHR recommended that the bill be amended to ensure that a CMP is only permitted as a last resort.[193] However, in the event a CMP is authorized, the JCHR recommended the bill be amended to ensure 'a full judicial balancing of interests' occurred.[194] It also recommended a statutory requirement to provide the excluded party

189 House of Commons Library, Research Paper 12/80, Justice and Security Bill, 14 December 2012, p. 13. See also discussion by JCHR, Fourth Report, Session 2012–2013, HL 59/HC 370, para 10.

190 Parliament of the United Kingdom, JCHR, Eight Report of Session 2012–2013, summary.

191 Parliament of the United Kingdom, JCHR, Fourth Report, Session 2012–2013, HL 59/HC 370, paras 60–61.

192 Parliament of the United Kingdom, JCHR, Twenty-Fourth Report of Session 2010–2013, HL 286/HC 1777, para 97.

193 Parliament of the United Kingdom, JCHR, Fourth Report, Session 2012–2013, HL 59/HC 370, para 67.

194 Ibid., para 71.

with the 'gist of the closed materials', sufficient to enable it to give effective instructions to the Special Advocate.[195]

The JCHR also reported that it did not accept it was consistent with the rule of law to remove the courts' jurisdiction to order disclosure of material relating to claims of wrongdoing when this involves sensitive information, and recommended certification based on the context of the information, which is subject to judicial control.[196] Given the committee's view that the effects of the bill would represent a radical departure from 'fundamental common law traditions', the JCHR recommended that the Secretary of State be required to regularly report to parliament about the use of the exceptional procedures the bill authorized, and also that the legislation be subject to independent review and annual renewal.[197]

In the House of Lords, peers tabled amendments that gave effect to many of the JCHR's concerns. These amendments included ensuring that judges decide whether a CMP should be used in any given case (in contrast to the original draft, which would have required a judge to order a CMP when materials impact on national security); that a CMP only be available as a procedure of last resort; and that courts be required to balance the interests of national security against the interests of fairness and open justice when deciding whether to agree to the use of a CMP.[198] However, even with these amendments, some members of the Lords (including members of the JCHR) indicated they were not convinced that closed material procedures should ever be used for civil trials because the government had not justified their use.[199]

Shortly before the substantially amended bill was introduced in the House of Commons on November 2012, Deputy Prime Minister Nick Clegg indicated that he was supportive of many of the JCHR's criticisms of the bill, and that the government would consider the Lords' amendments 'with an open and, in many respects, sympathetic mind'.[200]

[195] Parliament of the United Kingdom, JCHR, Fourth Report, Session 2012–2013, HL 59/HC 370, para 76.

[196] Ibid., para 96.

[197] Ibid., para 111.

[198] A. Home, 'Justice and Security Bill. Bill No 99 201203', Research Paper 12/80, 14 December 2012, House of Commons Library.

[199] Parliament of the United Kingdom, *Hansard*, HL, vol 740, col 1890, 21 November 2012 (Baroness Kennedy).

[200] O. Bowcott, 'Secret Courts Plans Savaged in the House of Lords', *The Guardian*, 21 November 2012, www.guardian.co.uk/law/2012/nov/21/secret-courts-house-of-lords

Clegg had earlier characterized his role as exerting 'a restraining influence on the security services' and acknowledged that he was 'struck' by the JCHR's critical reviews of the bill.[201] Yet despite this statement, Kenneth Clarke subsequently indicated that although the government was prepared to accept some of the amendments the JCHR proposed, the government was 'not wholly convinced that every one of the amendments is quite right'. He urged parliament to avoid assuming it should only support the bill on the condition the government had acceded to all of the JCHR's concerns.[202]

On the eve of the committee stage of the bill, the government introduced a number of amendments that overturned many of the changes made in the Lords. Although the government claimed that these amendments were sympathetic to the JCHR's concerns about respecting the principles of justice,[203] the JCHR subsequently disputed this assertion and criticized the government for having altered rights-protecting amendments made in the Lords without giving the JCHR adequate time to scrutinize and report on them.[204]

The committee published a second report on the bill restating its concern that CMPs should be used only as a last resort; that the legislation ensure 'a full judicial balancing of interests' always takes place within the CMP; and that there should be a statutory requirement to provide the excluded party the gist of the closed material so enable effective instructions for the Special Advocate. The JCHR also reiterated its recommendation for annual renewal,[205] which the House of Lords had not supported.

The JCHR was far from the only critic of the bill. An alliance of more than 100 human rights groups and human rights specialists also indicated strong concerns regarding the bill's effects on the right to a fair trial and the rule of law, and called on the House of Commons to vote against the bill. Some characterized the bill as having been motivated by an attempt to cover up British collusion in the abuse and rendition of terror

[201] 'Nick Clegg Demands Rethink on Secret Justice Plans', *The Guardian*, 4 April 2012, www.guardian.co.uk/law/2012/apr/04/human-rights-committee-hidden-justice

[202] Parliament of the United Kingdom, *Hansard*, HC, vol 555, col 714, 18 December 2012.

[203] Parliament of the United Kingdom, HM Government Response to the JCHR, Fourth Report, Session 2012–2013, Cm 8533 (2013).

[204] Parliament of the United Kingdom, JCHR, Eighth Report, Session 2012–2013, HL 128/HC 101, Summary.

[205] Ibid.

suspects, and felt that the idea of secret trials was a huge aberration from the idea that 'justice must be done and must be seen to be done'.[206]

Despite these criticisms, a substantial majority in the House of Commons approved the government's amended bill. When the bill returned to the Lords for final consideration, the conflict that might have been anticipated in light of the Lords' earlier stance on this issue fizzled out as the Lords backed down from their earlier insistence on amendments to the bill. The government was able to defeat new rights-inspired amendments, including a Labour-sponsored change that would have allowed the use of CMPs only if a judge determined it would be impossible to reach a fair verdict 'by any other means', by imposing a three-line whip on Liberal Democrat peers to support the government's preferred version of the bill.[207] The Labour amendment was narrowly defeated; 29 Liberal Democrats respected the three-line whip, while 26 defied it. A second amendment, suggested by Liberal Democrat Lord Marks – to require review of the legislation after four years – was also defeated; 31 Liberal Democrat peers supported the amendment and 22 voted against it.[208]

Conclusion

Both Labour and Coalition governments have demonstrated strong reluctance to allow concerns of compliance with the HRA to substantially constrain their ability to pass legislation directed at national security issues. Amendments have generally been considered only when politically necessary to save a bill from parliamentary defeat or substantial delay in the House of Lords. Governments do not act as if they accept an obligation to explain claims that legislation is compatible with Convention rights in the face of contestation from the JCHR, or to justify their disregard for the recommendations of specialized committees or independent overseers who recommend that respect for human rights requires the treatment of security issues within the normal framework of the criminal justice system.

[206] 'Campaigners United Against Secret Courts', *The Guardian*, 3 March 2013, www.guardian.co.uk/law/2013/mar/03/justice-and-security-mi5

[207] 'Last-ditch Bid to Dilute Secret Courts Plan Fails', *The Guardian*, 27 March 2013, www.guardian.co.uk/law/2013/mar/27/secret-courts-plan-fails

[208] C. Lindsay, 'Secret Courts Now a Reality After Lords Amendments Fall – How Did Liberal Democrats Vote?', 27 March 2013, www.libdemvoice.org/secret-courts-now-a-reality-after-lords-amendments-fall-how-did-liberal-democrats-vote-33875.html

Parliamentary deliberations and voting on national security issues also do not indicate that political behaviour in the Commons has been substantially reorientated to focus on compatibility issues, despite critical JCHR reports that contest ministerial claims of compatibility. Notwithstanding the JCHR's encouragement of parliament's assessing indefinite detention, control orders, TPIMs and the introduction of closed material procedures within a human rights framework, and the committee's repeated emphasis on the importance of justifying exceptions to traditional constitutional principles, the overwhelming majority of members in the House of Commons have remained largely indifferent to JCHR concerns. The Commons has been generally uninterested in adopting a compatibility-based framework and has approved the core elements of the governments' security agendas (with the exception of the Labour government's attempt to extend the pre-charge detention period to 90 days and then 42 days, and enhanced TPIMs). Although some members of the party in government have at times voted against their government's legislation, the number of rebels has generally been insufficient to compel the government to reconsider the legislation. Moreover, it is worth nothing that while rebel backbench members have invoked rights-based concerns, they have rarely been framed to emphasize compatibility with the HRA with Convention rights[209] or to engage JCHR reports in an effort to augment criticism of bills. Thus it is difficult to attribute these rebellious actions to the HRA or the idea of legislative rights review.

The idea that legislation should be compliant with the HRA has had far greater resonance in the House of Lords, where peers have consistently echoed many of the JCHR's concerns and have utilized these reports extensively to argue the justification of rights-improving amendments. The House of Lords defeated the attempt to substantially extend the pre-charge detention period, and was also able to force government to seek and attain parliamentary approval for the prolonged use of indefinite detention and control orders, and to accept limited judicial review. However, it is important to bear in mind that the government was nevertheless able to retain intact the core elements of its legislative agenda – indefinite detention, control orders and long periods of detention without charge – which, for critics, were the most problematic aspects of the governments' security agendas from a human rights perspective. Moreover, if the Lords' insistence on a renewal obligation

[209] D. Nicol, 'The Human Rights Act and the Politicians', (2004) 24 *Legal Studies* 462–64.

for indefinite detention and control orders had the intention of imposing a justificatory burden on government to demonstrate continued use of these coercive powers was warranted, it was spectacularly unsuccessful – the government subsequently found little difficulty in having these powers renewed, despite continued warnings by the JCHR that their prolonged use seriously undermines respect for human rights.

Despite a substantially stronger inclination in the Lords to address compatibility concerns, peers are not immune to substantial party influence. Thus, in the final vote on the Justice and Security Bill, a sufficient number of Liberal Democrat peers succumbed to party pressure to support the government and oppose an amendment intended to strengthen judicial oversight that the Lords had earlier approved, and which the JCHR strongly supported. Notwithstanding an earlier decision by a majority of Liberal Democrat delegates at a national convention to oppose the introduction of CMPs,[210] the party leadership imposed strong pressure on Liberal Democrat peers to vote against last-minute amendments intended to redress the severity of perceived rights infringements and to require review of the legislation by the next parliament. Thus, although peers normally have more liberty to vote against the government's agenda than do their elected partisan colleagues in the House of Commons, a majority of those Liberal Democrat peers who stayed long enough to vote in a late evening division respected a three-line whip to oppose these amendments so as to preserve the government's preferred version of the bill.[211] Liberal Democrat opposition to these amendments encouraged prominent human rights lawyers to resign their membership of the party and accuse it of having gone too far in its concern about the stability of the Coalition at the expense of the party's core principles.[212]

[210] R. Syal, 'Secret Courts Plan Receives Blow at Lib Dem Conference', *The Guardian*, 22 September 2012, www.guardian.co.uk/law/2012/sep/25/secret-courts-lib-dem-conference

[211] C. Lindsay, 'Secret Courts Now a Reality After Lords Amendments Fall'.

[212] P. Sands, 'I'm Leaving the Liberal Democrats Too', *The Guardian*, 11 March 2013, www.guardian.co.uk/commentisfree/2013/mar/11/justice-security-i-quit-the-lib-dems. Earlier, two other prominent members of the party, Dinah Rose QC and Jo Shaw QC, had also resigned because of the party's support for the bill. These resignations led to criticism from Liberal Democrat Lord Lester, a member of the JCHR, who characterized his former colleagues as 'fairweather friends' and argued that rather than quit the party they should have supported the work of the JCHR to build more safeguards into the bill. O. Bowcott, 'Lib Dem Peer Attacks "Fairweather Friends" Who Quit Over Secret Courts', *The Guardian*, 12 March 2013, www.guardian.co.uk/politics/2013/mar/12/lib-dem-peer-secret-courts

Although the habitual role of opposition parties is to demonstrate why their party is the better alternative to government, opposition party leaders have not incorporated compliance with Convention rights into their strategies for assessing bills relating to national security issues, by pressuring government either to explain why they are reporting that bills are consistent with Convention rights or to justify why its judgement on compatibility is more compelling than the JCHR's or other prominent voices contesting the government's assessment.

In short, the most effective constraint on government on national security issues has not arisen from parliamentary pressure but from judicial censure.

9

Parliamentary Review: Equality and Democratic Issues

This chapter examines governmental and parliamentary engagement with legislative bills that address a range of equality and democratic issues. The bills we examine entail the following: restrictions on election advertising; the recognition of civil partnerships and the subsequent decision to introduce same sex marriage; and the creation of identity cards and a national registry scheme. We also look at how government and parliament have responded to pressure to enact remedial measures after the European Court of Human Rights ruled that the UK's decision to deny all prisoners the right to vote violates the European Convention of Human Rights.

Our research reveals considerable variance in how rights-based concerns have influenced governmental behaviour and parliamentary assessments of legislative bills. Consistent with our analysis in the previous chapter, the House of Commons has generally exhibited a distinct lack of interest in assessing whether bills are compatible with Convention rights or engaging JCHR reports that contest ministerial claims of compatibility to pressure ministers into justifying or amending bills. Moreover, in those rare instances where JCHR reports are raised in the Commons, these are usually at the instigation of a member of the JCHR.[1] The parliamentary debates we examine here also reveal that a majority of elected members strongly resisted passing remedial measures to comply with European court rulings that parliament's ban on prisoners' voting is not compatible with Convention rights, despite JCHR warnings that such measures should be enacted as a matter of necessity.

Yet a lack of interest in the Commons in scrutinizing ministerial reports of compatibility or engaging JCHR concerns does not necessarily correspond to a lack of interest in the rights dimension of bills. For

[1] M. Hunt, H. Hooper and P. Yowell, 'Parliaments and Human Rights. Redressing the Democratic Deficit', AHRC Public Policy Series No. 5, 24, 2012. www.ahrc.ac.uk/News-and-Events/Publications/Documents/Parliaments-and-Human-Rights.pdf.

example, parliamentary deliberations about the introduction of legal recognition of same sex relationships and gay marriage were manifestly rights-based debates in which many members emphasized equality, non-discrimination and justice despite a lack of any obvious indication that these contributions were influenced by the language of Convention rights or the HRA's or JCHR's focus on compatibility with Convention rights. The same can be said about debates criticizing identity cards, where concerns of civil liberties and privacy were prominent. Moreover, depending on the issue, it is not necessarily the case that the House of Lords was the more rights-oriented chamber, as is evident in the amendments approved by the Lords that were intended to derail attempts to redress discrimination against gays and lesbians through civil partnership legislation.

We also find strong indications of strategic decision-making by governments. This is best exemplified by reactions to the European courts' rulings that the ban on prisoner voting is not consistent with Convention rights. Governments responded with stalling tactics and cost–benefit analyses of how to mitigate the political and fiscal consequences in the event of substantial judicially sanctioned fiscal remedies. At no time have either Labour or Conservative-led Coalition governments conceded that compatibility concerns justify amending the policy on prisoner voting. Labour failed to introduce any remedial measures, while the Coalition government made it abundantly clear that reforms were being considered only as a matter of political necessity in light of anticipated and substantial compensation costs. Labour's treatment of identity cards and a national registration regime also demonstrated that the government's acceptance of rights-inspired amendments was not because parliament had convinced it that these were justified, but because it was worried that opposition in the Lords would delay or block implementation of this legislation.

However, it would be inappropriate to characterize all governmental behaviour as being motivated by strategic considerations of how to manage the threat and consequences of judicial censure or legislative pressures that could delay or defeat bills in the absence of rights-improving amendments (primarily from the House of Lords). The Labour government's pursuit of civil partnership legislation and Conservative Prime Minister David Cameron's determination that parliament pass the bill on same sex marriage appeared to be inspired by genuine commitments to redress inequality in the legal treatment of gay men and lesbians, despite a lack of imminent judicial threat or parliamentary pressure to pursue rights-inspired reforms. Yet strategic assessments of the HRA were not irrelevant to how both governments managed potential opposition. What was particularly telling about government strategies in both cases was that despite pursuing substantive reforms motivated by concerns about equality, neither government invoked the HRA to champion its reform efforts. The most likely explanation is that party leaders' repeated criticisms of the HRA and the lack of strong public support for it rendered emphasis on the HRA an undesirable political resource for efforts to either build support for or challenge opposition related to these rights-inspired reforms.

I. Communications Act

The 2002 Communications Bill represented the first instance (and one of only two occasions) of a minister reporting under section 19(1)(b) an inability to state that the government's bill was compatible with protected rights at the time of introduction. The Communications Bill had several objectives, but relevant to discussion here is the question of whether a ban on paid political advertising on television and radio is compatible with the HRA. Paid political advertising on television or radio has not been permitted since the BBC came into operation in 1927, when its first Director General interpreted the corporation's responsibilities under the royal Charter as preventing the BBC from accepting payment for advertising, a decision that originated from Winston Churchill's request to broadcast a message about India in exchange for payment of £100. In 1954 the Television Act established the Independent Television Authority (subsequently renamed the Independent Broadcasting Authority) to oversee commercial broadcasting; it also accepted this ban on political advertising.[2]

Questions have subsequently arisen about the appropriateness of this ban, which has been defended as ensuring that 'the most powerful advertising medium is not available for purchase, no matter how much money a party is prepared to pay'.[3] The Committee on Standards in Public Life (Neill Committee) conducted an inquiry into the funding of political parties and, in 1998, recommended that the ban on paid political advertising on television and radio be maintained and the practice of

[2] M. Pinto-Duschinsky, *British Political Finance 1830–1980* (Washington: American Enterprise Institute for Public Policy Research, 1981), pp. 252–53.

[3] Ibid., p. 253.

broadcasters providing political parties with free airtime continued. The committee suggested that although it is difficult to discern the effects that paid advertising might have on an election, a ban is justified to ensure that elections are not extremely costly and to reduce parties' dependence on wealthy donors.[4] Although the committee recognized that a ban on political advertising constitutes a restriction on free expression, it concluded that the ban is appropriate and defensible as it protects 'the democratic right of UK citizens not to be subjected to a barrage of political propaganda at prime advertising time from the party with the richest backers'.[5]

The government introduced the Communications Bill in 2002, which maintained this ban on paid advertising. A draft version of the bill had already been subject to extensive scrutiny, including that of the JCHR, which reported that the complete ban on political advertising might not withstand judicial review and recommended the government find an alternative and proportionate way to maintain its objective.[6] The JCHR's recommendation was ignored and the bill proposed a ban on all advertising whose objects are political in nature, are directed toward a political end or have a connection with an industrial dispute.

Tessa Jowell, then Secretary of State for Culture, Media and Sport, reported to parliament that the government's decision to maintain the ban on political advertising prevented her from affirming that the bill was compatible with the HRA. She indicated that her interpretation of the section 19 reporting obligation on compatibility was influenced by the government's legal advisors' assessment of a European Court of Human Rights case involving the refusal to air a political advertisement on television. The case did not focus on whether a ban on all political party advertising was consistent with the ECHR, but addressed the issue of whether an advertisement could be banned on the basis of its content.[7]

Jowell explained that her inability to claim compatibility reflected the government's decision that positive reports of compatibility should be made only 'if it is more likely than not that the Bills' provisions would withstand a legal challenge on human rights grounds in both the

[4] Committee on Standards in Public Life (Neill Committee), Fifth Report, 'The Funding of Political Parties in the United Kingdom', Cm 4057-I (1998), R94, pp. 173–74.

[5] Ibid., pp. 174–75.

[6] Parliament of the United Kingdom, JCHR, Nineteenth Report, Session 2001–2002, HL 149/HC 1102, para 64.

[7] *Vgt Verein Gegen Tierfabriken* v. *Switzerland*, No. 24699/94 (28 June 2001).

domestic courts and the European Court of Human Rights'. Based on the legal advice she received, Jowell reported that she was unable to conclude that the bill was 'more likely than not' to be ruled consistent with Convention rights either in domestic courts or before the European Court.[8]

Although Jowell acknowledged uncertainty about how courts would rule on this issue, she stated that this acknowledgement should not be interpreted to mean the government accepted the bill was incompatible with Convention rights.[9] Yet Jowell also indicated that although the government would robustly defend the legislation, it would ultimately accept the verdict of the ECtHR should it lose. As she stated: 'Of course, if that defence subsequently failed before the domestic courts, we would need to reconsider our position. Beyond that, we take our international obligations extremely seriously and we would seek to amend the ban in accordance with any judgement of the European Court of Human Rights in Strasbourg that ruled against the UK legislation.'[10]

Jowell characterized the decision to proceed with a bill for which compatibility cannot be affirmed as constituting an 'obviously exceptional' circumstance, and stated that the decision to proceed was made 'only after careful deliberation and a full examination of both the legal arguments and the policy alternatives':[11]

> We looked hard at the current ban to see whether some minor changes would make it more certain that it was human rights compatible. Unfortunately, any such change would still allow substantial political advertising... By denying powerful interests the chance to skew political debate, the current ban safeguards the public and democratic debate, and protects the impartiality of broadcasters.[12]

As will become evident, this reluctance to claim compatibility because of uncertainty about how courts will rule distinguishes Jowell's interpretation of the reporting obligation from subsequent ministerial and cabinet interpretations of the section 19 statutory responsibility. This decision reflected close adherence to the Cabinet Office guidelines in place at the time, which, as discussed in Chapter 7, initially placed primacy on legal

[8] Parliament of the United Kingdom, JCHR, First Report, Session 2002–2003, HL 24/HC 191, Appendix 6.

[9] Parliament of the United Kingdom, *Hansard*, HC, vol 501, col 787–89, 3 December 2002 (Tessa Jowell).

[10] Ibid. [11] Ibid., col 787, 3 December 2002 (Tessa Jowell).

[12] Ibid., col 788, 3 December 2002 (Tessa Jowell).

interpretations of compatibility, but were subsequently replaced with criteria that allow far greater opportunity for value-based judgements to prevail over legal assessments of compatibility.

Although Jowell was forthcoming with respect to her uncertainty about how the ban would fare if litigated, she was less so on why the government had concluded that a complete ban was necessary to accomplish its goal of promoting fair elections and controlling election costs. Despite her assurances that the government had looked 'hard' for alternative ways to accomplish the policy objective of ensuring elections cannot be altered by substantial paid political advertising, Jowell did not explain to parliament the nature of these rejected options. For example, she stated that the government believed it was appropriate to prevent powerful groups from manipulating political debate,[13] but did not discuss the plausibility of spending restrictions rather than a total broadcast ban on paid political advertising, or the possibility of restricting paid political advertising only during the election period and not at other times. In an Explanatory Note for the House of Commons Library that was copied to the JCHR, she asserted without elaboration that an alternative scheme was not workable:

> Consideration was given to an alternative regime based on specific prohibitions, such as banning all party political advertising and all political advertising around the time of elections or referendums; coupled with other rules to avoid the predominance of any particular point of view on one channel, to provide visual or audible identification of political advertisements, and the control the scale of political advertising in terms both of broadcasting time and the proportion of advertising revenue that a broadcaster is permitted to derive from political
>
> The conclusion was reached, taking account of legal advice, that it would be very difficult to make such a scheme workable, and that in any event it would fall significantly short of the present outright ban, and allow a substantial degree of political advertising to be broadcast across a number of channels.[14]

Shortly after the report to parliament acknowledging uncertainty about how courts would rule, which was the basis for the government's belief

[13] Parliament of the United Kingdom, *Hansard*, HC, vol 501, col 787, 3 December 2002 (Tessa Jowell).

[14] Parliament of the United Kingdom, JCHR, First Report, Session 2002–2003, HL 24/HC 191, Appendix 6, paras 7–8.

that it was appropriate to acknowledge an inability to claim the bill was compatible with Convention rights, an independent Electoral Commission released a discussion paper that suggested the UK approach was likely to be upheld. The Electoral Commission reported that the UK's 'case for retaining the ban on paid advertising is persuasive' because it served the 'interests of the electorate and therefore the public interest', and 'would survive scrutiny under the ECHR and the HRA, at least if the regime of free and unmediated broadcasts is robust'.[15]

However, the JCHR was not as easily satisfied, reporting that any decision to pass legislation that cannot be claimed to be compatible with Convention rights 'requires strong justification as a matter of principle', which was lacking in this case.[16] Nevertheless, parliament passed the legislation, without addressing the JCHR's concerns or questioning the appropriateness of the ban.

Although Jowell indicated that the government would reconsider its position if unable to successfully defend the legislation,[17] the government benefited from a highly deferential judicial ruling from the House of Lords. The challenge was made by Animal Defenders International, an organization with the aim of lawful suppression of cruelty to animals, which was denied approval in 2005 to advertise its latest campaign[18] and subsequently applied for judicial review to seek a declaration under section 4 of the HRA that the ban on advertising was not compatible with freedom of expression under the ECHR. The group's claim was dismissed by the Queen's Bench Division[19] and was appealed to the House of Lords, which unanimously rejected the appeal. The Law Lords declared that the crucial issue was whether the restriction was necessary in a democratic society, and declared that great weight should be accorded to parliament's decision.[20] However, some have questioned

[15] European Commission, *Party Political Broadcasting: Report and Recommendations*, January 2003, p. 17, www.electoralcommission.org.uk/about-us/ppb.cfm.

[16] Parliament of the United Kingdom, JCHR, First Report, Session 2002–2003, HL 24/HC 191, paras 13–16.

[17] Ibid., Appendix 6, para 12.

[18] In 2005 the Broadcast Advertising Clearance Centre (an organization funded by commercial broadcasters to assess proposed advertisements to ensure they are in compliance with the law) decided not to permit the ADI advertising campaign on the basis it would breach s. 321(2) of the Communication Act 2003.

[19] *Animal Defenders International, R (on the application of)* v. *The Secretary of State for Culture, Media and Sport* [2006] EWHC 3069 (Admin).

[20] Ibid., para 18.

whether such deference was warranted, particularly in light of the JCHR's concerns that the government withheld from parliament a thorough explanation of the reasons why a ban was justified.[21]

Nevertheless, in April 2013 the Grand Chamber of the European Court of Human Rights narrowly ruled by the slimmest majority (9–8) that the UK's ban on political advertising does not constitute 'disproportionate interference' with the right of freedom of expression and therefore does not violate Article 10 of the Convention.[22]

Assessing the HRA's influence on the Communications Bill

The Communications Bill provides four interesting insights into political behaviour under the HRA. First, it reveals that on this issue, the Labour government was not willing to abandon legislation to which it was strongly committed simply because it recognized the possibility that a court might rule legislation incompatible with the HRA. Second, the government accorded primacy to case law-based risk assessments when determining the nature of the report it should issue to parliament. The government presented its section 19(1)(b) report acknowledging an inability to claim compatibility not because of its belief that the bill was incompatible with Convention rights, but because the legal advice it received suggested uncertainty about whether the government would be successful in defending the legislation. Third, the government's rejection of alternative and less restrictive options without discussing these or the reasons for their rejection, despite the JCHR's queries, indicates a thin commitment to political responsibility for justifying decisions where an affirmative compatibility report cannot be made. In this case, the issue was how to balance free speech and participation concerns with the promotion of equality and fair elections where money plays a decisive factor. Regardless of one's views of the merits of restricting political advertising, the question of whether and how to regulate money used for political advertising is one of the most contentious issues that liberal

[21] Tom Lewis and Peter Cumper question the appropriateness of judicial deference in this case, and suggest the more appropriate judicial finding would have been to issue a declaration of incompatibility under section 4 of the HRA. T. Lewis and P. Cumper, 'Balancing Freedom of Political Expression Against Equality of Political Opportunity: The Courts and the UK's Broadcasting Ban on Political Advertising', (2009) *Public Law* 89.

[22] European Court of Human Rights, Grand Chamber, *Animal Defenders International* v. *United Kingdom* (application no 48876/08 para 125).

democracies encounter. Finally, the fact that government's acknowledgement of an inability to claim compatibility did not provoke substantial parliamentary discussion, despite the JCHR's emphasis on the importance of considering more proportional ways to achieve the legislative objective, serves as a cautionary tale about assuming that the combination of ministerial reports on compatibility and scrutiny by a specialized parliamentary rights committee will alter how parliament reviews bills and/or compel government to justify decisions when interpretations of compatibility are contested.

II. Civil partnerships and same sex marriage

The United Kingdom has joined a growing number of nations reforming laws so as to recognize the legal union of same sex partners. The Civil Partnership Act was passed in 2004 and created a new legal category of state-recognized relationships: that of same sex partners in a registered civil partnership. Upon registration, same sex partners are treated similarly to those in traditional marriage with respect to inheritance taxes, pension benefits and responsibilities upon the dissolution of relationships. However, the legislation stopped short of allowing same sex partners to legally marry.

Historically, UK laws have regarded homosexuality as criminal and deviant behaviour,[23] and have denied same sex partners property rights of ownership upon the breakdown of a relationship,[24] protection for survivor's pensions, exemptions from inheritance tax,[25] compensation

[23] For a helpful discussion of oppression and attempts to implement reforms in the social, political and legal treatment of gay men and lesbians in the United Kingdom, see A. Grey, *Quest for Justice. Towards Homosexual Emancipation* (London: Sinclair-Stevenson, 1992).

[24] Not only did the law fail to recognize a guaranteed right to ownership of property upon the demise of a relationship; also, courts did not have the power to override legal ownership of property or divide it equitably upon the separation of a couple. The courts could only make orders based on determining the shares each member acquired in the property. Lorraine Conway and Catherine Fairbairn, 'The Civil Partnership Bill (HL): Background and Debate', Research Paper 04/64, House of Commons Library, 7 September 2004, p. 25.

[25] Same-sex partners could not rely on a former partner's contributions for state retirement pensions, in contrast to someone widowed or divorced. Stonewall, an organization promoting legislative reform to achieve equality and justice for gay men, lesbians and bisexuals, provided the following scenario to demonstrate the need to reform the law: 'Rex is 76. His partner, John, died after they had spent 45 years together. Their house was in both names and John left everything to Rex in his will. Rex faced a huge tax bill in

for partners in fatal accidents or recognition of them as their partner's next of kin[26] – resulting in exclusion from important decisions about medical treatment – and participation in decisions following the death of a partner.[27] The only relief same sex partners had from legislatively imposed discrimination occurred through inclusive judicial interpretations of statutory phrases to recognize same sex partners as constituting a 'member of the family'[28] or 'living as his or her husband or wife'.[29]

In addition to having to contend with discriminatory legislation, gay men and lesbians also had to confront state-sanctioned societal prejudices. As recently as the late 1980s, gay activists fought and lost a battle over the public portrayal of sexual orientation as deviant behaviour after the Conservative government enacted section 28 of the Local Government Act, which prohibited public authorities in England and Wales from 'promoting' homosexuality and referred to same sex unions as 'pretend' relationships. The controversial 1988 legislation has been described by gay and lesbian activists as 'the most notorious piece of anti-gay legislation' enacted in the UK in modern times.[30] The legislation is

order to be able to stay in his own home. He also lost John's pension. Had he married a woman for just one day, no tax would have been payable and Rex would have had a survivor pension.' Parliament of the United Kingdom, Civil Partnership Bill, Stonewall Briefing, House of Commons, Second Reading, Thursday 12 October 2004, p. 3, www.stonewall.org.uk/documents/oahq_Commons_Second_Reading_Sep_2004.doc

[26] Parliament of the United Kingdom, JCHR, Fifteenth Report, Session 2003–2004, HL 136/HC 885, para 7.

[27] Same-sex partners were not lawfully recognized as 'next of kin' and therefore could incur difficulty being recognized as a patient's partner, particularly when disagreements occurred between a patient's relatives and partner. L. Conway and C. Fairbairn, 'The Civil Partnership Bill (HL)', p. 26.

[28] *Fitzpatrick* v. *Sterling Housing Association* [2001] 1 AC 27. See Parliament of the United Kingdom, JCHR, Fifteenth Report, Session 2003–2004, HL 136/HC 885, para 6.

[29] *Ghaidan* v. *Godin-Mendoza* (FC) [2004] UKHL 30.

[30] Section 28 of the Local Government Act 1988 prohibited local authorities in England and Wales from 'promoting' homosexuality. The bill originated as a private member's bill introduced in the House of Lords in 1986, and was later championed by the National Council for Christian Standards in Society. The proposal was reintroduced to the House of Commons by a Conservative MP, and enacted by the Conservative government in 1988. Its repeal was supported by an extensive coalition, comprising children's organizations, teachers, school governors, local authorities, trade unions, health experts and lesbian, gay and bisexual groups, and a petition organized by Stonewall contained almost 25,000 signatures of support. For discussion, see Gay and Lesbian Humanist Association, www.pinktriangle.org.uk/glh/section28.html. See also Stonewall, www.stonewall.org.uk/information_bank/education/71.asp.

credited with helping to galvanize the modern gay rights movement, leading to increased pressure and protest rallies by activist groups such as OutRage![31] and Stonewall which are dedicated to fighting discrimination against LGBT people.[32] After Labour was elected in 1997 it tried twice to repeal section 28, only to encounter opposition from the House of Lords.[33] The controversial law was finally repealed in 2003,[34] in a decision supported by an extensive coalition that comprised teachers, school governors, local authorities, trades unions, health experts, LGBT groups and almost 25,000 signatories of a petition organized by Stonewall.[35]

Civil Partnership Bill

The Civil Partnership Bill followed two earlier failed initiatives to grant legal recognition to same sex partners.[36] In June 2003 the government published a consultation paper, *Civil Partnership – A Framework for the Legal Recognition of Same Sex Couples*, which discussed proposals for registering civil partnerships in England and Wales.[37] The Civil

[31] OutRage! is an organization of volunteers formed in 1990 and describes itself as committed to '[r]adical, non-violent direct action and civil disobedience' to 'assert the dignity and human rights of queers', 'fight homophobia, discrimination and violence directed against us'; and 'affirm our right to sexual freedom, choice and self-determination': http://outrage.org.uk/about/

[32] Audrey Gillan, 'Section 28 Gone … But Not Forgotten', *The Guardian*, 17 November 2003, www.guardian.co.uk/politics/2003/nov/17/uk.gayrights

[33] 'Government suffers s. 28 defeat', *BBC News*, 7 February 2000, http://news.bbc.co.uk/2/hi/uk_news/politics/633778.stm; 'Peers Vote to Keep Gay Ban', *BBC News*, 24 July 2000, http://news.bbc.co.uk/2/hi/uk_news/politics/849478.stm.

[34] Ben Summerskill, then executive and spokesperson for Stonewall, described its repeal as a 'triumph for 21st Century tolerance over 19th Century prejudice': 'Section 28 to be Repealed', *BBC News*, 18 September 2003, http://news.bbc.co.uk/2/hi/uk_news/politics/3120924.stm.

[35] For discussion, see Gay and Lesbian Humanist Association, www.pinktriangle.org.uk/glh/section28.html; Stonewall, www.stonewall.org.uk/information_bank/education/71.asp

[36] In 2001, Labour member Jane Griffiths introduced the Relationships (Civil Registration) Bill under the 10-minute rule (Bill 36), which would have provided civil registration of a relationship between two people who cohabitate, and also recognize certain legal rights. The following year, Lord Lester of the Liberal Democrats introduced a private member's bill to the House of Lords, the Civil Partnerships Bill, seeking to establish a legal framework for civil partnerships to include non-married opposite sex and same sex partners. Lord Lester, Press Release, 8 February 2002, as reported by The Odysseus Trust, www.odysseustrust.org/text/cpb/press.html.

[37] L. Conway and C. Fairbairn, 'The Civil Partnership Bill (HL)', p. 10.

Partnership Bill was introduced in 2004; the Labour government stated that it aimed to recognize the 'inherent value of committed same-sex relationships' and to grant 'respect, recognition and justice' for those so long denied.[38]

The Civil Partnership Bill was introduced in the House of Lords, where critics characterized the legislation as a 'gay marriage' bill[39] and argued that the new legal form of relationship was inconsistent with the nation's 'Christian tradition'.[40] Conservative peer Baroness O'Cathain proposed what has been referred to as a 'family members' amendment to change the definition of civil partnership to include family members and care-givers.[41] The amendment was significant for another reason beyond its fairly obvious intent to undermine legal recognition of same sex unions: by taking advantage of the legislation's intention to treat same sex partners similarly to opposite sex partners, the family members amendment would create a loophole through which more individuals could escape the legal requirement to pay inheritance taxes.

The government was extremely critical of this attempt to alter the purpose of the bill, and also argued the family members amendment would make it impossible for the government to report that the bill, as amended, was compatible with Convention rights.[42] The government also characterized the changes made in the Lords as unworkable and expensive.[43] The reduction in inheritance tax received as a result of extending the concept of civil partnership from same sex partners to other family members or care givers was estimated at more than £2 billion per year.[44]

[38] Department of Trade and Industry, 'Landmark Bill for Same-Sex Couples Published', P/2004/129, 31March 2004.

[39] *Hansard*, HL, vol 660, col 403, 22 April 2004.

[40] *Hansard*, HL, vol 662, col 1366, 24 June 2004.

[41] This attempt to change the legislation was harshly criticized by Stonewall. Also critical of the reforms was the Solicitors Family Law Association, which objected to the idea of using the concept of civil partnership to relieve carers and adult children of the burden of paying inheritance tax. It argued that broadening the concept of civil partnership from the intention of recognizing same sex partners to other familial relationships would distort the idea of a civil partnership and render it 'unworkable in the broader context of family law'. Civil Partnership Bill, Stonewall Briefing, House of Lords, Consideration of Commons Amendments, 7 November 2004, Stonewall, www.stonewall.org.uk/documents/Lords_Consideration_LLD.doc

[42] Parliament of the United Kingdom, The Civil Partnership Bill [HL], 5 July 2004, Explanatory Notes, paras 986–987, www.publications.parliament.uk/pa/cm200304/cmbills/132/en/04132x-o.htm

[43] Parliament of the United Kingdom, *Hansard*, HC, vol 425, col 199, 12 October 2004.

[44] Parliament of the United Kingdom, *Hansard*, HL, vol 663, cols. 393–4, 1 July 2004.

MPs from all parties criticized the Lords amendment for undermining the goal of legally recognizing same sex relationships and for exploiting attempts to gain equality for same sex partners to create an inheritance tax loophole.[45] Among the harshest criticism was levelled by Conservative member John Bercow, who admonished those Conservative peers who supported the amendment for their dishonesty and prejudice:

> Ultimately, the O'Cathain amendment is but a smokescreen. It is a smokescreen erected by its proposers in a determined but ultimately doomed attempt to conceal their deep-seated hostility to the very principle of gay equality. For in fact, of course, they simply cannot abide it. They despise it. They are frightened by it. The policy of the Bill's most vociferous opponents is driven not by consideration of reason, logic or fairness, but by considerations of paranoia and prejudice. Such an approach should be thoroughly denounced and rejected.[46]

The Commons removed the Lords' family amendment.[47] Another significant amendment made in the Commons related to more inclusive pension benefits for same sex partners. In the original version of the bill, survival benefits for occupational pension schemes were based only on contributions made after passage of the civil partnership legislation. The JCHR questioned whether the denial of benefits before this date was compatible with Convention rights and wrote to the minister to provide evidence of the justification for this distinction.[48] The government initially defended the decision on the basis that government had not earlier budgeted for same sex survivor benefits,[49] but later reversed its decision and announced that same sex couples would be entitled to survivor pensions in public service schemes from 1988, the same time that opposite sex couples became eligible.[50]

[45] As one member argued, '[T]he inheritance tax issues is a red herring when applied directly to the Bill, except in so far as it applies to same sex-partners… I believe that those who tabled the amendments in the Lords were seeking to wreck the Bill… [T]hose amendments would not even rectify the injustice that they believe to exist.' Parliament of the United Kingdom, *Hansard*, HC, vol 425, col 227, 12 October 2004.

[46] Parliament of the United Kingdom, *Hansard*, HC, vol 425, col 220, 12 October 2004.

[47] A proposed amendment to include family members as civil partners was defeated soundly in the Commons (381–74) Parliament of the United Kingdom, *Hansard*, HC, vol 426, col 781, 9 November 2004.

[48] Parliament of the United Kingdom, JCHR, Fifteenth Report, Session 2003–2004, HL 136/HC 885, paras 41, 46.

[49] Letter from Rt Hon Jacqui Smith MP, Minister of State for Industry and the Regions and Deputy Minister for Women and Equality, Department for Trade and Industry, JCHR, Twentieth Report, Session 2003–2004, HL 182/HC 1187, Appendix 1.

[50] Anne McGuire, Parliamentary Under-Secretary of State for Scotland, told parliament that in response to the considerable discussion in both houses about survivor pensions in

Although a substantial majority approved the bill in the Commons (426–79),[51] the debate was not devoid of criticisms that paralleled some of the objections raised in the House of Lords – claims that it was dishonest for the new civil partnership regime to be named other than 'gay marriage',[52] as well as that civil partnership would both undermine 'the uniqueness of marriage'[53] and also the 'Christian tradition' of opposite sex marriage.[54] Another contentious issue was whether civil partnerships should apply to Northern Ireland.[55] When the Bill returned to the House of Lords, another attempt was made to amend it by requiring its commencement be delayed until a parallel scheme was developed for family members. This was defeated by 251 to 136.[56]

Questions about compatibility

The Labour government responded to criticisms that the Civil Partnership Bill would undermine marriage by treading a strategic, though uneasy, path that: i) defended marriage as the most valued relationship in a hierarchy of relationship recognition, ii) denied that the legislation allows for gay marriage, and iii) characterized civil unions as analogous to marriage.[57] The tension inherent in denying same sex couples the ability to marry and yet characterizing same sex marriage as analogous to traditional marriage was particularly apparent in the government's explanation of why the bill should be considered compatible with Convention rights. In the Explanatory Notes for the bill, the government demonstrated unusual candour (although well hidden in the lengthy details provided) by acknowledging that the bill raises questions about

public service schemes, the government had decided to make the change, which could be achieved by means of regulations, rather than formal amendment to the Bill. Parliament of the United Kingdom, *Hansard*, HC, vol 425, cols. 249–250, 12 October 2004.

51 Parliament of the United Kingdom, *Hansard*, HC, vol 425, col 250, 12 October 2004.

52 Parliament of the United Kingdom, *Hansard*, HC, vol 426, col 731, 9 November 2004.

53 Parliament of the United Kingdom, *Hansard*, HC, vol 425, col 201, 12 October 2004.

54 Gerald Howarth criticized the government for trying to 'force a cultural change on our society' and characterized the decision to alter the nature of marriage as oppressive and dictatorial. Parliament of the United Kingdom, *Hansard*, HC, vol 425, col 239, 12 October 2004.

55 Parliament of the United Kingdom, *Hansard*, HC, vol 425, col 176, 12 October 2004 (Rev Ian Paisley).

56 Parliament of the United Kingdom, *Hansard*, HL, vol 666, col 1481, 17 November 2004.

57 Parliament of the United Kingdom, *Hansard*, HC, vol 426, col 776, 9 November 2004 (Jacqui Smith).

whether discrimination occurs both with respect to denying marriage for same sex partners[58] as well as by denying opposite sex couples the opportunity to become civil partners. The government ultimately concluded it was satisfied that an affirmative compatibility report was warranted.[59]

The explanation for the government's belief that the bill should be interpreted as compatible with Convention rights was premised on the government's view that marriage provides the best framework for stable family relationships.[60] Since same sex partners are prevented from having their relationships legally recognized, the government asserted it was justifiable to focus exclusively on same sex couples to redress the discrimination they experience[61] and to establish a new legal form of relationship[62] that is 'akin to marriage'.[63] The government also asserted that opposite sex couples who cohabit but choose not to marry are not in an analogous position to same sex couples[64] because they have voluntarily opted for a lesser degree of legal recognition[65] as a matter of choice.[66]

Lacking in the government's statement explaining its assessment of compatibility is any justification for denying same sex partners the opportunity to marry. Although the government claimed that the legitimate aims of the bill represent 'objective justification' for the legislation,[67] it did not actually explain why the decision to deny same sex marriage is not discriminatory. The government postulated that marriage is the most valuable form of relationship but did not explain why this should be denied as an option for same sex couples. Nor did it substantively justify its belief that marriage provides more stability for family

[58] Parliament of the United Kingdom, The Civil Partnership Bill [HL], 5 July 2004, Explanatory Notes, para 990.

[59] Ibid., para 989–991. [60] Ibid., para 990. [61] Ibid. [62] Ibid., 991.

[63] Parliament of the United Kingdom, *Hansard*, HC, vol 426, col 776, 9 November 2004 (Jacqui Smith).

[64] Parliament of the United Kingdom, The Civil Partnership Bill [HL], 5 July 2004, Explanatory Notes, para 703.

[65] In the UK, cohabitation of opposite sex couples who live together in a long-term sexual relationship does not confer legal status to the couple, unlike marriage, which confers legal rights and duties. See House of Commons Library, The Relationships (Civil Registration) Bill and the Civil Partnerships Bill, Research Paper 02/17, 19 March 2002.

[66] Parliament of the United Kingdom, JCHR, Fifteenth Report, Session 2003–2004, HL 136/HC 885, para 21.

[67] JCHR, Fifteenth Report, para 23.

relationships or why this assumption justifies privileging marriage ahead of other forms of relationship recognition, particularly as substantial state-sanctioned benefits flow from marriage and yet a significant number of those in committed unions choose not to marry (and those in same sex unions might reject marriage even if given the option).

Despite the government's candour in acknowledging its uncertainty about interpreting the compatibility assessment, along with its failure to address the question of why it is not discriminatory to deny same sex partners the opportunity to marry, the compatibility issue did not influence parliamentary debate. Neither the JCHR nor parliament pressed the government to explain why denial of the ability to marry should not be considered discriminatory; however, the JCHR did raise the question of whether courts might decide discrimination has occurred in denying opposite sex couples the opportunity to register as civil partners.[68] As will be argued, this denial would become substantially more contentious a few years later.

The marriage question

The lack of formal recognition of same sex marriage was not overly controversial at the time the legislation was debated, for two key reasons.[69] The first was the success of the Labour government's strategic approach to the matter, portraying civil partnerships as analogous to marriage without actually recognizing the legality of same sex marriage. This political strategy produced an outcome that satisfied, or at least did not alienate, key divisions within gay and lesbian communities, while also mitigating the force of criticism from opponents of same sex marriage. Carl Stychin describes the generally positive reaction to the legislation within gay and lesbian communities as a 'victory for the politics of

[68] Parliament of the United Kingdom, JCHR, Civil Partnership Bill, Fifteenth Report of Session 2003–2004, l, HL 136, HC 885, para 24.

[69] This does not mean the legislation was immune to criticism, particularly from academics. The legislation has been criticized as an 'unqueer' text that is 'deeply assimilationist' and, by mimicking the marriage model, foregoes 'the perfect opportunity to rethink in a radical way the institution of the family in law'. Yet at the same time, commentators such as Carl Stychin recognize that the legislation helps promote an improved political climate for gay men and lesbians, particularly as contrasted with the 1980s, and suggest 'it would be churlish not to recognize the changed legal and political reality for lesbians and gay men in the U.K.' C.F. Stychin, 'Sexuality: Couplings: Civil Partnership in the United Kingdom', (2005) 8 *New York City Law Review*, 543 pp. 545, 570–71.

compromise': it delivered an outcome that satisfied those who wanted legal recognition and protection for their relationships, without causing serious dissent among those who opposed same sex marriage.[70] For Stychin, the genius of the government's approach was that it produced the legal status of 'civil partner' in a form that 'does not depend upon marriage, but which displays virtually all of the characteristics of a civil marriage'.[71] The second reason why the emphasis on civil union and lack of recognition for same sex marriage was not overly controversial was because the political strategies of gay and lesbian activists reflected ambivalence on the marriage question.[72] Stonewall did not press the government to adopt marriage, not only because its polling revealed the issue of marriage was considered a lower priority for gay and lesbian communities, but also because the organization believed it had a better chance of convincing parliament to support civil union and anticipated major political controversy would arise should it pursue marriage.[73]

Although many supporters of the Civil Partnership Act did not press for marriage at the time the bill was debated, the Civil Partnership Act was subsequently subject to legal challenge for discriminating against

[70] C.F. Stychin, 'Not (Quite) A Horse and Carriage: The Civil Partnership Act 2004', (2006) 14 *Feminist Legal Studies* 79.

[71] Stychin characterizes the British approach as a culturally unique approach to the issue of same sex relationships. C.F. Stychin, 'Sexuality: Couplings', 543 at 550. Other commentators also discuss the significance of cultural differences to explain different forms of relationship recognition. Comparative scholars note the general acceptance of civil union over marriage distinguishes the UK from the United States and Canada. Ken Norrie characterizes the Canadian focus on same sex marriage as a peculiarly North American debate, where civil partnership is treated as a second-rate alternative to marriage. K. Norrie, 'Marriage and Civil Partnership for Same-Sex Couples: The International Imperative', (2005) 1 *Journal of International Law and International Relations* 249–60.

[72] This ambivalence was reflected in the relative absence of lesbian feminist voices in the debates, which some believe contributed to the dominance of arguments for liberal equality in the discourse. Critics or sceptics of same sex marriage draw upon feminist and gay liberationist critiques of marriage and family in arguing that same sex marriage suffers the problem of importing heterosexual and paternal standards, while undermining the significance and unique value of lesbian and gay cultures and communities. For insights on debates about same-sex marriage, see N. Barker, 'Not the Marrying Kind: Feminist Critiques of Marriage and Legal Recognition of Same-sex Relationships', PhD Thesis, University of Keele (2008); V. Clarke and S.J. Finlay, '"For Better or Worse?' Lesbian and Gay Marriage', (2004) 14 *Feminism and Psychology* 17.

[73] Interview.

both same sex couples because of their inability to marry[74] and opposite sex couples because of their inability to register as civil partners.[75]

In the lead-up to the 2010 election, David Cameron indicated his willingness to 'consider gay marriage',[76] while the Liberal Democrats announced their support for legal recognition of same sex marriage a few months later.[77] Soon after the Coalition government was formed, it announced it would legislate to allow civil union ceremonies to be performed in churches that did not oppose the idea, which some interpreted as a prelude to legislating formal legal recognition of marriage.[78] In March 2012 the government initiated a consultation process with regard to legislating marriage for same sex couples,[79] during which Cameron indicated that he was 'absolutely determined' to allow same sex couples to marry.[80] The consultation paper also indicated that government was not interested in altering the civil partnership legislation to allow opposite sex couples to marry.[81]

Marriage (Same Sex Couples) Bill

The Coalition government introduced the Marriage (Same Sex Couples) Bill to the House of Commons in January 2013. The bill sought to extend civil marriage to same sex couples and would also allow religious

74 Several applications were made as part of an initiative labelled 'Equal Love' to try and repeal the ban on same sex marriage. See 'Gay Marriage Bid Rejected. Lesbian Couple will Now Take Legal Action', (2010) 10 November, www.ukgaynews.org.uk/Archive/10/Nov/0201print.htm.

75 'Heterosexual Couple Begin Legal Fight After Being Refused Civil Partnership', *The Guardian*, 17 November 2009, www.guardian.co.uk/lifeandstyle/2009/nov/24/heterosexual-couple-refused-civil-partnership

76 'George Osborne Says Tories will 'Consider Gay Marriage', *BBC News*, 11 April 2010, http://news.bbc.co.uk/2/hi/uk_news/politics/election_2010/8614235.stm

77 H. Mulholland, 'Liberal Democrats Back Same-sex Marriage Motion', *The Guardian*, 21 September 2010, www.guardian.co.uk/politics/2010/sep/21/liberal-democrats-same-sex-marriage

78 T. Ross, 'Coalition Ministers Consider Gay Marriage Plans', *The Telegraph*, 24 December 2010, www.telegraph.co.uk/news/religion/8221964/Coalition-ministers-consider-gay-marriage-plans.html

79 Government Equalities Office, 'Equal Civil Marriage: A Consultation', 15 March 2012.

80 C. Hope, 'We will Legalise Gay Marriage by 2015, Says David Cameron', *The Telegraph*, 24 July 2012, www.telegraph.co.uk/news/politics/9425174/We-will-legalise-gay-marriage-by-2015-says-David-Cameron.html

81 Government Equalities Office, 'Equal Civil Marriage', p. 5.

organizations to decide whether they were willing to conduct religious ceremonies. The bill was extremely controversial, not only because a sizeable faction of the Conservative party opposed gay marriage, but also because many critics argued that the government should also reform civil partnership legislation to allow opposite sex couples the opportunity to register as civil partners. Although a vote against the bill receiving second reading was defeated, the government had to rely on support from Labour, as more than half of the Conservative members in the Commons either abstained from the vote or opposed the bill (including two cabinet ministers, eight junior ministers and eight whips).[82]

The JCHR conducted two sessions to obtain evidence. In its review of the bill, the JCHR deliberately chose against reporting on the merits or justification of gay marriage, which it interpreted as 'a matter of individual conscience', and acknowledged this was an issue of differing opinions among members of the committee.[83] It nevertheless noted that government has an obligation to protect freedom of thought, conscience and religion, particularly with respect to religious organizations that decide against conducting same sex marriage, and indicated it was not convinced the government had justified its reasoning for not extending civil partnerships to opposite sex couples.[84]

At committee stage, members considered a number of amendments to extend civil partnerships to opposite sex couples and recognize conscientious objections from those not wanting to conduct same sex marriages.[85] Although the Conservative government initially appeared to be in danger of being defeated in the House of Commons, a last-minute agreement with Labour salvaged the legislation after Labour agreed not to support what was considered a wrecking amendment. The amendment was introduced by a Conservative member who opposed gay marriage and, if approved, would have altered the legal definition of civil partnerships to include opposite sex couples; however, such a substantial change to the scope of the bill was expected to significantly delay the passage of gay marriage legislation, and some speculated it could even result in the

[82] 'Gay Marriage: MPs Back Bill Despite Conservative Backbench Opposition' *BBC News*, 5 February 2013, www.bbc.co.uk/news/uk-politics-21346220

[83] Parliament of the United Kingdom, JCHR, Second Report of Session 2013–2014, L 24, HC 157, para 1.

[84] Ibid., pp. 3–5.

[85] E. Scott, 'Marriage (Same Sex Couples) Bill (HL Bill 29 of 2013–14)', House of Lords Library Note, LLN 2013/011, p. 1.

legislation being scrapped.[86] In exchange for Labour's decision to back away from this amendment, Cameron agreed that the government would follow up by reviewing the Civil Partnership Act in light of pressure to allow opposite sex couples to choose this form of relationship recognition, which Labour now supported despite its earlier opposition to the idea in 2004.[87]

Although the Commons approved the marriage bill by 366 to 161,[88] same sex marriage was opposed by a significant proportion of Cameron's own party,[89] as many Conservative members criticized the legislation as unnecessary, divisive, a threat to freedom of religion and inconsistent with the party's manifesto. Sir Gerald Howarth's criticism of the bill at an earlier stage aptly sums up the position of Conservative opponents:

> I am not a Tory moderniser, for I believe that marriage can only be between a man and a woman. I shall not surrender my principles. I believe that this Bill is wrong and that the consultation process was a complete sham. The Bill is opposed by the established Church and has caused deep and needless divisions within the Conservative party. There is no mandate for it and it has huge potential consequences, not least the prospect of endless legal challenge. The nation faces much more serious challenges that the Government need to address. I therefore hope and pray that this measure will be rejected, if not in this place, then in the other place.[90]

Serious opposition was anticipated in the House of Lords, yet despite expectation that the vote on same sex marriage would be too close to call,[91] the legislation easily passed in the House of Lords without a formal vote. The relative speed at which the bill passed provoked accusations from opponents that the government was using a parliamentary

86 T. Ross, 'David Cameron Facing Commons Defeat Over Gay Marriage Plans', *The Telegraph*, 20 May 2013, www.telegraph.co.uk/news/politics/conservative/10067511/David-Cameron-facing-Commons-defeat-over-gay-marriage-plans.html

87 N. Watt, 'Labour Saves David Cameron's Gay Marriage Bill', *The Guardian*, 21 May 2013, www.guardian.co.uk/society/2013/may/21/labour-cameron-gay-marriage-bill

88 Parliament of the United Kingdom, *Hansard* HC 5 673, c. 1160.

89 N. Watt, 'Gay Marriage: MPs' Vote in Favour Leaves Cameron Adrift from Tories', *The Guardian*, 6 February 2013, www.guardian.co.uk/society/2013/feb/05/gay-marriage-vote-cameron-adrift

90 Parliament of the United Kingdom, *Hansard*, HC, vol 558, col 185, 5 February 2013 (Sir Gerald Howarth).

91 A. Sparrow, 'Peers Back Gay Marriage Bill by Majority of 242: Politics Live Blog', *The Guardian* 4 June 2013 www.guardian.co.uk/politics/blog/2013/jun/04/lords-gay-marriage-vote-live-blog

'bulldozer' to speed through the process.[92] Despite the bill's passing, opponents engaged in spirited arguments against the recognition of same sex marriage: some of the more controversial interventions included statements that although 'homosexuals are often very delightful, artistic and loving people', marriage 'is not just about just love',[93] and that agreeing to same sex marriage could lead to uncertainty about who should inherit the throne if a future Queen were to be lesbian and she and her partner bore children fathered by an anonymous sperm donor.[94]

Assessing the HRA's influence on the civil partnership and marriage bills

The enactment of the civil partnership legislation in 2004 repudiated the Thatcher government's message that same sex relationships are both deviant and unworthy of state recognition. The enactment of this legislation a mere four years after the Human Rights Act came into force raises the obvious question of whether the HRA influenced the decision to reform legal recognition of same sex relationships and the subsequent decision to pass same sex marriage legislation. However, it is difficult to attribute political behaviour in these legislative decisions to the influence of the HRA. For example, government decisions to pursue reforms were not driven by concerns of imminent threat of judicial censure. Although a body of jurisprudence was emerging that conveyed a strong signal that failing to recognize same sex partners as family members or spouses was discriminatory, the threat to existing legislation was neither sufficiently imminent nor substantial enough to provoke government leaders into pursuing legislation they did not support. Before the civil partnership legislation was introduced, the Labour government had already passed legislation to remedy a 2002 ruling by the European Court of Human Rights that the UK had breached the rights of two transsexual people under Article 8 (the right to respect for private life) and 12 (the right to marry).[95] At the time, transsexual individuals were not recognized in their acquired gender. They could obtain some official documents under their new name and acquired gender, but they could not obtain new birth

[92] J. Bingham, 'Gay Marriage Clears the House of Lords', *The Telegraph*, 15 July 2013, www.telegraph.co.uk/news/politics/10180552/Gay-marriage-clears-the-House-of-Lords.html

[93] Parliament of the United Kingdom, *Hansard*, HL, vol 745, col 985, 3 June 2013 (Baroness Knight).

[94] Ibid., col 1018, 3 June 2913 (Lord Tebbit).

[95] *Goodwin* v. *The United Kingdom* (2002) 35 EHRR 18.

certificates or enjoy all rights conferred on those assigned that gender at birth. The Labour government responded in 2004 by passing the Gender Recognition Act, which provided transsexual individuals with legal recognition for their acquired gender.[96]

Although other judicial decisions underscored that discrimination occurs when same sex partners are not interpreted as constituting spouses or family members,[97] these rulings did not indicate that the necessary remedy was comprehensive legislative reform. Even if the Labour government was uncertain about how long it could afford to delay introducing substantive legislative reforms, it did not face imminent legal pressure to give priority to legislation that introduced new legal recognition for same sex partners. Had the government been opposed to the idea of introducing a new form of relationship recognition, it could have passed the burden of reform to litigants and courts, to challenge and reinterpret existing entitlements or rules about responsibility on a case-by-case basis.

Political support for the Civil Partnership Act is best explained by the Labour government's political commitment to redress legislative discrimination against gay men and lesbians. Labour government websites proudly proclaimed advances in the treatment of gay men and lesbian for which the government sought credit.[98] In his final appearance as Prime Minister before a Labour party congress, Blair identified greater equal rights for the gay community as a highlight of his tenure as Prime Minister.[99]

It is also difficult to characterize David Cameron's promotion of same sex marriage as having been motivated by risk-averse strategies to cope with the threat of imminent judicial censure. In 2006 a Family Division judge rejected the argument that the lack of recognition for same sex

[96] Gender Recognition Act, 2004 (UK), c 7, Explanatory Notes, www.opsi.gov.uk/acts/acts2004/en/ukpgaen_20040007_en_1.

[97] See for example, *Karner* v. *Austria* (2003) 38 EHRR 24; *Fitzpatrick* v. *Sterling Housing Association Ltd* [2001] 1 AC 27; *Ghaidan* v. *Mendoza* [2002] EWC Civ 1533.

[98] These include the Adoption and Children Act, 2002 (UK), c 38, allowing same sex couples to adopt a child jointly; paternity leave and flexible working practices that apply to same sex partners; anti-discrimination legislation that includes sexual orientation in employment and training; repeal of s. 28 of the Local Government Act; the lowering of the age of consent to 16 for gay men; the inclusion of same sex partners in the Criminal Injuries Compensation Scheme; and amendments to immigration rules to improve the situation for same sex partners. Department of Trade and Industry, Women and Equality Unit, Sexual Orientation, www.equalities.gov.uk/lgbt/what_done.htm

[99] Marc Shoffman, 'Gay Rights Highlight for Blair Career', *Pink News*, 26 September 2006, www.pinknews.co.uk/news/articles/2005-2568.html

marriage breached protected rights (Articles 8, 12 and 14 of the ECHR),[100] and in 2010 the ECtHR ruled that states have no obligation to recognize same sex marriages.[101] Moreover, Cameron's indication that he would support same sex marriage preceded the announcement of a new legal challenge before the ECtHR stating that the civil partnership scheme discriminates against both same sex partners (who are denied the right to marry) and opposite sex couples (who are denied the opportunity to form civil partnerships).[102] A better explanation for Cameron's promotion of same sex marriage is the strength of his commitment to marriage, his acceptance of an inclusive definition of this relationship and his willingness to use his position as leader and Prime Minister to give priority to an issue his party opposed.[103] Although same sex marriage was strongly supported by the Liberal Democrat wing of the Coalition government, Conservative party critics of same sex marriage tried to dissuade Cameron from pursuing same sex marriage, arguing that it was not part of the party's mandate, that it would be extremely divisive and that it would weaken the party's electoral support and alienate donors. Some Conservative critics of the legislation went so far as to speculate that Cameron's willingness to defy his party's core values could result in him being ousted as leader, particularly as it was occurring while his political capital within the party was said to be in decline.[104] Cameron also had to withstand strong pressure and criticism from religious officials including Lord Carey, former Archbishop of Canterbury, who accused the Prime Minister of alienating Christian voters and promoting an 'aggressive secularist' approach that threatened the link between church and state.[105]

[100] *Wilkinson* v. *Kitzinger* [2006] EWHC 2022 (Fam), [2007] 1 FLR 295.

[101] *Schalk and Kopf* v. *Austria*, No. 30141/04, [2010] ECHR 995 (24 June 2010).

[102] J. Bingham, 'Heterosexual Couples Challenge "Discriminatory" Civil Partnerships Bar', *The Telegraph*, 16 February 2013 www.telegraph.co.uk/news/uknews/law-and-order/9873404/Heterosexual-couples-challenge-discriminatory-civil-partnerships-bar.html

[103] Months before introducing legislation, Cameron spoke to a lesbian, gay, bisexual and transsexual community at a reception at 10 Downing Street, where he defended marriage as 'a great institution' and argued that he felt passionately about redefining marriage to include same sex partners. C. Hope, 'We Will Legalise Gay Marriage by 2015'.

[104] A. Osborn, 'British PM's Party Split as First Gay Marriage Vote Passes', *Reuters*, 5 February 2013, www.reuters.com/article/2013/02/05/us-britain-cameron-idUSBRE91400820130205; R. Watts, 'Conservative Party Ripped Apart by Gay Marriage Vote', *The Telegraph*, 2 February 2013, www.telegraph.co.uk/news/politics/9844514/Conservative-party-ripped-apart-by-gay-marriage-vote.html

[105] 'Cameron 'Alienating' Christians by Promoting Gay Marriage', *The Irish Times*, 30 March 2013, www.irishtimes.com/news/world/uk/cameron-alienating-christians-by-promoting-gay-marriage-1.1344454

To the extent that either government engaged in strategic behaviour, this occurred in the sense of anticipating objections and forging appropriate strategies to pass the legislation. Thus, in 2004 Labour deliberately fostered ambiguity about the definition of marriage by disputing allegations that civil partnership legislation constitutes marriage, while at the same time presenting civil partnership as akin to marriage. As for strategic behaviour by the Conservative government, Cameron agreed to review the question of whether civil partnerships should include opposite sex couples as a necessary concession so Labour would not support a wrecking amendment, despite his earlier reluctance to endorse this option. Although these kinds of strategic decisions are the regular stuff of day-to-day politics, they are not obviously shaped by the HRA; nor do they represent the kind of strategic calculations to which we referred earlier, in which governments consider the risks and consequences of judicial censure or political pressures for amendments when determining whether to act in a risk-averse or risk-taking manner on bills for which the issue of compatibility is in doubt. To the extent that these strategic decisions were related to the HRA, the relevant strategies focused on how to frame the debate. Neither the Labour nor the Conservative government invoked the HRA to justify their intended legislative reforms, despite the reliance of both on normative and rights-based reasons for supporting legislation. Public ambiguity and inter-party dissent about the merits of the HRA likely weakened the perceived political utility of framing the debate in terms of compliance with the normative values in the HRA.

It is also difficult to discern any obvious impact of the HRA on parliamentary behaviour. One strong indication that the HRA was relatively peripheral to the debate on civil partnership legislation was that the Labour government's acknowledgement that two aspects of the bill raised questions about their compatibility with Convention rights had no discernable impact on parliamentary deliberations or the vote.[106] Parliamentary debates on both bills were manifestly rights-based. However, deliberations were not framed in the language of Convention rights or influenced by the HRA's emphasis on compatibility. Arguments in support of the Civil Partnership Bill reflected normative claims about the

[106] Parliament of the United Kingdom, The Civil Partnership Bill [HL], 5 July 2004, Explanatory Notes, paras 989–991.

need for reform to address 'outdated' grave injustices[107] that were barbaric and inhuman,[108] and the moral importance of according same sex partners recognition and respect.[109] Supporters of the bill also defended the legislation's objectives to promote equality and social justice for same sex partners,[110] reduce prejudice and homophobic violence[111] and overcome bigotry and ignorance.[112] Similarly, supporters of the marriage bill justified same sex marriage as essential to promote equality and fairness and to overcome long-standing discrimination against gay men and lesbians[113] (although critics disputed the idea that equality was at stake,[114] and expressed outrage at the portrayal of their defence of traditional marriage as homophobic or bigoted).[115] To the extent that parliamentary debate was structured as a debate about compatibility with Convention rights, this occurred principally among opponents of the marriage bill who argued that legal recognition of same sex marriage could lead to discrimination and persecution of those whose religious beliefs oppose same sex marriage, and could encourage courts to rule that churches discriminate when refusing to allow same sex marriages.[116]

Political behaviour around the Civil Partnership Act and the marriage bill reinforces the need for caution about attributing too much influence to a bill of rights when trying to account for legislative reforms.[117] Both

[107] Parliament of the United Kingdom, *Hansard*, HC, vol 425, col 216, 12 October 2004 (John Bercow).

[108] Ibid., col 233, 12 October 2004 (Charles Hendry).

[109] Ibid., col 182, 12 October 2004 (Jacqui Smith).

[110] Ibid., col 191, 12 October 2004 (Barbara Roche).

[111] Ibid., col 207, 12 October 2004 (Robert Kay).

[112] Ibid., col 197, 12 October 2004 (Angela Eagle).

[113] Parliament of the United Kingdom, *Hansard*, HC, vol 558, col 185, 5 February 2013 (Emma Reynolds); vol 558, col 204, 5 February 2013 (Sarah Wollaston); vol 558, col 208, 5 February 2013 (William Bain); vol 558, col 189, 5 February 2013 (Mark Durkan).

[114] Ibid., col 196, 5 February 2013 (David Burrowes); vol 558, col 183, 5 February 2013 (Sir Gerald Howarth).

[115] Ibid., col 190, 5 February 2013 (John Glenn).

[116] Ibid., col 180, 5 February 2013 (Michael McCann); *Hansard*, HC, vol 558, col 199, 5 February 2013 (William McCrea); *Hansard*, HC, vol 558, col 196, 5 February 2013 (David Burrowes).

[117] G.N. Rosenberg, *The Hollow Hope. Can Courts Bring About Social Change?* 2nd edition (University of Chicago Press, 2008). Charles Epp also argues that unless a polity has support structures in place that are willing and capable of legal uses of rights to pressure for change, a bill of rights will not be as effective as it would otherwise in creating pressure for change: C.R. Epp, *The Rights Revolution: Lawyers, Activists, and Supreme Courts in Comparative Perspective* (Chicago: University of Chicago Press, 1998), p. 23.

debates suggest that the HRA was largely irrelevant to the motivation to introduce legislation or to how parliamentary deliberations unfolded.

III. Identity cards

Identity cards were used during the two World Wars, but this practice lapsed in 1952.[118] The Blair government introduced legislation to create a new system of identity cards in November 2004, which it defended as serving a medley of purposes: to regulate access to social programmes and other entitlements; expose fraud and track illegal employment;[119] and assist in the fight against terrorism and organized crime.[120] The Identity Cards Bill proposed a regulatory framework to introduce a national compulsory identity card scheme based on secure, biometric information and to set up a National Identity Registry. The bill was subject to substantial critical scrutiny by the JCHR[121] and received a raucous parliamentary reception.

Although the JCHR did not dispute the possibility of developing an identity card scheme in a manner compatible with Convention rights, the committee was troubled by the extensive reliance on secondary legislation for setting out details of how the legislation would operate.[122] The JCHR reported concerns regarding how personal information would be gathered, stored and disclosed, and advised parliament that intrusion into privacy rights would be even greater when the compulsory scheme came into effect. The committee also warned parliament that the immediate compulsory dimension of the scheme could be interpreted as discriminatory because it applied only to non-national subjects.[123]

The bill reached second reading stage in the House of Lords, but died with the dissolution of parliament in April 2005.[124] Despite this set-back,

118 House of Commons Library, The *Identity Cards Bill*, Bill 9 of 2005–06, Research Paper 05/43, p. 7.

119 Parliament of the United Kingdom, *Hansard*, HC, vol 379, col 872-3W, 5 February 2002 (David Blunkett).

120 Home Office, http://webarchive.nationalarchives.gov.uk/+/www.homeoffice.gov.uk/comrace/identitycards/faq.html#2

121 Parliament of the United Kingdom, JCHR, Fifth Report, Session 2004–2005, HL 35/HC 283.

122 Parliament of the United Kingdom, JCHR, Eighth Report, Session 2004–2005, HL 60/HC 388, paras 1.2–1.24.

123 JCHR, Fifth Report, Session 2004–2005, HL 35/HC 283, paras 23–25.

124 House of Commons Library, Identity Cards Bill, Bill 9 of 2005–2006, Research Paper 05/43.

Labour promised in its 2005 election manifesto to introduce identity cards and a national register.[125] Following its 2005 election victory, it quickly reaffirmed its intention to establish identity cards in the first Queen's Speech of the new parliament.[126]

The second Identity Cards Bill was introduced to the House of Commons in 2005, and once again took the form of framework legislation that set out broad elements of the scheme but left most of the detail dependent on subsequent regulations.[127] The bill established the National Identity Register, mandated that driving licences and passports be based on biometric technology, authorized public and private organizations to verify identities against the National Identity Register and created criminal offences for possession of false identity documents. The first stage for registration was presented as being voluntary other than in the case of those foreign nationals who wished to stay in the UK for more than three months, yet this characterization was contested because anyone seeking or renewing a passport would be required to obtain an identity card and would be included in the National Register.[128] The second stage, which was anticipated but not authorized in the bill, would be a fully compulsory scheme (the government anticipated that most people in the UK would have obtained biometric ID cards by 2013).[129]

The JCHR reported similar concerns as it had with the earlier bill: largely that privacy would be infringed and that the legislation would have discriminatory effects because it subjected foreign nationals to compulsory registration, while purporting to be voluntary for UK citizens.[130] Nevertheless, these objections did not persuade government to alter its position either with respect to the distinction between the legislation's application to foreign nationals vs citizens or to the decision

[125] Labour Party, *Britain Forward Not Back: The Labour Party Manifesto 2005*, pp. 52–53, http://newsimg.bbc.co.uk/1/shared/bsp/hi/pdfs/LAB_uk_manifesto.pdf

[126] House of Commons Library, *Identity Cards Bill*, Bill 9 of 2005–2006, Research Paper 05/43, p. 101.

[127] Ibid.

[128] Parliament of the United Kingdom, Home Affairs Committee, Fourth Report, Session 2003–2004, HC 130-I, para 135.

[129] House of Commons Library, *Identity Cards Bill*, Bill 9 of 2005–2006, Research Paper 05/43.

[130] Parliament of the United Kingdom, JCHR, First Report, Session 2005–2006, HL 48/HC 560, para 4.14.

to rely heavily on secondary legislation to flesh out the details of the scheme. Rights-based objections were also raised by the Law Society, which objected to 'unnecessary and undesirably wide powers to record, retain and disseminate personal data'.[131] The proposal to issue identity cards also generated substantial negative attention from prominent civil liberties organizations and launched a single-issue group (No2ID) dedicated to defeating the bill.[132] No2ID criticized the scope of the data collected, and warned of threats to privacy and other rights.[133]

The 2005 bill had a rocky reception in the House of Commons, where the government encountered strong opposition from the Conservative and Liberal Democrat parties, as well as from a sizeable and vocal group of Labour backbench members who argued that the legislation violated civil liberties[134] and was too expensive.[135] Labour backbench members were unusually scathing of the government bill: one member described the issue as 'more serious than the decision to go to war', while another likened then Home Secretary Charles Clarke's defence of identity cards to a snake-oil salesman offering a cure for all ills.[136]

Despite substantive rights-based objections to the bill, it was not obvious that the HRA or JCHR reports influenced debate in the House of Commons. MPs did not refer to the JCHR's concerns in second or third reading debates, and did not frame their objections to the bill in the specific language of Convention rights or the HRA's particular emphasis on legal compatibility.[137] Instead, MPs' criticisms of the bill utilized

131 Parliament of the United Kingdom, JCHR, First Report, Session 2005–2006, HL 48/HC 560, Appendix 3(a), Submission from the Law Society.

132 Prominent civil liberties groups such as Liberty raised objections to the scheme: www.liberty-human-rights.org.uk/issues/3-privacy/31-id-cards/why-liberty-opposes-id-cards.shtml. The idea of identity cards was also criticized by NO2ID, a single-issue group organized to campaign against the 'rapid growth of the database state': www.no2id.net.

133 Parliament of the United Kingdom, JCHR, First Report, Session 2005–2006, HL 48/HC 560, Appendix 3(b), Submission from NO2ID.

134 R. Whitaker, 'Backbench Influence on Government Legislation? A Flexing of Parliamentary Muscles at Westminster', (2006) 59 *Parliamentary Affairs* 350.

135 Some members raised both concerns simultaneously, as evident in Conservative member David Davis' criticism of the government's failure to find 'a better, cheaper and more cost-effective solution that does not threaten to remove the long-held and fought-for freedoms of the British people.' Parliament of the United Kingdom, *Hansard*, HC, vol 435, col 1181, 28 June 2005.

136 D. Charter, 'Plastic Poll Tax Scheme may Haunt the Party', *The Times*, 29 June 2005, www.thetimes.co.uk/tto/news/uk/article1934761.ece

137 One exception was a statement made by Conservative MP William Cash, who referred to the Information Commissioner's remarks that the 'data trail of identity checks on

broader, more philosophically grounded arguments. For example, critics argued that the bill would introduce a 'fundamental shift in the balance of power between the citizen and state' and represent another step toward a 'surveillance society' that undermines respect for liberty and freedom. Nick Clegg, then Home Affairs spokesperson for the Liberal Democrats, claimed that the introduction of identity cards would 'usher in one of the most far-reaching changes in British public life in recent times', which would revolutionize the capacity of the state to monitor the movements and behaviour of citizens, and that the scheme would erode privacy and curtail freedom.[138] Despite these criticisms, the Labour government's majority was sufficient for the bill to pass in the House of Commons; albeit by a narrow 309–284 margin.[139]

The proposed legislation encountered substantial resistance in the House of Lords. Peers similarly objected to the bill's adverse implications for civil liberties, and also raised the estimated costs associated with the scheme. Opponents also challenged the idea that the scheme was voluntary and warned that the rights to liberty and privacy should not be 'carelessly thrown away'.[140] However, unlike in the debate in the Commons, the HRA was far more prominent in how objections were framed. Peers referred to JCHR reports more than two dozen times (some of these references were made by a member of the JCHR) and also to the Select Committee on the Constitution, which reported that the constitutional significance of the bill was that it 'adjusts the fundamental relationship between the individual and the state', and warned of the importance of 'adequate safeguards' to protect individuals from 'excessive intrusion into their affairs'.[141]

The House of Lords proposed significant amendments at report stage that would delay the legislation's coming into effect until the government had made the costs of the scheme public, emphasize the voluntary

individuals risk an unnecessary and disproportionate intrusion into individuals' privacy' and asked Home Secretary Charles Clarke how he could 'sign off the Bill as being compatible with the European convention on human rights': Parliament of the United Kingdom, *Hansard*, HC, vol 435, col 1152, 28 June 2005.

[138] Parliament of the United Kingdom, *Hansard*, HC, vol 444, col 1004, 29 March 2006 (Nick Clegg).

[139] 'Labour Survives ID Card Rebellion', *BBC News*, 18 October 2005, http://news.bbc.co.uk/2/hi/4354886.stm

[140] 'MPs Again Reject Lords ID Card Amendments', *The Guardian*, 16 March 2006, www.guardian.co.uk/politics/2006/mar/16/immigrationpolicy.idcards

[141] Parliament of the United Kingdom, House of Lords, Select Committee on the Constitution, Fifth Report of Session 2004–2005, HL Paper 82, para 4.

element of the scheme, increase security for data that was held on the National Identity Register and limit the requirement that citizens have an identity card in order to access public services. The House of Commons overturned Lords amendments on voluntary inclusion in the identity database and governmental disclosure of the costs before the legislation was enacted.[142]

In the ensuing volley of amendments and defeats, the government accused the House of Lords of violating the Salisbury Convention – the idea that the Lords does not defeat a bill at second and third reading, when the bill represents the government's election manifesto, but instead tables reasoned amendments to suggest its dissent.[143] Peers responded to this claim by arguing that the House of Lords was acting appropriately to defend ancient liberties.[144] Despite a threat by Charles Clarke to invoke the Parliament Act to resolve the disagreement,[145] and competing claims about which House was representing the interests and rights of the nation,[146] a compromise was finally achieved between both houses. Under this compromise, anyone applying for a passport before 2010 would have the option to opt out of having an identity card, but his or her personal information would still be included in the identity register.[147]

This compromise did not silence criticism of the bill, which increasingly focused on the escalating costs associated with the scheme.[148] The Regulatory Impact Assessment for the legislation estimated the annual cost of issuing passports and ID cards to UK nationals at £584 million.[149] Critics argued that the government had seriously underestimated costs,[150]

142 R. Whitaker, 'Ping-Pong and Policy Influence: Relations between the Lords and Commons, 2005–06', (2006) 59 *Parliamentary Affairs*, p. 540.

143 H. Mulholland, 'Lords Reject ID Cards Bill for Third Time', *The Guardian*, 15 March 2006, www.guardian.co.uk/politics/2006/mar/15/lords.idcards/print

144 W. Woodward and A. Travis, 'ID Cards to be Compulsory with Passports Issued from 2010', *The Guardian*, 30 March 2006, www.guardian.co.uk/politics/2006/mar/30/idcards.immigrationpolicy

145 N. Assinder, 'Where Now for ID Cards?' *BBC News*, 16 March 2006, http://news.bbc.co.uk/2/hi/uk_news/politics/4804528.stm

146 W. Woodward and A. Travis, 'ID Cards to be Compulsory with Passports Issued from 2010'.

147 R. Whitaker, 'Backbench Influence on Government Legislation?' p. 541.

148 House of Commons Library, *Identity Cards Bill*, Bill 9 of 2005–2006, Research Paper 05/43, p. 33.

149 House of Commons Library, *Identity Cards Bill*, Bill 9 of 2005–2006, Research Paper 05/43, p. 34.

150 See for example, Parliament of the United Kingdom, *Hansard*, HC, vol 428, col 627, 1 December 2004.

a charge reinforced by research by the London School of Economics, which in 2005 estimated that the true cost of implementing and running the scheme was more likely £12–18 billion.[151]

In the 2010 general election, both the Conservative and Liberal Democrat parties criticized the legislation's invasion of privacy and interference with individuals' liberty, as well as the mounting costs associated with the scheme. After Labour lost the election, the new Coalition government indicated it would repeal the legislation as one of its first orders of business. In December 2010 the Identity Document Act was passed to repeal the legislation, cancel the estimated 15,000 identification cards already issued[152] and order that information in the National Identity Register be destroyed.[153]

Assessing the HRA's influence on identity card bills

In addition to shared concerns about financial costs, debate in both houses was heavily influenced by criticism that rights were being infringed. However, parliamentary debate on the identity card scheme confirms distinct differences between the houses of parliament on the relevance of the HRA for parliamentary deliberations. Whereas references to JCHR reports were extremely prevalent in the House of Lords and framed criticisms and arguments for amendments, they were absent in the House of Commons; yet while MPs showed a distinct lack of interest in invoking the language of Convention rights or the compatibility emphasis in JCHR reports, they emphasized civil liberties in more general and abstract terms. However, despite the significant number of rights-based objections from within the House of Commons, which included a significant number of Labour MPs, the Labour government had a sufficient majority to ensure passage of the bill, albeit with forced concessions because of robust opposition from the Lords. The debate also revealed that although government was willing to make the necessary concessions to save the bill, it did not

[151] 'ID Card Scheme May Cost £18 bn', *BBC News*, 29 May 2005, http://news.bbc.co.uk/2/hi/uk_news/politics/4590817.stm

[152] House of Commons Library, Identity Documents Bill, Research Paper 10/41, 4 June 2010.

[153] The bill also re-enacts some aspects of the 2006 Act that are unrelated to ID cards, addressing issues such as the possession and manufacture of false identity documents and data-sharing provisions in support of passport applications.

acknowledge or embrace these as justifiable changes to ensure that legislation was compatible with Convention rights.

IV. Disenfranchisement of prisoners[154]

The final legislative debate we examine differs from the others in that it arose from pressure to revisit legislation following the ECtHR ruling that the UK's practice of denying prisoners the right to vote is not consistent with Convention rights.[155] The majority of prisoners in the UK have not been able to vote for more than a century.[156] Initially, disenfranchisement occurred because convicted traitors forfeited their land and therefore did not satisfy the property requirement to vote, or because convicted criminals' custodial sentences prevented them from satisfying residency requirements for registering to vote.[157] In 1969 parliament passed the Representation of the People Act, which denied the vote to those detained in penal institutions. The legislation did not distinguish between those on remand and those already convicted. In 1983, parliament passed the Representation of the People Act, which continued the practice of disenfranchising prisoners. The legislation was amended in 1990 to allow those on remand and not yet subject to custodial sentence to vote.[158]

In 2001 John Hirst challenged his inability to vote while incarcerated following his conviction for manslaughter. Hirst's claim initially failed in the High Court,[159] but it succeeded in 2004 before the European Court of Human Rights. The Labour government unsuccessfully argued that denying prisoners the right to vote is a justified way of enhancing civic

[154] The discussion of the background and government responses to ECtHR rulings draws heavily from J. Hiebert, 'The HRA: Ambiguity about Parliamentary Sovereignty' (2013) 14 *German Law Journal*, pp. 2251–54.

[155] *Hirst* v. *United Kingdom* (2004) 38 EHRR 40.

[156] An assessment of the history of prisoner disenfranchisement in the United Kingdom by Colin Murray challenges assumptions that disenfranchisement of prisoners has been 'an ever-present feature' of the electoral system and argues that by the middle of the twentieth century, restrictions on the franchise were subject to extensive exceptions: C.R.G. Murray, 'A Perfect Storm: Parliament and Prisoner Disenfranchisement', (2012) *Parliamentary Affairs* 1, pp. 6–11.

[157] Department of Justice, 'Voting Rights of Convicted Prisoners Detained within the United Kingdom', CP29/06 (2006).

[158] I. White and V. Miller, 'Prisoners' Voting Rights', 8 March 2011, SN/PC/01764, House of Commons Library, pp. 8–11.

[159] *Hirst* v. *Attorney General* [2001] EWHC Admin 239.

responsibility and respect for the rule of law,[160] and that the issue should be decided by parliament, not the judiciary.[161] The ECtHR ruled that the ban on prisoners' voting breached Article 3 of protocol 1 of the European Convention on Human Rights, which protects 'free elections . . . under conditions which will ensure the free expression of the opinion of the people in the choice of the legislature'.[162] The Grand Chamber confirmed this outcome in 2005.[163] The Court described the legislation as a blunt instrument that falls outside any acceptable margin of appreciation,[164] and faulted the UK parliament for not weighing 'the competing interests or to assess the proportionality of a blanket ban on right of a convicted prisoner to vote' or reassessing the continued practice of prisoner disenfranchisement in light of 'current human rights standards'.[165]

The decision to deny prisoners the vote affects prisoners throughout the UK. Courts in Scotland and Northern Ireland have also heard rights-based challenges to prisoners' disenfranchisement. In Scotland, the Registration Appeal Court ruled that the blanket ban on prisoner voting was incompatible with human rights;[166] in Belfast, the High Court rejected an application to postpone the 2007 election until two prisoners' names were added to the electoral register. The UK government responded to these challenges by arguing that the issue of enfranchisement of prisoners is only relevant for the Westminster and European parliament elections, and that elections to the Northern Ireland Assembly fall outside the scope of the right to free and fair elections in Article 1 of Protocol 3 of the ECHR.[167]

Both Labour and Conservative-led governments have defended the ban on prisoners voting and have engaged in delaying tactics to avoid passing remedial measures, despite strong and persistent criticism from the JCHR and rebuke from the Council of Europe (to be discussed).[168]

160 Department of Justice, 'Voting Rights of Convicted Prisoners Detained within the United Kingdom', CP29/06 (2006).

161 Ibid., p. 12.

162 *Hirst* v. *United Kingdom* (2004) 38 EHRR 40.

163 *Hirst* v. *United Kingdom* (No. 2), [2005] ECHR 68, (2006) 42 EHHR 41, [GC].

164 Ibid., para 82. 165 Ibid., [GC], para 79.

166 *William Smith (AP)* v. *KD Scott Electoral Registration Officer* [2007] CSIH 9

167 Parliament of the United Kingdom, *Hansard* HC, vol 522, col 990W 4 February 2011 (Mark Harper).

168 Parliament of the United Kingdom, JCHR, Eleventh Report, Session 2005–2006, HL 115/HC 899; Parliament of the United Kingdom, JCHR, Thirteenth Report, Session 2005–2006, HL 133/HC 954; Parliament of the United Kingdom, JCHR, Sixteenth Report, Session 2006–2007, HL 128/HC 728; Parliament of the United Kingdom, JCHR,

These delaying tactics have also included cost/benefit assessments of the consequences for failing to comply.

The Labour government responded to the ECtHR rulings with two consultation processes, but refused to introduce remedial legislation. The first consultation exercise was initiated a year after the Grand Chamber ruling, and was prefaced by a position paper that defended the very arguments in support of the ban which the ECtHR had earlier rejected.[169] The second consultation process did not begin until 2009; in this the government repeated its disapproval of allowing prisoners to vote and indicated it was only considering reforms because the European courts had made it clear that remedies were 'legally unavoidable'.[170] The government proposed making the right to vote contingent upon the length of the custodial sentence (options ranged from less than one year to less than four years) or alternatively that all prisoners should require judicial permission to vote.[171]

The JCHR has forcefully criticized government delays in redressing the ban. The committee has raised the issue of the government's obligations to respond in at least eight reports,[172] and has stressed the urgency of redressing the issue, particularly after the Registration Appeal Court in Scotland made a declaration of incompatibility in respect of section 3 of

Thirty-First Report, Session 2007–2008, HL 173/HC 1078; Parliament of the United Kingdom, JCHR, Fourth Report, Session 2008–2009, HL 23/HC 204; Parliament of the United Kingdom, JCHR, Seventeenth Report, Session 2008–2009, HL 104/HC 592; Parliament of the United Kingdom, JCHR, Fifteenth Report, Session 2009–2010, HL 85/HC 455; and Parliament of the United Kingdom, JCHR, Sixth Report, Session 2010–2011, HL64/HC 640.

[169] Department of Justice, 'Voting Rights of Convicted Prisoners Detained within the United Kingdom', CP29/06 (2006).

[170] R. Winnett and T. Whitehead, 'Prisoners to get Right to Vote After 140 Years Following European Ruling', *The Telegraph*, 9 April 2009, www.telegraph.co.uk/news/uknews/law-and-order/5126647/Prisoners-to-get-right-to-vote-after-140-years-following-European-ruling.html

[171] Ibid.

[172] Parliament of the United Kingdom, JCHR Eleventh Report of Session 2005–2006, HL 115/HC 899; Parliament of the United Kingdom, Thirteenth Report, Session 2005–2006, HL 133/HC 954; Parliament of the United Kingdom, Sixteenth Report of Session 2006–2007, HL 128/HC 728; Parliament of the United Kingdom, Thirty-First Report of Session 2007–2008, HL 173/HC 1078; Parliament of the United Kingdom, Fourth Report of Session 2008–2009, HL 23/HC 204; Parliament of the United Kingdom, Seventeenth Report of Session 2008–2009, HL 104/HC 592; Parliament of the United Kingdom, Fifteenth Report of Session 2009–2010, HL 85/HC 455; and Parliament of the United Kingdom, Sixth Report of Session 2010–2011, HL64/HC 640.

the Representation of the People Act 1983[173] which meant that without a change to the legislation, the upcoming election for the Scottish Parliament would 'take place in a manner which was not 'Convention-compliant'.[174] The JCHR disputed the Labour government's explanation for the continued delay in remedying the situation (that the government considered the issue complex and difficult, particularly in light of opposition to removing the ban on prisoners' ability to vote).[175] As the JCHR reported:

> We consider that the time taken to publish the Government's consultation paper and the time proposed for consultation is disproportionate. While the issues involved give rise to political controversy, they are not legally complex. The continued failure to remove the blanket ban, enfranchising at least part of the prison population, is clearly unlawful... We would be disappointed if a legislative solution were not in force in adequate time to allow the necessary preparations to be made for the next general election.[176]

In the absence of legislation to implement these suggestions, the JCHR upgraded its warning of the importance of remedying the situation as a matter of urgency, so that prisoners would be entitled to vote in the next general election.[177] Nevertheless, the government did not act and there was little pressure from parliament to introduce remedial action. The Conservative Shadow Justice Secretary of the period, Dominic Grieve, argued remedial measures should not be considered because the 'principle that those who are in custody after conviction should not have the opportunity to vote is a perfectly rational one'.[178] Although the Liberal Democrats criticized the government for its delays and for lacking

[173] *William Smith* v. *Electoral Registration Officer* [2007] CSIH 9 XA33/04 (24 January 2007), paras 55–56.

[174] In 2008 the JCHR called on the government to publish the responses to its earlier consultation, as well as publish its proposals for reform, without further delay. It indicated the need for urgency because without finding a legislative solution before the next general election, 'part of the prison population will be unlawfully disenfranchised': Parliament of the United Kingdom, JCHR 31st Report of Session 2007–2008, para 63.

[175] Parliament of the United Kingdom, Thirty-First Report, Session 2006–2007, Appendix 13, Letter dated 27 March from the Rt Hon Lord Falconer of Thoroton QC, Secretary of State and Lord Chancellor, Department for Constitutional Affairs, re Implementation of judgments of the European Court of Human Rights, Human Rights Act: Declarations of Incompatibility, *William Scott* v. *Electoral Registration Officer*.

[176] Parliament of the United Kingdom, JCHR, Sixteenth Report, Session 2006/06, para 78–79.

[177] Parliament of the United Kingdom, JCHR, Fifteenth Report, Session 2008–2009, HL 85/ HC 455, para 113.

[178] R. Winnett and T. Whitehead, 'Prisoners to get Right to Vote After 140 Years Following European Ruling'.

the courage to lift the ban,[179] the party lacked sufficient parliamentary support to compel the government to act.

Late in 2009, the Council of Europe noted the 'substantial delay' in complying with the *Hirst* judgment,[180] and a few months later it advised the government to take urgent measures, if only of an 'interim nature', to address the situation before the next election.[181] The government ignored these calls, and the 2010 election proceeded without remedial measures in place. Prisoners' inability to vote in the 2010 - election resulted in a significant increase in the number of applications to the ECtHR, prompting the Chair of the Committees for the Council of Europe to urge the UK to 'prioritise the implementation of [the Hirst] judgment'.[182]

New government responsible for remedial measures

Labour's defeat in the 2010 election meant that the new Conservative-lead Coalition government would have to address this issue – a challenge made more difficult by the profoundly different views held by the two parties regarding the merits of disenfranchising prisoners. While in opposition, Liberal Democrats had to endure accusations that their support for the vote for prisoners meant they were 'soft on criminals'.[183] As the junior Coalition partner, the party had to decide what weight to attach to introducing remedial action, given its substantive differences with the Conservatives on a range of other issues and the fact that the Conservative party repudiates the merits of allowing prisoners to vote. It is unlikely that the potential fragility of the coalition agreement was the only influence on Liberal Democrat strategies. Now in government, the party leadership's commitment to redress the issue of prisoner voting was also certainly

[179] 'Some Inmates to get Voting Rights', *BBC News*, 9 April 2009, http://news.bbc.co.uk/2/hi/uk_news/politics/7992045.stm

[180] Interim Resolution CM/ResDH(2009) 160, 'Execution of the Judgment of the European Court of Human Rights Hirst against the United Kingdom No. 2', https://wcd.coe.int/wcd/ViewDoc.jsp?id=1556821&Site=CM.

[181] CM/Del/Dec (2010) 1078.

[182] 'Communication on the Activities of the Committee of Ministers, Report by the Chair of the Committee of Ministers to the Parliamentary Assembly', CM/AS(2010)7 rev 4, para 16, https://wcd.coe.int/wcd/ViewDoc.jsp?id=1678647&Site=CM&BackColorInternet=C3C3C3&BackColorIntranet=EDB021&BackColorLogged=F5D383

[183] 'Some Inmates to get Voting Rights', *BBC News*.

influenced by the strong public opposition to prisoner voting,[184] estimated at more than 60 per cent, and even higher among older voters.[185]

As discussed in Chapter 7, the prolonged delay in implementing remedies meant that the government had to acknowledge the inability to claim that its House of Lords Reform Bill 2012–13 was compatible with Convention rights. This bill sought to reform the composition of the House of Lords, and thus the question of prisoner voting was relevant when addressing the franchise.[186]

The strongest incentive for the Conservative leadership to consider remedial legislation arose not, it would seem, from political pressure on the part of the Liberal Democrats, but rather from apprehension of the substantial costs of litigation and compensation associated with the failure to enact remedial measures. Attenuating this concern was the November 2010 judgment in *Greens and M.T.* v. *the United Kingdom*, in which the government received a blunt warning that unless remedial legislation was introduced within six months, the court would reinstate approximately 2,500 similar applications. This reinstatement would significantly escalate the litigation and compensation costs for which the government might be responsible – not only for these reinstated applications, but also for new actions (approximately 100,000 UK prisoners had been affected by the ban on voting).[187] On the eve of the 2010 Christmas break, the Coalition government announced it would introduce legislation to allow any prisoner serving a sentence of under four years to be eligible to vote; this was expected to include more than 28,000 prisoners.[188]

[184] Media reports speculated that although Liberal Democrat ministers still support compliance with the ECHR, 'they no not want to be seen any longer to be in the vanguard on an issue that is likely to make them deeply unpopular': P. Wintour and A. Sparrow, 'I Won't Give Prisoners the Vote, Says David Cameron', *The Guardian*, 24 October 2012, www.guardian.co.uk/society/2012/oct/24/prisoners-vote-david-cameron.

[185] See Angus Reid Public Opinion, 'Most Britons Believe Prisoners Should Not Vote in Elections', www.angus-reid.com/wp-content/uploads/2010/11/2010.11.22_Prisoner_BRI.pdf

[186] The government subsequently announced it would not proceed with the legislation because of apprehension of defeat in the Commons, after more than 100 Conservative MPs threatened to join Labour and vote against the bill. R. Prince, 'Lords Reform: Government Scraps Vote to Save Legislation', *The Telegraph*, 10 July 2012, www.telegraph.co.uk/news/9389232/Lords-reform-Government-scraps-vote-to-save-legislation.html

[187] *Greens and M.T.* v. *The United Kingdom*, No. 60041/08 (23 Nov 2010).

[188] J. Kirkup, '30,000 Prisoners will be Able to Vote', *The Telegraph*, 6 January 2011, www.telegraph.co.uk/news/uknews/law-and-order/8241920/30000-prisoners-will-be-able-to-vote.htm

Cameron explained that the legislation was unavoidable because of the possibility of crippling financial costs of failure to comply – reported to be in excess of £160 million – but declared that the idea of allowing prisoners to vote left him feeling physically ill.[189] However, before the legislation was introduced, parliament made it clear that it opposed any form of remedial legislation. This opposition was expressed in a backbench members' vote on a motion in February 2011 in which a 234–22 majority voted to maintain the current situation (neither the government nor opposition front benches participated).[190] The motion was initiated by Jack Straw (the former Secretary of State for Justice, with responsibility for the Labour government's earlier failure to comply with the Hirst ruling) and Conservative member David Davis.[191]

Although this spirited debate invoked constitutional arguments, the emphasis was not on compatibility with Convention rights or assessments of the JCHR recommendations, but on bold claims invoking the rule of law, the sovereignty of parliament and the separation of powers.[192] The parliamentary vote provoked mixed responses as to whether the government should withdraw plans to introduce remedies. Although Justice Secretary Ken Clarke rejected the position that the government should abandon remedial measures, arguing that the UK government 'does not defy the ruling of courts whose jurisdiction it has always accepted',[193] other Conservatives argued that parliament's will

[189] 'Prison Votes will be Kept to a Minimum', *BBC News*, 20 January 2011, www.bbc.co.uk/news/uk-politics-12233938

[190] The full wording of the motion was: 'That this House notes the ruling of the European Court of Human Rights in *Hirst v. United Kingdom* in which it held that there had been no substantive debate by members of the legislature on the continued justification for maintaining a general restriction on the right of prisoners to vote; acknowledges the treaty obligations of the UK; is of the opinion that legislative decisions should be a matter for democratically elected lawmakers; and supports the current situation in which no prisoner is able to vote except those imprisoned for contempt, default or on remand.' Parliament of the United Kingdom, *Hansard*, HC, vol 523, col 483, 10 February 2011.

[191] This opportunity is a result of the decision to establish a backbench business committee. See www.parliament.uk/business/committees/committees-a-z/commons-select/backbench-business-committee

[192] D. Nicol, 'Legitimacy of the Commons Debate on Prisoner Voting', (2011) *Public Law* 681, p. 683.

[193] 'No Votes for Jailed Murderers and Rapists – Ken Clarke', *BBC News*, 9 February 2011, www.bbc.co.uk/news/uk-politics-12402704?print=true

should prevail over that of Strasbourg, and speculated that the consequences for defying Strasbourg would be negligible.[194]

Clarke's position that the government must not ignore its responsibility to comply with the Convention did not convince the government, as was made evident in its decision to engage in a cost–benefit analysis of its options. Advice prepared for Deputy Prime Minister Nick Clegg and subsequently leaked to the press discussed the fiscal and political implications of defying Strasbourg and speculated about ways to mitigate the consequences of failure to remedy prisoner disenfranchisement.[195] This advice suggested that failure to comply would be unlikely to result in the UK's suspension or expulsion from the Council of Europe, although the government would be exposed to continued criticism from the Committee of Ministers in Strasbourg and the country's international credibility in terms of commitment to human rights would be undermined. The advice also indicated that the dangers of suspension could be significantly reduced if the government introduced remedial measures, even if parliament refused to pass these,[196] prompting speculation that the government might actually facilitate the defeat of legislation by allowing members a free vote.[197] Finally, the advice suggested that the government could substantially lower the fiscal consequences of any compensation award by 'confiscating' compensation and levying it against a new 'fee for accommodation in prison'. The government was advised that even if it was unsuccessful in passing remedial legislation, the very fact of its trying would be likely to reduce the number of cases heard and compensation awards provided.[198]

In addition to engaging in cost–benefit analysis of its options, which included the idea of clawing back compensation awards by charging rent

[194] D. Raab, 'What Happens if We Defy Europe – Nothing', *The Telegraph*, 2 February 2011, www.telegraph.co.uk/news/politics/8299615/What-happens-if-we-defy-Europe-Nothing.html

[195] T. Shipman, 'Cameron CAN Defy Euro Court Diktats: UK "May Deny Votes for Inmates Without Penalty"', *The Daily Mail*, 18 February 2011, www.dailymail.co.uk/news/article-1358199/Cameron-CAN-defy-Euro-court-diktats-UK-deny-votes-inmates-penalty.html

[196] Ibid.

[197] House of Commons Library, Vaughne Miller, 'European Court of Human Rights rulings: are there options for governments?' SN/IA/5941, 18 April 2011, p. 5, www.parliament.uk/business/publications/research/briefing-papers/SN05941/european-court-of-human-rights-rulings-are-there-options-for-governments

[198] 'Prisoner Voting – Consequences of Non-compliance', *The Times*, 18 February 2011, www.thetimes.co.uk/tto/multimedia/archive/00118/mojlegaladvice0001n_118733a.pdf

to prisoners, the government tried once again to convince the Grand Chamber to accept the UK's position. The government argued that the result of the parliamentary vote in February 2011 would make it extremely difficult to pass remedial legislation,[199] and urged the court to reconsider its assessment of the margin of appreciation to recognize parliament's strong view that the ban was justified.[200] In April 2011 the Grand Chamber rejected the UK government's request to rehear the case, which triggered a six-month deadline for the government to introduce legislation to ensure compliance with the court's jurisprudence (dating from 11 April 2011).[201] However, the government was able to gain yet another delay after Conservative Attorney General Dominic Grieve made a submission as a third party in *Scoppola* v. *Italy*, which also addressed restrictions on prisoner voting, and which urged the court to avoid imposing 'uniform solutions' to this issue.[202] The government was not successful, however, and was granted a six-month extension (from the date of the *Scoppola* judgment on 22 May 2012) to introduce legislation to end the blanket ban on prisoners voting.[203] The ruling indicated that the UK could be compliant without necessarily allowing all prisoners to vote and would be afforded a wide margin of appreciation when deciding the specific scope of the right to vote.[204]

Despite the failure to convince the court to defer to the UK's earlier decision to deny all prisoners the vote, and the indication that the European Court would be receptive to some restrictions on prisoner voting, Prime Minister Cameron declared that he would support parliament's earlier opinion on the issue, and pledged that the issue would be

199 Communication from the government in the case of Hirst No. 2 against the United Kingdom (Application No. 74025/01), 1 March 2011, https://wcd.coe.int/ViewDoc.jsp?id=1753877&Site=CM

200 Ibid.

201 European Court of Human Rights, Press Release no. 328, 12 April 2011, http://adam1-cor.files.wordpress.com/2011/04/referral-to-grand-chamber-rejected-greens-and-m-t-v-the-united-kingdom-12-04-11-2.pdf

202 R. Mason, 'Government Tells European Judges No Right to Meddle with UK Prisoner Vote Policy', *The Telegraph*, 2 November 2011, www.telegraph.co.uk/news/8865204/Government-tells-European-judges-no-right-to-meddle-with-UK-prisoner-vote-policy.html

203 Ministry of Justice, 'Responding to Human Rights Judgment: Report of the Joint Committee on Human Rights on the Government's Response to Human Rights Judgments 2010–11', Cm 8162 (2011), p. 18.

204 *Scoppola* v. *Italy (No. 3)*, No. 126.05, [2012] ECHR 868 (22 May 2012) [GC].

decided by parliament and 'not a foreign court';[205] an assurance he repeated in October 2012, shortly before the deadline lapsed.[206] The government's continued refusal to introduce remedial legislation prompted the November 2012 publication in *The Times* of a letter to the Prime Minister written by several legal academics and judges, including former Conservative Lord Chancellor Lord Mackay and former Lord Chief Justice Lord Woolf. The letter warned the Prime Minister that he 'appears set upon a course which is clearly unlawful' and that continued disregard for the European Convention could encourage non-compliant behaviour by 'those nations whose commitment to the rule of law is tenuous'.[207]

A few weeks later, Lord Chancellor Chris Grayling made a statement to the House of Commons that the government was proceeding with a draft bill – the Voting Eligibility (Prisoners) Draft Bill – for examination by a joint committee of both houses, setting out three options for parliament: a ban for prisoners who are sentenced to four years or more; a ban for prisoners sentenced to more than six months; and a ban for all convicted prisoners.[208] The Explanatory Notes for the bill acknowledged that, should parliament endorse the third option of a total ban, the minister would not be able to claim it as compatible with Convention rights.[209] In December 2012, the Council of Europe's Committee of Ministers indicated that although it welcomed the government's indication that it was introducing remedial measures, the option for a blanket ban on voting by prisoners 'cannot be considered compatible' with the ECHR.[210]

Some speculated that this draft bill was another stalling tactic, because of the length of time before legislation will be passed. An unnamed senior Whitehall spokesperson indicated that because the *Scoppola* ruling does

[205] R. Mason and T. Whitehead, 'David Cameron: Britain will Decide on Votes for Prisoners, Not A "Foreign Court"', *The Telegraph*, 23 May 2012, www.telegraph.co.uk/news/politics/9284892/David-Cameron-Britain-will-decide-on-votes-for-prisoners-not-a-foreign-court.html

[206] P. Wintour and A. Sparrow, 'I Won't Give Prisoners the Vote, Says David Cameron'.

[207] F. Gibb, 'Warning to Cameron on Prisoner Votes', *The Times*, 2 November 2012, www.thetimes.co.uk/tto/law/article3587961.ece

[208] Ministry of Justice, The Voting Eligibility (Prisoners) Draft Bill, Cm 8499 (2012).

[209] Voting Eligibility (Prisoners) Draft Bill, Ministry of Justice, November 2012, para 58, Cm 8499.

[210] O. Bowcott, 'Votes for Prisoners: UK Told it Must Implement ECHR Decisions', *The Guardian*, 11 December 2012, www.theguardian.com/politics/2012/dec/10/votes-for-prisoners-uk-delaying-tactics/print

not require that all prisoners be given the vote, governments will be able to delay implementing the judgment for years, by drawing up consultations and draft laws.[211] The idea of introducing draft legislation as a stalling tactic is also consistent with the earlier leaked legal advice suggesting that political and fiscal consequences of the delay in remedying the ban on voting would likely be reduced if the government at least introduced legislation, even if its passage was ultimately unsuccessful.

However, quite separate from the potential costs government could incur if the courts do not interpret the draft bill as satisfying the UK's requirements for compliance, there are serious potential political consequences arising from Cameron's political handling of the case. Cameron's pledge not to allow prisoners to vote could prove politically costly if parliament subsequently approves affording some prisoners the opportunity to vote, particularly if opponents and the press criticize Cameron for having backed down from his earlier hard-line position. As an editorial comment in the *Daily Mail* stated with regard to Cameron's response to the *Scoppola* ruling:

> With a single word yesterday, David Cameron seized an opportunity that could work wonders to restore his battered fortunes. That word was 'Yes'. He had been asked if he would give an undertaking not to succumb to the diktat from the European Court of Human Rights, demanding that prisoners should be given the right to vote. Further, would he stand up for the sovereignty of Parliament and the British people by upholding the huge Commons vote in support of the blanket ban? Mr. Cameron replied: 'Well, the short answer to that is yes'. Now his real test begins. For he must prove he meant it. So, there can be no compromise with the court – no clever-Dick move to satisfy the letter of its ruling by giving the vote to the barest minimum of prisoners. Without our sovereignty at stake – and an opportunist Labour party pledging its support – the blanket ban must remain. And if the judges then order Mr. Cameron to compensate prisoners, he should consign their demands to the bin.[212]

The issue of prisoner voting returned to British courts in 2013, when two prisoners serving life sentences for murder challenged the blanket ban on voting by prisoners. Although the Supreme Court unanimously dismissed

[211] R. Mason and T. Whitehead, 'David Cameron: Britain Will Decide on Votes for Prisoners, Not a "Foreign Court"'.

[212] 'Cameron's Chance to Deliver for Britain', *The Daily Mail*, 23 May 2012, www.dailymail.co.uk/debate/article-2148987/Prisoner-voting-rights-David-Camerons-chance-deliver-Britain.html?ito=feeds-newsxml

both appeals, it also rejected the government's argument that it should 'refuse to follow and apply the approach taken by the European Court of Human Rights in Hirst (No 2) and Scoppola'.[213] As Lord Sumpton stated, '[I]t would be neither wise nor legally defensible for an English court to say that Article 3 of the First Protocol has a meaning different from that which represents the settled view of the principal court charged with its interpretation, and different from that which will consequently apply in every other state party to the Convention.'[214] David Cameron initially responded to the outcome by tweeting that he welcomed the ruling as a 'victory for common sense'. However, when Conservatives more closely read the court's ruling and, in particular, the part indicating its refusal to ignore the ECtHR, political reaction was significantly different, as evident in backbencher Dominic Raab's criticism of the Supreme Court for what he characterized as its 'spineless capitulation' to the ECtHR through failing to protect British laws from 'foreign judicial legislation'. As Raab wrote in an editorial statement in the Daily Mail:

> The Human Rights Act is bad enough. But, at least it states plainly that our courts only have to 'take into account' Strasbourg case law, rather than slavishly bow to it. Yesterday the Supreme Court shifted the goal posts, ruling that British courts must comply with Strasbourg rulings unless it involves 'some truly fundamental principle' or an 'egregious oversight or misunderstanding' of UK law.[215]

Compounding the testy political environment for this issue was the statement from the Council of Europe's human rights commissioner before the joint parliamentary committee to study the draft bill, who stated that the UK should not try to cherry-pick which decisions of the European Court of Human Rights it was prepared to accept, but should instead be prepared to withdraw from the Council of Europe if it chooses not to comply with the ECtHR.[216]

[213] *R (on the application of Chester) (Appellant)* v. *Secretary of State for Justice (respondent), McGeoch (AP) (Appellant)* v. *The Lord President of the Council and another (respondents) (Scotland)* (2013) UKSC, para 29.

[214] Ibid., para 138.

[215] D. Raab, 'Even When We Win . . . We Still Lose', *Daily Mail Online*, 16 October 2013, www.dailymail.co.uk/news/article-2462774/David-Camerons-delight-Supreme-Court-ruling-prisoners-NOT-vote.html

[216] O. Bowcott, 'UK "Should Leave Council of Europe" if it Defies Ruling on Prisoner Voting Rights', *The Guardian*, 18 October 2013, www.theguardian.com/politics/2013/oct/17/uk-council-of-europe-prisoner-votes-human-rights

The bill was reviewed by a joint committee of both houses, which was required to report to parliament late in 2013. Several months before the Committee reported, the ECtHR dismissed applications made by two prisoners claiming that their rights were violated because of their inability to vote in the European parliamentary elections in 2009, the UK general election in 2010, elections to the Scottish Parliament in 2011, the AV referendum in 2011, local government and future elections. The court ruled that the complaint was lodged more than six months after the most recent election had taken place, thus rendering it inadmissible. It also held that complaints related to elections that are not covered by the European Convention. Finally, the court indicated that little was to be gained from considering the applications with respect to future elections because of ongoing political developments with respect to this issue, but suggested that if legislation addressing this issue is not in place at the time of future elections, the applicants could lodge a new application.[217]

The joint committee examining the draft bill offered a divided report, in which the majority urged compliance with the European court and warned of the grave implications for non-compliance. The majority recommended that all prisoners serving sentences of 12 months or less be entitled to vote in all UK parliamentary local and European elections, and that prisoners should be entitled to apply up to six months before their scheduled release date to register to vote in the constituency into which they are due to be released.[218] The minority view argued that despite the serious consequences of non-compliance, parliament's obligation to comply was set aside by the perception that the ECtHR had exceeded its mandate 'in seeking to dictate to a democratically elected legislature the detailed arrangements regarding prisoner voting'; these committee members also considered the Court's recent jurisprudence on the issue as 'internally incoherent, clearing demonstrating the dangers of judicial law-making'.[219] At the time of writing, the issue has not been resolved.

[217] ECtHR, Press Release, ECHR 195 (2013) June 28 2013.

[218] Joint Committee on the Daft Voting Eligibility (Prisoners) bill, Report, Session 2013–2014, HL 103, HC 924, para 228.

[219] Ibid., para 227.

Assessing the HRA's influence on prisoner voting

Although bills of rights can alter how contentious issues are interpreted and debated, they do not necessarily change political judgement about contested issues. The political response to whether and how to remedy prisoner disenfranchisement demonstrates deep political discomfort with the idea that ECtHR rulings should prevail over parliament's judgement on an issue about which parliament has particularly strong opinions. It also demonstrates the significance of financial costs as a driving factor in government's strategies to respond to judicial rulings where substantive remedial action is required. After years of delay, the government's willingness to introduce remedial legislation has not come about because of the impact of persistent critical reports by the JCHR and its strong recommendations to introduce remedial measures, or because the HRA has encouraged parliament to pressure government into ensuring legislation is compatible with Convention rights; instead, the principal factors motivating the government to introduce remedial measures appear to be apprehension of the significant costs associated with continued non-compliance and also political concerns regarding the consequences of non-compliance with treaty obligations. However, these concerns have far greater resonance for government than for parliament. Moreover, the strong rhetorical arguments by governments contesting the legitimacy of the European courts' rulings only compounds the difficulty of engaging in a debate about whether the HRA compels parliament to revisit the merits of its earlier positions on this issue.

To the extent that the HRA influenced political arguments about prisoner voting, the focus was on parliamentary sovereignty rather than on the JCHR's emphasis on compatibility with protected rights or broader political expectations of compliance with Convention rights. As Danny Nicol argues, parliamentary backbench debate was 'replete with references to parliamentary sovereignty' in which MPs adopted a 'looser, more political conception' than that usually understood by constitutional scholars, and focused principally on the idea 'that the latest expression of Parliament's will should prevail'.[220] In making these arguments MPs emphasized the idea of the democratic accountability of the legislature as an essential justification for parliament's will prevailing

[220] D. Nicol, 'Legitimacy of the Commons Debate on Prisoner Voting', (2011) *Public Law* 681, p. 681, 683.

over that of the European court.[221] Some might interpret this debate as echoing what Jeremy Waldron has referred to as 'the right of rights';[222] the judgement of the people, as interpreted via the judgement of their elected representatives.

However, defenders of legislation that gives primacy to parliament's view on this issue failed to confront a serious tension between claims that parliamentary supremacy justifies parliament's will prevailing on this particular issue and the deliberate exclusion of a specific segment of the adult polity from voting for their elected representatives. Waldron had occasion to alert parliamentarians to this tension in evidence given to the JCHR, when he explicitly addressed the issue of whether parliamentary sovereignty justifies a parliamentary decision to deny prisoners the right to vote. Waldron advised the JCHR that he believed disenfranchisement to be 'a serious mistake'.[223] As he stated:

> The position that I defend, the misgivings I have about judicial review and the democratic basis that I embrace as a foundation ... run into their deepest challenge when the majoritarian institution is actually addressing the basis of its own electoral credentials. It runs into the deepest challenge where the parliament is actually addressing the right to vote and the integrity and continuance of the electoral and democratic process... Parliament's legitimacy and supremacy in our constitution is not based upon history and is not an abstract proposition; it is based on the fact that the leading part of Parliament has electoral credibility. Parliamentary decision-making and legislation is legitimate because people have the right to vote, not the other way round.[224]

It remains to be seen whether parliament will reflect upon this tension regarding the scope of parliamentary sovereignty, and how it implicates the issue of participation, when choosing which remedial option to approve.

Conclusions

Notwithstanding the HRA's quasi-constitutional status, it has not displaced the two central characteristics that shape how the UK's

[221] Ibid., pp. 685–86.

[222] Waldron borrows the phrase 'right of rights' from a much earlier discussion by William Cobbett, *Advice to Young Men* (London: 1829), as referred to by J. Waldron, *Law and Disagreement* (Oxford: Oxford University Press, 1999), p. 232.

[223] Parliament of the United Kingdom, JCHR, Oral Evidence, 15 March 2011, Q 58.

[224] Ibid., Q53.

Westminster parliamentary system operates: executive dominance of parliament and the centrality of cohesive political parties. The HRA also has not displaced a key focus of any government, which is to protect its legislative agenda from potential obstacles and anticipate and manage challenges that could result in the governing party losing outright or incurring a substantially diminished majority in the next election.

Regardless of which party wins a general election, a government's legislative agenda is generally shaped by a variety of factors: problems the leaders and members of the governing party believe should be redressed; their philosophical understandings of the public interest, equality, liberty and other substantive values; political assumptions about the appropriate role of the state in redressing social problems and inequalities in power, as well as the appropriate institutional division of labour between courts and parliament for resolving contested issues; partisan and electoral considerations relating to how to maintain party cohesion and retain power; and strategic factors such as anticipation of political obstacles that could delay, alter or defeat a government's legislative agenda.

The HRA complicates rather than changes how governments conceive and pursue their legislative priorities. Contrary to political claims that the HRA would facilitate a proactive rights culture wherein government would be compelled to explain and defend the merits of proposed legislation before parliament with respect to questions of compatibility, and where parliament would satisfy itself that legislation is justified in light of its implications for rights (particularly when advised by the JCHR about compatibility issues), our research supports the conclusion that political behaviour under the HRA is better explained by governments' strategic assessments of how to manage the risks and consequences associated with the HRA, as well as by the House of Commons' relative indifference to compatibility-based assessments.

This does not mean that the HRA is incidental to legislative decision-making. On the contrary, the HRA complicates political decision-making by emphasizing that notwithstanding how government defines and justifies the importance of its legislative agenda, Convention rights function as distinct yet often contested criteria against which legislation will now also be assessed – by vocal and influential parliamentary actors (principally the JCHR and the House of Lords), by civil liberties organizations, academic commentators and the media and ultimately by domestic and European courts. Thus, the HRA influences government behaviour by introducing an additional set of considerations that enter into a government's strategic calculus about the vulnerability of its political agenda to defeat or change, and how to best to improve its chances of achieving its legislative and political goals.

As we argued in Chapter 7, governments have a strong interest in ensuring that legislation is not unnecessarily vulnerable to judicial censure, particularly when legal problems can be anticipated and rectified without significantly impacting upon the government's legislative agenda. At the same time, governments might be strongly committed to legislative initiatives in which the risk of a negative judicial ruling cannot be mitigated without significantly altering the government's legislative intentions. Risk aversion and risk-taking occupy either end of a continuum of political responses to governing under the HRA.

We interpret government behaviour as frequently occupying the risk-taking end of this continuum. As we argued in Chapter 7, both Labour and Conservative-led coalition governments have appeared willing to introduce risky legislation. The frequency with which the JCHR contests ministerial claims of compatibility, and the message conveyed to us – that JCHR concerns rarely come as a surprise due to the multiple occasions in which legislative initiatives are assessed for compatibility before their approval as bills for introduction to parliament – strongly indicate that governments knowingly introduce legislation which they have been advised stands a reasonable chance of being successfully litigated on compatibility grounds. Yet governments have rarely felt compelled to disclose to parliament the fact that they are fully aware of the contested nature of compatibility claims or the extent to which legislation is vulnerable to judicial censure, or to defend their judgement about why legislation is reasonable or justified in light of its possible adverse implications for protected rights.

Our case studies here and in Chapter 8 reinforce our interpretation that government strategies often lie closer to the risk end of the continuum. Governments' frequent dismissals of JCHR concerns and determination to overturn rights-compliant amendments in the House of Lords suggest a willingness to roll the dice in terms of whether courts will rule that legislation is compatible with Convention rights. Specific examples of risk-taking are evident in governments' decisions to ignore JCHR concerns and authorize indefinite detention for foreign terrorist suspects, refusal to authorize stronger judicial safeguards to review the basis for control orders and TPIMs and willingness to authorize closed material procedures for civil trials despite strong criticism that the government had not justified their use or adopted sufficient safeguards to prevent abuse. Risk-taking is also indicated by governmental delay of remedial measures for the disenfranchisement of all prisoners, despite persistent pressure from the JCHR, and by cost–benefit assessments of the consequences of non-compliance.

However, we also recognize the need to introduce a significant caveat to our characterization of government behaviour. Not all legislative bills are appropriately interpreted as strategic attempts to manage the new challenges of governing under the HRA. Both the civil partnership and the marriage bills are difficult to attribute to strategic assessments or political cost–benefit analyses related to compliance with Convention rights. The Labour government's decision to promote the civil partnership legislation appears to have been influenced more by a genuine commitment to redress discrimination against same sex partners than by a substantial and imminent legal imperative to introduce a new form of relationship recognition. David Cameron's support for same sex marriage is even more difficult to characterize in terms of strategic decision-making with respect to compliance with the HRA, because not only was his support for the Marriage Bill not prompted by apprehension of immediate judicial censure; it also provoked substantial and frequent warnings from within his own party that promoting gay marriage would seriously undermine his party's political and electoral base and lead to political questions about his future as party leader. Cameron's determination to push ahead with same sex marriage appears to reflect his commitment to an inclusive understanding of marriage, and his willingness to use his position as party leader and Prime Minister to pass legislation his party did not support.

Notwithstanding the civil partnership and marriage bills, governmental willingness to act in a strategic and high-risk manner prompts the following questions: What can explain why the HRA is not evolving in the manner associated with the idea of a proactive rights-protecting environment? Why do governments not make more concerted efforts to ensure that their bills are compatible with Convention rights? However, we believe the more relevant question is: why is government able to frequently adopt risk-taking strategies?

As political strategy, risk-taking is made easier by the lack of broad public and party support for the HRA. Although Labour introduced the HRA, once confronted with the stark realities of what governing under a rights regime entails, Labour government leaders appeared to rapidly lose enthusiasm for the HRA.[225] The Labour government rarely

[225] Interviews.

presented itself as a champion of the HRA, or promoted its role as the government that introduced the HRA. For example, even when arguing about the need to promote equality and protect same sex partners from historical discrimination, the government did not invoke the HRA to support the Civil Partnership Bill. More pointedly, when the Labour government was criticized for promoting legislation that infringes upon rights, it rarely acknowledged that rights-based concerns justify amendments and, depending on the issue, responded to many such criticisms with hostility and contempt (most evident in its response to critics of its anti-terrorist measures). Its complete absence from a Labour party statement of its top 50 achievements since being elected in 1997 is a strong indication of how Labour views the significance of the HRA.[226]

Risk-taking is a potentially more complicated strategy for the Coalition government, because the Liberal Democrats support the HRA whereas the Conservative party has actively campaigned to repeal it. However, the Liberal Democrats' power within the Coalition has been insufficient to ensure compliance with Convention rights, as evident in the government's prolonged delay in introducing remedial measures for prisoner voting and the ability of a three-line Whip in the House of Lords to compel Liberal Democrat peers' support for the government's version of the Justice and Security Bill, notwithstanding the party's earlier renunciation of authorizing the use of closed material procedures in civil trials because of concerns they are not consistent with constitutional principles.[227]

How governments broach the HRA is only one element in the equation when assessing how it influences legislation. A related dimension is how parliament evaluates bills that implicate rights and whether it pressures government to justify or amend bills where compatibility is contested. Political proponents of the HRA emphasized that parliament itself would play an important rights-protecting role under the HRA – a role facilitated by the new requirement that ministers alert parliament to whether bills are compatible with Convention rights, along with the creation of a specialized parliamentary rights committee (the JCHR).

[226] J. Isaby, 'Are These Labour's Top Achievements?', *The Telegraph*, 21 February 2008, http://blogs.telegraph.co.uk/news/jonathanisaby/3669111/Are_these_Labours_top_achievements/

[227] R. Syal, 'Secret Courts Plan Receives Blow at Lib Dem Conference', *The Guardian*, 26 September 2012, www.guardian.co.uk/law/2012/sep/25/secret-courts-lib-dem-conference

UK parliamentary resources for engaging in rights-based scrutiny far exceed those available to other Westminster-based parliaments such as those of Canada and New Zealand, which have similarly adopted statutory obligations for government to report on whether bills are compatible with protected rights. The UK parliament has access to the timely and comprehensive reports of a specialized rights committee whose reputation for principled and robust parliamentary scrutiny is widely respected, and which is prepared to conduct evidence-based hearings when government claims for new coercive powers are not substantiated or where government has not presented evidence to justify deviating from the norms of the criminal justice system. The JCHR's robust approach to its scrutiny function and its impressive work ethic ensure that parliament has access to critical analysis of how bills implicate rights at a stage in which the bill is being debated before at least one house of parliament, and thus parliament can demand amendments if it is convinced that legislation imposes an unwarranted or unjustified restriction on rights. Finally, the transparent nature of the committee's proceedings allows parliament to be privy to written correspondence between the committee, ministers and department officials about the reasons for and potential consequences of the legislative initiative and possible amendments. If one's mission were to identify the kinds of resources required for effective parliamentary rights scrutiny, it would be difficult to conclude that those offered the UK parliament fall seriously short.[228] As Stephen Gardbaum characterizes the JCHR, it represents a gold standard for emulation by other jurisdictions.[229]

However, having the necessary resources for robust legislative rights review does not guarantee that parliament will necessarily utilize these or hold government to account for decisions that potentially implicate rights in an adverse manner. In our research, we uncovered several reasons why the JCHR's frequent contestations of government claims of compatibility do not more regularly influence a government's decision to revise legislation. These include: the fact that JCHR assessments of compatibility occur after government has already grappled with the issue and determined how much risk it is prepared to tolerate, which makes

[228] This doesn't mean one can't quibble with the reporting style of the JCHR: its assessments are often fairly dense and legalistic and thus require considerable energy on the part of the reader (a potential problem for busy elected members and their overworked staff).

[229] S. Gardbaum, *The New Commonwealth Model of Constitutionalism: Theory and Practice* (New York: Cambridge University Press, 2013), p. 225.

it difficult politically for government to step back or consider substantial amendments to the scope of a bill; that government interprets JCHR opinion on compatibility as simply a different perspective on proportionality, and therefore government does not accept that its own judgment is inappropriate (particularly as it will include opinions from the office of the Attorney General); that government does not always accept the need to include safeguards in legislation because of the legal obligation on public authorities to act in a compliant manner; and that government is generally confident in its ability to control the House of Commons where voting is rarely influenced by JCHR concerns of compatibility.[230]

Although all of the preceding factors are important in understanding how and why governments are so reluctant to revisit the scope of legislative bills in order to address compatibility issues that are subsequently raised, our research underscores the significance of the last reason. Governments have been able to frequently utilize risk-taking strategies because of parliament's continued weakness relative to the executive, as well as the House of Commons' reluctance to address compatibility questions when debating or voting on bills. The House of Commons does not challenge government's claims of compatibility, or demand more substantive explanations to justify the introduction of powers or use of legislative means that the JCHR reports are problematic from a compatibility perspective. Nor has the House of Commons put pressure on government to justify or alter its approach to interpreting compatibility for statutory reporting purposes. Consequently, ministers do not acknowledge the contested nature of their conclusions about compatibility, or explain what assumptions were used for determining that the bill is compatible with Convention rights.

The House of Commons might engage in rights talk, but parliamentary rights discourse is not influenced by the legal language of Convention rights and therefore does not reflect the HRA's and JCHR's emphasis on compatibility. Thus, despite its earnest reviews and the considerable energy the JCHR invests in trying to steer parliamentary debate toward evaluation of the government's claims of compatibility, to date government has had little reason to fear that rights-based concerns in the House of Commons will rise to the level of being marshalled to defeat or amend legislation.

[230] Interviews.

For the House of Commons to play a more active role in assessing whether bills are compatible with Convention rights would require opposition leaders to significantly adjust their political strategies to accord more attention to questions of how the HRA appropriately guides or constrain legislative bills and whether proposed legislation is compatible with Convention rights, and to integrate compatibility-based arguments into their more conventional foci on philosophical and policy differences that distinguish their party from the government party, the relative merits of leaders' and parties' track records on particular issues and how to exploit these differences for political and electoral advantages. However, whether due to genuine disagreement about the merits of compatibility-based assessments structuring or influencing the vote or to strategic consideration of what kind of arguments are most useful for political and electoral purposes, neither Conservative nor Labour party leaders have embraced the idea of incorporating an emphasis on compatibility with Convention rights in their political agendas.[231] Instead of emphasizing HRA compliance, Conservative and Labour party strategies often promote antagonistic positions toward the HRA, which exploit public concerns and ambivalence about the merits of the HRA; promote Convention rights and public safety in oppositional terms; and engage in anti-HRA rhetoric so as to gain political traction from the deep hostility toward the HRA expressed by the tabloid press.

If party leaders continue to ignore compatibility-based assessments in their reviews of legislative bills, this norm of rights-based justification for legislation will only shape parliamentary behaviour in the House of Commons where significant numbers of elected members exert greater independence from their party leadership. Although a substantial number of government backbench members frequently exert autonomy from party whips, government control over its parliamentary caucus in the House of Commons has generally been sufficiently robust to minimize the number of defeats encountered by the government (particularly when it has a majority). In any event, the lack of broad political support for the HRA undermines interest and utility in calling upon government to defend its perspectives in terms of their consistency with Convention rights.

As evident in the legislative bills examined here and in the previous chapter, the HRA is considerably more prominent in House of Lords debates. The House of Lords has been significantly more willing (and

[231] 'Prison votes will be Kept to a Minimum', *BBC News*.

capable) than the House of Commons to amend or defeat government bills, and regularly engages JCHR reports when arguing for rights-based changes. The non-elected nature of membership in the House of Lords provides peers greater independence from party and public pressures. Analysis of the House of Lords after the 1999 reform that removed the majority of hereditary peers suggests this was a significant factor in changing how the House of Lords performs. The reform not only created the confidence necessary for peers (and the public) to accept their legitimacy in the political process, but also reduced the ability of any party to control the chamber, which resulted in Liberal Democrats (the party most sympathetic to the ECHR) gaining more importance in British politics.[232]

Although government has frequently been compelled to accept rights-inspired amendments in the Lords, such as the introduction of safeguards to the anti-terrorism legislation and identity card bills, the influence of the Lords is often constrained by party leaders' ability to call upon disciplined voting in the Commons to defeat these amendments. Moreover, no matter how robust or rights-orientated the opposition to the anti-terrorism scheme, the House of Lords was not able to defeat the essential objective of indefinite detention or highly restrictive control orders. Finally, it cannot necessarily be assumed that amendments made in the Lords will be inspired by rights-protecting motives, as was evident in debate about civil partnership legislation, where amendments were inspired by an explicit attempt to undermine the legal recognition of same sex relationships.

The HRA's limited impact on parliamentary decision-making, particularly in the House of Commons, represents a substantial gap in a rights project that is predicated on the idea that parliamentary discourse will occur around the issue of compatibility and in a manner that challenges government to explain and justify the passage of bills that raise compatibility concerns. This gap is all the more significant in light of the broad discretion ministers exercise when determining the level of risk they are willing to take in introducing measures that stand a reasonably strong chance of being subject to judicial censure, and their refusal to acknowledge to parliament the nature or degree of this risk. Keith Ewing aptly characterizes the problem of parliament's ability to hold the government

232 M. Russell and M. Sciara, 'Why Does the Government get Defeated in the House of Lords? The Lords, the Party System and British Politics', (2007) 2 *British Politics* 299.

to account by warning that parliamentary control 'can only be as effective as parliament is powerful'.[233] We would add the following observation. Even assuming parliament were sufficiently powerful to hold the government to account, parliament's rights-protecting role can only be effective if party leaders take seriously the idea that legislation should be subject to compatibility-based assessments.

[233] K. Ewing, 'The Political Constitution of Emergency Powers: A Comment', (2008) 3 *International Journal of Law in Context* 316.

10

Conclusion

Both the New Zealand Bill of Rights Act and the United Kingdom's Human Rights Act were defended as bills of rights that would challenge core assumptions about how and why a bill of rights influences legislation. Contrary to more conventional expectations that a bill of rights functions principally in a reactive sense, by empowering courts to review whether legislation is consistent with protected rights and to provide appropriate remedies where rights have been violated, both of these statutory rights instruments were expected to facilitate a significantly more prominent and proactive role for parliament to protect rights while also constraining the scope of judicial interpretative and remedial powers.

Political framers of the NZBORA and HRA had ambitious views of the potential significance of creating a new statutory requirement to alert parliament when government bills appear to be inconsistent with protected rights. The requirement to both confront and acknowledge how legislative bills implicate rights was expected to alter the norms of legislative decision-making by making bureaucrats, government and parliamentarians more sensitive to the rights dimension of legislative choices, and also by directing greater parliamentary attention to issues of compatibility when evaluating bills and determining whether to support, revise or defeat the government's legislative initiatives.

Yet despite political arguments that these bills of rights strike a reasonable balance between reconciling democratic concerns with greater sensitivity for ensuring that legislation complies with protected rights or, alternatively, promoting more informed and thoughtful decisions about the circumstances or conditions that justify restricting protected rights, neither the NZBORA nor the HRA have fundamentally altered the political dynamics that shape how the New Zealand and United Kingdom parliamentary systems operate. These dynamics continue to be characterized by the executive domination of parliament (notwithstanding New Zealand's electoral system of MMP that virtually guarantees minority or coalition governments will be produced) and the centrality of political parties in structuring how parliament votes.

These factors hinder these bills of rights from operating as instruments to discourage government from promoting rights-infringing legislation, encourage parliament to hold government to account for legislative decisions that engage rights or establish the context for reasoned deliberations about the justification of legislation from a rights perspective. Governments are not necessarily prepared to abandon legislative initiatives that engage rights, or to explain or attempt to justify why they should infringe upon rights; opposition party leaders do not focus on compatibility as a political strategy in their perpetual efforts to demonstrate why their party is a better choice for government; and the cohesiveness of political parties undermines incentives for independent voting that contradicts leaders' political strategies. Although party behaviour is far less cohesive in the UK parliament than in New Zealand, backbench rebellions do not occur frequently enough to regularly block the government's ability to pursue its legislative agenda, and even when these occur, they rarely focus on questions of compatibility.

Although shared institutional factors undermine parliamentary capacity and willingness to hold governments to account for decisions that implicate rights in an adverse manner, important institutional variations also exert distinct influences on how and why these bills of rights affect political behaviour. In New Zealand, the change of electoral system to MMP has encouraged attempts to find ways to manage the potential instability associated with an electoral system that regularly produces minority or coalition governments. Political attempts to bolster the stability of government under MMP have resulted in political agreements that led to the formation of governing coalitions based on supply and confidence arrangements, as well as changes made to the Standing Orders of the House of Representatives that emphasize the party vote over the preferences of individual members. However, the promotion of stability comes at the price of accountability, in the sense of weaker institutional capacity for parliament to hold government to account for legislative bills that adversely implicate rights.

The combination of coalition formations for specific policy issues and rules that emphasize the party vote substantially weakens parliamentarians' capacity to demand that government justify legislative bills where rights are implicated adversely. The *quid pro quo* effect encouraged by these coalition arrangements discourages coalition members from engaging in robust scrutiny that could undermine the stability of these political arrangements. Moreover, the political concern about member placement on the party list for selection purposes operates as a strong disincentive for members to focus on compatibility issues if so doing is seen as contradicting party leaders' electoral or political strategies. Finally, the lack of a specialized rights committee to direct attention explicitly to issues of compatibility, and engage ministers and department officials in public accounting for their reasons and justifications for pursuing rights-infringing legislation, deprives parliament of a valuable resource to assess and debate whether legislation should be amended or is otherwise justified despite its adverse implications for rights. The absence of this important resource, combined with members' discretion to nominate which select committee will review a bill and the lack of any requirement to address the issues that give rise to a section 7 report by the Attorney General, undermine the idea of justifying legislation in terms of its implication for rights. These factors also encourage a disproportionate focus on the bills' objectives without sufficient consideration of whether these objectives or the means adopted to pursue them are justified or should be revised in light of their adverse implications for protected rights.

In the UK, political responses to the HRA are influenced by bicameralism as well as by the role of a specialized parliamentary committee that focuses heavily on rights and compatibility. Both the House of Lords and the JCHR enhance parliamentary attention to the rights dimension of bills and focus awareness on the potentially contested nature of affirmative ministerial reports of compatibility. The House of Lords has demonstrated strong interest in and capacity to press for rights-improving reforms, and has drawn support from the JCHR, which has earned considerable respect for the robust manner in which it addresses compatibility issues.

Political variables are only one dimension of the differences that account for how these bills of rights influence political behaviour. The other important dimension is the scope of judicial authority. Unlike in New Zealand, where courts lack the power to declare legislation inconsistent with rights, UK courts' authority to declare that legislation is incompatible with protected rights, along with expectations of compliance with these norms, operate to discourage government from acknowledging that judgement about compatibility is contested or reporting the inability to claim that bills are compatible with protected rights. Acknowledging an inability to report that a bill is compatible with protected rights exposes UK legislation to a greater risk of judicial censure because it makes it potentially more difficult to subsequently defend legislation as compatible with Convention rights in the event legislation is challenged through litigation. Moreover, anticipation of robust scrutiny by the JCHR and the willingness in the House of Lords to press for rights-improving amendments reinforce governmental reluctance to admit to doubts about compatibility or to acknowledge that assumptions about compatibility are likely to be contested. Such acknowledgements would augment the pressure associated with criticisms in the House of Lords or the force of JCHR reports where these call for amendments to redress compatibility problems.

An obvious indication of differences in the interpretation of reporting obligations on compatibility is the frequency of negative reports on consistency in New Zealand, contrasted with relatively few reports in the UK. In New Zealand, more than 60 reports that a bill appears to be inconsistent with protected rights have been made, almost half of which involve government bills, whereas in the UK ministers have made only four reports acknowledging an inability to claim compatibility (including two as a result of amendments made in the House of Lords). At first glance, this discrepancy suggests one or both of the following explanations. One possibility is that the New Zealand policy process is far more rigorous in identifying possible inconsistencies than the UK process is. An alternative explanation is that the compatibility-reporting exercise exerts a more substantial influence on a UK government's legislative agenda, and thus UK governments are more likely than New Zealand governments to address compliance problems before bills are introduced to parliament.

However, our research suggests a more complex explanation for these different levels of reporting on inconsistency with rights, associated with the distinct political and judicial consequences that accrue from rendering an adverse report on compatibility. In New Zealand, four factors help explain the frequency of adverse reports on inconsistency. First, as compatibility reports are made by the Attorney General rather than by individual ministers, this helps ensure that interpretations of prevailing legal norms are not subject to the same political filters that would be required if these judgements were both decentralized and also subject to cabinet input, as occurs in the UK. Second, the limited scope of judicial review and more heavily constrained judicial remedial powers in New Zealand provide more fertile conditions for allowing forthright and transparent accounts about whether and how bills implicate rights than would be the case if this judgement occurred in a political environment that combines stronger judicial remedial powers with an expectation of political compliance with judicial rulings, as is the situation in the UK. Reporting an inability to claim compatibility in New Zealand does not render legislation significantly more vulnerable to judicial censure, because of the weak manner in which judicial review is authorized in the NZBORA. Moreover, these negative reports do not convey the implicit message that the bill will likely have to be revisited or revised down the road, as such a report would indicate in the UK.

Third, the changes made to manage the potential political instability associated with MMP have emphasized the importance of party votes over the preferences of individual members, diminishing the incentives and capacity for parliamentarians to demand that government justify legislative bills where rights are implicated adversely. Finally, the lack of a specialized parliamentary committee in New Zealand – particularly given the absence of an explicit or implicit mandate for select committees to address Attorney General section 7 reports, and the discretion of members to nominate the particular committee that reviews the bills whose sympathies might be geared more toward the policy area of a bill rather than to its implications for rights – discourage focusing attention on whether it is appropriate to pass bills that may not be consistent with rights. Thus, it is not surprising that reports of an inability to claim consistency are more regularly made than in the UK, or that New Zealand governments incur little pressure to explain or justify passing legislation that has been subject to a section 7 report.

In the UK, considerably higher political and judicial consequences arise from acknowledging an inability to report that bills are compatible with protected rights, which have influenced how this reporting obligation is broached. The combination of a stronger judicial interpretive and remedial authority, along with a high expectation of compliance with European and domestic courts, create strong political incentives for governments to manage the potential effects the statutory reporting obligation on compatibility will have for their legislative agendas. These factors have effectively transformed the compatibility-reporting obligation into an exercise in risk assessment and risk management.

UK governments have responded in three ways to perceived threats to their legislative agendas. First, government party leaders have sanctioned an interpretation of the statutory reporting obligation that encompasses a low threshold for claiming that a bill is compatible with the HRA, even when almost certainly aware that an affirmative compatibility report will be contested and/or advised that legislation stands a reasonably high risk of judicial censure in the event of litigation. Second, ministers rarely acknowledge the merits of rights-improving amendments, which are often agreed to only at the point of serious apprehension that the bill will be defeated or will be subject to substantial amendments and/or serious delays, which usually occurs in the House of Lords. However, a perceptible lack of interest by opposition party leaders in focusing on the issue of compatibility has resulted in the under-utilization of JCHR reports in the House of Commons, which, along with government's ability to rely on cohesive party voting in a majority or relatively stable coalition setting, has influenced government strategies to not only resist JCHR calls for additional changes, but also orchestrate the defeat of rights-improving amendments made in the House of Lords. Third, approaching the HRA as a form of risk management encourages government leaders to strategize about how much risk they are prepared to tolerate and whether and how to acknowledge the nature of this risk to parliament, both in the reporting requirement and in responding to calls for amendments made by the JCHR or in the House of Lords. This orientation also inevitably influences how political officials perceive their role by emphasizing the need to develop arguments to justify rights-infringing decisions.

Although a government has every reason to want to be advised of possible political and judicial obstacles to the successful pursuit of its legislative agendas before introducing bills to parliament, the House of Commons' general lack of interest in questions of compatibility, along with government capacity to frequently overturn rights-protecting reforms made in the House of Lords, provide governmental leaders considerable latitude to decide whether to pursue risky legislation, even if aware that they, or a future government, will eventually incur pressure to enact remedial measures. Among the most likely considerations that influence these decisions, which do not occur or do not occur to the same extent in New Zealand, are:

- What effects would reporting to parliament that government is not confident the bill is compatible with protected rights have on the government's ability to pass the legislation without substantive amendments?
- How will risky or risk-averse legislation play out for caucus, the government's political and electoral constituencies, and the media (and in particular the tabloid press)?

- Will government be able to leverage losing a case to subsequently argue to caucus or its electoral base that it was forced to adopt controversial measures for which it earlier lacked sufficient support?
- What is the estimated strength of lobbying efforts in support or in opposition to the legislative initiative in question?
- Would acknowledging an inability to claim compatibility undermine the government's ability to successful defend the legislation if subject to litigation?
- How long would government likely have from the time of passage and pressure to introduce remedial measures?
- How much deference might courts exercise when reviewing any remedial measures?

Although neither the BORA nor the HRA have functioned in a manner that substantially increases parliaments' willingness and capacity to hold governments to account for decisions that implicate rights adversely, we do not conclude these bills of rights have had no significant effects on legislative development. Public officials in both countries confirm that the statutory requirement for reporting on compatibility has influenced policy development by encouraging more rational approaches to policy development. The very act of confronting whether a legislative initiative is compatible with rights directs more attention to the importance of justification, and the necessity to develop compliant ways to achieve legislative objectives.

These concerns about developing legislative initiatives in a rights-compliant manner are reinforced in the UK through informal and formal correspondence with the JCHR (the latter occurring through critical reports), and in both countries by queries from legislative draftspersons. Interviews in both countries reinforce the message that professional reputations are at stake if advisors neglect to inform senior department officials and ministers about compatibility issues that are subsequently identified or questioned, and that time management issues are also raised. However, these pressures are considerably higher in the UK because of the existence of a dedicated parliamentary rights committee whose frequent questions related to compatibility issues regularly compel ministers and departments to respond to queries and explain their earlier decisions and assumptions. The extra resources required for engaging in ongoing and often prolonged correspondences are incentives for public officials to anticipate such queries in an effort to minimize the likelihood of having to spend additional time responding to JCHR questions, particularly if these could have been earlier avoided without seriously challenging the ministers' legislative initiatives.

At the same time, it is important to emphasize that neither the NZBORA nor the HRA have discouraged or prevented governments from passing legislation that is inconsistent with protected rights, whether as admitted to in an adverse report by the New Zealand Attorney General or as alleged in the UK through review by the JCHR and scrutiny by the House of Lords. Governments might be prepared to accept bureaucratic advice that emphasizes more rights-compliant ways of conceiving legislative initiatives early in the legislative process, particularly where so doing does not fundamentally constrain or alter a government's legislative initiative. However, by the time the government has committed itself publicly to the initiative in question by introducing it as a legislative bill, it is extremely difficult politically for the government to subsequently agree to substantive amendments that are portrayed through partisan debate and in the media as a sign of weakness.

Bureaucratic advice about compatibility is not binding and is one of many considerations relied upon when rendering political judgement about how government leaders define and decide to proceed with their legislative agenda. This judgement is generally shaped by political leaders' philosophical understandings of the public interest, equality, liberty and other substantive values; political assumptions about the appropriate role of the state to redress social problems and inequalities in power, as well as the appropriate institutional division of labour between courts and parliament for resolving contested issues; partisan and electoral considerations relating to how to maintain party cohesion and retain power; and strategic factors such as anticipation of political obstacles that could delay, alter or defeat a government's legislative agenda. In the case of New Zealand, or coalition situations in the UK, the latter considerations also include factors related to how to maintain stability between political partners who were earlier rivals, and will be again in upcoming elections, and thus involve a delicate balancing exercise between short-term interests and parties' future electoral prospects.

Our explanation of the reasons impeding the NZBORA and HRA's functioning in the optimistic and proactive manner intended by their framers raises the following question: is it appropriate or helpful to characterize the NZBORA and HRA as constituting a distinct model of constitutionalism?

Our research reinforces the instability that Mark Tushnet earlier associated with parliamentary bills of rights, which he characterizes as a weak-form model. Tushnet argues these bills of rights are vulnerable to instability at both ends of the continuum distinguishing weak from strong-form systems. At one end of the continuum, bills of rights with constrained judicial review and remedial powers could effectively relapse into a situation where government neither has a strong commitment to integrate rights-based norms into legislative decisions nor is subject to parliamentary pressure or robust judicial oversight to comply with rights-based norms. At the other end of the continuum, these systems could evolve to resemble the judicial dominance associated with the United States, particularly if there is judicial insistence on increasingly precise requirements to ensure legislation is compliant with protected rights and political practices that emphasize compliance with judicial rulings.[1] Our research reinforces the notion of instability. New Zealand political leaders incur weak pressure to justify why legislation should be passed where it has been reported as inconsistent with protected rights, because of weak judicial and political consequences that accrue from promoting inconsistent legislation. In addition, legislation that is considered by the Attorney General to be inconsistent with the NZBORA frequently affects the rights of people accused of crimes or those already incarcerated, which significantly reduces the willingness of parliamentarians to demand rights-friendly amendments. In the UK, political leaders incur substantially stronger pressures to remedy perceived compatibility issues because of the treaty character of protected rights. Nevertheless, despite a strong expectation of compliance, government leaders are often prepared to roll the dice in terms of promoting legislation which they can reasonably anticipate will be subject to judicial censure, even if aware that remedial measures might eventually be required.

Stephen Gardbaum has also addressed the potential instability of these bills of rights in his comparative assessment of what he has influentially coined the Commonwealth model. Yet Gardbaum argues that despite considerable variance in the function of bills of rights in Canada, New Zealand, the United Kingdom and Australia, this model encapsulates optimal techniques for protecting rights and as such constitutes a distinct model of constitutionalism that combines the strengths of both polar

[1] M. Tushnet, 'New Forms of Judicial Review', (2003) 38 *Wake Forest Law Review*, 813; M. Tushnet, *Weak Courts, Strong Rights. Judicial Review and Social Welfare Rights in Comparative Constitutional Law* (Princeton University Press, 2008).

models while avoiding each of their principal weaknesses. Gardbaum uses the metaphor of constitutional engineering to convey what he considers the normative significance of this model, which he sees as striking a more 'optimal institutional form of constitutionalism within a democratic polity' than is offered by the rival models of parliamentary sovereignty and judicial supremacy, by recalibrating the power between the judiciary and parliament to create a greater balance by denying 'too much power to either'.[2]

Our research has left us reluctant to characterize the NZBORA or HRA as constituting a distinct model, at least to the extent that these bills of rights are considered to represent fundamental reforms to how the Westminster-based parliamentary systems operate. As we have argued throughout, New Zealand and the UK have shared political and institutional characteristics which undermine the idea that parliament will function to hold government to account for legislative decisions that implicate rights. Westminster-influenced variables of executive domination of parliament and the centrality of highly disciplined political parties continue to influence how both parliaments function. This Westminster context is so significant that we believe the more prudent way to characterize these new rights instruments is to refer to them as parliamentary bills of rights, rather than as part of a Commonwealth model. At the same time, important institutional variations also suggest that these bills of rights will not necessarily function in a similar manner, because they influence how the statutory compatibility exercise is broached, the pressures on government to address compatibility problems and also the nature and force of parliamentary and judicial pressure. These variations are substantial enough that they give us pause with regard to the question of whether it is useful to consider these bills of rights in practice as constituting a distinct and new normative model for a bill of rights.

We are even more sceptical about interpreting these reforms via the metaphor of constitutional engineering, which Gardbaum utilizes. Although we appreciate the difficulty of overcoming conventional wisdom that assumed the principle of parliamentary sovereignty was a serious impediment to Westminster-based systems' adoption of a bill of rights, and also the political significance of the idea of conceiving an alternative view of how a bill of rights functions, we are troubled by the

[2] S. Gardbaum, *The New Commonwealth Model of Constitutionalism. Theory and Practice* (Cambridge: Cambridge University Press, 2013), p. 52.

implicit assumption that the introduction of a bill of rights will necessarily transform political behaviour in the way the 'engineering' metaphor implies. It is not necessarily the case that rights-inspired arguments are absent from parliamentary deliberations. However, there is little indication that the NZBORA or the HRA have framed or otherwise influenced these debates, or that they occur frequently enough to regularly challenge governments' capacity to implement their legislative agendas.

Although our initial interest in these bills of rights was inspired by the potential benefits of parliament playing a more substantial role when rendering judgement about rights appropriately guide and constrain legislative actions,[3] our research into how the compatibility requirement in NZBORA and HRA is broached by legal advisors, the relationship between this advice and governmental decision-making and the influence this has on parliamentary engagement with rights reinforces the necessity of grounding assessments of bills of rights in the actual political and institutional contexts in which these political systems operate.

What most troubles us about the reformist vision associated with this metaphor is the apolitical conception of this reform agenda. As our research demonstrates, lower houses of parliament do not seem to be an effective venue for elected members to engage in independent, moral judgements about the scope of rights, or how rights-based or compatibility-based considerations should guide or constrain legislation. Instead, debate and voting in these parliamentary venues is heavily constrained by government domination, norms of party cohesion and an 'us vs. them' focus that emphasizes criticism of the government's legislative agenda rather than seeking the best way to ensure legislation is compliant with protected rights. Equally difficult for the purpose of associating these parliamentary bills of rights with the reformist metaphor of constitutional engineering is the inability to explain what incentives exist for government to accept rights-based constraints on its legislative agenda when such considerations would alter or impair the

[3] See in particular J. Hiebert, 'New Constitutional Ideas: Can New Parliamentary Models Resist Judicial Dominance When Interpreting Rights?', (2004) 82 *Texas Law Review* 1963; J. Hiebert, 'Parliamentary Bills of Rights. An Alternative Model?' (2006) 69 *Modern Law Review* 7; J. Hiebert 'Constitutional Experimentation: Rethinking How a Bill of Rights Functions', in T. Ginsburg and R Dixon (eds.) *Comparative Constitutional Law* (Cheltenham: Edward Elgar, 2011), pp. 298–320.

governing party's interpretation of the public interest or its own party political interests in a political environment in which government has the political capacity to ensure passage of its preferred legislative agenda in parliament, and where judicial review either does not present a serious threat to a government's agenda, or encourages political strategies about how to manage the political consequences associated with judicial censure.

Appendix 1

Section 7 reports to the New Zealand Parliament, 1990–2014

I. Non-government bills (Members' and Local)		Vote	Type	AG	Year	Passed	Amended*	Act(s)
1	Kumeu District Agricultural and Horticultural Bill	SMP	Members'	East	1991	Yes	Yes	Kumeu District Agricultural and Horticultural Act
2	Napier City Council (Control of Skateboards) Empowering Bill	SMP	Local	East	1991	No		
3	Rights of Prisoners to Vote Bill	SMP	Members'	McGrath	1992	No		
4	Technology and Crimes Reform Bill	SMP	Members'	East	1994	No		
5	Disclosure of Political Donations and Gifts Bill	SMP	Members'	East	1995	No		
6	Degrees of Murder Bill	SMP	Members'	East	1996	No		
7	Resource Management (Cellsite Moratorium) Amendment Bill	MMP	Members'	East	1997	No		
8	Trade in Endangered Species Amendment Bill	MMP	Members'	East	1997	Yes	Yes	Trade in Endangered Species Amendment Act 1998
9	Animal Welfare Bill	MMP	Members'	East	1997	No		
10	Crimes (Bail Reform) Bill	MMP	Members'	Graham	1999	No		
11	Summit Road (Canterbury) Protection Bill	MMP	Local	Wilson	2000	Yes	Yes	Summit Road (Canterbury) Protection Act 2001
12	Sale of Liquor (Health Warnings) Amendment Bill	MMP	Members'	Wilson	2000	No		
13	Electoral (Public Opinion Polls) Amendment Bill	MMP	Members'	Wilson	2000	No		

14	Criminal Justice (Parole Offenders) Amendment Bill	MMP	Members'	Wilson	2000	No		
15	Volunteers Employment Protection Amendment Bill	MMP	Members'	Wilson	2000	No		
16	Films, Videos, and Publications Classification (Child Pornography) Amendment Bill	MMP	Members'	Wilson	2000	No		
17	Death with Dignity Bill	MMP	Members'	Wilson	2003	No		
18	Sentencing (Community Sentencing to Fit the Crime) Amendment Bill	MMP	Members'	Wilson	2004	No		
19	Marriage (Gender Classificaton) Amendment Bill	MMP	Members'	Cullen	2005	No		
20	Manukau City Council (Control of Graffiti) Bill 2005	MMP	Local	Parker	2005	Yes	No	Manukau City Council (Control of Graffiti) Act 2008
21	Manukau City Council (Control of Prostitution) Bill 2005	MMP	Local	Parker	2005	No		
22	Human Tissue (Organ Donation) Amendment Bill	MMP	Members'	Cullen	2006	No		
23	Human Rights (One Law for All) Amendment Bill	MMP	Members'	Cullen	2006	No		
24	Auckland Regional Amenities Funding Bill	MMP	Members'	Cullen	2007	Yes	Yes	Auckland Regional Amenities Funding Act 2008
25	Wanganui District Council (Prohibition of Gang Insignia) Bill	MMP	Local	Cullen	2008	Yes	Yes	Wanganui District Council (Prohibition of Gang Insignia) Act 2009

(*cont.*)

I. Non-government bills (Members' and Local)		Vote	Type	AG	Year	Passed	Amended*	Act(s)
26	Eden Park Trust Amendment Bill	MMP	Local	Finlayson	2009	Yes	Yes	Eden Park Trust Amendment Act 2009
27	Liquor Advertising (Television and Radio) Bill	MMP	Members'	Finlayson	2009	No		
28	Electoral (Disqualification of Convicted Persons) Amendment Bill	MMP	Members'	Finlayson	2010	Yes	No	Electoral (Disqualification of Sentenced Prisoners) Amendment Act 2010
29	Head of State Referenda Bill	MMP	Members'	Finlayson	2010	No		
30	Local Electoral (Māori Representation) Amendment Bill	MMP	Members'	Finlayson	2010	No		
31	Smoke-free Environments (Removing Tobacco Displays) Amendment Bill	MMP	Members'	Finlayson	2010	No		
32	Lobbying Disclosure Bill	MMP	Members'	Finlayson	2011	In progress		
33	Land Transport (Admissibility of Evidential Breath Tests) Amendment Bill	MMP	Members'	Finlayson	2012	In progress		

II. Government bills		Vote	Type	AG	Year	Passed	Amended*	Act(s)
1	Transport Safety Bill	SMP	Govt	East	1991	Yes	No	Transport Amendment Act 1992
2	Films, Videos, and Publications Classification Bill	SMP	Govt	East	1992	Yes	No	Films, Videos, and Publications Classification Act 1993
3	Children, Young Persons and their Families Amendment Bill	SMP	Govt	Graham	1993	Yes	Yes	Children, Young Persons and their Families Amendment Act 1994
4	Casino Control (Moratorium) Amendment Bill	MMP	Govt	East	1997	Yes	No	Casino Control (Moratorium) Amendment Act 1998
5	Land Transport Bill	MMP	Govt	East	1997	Yes	No	Land Transport Act 1998
6	Housing Restructuring (Income Related Rents) Amendment Bill	MMP	Govt	Wilson	2000	Yes	No	Housing Restructuring (Income Related Rents) Amendment Act 2000
7	Social Security (Residence of Spouses) Amendment Bill	MMP	Govt	Wilson	2001	Yes	No	Social Security Amendment Act (No 2) 2001
8	Electoral Amendment Bill (No.2)	MMP	Govt	Wilson	2001	Yes	Yes	Electoral Amendment Act 2002
9	War Pensions Amendment Bill	MMP	Govt	Wilson	2001	Yes	No	War Pensions Amendment Act 2003
10	Income Tax Bill 2002	MMP	Govt	Wilson	2002	Yes	No	Income Tax Act 2004
11	Land Transport (Street and Illegal Drag Racing) Amendment Bill	MMP	Govt	Wilson	2002	Yes	No	Land Transport (Unauthorised Street and Drag Racing) Amendment Act 2003
12	Social Security (Long-term Residential Care) Amendment Bill	MMP	Govt	Wilson	2003	Yes	No	Social Security (Long-term Residential Care) Amendment Act 2006
13	Taxation (Annual Rates, GST, Trans-Tasman Imputation and Miscellaneous Provisons) Bill 2003	MMP	Govt	Hodgson	2003	Yes	No	Taxation (GST, Trans-Tasman Imputation and Miscellaneous Provisions) Act 2003; Taxation (Annual Rates of Income Tax Bill 2003–2004) Act 2003; Student Loan

II. Government bills		Vote	Type	AG	Year	Passed	Amended*	Act(s)
								Scheme Amendment Act (No. 2) 2003; Child Support Amendment Act (No.2) 2003
14	Care of Children Bill	MMP	Govt	Wilson	2003	Yes	No	Care of Children Act 2004
15	Parole (Extended Supervision) and Sentencing Amendment Bill	MMP	Govt	Wilson	2003	Yes	No	Parole (Extended Supervision) Amendment Act 2004 and Sentencing Amendment Act 2004
16	Future Directions (Working for Families) Bill	MMP	Govt	Wilson	2004	Yes	No	Social Security (Working for Families) Amendment Act 2004; Taxation (Working for Families) Act 2004
17	Relationships (Statutory References) Bill	MMP	Govt	Wilson	2004	Yes	No	Relationships (Statutory Reference) Act 2005; Adminstration Amendment Act 2005; Care of Children Amendment Act 2005; Child Support Amendment Act 2005; Deaths by Accidents Compensation Act 2005; Estates and Gift Duties Amendment Act 2005; Goods and Servies Tax Amendment Act 2005; Government Superannuation Fund Amendment Act 2005; Income Tax Amendment Act 2005; Injury, Prevention, Rehabilitation, and Compensation Amendment Act 2005; Interpretation Amendment Act 2005; Life Insurance Amendment Act 2005;

								Marriage Amendment Act 2005; Minors' Contracts Amendment Act 2005; New Zealand Superannuation Amendment Act 2005; Parental Leave and Employment Protection Act 2005; Property (Relationships) Amendment Act 2005; Real Estate Agents Amendment Act 2005; Social Security Amendment Act 2005; Tax Administration Amendment Act 2005; Trustee Amendment Act 2005; War Pensions Amendment Act 2005; Wills Amendment Act 2005
18	Criminal Procedure Bill	MMP	Govt	Wilson	2004	Yes	No	Crimes Amendment Act (no 2) 2008; Criminal Disclosure Act 2008; District Courts Amend Act (No 2) 2008; Juries Amendment Act 2008; Summary Proceedings Amendment Act (No 2) 2008; Victims' Rights Amendment Act 2008
19	Misuse of Drugs (Classification of BZP) Amendment Bill	MMP	Govt	Cullen	2007	Yes	No	Misuse of Drugs (Classification of BZP) Amendment Act 2008
20	Criminal Investigations (Bodily Samples) Amendment Bill	MMP	Govt	Finlayson	2009	Yes	No	Criminal Investigations (Bodily Samples) Amendment Act 2009
21	Sentencing and Parole Reform Bill	MMP	Govt	Finlayson	2009	Yes	No	Sentencing and Parole Reform Act 2010
22	Parole (Extended Supervision Orders) Amendment Bill	MMP	Govt	Finlayson	2009	Yes	No	Parole (Extended Supervision Orders) Amendment Act 2009
23	Misuse of Drugs Amendment Bill	MMP	Govt	Finlayson	2010	Yes	No	Misuse of Drugs Amendment Act (No 2) 2011
24	Criminal Procedure (Reform and Modernization) Bill	MMP	Govt	Finlayson	2010	Yes	No	Criminal Procedure Act 2011; Bail Amendment Act 2011; Children, Young

II. Government bills		Vote	Type	AG	Year	Passed	Amended*	Act(s)
								Persons, and Their Families Act (No 2) 2011; Corrections Amendment Act 2011; Crimes Amendment Act (No 4) 2011; Criminal Disclosure Amendment Act 2011; Criminal Procedure (Mentally Impaired Persons) Amendment Act 2011; District Courts Amendment Act (No 2) 2011; Evidence Amendment Act 2011; Juries Amendment Act 2011; Justices of the Peace Amendment Act 2011; New Zealand Bill of Rights Amendment Act 2011; Sentencing Amendment Act (No 2) 2011; Summary Proceedings Amendment Act (No 2) 2011; Victims' Rights Amendment Act 2011
25	New Zealand Bill of Rights Act section 24(e) Amendment Bill	MMP	Govt	Finlayson	2010	Yes	No	New Zealand Bill of Rights Amendment Act 2011
26	Social Assistance (New Work Tests, Incentives, and Obligations) Amendment Bill	MMP	Govt	Finlayson	2010	Yes	No	Children, Young Persons, and Their Families Amendment Act 2010; Education Amendment Act (No 2) 2010; Taxation (Definitions of Dependent Child) Act 2010; Social Security (New Work Tests, Incentives, and Obligations) Amendment Act 2010; War Pensions Amendment Act (No 2) 2010

27	Alcohol Reform Bill	MMP	Govt	Finlayson	2010	Yes	No	Sale and Supply of Alcohol Act 2012; Local Government (Alcohol Reform) Amendment Act 2012; Summary Offences (Alcohol Reform) Amendment Act 2012
28	New Zealand Public Health and Disability Amendment Bill (No2) 2013	MMP	Govt	Finlayson	2013	Yes	No	New Zealand Public Health and Disability Amendment Act (No2) 2013
29	Taxation (Income-sharing Tax Credit) Bill	MMP	Govt	Finlayson	2010	In progress		
30	Prisoners' and Victims' Claims (redirecting Prisoner Compensation) Amendment Bill	MMP	Govt	Finlayson	2011	In progress		
31	Land Transport Admendment Bill	MMP	Govt	Finlayson	2013	In progress		
32	Parole (Extended Supervision Orders) Amendment Bill	MMP	Govt	Finlayson	2014	In progress		

*Whether amended to address NZBORA concerns raised by the Attorney General's section 7 report.

BIBLIOGRAPHY

Parliamentary and Government Documents

Cabinet Office (United Kingdom) 1987. 'The Judge Over Your Shoulder: Judicial Review of Administrative Decisions'. (MPO) Training Division. London: Cabinet Office

Cabinet Office (New Zealand) 2008. Department of the Prime Minister and Cabinet. *Cabinet Manual 2008*. Wellington, New Zealand. cabinetmanual.cabinetoffice.govt.nz

Cabinet Office (United Kingdom) 2014. 'Guidelines for Making Legislation' (July). https://www.gov.uk/government/uploads/system/uploads/attachment_data/file/328408/Guide_to_Making_Legislation_July_2014.pdf

Civil Partnership Bill 2004. Stonewall Briefing, House of Lords, Consideration of Commons Amendments (7 November). www.stonewall.org.uk/documents/Lords_Consideration_LLD.doc

Conway, Lorraine, and Catherine Fairbairn 2004. 'The Civil Partnership Bill (HL): background and debate'. House of Commons Library, Research Paper 04/64 (7 September).

Council of Europe, Committee of Ministers 2009. 'Execution of the Judgment of the European Court of Human Rights Hirst Against the United Kingdom No. 2', Interim Resolution CM/ResDH. wcd.coe.int/wcd/ViewDoc.jsp?id=1556821&Site=CM

2010. 'Communication on the Activities of the Committee of Ministers, Report by the Chair of the Committee of Ministers to the Parliamentary Assembly', CM/AS(2010)7 rev, 4 October. wcd.coe.int/wcd/ViewDoc.jsp?id=1678647&Site=CM&BackColorInternet=C3C3C3&BackColorIntranet=EDB021&BackColorLogged=F5D383

2011. 'Communication from the Government in the Case of Hirst No. 2 Against the United Kingdom' (Application No. 74025/01) 1 March. https://wcd.coe.int/ViewDoc.jsp?id=1753877&Site=CM

Crown Law Office (New Zealand) 1992. 'Rights of Prisoners to Vote' (17 November). www.crownlaw.govt.nz/uploads/Prisoners.pdf

Department for Constitutional Affairs (United Kingdom) 2006. 'Guidance Section 19 statements: Revised Guidance for Departments', www.humanrights.gov.uk/guidance/guide-updated.htm

2006. 'Review of the Human Rights Act' (July). www.webarchive.nationalarchives.gov.uk/+/http:/www.dca.gov.uk/peoples-rights/human-rights/pdf

Department of Corrections (New Zealand) 2010. 'Electoral (Disqualification of Convicted Prisoners) Amendment Bill', *Initial Briefing for the Law and Order Committee* (26 June). www.parliament.nz/resource/0000129281

2010. 'Electoral (Disqualification of Convicted Prisoners) Amendment Bill', *Departmental Report for the Law and Order Committee* (16 August). www.parliament.nz/resource/0000129277

2013. Regulatory Impact Statement—Enhanced Extended Supervision Orders (21 November). www.treasury.govt.nz/publications/informationreleases/ris/pdfs/ris-corr-ees-apr14.pdf

Department of Justice (New Zealand) 1992. Consistency Between the Bill of Rights Act 1990 and Restrictions on Prisoners' Voting Rights (17 November). www.crownlaw.govt.nz/uploads/Prisoners.pdf

Department of Trade and Industry (United Kingdom) 2004. 'Landmark Bill for Same-sex Couples Published', P/2004/129

2012. Women and Equality Unit, Sexual Orientation. www.equalities.gov.uk/lgbt/what_done.htm

Expert Advisory Committee on Drugs 2003. 'Advice to the Minister of Health on Pseudoephedrine', Government of New Zealand (June). www.ndp.govt.nz/moh.nsf/pagescm/569/$File/eacdpseudoephedrine.pdf

2003. 'Advice to the Minister of Health on Ephedrine', Government of New Zealand (November). www.ndp.govt.nz/moh.nsf/pagescm/569/$File/eacdephedrine.pdf

2004. 'The Expert Advisory Committee on Drugs (EACD) Advice to the Minister on Benzylpiperazine (BZP)', Government of New Zealand (April). www.ndp.govt.nz/moh.nsf/pagescm/569/$File/eacdbzp.pdf

2006. 'Report for the Ministry of Health: The Benzylpiperazine (BZP)/Trifluoromethylphenylpiperazine (TFMPP) and Alcohol Safety Study', Government of New Zealand (24 November). www.ndp.govt.nz/moh.nsf/indexcm/ndp-publications-bzp-tfmpp-alcohol-safety-study/$File/bzp-report-08.pdf

2006. 'Advice to the Minister on Benzylpiperazine (BZP)', Government of New Zealand (9 December). www.ndp.govt.nz/moh.nsf/Files/ndp-advice-docs/$file/bzp-eacd-dec-2006.pdf

2009. 'Classification of Pseudoephedrine and Ephedrine Under the Misuse of Drugs Act 1975', Government of New Zealand (15 July). www.ndp.govt.nz/moh.nsf/Files/ndp-advice-docs/$file/advice-to-minister-pseudoephedrineandephedrine-july-2009.pdf

2009. 'EACD Recommendations in Relation to Pseudoephedrine and Ephedrine', Government of New Zealand (6 November). www.ndp.govt.nz/moh.nsf/Files/ndp-advice-docs/$file/advice-to-minister-pseudoephedrine-and-ephedrine-nov09.pdf

European Commission 2003. 'Party Political Broadcasting: Report and Recommendations (January)'. www.electoralcommission.org.uk/about-us/ppb.cfm

Government Equalities Office 2012. 'Equal Civil Marriage: A Consultation' (15 March).

Government of the United Kingdom 2011. 'Draft Enhanced Terrorism Prevention and Investigation Measures Bill', Cm 8166 (September). www.gov.uk/government/uploads/system/uploads/attachment_data/file/98424/etpim-draft-bill.pdf

Home, Alexander 2012. 'Justice and Security Bill: Bill No 99 2012–13', Research Paper 12/80, House of Commons Library (14 December).

Home Office (United Kingdom) 1997. 'Rights Brought Home: The Human Bill of Rights', Cm 3782.

2005. 'Community and Race: Frequently Asked Questions'. www.webarchive.nationalarchives.gov.uk/+/www.homeoffice.gov.uk/comrace/identitycards/faq.html#2

2007. 'Pre-charge Detention of Terrorist Suspects' (December). www.loc.gov/law/help/uk-pre-charge-detention.php

2010. 'Written Ministerial Statement on Control Orders: 11 March–10 June 2010'. www.homeoffice.gov.uk/publications/written-ministerial-statement/control-orders-june2010-wms/?view=Standard&pubID=818801

Horne, Alexander and Gavin Berman 2012. 'Pre-Charge Detention in Terrorism Cases', House of Commons Library (15 March) SN/HA/5364.

Hunt, M., H. Hooper and P. Yowell, 'Parliaments and Human Rights. Redressing the Democratic Deficit', AHRC Public Policy Series No. 5, 24, www.ahrc.ac.uk/News-and-Events/Publications/Documents/Parliaments-and-Human-Rights.pdf

Legislation Advisory Committee (New Zealand) 2012. 'Legislation Advisory Committee Annual Report', Government of New Zealand. www2.justice.govt.nz/lac/pubs/2012/LAC_Annual_Report_2012.pdf

Lord MacDonald 2011. 'Review of Counter-Terrorism and Security Powers: A Report by Lord Macdonald of River Glaven QC', (January) Cm 8003.

Miller, Vaughne 2011. 'European Court of Human Rights Rulings: Are There Options for Governments?', House of Commons Library, SN/IA/5941 (18 April) www.parliament.uk/briefingpapers/commons/lib/research/briefings/snia-05941.pdf

Ministry of Health (New Zealand) 2009. 'Advice to the Expert Advisory Committee on Drugs on: The Presumption of Supply of Pseudoephedrine and Ephedrine', Government of New Zealand (October). www.ndp.govt.nz/moh.nsf/Files/ndp-advice-docs/$file/advice-to-eacd-pseudoephedrineandephedrine-october-2009.pdf

2010. 'Regulating and Controlling Drugs: Ministry of Health Submission to the Law Commission' (April). www.parliament.nz/resource/0000138330

2011. 'Controlling and Regulating Drugs—A Review of the Misuse of Drugs Act 1975', Government Response to the Law Commission's Report (8 September). www.health.govt.nz/about-ministry/legislation-and-regulation/regulatory-impact-statements/government-response-law-commissions-report-controlling-and-regulating-drugs-review-misuse-drugs-act

Ministy of Justice (New Zealand) 2002. 'Sentencing Act 2002 Parole Act 2002' (May). www.justice.govt.nz/publications/publications-archived/2002/sentencing-act-2002/sentencing-act-2002

2002. 'How Does the Legislation Respond to the 1999 Referendum on Criminal Justice?', Sentencing Act 2002. www.justice.govt.nz/publications/publications-archived/2002/sentencing-act-2002/how-does-the-legislation-respond-to-the-1999-referendum-on-criminal-justice

2004. 'The Guidelines on the New Zealand Bill of Rights Act 1990: A Guide to the Rights and Freedoms in the Bill of Rights Act for the Public Sector'. www.justice.govt.nz/publications/global-publications/t/the-guidelines-on-the-new-zealand-bill-of-rights-act-1990-a-guide-to-the-rights-and-freedoms-in-the-bill-of-rights-act-for-the-public-sector

2009. 'Criminal Investigations (Bodily Samples) Amendment Bill—Initial Briefing' (28 April). www.parliament.nz/en-nz/pb/sc/documents/advice/49SCJE_ADV_00DBHOH_BILL9027_1_A29076/initial-briefing

2009. 'Initial Briefing to Law and Order Select Committee', Sentencing and Parole Reform Bill. (29 April). www.parliament.nz/NR/rdonlyres/601496A6-8045-414C-9357-8C50C226C4FB/125958/49SCLO_ADV_00DBHOH_BILL9040_1_A15563_Initialbriefi.pdf

2009. 'Criminal Investigations (Bodily Samples) Amendment Bill—Additional Information' (18 June). www.parliament.nz/en-nz/pb/sc/documents/advice/49SCJE_ADV_00DBHOH_BILL9027_1_A29079/ministry-of-justice-additional-information

2009. 'Sentencing and Parole Reform Bill—Initial Briefing to the Law and Order Committee' (29 April). www.parliament.nz/en-nz/pb/sc/documents/advice/49SCLO_ADV_00DBHOH_BILL9040_1_A15563/initial-briefing

2009. 'Departmental Report for the Justice and Electoral Committee. Criminal Investigations (Bodily Samples) Amendment Bill' (18 June).

Ministry of Justice (United Kingdom) 2006. 'Voting Rights of Convicted Prisoners Detained within the United Kingdom', CP29/06.

2010. 'Responding to Human Rights Judgment: Report of the Joint Committee on Human Rights on the Government's Response to Human Rights Judgments 2010–11', Cm 8162.

2011. 'Justice and Security Green Paper', Cm 8194.

2012. 'Voting Eligibility (Prisoners) Draft Bill', Cm 8499.

2012. 'The Commission on a Bill of Rights, A UK Bill of Rights? The Choice Before Us', (18 December). www.justice.gov.uk/cbr/index.htm

New Zealand Human Rights Commission 2009. 'Submission of the Human Rights Commission on Criminal Investigations (Bodily Samples) Amendment Bill to the Justice and Electoral Committee' (6 April). www.parliament.nz/resource/0000088692

2009. 'Submission of the Human Rights Commission on Sentencing and Parole Reform Bill' (24 April). www.parliament.nz/en-nz/pb/sc/documents/evidence/49SCLO_EVI_00DBHOH_BILL9040_1_A21935/human-rights-commission

2010. 'Sentencing and Parole Reform Bill' (5 March). www.hrc.co.nz/hrc_new/hrc/cms/files/documents/19-Mar-2010_15–38-41_Sentencing_and_Parole_Reform_Submission_2__Final.pdf

2010. 'Electoral (Disqualification of Convicted Prisoners) Bill', Submission by the Human Rights Commission to the Law and Order Committee (11 June). www.parliament.nz/resource/0000112104

2010. 'Misuse of Drugs Amendment Bill', Submission by the Human Rights Commission to the Health Committee. (27 September). www.parliament.nz/resource/0000129898

New Zealand Law Commission 2010. 'Controlling and Regulating Drugs', Issue Paper 16 (11 February). www.lawcom.govt.nz/sites/default/files/publications/2010/02/Publication_143_455_IP16%20-%20Controlling%20and%20Regulating%20Drugs.pdf

2011. 'Controlling and Regulating Drugs', *A Review of the Misuse of Drugs Act* 1975 (3 May). www.lawcom.govt.nz/project/review-misuse-drugs-act-1975/publication/report/2011/controlling-and-regulating-drugs-review

New Zealand Law Society 2003. 'Submissions on Parole (Extended Supervision) and Sentencing Amendment Bill'. www.lawsociety.org.nz/news-and-communications/law-reform-submissions/submissions-on-bills

2009. 'Submission on Criminal Investigations (Bodily Samples) Amendment Bill' (3 April). www.parliament.nz/en-nz/pb/sc/documents/evidence/49SCJE_EVI_00DBHOH_BILL9027_1_A28808/new-zealand-law-society

2010. 'Submission on Sentencing and Parole Reform Bill (Revised)'. www.lawsociety.org.nz/__data/assets/pdf_file/0018/20817/sentencing-and-parole-reform-bill.pdf

2010. 'Submission on Sentencing and Parole Reform Bill' (23 March). www.lawsociety.org.nz/news-and-communications/law-reform-submissions/submissions-on-bills

2010. 'Submission on Electoral (Disqualification of Convicted Prisoners) Amendment Bill 2010' (16 June). www.parliament.nz/resource/0000112144

New Zealand Law Society (Human Rights and Privacy Committee) 2013. 'Submission to the 18th Session of the Human Rights Council—Shadow Report to New Zealand's 2nd Universal Periodic Review' (17 June), 3–5. www.lawsociety.org.nz/__data/assets/pdf_file/0006/68541/United-Nations,-Universal-Periodic-Review-17–6-13.pdf

New Zealand Parliamentary Library 2003. 'Bills Digest No. 1039—Parole (Extended Supervision) and Sentencing Amendment Bill 2003' (11 November). www.parliament.nz/resource/0000013603

2003. 'Bills Digest No. 1115—Parole (Extended Supervision) and Sentencing Amendment Bill 2003' (14 June). www.parliament.nz/resource/0000016538

2009. 'Bills Digest No. 1675—Parole (Extended Supervision Orders) Amendment Bill' (02 April). www.parliament.nz/en-nz/pb/legislation/bills/digests/49PLLawBD16751/parole-extended-supervision-orders-amendment-bill-2009

New Zealand Police Association 2009. 'Criminal Investigations (Bodily Samples) Amendment Bill'. Submission of the New Zealand Police Association. Submitted to the Justice and Electoral Committee (6 April). www.parliament.nz/en-nz/pb/sc/documents/evidence/49SCJE_EVI_00DBHOH_-BILL9027_1_A28800/new-zealand-police-association

New Zealand Police 2010. 'Changes to the Sentencing and Parole Reform Bill. Presentation to the Law and Order Committee' (17 February). www.parliament.nz/en-nz/pb/sc/documents/advice/49SCLO_ADV_00DBHOH_BILL9040_1_A35171/nz-police-briefing-on-proposed-amendments-100215

2010. 'Sentencing and Parole Reform Bill—Departmental Report' (12 March). www.parliament.nz/en-nz/pb/sc/documents/advice/49SCLO_ADV_00DBHOH_BILL9040_1_A38119/departmental-report-100312

New Zealand Privacy Commissioner 2009. 'Criminal Investigations (Bodily Samples) Amendment Bill. Submission by the Privacy Commissioner to the Justice and Electoral Committee' (6 April). www.parliament.nz/en-nz/pb/sc/documents/evidence/49SCJE_EVI_00DBHOH_BILL9027_1_A28788/privacy-commissioner-supp-1

New Zealand Treasury 2009. Regulatory Impact Statement. Sentencing and Parole Reform Bill (February). www.justice.govt.nz/publications/global-publications/c/cabinet-papers-relating-to-the-sentencing-and-parole-reform-bill/documents/Paper-2.pdf

Office of Hon. Judith Collins 2010. 'Letter to Sandra Goudie MP, Chair, Law and Order Committee' (19 January). www.parliament.nz/en-nz/pb/sc/documents/advice/49SCLO_ADV_00DBHOH_BILL9040_1_A30868/advisors-and-changes-to-the-bill-hon-judith-collins-100119

Office of the Clerk of the House of Representatives (New Zealand) 2009. 'Criminal Investigations (Bodily Samples) Amendment Bill:

Summary of Submissions' (7 May) www.parliament.nz/en-nz/pb/sc/documents/advice/49SCJE_ADV_00DBHOH_BILL9027_1_A28954/summary-of-submissions

Office of the Minister of Justice (New Zealand) 2008. 'Cabinet Business Committee. No Parole for Worst Repeat Offenders and Worst Murder Cases (5 December). www.justice.govt.nz/publications/global-publications/c/cabinet-papers-relating-to-the-sentencing-and-parole-reform-bill/documents/Paper-3.pdf

2008. 'Cabinet. Sentencing and Parole Reform Bill: Approval for Introduction' (11 December). www.justice.govt.nz/publications/global-publications/c/cabinet-papers-relating-to-the-sentencing-and-parole-reform-bill/documents/Paper-4.pdf

2009. 'Cabinet. Final Approval for Introduction of Sentencing and Parole Reform Bill' (20 January). www.justice.govt.nz/publications/global-publications/c/cabinet-papers-relating-to-the-sentencing-and-parole-reform-bill/documents/Paper-6.pdf

2009. 'Cabinet Business Committee. Final Approval for Introduction of Sentencing and Parole Reform Bill' (22 January). www.justice.govt.nz/publications/global-publications/c/cabinet-papers-relating-to-the-sentencing-and-parole-reform-bill/documents/Paper-5.pdf

2009. 'Cabinet Domestic Policy Committee. Worst Repeat Violent Offender Policy' (5 February). www.justice.govt.nz/publications/global-publications/c/cabinet-papers-relating-to-the-sentencing-and-parole-reform-bill/documents/Paper-7.pdf

2009. 'Cabinet. Sentencing and Parole Reform Bill: Final Approval for Introduction' (12 February). www.justice.govt.nz/publications/global-publications/c/cabinet-papers-relating-to-the-sentencing-and-parole-reform-bill/documents/Paper-8.pdf

Parker, David 2005. 'The Attorney General's Reporting Function Under Section 7 of the New Zealand Bill of Rights Act 1990'. www.justice.org.nz/policy-and-consultation/legislation/bill-of-rights/the-attorney-generals-reporting-function-under-section-7-of-the-new-zealand-bill-of-rights-act-1990

Parliament of New Zealand 1985. 'A Bill of Rights for New Zealand—A White Paper'. New Zealand, House of Representatives.

1986. 'Towards a Better Democracy', Report of the Royal Commission on the Electoral System (December 1986). www.elections.org.nz/sites/default/files/bulk-upload/documents/Royal%20Commission%20Report%20Contents.pdf

1987. Justice and Law Reform Select Committee. 'Inquiry into the White Paper—A Bill of Rights for New Zealand'. New Zealand: House of Representatives.

1987. Interim Report of the Justice and Law Reform Select Committee. 'Inquiry into the White Paper—A Bill of Rights for New Zealand'. Second Session, Forty-First Parliament (July).

1988. Final Report of the Justice and Law Reform Committee. '*A White Paper on a Bill of Rights for New Zealand*'. New Zealand: House of Representatives.

1989. 'New Zealand Parliamentary Debates' (Hansard). (10 October). Wellington: Government Printer.

1990. 'New Zealand Parliamentary Debates' (Hansard). Volume 509 (10 July to 21 August). Wellington: Government Printer.

2003. Parole (Extended Supervision) and Sentencing Amendment Bill 2003. Explanatory Note. www.parliament.nz/resource/0000058455

2004. Parole (Extended Supervision) and Sentencing Amendment Bill. As reported from the Justice and Electoral Committee (14 June). www.parliament.nz/resource/0000019160

2005. Misuse of Drugs Amendment Bill (No 3). As reported from the Health Committee (23 May) www.parliament.nz/NR/rdonlyres/59D9ADFB-A51C-44A1-9B42-653870594D1C/48118/DBSCH_SCR_3118_31693.pdf

2007. Misuse of Drugs (Classification of BZP) Amendment Bill 2007. Report of the Health Committee (15 November). www.parliament.nz/NR/rdonlyres/4F36FA79-8AD6-4845-B3EC-179DAD6AAAB0/94014/DBSCH_SCR_3903_6327.pdf

2008. 'Standing Orders of the House of Representatives 2008'. www.parliament.nz/NR/rdonlyres/81D0893A-FFF2-47A3-9311-6358590BEB3D/100828/standingorders2008_5.pdf

2009. Criminal Investigations (Bodily Samples) Amendment Bill. Explanatory Note. www.legislation.govt.nz/act/public/2013/0112/latest/versions.aspx

2009. Sentencing and Parole Reform Bill. Explanatory Note. www.legislation.govt.nz/bill/government/2009/0017/11.0/DLM1845301.html

2009. Parole (Extended Supervision Orders) Amendment Bill. Explanatory Note. www.legislation.govt.nz/bill/government/2009/0024/latest/whole.html

2009. Criminal Investigations (Bodily Samples) Amendment Bill. As reported from the Justice and Electoral Committee (24 August). www.parliament.nz/en-nz/pb/sc/documents/reports/49DBSCH_SCR4477_1/criminal-investigations-bodily-samples-amendment-bill

2009. Sentencing and Parole Reform Bill. Explanatory Note. www.legislation.govt.nz/bill/government/2009/0017/11.0/DLM1845301.html

2009. Sentencing and Parole Reform Bill. As reported from the Law and Order Committee. www.parliament.nz/en-nz/pb/sc/documents/reports/49DBSCH_SCR4671_1/sentencing-and-parole-reform-bill-17-2-and-petition-20084

2010. Electoral (Disqualification of Convicted Prisoners) Amendment Bill. Explanatory Note (10 February) www.legislation.govt.nz/bill/member/2010/0117/3.0/DLM2739702.html

2010. Sentencing and Parole Reform Bill. As reported from the Law and Order Committee (26 March). www.parliament.nz/NR/rdonlyres/B3CC33ED-81B0-4E4B-A7F3-DC8E0DA5889E/137271/DBSCH_SCR_4671_SentencingandParoleReformBill172and.pdf

2010. Sentencing and Parole Reform Bill. As reported by the Law and Order Committee (26 March). www.parliament.nz/en-nz/pb/sc/documents/reports/49DBSCH_SCR4671_1/sentencing-and-parole-reform-bill-17–2-and-petition-20084

2010. Electoral (Disqualification of Convicted Prisoners) Amendment Bill. As Reported from the Law and Order Committee (17 September). www.legislation.govt.nz/bill/member/2010/0117/latest/DLM2739702.html

2010. Misuse of Drugs Amendment Bill. Report of the Health Committee (November 29). www.parliament.nz/resource/0000166941

2011. 'Standing Orders of the House of Representatives'. www.parliament.nz/en-NZ/PB/Rules/StOrders/b/a/e/00HOHPBReferenceStOrders3-Standing-Orders-of-the-House-of-Representatives.htm

Parliament of the United Kingdom 2000. 'Local Government Bill, (Session 1999–2000)', House of Commons. //www.publications.parliament.uk/pa/cm199900/cmbills/087/2000087.htm

2002. House of Commons Library. 'The Relationships (Civil Registration) Bill and the Civil Partnerships Bill', Research Paper 02/17 (19 March).

2005. House of Commons Library. 'The Identity Cards Bill, Bill 9 of 2005–06', Research Paper 05/43.

2010. House of Commons Library. 'Identity Documents Bill', Research Paper 10/41 (4 June).

2012. House of Commons Library. 'Justice and Security Bill', Research Paper 12/80 (14 December).

2012. House of Lords. Reform Bill 2012–13, Explanatory Notes, Bill 52 –EN. www.publications.parliament.uk/pa/bills/cbill/2012–2013/0052/en/13052en.htm

Report of the Attorney General under the New Zealand Bill of Rights Act 1990 on the Criminal Investigations (Bodily Samples) Amendment Bill 2009. www.parliament.nz/en-nz/pb/presented/papers/49DBHOH_PAP17701_1/attorney-general-report-of-the-under-the-new-zealand

Report of the Attorney General under the New Zealand Bill of Rights Act 1990 on the Eden Trust Amendment Bill. www.parliament.nz/NR/rdonlyres/6840F27A-8200–432A-AA61-4B7FC25E8FF8/101713/DBHOH_PAP_17966_6596.pdf

Report of the Attorney General under the New Zealand Bill of Rights Act 1990 on the Electoral (Disqualification of Convicted Prisoners) Amendment Bill 2010. www.parliament.nz/NR/rdonlyres/AD4ED20E-03EA-4186-B2C1-FF985E92ED38/131504/DBHOH_PAP_19503_AttorneyGeneralReportoftheunderthe.pdf

Report of the Attorney General under the New Zealand Bill of Rights Act 1990 on the Misuse of Drugs (Classification of BZP) Amendment Bill 2007. www.parliament.nz/en-NZ/PB/Presented/Papers/d/6/a/48DBHOH_PAP15548_1-Attorney-General-Report-of-the-under-the-New-Zealand.htm

Report of the Attorney General under the New Zealand Bill of Rights Act 1990 on the Misuse of Drugs Amendment Bill 2010. www.parliament.nz/en-NZ/PB/Presented/Papers/4/7/c/49DBHOH_PAP19705_1-Attorney-General-Report-of-the-under-the-New-Zealand.htm

Report of the Attorney General under the New Zealand Bill of Rights Act 1990 on the Parole (Extended Supervision) and Sentencing Amendment Bill 2003. www.parliament.nz/en-NZ/PB/Presented/Papers/5/3/0/47DBHOH_PAP9852_1-Attorney-General-Report-under-the-New-Zealand-Bill.htm

Report of the Attorney General under the New Zealand Bill of Rights Act 1990 on the Parole (Extended Supervision Orders) Amendment Bill 2009. www.parliament.nz/en-nz/pb/presented/papers/49DBHOH_PAP17945_1/attorney-general-report-of-the-under-the-new-zealand

Report of the Attorney General under the New Zealand Bill of Rights Act 1990 on the Parole (Extended Supervision Orders) Amendment Bill 2014. www.parliament.nz/en-nz/pb/presented/papers/50DBHOH_PAP26129_1/attorney-general-report-of-the-under-the-new-zealand

Report of the Attorney General under the New Zealand Bill of Rights Act 1990 on the Sentence and Parole Reform Bill 2009. www.parliament.nz/en-nz/pb/presented/papers/49DBHOH_PAP17759_1/attorney-general-interim-report-of-the-under-the-new

Scott, Edward 2013. 'Marriage (Same Sex Couples) Bill (HL Bill 29 of 2013–14)', House of Lords Library Note, LLN 2013/011.

Secretary of State for the Home Department (United Kingdom) 2004. 'Reconciling Security and Liberty in an Open Society', Cm 6147.

Sensible Sentencing Trust. 2009. 'Submission on the Sentencing and Parole Reform Bill'. www.safe-nz.org.nz/Submissions/sprbjwalsh.htm

Sensible Sentencing Trust Nelson 2010. 'Sentencing and Parole Reform Bill' (3 March). www.parliament.nz/en-nz/pb/sc/documents/evidence/49SCLO_EVI_00DBHOH_BILL9040_1_A37589/sensible-sentencing-trust-nelson

Thorp, Arbella 2000. 'The Local Government Bill [HL]: The "Section 28" Debate', House of Commons Library, Research Paper 00/47 (6 April).

Tobin, James 2011. 'Terrorism Prevention and Investigation Measures Bill (HL Bill 91 of 2010–12)', House of Lords, Library Notice, (19 September) LLN 2011/027.

White, Isobel, and Vaughne Miller 2011. 'Prisoners' Voting Rights', House of Commons Library, SN/PC/01764 (8 March).

'Rights Brought Home', Preface by the Prime Minister, 1987, Cm 3782.

Party Documents

ACT New Zealand 2011. 'Law and Order'. www.act.org.nz/policies/law-and-order

2002. 'Policy 2002: Our Vision'. Accessed at https://manifesto-project.wzb.eu/countries/New%20Zealand

Brash, Don 2011. 'Law and Order: Protecting New Zealanders from Crime', transcript, ACT New Zealand, ACT Party Speech (25 September) Waipuna Lodge, Auckland. www.act.org.nz/posts/law-and-order-protecting-new-zealanders-from-crime

British Labour Party 1970. *Charter of Human Rights*. British Labour Party

1992. Labour Party Manifesto, 1992, 'It's Time to get Britain Working Again'. www.politicsresources.net/area/uk/man/lab92.htm1992

Cabinet Office (New Zealand) 2012. 'National-led Administration: Consultation and Operating Arrangements', Circular (01 May). www.dpmc.govt.nz/cabinet/circulars/co12/3

Clark, Helen 1999. 'Coalition Agreement between Labour and the Alliance', transcript, Speech notes and Coalition Agreement, *Scoop: Parliament* (06 December). www.scoop.co.nz/stories/PA9912/S00021.htm

Coalition Agreement 2002. *Coalition Agreement*, Labour and Progressive Coalition Parties in Parliament (08 August). www.beehive.govt.nz/sites/all/files/ACF1BA.pdf

Confidence and Supply Agreement 2002. *Confidence and Supply Agreement*, Labour/Progressive and United Future (08 August). www.beehive.govt.nz/sites/all/files/conf-and-supply-govt-and-UF.pdf

2005. *Confidence and Supply Agreement*, New Zealand Labour and New Zealand First (17 October). www.beehive.govt.nz/sites/all/files/NZFirst.pdf

2005. *Confidence and Supply Agreement*, New Zealand Labour and United Future (17 October). www.beehive.govt.nz/sites/all/files/United.pdf

2008. *Confidence and Supply Agreement*, National and United Future (14 November). www.national.org.nz/files/agreements/National-UF_agreement.pdf

2008. *Confidence and Supply Agreement*, National and ACT New Zealand (14 November). www.national.org.nz/files/agreements/National-Act_Agreement.pdf

2008. *Confidence and Supply Agreement*, Relationship Accord, National and Māori Party. (16 November). www.national.org.nz/files/agreements/National-Maori_Party_agreement.pdf

2011. *Confidence and Supply Agreement*, National and ACT New Zealand (05 December). www.parliament.nz/NR/rdonlyres/5634F13B-7744–4D03-A9F9-EBB0E4F83621/207925/NationalACT_Confidence_and_Supply_Agreement0512201.pdf

2011. *Confidence and Supply Agreement*, National and United Future New Zealand (05 December). www.parliament.nz/NR/rdonlyres/5E74E888-B2FF-

4663-906D-C551BE4E252D/207945/United_Future_Confidence_and_Supply_Agreement05122.pdf

2011. *Confidence and Supply Agreement*, Relationship Accord, National and Māori Party. http://ourhouse.parliament.nz/NR/rdonlyres/268FB129-6DC2-4FCF-B3FE-281C4A473DAB/269075/RelationshipAccordandConfidenceandSupplyAgreementw.pdf

Conservative Party 1979. General Election Manifesto, 1979. www.margaretthatcher.org/document/110858

Labour Party 2005. 'Britain Forward Not Back: The Labour Party Manifesto 2005'. http://newsimg.bbc.co.uk/1/shared/bsp/hi/pdfs/LAB_uk_manifesto.pdf

Lindsay, Caron 2013. 'Secret Courts Now a Reality After Lords Amendments Fall – How Did Liberal Democrats Vote?' Liberal Democratic Voice (27 March). www.libdemvoice.org/secret-courts-now-a-reality-after-lords-amendments-fall-how-did-liberal-democrats-vote-33875.html

New Zealand First 2002. 'Keeping New Zealand First 2002'. https://manifesto-project.wzb.eu/countries/New%20Zealand

2011. 'New Zealand First Election Manifesto 2011'. https://manifesto-project.wzb.eu/countries/New%20Zealand

New Zealand Labour Party 2011. 'Labour Party Manifesto 2011 – Own Our Future'. https://www.labour.org.nz/sites/default/files/2011%20Labour%20Party%20Manifesto.pdf

New Zealand National Party 2008. 'National's Post-Election Action Plan 2008'. www.national.org.nz/web/post_election_action_plan.pdf

2011. 'Law & Order: Victims. Building a Safer New Zealand', *Policy* 2011. www.national.org.nz/files/2011/Victims_policy.pdf

2011. 'Law & Order: Protecting Communities. Building a Safer New Zealand', *Policy* 2011. www.national.org.nz/pdf_general/protecting_communities_policy.pdf

2011. 'Law & Order: Bail. Building a Safer New Zealand', Policy 2011. www.national.org.nz/PDF_General/Bail_policy.pdf

2011. 'National's Post-Election Action Plan 2011'. www.parliament.nz/resource/0001691449

Press Releases

Collins, Judith 2010. 'National and ACT Agree to Three-strikes Regime' (19 January) www.beehive.govt.nz/release/national-and-act-agree-three-strikes-regime

Goff, Phil 2001. 'Goff Introduces Sentencing and Parole Reform Bill' (7 August). www.beehive.govt.nz/node/11402

2003. 'Goff Unveils Supervision Regime for Sex Offenders' (11 November). www.beehive.govt.nz/node/18342

2004. 'Tougher Laws Driving Up Prison Population' (9 March). www.beehive.govt.nz/node/19112

2005. 'Tougher Laws, Better Policing Push Up Job Numbers' (23 January). www.beehive.govt.nz/node/22025

Lord Lester 2002. 'Press Release', The Odysseus Trust (8 February) www.odysseustrust.org/text/cpb/press.html

Rt. Hon. Tony Blair 2005. 'PM's Press Conference' (5 August) http://webarchive.nationalarchives.gov.uk/20040105034004/number10.gov.uk/page8041

Power, Simon 2009 'Government Closes Loopholes in Child-sex Law' (2 April) http://beehive.govt.nz/release/government-closes-loopholes-child-sex-law

2009 'Government Introduces Bill for Modern-day Fingerprint' (10 February) www.beehive.govt.nz/release/government-introduces-bill-modern-day-fingerprint

Tolley, Anne 2014. 'Extended Supervision Orders to be Expanded' (17 January 2014) www.beehive.govt.nz/release/extended-supervision-orders-be-expanded

Newspaper Articles

Anderson, Bruce 2001. 'Don't Pity Those Foreigners Who Exploit Our Generosity', *The Independent* (12 November) www.highbeam.com/doc/1P2–5206859.html.

Assinder, Nick 2006. 'Where Now for ID Cards?', *BBC News* (16 March). http://news.bbc.co.uk/2/hi/uk_news/politics/4804528.stm

BBC News 2000. 'Government Suffers s. 28 Defeat' (7 February) http://news.bbc.co.uk/2/hi/uk_news/politics/633778.stm

2000. 'Peers Vote to Keep Gay Ban' (24 July) http://news.bbc.co.uk/2/hi/uk_news/politics/849478.stm

2001. 'Anti-Terror Defeats for Government' (6 December) http://news.bbc.co.uk/2/hi/uk_news/politics/1696047.stm

2001. 'Labour MPs Rebel on Terror Bill' (22 November) http://news.bbc.co.uk/2/hi/uk_news/politics/1669175.stm

2003. 'Section 28 to be Repealed' (18 September) http://news.bbc.co.uk/2/hi/uk_news/politics/3120924.stm

2005. 'Howard Warns Judges Over Terror' (10 August) http://news.bbc.co.uk/1/hi/uk_politics/4136940.stm

2005. 'ID Card Scheme May Cost £18 bn' (29 May) http://news.bbc.co.uk/2/hi/uk_news/politics/4590817.stm

2005. 'Labour Survives ID Card Rebellion' (18 October) http://news.bbc.co.uk/2/hi/4354886.stm

2005. 'UK Criticized Over Human Rights' (8 June) http://news.bbc.co.uk/2/hi/uk_news/politics/4071968.stm

2005. 'Wilmshurst Resignation Letter' (24 March) www.globalpolicy.org/security/issues/iraq/attack/law/2005/0324wilmshurst.htm

2006. 'Lords Back Down on Glorification' (22 March) http://news.bbc.co.uk/2/hi/uk_news/politics/4834738.stm

2007. 'Smith Plans 42-day Terror Limit' (6 December) http://news.bbc.co.uk/1/hi/uk_politics/7130072.stm

2008. 'Brown Wins Crunch Vote on 42 Days' (11 June) http://news.bbc.co.uk/2/hi/uk_news/politics/7449268.stm

2009. 'Some Inmates to Get Voting Rights' (9 April) http://news.bbc.co.uk/2/hi/uk_news/politics/7992045.stm

2010. 'Coalition Faces Major Problem on Control Orders – Davis' (1 November) www.bbc.co.uk/news/uk-politics-11664408

2010. 'George Osborne Says Tories will "Consider Gay Marriage"' (11 April) http://news.bbc.co.uk/2/hi/uk_news/politics/election_2010/8614235.stm

2011. 'No Votes for Jailed Murderers and Rapists – Ken Clarke' (9 February) www.bbc.co.uk/news/uk-politics-12402704?print=true

2011. 'Prison Votes Will be Kept to a Minimum' (20 January) www.bbc.co.uk/news/uk-politics-12233938

2013.'Gay Marriage: MPs Back Bill despite Conservative Backbench Opposition' (5 February) www.bbc.co.uk/news/uk-politics-21346220

Bingham, John 2013. 'Gay Marriage Clears the House of Lords', *The Telegraph* (15 July) www.telegraph.co.uk/news/politics/10180552/Gay-marriage-clears-the-House-of-Lords.html

2013. 'Heterosexual Couples Challenge "Discriminatory" Civil Partnerships Bar', *The Telegraph* (16 February) www.telegraph.co.uk/news/uknews/law-and-order/9873404/Heterosexual-couples-challenge-discriminatory-civil-partnerships-bar.html

Brogan, Benedict 2001. 'Blunkett Puts War Before Concerns for Human Rights', *The Daily Telegraph* (24 September) www.telegraph.co.uk/news/uknews/1341426/Blunkett-puts-war-before-concerns-for-human-rights.html.

Brown, Colin 2007. 'MI5 Chief: Children are Being Taught to Become Terrorists', *The Independent* (6 November) www.independent.co.uk/news/uk/politics/mi5-chief-children-are-being-taught-to-become-terrorists-399171.html

Bowcott, Owen 2012. 'Secret Courts Plans Savaged in the House of Lords', *The Guardian* (21 November) www.guardian.co.uk/law/2012/nov/21/secret-courts-house-of-lords

2012. 'Votes for Prisoners: UK Told It Must Implement ECHR Decisions', *The Guardian* (11 December) www.theguardian.com/politics/2012/dec/10/votes-for-prisoners-uk-delaying-tactics/print

2013. 'Lib Dem Peer Attacks "Fairweather Friends" Who Quit Over Secret Courts', *The Guardian* (12 March) www.guardian.co.uk/politics/2013/mar/12/lib-dem-peer-secret-courts

2013. 'UK 'Should Leave Council of Europe' if it Defies Ruling on Prisoner Voting Rights', *The Guardian* (18 October) www.theguardian.com/politics/2013/oct/17/uk-council-of-europe-prisoner-votes-human-rights

Bowcott, Owen and Ian Cobain 2012. 'Ken Clarke Unsettled by Criticism of Secret Court Plan', *The Guardian* (6 March) www.guardian.co.uk/politics/2012/mar/06/ken-clarke-secret-courts-plan-criticised

Campbell, Duncan and Afua Hirsch 2008. 'Council of Europe report criticizes 42-day detention', *The Guardian* (1 October) www.guardian.co.uk/uk/2008/oct/01/civilliberties.justice/print

Carlin, Brenden, John Steele and Duncan Gardham 2005. 'Howard Attacks Courts on Terrorism', *The Telegraph* (16 August) www.telegraph.co.uk/news/uknews/1495880/Howard-attacks-courts-on-terrorism.html

Chakrabarti, Shami 2005. 'The Price of a Chilling and Counterproductive Recipe', *The Guardian* (8 August) www.guardian.co.uk/comment/story/0,,1544581,00.html

Charter, David 2005. 'Plastic Poll Tax Scheme May Haunt the Party', *The Times* (29 June) www.thetimes.co.uk/tto/news/uk/article1934761.ece

Cheng, Derek 2010. 'Upset MPs Stage Walkout', *The New Zealand Herald* (1 July) www.nzherald.co.nz/politics/news/article.cfm?c_id=280&objectid=10655608

2011. 'Ex PM: 'Fix It' Bill Oppressive', *The New Zealand Herald* (29 September) www.nzherald.co.nz/nz/news/article.cfm?c_id=1&objectid=10755129

Clegg, Nick 2007. 'This is a Fork in the Road', *The Guardian* (21 February) www.guardian.co.uk/commentisfree/2007/feb/21/comment.terrorism

Crossman, Gareth 2005. 'Terrorism Bill: Liberty's Briefing for Second Reading in the House of Lords', Liberty (November) www.liberty-human-rights.org.uk/pdfs/policy05/terrorism-bill-2nd-reading-lords.pdf

Daily Mail 2012. 'Cameron's Chance to Deliver for Britain' (23 May) www.dailymail.co.uk/debate/article-2148987/Prisoner-voting-rights-David-Camerons-chance-deliver-Britain.html?ito=feeds-newsxml

2012. 'Tories Turn Up Heat on Human Rights Act as Seven Former Ministers Call on Cameron to Repeal the Law' (5 December) www.dailymail.co.uk/news/article-2243161/Tories-turn-heat-Human-Rights-Act-seven-ministers-Cameron-repeal-law.html

Davies, Lizzy and Nicholas Watt 2012. 'David Cameron Defends Secret Courts and Surveillance Plans', *The Guardian* (4 April) www.guardian.co.uk/law/2012/apr/04/clarke-defends-secret-courts-plans-clegg

Dyer, Clare 2005. 'Law Lord Hits Back at Politicians After Attacks on Judges', *The Guardian* (15 September) http://politics.guardian.co.uk/homeaffairs/story/0,11026,1570247,00.html

Gibb, Frances 2003. 'Blunkett vs. the Bench: the Battle has Begun', *The Times* (4 May) http://business.timesonline.co.uk/tol/business/law/article1115351.ece

2012. 'Warning to Cameron on Prisoner Votes', *The Times* (2 November) www.thetimes.co.uk/tto/law/article3587961.ece

Gibb, Frances, and Philip Webster 2005. 'We Won't Heed Blair, Say Judges', *The Times* (28 July) www.thetimes.co.uk/tto/news/uk/article1936100.ece

Gillan, Audrey 2003. 'Section 28 Gone ... But Not Forgotten', *The Guardian* (17 November) www.guardian.co.uk/politics/2003/nov/17/uk.gayrights

Gower, Patrick 2009. 'Finlayson 'Just Doing My Duty' on Crime Bills', *The New Zealand Herald* (04 March) www.nzherald.co.nz/politics/news/article.cfm?c_id=280&objectid=10559835

The Guardian 2005. 'Terror Bill Rebellion Defeated by One Vote' (2 November) http://politics.guardian.co.uk/terrorism/story/0,15935,1607043,00.html

2006. 'MPs Again Reject Lords ID Card Amendments' (16 March) www.guardian.co.uk/politics/2006/mar/16/immigrationpolicy.idcards

2006. 'Cameron Calls for Repeal of Human Rights Act' (12 May) www.guardian.co.uk/politics/2006/may/12/immigrationpolicy.immigration

2009. 'Heterosexual Couple Begin Legal Fight After Being Refused Civil Part nership' (17 November) www.guardian.co.uk/lifeandstyle/2009/nov/24/heterosexual-couple-refused-civil-partnership

2012. 'Nick Clegg Demands Rethink on Secret Justice Plans' (4 April) www.guardian.co.uk/law/2012/apr/04/human-rights-committee-hidden-justice

2013. 'Campaigners United Against Secret Courts' (3 March) www.guardian.co.uk/law/2013/mar/03/justice-and-security-mi5

2013. 'Last-ditch Bid to Dilute Secret Courts Plan Fails' (27 March) www.guardian.co.uk/law/2013/mar/27/secret-courts-plan-fails

Hartevelt, John and Ian Steward 2010. 'Three Strikes and Then It's Life', *The Dominion Post* (20 January) www.stuff.co.nz/dominion-post/news/politics/3243334/Three-strikes-and-then-its-life

Herman, Michael, and PA 2007. 'Judges Order Rethink on Control Orders', *The Times* (31 October) www.thetimes.co.uk/tto/law/article2210262.ece

Hope, Christopher 2012. 'We Will Legalise Gay Marriage by 2015, says David Cameron', *The Telegraph* (24 July) www.telegraph.co.uk/news/politics/9425174/We-will-legalise-gay-marriage-by-2015-says-David-Cameron.html

Isaby, Jonathan 2008. 'Are These Labour's Top Achievements?', *The Telegraph* (21 February) http://blogs.telegraph.co.uk/news/jonathanisaby/3669111/Are_these_ Labours_top_achievements/

The Irish Times 2013. 'Cameron 'Alienating' Christians by Promoting Gay Marriage' (30 March) www.irishtimes.com/news/world/uk/cameron-alienating-christians-by-promoting-gay-marriage-1.1344454

Jeffrey, Simon 2005. 'The Rules of the Game are Changing', *The Guardian* (5 August) www.guardian.co.uk/attackonlondon/story/0,16132,1543359,00.html

Johnston, Kirsty 2013. 'Criminals Seek to Overturn Voting Ban', *Stuff.co.nz* (6 September) www.stuff.co.nz/national/crime/9134868/Criminals-seek-to-overturn-voting-ban

Johnston, Philip 2005. 'Clarke Urges EU to Rethink Rights Laws on Deportation', *The Telegraph* (20 October) www.telegraph.co.uk/news/1497789/Clarke-urges-EU-to-rethink-rights-laws-on-deportation.html

Jones, George 2005. 'Blair's on Collision Course Over Laws to Beat Terrorism', *The Telegraph*, (27 July) www.telegraph.co.uk/news/uknews/1494869/Blairs-on-collision-course-over-laws-to-beat-terrorism.html

2005. 'Blair to Curb Human Rights in War on Terror', *The Telegraph* (6 August) www.telegraph.co.uk/news/uknews/1495605/Blair-to-curb-human-rights-in-war-on-terror.html

2005. 'We Must Put Safety Before Liberty, Says Blair', *The Telegraph* (24 February) www.telegraph.co.uk/news/uknews/1484284/We-must-put-safety-before-liberty-says-Blair.html

Kay, Martin 2010. 'Three Strikes Law Passes', *The Dominion Post* (25 May) www.stuff.co.nz/dominion-post/news/politics/3736399/Three-strikes-law-passes

King, Oliver and Matthew Tempest 2005. 'Government to Offer Terror Bill Compromise', *The Guardian* (7 November) www.guardian.co.uk/politics/2005/nov/07/uksecurity.terrorism1

Kirkup, James 2011. '30,000 Prisoners Will Be Able to Vote', *The Telegraph* (6 January) www.telegraph.co.uk/news/uknews/law-and-order/8241920/30000-prisoners-will-be-able-to-vote.html

Klug, Francesca 2000. 'Target of the Tabloids', *The Guardian* (14 July).

Liberty 2005. 'New Anti Terror Bill Published', (15 September) www.liberty-human-rights.org.uk/media/press-releases/new-anti-terrori-bill-published

2010. 'Charge or Release', www.liberty-human-rights.org.uk/sites/default/files/comparative-law-study-2010-pre-charge-detention.pdf

2011. 'Anyone for TPIMs – Control Orders with a Twist?' (2 September) www.liberty-human-rights.org.uk/news/2011/anyone-for-tpims-control-orders-with-a-twist-.php

Mason, Rowena 2011. 'Government Tells European Judges No Right to Meddle with UK Prisoner Vote Policy', *The Telegraph* (2 November) www.telegraph.co.uk/news/8865204/Government-tells-European-judges-no-right-to-meddle-with-UK-prisoner-vote-policy.html

Mason, Rowena and Tom Whitehead 2012. 'David Cameron: Britain Will Decide on Votes for Prisoners, Not a "Foreign Court"', *The Telegraph* (23 May) www.telegraph.co.uk/news/politics/9284892/David-Cameron-Britain-will-decide-on-votes-for-prisoners-not-a-foreign-court.html

Mulholland, Hélène 2006. 'Lords Reject ID Cards Bill for Third Time', *The Guardian* (15 March) www.guardian.co.uk/politics/2006/mar/15/lords.idcards/print

2010. 'Liberal Democrats Back Same-sex Marriage Motion', *The Guardian* (21 September) www.guardian.co.uk/politics/2010/sep/21/liberal-democrats-same-sex-marriage

New Zealand Herald 2010. 'Labour Views Left Out of Law and Order Reports' (2 July) www.nzherald.co.nz/nz/news/article.cfm?c_id=1&objectid=10656089

Osborn, Andrew 2013. 'British PM's Party Split as First Gay Marriage Vote Passes', *Reuters* (5 February) www.reuters.com/article/2013/02/05/us-britain-cameron-idUSBRE91400820130205

Otago Daily Times 2014. 'Labour Questions Minister's Commitment to Bill' (17 February). www.odt.co.nz/news/politics/94003/labour-questions-minister039s-commitment-bill

Prince, Rosa 2012. 'Lords Reform: Government Scraps Vote to Save Legislation' *The Telegraph* (10 July) www.telegraph.co.uk/news/9389232/Lords-reform-Government-scraps-vote-to-save-legislation.html

Raab, Dominic 2011. 'What Happens if We Defy Europe – Nothing', *The Telegraph* (2 February) www.telegraph.co.uk/news/politics/8299615/What-happens-if-we-defy-Europe-Nothing.html

2013. 'Even When We Win ... We Still Lose', *The Daily Mail* (16 October) www.dailymail.co.uk/news/article-2462774/David-Camerons-delight-Supreme-Court-ruling-prisoners-NOT-vote.html

Ross, Tim 2010. 'Coalition Ministers Consider Gay Marriage Plans', *The Telegraph* (24 December) www.telegraph.co.uk/news/religion/8221964/Coalition-ministers-consider-gay-marriage-plans.html

2013. 'David Cameron Facing Commons Defeat Over Gay Marriage Plans', *The Telegraph* (20 May) www.telegraph.co.uk/news/politics/conservative/10067511/David-Cameron-facing-Commons-defeat-over-gay-marriage-plans.html

Rozenberg, Joshua 2005. '90-day Detention of Suspects "Unlawful"', *The Telegraph* (21 October) www.telegraph.co.uk/news/uknews/1500305/90-day-detention-of-suspects-unlawful.html

Ryder, Matthew 2011. 'Control Orders Have Been rebranded: Big Problems Remain' *The Guardian* (11 January) www.guardian.co.uk/commentisfree/libertycentral/2011/jan/28/control-orders-protection-of-freedoms-bill

Sands, Phillippe 2013. 'I'm Leaving the Liberal Democrats Too', *The Guardian* (11 March) www.guardian.co.uk/commentisfree/2013/mar/11/justice-security-i-quit-the-lib-dems

The Scotsman 2008. 'Brown Survives Labour Revolt on 42-day Detention' (12 June).

Shipman, Tim 2011. 'Cameron CAN Defy Euro Court Diktats: UK "May Deny Votes for Inmates Without Penalty"', *The Daily Mail* (18 February) www.dailymail.co.uk/news/article-1358199/Cameron-CAN-defy-Euro-court-diktats-UK-deny-votes-inmates-penalty.html

Shipman, Tim, and Kirsty Walker 2011. 'Cameron's War on Feckless Families: PM Attacks the Human Rights Laws and Backs National Service', *The Daily Mail* (17 August) www.dailymail.co.uk/news/article-2026163/David-Cameron-UK-riots-speech-PM-attacks-human-rights-laws-backs-national-service.html

Shoffman, Marc 2006. 'Gay Rights Highlight for Blair Career', *Pink News* (26 September) www.pinknews.co.uk/news/articles/2005–2568.html

Sparrow, Andrew 2013. 'Peers Back Gay Marriage Bill by Majority of 242: Politics Live Blog', *The Guardian* (4 June) www.guardian.co.uk/politics/blog/2013/jun/04/lords-gay-marriage-vote-live-blog

Syal, Rajeev 2012. 'Secret Courts Plan Receives Blow at Lib Dem Conference', *The Guardian* (26 September) www.guardian.co.uk/law/2012/sep/25/secret-courts-lib-dem-conference

The Telegraph 2001. 'Blunkett Puts War Before Concerns for Human Rights' (24 September) www.telegraph.co.uk/news/main.jhtml?xml=/news/2001/09/24/nblunk24.xml

Tempest, Matthew 2001. 'No. 10: Antiterror Bill Opponents are Naïve', *The Guardian* (7 December) www.guardian.co.uk/world/2001/dec/07/september11.usa1

2005. 'Howard Warns Against "Judicial Activism"', *The Guardian* (10 August) www.guardian.co.uk/politics/2005/aug/10/uksecurity.terrorism

The Times 2005. 'Full Text of Blair Statement on Extremism' (5 August) www.thetimes.co.uk/tto/news/uk/article1936508.ece

2008. '42 Days: Westminster for Sale' (12 June) www.thetimes.co.uk/tto/opinion/leaders/article2091189.ece

2011. 'Prisoner Voting – Consequences of Non-compliance' (18 February) www.thetimes.co.uk/tto/multimedia/archive/00118/mojlegaladvice0001n_118733a.pdf

Travis, Alan 2001. 'Blunkett to Face Rough Ride Over Terror Law', *The Guardian* (19 November) http://politics.guardian.co.uk/attacks/story/0,1320,597231,00.html

2009. 'Cameron Pledges Bill to Restore British Freedoms', *The Guardian* (28 February) www.guardian.co.uk/politics/2009/feb/28/conservatives-human-rights

2010. 'Control Order Ban Central to Coalition Civil Rights Policy, Warn Lib Dems', *The Guardian* (29 October) www.guardian.co.uk/law/2010/oct/29/control-order-ban-coalition-rights

2011. 'Judges Tell Theresa May to Revoke 'Flawed' Control Order on Terror Suspect', *The Guardian* (5 April) www.guardian.co.uk/law/2011/apr/05/judges-theresa-may-control-order

Walters, Simon 2013. 'A Great Day for British Justice: Theresa May Vows to Take UK Out of the European Court of Human Rights', *Mail Online* (4 March) www.dailymail.co.uk/news/article-2287183/A-great-day-British-justice-Theresa-May-vows-UK-European-Court-Human-Rights.html

Watt, Nicholas 2013. 'Gay Marriage: MPs' Vote in Favour Leaves Cameron Adrift from Tories', *The Guardian* (6 February) www.guardian.co.uk/society/2013/feb/05/gay-marriage-vote-cameron-adrift

2013. 'Labour Saves David Cameron's Gay Marriage Bill', *The Guardian* (21 May) www.guardian.co.uk/society/2013/may/21/labour-cameron-gay-marriage-bill

Watts, Robert 2013. 'Conservative Party Ripped Apart by Gay Marriage Vote', *The Telegraph*, (2 February) www.telegraph.co.uk/news/politics/9844514/Conservative-party-ripped-apart-by-gay-marriage-vote.html

White, Michael 2005. 'Labour MPs Attack Blair's 12-point Plan', *The Guardian* (9 August) http://politics.guardian.co.uk/terrorism/story/0,15935,1545190,00.html

Winnett, Robert, and Tom Whitehead 2009. 'Prisoners to Get Right to Vote after 140 Years Following European Ruling', *The Telegraph* (9 April) www.telegraph.co.uk/news/uknews/law-and-order/5126647/Prisoners-to-get-right-to-vote-after-140-years-following-European-ruling.html

Wintour, Patrick 2001. 'Blunkett Rejects 'Airy Fairy' Fears', *The Guardian* (2 November) www.guardian.co.uk/politics/2001/nov/12/uk.september11/print

2005. 'After Eight Years in Power Tony Blair Hears a New Word: Defeat', *The Guardian* (10 November) http://politics.guardian.co.uk/terrorism/story/0,15935,1639028,00.html

2011. 'Control Orders Set to Split All Three Parties', *The Guardian* (6 January) www.guardian.co.uk/politics/wintour-and-watt/2011/jan/06/control-orders-split-all-three-parties

Wintour, Patrick, and Andrew Sparrow 2012. 'I Won't Give Prisoners the Vote, Says David Cameron', *The Guardian* (24 October) www.guardian.co.uk/society/2012/oct/24/prisoners-vote-david-cameron

Wolf, Marie 2005. 'Was the Attorney General Leant On to Change His Mind?', *The Independent* (24 March) www.independent.co.uk/news/uk/politics/was-the-attorney-general-leant-on-to-change-his-mind-6149914.html

Woodward, Will, and Alan Travis 2006. 'ID Cards to be Compulsory with Passports Issued from 2010', *The Guardian* (30 March) www.guardian.co.uk/politics/2006/mar/30/idcards.immigrationpolicy

Young, Hugo 2001. 'David Blunkett Holds Liberty and the Judges in Contempt', *The Guardian* (15 November) www.guardian.co.uk/world/2001/nov/15/september11.britainand911

Books and Articles

A British Bill of Rights, 2nd edition. London: Institute of Public Policy Research, 1996

Allan, James 2000. 'Turning Clark Kent into Superman: The New Zealand Bill of Rights Act 1990', *Otago Law Review* 9: 613–32

2001. 'The Effect of a Statutory Bill of Rights where Parliament is Sovereign: The Lesson from New Zealand', in Tom Campbell, K. D. Ewing and Adam Tomkins (eds.), *Sceptical Essays on Human Rights*. Oxford: Oxford University Press, pp. 375–90

Allan, James and Andrew Geddis 2006. 'Waldron and Opposing Judicial Review – Except, Sort Of, in New Zealand', *New Zealand Law Journal* April: 94–96

Allan, Trevor 1997. 'Parliamentary Sovereignty: Law, Politics, and Revolution', *Law Quarterly Review* 113: 443–52

Ajzenstat, Janet 1997. 'Reconciling Parliament and Rights: A.V. Dicey Reads the Canadian Charter of Rights', *Canadian Journal of Political Science* 30: 645–662

Angus Reid Public Opinion 2010. 'Most Britons Believe Prisoners Should Not Vote in Elections', www.angus-reid.com/wp-content/uploads/2010/11/2010.11.22_Prisoner_BRI.pdf

Archer, Carolyn and Gaze Burt 2004. 'Section 7 of the Bill of Rights Act', *New Zealand Law Journal* August: 320–23

Arnold, Terrence 2005. 'Parliament and the Courts: Arm Wrestle or Handshake?', *New Zealand Journal of Public and International Law* 3: 45–61

Aroney, Nicholas and Steve Thomas 2012. 'A House Divided: Does MMP Make an Upper House Unnecessary in New Zealand?', *New Zealand Law Review* 403–41

Barker, Fiona and Elizabeth McLeay 2000. 'How Much Change?: An Analysis of the Initial Impact of Proportional Representation on the New Zealand Parliamentary party System', *Party Politics* 6: 131–54

Barker, Fiona and Stephen Levine 1999. 'The Individual Parliamentary Member and Institutional Change: The Changing Role of the New Zealand Member of Parliament', *The Journal of Legislative Studies* 5: 105–30

Barker, Nicola 2008. 'Not the Marrying Kind: Feminist Critiques of Marriage and Legal Recognition of Same-sex Relationships', PhD Thesis, University of Keele

Bartlett, Tess 2009. The Power of Penal Populism: Public Influences on Penal and Sentencing Policy from 1999 to 2008, unpublished Masters Thesis, Victoria University of Wellington

Bassett, Michael 2008. *Working with David: Inside the Lange Cabinet.* Auckland: Hachette Livre NZ

Bellamy, Richard 2007. *Political Constitutionalism: A Republican Defence of the Constitutionality of Democracy.* Cambridge: Cambridge University Press

2011. 'Political Constitutionalism and the Human Rights Act', *International Journal of Constitutional Law* 9: 86–111

Bennion, Tom, Birdling, Malcolm and Paton, Rebecca 2004. 'Making Sense of the Foreshore & Seabed', *The Māori Law Review* 1–131

Berryman, Jeff 1988. 'A Bill of Rights for New Zealand', *Political Science* 40:39–56

Bingham, T.H. 1993. 'The European Convention on Human Rights: Time to Incorporate', *Law Quarterly Review* 109: 390–400

Blackburn, Robert, 1999. *Towards a Constitutional Bill of Rights for the United Kingdom.* London, Pinter Publishers

Black-Branch, Jonathan L. 2002. 'Parliamentary Supremacy or Political Expediency? The Constitution Position of the Human Rights Act under British Law', *Statute Law Review* 23: 59–91

Black Jr., Charles L. 1973. 'Is There Already a British Bill of Rights?', (1973) 89 *Law Quarterly Review* 89: 173

Blanchard, Peter 2008. 'The New Zealand Bill of Rights: Where Have We Got To After 16 Years?', *New Zealand Universities Law Review* 263–282

2008. 'The Early Experiences of the New Zealand Supreme Court', *New Zealand Journal of Public and International Law* 6: 175–96

Blick, Andrew, and Stuart Weir 2005. 'The Rules of the Game: The Terrorism Bill 2005', Democratic Audit (27 June) www.jrrt.org.uk/publications/rules-game-terrorism-bill-2005-scoping-report

Bogdanor, Vernon 2009. *The New British Constitution.* Oxford: Hart Publishing Ltd

Boston, Jonathan 1987. 'Thatcherism and Rogernomics: Changing the Rules of the Game – Comparisons and Contrasts', *Political Science* 39: 129–52

Boston, Jonathan, Levine, Stephen, McLeay, Elizabeth and Roberts, Nigel S. 1999. *Electoral and Constitutional Change in New Zealand: An MMP Source Book.* Palmerston North: Dunmore Press Ltd

Boston, Jonathan, Stephen Church and Tim Bale 2003. 'The Impact of Proportional Representation on Government Effectiveness: The New Zealand Experience', *Australian Journal of Public Administration* 62: 7–22

Boston, Jonathan and Bullock, David 2009. 'Experiments in Executive Government under MMP in New Zealand: Contrasting Approaches to Multiparty Governance', *New Zealand Journal of Public and International Law* 7: 39–75

Bradbury, Jonathan 2009. 'The Best of Both Worlds? MMP Electoral Reform and Constitutional Development in Scotland and Wales', *New Zealand Journal of Public and International Law* 7: 157–83

Bradley, A.W. and K.D. Ewing 2003. *Constitutional and Administrative Law*, 13th edition. New York: Pearson Education Limited

Bromwich, Tessa 2009. 'Parliamentary Rights-vetting Under the NZBORA', *New Zealand Law Journal* 189–92

Brookbanks, Warren J. 2012. 'Punishing Recidivist Offenders in New Zealand Using Three Strikes Legislation: Sound Policy or Penal Excess?', *US–China Law Review* 9: 1–19

Brookbanks, Warren and Richard Elkins 2010. *Criminal Injustice and the Proposed 'Three Strikes' Law*. Maxim Institute: New Zealand

2010. 'The Case Against the "Three Strikes" Sentencing Regime', *New Zealand Law Review* 689–724

Brown, Mark and Warren Young 2000. 'Recent Trends in Sentencing and Penal Policy in New Zealand', *International Criminal Justice Review* 10: 1–31

Butler, Andrew 1997. 'The Bill of Rights Debate: Why the New Zealand Bill of Rights Act 1990 is a Bad Model for Britain', *Oxford Journal of Legal Studies* 17: 323–45

2000. 'Strengthening the Bill of Rights', *Victoria University of Wellington Law Review* 31: 129–47

2000. 'Judicial Invalidations of Inconsistency – A New Weapon in the Bill of Rights Armoury', *New Zealand Law Review* 43–60

2001. 'Implied Repeal, Parliamentary Sovereignty and Human Rights in New Zealand', *Public Law* 586–98

2002. 'Judicial Review, Human Rights and Democracy', in Grant Huscroft and Paul Rishworth (eds.), *Litigating Rights: Perspectives from Domestic and International Law*. Oxford: Hart Publishing, pp. 47–72

Butler, Andrew and Petra Butler 2005. *The New Zealand Bill of Rights Act: A Commentary*. Wellington, LexisNexis

Butler, Petra 2004. 'Human Rights and Parliamentary Sovereignty in New Zealand', *Victoria University of Wellington Law Review* 35: 341–66

2006. '15 Years of the NZ Bill of Rights: Time to Celebrate, Time to Reflect, Time to Work Harder?', *Human Rights Research Journal* 4: 1–31 http://papers.ssrn.com/sol3/papers.cfm?abstract_id=2022681

2010. 'It Takes Two to Tango: Have They Learned Their Steps?' University of Sydney Workshop on 'Judicial Supremacy or Inter-institutional Dialogue'? *Political Responses to Judicial Review (May 18–19)* http://papers.ssrn.com/sol3/papers.cfm?abstract_id=2022681

2013. 'Cross-fertilization of Constitutional Ideas: The Relationship between the UK Human Rights Act 1998 and the New Zealand Bill of Rights Act 1990', in Roger Masterman and Ian Leigh (eds.), *The United Kingdom's Statutory*

Bill of Rights: Constitutional and Comparative Perspectives. Oxford: Oxford University Press, pp. 251–78

Campbell, Tom 2001. 'Incorporation through Interpretation', in Tom Campbell, K.D. Ewing, and Adam Tomkins (eds.), *Sceptical Essays on Human Rights*. New York: Oxford University Press, pp. 79–101

Charters, Claire 2006. 'Responding to Waldron's Defence of Legislatures: Why New Zealand's Parliament Does Not Protect Rights in Hard Cases', *New Zealand Law Review* 621–63

Chen, Mai 1993. 'Remedying New Zealand's Constitution in Crisis: Is MMP Part of the Answer?', *New Zealand Law Journal* 22–39

Chen, Mai and Sir Geoffrey Palmer 1993. *Public Law in New Zealand: Cases, Materials, Commentary, and Questions*. Melbourne: Oxford University Press

Chesterman, John and Brian Galligan 2009. 'The Politics of Rights Protection in Western Democracies', *Australian Journal of Political Science* 44: 29–40

Christie, Nigel 2001. 'The New Zealand Same-Sex Marriage Case: From Aotearoa to the United Nations', in Robert Wintemute and Mads Andenaes (eds.), *Legal Recognition of Same-Sex Partnerships*. Oxford: Hart Publishing, pp. 317–35

Choudhry, Sujit 2009. 'Bills of Rights as Instruments of Nation Building in Multinational States: The Canadian Charter and Quebec Nationalism', in James B. Kelly and Christopher P. Manfredi (eds.), *Contested Constitutionalism: Reflections on the Canadian Charter of Rights and Freedoms*. Vancouver: UBC Press, pp. 233–50

Clarke, Victoria and Sara-Jane Finlay 2004. "For Better or Worse?' Lesbian and Gay Marriage'. *Feminism and Psychology* 14: 17–23

Clements, Luke 2005. 'Winners and Losers', *Journal of Law and Society* 32: 34–50

Cooper, Jonathan, and Adrian Marshall-Williams 2000. *Legislating for Human Rights: The Parliamentary Debates on the Human Right Bill*. Oxford: Hart Publishing

Corlett, Marc 1994. 'The New Zealand Bill of Rights Act and the Right to Counsel', *Auckland University Law Review* 7: 579–600

Cowley, Philip 2002. *Revolts and Rebellions: Parliamentary Voting under Blair*. London: Politico's

2005. *The Rebels. How Blair Mislaid His Majority*. London: Politico's

Croft, J. 2000. 'Whitehall and the Human Rights Act', The Constitution Unit, UCL (September), www.ucl.ac.uk/spp/publications/unit-publications/61.pdf

Danswan, Chadleigh 2004. 'New Zealand's Evidence Exclusion Rule: Assessment of *R. v. Shaheed* in 2003', *Auckland University Law Review* 10: 174–211

Davis, Fergal F., and Fiona de Londras 2014. 'Counter-Terrorist Judicial Review: Beyond Dichotomies', in Fergal F. Davis and Fiona de Londras (eds.), *Critical Debates on Counter-Terrorist Judicial Review*. Cambridge: Cambridge University Press

Debeljak, Julie 2003. 'Rights and Democracy: A Reconciliation of the Institutional Debate', in Tom Campbell, Jeffrey Goldsworthy, and Adrienne Stone (eds.), *Protecting Human Rights*. Oxford: Oxford University Press, 135–57

de Londras, Fiona 2011. *Detention in the 'War on Terror': Can Human Rights Fight Back?* New York: Cambridge University Press

Dicey, A.V. 1960. *An Introduction to the Study of the Law of the Constitution*, 10th edition. London: Macmillan

Dixon, Rosalind 2001. 'Weak-form Judicial Review and American Exceptionalism', *Oxford Journal of Legal Studies* 32: 487–506

2007. 'Creating Dialogue about Socioeconomic Rights: Strong-form versus Weak-form Judicial Review Revisited', *International Journal of Constitutional Law* 5: 391–418

Driedger, Elmer A. 1977. 'The Meaning and Effect of the Canadian *Bill of Rights:* A Draftsman's Viewpoint', 9 *Ottawa Law Review* 9: 303–20

Dugdale, D.F. 1986. 'Common Sense about the Bill of Rights: A Criticism of Geoffrey Palmer's Super-law', *New Zealand Law Journal* April: 127–28

2000. 'Framing Statutes in an Age of Judicial Supremacism', *Otago Law Review* 9: 603–11

East, Paul 1991. 'Monitoring Bills for Compliance with the New Zealand Bill of Rights Act 1990', in Mai Chen and Geoffrey Palmer (eds.), *Public Law in New Zealand*. Auckland: Oxford University Press, 556–563.

1995. 'The Role of the Attorney General', in Philip A. Joseph (ed.), *Essays on the Constitution*. Wellington: Brooker's, pp. 184–213

Eichbaum, Chris and Richard Shaw 2007. 'Ministerial Advisers, Politicization and the Retreat from Westminster: The Case of New Zealand', *Public Administration* 85: 609–40

Elkind, Jerome B. 1987. 'The Bill of Rights', in Jonathan Boston and Martin Holland (eds.), *The Fourth Labour Government: Radical Politics in New Zealand*. Melbourne: Oxford University Press, pp. 54–71

Elkind, Jerome B., and Anthony Shaw 1986. *A Standard for Justice: A Critical Commentary on the Proposed Bill of Rights for New Zealand*. Auckland: Oxford University Press

Elliott, Mark 2002. 'Parliamentary Sovereignty and the New Constitutional Order: Legislative Freedom, Political Reality and Convention', *Legal Studies* 22: 340–376

2004. 'United Kingdom: Parliamentary Sovereignty Under Pressure', *International Journal of Constitutional Law* 2: 545–627

Epp, Charles R. 1998. *The Rights Revolution: Lawyers, Activists, and Supreme Courts in Comparative Perspective*. Chicago: University of Chicago Press

Erdos, David 2007. 'Aversive Constitutionalism in the Westminster World: The Genesis of the New Zealand Bill of Rights Act 1990', *International Journal of Constitutional Law* 5: 343–69

2008. 'Elite Supply "Blockages" and the Failure of National Bill of Rights Initiatives in Australia: A Comparative Westminster Analysis', *Commonwealth & Comparative Politics* 46: 341–64

2009. 'Ideology, Power Orientation and Policy Drag: Explaining the Elite Politics of Britain's Bill of Rights Debate', *Government and Opposition* 44: 20–41

2009. 'Judicial Culture and the Politicolegal Opportunity Structure: Explaining Bill of Rights Legal Impact in New Zealand', *Law and Social Inquiry* 34: 95–127

2009. 'Postmaterialist Social Constituencies and Political Triggers: Explaining Bill of Rights Genesis in Internally Stable, Advanced Democracies', *Political Research Quarterly* 62: 798–810

2010. *Delegating Rights Protection: The Rise of Bills of Rights in the Westminster World.* Oxford: Oxford University Press

Evans, Carolyn and Simon Evans 2011. 'Messages from the Front Line: Parliamentarians' Perspectives on Rights Protection', in Tom Campbell, K.D. Ewing and Adam Tomkins (eds.), *The Legal Protection of Human Rights: Sceptical Essays.* Oxford: Oxford University Press, pp. 329–46

Ewing, Keith, and Conor Gearty 1990. *Freedom Under Thatcher: Civil Liberties in Modern Britain.* Clarendon Press: Oxford

Ewing, Keith 2000. 'The Politics of the British Constitution', *Public Law* 436.

2001. 'The Unbalanced Constitution', in Tom Campbell, K.D. Ewing, and Adam Tomkins (eds.), *Sceptical Essays on Human Rights.* New York: Oxford University Press, pp. 103–117

2003. 'The Case for Social Rights', in Tom Campbell, Jeffrey Goldsworthy and Adrienne Stone (eds.), *Protecting Human Rights: Instruments and Institutions.* New York: Oxford University Press, pp. 323–337

2008. 'The Political Constitution of Emergency Powers: a Comment' *International Journal of Law in Context* 3: 316

2010. *Bonfire of the Liberties: New Labour, Human Rights, and the Rule of Law.* Oxford: Oxford University Press

Ewing, Keith and Joo-Cheong Tham 2008. 'The Continuing Futility of the Human Rights Act', *Public Law* 670

Favoreau, Louis 1982. 'Décentralisation et Constitution', *Revue du droit public* 98: 1259–95

Feldman, David 2002. 'Parliamentary Scrutiny of Legislation and Human Rights', *Public Law* 323–48

2004. 'The Impact of Human Rights on the UK Legislative Process', *Statute Law Review* 25: 91–115

2007. 'Institutional Roles and Meanings of "Compatibility"', in Helen Fenwick, Helen, Gavin Phillipson, and Roger Masterman (eds.), *Judicial Reasoning Under the UK Human Rights Act.* Cambridge: Cambridge University Press, pp. 87–113

Fenwick, Helen 2002. 'Anti-Terrorism, Crime and Security Act 2001: A Proportionate Response to 11 September?', *Modern Law Review* 65: 742–62

Fenwick, Helen, and Gavin P. Phillipson, 2005. 'Legislative Over-breadth, Democratic Failure and the Judicial Response: Fundamental Rights and the UK's Anti-terrorist Legal Policy', in Victor Ramraj, Michael Hor, and Kent Roach (eds.), *Global Anti-Terrorism Law and Policy*. Cambridge: Cambridge University Press, pp. 455–89

Fitzgerald, Paul 1992. 'Section 7 of the New Zealand Bill of Rights Act 1990: A Very Practical Power or A Well-intentioned Nonsense', *Victoria University of Wellington Law Review* 22: 135–58

Franks, C.E.S. 1987. *The Parliament of Canada*. Toronto: University of Toronto Press

Foster, Christopher 2005. *British Government in Crisis*. Portland: Hart Publishing

Galligan, Brian and F.L. Morton 2006. 'Australian Exceptionalism: Rights Protections Without a Bill of Rights', in Tom Campbell, Jeffrey Goldsworthy, and Adrienne Stone (eds.), *Protecting Rights Without a Bill of Rights*. London: Ashgate, pp. 17–39

Gardbaum, Stephen 2001. 'The New Commonwealth Model of Constitutionalism', *American Journal of Comparative Law* 29: 707–60

2010. 'Reassessing the New Commonwealth Model of Constitutionalism', *International Journal of Constitutional Law* 8: 167–206

2011. 'How Successful and Distinctive is the Human Rights Act? An Expatriate Comparativist's Assessment', *Modern Law Review* 74: 195–215

2013. *The New Commonwealth Model of Constitutionalism: Theory and Practice*. Cambridge: Cambridge University Press

Gay and Lesbian Humanist Association 2009. www.pinktriangle.org.uk/glh/section28.html

Gearty, Conor 1999. 'Terrorism and Human Rights: A Case Study of Impending Legal Realities', *Legal Studies* 19: 367–79

2001. 'Reflections on Human Rights and Civil Liberties in Light of the United Kingdom's Human Rights Act 1998', *University of Richmond Law Review* 35: 1–26

2004. *Principles of Human Rights Adjudication*. Oxford: Oxford University Press

2005. 'Human Rights in an Age of Counter-Terrorism: Injurious, Irrelevant or Indispensable?', *Current Legal Problems* 58: 25–46

Geddis, Andrew 2008. 'New Zealand's Electoral Finance Act 2007 and its Discontents', *Public Law Review* 19: 215–33

2009. 'The Comparative Irrelevance of the NZBORA to Legislative Practice', *New Zealand Universities Law Review* 43: 465–88

2011. 'Inter-institutional 'Rights Dialogue' Under the New Zealand Bill of Rights Act,' in Tom Campbell, K.D. Ewing and Adam Tomkins, (eds.),

The Legal Protection of Human Rights: Sceptical Essays. Oxford: Oxford University Press, pp. 87–107

2011. 'Prisoner Voting and Rights Deliberation: How New Zealand's Parliament Failed', *New Zealand Law Review* 443–474

Geddis, Andrew and Bridget Fenton, 2008. 'Which is to be Master?' – Rights-Friendly Statutory Interpretation in New Zealand and the United Kingdom', *Arizona Journal of International and Comparative Law* 25: 733–78

Geiringer, Claudia 2007. 'The Dead Hand of the Bill of Rights? Is the New Zealand Bill of Rights Act 1990 a Substantive Legal Constraint on Parliament's Power to Legislate?', *Otago Law Review* 11: 389–415

2008. 'The Principle of Legality and the Bill of Rights Act: A Critical Examination of R. v. Hansen', *New Zealand Journal of Public and International Law* 6: 59–93

2009. 'On a Road to Nowhere: Implied Declarations of Inconsistency and the New Zealand Bill of Rights Act', *Victoria University of Wellington Law Review* 40: 613–47

2009. 'Declarations of Inconsistency Dodged Again', *New Zealand Law Journal* 232–35

Geiringer, Claudia and Matthew Palmer 2007. 'Human Rights and Social Policy in New Zealand', *Social Policy Journal of New Zealand* 30: 12–41

Geiringer, Claudia, Polly McLeay and Elizabeth McLeay 2011. *What's the Hurry? Urgency in the New Zealand Legislative Process*. Wellington: Victoria University of Wellington Press

Ginsburg, Tom 2003. *Judicial Review in New Democracies*. Cambridge University Press

Goldsworthy, Jeffrey 2003. 'Homogenizing Constitutions', *Oxford Journal of Legal Studies* 23: 482–505

2003. 'Judicial Review, Legislative Override, and Democracy', in Tom Campbell, Jeffrey Goldsworthy, and Adrienne Stone (eds.), *Protecting Human Rights*. Oxford: Oxford University Press, pp. 263–79

Grau, Karen 2002. 'Parliamentary Sovereignty: New Zealand – New Millenium', *Victoria University of Wellington Law Review* 33: 351–77

Grey, Antony 1992. *Quest for Justice. Towards Homosexual Emancipation*. London: Sinclair-Stevenson

Griffith, J.A.G., and Michael Ryle 1989. *Parliament: Functions, Practice and Procedures*. London: Sweet & Maxwell

Harris, B. V. 2004. 'The Constitutional Future of New Zealand', *New Zealand Law Review* 269–313

Harris, Bruce 2008. 'Judicial Activism in New Zealand's Appellate Court', in Brice Dickson (ed.), *Judicial Activism in Common Law Supreme Courts*. Oxford: Oxford University Press, pp. 273–322

Harrison, Kevin, and Tony Boyd 2006. *The Changing Constitution*. Edinburgh: Edinburgh University Press

Hawke, Gary 2008. 'Lawyers in the Policy Process', *New Zealand Journal of Public and International Law* 6: 161–73

Hiebert, Janet 2002. *Charter Conflicts: What is Parliament's Role?* Montreal: McGill-Queen's University Press

2003. 'Parliament and Rights', in Tom Campbell, Jeffrey Goldsworthy, and Adrienne Stone (eds.), *Protecting Human Rights*. Oxford: Oxford University Press, pp. 231–46

2004. 'Is It Too Late to Rehabilitate Canada's Notwithstanding Clause?', *Supreme Court Law Review* 23: 169–89

2004. 'New Constitutional Ideas: Can the New Parliamentary Models Resist Judicial Dominance When Interpreting Rights?' *Texas Law Review* 82: 1963–87

2005. 'Interpreting a Bill of Rights: The Importance of Legislative Rights Review', *British Journal of Political Science* 35: 235–55

2005. 'Rights-vetting in New Zealand and Canada: Similar Ideas, Different Outcomes', *New Zealand Journal of Public and International Law* 63–105

2006. 'Parliamentary Bills of Rights: An Alternative Model?', *Modern Law Review* 69: 7–28

2006. Parliament and the Human Rights Act: Can the JCHR Help Facilitate A Culture of Rights?', *International Journal of Constitutional Law* 4: 1–38

2011. 'Constitutional Experimentation: Rethinking How a Bill of Rights Functions', in Tom Ginsburg and Rosalind Dixon, (eds.), *Comparative Constitutional Law*. Northhampton: Edward Elgar, pp. 298–320

2011. 'Governing Like Judges?', in Tom Campbell, K.D. Ewing and Adam Tomkins (eds.), *The Legal Protection of Human Rights: Sceptical Essays*. Oxford: Oxford University Press, pp. 40–65

2012. 'Governing Under the Human Rights Act: The Limitations of Wishful Thinking', *Public Law* 26–49

2012. 'Parliamentary Engagement with the Charter: Rethinking the Idea of Legislative Rights Review', *Supreme Court Law Review* 58: 87–107

2013. 'The HRA: Ambiguity about Parliamentary Sovereignty', *German Law Journal* 14: 2251–2254

2015. 'Legislative Rights Review: Addressing the Gap between Ideals and Constraints', in Murray Hunt, Hayley Hooper, and Paul Yowell (eds.) *Parliament and Human Rights: Redressing the Democratic Deficit*. Oxford: Hart Publishing

Hirschl, Ran 2000. 'The Political Origins of Judicial Empowerment through Constitutionalization: Lessons from Four Constitutional Revolutions', *Law and Social Inquiry* 91–149

2004. *Toward Juristocracy*. Cambridge: Harvard University Press

Hirst, Paul 1989. *After Thatcher*. London: Collins

Hogg, Peter W. 2007. 'Constitutional Dialogue under a Bill of Rights', *National Journal of Constitutional Law* 23: 127–38

2008. 'Judges and Legislators: Constitutional Dialogue under a Bill of Rights', in Claudia Geiringer and Dean R. Knight (eds.), *Seeing the World Whole: Essays in Honour of Sir Kenneth Keith*. Wellington: Victoria University Press, pp. 311–319

Hogg, Peter W., Allison A. Bushell Thorton and Wade K. Wright 2007. 'Charter Dialogue Revisited – or 'Much Ado About Metaphors', *Osgoode Hall Law Journal* 45: 2–65

Hunt, M. 2007, 'Reshaping Constitutionalism', in John Morrison, Kieran McEvoy, and Gordon Anthony (eds.), *Judges, Transition, and Human Rights*. Oxford: Oxford University Press, pp. 467–77

Huscroft, Grant 1995. 'The Attorney-General, the Bill of Rights, and the Public Interest', in Grant Huscroft and Paul Rishworth (eds.), *Rights and Freedoms: The New Zealand Bill of Rights Act 1990 and the Human Rights Act 1993*. Wellington: Brookers, pp. 133–70

1999. 'Politics and Principle in Public Law Advocacy – The Role of the Solicitor General', *New Zealand Universities Law Review* 18: 585–96

2002. 'Protecting Rights and Parliamentary Sovereignty: New Zealand's Experience with a *Charter*-Inspired, Statutory Bill of Rights', *Windsor Yearbook of Access to Justice*, 21: 111–27

2003. 'Is the Defeat of Health Warnings A Victory for Human Rights? The Attorney-General and Pre-legislative Scrutiny for Consistency with the New Zealand Bill of Rights', *Public Law Review* 14: 109–21

2007. 'Constitutionalism from the Top Down', *Osgoode Hall Law Journal* 45: 91–104

2009. 'Reconciling Duty and Discretion: The Attorney General in the Charter Era', *Queen's Law Journal* 34: 773–811

Huscroft, Grant, Scott Optican and Paul Rishworth 2001. *The Bill of Rights – Getting the Basics Right*. Wellington: New Zealand Law Society

Huscroft, Grant and Paul Rishworth 2009. '"You Say You Want a Revolution": Bills of Rights in the Age of Human Rights', in David Dyzenhaus, Murray Hunt, and Grant Huscroft (eds.), *A Simple Common Lawyer: Essays in Honour of Michael Taggart*. Oxford: Hart Publishing, pp. 123–50

Jackson, K. 1987. *The Dilemma of Parliament*. Auckland: Allen and Unwin

Jackson, Sara 2007. 'Designing Human Rights Legislation: "Dialogue", the Commonwealth Model and the Roles of Parliaments and Courts', *Auckland University Law Review* 13: 89–115

Jaconelli, Joseph 1980. *Enacting a Bill of Rights: The Legal Problems*. London: Oxford University Press

Jaensch, Dean 1992. *The Politics of Australia*. Melbourne: Macmillan Australia

Joseph, Phillip 1986. 'The Challenge of a Bill of Rights: A Commentary', *New Zealand Law Journal* December: 416–22

1999. 'The New Zealand Bill of Rights Experience', in Philip Alston (ed.), *Promoting Human Rights Through Bills of Rights*. Oxford: Oxford University Press, pp. 283–317

Joseph, Philip A. 2004. 'Parliament, the Courts and the Collaborative Enterprise', *King's College Law Journal* 15: 321–45

2009. 'MMP and the Constitution', *New Zealand Journal of Public and International Law* 7: 111–34

Kahana, Tsvi 2002. 'The Notwithstanding Mechanism and Public Discussion: Lessons from the Ignored Practice of Section 33 of the Charter', *Canadian Public Administration* 44: 255–91

Kaiser, Andre 2009. 'MMP, Minority Governments and Parliamentary Opposition', *New Zealand Journal of Public and International Law* 7: 77–91

Kaiser, Andre and Thomas Brechtel 1999. 'Party System, Bargaining Power and Coalition Formation After the 1999 New Zealand General Election', *Political Science* 51: 182–86

Kam, Christopher J. 2009. *Party Discipline and Parliamentary Politics*. Cambridge: Cambridge University Press

Kavanagh, Aileen 2009. *Constitutional Review Under the UK Human Rights Act*. Cambridge: Cambridge University Press

2010. 'Special Advocate, Control Orders and the Right to a Fair Trial', *Modern Law Review* 73: 836–57

2011. 'Constitutionalism, Counterterrorism, and the Courts: Changes in the British Constitutional Landscape', *International Journal of Constitutional Law* 9: 172–99

Keith, Kenneth J. 2000. '"Concerning Change": The Adoption and Implementation of the New Zealand Bill of Rights Act 1990', *Victoria University of Wellington Law Review* 31: 721–46

2003. 'Public Law in New Zealand', *New Zealand Journal of Public and International Law* 1: 3–24

Kelly, James B. 2005. *Governing with the Charter: Legislative and Judicial Activism and Framers' Intent*. Vancouver: UBC Press

2009. 'Legislative Activism and Parliament Bills of Rights: Institutional Lessons for Canada', in James B. Kelly and Christopher P. Manfredi (eds.), *Contested Constitutionalism: Reflections on the Canadian Charter of Rights and Freedoms*. Vancouver: UBC Press, pp. 86–106

2011. 'Judicial and Political Review as Limited Insurance: The Functioning of the New Zealand Bill of Rights Act in "Hard" Cases', *Commonwealth & Comparative Politics* 49: 295–317

2011. 'A Difficult Dialogue: Statements of Compatibility and the Victorian *Charter of Human Rights and Responsibilities Act*', *Australian Journal of Political Science* 46: 257–79

Kelly, James B. and Matthew A. Hennigar, 2012. 'The Charter of Rights and the Minister of Justice: Weak-form Review Within a Constitutional Charter of Rights', *International Journal of Constitutional Law* 10: 35–68

Kinley, David 1999. 'Parliamentary Scrutiny of Human Rights: A Duty Neglected?', in Philip Alston (ed.), *Promoting Human Rights Through Bills of Rights*. Oxford: Oxford University Press, pp. 158–84

Klinger, Sophie 2009. 'Legislation Note: Three Strikes for New Zealand? Repeat Offenders and the Sentencing and Parole Reform Bill 2009', *Auckland University Law Review* 15: 248–57

Klug, Francesca 2000. *Values for a Godless Age: The Story of the United Kingdom's New Bill of Rights*. London: Penguin Books

2006. 'The Long Road to Human Rights Compliance', *Northern Ireland Legal Quarterly* 57: 189–204

2007. 'A Bill of Rights: Do We Need One or Do We Already Have One?', *Public Law* 701–19

2007. 'A Bill of Rights: What For?' in Chris Bryant (ed.), *Towards a New Constitutional Settlement*. London: Smith Institute, www2.lse.ac.uk/humanRights/articlesAndTranscripts/FK_SmithInstitute_07.pdf

n.d. 'The United Kingdom Experience', www.lse.ac.uk/humanRights/articlesAndTranscripts/The_UK_Experience.pdf

Kumarasingham, Harshan 2010. 'Executive Power 60 Years On: Has Anything Changed?' *Policy Quarterly* 6: 46–52

Lacey, Nicola 2011. 'The Prisoners' Dilemma and Political Systems: The Impact of Proportional Representation on Criminal Justice in New Zealand', *Victoria University of Wellington Law Review* 42: 615–37

2012. 'Political Systems and Criminal Justice: The Prisoners' Dilemma After the Coalition', *Current Legal Problems* 65: 203–39

Landfried, Christine 1984. *Bundesverfassungsgericht und Gesetzgeber*. Baden-Baden: Nomos, 1984

1992. 'Judicial Policymaking in Germany: The Federal Constitutional Court', *West European Politics* 15: 50–67

Laskin, Bora 1958. *The Proposed Bill of Rights*. The National Human Rights Conference (December 10)

Laws, John 1993. 'Is the High Court the Guardian of Fundamental Constitutional Rights?', *Public Law* 50

1996. 'Law and Democracy', *Public Law* 72

Leane, G.W.G. 2004. 'Enacting Bills of Rights: Canada and the Curious Case of New Zealand's "Thin" Democracy', *Human Rights Quarterly* 26: 152–88

Leigh, Ian and Roger Masterman 2008. *Making Rights Real: The Human Rights Act in its First Decade*. Oxford: Hart Publishing

Lester, Anthony 1968. 'Democracy and Individual Rights', *Fabian Tract no.* 390 London: Fabian Society

Lord Lester 1997. 'First Steps Towards a Constitutional Bill of Rights', *European Human Rights Law Review* 2: 124–31

Lord Lester and David Pannick 2004. *Human Rights Law and Practice*, 2nd edition. London: LexisNexis

Levine, Stephen 1991. 'Bills of Rights in Parliamentary Settings: New Zealand and Israeli Experience', *Parliamentary Affairs* 337–52

2004. 'Parliamentary Democracy in New Zealand', *Parliamentary Affairs* 75: 646–65

Lewis, Tom and Peter Cumper 2009. 'Balancing Freedom of Political Expression Against Equality of Political Opportunity: The Courts and the UK's Broadcasting Ban on Political Advertising', *Public Law* 89–111.

Liberty n.d. www.liberty-human-rights.org.uk/issues/3-privacy/31-id-cards/why-liberty-opposes-id-cards.shtml

Lippman, Matthew 1980. 'The Debate Over a Bill of Rights in Great Britain: The View from Parliament', *Universal Human Rights* 2: 25–42

Lord Falconer, 2004. Speech to the Law Society and Human Rights Lawyers' Association, London (17 February)

Lord Hailsham 1976. 'Elective Dictatorship', *The Listener* (21 October).

Lord Woolf 1994. 'Droit Public – English Style', *Public Law*: 57

Lundberg, Thomas Carl 2013. 'Politics is Still an Adversarial Business: Minority Government and Mixed-Member Proportional in Scotland and in New Zealand', *British Journal of Politics and International Relations* 15: 609–25

Macdonald, John 1969. *Bill of Rights*. London: Liberal Publications Department

MacFarlane, Emmett 2013. 'Dialogue or Compliance? Measuring Legislatures' Policy Response to Court Rulings on Rights', *International Political Science Review* 34: 39–56

MacLennan, Christopher 2003. *Toward the Charter: Canadians and the Demand for a National Bill of Rights, 1929–1960*. Montreal: McGill-Queen's University Press

Malone, Ryan 2008. *Rebalancing the Constitution: The Challenge of Government Law-Making under MMP*. Wellington: Milne Printers

2009. '"Who's the Boss?" Executive–Legislature Relations in New Zealand Under MMP', *New Zealand Journal of Public and International Law* 7: 1–20

Manfredi, Christopher P. 2001. *Judicial Power and the Charter: Canada and the Paradox of Liberal Constitutionalism*, 2nd edition. Toronto: Oxford University Press

2006. 'The Unfulfilled Promise of Dialogic Constitutionalism: Judicial-Legislative Relationships Under the Canadian Charter of Rights and Freedoms', in Tom Campbell, Jeffrey Goldsworthy, and Adrienne Stone (eds.), *Protecting Rights Without a Bill of Rights*. London: Ashgate, pp. 239–59

2007. 'The Day the Dialogue Died: A Comment on *Sauve v. Canada*', *Osgoode Hall Law Journal* 45: 105–23

2009. 'In Defense of Prisoner Disenfranchisement', in Alec C. Ewald and Brandon Rottinghaus (eds.), *Criminal Disenfranchisement in an International Perspective*. New York: Cambridge University Press, pp. 259–80

Manfredi, Christopher P., and James B. Kelly, 1999. 'Six Degrees of Dialogue: A Response to Hogg and Bushell', *Osgoode Hall Law Journal* 37: 513–27

Mathieson, D.L. 1986. 'Interpreting the Proposed Bill of Rights (I)', *New Zealand Law Journal April*: 129–36

1986. 'Interpreting the Proposed Bill of Rights (II)', *New Zealand Law Journal May*: 160–64

McClelland, Sarah 1996. 'The Right to Vote: Implications of New Zealand's International Legal Obligations and the New Zealand Bill of Rights Act', *Victoria University of Wellington Law Review* 26: 575–94

McDonald, Leighton 2004. 'Rights, "Dialogue" and Democratic Objections to Judicial Review', *Federal Law Review* 32: 1–28

McGee, David 2005. *Parliamentary Practice in New Zealand*. Wellington: Dunmore Publishing

2007. 'Concerning Legislative Process', *Otago Law Review* 11: 417–31

McHugh, Paul 2005. 'Setting the Statutory Compass: The Foreshore and Seabed Act 2004', *New Zealand Journal of Public and International Law* 3: 255–83

McKeever, David 2010. 'The Human Rights Act and Anti-Terrorism in the United Kingdom: One Great Leap Forward by Parliament, But Are the Courts Able to Slow the Steady Retreat that has Followed?', *Public Law* 117

McLean, Janet 2001. 'Legislative Invalidation, Human Rights Protection and s. 4 of the New Zealand Bill of Rights Act', *New Zealand Law Review* 421–48

McLeay, Elizabeth 1987. 'Selection Versus Election: Choosing Cabinets in New Zealand', in Harold D. Clarke and Moshe M. Czudnowski, (eds.), *Political Elites in Anglo-American Democracies*. Dekalb: Northern Illinois University Press, pp. 279–306

1995. *The Cabinet & Political Power in New Zealand*. Melbourne: Oxford University Press

2001. 'Parliamentary Committees in New Zealand: A House Continuously Reforming Itself?', *Australasian Parliamentary Review* 16: 121–39

2006. 'Leadership in Cabinet under MMP', in Raymond Miller and Michael Mintrom (eds.), *Political Leadership in New Zealand.* Auckland: Auckland University Press, pp. 92–112

McQueen, Hamish 2010. 'Parliamentary Business: A Critical Review of Parliament's Role in New Zealand's Law-Making Process', *Auckland University Law Review* 32: 1–25

McRae, Tom 1994. *A Parliament in Crisis: The Decline of Democracy in New Zealand.* Wellington: Sheildag Publishing

Mueller, Sacha 2011. 'Where's the Fire? The Use and Abuse of Urgency in the Legislative Process', *Canterbury Law Review* 17: 316–30

2011. 'The Busy House: Alternatives to the Urgency Motion', *New Zealand Journal of Public and International Law* 9: 167–91

Mullan, David 2004. 'The Role for Underlying Constitutional Principles in a Bill of Rights World', *New Zealand Law Review* 9–38

Murray, C.R.G. 2012. 'A Perfect Storm: Parliament and Prisoner Disenfranchisement', *Parliamentary Affairs* 1: 511–539

Nicholls, Colin 2002. 'The UK Anti-Terrorism Crime & Security Act 2001: Too Much ... Too Soon', *Commonwealth Human Rights Initiative Newsletter (February)*: 9

Nicol, Danny 2004. 'The Human Rights Act and the Politicians', (2004) *Legal Studies* 24: 451–79

2011. 'Legitimacy of the Commons Debate on Prisoner Voting', *Public Law* 681–91

NO2ID Campaign 2014. 'NO2ID: Stop the Database State', www.no2id.net

Norrie, Kenneth 2005. 'Marriage and Civil Partnership for Same-Sex Couple: The International Imperative' *Journal of International Law and International Relations* 1: 249–260

Norton, Philip 1975. *Dissention in the House of Commons: Intra-party Dissent in the House of Commons Division Lobbies 1945–1974.* London: MacMillan

1980. *Dissension in the House of Commons, 1974–1979.* New York: Oxford University Press

Norton, Philip 1985. 'Behavioural Changes: Backbench Independence in the 1980s', in Philip Norton (ed.), *Parliament in the 1980s.* Oxford: Basil Blackwell, 22–47

Oliver, Dawn 2004. 'Constitutional Scrutiny of Executive Bills', *Macquarie Law Journal* 4: 33–55

2006. 'Improving the Scrutiny of Bills: The Case for Standards and Checklists', *Public Law* 2006: 219–46

Palmer, Geoffrey 1968. 'A Bill of Rights for New Zealand?', in K.J. Keith (ed.) *Essays on Human Rights.* Wellington: Sweet & Maxwell Ltd., pp. 106–31

1979. *Unbridled Power: An Interpretation of New Zealand's Constitution and Government.* Melbourne: Oxford University Press

1987. 'The New Zealand Legislative Machine', *Victoria University of Wellington Law Review* 17: 285–06

1987. *Unbridled Power*, 2nd edition. Melbourne: Oxford University Press

1988. 'Human Rights – The Proposed New Zealand Bill of Rights', *The Parliamentarian: Journal of the Parliaments of the Commonwealth* January: 10–13

1992. *New Zealand's Constitution in Crisis.* Dunedin: McIndoe

2000. 'The Provision of Legal Services to Government', *Victoria University of Wellington Law Review* 31: 65–76

2002. 'The Hazards of Making Constitutions: Some Reflections on Comparative Constitutional Law', in David Carter and Matthew Palmer (eds.) *Roles and Perspectives in the Law: Essays in Honour of Sir Ivor Richardson.* Wellington: Victoria University Press, pp. 209–38

2004. 'Muldoon and the Constitution', in Margaret Clark (ed.), *Muldoon Revisited.* Palmerston North: Dunedin Press, pp. 167–214

2006. 'Law Reform and the Law Commission in New Zealand After 20 Years – We Need to Try a Little Harder', Address to the New Zealand Centre for Public Law, Victoria University of Wellington (30 March)

2006. 'The Bill of Rights Fifteen Years On', Keynote Speech Ministry of Justice Symposium: The New Zealand Bill of Rights Act (10 February)

2007. 'Improving the Quality of Legislation – the Legislation Advisory Committee, the Legislation Design Committee and What Lies Beyond', *Waikato Law Review* 15: 12–22

2008. 'Government and Advice: Reflections upon the Wellington Policy-Making Culture', in Claudia Geiringer and Dean R. Knight (eds.) *Seeing the World Whole: Essays in Honour of Sir Kenneth Keith.* Wellington: Victoria University Press, pp. 274–97

Palmer, Geoffrey and Palmer, Matthew 2004. *Bridled Power.* Melbourne: Oxford University Press

Palmer, Matthew 2002. 'Counter-Terrorism Law', *New Zealand Law Journal* December: 456–64

2006. 'Using Constitutional Realism to Identify the *Complete* Constitution: Lessons from an Unwritten Constitution', *American Journal of Comparative Law* 54: 587–36

2006. 'What Is New Zealand's Constitution and Who Interprets It? Constitutional Realism and the Importance of Public Office-holders', *Public Law Review* 17: 133–63

2006. 'Resolving the Foreshore and Seabed Dispute', in Raymond Miller and Michael Mintrom (eds.), *Political Leadership in New Zealand.* Auckland: Auckland University Press, pp. 197–214

2007. 'New Zealand's Constitutional Culture', *New Zealand Universities Law Review* December: 565–97

2008. *The Treaty of Waitangi in New Zealand's Law and Constitution*. Wellington: Victoria University Press

2011. 'The Law Officers and Departmental Lawyers', *New Zealand Law Journal* November: 333–38

Parry, Stephen 2011. 'The Road to Nowhere: An Account of the Increase in New Zealand's Rate of Incarceration between 1999 and 2009', *Auckland University Law Review* 17: 88–118

Perry, Michael J. 2003. 'Protecting Human Rights in a Democracy: What Role for the Courts?', *Wake Forest Law Review* 38: 635–695

Petter, Andrew 2007. 'Taking Dialogue Theory Much Too Seriously (Or Perhaps Charter Dialogue Isn't Such a Good Thing After All)', *Osgoode Hall Law Journal* 45: 147–67

Phillipson, Gavin P. 2007. 'Defence, Discretion, and Democracy in the Human Rights Era', *Current Legal Problems* 60: 40–78

Pinto-Duschinsky, Michael 1981. *British Political Finance 1830–1980*. Washington, DC: American Enterprise Institute for Public Policy Research

Pratt, John 2006. 'The Dark Side of Paradise', *British Journal of Criminology* 46: 541–60

2007. *Penal Populism*. London: Routledge

2008. 'When Penal Populism Stops: Legitimacy, Scandal and the Power to Punish in New Zealand', *Australian and New Zealand Journal of Criminology* 41: 364–83

Pratt, John and Marie Clark, 2005. 'Penal Populism in New Zealand', *Punishment & Society* 7: 303–22

Reidy, Aisling 1999. 'The House of Lords in Defence of Human Rights?' UCL Constitution Unit (October), www.ucl.ac.uk/constitution-unit/publications

Renwick, Alan 2011. 'House of Lords Reform: A Briefing Paper', *Political Studies Association* (11 July)

Rhodes, R.A.W., John Wanna and Patrick Weller 2009. *Comparing Westminster*. Oxford: Oxford University Press

Rishworth, Paul 1985. 'The Birth and Rebirth of the New Zealand Bill of Rights Act', in Grant Huscroft and Paul Rishworth, (eds.), *Rights and Freedoms: The New Zealand Bill of Rights Act 1990 and the Human Rights Act 1993*. Wellington: Brookers, pp. 1–35.

1989. 'A Canadian Bill of Rights for New Zealand? The Justice and Law Reform Committee's Final Report', *New Zealand Recent Law Review* 83–104

1992. 'The New Zealand Bill of Rights 1990: The First Fifteen Months', *Essays on the New Zealand Bill of Rights Act 1990* 7–39

2007. 'Changing Times, Changing Minds, Changing Law – Sexual Orientation and New Zealand Law, 1960 to 1985', *International Journal of Human Rights* 11: 85–107

2010. 'The Bill of Rights and "Rights Dialogue" in New Zealand: After 20 years, What Counts as Success?' University of Sydney Workshop on "Judicial Supremacy or Inter-institutional Dialogue? Political Responses to Judicial Review' (May 18–19)

Rishworth, Paul, Grant Huscroft, Scott Optican and Richard Mahoney 2003. *The New Zealand Bill of Rights*. Melbourne: Oxford University Press

Roach, Kent 2000. 'The Attorney General and the Charter Revisited', *University of Toronto Law Journal* 50: 1–40

2006. 'Dialogue or Defiance: Legislative Reversals of Supreme Court Decisions in Canada and the United States', *International Journal of Constitutional Law* 4: 347–70

2006. 'Not Just the Government's Lawyer: The Attorney General as the Defender of the Rule of Law', *Queen's Law Journal* 31: 598–642

2007. 'Sharpening the Dialogue Debate: The Next Decade of Scholarship', *Osgoode Hall Law Journal* 45: 169–91

2011. *The 9/11 Effect: Comparative Counter-Terrorism*. New York: Cambridge University Press

Roberts, Julian V. 2003. 'Sentencing Reform in New Zealand: An Analysis of the Sentencing Act 2002', *Australian and New Zealand Journal of Criminology* 36: 249–71

Robins, Greg 2006. 'The Right of Prisoners to Vote: A Review of Disenfranchisement in New Zealand', *New Zealand Journal of Public and International Law* 4: 165–95

Rumbles, Wayne 2011. '"Three Strikes" Sentencing: Another Blow for Māori', *Waikato Law Review* 19: 108–16

Russell, Meg, and Maria Sciara 2007. 'Why Does the Government get Defeated in the House of Lords? The Lords, the Party System and British Politics', *British Politics* 2: 299–322

Sedley, S. 1995. 'Human Rights: A Twenty-First Century Agenda', *Public Law* 385.

Skene, Geoff 1987. 'Parliamentary Reform', in Jonathan Boston and Martin Holland (eds.), *The Fourth Labour Government: Radical Politics in New Zealand*. Melbourne: Oxford University Press, pp. 72–88

Seuffert, Nan 2006. 'Sexual Citizenship and the Civil Union Act 2004', *Victoria University of Wellington Law Review* 37: 281–301

Shapiro, Martin and Alec Stone Sweet 2002. *On Law, Politics, and Judicialization*. New York: Oxford University Press

Stemplewitz, Jan 2002. 'Section 6 of the Bill of Rights Act 1190: A Case for Parliamentary Responsibility for Human Rights and Freedoms', *Victoria University of Wellington Law Review* 33: 409–23

Straw, Jack 1999. 'Building a Human Rights Culture', address to Civil Service College Seminar (19 December) www.nationalarchives.gov.uk/ERORecords/HO/415/1/hract/cscspe.htm

Straw, Jack and Paul Boateng 1997. 'Bringing Rights Home: Labour's Plans to Incorporate the European Convention on Human Rights into U.K. Law', *European Human Rights Law Review*: 71–80

Stone Sweet, Alec 2000. *Governing with Judges: Constitutional Politics in Europe*. New York: Oxford University Press

Stonewall, www.stonewall.org.uk/information_bank/education/71.asp

Stychin, Carl F. 2005. 'Sexuality: Couplings: Civil Partnership in the United Kingdom', *New York City Law Review* 8: 543

2006. 'Not (Quite) A Horse and Carriage: The Civil Partnership Act 2004', *Feminist Legal Studies* 14: 79–86

Thayer, J.B. 1893. *The Origin and Scope of the American Doctrine of Constitutional Law*. Boston: Little, Brown and Company

Tremblay, Luc 2005. 'The Legitimacy of Judicial Review: The Limits of Dialogue Between Courts and Legislatures', *International Journal of Constitutional Law* 3: 617–48

Tomkins, Adam 2005. *Our Republican Constitution*. Oxford: Hart Publishing

2010. 'National Security and the Role of the Court: A Changed Landscape?', *Law Quarterly Review* 126: 543–67

2011. 'Parliament, Human Rights and Counter-Terrorism', in Tom Campbell, K.D. Ewing and Adam Tomkins (eds.), *The Legal Protection of Human Rights: Sceptical Essays*. Oxford: Oxford University Press, pp. 44–65

2014. 'Justice and Security in the United Kingdom', *Israel Law Review* 47: 305–329

Tushnet, Mark 1999. *Taking the Constitution Away from the Courts*. Princeton, NJ: Princeton University Press

2003. 'Alternative Forms of Judicial Review', *Michigan Law Review* 101: 2781–802

2003. 'Non-judicial Review', in Tom Campbell, Jeffrey Goldsworthy, and Adrienne Stone (eds.), *Protecting Human Rights*. Oxford: Oxford University Press, pp. 213–29

2003. 'New Forms of Judicial Review', *Wake Forest Law Review* 38: 813–38

2004. 'Weak-form Judicial Review: Its Implications for Legislatures', *New Zealand Journal of Public and International Law* 2: 7–23

2008. *Weak Courts, Strong Rights: Judicial Review and Social Welfare Rights in Comparative Constitutional Law*. Princeton: Princeton University Press

2010. 'How Different Are Waldron's and Fallon's Core Cases For and Against Judicial Review?', *Oxford Journal of Legal Studies* 30: 49–70

2011. 'The Political Institutions of Rights-Protection', in Tom Campbell, K.D. Ewing and Adam Tomkins (eds.), *The Legal Protection of Human Rights: Sceptical Essays*. Oxford: Oxford University Press, pp. 297–311

Uhr, John 2006. 'The Performance of Australian Legislatures in Protecting Rights', in Tom Campbell, Jeffrey Goldsworthy, and Adrienne Stone, (eds.), *Protecting Rights Without a Bill of Rights*. London: Ashgate, pp. 41–59

Varuhas, Jason N.E. 2009. 'Courts in the Service of Democracy: Why Courts Should Have a Constitutional (But Not Supreme) Role in Westminster Legal Systems', *New Zealand Law Review* 3: 481–518

Wade, William 1996. 'Sovereignty: Revolution or Evolution?', 112 *Law Quarterly Review* 568–75

Wadham, John 1996. 'Why Incorporation of the European Convention on Human Rights is Not Enough', in Richard Gordon and Richard Wilmot-Smith (eds.), *Human Rights in the United Kingdom*. Oxford: Oxford University Press, pp. 25–45

1997. 'Bringing Rights Half-way Home' (1997) 2 *European Human Rights Law Review* 2: 141–45

Wagner, Adam 2011. 'Anti-terrorism Powers for a Rainy Day', *UK Human Rights Blog* (4 September) http://ukhumanrightsblog.com/2011/09/04/anti-terrorism-powers-for-a-rainy-day/

Waldron, Jeremy 1999. *The Dignity of Legislation*. Cambridge: Cambridge University Press

1999. *Law and Disagreement*. New York: Oxford University Press

2005. 'Compared to What? Judicial Activism and New Zealand's Parliament', *New Zealand Law Journal* December: 441–45

2008. 'Parliamentary Recklessness: Why We Need to Legislate More Carefully', Maxim Institute John Graham Lecture, 1–48

2006. 'The Core of the Case Against Judicial Review', *Yale Law Journal* 115: 1346–406

Wallington, Peter, and Jeremy McBride, 1976. *Civil Liberties and a Bill of Rights*. London: Cobden Trust

Walker, Clive 2006. 'Clamping Down on Terrorism in the United Kingdom', *Journal of International Criminal Justice* 4: 1137–1151

2010. 'The Threat of Terrorism and the Fate of Control Orders', *Public Law* 4: 3–15

Walker, Clive, and Stuart Osborne (eds.) 2009. *Blackstone's Guide to The Anti-Terrorism Legislation*. Oxford: Oxford University Press

Watson, Jenny 2002. 'Something for Everyone: The Impact of the Human Rights Act and the need for a Human Rights Commission', *The British Institute of Human Rights*

2006. 'Backbench Influence on Government Legislation? A Flexing of Parliamentary Muscles at Westminster', *Parliamentary Affairs* 59: 350–59

Whitaker, Richard 2006. 'Ping-Pong and Policy Influence: Relations between the Lords and Commons, 2005–06', *Parliamentary Affairs* 59: 536–45

Whittington, Keith E. 2007. *Political Foundations of Judicial Supremacy*. Princeton, NJ: Princeton University Press

Williams, George 2006. 'The Victorian *Charter of Human Rights and Responsibilities*: Origins and Scope', *Melbourne University Law Review* 30: 880–905

Young, Alison L. 2002. 'Judicial Sovereignty and the Human Rights Act 1998', *Cambridge Law Journal* 61: 53–65

2009. *Parliamentary Sovereignty and the Human Rights Act*. Oxford: Hart Publishing Ltd

2011. 'Is Dialogue Working Under the Human Rights Act 1998?', *Public Law* 773–800

Zander, Michael 1985. *A Bill of Rights?* 3rd edition. London: Sweet & Maxwell

INDEX

CPSIA information can be obtained at www.ICGtesting.com
Printed in the USA
BVOW08*0442190115

383803BV00004B/19/P

9 781107 076518